web publishing
with Microsoft FrontPage 97

web publishing
with Microsoft FrontPage 97

Charles Brannon

VENTANA

Web Publishing With Microsoft FrontPage 97
Copyright © 1997 by Charles Brannon

All rights reserved. This book may not be duplicated in any way without the expressed written consent of the publisher, except in the form of brief excerpts or quotations for the purposes of review. The information contained herein is for the personal use of the reader and may not be incorporated in any commercial programs, other books, databases, or any kind of software without written consent of the publisher or author. Making copies of this book or any portion for any purpose other than your own is a violation of United States copyright laws.

Library of Congress Cataloging-in-Publication Data

Brannon, Charles.
    Web Publishing with Microsoft Frontpage 97 / Charles Brannon. — 1st ed.
   p. cm.
Includes index.
ISBN 1-56604-478-2
1. Web sites. 2. Frontpage(Computer file) 3. Web publishing.
TK5105.888.B725 1996
005.7'2—dc21   96-37901

First Edition 9 8 7 6 5 4 3 2 1

Printed in the United States of America

Ventana Communications Group
P.O. Box 13964
Research Triangle Park, NC 27709-3964
919.544.9404
FAX 919.544.9472
http://www.vmedia.com

Ventana Communications Group is a division of International Thomson Publishing.

Limits of Liability & Disclaimer of Warranty
The author and publisher of this book have used their best efforts in preparing the book and the programs contained in it. These efforts include the development, research, and testing of the theories and programs to determine their effectiveness. The author and publisher make no warranty of any kind, expressed or implied, with regard to these programs or the documentation contained in this book.
    The author and publisher shall not be liable in the event of incidental or consequential damages in connection with, or arising out of, the furnishing, performance or use of the programs, associated instructions and/or claims of productivity gains.

Trademarks
Trademarked names appear throughout this book and on the accompanying compact disk, if applicable. Rather than list the names and entities that own the trademarks or insert a trademark symbol with each mention of the trademarked name, the publisher states that it is using the names only for editorial purposes and to the benefit of the trademark owner with no intention of infringing upon that trademark.

President
Michael E. Moran

**Vice President of
Content Development**
Karen A. Bluestein

**Director of Acquisitions
and Development**
Robert Kern

Managing Editor
Lois J. Principe

Production Manager
John Cotterman

Art Director
Marcia Webb

**Technology Operations
Manager**
Kerry L. B. Foster

Brand Manager
Jamie Jaeger Fiocco

Creative Services Manager
Diane Lennox

Acquisitions Editor
Neweleen A. Trebnik

Project Editor
Amy E. Moyers

Development Editor
Lisa Bucki

Copy Editor
Judy Flynn

CD-ROM Specialist
Ginny Phelps

Technical Director
Dan Brown

Technical Reviewer
Russ Mullen

Desktop Publisher
Kristin Miller

Proofreader
Tom Collins

Indexer
Ann Norcross

Cover Designers
Tom Draper Design
Laura Stalzer

About the Author

Charles Brannon is a contributing writer for Imagine Publications and a founding member of the Windows User Group Network (WUGNET) Advisory Panel. He previously served as Program Editor for Compute Publications. With his popular books and hundreds of magazine articles, Charles has taught millions of computer users how to get the most out of their machines. Charles is coauthor of *The Windows 95 Book* and *Microsoft Windows NT4 Workstation Desktop Companion* (both published by Ventana) and has contributed to several other Ventana titles.

Acknowledgments

First I want to give special credit to Evangelos Petroutsos, who played a crucial role in developing Chapter 9 of this book. Also kudos to the friends and colleagues who helped test my chapters, offered advice, and helped buoy my confidence, including Martin Beste, Randy Fosner, Richard Mansfield, Jennifer Pearson, Dallas Peoples, and Mike Young. I also want to extend my appreciation to all the participants in the Microsoft FrontPage newsgroup, especially Cathy J., Jens Peter Carlson, D. E. Dorgan, , R. W. Gerling, M.D., and Peter Perchansky. I want to emphasize my gratitude and appreciation to family members Bill Brannon, Suzanne Ramsey, Lori Herron, Michael Brannon, and Wendy Brannon, and my niece and nephews for their support, encouragement, and humor. Thanks to Margaret Sullivan for her patience and kindness. Also a big round of applause for the excellent editorial support at Ventana, especially Amy Moyers, Russ Mullen, Lisa Bucki, Judy Flynn, Kristin Miller, Lois Principe, and Neweleen Trebnik, without whom there would be no way to acknowledge anyone else.

Dedication

This book is dedicated to Logan and Brynn McChesney.

Contents

Introduction xix

1 Getting Started: Inside FrontPage 97 1

Introducing FrontPage 1

Webtop Publishing 3

The World Wide Web & the Internet 5
   About the Internet ■ Inside the Net: TCP/IP ■ About the
   World Wide Web ■ HTTP: The Internet Connection ■ Related
   Technologies ■ About Webs & Web Servers

What About HTML? 12
   HTML: The Language of the Web ■ A Simple HTML Page
   ■ Dissecting the Greetings Page ■ The Power of HTML ■ Forget
   HTML!

FrontPage Quick Tour 21
   The FrontPage Editor ■ FrontPage Explorer ■ Templates
   ■ Wizards ■ WebBots

The Art of Webtop Publishing 35
   The Seven Elements of a Web Page ■ Other Page Elements

2 Your First FrontPage Project 53

Getting Started 53

Wizards at Work 54
Choosing a Wizard or Template ■ Choosing a Server & Naming the Web ■ Pages & Topics to Include ■ Consistency Considerations ■ Substitution Settings ■ It's Alive

Planning & Delegating Web Work 71

Creating a Custom Logo 73
How It Works ■ Inserting Graphics ■ The Eraser Tool ■ Save the Logo

Race to the Finish 82

First Impressions 83
Web Page Properties ■ Importing Text & Word Processing Documents ■ Mission (Almost) Accomplished

Customizing Pages: A Closer Look 92
Editing & Creating Links ■ Are We There Yet?

Introducing Forms 100
Forming Fields ■ How It Works

Mission Accomplished 102
Taking a Peek ■ Why Worry?

3 Enhancing Your Site: FrontPage Techniques 105

Creating a Custom Page Background 105
Company Literature Suggests a Design ■ Introducing Microsoft Image Composer ■ Using Image Composer to Create the Background ■ Applying the Custom Background ■ Don't Cross the Border

Aligning Text With Tables 120
Cell Properties ■ Changing the Column Widths ■ Moving the Content Into the Table ■ Update the Other Pages, Too

Creating a Blank Page 128

Creating a Contacts Page 129

Linking the Web Together 135

Contents xv

Building an Animated Graphic for Use as a Navigation Bar 136
Options Tab ■ Animation Tab ■ Image Tab

Converting the Animation to a Navigation Bar With Hot Spots 146
The Old Way ■ A Better Way ■ Inserting the Animation
■ Mapping Hot Spots ■ Image Toolbar Commands ■ Updating
the Navigation Links ■ Right at Home

4 Building an Interactive Web Site: Forms & Form Handlers 157

Planning a Form 158

Modeling the Form 159

Choosing Form Fields 160

Designing the Census Form 161

Laying Out the Census Form 164
Inserting Text Fields ■ Enforcing Data Entry With Validation
Rules ■ Building the Census Table ■ Laying Out the Census
Entries ■ Filling the Rest of the Census Table ■ Adding a Form
Handler ■ Creating a Custom Confirmation Page ■ Alternatives
to Save Results

5 Reaching Your Audience: FrontPage Publishing 209

Webs Online 210
Master of Your Domain ■ The Need for Speed

Finding a Home 219
FrontPage Web Presence Providers ■ Where to Shop
■ Determine Your Requirements ■ Ordering Your Account

Publishing to a Non-FrontPage Server 227
WebBot Limitations on a Non-FrontPage Server ■ Uploading
Your Web With the File Transfer Protocol ■ Uploading Withthe
Web Publishing Wizard

Publishing to a FrontPage Server 237
Preparing Your Web for the World Wide Web ■ Publishing to
the Internet Web Server

Web Site Maintenance 242
    Team Web Development ■ Security Issues ■ Is the Registration
    WebBot Worth the Trouble? ■ Versioning & Backup Security
    ■ Advanced Recovery

Promoting Your Site 253

6 FrontPage Configuration & Server Issues 257

Why Web Servers? 258
    Why Web Servers? Why Not? ■ Local Authoring
    ■ Introduction to Web Security

Microsoft Web Servers Overview 264

All In the Family 264

A Fork in the Road 267

Microsoft Personal Web Server for Windows 95 267
    Installing Microsoft PWS ■ The FrontPage 97 Server
    Administrator ■ Microsoft PWS Administration ■ Microsoft
    Personal Web Server Administration ■ Microsoft Personal Web
    Server Security ■ Enabling & Maintaining the FTP Server
    ■ MS PWS Intranet FTP Applications ■ Restricting FTP Access
    on a Per-User Basis ■ The Little Server That Could

Microsoft Internet Information Server for Windows NT 305
    Installing NT Peer Web Services ■ Installing Peer Web Services
    ■ The FrontPage 97 Server Administrator ■ NT Workstation PWS
    Administration ■ Peer Web Services Security ■ Enabling &
    Maintaining the FTP Server ■ IIS & Peer Web Services Intranet
    FTP Applications ■ Restricting FTP Access on a Per-User Basis

7 Private Webs: Deploying a Corporate Intranet ... 335

Intranet Fundamentals 336

Getting Started With a Disk-Based Web 338
    Creating a Hypertext FAQ ■ Testing the Disk-Based Web
    ■ Limitations of Disk-Based Webs

Setting Up Intranetworking 344
    Installing TCP/IP Support ■ Windows NT 4.0 Workstation
    TCP/IP Setup

Contents

Planning a Corporate Intranet 356
Implementing the Corporate Intranet 358
Deploying the Browser 358
    Designing the Home Page
Designing Intranet Content 370
    Access Intranet Documents ■ Run Software ■ Employee
    Resources

8 Database Publishing With The Internet Database Connector 391

Intranet Database Applications 392
    Overview: Using the Internet Database Connector With
    FrontPage ■ What About Active Server Pages?

IDC Intranet Examples 395
    Getting Ready for IDC ■ Work With Address Book ■ How to
    Create an IDC Query ■ Building a Results Page ■ Completing
    the Purchase Requisition Form

Advanced Database Examples 426
    Query by Example ■ Updating Records ■ Deleting Records
    ■ Adding Records

9 Advanced FrontPage Techniques 431

A Few Active Pages 432
Getting Input & Displaying Output 437
    Building a Better User Interface ■ Metric Conversion Revisited
    ■ Where Is the Script?

Form Validation Techniques 449
Browsing For Methods 453
Updating & Reading Form Field Controls 455
    Activating the Page ■ Variable Declaration ■ Calculating the
    Total ■ Responding to User Input

Floating Frames 470
Floating Images 474

Web Publishing With FrontPage 97

The Story of ActiveX 476
Inserting ActiveX Controls 477
   Where to Find ActiveX Controls ■ Using the ActiveX Marquee
   Control ■ Exploiting the Timer Control ■ Displaying Status
   Messages
More VBScript Techniques 493
   Color Animation ■ Experimenting With VBScript
The Game of Life ActiveX Control 498
Inserting Java Applets 501
   Acquiring Java Classes/Applets ■ Inserting a Java Applet
Java or ActiveX? 506

10 FrontPage 97 Visual Reference Guide 509

FrontPage Menu Reference 510
   FrontPage Explorer (Link View) Toolbar Reference
   ■ FrontPage Explorer (Folder View) Toolbar Reference
   ■ FrontPage Explorer - File Menu ■ FrontPage Explorer - Edit
   Menu ■ FrontPage Explorer - View Menu ■ FrontPage Explorer
   - Tools Menu ■ FrontPage Explorer and Editor - Help Menu
   ■ FrontPage Editor - Toolbar Reference ■ FrontPage Editor - File
   Menu ■ FrontPage Editor - Edit Menu ■ FrontPage Editor -
   View Menu ■ FrontPage Editor - Insert Menu ■ FrontPage
   Editor - Tools Menu ■ FrontPage Editor - Table Menu
FrontPage WebBot Reference 532
FrontPage Template Reference 534

A About the Companion CD-ROM 549

B FrontPage 97 Internet Resources 557

Index 569

Introduction

Believe it or not, the World Wide Web is just four years old in 1997. In "normal time," that's the span of a Presidential term, the amount of time we wait for the next Summer Olympics, or the life span of a household gerbil or guppy. But "Internet time," a term coined to describe the onrush of new technologies and industry turnovers that accompany the unprecedented growth of the Internet and World Wide Web (WWW), has a pace that seems to defy conventional standards for measuring progress.

A lot has changed in four years. The original freeware Mosaic web browser has given way to commercial offerings from Microsoft and Netscape. The competition has led to increasing sophistication in browser features and WWW standards. Recently Microsoft, who makes the Internet Explorer web browser, and Netscape, inventor of Navigator and Communicator, have called a truce of sorts, declaring full support for one another's browser conventions and HTML extensions. (Of course, the competition continues, with Netscape adding yet another nonstandard but desirable HTML extension, the ability to display web page components in layers.)

The display of text, tables, and graphics in the web browser environment is generated by the web browser as it interprets HyperText Markup Language codes that it pulls from an Internet or intranet web server. The HTML codes look like gibberish to the layman, which is why HTML itself is never seen by someone browsing the Web; he or she only sees the output produced by the HTML tags and attributes.

In 1993 and early 1994, it was possible to produce competitive web pages with a simple text editor like the Windows Notepad. Initially taken up by programmers and later taught to reluctant designers, hand-coding with HTML was really the only way to build effective web sites.

As the race to the Web accelerated in 1995 and 1996, it became clear that hand-coding HTML was not efficient or productive. Although there have always been simple programs to automate insertion and verification of HTML tags and to provide a crude preview of the results of using them, what designers really needed was a graphical page-layout program, a kind of a word processor for webs.

The Evolution of FrontPage

In 1996, several companies finally answered this need. Adobe's PageMill and Vermeer FrontPage took the lead with a true What You See Is What You Get (WYSIWYG) web page editor. It was clear that FrontPage had the edge in its faithfulness to the HTML standard, although the product was a little rough around the edges.

Further, whereas PageMill focused only on web page design (later complemented by Adobe SiteMill), FrontPage included full-featured site management tools, including a visual FrontPage Explorer that graphically depicted the relationships (links) between all the pages in a web site. What's better, FrontPage also included ready-to-use WebBots that performed interactive web functions, like site search, forms storage, and table of contents generation, that would normally require expensive custom programming with the Common Gateway Interface (CGI).

The FrontPage software was rounded out with a set of time-saving templates and intelligent Wizards to quickly prototype pages and even entire web sites. The user could build complex pages and sites simply by answering a series of questions.

Microsoft's Challenge

In 1995, Microsoft was beginning to founder for the first time in its existence. Bill Gates had incorrectly surmised that using the Internet was a frustrating, difficult, and intimidating experience that would never be able to compete with using a well-designed and easy-to-operate commercial online system. Taking inspiration from America Online and CompuServe (both of whom now risk being swept aside by Internet mania), Microsoft decided to focus its online efforts on The Microsoft Network.

It was indeed a mistake, as other computer companies quickly moved to take advantage of the new opportunities spawned by the sudden success of the World Wide Web. Thanks to the WWW, interest in the Internet shifted from mere curiosity to a public fascination. Sudden media infatuation with something new and different soon led to newscasters awkwardly instructing television viewers to "tune into aitch-tee-tee-pee, forward slash, forward slash, double-yew double-yew double-yew dot whatever dot com."

For a myriad of reasons, the World Wide Web was the catalyst of the Internet's maturation. Not only was the public fascinated, the WWW caught the fancy of advertisers, marketeers, and businesses worldwide, first as a vehicle for promotion, then as an elusive holy grail for online commerce. Thar's gold 'n them thar webs!

Microsoft's Solution

As Netscape's star rose amid Wall Street Internet frenzy, Bill Gates knew he had miscalculated. Putting The Microsoft Network in a holding pattern, Microsoft made an abrupt shift in its product plans and even reorganized the entire company around plans to exploit the Internet. Add-ons appeared for Microsoft Office to give it basic web publishing capabilities, with even more promised for Office 97. Windows NT Server was beefed up and positioned as a top-notch web server with the free addition of Internet Information Server (IIS) and other Internet-related BackOffice components. The Microsoft Network was scrapped and sent back to the drawing board to reemerge as an Internet Service Provider with enhanced content via the WWW.

Yet Microsoft still had no flagship web site creation tool.

That's where FrontPage came back into the picture. With its acquisition of Vermeer Technologies, Microsoft had its plum, a premiere WYSIWYG web editor and site management tool. Quickly relabeled and repackaged with a slightly revised user interface, Microsoft FrontPage 1.1 hit the store shelves in the second quarter of 1996.

Crucial to the success of FrontPage was the ability of Internet web servers to support the FrontPage WebBots, without which FrontPage was merely a great page editor. At first, FrontPage Web Presence Providers (WPPs) were few and far between, but as this book went to press, there were well over 150 WPPs, with the number reaching toward the 200 mark.

The initial release of FrontPage 1.1 was "underwhelming" to early FrontPage users, basically just icing on the cake with a few new table features and a frames wizard. It wasn't until the January 1997 release of FrontPage 97 that the product really hit its stride.

Introducing FrontPage 97

Now a fully compliant member of the Office product line, FrontPage 97 supports every advanced feature of HTML 3.2 plus several Microsoft innovations such as ActiveX controls and the Internet Explorer Marquee. In addition, it supports Netscape plug-ins, Java applets, and client-side web scripting with both VBScript and JavaScript.

Refinements to the user interface include a configurable toolbar, color-coded HTML editing, resizable graphics, scriptless database programming with the Internet Database Connector, a Preview in Browser command, and an Explorer-style folder view for the FrontPage Explorer with support for drag-and-drop file operations. Improvements to the core functionality of FrontPage include enhanced forms processing with form field validation, cross-web spell checking, cross-web search and replace, Secure Sockets Layer (SSL) support, conversion of Office documents, and integration with Microsoft Visual SourceSafe for version control.

Other goodies introduced with FrontPage 97 include the ability to prepare and upload webs to servers without FrontPage extensions and to support disk-based webs without a web server at all, faster operation via the Internet Server application programming interface (ISAPI), more control over security access, an Import Wizard for integrating existing web pages and other document content, Microsoft Image Composer with web clip art and animated graphics, and a powerful new Personal Web Server for Windows 95.

About This Book

Many of the FrontPage books on the store shelves were written during the beta testing of FrontPage 1.1 and are, quite frankly, rehashes of the product documentation and hastily thrown-together tutorials. Some of them have been patched up to be relevant to FrontPage 97. There are books that may have been written specifically for FrontPage 97, but they were also thrown together quickly in order to be the first on the shelves and were often limited to discussing only the features available in the beta versions.

This book is different. It was developed over a long period of time, starting with the release of FrontPage 1.1 and evolving during the FrontPage 97 beta testing program. The book is tested against the release version of FrontPage 97, and in fact, some material was updated and improved at the last minute even after FrontPage 97 reached store shelves.

I've used FrontPage for nearly two years now (half the life span of the WWW), and because I thoroughly understand the features and potential of this software, I believe I'm uniquely qualified to pass along this mastery to you, the reader.

Unlike the other books, *Web Publishing With FrontPage 97* does not focus on product features or components, nor on simple lessons, but instead emphasizes a practical, hands-on approach. With both clear and lucid explanations and step-by-step tutorials, you'll develop several real-world web applications as you master both the basic and advanced capabilities of FrontPage 97.

Because of this approach, this book is relevant to the web novice, intermediate readers familiar with HTML and other web authoring tools, and users upgrading from FrontPage 1.1. Even advanced readers will pick up several techniques to round out their web skills and will find the lessons valuable for teaching others in the organization how to use FrontPage 97.

Conventions Used in This Book

There are two conventions common to Ventana books and computer books in general that I want to point out. Although they are fairly obvious, a brief explanation is in order.

Vertical Lines Indicate Menu Items

When I describe a menu choice, the menu name and menu items are separated by the pipe symbol (a vertical line). Menu choices will look like this: To switch to Link View in the FrontPage Explorer, choose View | Link View. That translates to: Click on View on the menu bar, and then when the menu drops down, click on the Link View menu choice. Some menus have a third level, as in File | New | FrontPage Web, which means: Click on the File menu, click the New choice to display the flyout menu, and then choose FrontPage Web from the flyout menu.

Dialog Descriptions Are Capitalized

Each word is capitalized in text that appears as labels of program features in property sheet windows and dialog boxes, even if the text on the screen is not capitalized. For instance, Show Getting Started Dialog is the label of a check box in the General tab of the FrontPage Explorer options dialog box. Therefore, I will refer to it as the Show Getting Started dialog box. (The term *property sheet* has begun to replace the more generic term, *dialog box*, which is usually only a single window with limited options. Since most property sheets are tabbed pages in a set of property sheets, however, I feel it's more clear to refer to the entire collection as a dialog box.)

Reader Options

If you're in a hurry to learn as much about FrontPage as possible, you can probably skim through this book in just a few days, relying on the numerous illustrations and screen shots that parallel the book discussion. You can import the sample project webs that are included in the Companion CD-ROM directly into FrontPage Explorer to see how they tick.

To get more out of the book, I recommend taking a somewhat more leisurely approach by trying out each lesson, even if you feel you already understand some of the concepts mentioned. You'll also benefit from tips and notes.

TIP

Tips like this appear throughout the book and are an amplification of the main discussion or offer up some tidbit, trick, or special technique. Tips are optional reading.

Note: Notes are often provided as a warning about potential problems or risks or to draw your attention to a crucial point. Sometimes, however, a note simply inserts a clarification that is peripheral to the main discussion. Nevertheless, the notes contain important information and you should read them.

Sidebars
Sidebars provide a way to go into more detail on a particular topic without interrupting the flow of the discussion in the text. If you want to learn all you can about FrontPage and web authoring, you'll want to examine the sidebars carefully. However, they are not essential to any discussion, and you can skip them if you like, perhaps coming back to them at a later time.

What's the Plan?

Let's examine the way this book is laid out. You need not read the book cover to cover, or even sequentially, since each chapter includes numerous cross-references to relevant topics in other chapters. However, the layout of this book was carefully planned to progress from easy topics to more sophisticated topics and to anticipate your needs as you begin to understand and work with FrontPage. Those of you who are new users should focus on the first four chapters. If you are a more experienced user, you may wish to skim these chapters and perhaps return to them to pick up tips and techniques, but delve into the more advanced chapters toward the end of the book.

At any point, you can check out the reference section (Chapter 10 and the appendices) as needed to support your FrontPage authoring efforts.

Inside *Web Publishing With FrontPage 97*

Chapter 1 further delves into the history, evolution, and future of the Internet and the World Wide Web, providing the background you need to appreciate the automatic HTML-generation capabilities of FrontPage. Chapter 1 is ideal for new users of FrontPage because it introduces the FrontPage Editor and FrontPage Explorer with an overview of the noteworthy features of each. You'll learn the art of webtop publishing, including the "do's and don'ts" of fundamental web design. The chapter wraps up with some advice on integrating multimedia elements into your pages.

In Chapter 2, you'll see how to quickly prototype a corporate web site (sometimes called a company home page) with the easy FrontPage Corporate Presence Wizard and begin to move beyond the generic by customizing the pages for your particular business. To keep the focus on the practical, you'll develop a version of the actual web site employed by Group US, Inc., a group insurance wholesaler.

This project continues in Chapter 3, where you'll further customize the Company web with background textures, see how to align text and graphics with tables, and put together an animated navigation bar.

You'll wrap up the Company web project in Chapter 4, which shows you how to use the FrontPage Save Results WebBot to build a full-featured electronic data collection form with form-field error checking (validation) and online forms storage.

Chapter 5 gives you all the information you need to know to publish your web on the World Wide Web, including step-by-step techniques for uploading content via File Transfer Protocol (FTP), the Microsoft Web Publishing Wizard, and the FrontPage Explorer Publish Web command. You'll learn how to take advantage of free web hosting, how to shop for a commercial FrontPage Web Presence Provider, and some techniques for authoring webs either locally or remotely—both on your own or as part of a team.

Chapter 6 provides the technical background you may need if you're deploying a workgroup or corporate web server for intranet applications with Internet Information Server, NT Workstation Peer Web Services, or the new Microsoft Personal Web Server for Windows 95. In fact, this chapter offers one of the few good tutorials on using the Windows 95 PWS. Even if you only use your web server for local authoring, you'll appreciate knowing how to set up, configure, and optimize the server end of things. You'll also learn how to take advantage of direct-to-web publishing with Office 97 via its FTP interface.

Since the World Wide Web is only part of the story (albeit the most visible), Chapter 7 focuses on corporate intranet applications. Although intranet web development is easily a book-length topic in itself, you'll learn all you need to know to quickly set up a basic company intranet with accessible employee resources such as a policy manual and employee directory, quick program launching, integration of existing network documents, and client-server web front ends for electronic forms.

The intranet discussion continues in Chapter 8, but the real focus here is on web database integration using the Internet Database Connector (IDC). FrontPage 97 includes special support for IDC with the IDC Wizard, but you'll need this chapter to make sense of how to implement IDC queries with the Structured Query Language, integrate your pages with Microsoft Access, and put together useful data collection forms with updatable results pages. The lessons you learn here will put you on the right track for intranet database applications, but you'll also be able to apply this knowledge to Internet webs, including the basis for electronic commerce.

Chapter 9 introduces you to state-of-the-art features of FrontPage 97 that permit you to create intelligent, active web pages with the ease of Visual Basic scripting (VBScript), techniques that are also applicable to JavaScript. What's more, you'll learn how to "turbocharge" your web with ready-to-use ActiveX controls that add interactivity, animation, and even custom applications that run within a window on the browser. If ActiveX isn't your cup of tea, I'll also show you how to plug in Java applets to accomplish similar goals.

Chapter 10 is what makes this book a durable and lasting resource because it offers an innovative visual map of virtually every FrontPage menu, toolbar, dialog box, and property sheet. You can see where to find an elusive program option at a glance, and it lets you quickly understand the product's features and capabilities. There's also a quick reference to the FrontPage templates and page wizards, so you can instantly decide which one is right for your next project.

Since not every topic could be squeezed into 10 chapters, the Appendices provide you with additional reference material, including links to over 100 FrontPage-related web sites.

In Appendix A, you'll find detailed instructions on using this book's Companion CD-ROM, which features both commercial and shareware software for your evaluation; they are ideal for building up your Internet toolkit. The Companion CD-ROM also includes all the projects developed in this book to save you typing and ensure that you have a working reference for the techniques explained in the book.

Provided in Appendix B are links to other web authoring resources as well as additional information on FrontPage 97.

Finally, don't forget that the index is always waiting for you like a faithful servant, ready to provide instant reference to any topic, term, or technique. The index provides a great way to use this book as an ongoing reference or to jog your memory.

Welcome to the Web!

As you continue your journey toward webmaster status, you'll appreciate the collection of material I've put together for readers of this book on my web site. Please visit http://www.WebsFrontPage.com to try out the example webs and explore additional tutorials and links to other FrontPage and web authoring resources. You'll also find a special offer for FrontPage hosting should you be shopping for a home for your webs. I look forward to visiting with you online!

Charles Brannon
February 21, 1997

chapter 1

Getting Started: Inside FrontPage 97

Microsoft FrontPage is a powerful yet uniquely easy-to-use application for creating web pages and entire web sites. This book is your gateway to mastering this manageable and yet complex tool. In this chapter, I want to introduce to you the concepts of FrontPage authoring and show you what FrontPage can do for you. Subsequent chapters will delve into more detail on various topics, but you'll learn a lot from this chapter right off the bat.

Introducing FrontPage

An introduction to Microsoft FrontPage may seem a bit odd. After all, you've probably already paid for the software or are seriously considering it, or why would you be reading this book? Nevertheless, while you may have "met" FrontPage, perhaps you haven't been properly introduced. To start off on the right foot, I'm not going to make any assumptions about your level of expertise or experience with FrontPage. As mentioned in the introduction, this book was written to serve both beginning and intermediate FrontPage and Internet users. Even advanced users will learn valuable techniques in the latter chapters, yet that same material is designed to be accessible to anyone who completes the earlier tutorial chapters.

The primary goal of FrontPage is to free you from the tedious process of understanding and hand-coding page layout with the HyperText Markup Language (HTML). This is achieved by the FrontPage Editor, a true What You See Is What You Get (WSYIWYG) visual editor for web pages. Virtually any page that can be constructed with HTML statements can instead be created as easily as a word processing document. Furthermore, numerous design templates and automated web site wizards let you quickly prototype pages and entire web sites, then customize to suit.

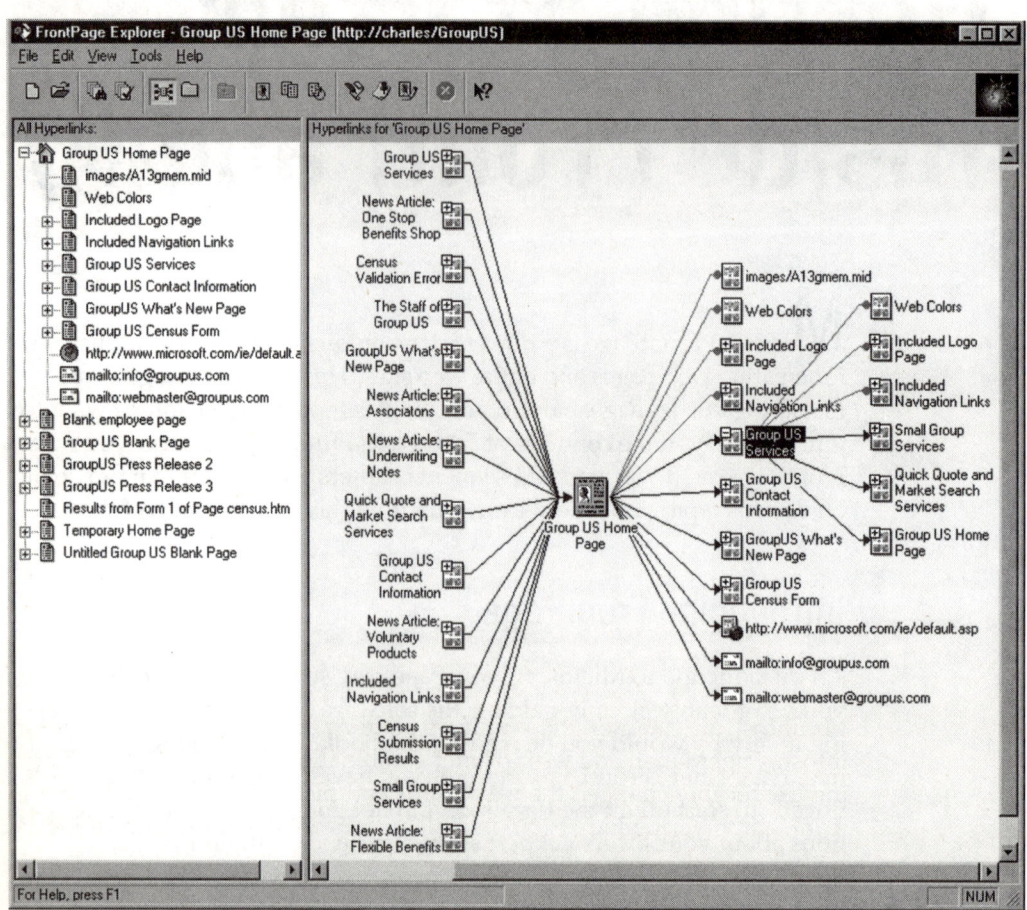

Figure 1-1: The FrontPage Explorer allows you to visualize the relationships between pages in a complex site.

FrontPage is also intended to give web authors an easy-to-use tool to visualize the layout of a site, a tool that gives you a graphical map of pages and the linkages between pages. This is accomplished with the FrontPage Explorer, which resembles the Windows 95/NT 4 Explorer user interface that is already familiar to anyone who has worked with hard disk or network files and folders. FrontPage Explorer lets you view your webs either as traditional files and folders or as a network of connections between pages. See Figure 1-1 for a sneak preview of the FrontPage Explorer interface. (It may seem daunting, but imagine trying to visualize these linkages in your head without any help from FrontPage Explorer!)

Finally, FrontPage lets users of every experience level take advantage of powerful web site capabilities such as forms storage, table of contents generation, search forms, discussion groups, and more without resorting to the arcane art of custom programming. All this power is enabled by the FrontPage WebBots, self-contained software "robots" that do all the work for you.

 Webtop Publishing

Vermeer Technologies coined the term *webtop publishing* with the release of FrontPage 1.0. (Microsoft was so impressed with the potential for FrontPage, it quickly moved to acquire Vermeer and move its staff of talented programmers to Microsoft headquarters.) Although the term has its limitations, it's worth exploring what webtop publishing is all about.

Clearly the term is related to desktop publishing, the computer publishing revolution of the 1980s made possible by the low-cost, high-quality laser printer and the advent of powerful and graphical page layout software, pioneered by Aldus (now Adobe) PageMaker on the Macintosh and later on the Windows platform. So potent was the Macintosh, PageMaker, and laser printer combination, that desktop publishing irrevocably changed the way words and pictures were brought to print, empowering individuals, small businesses, and large publishing houses alike. In fact, the success of desktop publishing gave the Macintosh a crucial boost in its formative years, and the Macintosh is even now the leading platform for graphic designers and publishers despite its dwindling share of the personal computer market.

 Web Publishing With FrontPage 97

If desktop publishing was the craze of the '80s, and multimedia and CD-ROM the rage of the early '90s, then clearly the Internet and the World Wide Web is where it's at in the late '90s and into the 21st century. PageMaker and the Macintosh graphical user interface brought about the sea change of desktop publishing. Low-cost multimedia PCs and non-technical authoring software, such as Asymetrix Multimedia Toolbook, ushered in the CD-ROM era. Yet until FrontPage came along, there was no easy-to-master, powerful software package and publishing solution for web site creation.

When it comes to webtop publishing, FrontPage fits the bill. The FrontPage Editor makes it a snap to design attractive and functional web pages, complete with formatted text, graphics, and multimedia elements such as music, sound, and video. The FrontPage Editor gives you visual tools to design electronic data collection forms and ready access to advanced features such as scripting, Java, ActiveX Controls, and plug-ins. FrontPage Explorer goes beyond mere web page design to help you manage entire web sites with visualization of links between pages, drag-and-drop file management, and one-step web publishing to your choice of Internet web servers.

It's true that there are other credible software packages for graphical web design, including Adobe SiteMill and NetObjects Fusion, but neither of these include the crucial mix of ingredients that will ensure the success of FrontPage. I already mentioned the important advantages of the FrontPage Editor and FrontPage Explorer. The key advantage of FrontPage is Microsoft's effort to make web publishing a point-and-click affair, thanks to the development of FrontPage server extensions for nearly every web server currently operated on the Internet.

By choosing from one of over 150 FrontPage Web Presence Providers, you can author and test your entire site on your local computer and upload it with just one menu command to your site on the Internet. You can maintain the site on the local computer and republish only the pages that have changed, or you can edit and update the material directly on the web server.

Thanks to the FrontPage server extensions, you're not locked into subscribing to a proprietary or Microsoft-only solution. The server extensions are based on open Internet standards and are freely available to all Web Presence Providers and other interested providers. Sites designed with FrontPage can be accessed by any web browser, including Netscape Navigator and Communicator, not just Microsoft Internet Explorer.

Furthermore, the FrontPage server extensions support the FrontPage WebBots transparently; that is, you don't need to know how the extensions work. You just insert the WebBots on a page or take advantage of web creation wizards that themselves rely on WebBot functionality.

Combined, all these features and capabilities vault FrontPage into the spotlight as the preeminent solution for "drag-and-drop" web publishing, that is, webtop publishing.

For more about Microsoft's point of view on webtop publishing, browse the location http://www.microsoft.com/frontpage/documents/webtop.htm.

The World Wide Web & the Internet

Although you can take advantage of FrontPage without understanding very much about how the World Wide Web works on the Internet, there will always be some nagging questions in the back of your mind about what's going on behind the curtains, so to speak. Let's examine some of these standards and technologies to provide the underpinning for your understanding of FrontPage web publishing.

About the Internet

There are very few people these days who aren't familiar with the Internet, and I'd be shocked if you, as a reader of this book, aren't already fairly conversant, at least in terms of using a web browser and Internet mail. So I won't get too fundamental here. However, you may have taken a lot of this technology for granted up to now, so let's examine what this Internet thing is all about.

As you've probably heard, the Internet arose as the ARPANet during a time of cold war paranoia and out of a legitimate concern about the survivability of military computer communications in the event of a nuclear strike. The idea was that instead of depending on a monolithic "master control computer" (shades of Tron), the computer network would be distributed all over the country. Any computer surviving the attack would be able to operate on its own and connect up with any other surviving computers on the network.

There's something apocryphal about this story. Surely no one really believed that the nation's infrastructure could withstand a full-scale nuclear war, and very few believed that a limited nuclear exchange would not inevitably escalate to full-blown planetary obliteration. It's more likely that the threat of nuclear war and cold war paranoia served to inspire the necessary funding to establish expensive new research projects and government agencies.

While it's questionable whether a distributed network like the original ARPANet could survive a series of thermonuclear explosions, the plan did make sense as a defense against more modest failures, such as power outages, severed cabling, network downtime, and server overload. By redundantly distributing the work of the Internet among many computer systems, the entire network is more reliable and less prone to interruption of service.

The success of the ARPANet experiment was the basis for the development of the National Science Foundation's NSFNET, employed to tie researchers and educational institutions into any of five supercomputing centers. These institutions were intranetworked in clusters, and the clusters were internetworked together. Other organizations joined the internetwork, including NASA Science Internet (NSI), the Swiss Academic and Research Network (SWITCH), and the Australian Academic and Research Network (AARNet).

Over time, the success of this scheme lead to the Internet we know today, although it's no longer controlled by a government agency, but by cooperation between the various companies and organizations that own or manage facets of the interconnected network. There are dozens of organizations that subdivide the task of running the Internet, including the Internet Engineering Task Force (IETF), Internet Research Task Force (IRTF), the Internet Society (ISOC), the Internet Architecture Board (IAB), the Network Information Center (NIC), and the InterNIC.

Fortunately, we can let the experts do their job, and enjoy the fruits of this enterprise. As the saying goes, "if it ain't broke, don't fix it," so the Internet community has fiercely resisted efforts by the rich and powerful to "privatize" the Internet, which would amount to a strategic takeover of an unbiased, disinterested system, putting it squarely in the hands of commercial interests.

Whatever your opinion on the virtues of capitalism, no one has ever claimed altruism as one of its benefits. Likewise, any attempts by a government to take the reins of Internet management will surely only bloat and corrupt a system that is owned by no one, is controlled by no one, yet truly belongs to everyone in the world.

Inside the Net: TCP/IP

Information sent via the Internet is broken up into myriad tiny blocks of data, called *packets*. Each packet is inserted into a virtual "envelope," stamped with a destination address and return address. These addresses are a series of four octets, as in 207.68.156.58, the IP address of Microsoft's domain. (A *domain* is a name listed in the Internet's Domain Name System. Each name is translated to an IP address that can be used to contact a server computer.)

Communication on the Internet is routed and encoded using the Transmission Control Protocol/Internet Protocol (TCP/IP). A *protocol* is an agreed-upon standard for accomplishing a task, network communication in this case. As with a diplomatic protocol, the universal TCP/IP protocol enables communication between every type of computer system.

When a computer sends a packet on to the network, it is the responsibility of each computer the packet passes through to forward it, until the packet reaches the computer that is geographically closest to its destination. Along the way, if a particular server computer fails or refuses to forward the packet, the previous computer reroutes the packet to another computer. That way, a failure along any point in the network can be overcome, and no computer has to service more than its fair share of packets.

As you're no doubt well aware, congestion on the Internet is slowing things down. Overloaded Internet routing computers are refusing packets, some of which never do go through. This requires the source computer to resend dropped packets. This in turn means that a message has to be reconstructed at the destination from all the packets, some of which arrive out of order. For some types of traffic, such as audio, it's OK to put up with some noise by ignoring lost packets and avoiding retransmission, which is what makes real-time Internet audio feasible, such as Progressive Networks's RealAudio and Internet telephony products.

The computers discussed so far are run by large telecommunications companies such as Sprint, MCI, and America Online and by nonprofit institutions. These are the only computers that are actually "on the Internet." Everyone else, including yourself, your Internet Service Provider, and your Web Presence Provider, subscribes to the services of the commercial network providers via secondary networks. You have full access to the Internet, but you're not really "on the Internet."

About the World Wide Web

For most of its life span, the Internet was largely ignored. Only academia, students, and scientists had any use for it. The applications included *Telnet*, for tying into a remote mainframe or minicomputer via a text-only terminal emulator interface; the *File Transfer Protocol* (FTP) for uploading and downloading files; the *Internet Relay Chat* for real-time typed conversations; USENET, which provided a way to take part in offline discussion newsgroups; and *Gopher* servers for access to databases and white pages. *Archie* servers allowed Internet users to search FTP sites for files.

By far, the most popular application for the Internet has been electronic mail (e-mail). The Internet ties together disparate mail systems from proprietary services (like CompuServe, Prodigy, America Online), corporate mail systems, and educational mail systems so that you can send electronic mail to virtually anyone with an e-mail address. The success of Internet gateways for electronic mail helped to boost interest in and investment in the Internet infrastructure, paving the way for the next new Internet application that would quickly cause the popularity of the Internet to skyrocket.

In 1980, Tim Berners-Lee, working with other researchers at European Laboratory for Particle Physics (CERN), advanced the idea of a system for displaying documents retrieved from Internet servers. These would not be stand-alone documents, but rather documents with embedded links to other documents, based on the principles of hypertext.

If fully implemented, hypertext would let you browse any topic, and while reading, let you instantly jump to related information. If you're curious about a particular word, bibliographical reference, or author, you can jump to another linked document. You can back up at any point to the previous level. It's not really necessary to belabor this further; you've already seen hypertext at work on the World Wide Web (WWW). So far, hypertext has not lived up to its full potential, largely due to the daunting task of researching and linking together so many disparate documents. (To see hypertext as it really should work, look at a CD-ROM encyclopedia like Microsoft Encarta.)

The first real application of this idea took the form of the Mosaic web browser. First released in 1993, it was developed at the National Center for Supercomputing Applications (NCSA) by a team led by Marc Andreesson, who later founded Netscape Communications. Netscape's improved Mosaic became known as Netscape Navigator. Meanwhile, Mosaic was commercialized and was eventually licensed to Microsoft, who rewrote it as the first release of Microsoft Internet Explorer.

With support for enhanced text presentation, graphics, and user interface elements, in addition to the ubiquitous hyperlinks, the World Wide Web became the "killer application" for the Internet. The growth of the WWW since then has defied all description, starting from a modest network of 200 hosts (web servers) in 1993 and growing to over 897,612 hosts by the end of 1996. Estimates of users connected to the Internet today (in the United States alone) via online services and Internet Service Providers range from a conservative 5 million to as many as 25 million active users. (Worldwide estimates are even harder to come by, but should at least double the U.S. figures.)

HTTP: The Internet Connection

Documents on the WWW (and on private intranets) are stored on dedicated computer systems called web servers. A *web server* is a computer with enough hard disk storage to hold the documents for one or more webs or web sites. Documents are delivered to end users running web browsers that use the Internet HyperText Transfer Protocol (HTTP), which runs "on top" of the TCP/IP protocol. Should the browser need to send information back to the server (such as form data), this communication also occurs over an HTTP connection.

Keep in mind the separate roles played by the web server and the web browser. The web server simply delivers files to the browser, which formats the content of the file to display it on the screen. None of the visual layout of the page is generated by the server. The server is responsible for processing or storing information sent to it by the browser, such as the contents of form fields like text boxes, but the browser initiates this process only when it detects that the user has clicked on a Submit button. The web server is not in control of the computer running the web browser, nor can the web browser directly control the web server. It's really just an orchestrated form of communication using the HTTP protocol.

You really shouldn't care how information is sent. However, keep in mind that the web server and the client browser must negotiate a separate HTTP connection for each object on your page. The text is all one object, but each graphic is a separate object, and the more objects on the page, the slower it will be to access. It's just as important to keep the total number of graphics to a minimum as it is to minimize the file length and size of the images.

Related Technologies

Many sites will benefit from access to an FTP server for storing files that can be downloaded. While files can also be downloaded using the HTTP protocol, this can keep the server so busy sending files that it can't keep up with web page requests. The File Transfer Protocol (mentioned earlier) is optimized for sending and receiving files. You can provide a publicly accessible download directory for publishing program files, documents in word processor format, artwork, and other content such as pictures. A private download directory can be used to supply customer-only information, documents, spreadsheets, and the like. An upload directory lets your users send you submissions, documents, pictures, and so forth, although most web browsers don't include FTP upload capability. (The Companion CD-ROM includes two full-featured FTP clients: WS_FTP32 and CuteFTP32. See Appendix A.)

Java and ActiveX are two new web publishing technologies that are making big waves on the WWW. Java is a programming language and method for attaching program objects (applications, or applets) that go way beyond the plain text abilities of HTML.

So that the open nature of the WWW can be fully exploited, Java programs are capable of running as is on nearly every computing platform in common use. ActiveX Controls similarly encapsulate program features and special effects into modules that can be inserted into your pages or linked to from your pages. With Java or ActiveX, your pages can display active content such as scrolling banners, stock tickers, and animated graphics and provide true interactivity via games, whiteboard collaboration, live chats, and applications that include financial calculators, DNA analysis, and of course, electronic commerce.

Scripting lets you embed simple programming directly onto your pages to jazz them up with special effects, to test form data for validity, or to create a custom user interface, among just a few of the possibilities. Consult Chapter 9 for more on Java, ActiveX, and scripting.

About Webs & Web Servers

FrontPage lets you prototype your web pages and web sites on your local machine. To do this, you need to be running a FrontPage-enabled web server. The server software is usually installed on your own computer, unless you're part of an authoring team for a larger company, which may maintain a separate machine running a local web server or intranet server.

The local web server stores your web pages on its hard drive, but you can't (or shouldn't) access the hard drive directly. Instead, the FrontPage Editor requests pages and submits changes to the FrontPage Explorer, which relays these actions to the web server. This means that the software works the same way when you are developing your webs locally or when you are directly maintaining a site on the Internet.

You create new web projects using the FrontPage Explorer. Each new project is stored as a FrontPage web, a collection of web pages and other content like graphics. There is also a special web location called the *root web*, which you can use for your primary (or only) web project, although it can be advantageous to use a separate web for each project you develop. Since I'll walk you through the creation or analysis of several sample webs in this book, you should always create (or import from the Companion CD-ROM, see Appendix A) each project as a new web.

The relationship between the root web and other webs (called *child webs*) has been the source of much frustration and head-scratching for FrontPage users. We'll examine this issue more closely in "FrontPage Explorer" later in this chapter.

In any case, you'll develop your web projects (webs) on your local computer and then publish them to an Internet Web Presence Provider (see Chapter 5) or on an intranet web server. (See Chapter 7 for details on intranet applications.)

The FrontPage installation diskettes or CD-ROM include two personal web servers: the FrontPage Personal Web Server, and the Microsoft Personal Web Server for Windows 95. The former is only intended as a trivial upgrade path for FrontPage users upgrading from an earlier version of FrontPage. The Microsoft PWS is much more powerful and suitable for both local web authoring and small-scale intranet publishing. It's also possible to connect the personal web server to the Internet, so that others on the Internet can browse the pages on your computer. This is a fine solution for trivial web applications, like transient "See? My web page is on the Internet!" home pages, but isn't a practical solution for true Internet publishing.

Microsoft Windows NT Workstation 4.0 is a near-ideal platform for both local web authoring and intranet publishing. It includes the NT Workstation version of Microsoft Internet Information Server, called Peer Web Services. NT Workstation is limited by the Microsoft license agreement to 10 simultaneous TCP/IP connections (yes, I know, it's ludicrous, but it's in the fine print), so it too is only suitable for workgroup intranet publishing or as a temporary Internet web server. The Microsoft Personal Web Server for Windows 95 will not run on Windows NT, and that's no problem, since Peer Web Services is an even better choice.

The Internet Information Server in Windows NT Server 4.0 is a true industrial-scale web server. If the machine running NT Server is connected to the Internet with a high-speed, dedicated connection and with an assigned domain name, such as www.yourcompany.com, IIS fits the bill for any level of web publishing.

All these servers support the FrontPage server extensions, special software modules that let the FrontPage Explorer communicate directly with the web server using the HTTP protocol. The server extensions also support ready-to-use program modules called *WebBots* that can automate many common web site tasks and include the ability to collect data from web-based electronic forms and store it as a page on the web site.

You will most likely choose a third-party company to host your web sites. These companies may be running any one of a number of web server solutions, but as long as they have installed the FrontPage server extensions, you can publish your web with just one menu command and work with your site remotely as if the web site were located on your local computer.

See Chapter 5 for more information on publishing to a third-party Internet web server or Chapter 6 for more details on setting up, configuring, and optimizing the local web server.

What About HTML?

The most obvious and visible components of a web site are the text, graphics, and tables you see on your screen. These elements are formatted with the HyperText Markup Language, a standard for specifying the attributes of text, such as boldface, italic, font type, and relative font size. These codes are interpreted by the web browser to assemble the page layout; you normally never see the raw HTML source code. (Most browsers have a way to view the HTML for the current page, however.)

With FrontPage, you never need to view or modify HTML; just type on the screen like using a word processor. FrontPage does the dirty work behind the scenes. Nevertheless, an explanation of HTML is necessary to truly understand and appreciate FrontPage.

HTML: The Language of the Web

In effect, HTML is the lingua franca of the World Wide Web. It's not really a programming language like Visual Basic or C++, but a simplistic typesetting specification. HTML is derived from the much more complex Standardized General Markup Language (SGML), a relatively obscure document-formatting specification that was used before its progeny HTML took center stage on the Internet.

HTML tags are used to turn on or off formatting commands. For example, consider the following sentence: The *quick brown fox* jumped over the **lazy dogs**. This would be formatted in HTML as:

```
The <I>quick brown fox</I> jumped over the <B>lazy dogs</B>.
```

That certainly looks easy enough, and many web authors cut their teeth by typing HTML tags into a text editor; it can even be an enjoyable pastime to build pages with raw HTML codes. In fact, to help you understand the basis for FrontPage, let's design a simple HTML document using the Windows Notepad text editor.

A Simple HTML Page

HTML files are plain text files. The formatting is not applied with a tool like a word processor, but by adding HTML tags in angled brackets (also known as the less-than and greater-than symbols). Consider the web page shown in Figure 1-2. Here's how you build the page:

1. Start Windows Notepad from Start | Programs | Accessories.

2. Type the following text into Notepad:

   ```
   <html>

   <head>
   <title>Greetings Page</title>
   </head>

   <body>

   <h1>Greetings Lifeform!</h1>

   <p>This is a simple web page that demonstrates how HTML
   works.</p>
   ```

```
<h2>Click on a link below:</h2>

<ul>
    <li>Visit the author's site at <a
        href="http://
www.websfrontpage.com">www.websfrontpage.com</a></li>
    <li>Visit the <a href="www.microsoft.com">Microsoft</a> web
        site</li>
    <li>View <a href="morelinks.htm">more links</a></li>
</ul>
</body>
</html>
```

3. Save the page as Greetings.htm in the Windows Desktop folder. (It will appear as an icon on your desktop.)
4. To view the page with your web browser, double-click the Greetings icon on the desktop.

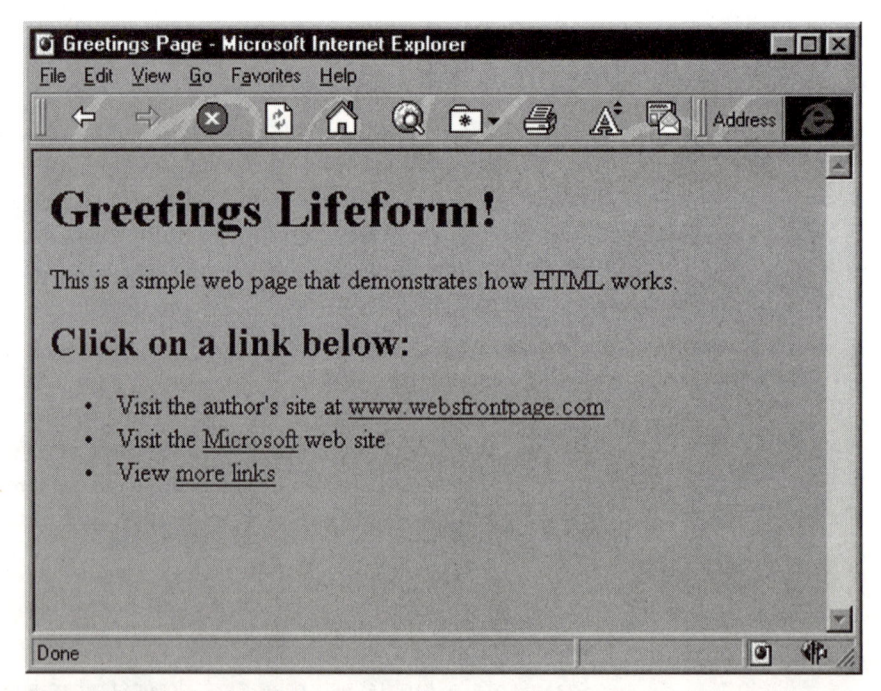

Figure 1-2: This simple web page requires 15 lines of HTML code or a few second's worth of typing using the FrontPage Editor.

Dissecting the Greetings Page

Every HTML page has a few tags in common. The page must begin with the <html> tag to indicate that the document is coded using the HTML specification. The HTTP transport can send other types of files besides HTML, and basically, this tag tells the web browser to interpret the file as a web page. The last line is </html>, read "end HTML." So the page is bracketed by the <html> and </html> tags. Many HTML tags are used in pairs like this.

You next encounter the <head> and </head> tags, which bracket the <title> and </title> tags. The <title> tags, in turn, surround the text that is the title of the web page. This is the "name" of the page displayed in the title bar of the web browser. It has no relation to the filename of the page, which can be renamed without affecting the content of the page. After the header comes the body of the HTML page. The <body> and </body> tags encapsulate the visible content of the page. The <body> tag comes after the </head> and the </body> tag always appears prior to the </html> tag. So you have this kind of structure:

```
HTML
     HEAD/ENDHEAD
     BODY
         PAGE CONTENT
ENDBODY
ENDHTML
```

Formatting Tags

The first true formatting tag you encounter in the sample HTML is the <h1> tag. Anything after an <h1> tag and prior to the </h1> tag is interpreted by the web browser as a Heading 1 section. Most web browsers display a level 1 heading in bold using a large font size (several points larger than the body text). You can't choose the exact size with standard HTML; the range of font sizes is a user preference, and depends on the display capabilities of the computer hosting the browser. The default proportional font for most web browsers is Times Roman, a serif font, and there is no way to specify the exact font name with standard HTML.

> **Font Specs**
>
> A *proportional font*, like the text you're reading now, varies the spacing between characters so that a *W* occupies more space on a line than an *I* does. This is more visually pleasing that a nonproportional font, like the font used for the HTML text shown earlier. The only advantage of a nonproportional font is that you can line up text tables by using spaces; numbers in columns also line up neatly, since every character occupies a standard width that is equivalent to the width of the letter *M*. This type of font is available by using the <pre> and </pre> tags, which are equivalent to the Formatted paragraph style in the FrontPage Editor.
>
> The proportional font in most web browsers defaults to some variation of Times Roman (such as Times New Roman), and the nonproportional, or *fixed* font defaults to Courier (or Courier New). Many browsers allow the user to specify these fonts as a user preference, so you have no guarantee that the typeface will be sans serif (without embellishments on the letter edges like the bars on the edges of the letter *T*) or serif.
>
> Both Microsoft and Netscape have extended the basic HTML specification to allow a choice of fonts and sizes (even down to the exact point size). The FrontPage Editor gives you this ability with the Format|Font menu choice, but be careful. The fonts you have on your computer probably aren't available on every other computer on the Internet. Microsoft and Netscape have developed competing specifications to allow font distribution on the Internet, but if you want your pages to be truly portable, stick with the standard methods of formatting text, such as the drop-down menu on the FrontPage Editor's formatting toolbar, which lets you choose from the various paragraph styles.

Keep in mind that the default settings of various browsers, and the preferences of individual users, will determine how the heading appears on the page. You have no control over this. You only know that a level 1 heading will be large and bold. This is not considered a deficiency by many Internet purists, since it ensures that web pages will be usable no matter what kind of computer, display mode, or desktop resolution is in effect.

After the heading text is the end heading tag, <h1>, and on the next line, a new tag, <p>, which indicates a standard paragraph. Anything between <p> and </p> is displayed using the default proportional font (usually Times Roman) at a "normal" size, with no boldface or italics. Again, the actual size of the text will vary depending on the browser and user preferences.

You next encounter the <h2> and </h2> (Heading 2) tags that display the instruction "Click on a link below" using the default proportional font in a smaller size than the level 1 heading. That's clear enough.

Bulleted Lists

The bulleted list deserves closer inspection.

```
<ul>
    <li>Visit the author's site at <a
        href="http://www.websfrontpage.com">www.websfrontpage.com
</a></li>
    <li>Visit the <a href="www.microsoft.com">Microsoft</a> web
        site</li>
    <li>View <a href="morelinks.htm">more links</a></li>
</ul>
```

TIP

Notice that two of the list items are broken into two lines. This doesn't faze the web browser, which ignores any manual paragraph formatting. It only starts a new line when it encounters a new paragraph tag or an HTML line break, <br>, which does not require a corresponding </br> tag.

The entire bulleted list section is enclosed in <ul> and </ul> tags. Each bulleted item (list item) is bracketed by <li> and </li> tags. Each of these bulleted items contains both ordinary text and a *hyperlink* that points to another location on the Internet.

Inside the Hyperlink

A *hyperlink* embeds the Internet address of a web page or web site on the current web page. It appears as blue and underlined by default (unless, again, the user has customized these settings). The Internet address is also known as a Uniform Resource Locator, or URL (pronounced earl).

A hyperlink URL can point to a single web page located within the same web as the current page (a relative URL) and takes the form of the name of that page, usually ending with the characters .HTM or .HTML. A URL can be a fully qualified domain name (FQDN) such as http://www.microsoft.com, in which case the web browser opens the default document from that location, index.htm or default.htm. An Internet URL can also point to other types of files, such as graphic images, sounds, or other types of Internet addresses, such as ftp://ftp.microsoft.com, which takes you to the Microsoft File Transfer Protocol server. I go into a deeper explanation of URLs in Chapter 2 in the section, "Links & URLs."

The links in the bulleted items in the preceding section are in the form <a href="destinationURL">link text</a>, where *destinationURL* is the Internet address that the browser will switch to when the link is clicked upon, and *link text* is what's shown on the screen as the blue underlined link.

Another variation lets you use icons or other graphics as hyperlink buttons. In this case, the link is in the form <a href="destinationURL"><img src="imageURLl"></a>, where *imageURL* points to the Internet location of a graphic file, such as images/redball.gif.

The Power of HTML

It's easy to get sucked into HTML coding, especially since it seems so easy and so effective. Indeed, the HTML specification is an extremely powerful way to format pages, embed hyperlinks and graphics, and much more. There are tags for six levels of headings and many common paragraph styles, including automatic numbered lists, glossary definitions, menu lists, directory lists, and addresses. There are additional tags for page background colors, page texture, and music. There are new tags for blinking text (abhorrent) and other special effects. Speaking of new tags, both Microsoft and Netscape continue to extend the abilities of HTML with new additions to the specification; some, such as Netscape frames or Microsoft cascading style sheets, are eventually accepted by the World Wide Web Consortium (W3C), while others remain as proprietary tags that only work with a particular browser.

Before you become too enamored of manual HTML (although I doubt too many readers will be seduced by Notepad when the FrontPage Editor is close at hand), consider this fragment of HTML required for a more sophisticated HTML page, shown in Figure 1-3:

```html
<h1 align="center"><font color="#0000A0">Lori Herron</font></h1>

<table border="2" cellpadding="2" cellspacing="1" width="620">
    <tr>
        <td valign="top" rowspan="5" width="130"><img
        src="images/lori.gif" width="128" height="185"></td>
        <th align="left" width="150">Title</th>
        <td width="340"><em>Marketing Specialist</em></td>
    </tr>
    <tr>
        <th align="left" width="150">Telephone</th>
        <td width="340">(910) 294-4440, extension 124</td>
    </tr>
    <tr>
        <th align="left" width="150">Years in Insurance</th>
        <td width="340">18</td>
    </tr>
    <tr>
        <th align="left" width="150">Responsibilities</th>
        <td width="340">Flexible benefits, marketing,
        communications</td>
    </tr>
    <tr>
        <th align="left" width="150">Email:</th>
        <td width="340"><a
href="mailto:LoriHerron@groupus.com">LoriHerron@groupus.com</a></td>
    </tr>
</table>
```

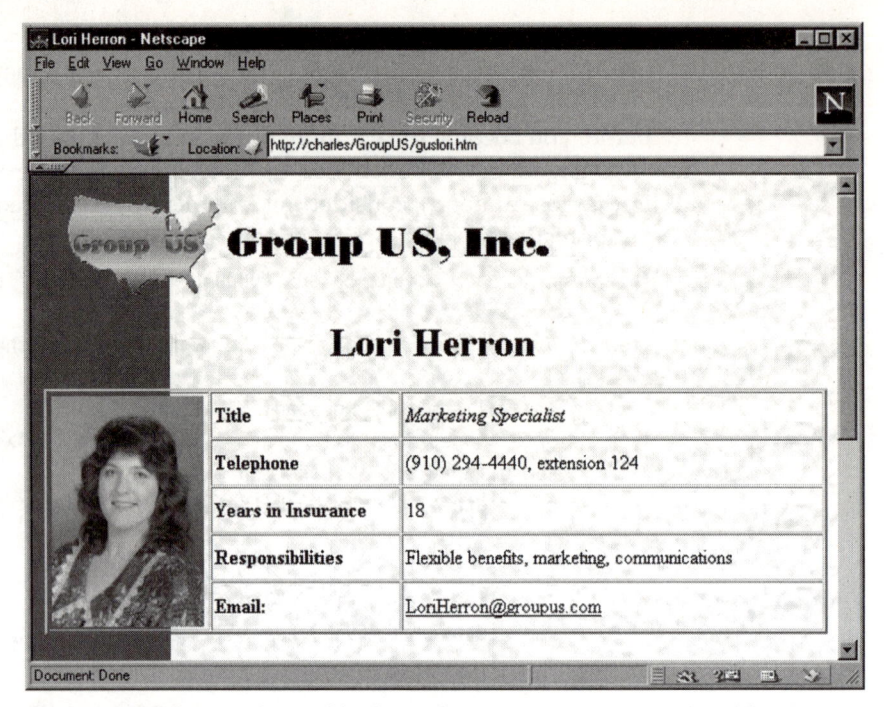

Figure 1-3: While a simple page like the one in Figure 1-2 is easy to write with raw HTML code, a page like this requires much patience and ingenuity to hand-code, or about a half hour of casual FrontPage editing.

Forget HTML!

The days when a web designer could rely on Notepad and HTML to design sites are numbered, if not long gone. Certainly an expert with HTML could reproduce anything you can do with FrontPage, but I'd love to see a contest, like the famous contests of the 1890s between a savant with an abacus and an engineer with a steam-driven calculator, that would prove who is going to get more work done in the least amount of time. Moreover, the time you save can be plowed back into more practical tasks such as building a useful site or improving the visual design with the FrontPage editor's desktop publishing style tools.

Something similar happened with other formatting languages. When Adobe introduced the Postscript page design language for typesetters and laser printers, there were technical types (geeks) that would show off their carefully crafted and very clever PostScript programs to produce beautiful designs and attractive layouts. Imagine the dismay on their faces when they saw the typical output of PageMaker documents designed by a graphic artist. The real merit is in the design work and the organization of the work; let the computers speak computer languages to one another.

As you'll see in the tutorials and examples in this book, FrontPage gives you the full power of HTML without writing a single line of HTML code. If you're still interested in programming, save your neurotransmitters for a more suitable challenge, such as adding scripts or Java to your pages. (If you can't wait, jump to Chapter 9.)

FrontPage Quick Tour

I'm not going to attempt to teach you all about FrontPage in a single chapter, nor am I going to try to replace the user's manual for FrontPage, which is readable and usable given its modest goals. You also have the FrontPage help at your disposal, although I'll admit it's pretty skimpy.

Instead, I want to show you what FrontPage can do so that when you're designing pages or working with the tutorials, you'll know ahead of time what's possible, to better inspire you to strive for excellence in your web design.

The FrontPage Editor

The FrontPage Editor, while incredibly easy to use, is no mere entry-level HTML tool; it fully supports virtually every HTML 3.2 specification, thanks to the graphical user interface that lets you drag and drop text and graphics, choose paragraph styles and text formatting with menus and toolbar buttons, format text and columnar information with tables, and insert form elements and database links. Even the complexities of frame-based navigation are made simple with the FrontPage Frames Wizard. (See Chapter 7 for a tutorial on adding frames-based navigation to your site.)

A Word Processor for Webs?

If you want to follow along with this discussion, double-click the FrontPage Explorer icon on your desktop, or choose it from the Start menu. Once running, choose Tools | FrontPage Editor to switch to the FrontPage Editor application. You can also simply refer to the figures to enjoy an executive overview of how the FrontPage Editor works.

> **TIP**
>
> *If you like to use the FrontPage Editor by itself (perhaps to edit simple pages), you can find a shortcut icon for it in the same folder where FrontPage is installed, such as C:\Program Files\Microsoft FrontPage 97\. Copy this shortcut and paste it onto your desktop for quick access in the future.*

Figure 1-4 shows the FrontPage Editor at work on the same page displayed in the browser in Figure 1-3. Basically, the FrontPage Editor is like a word processor for HTML documents. In fact, it has many of the same menu commands and toolbar items as Microsoft Word. To get started with your own documents, just start typing and then learn how to format your text.

The most obvious graphical user interface element is the toolbar at the top of the screen, which gives you one-click access to the most common menu commands and formatting features. Actually, there are several toolbars, and a few more are available as choices that you can enable on the View menu, including the Forms toolbar (which appears automatically if you insert any form fields) and the Image toolbar (which shows up automatically when you insert or select a graphic image). You can also display an advanced toolbar with buttons for inserting scripts, plug-ins, video, Java, and ActiveX Controls.

The standard toolbar (left to right at the top of the screen) includes buttons for New Page, Open, Save, Print, Preview in Browser, Spell Check, Cut, Copy, Paste, Undo, Redo, Show FrontPage Explorer, Show To Do List, Insert WebBot, Insert Table, Insert Image, Create or Edit Hyperlink, Back, Forward, Refresh, Stop, Show/Hide Marks, and Help.

You don't have to memorize the buttons; just let the mouse hover over any button (without clicking) and a tool tip appears with the name of the button. You can also access most of these functions from one of the FrontPage menus, which drop down from the menu bar just above the toolbar. And you can click the Help button at the far right of the toolbar; then use the Help pointer to click on any toolbar or to choose any menu command for quick help on any feature.

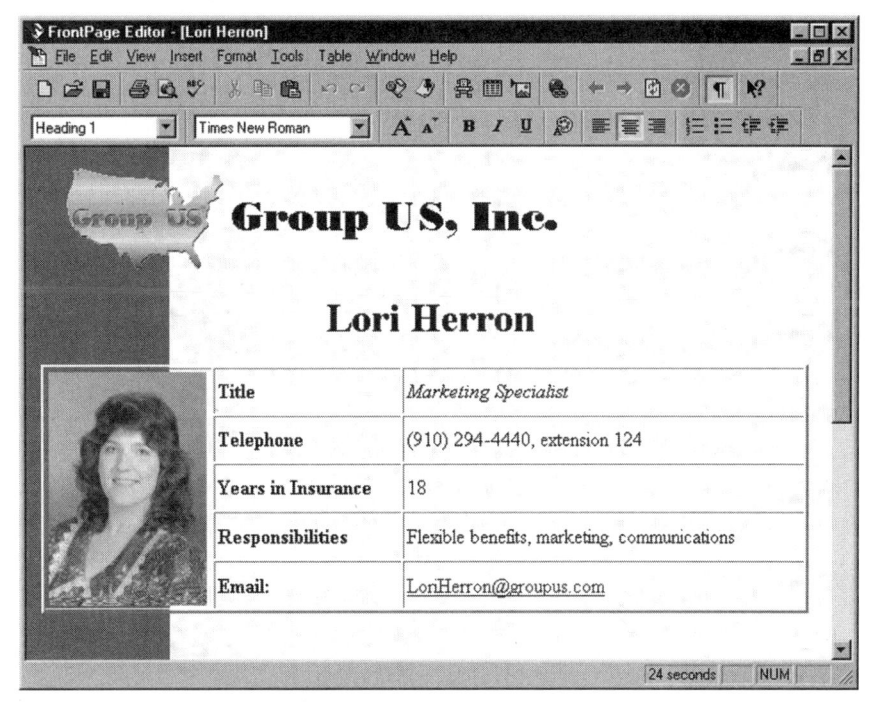

Figure 1-4: The FrontPage Editor works much like a powerful word processor with powerful web tools built in.

Many of these toolbar options are obvious, others are explained in the various chapters of this book where appropriate. You can also find a complete reference for all toolbars and menu commands in Chapter 10.

The formatting toolbar is where you'll click the most. First select some text that you want to format by dragging across it with the mouse. You can select an entire line by positioning the mouse pointer to the far left of the line and clicking or use other standard selection techniques (click and Shift+click or hold down the Shift key while pressing the arrow keys or other keys such as Home, End, Page Up, and Page Down). You can then click the B button for boldface or the I button for italics, or you can choose from the paragraph style or font drop-down menus. Let's take a closer look.

At the left of the formatting toolbar is a drop-down menu containing choices for the various ways you can format paragraphs. This is much like the Style menu in a word processor, with choices for Address, Bulleted List, Defined Term, Definition, Directory List, Formatted, Heading 1, Heading 2, Heading 3, Heading 4, Heading 5, Heading 6, Menu List, Normal, and (whew!) Numbered List.

Each of the choices corresponds to a standard HTML paragraph tag, of interest to those of you who are already familiar with HTML. For the rest of us, the best way to learn about them is to type some text and try each of the paragraph styles. Just position the text insertion point anywhere within a line of text and choose a style from the drop-down menu.

To the right of the paragraph style list is a drop-down menu with choices for the various fonts installed on your computer. Don't touch this list if you want to create pages that can be viewed on any web browser; the HTML extensions for font specifications aren't standard on all web browsers, and some listed fonts won't even exist on the end user's computer. The worst that can happen, though, is that either your preferred font will be ignored or the closest available font style is chosen. For example, if you choose Arial, a Macintosh web browser will probably display the text using Helvetica. On the other hand, if you're creating documents for an intranet, and you can make sure the fonts you prefer are installed on every computer (or if you restrict yourself to the common Windows fonts such as Arial, Times New Roman, Courier, and WingDings, along with the Internet Explorer fonts Comic Sans and Verdana), feel free to use these fonts for your text.

> **TIP**
>
> *For complete control over both font choices and HTML type styles, select some text and choose Font from the Format menu. The Special Styles tab lets you choose from text effects, including the infamous blinking text tag that will surely drive your visitors nuts after a few minutes.*

The buttons on the formatting toolbar are Increase Text Size, Decrease Text Size, Bold, Italic, Underline, Text Color, Align Left, Align Center, Align Right, Numbered List, Bulleted List, Decrease Indent, and Increase Indent.

Again, most of these options are either obvious or will be after you try them out. Even if you've never used a word processor (let alone a web page editor) before, you can't go wrong.

I'll discuss some other issues relating to paragraph styles and text formatting in "The Art of Webtop Publishing" later in this chapter.

Web Processing: Beyond Word Processing

Once you've gotten the knack of typing and formatting text (guaranteed to be HTML compatible, FrontPage won't let you go beyond the capabilities of HTML, as frustrating as this can be sometimes), you'll want to explore the features of the FrontPage Editor that make it a powerful web page editor.

The most important command is the Edit | Hyperlink menu option, which is shown as the Hyperlink symbol on the standard toolbar and has a keyboard shortcut of Ctrl+K. You'll use this feature whenever you want to create a link from one page to another. In general, try to keep your web pages short, so that the user doesn't have to scroll too much, and break up your information into numerous pages. Each page is usually saved to the same folder or web. To create a link, type some text explaining the link to the user, or select a part of a sentence or phrase that implies a link, such as "Try our online census form to request a quick quote." Then press Ctrl+K and choose the destination web page from the Edit Hyperlink dialog box, shown in Figure 1-5.

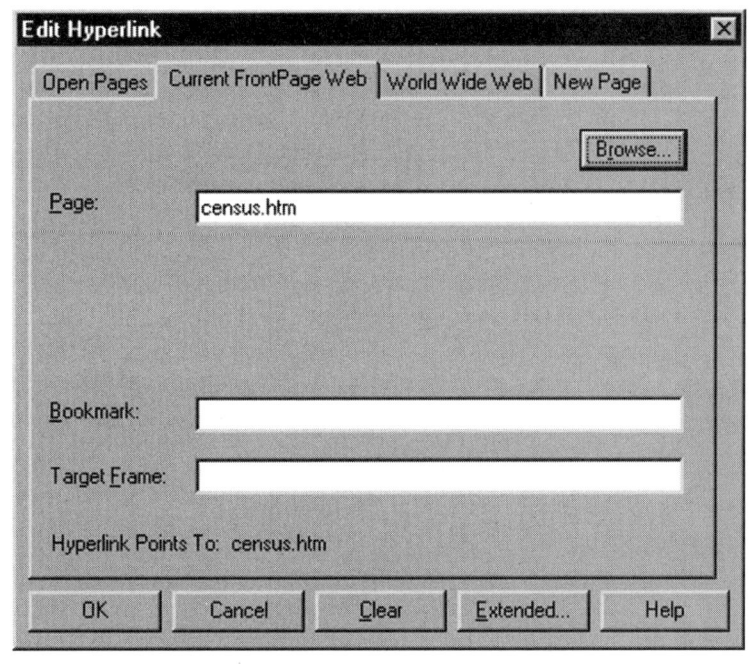

Figure 1-5: Type the name of a page or use Browse to find it in your current web. Ignore the options for Bookmark and Target Frame for now.

You can see the Current FrontPage Web tab heading in Figure 1-5. You can click the Browse button to choose a page from a list of the pages you've already developed. If the page you want to link to is already loaded by the FrontPage Editor, find it on the Open Pages tab. Use the World Wide Web tab to link to a location on the Internet, or use the New Page tab if you want to create a link to a page that doesn't exist yet. These options are more thoroughly explored in subsequent chapters.

FrontPage can also create hyperlinks automatically as you type. It recognizes common links (www.companyname.com, http://webname.net/page.htm) and other URLs (mail links such as the LoriHerron@groupus.com link shown in Figure 1-4). A Mailto link, when clicked on by your web visitor, opens the e-mail client on that person's computer; the e-mail address is already entered into the To (destination) box, ready to type a message. Mailto links are a great way to expand the presentation of your site to a two-way dialog between yourself and your visitors.

Note: The user's browser may or may not be configured for e-mail. The mailto link only tells the browser to open a new mail message with the TO box already filled in.

The Table | Insert Table command (and its counterpart, the Insert Table toolbar button) is the easiest way to create HTML tables, with or without gridlines. Without gridlines, a table is the best way to line up text in columns, since you can't use the Tab character or even multiple spaces with HTML. HTML tables greatly resemble tables in a word processor. With gridlines, a table is ready for formatting lists, charts, and columnar data such as spreadsheets. (You can even insert Excel spreadsheets with Cut and Paste or the Insert | File command, and FrontPage will convert it to a table, with varying degrees of success. The reverse method is to save a range of cells or a spreadsheet as HTML from Excel 97, and paste the generated HTML into your page.)

Use the Insert Image button to choose a graphic from the FrontPage clip-art library or from a directory on your hard drive or a CD-ROM clip-art collection. FrontPage understands most types of graphics and will automatically convert them to one of two standard web graphics formats: GIF (for images with less than 256 colors) or JPEG (for images with more than 256 colors, such as color photos). FrontPage temporarily stores the converted graphic with your page, but when you save the page, you're prompted to save the graphic to your web.

FrontPage Explorer

You develop individual web pages with the FrontPage Editor, but the collection of web pages and attached graphics, multimedia objects, and WebBot components together make up something called a FrontPage web. In effect, a FrontPage web is equivalent to a web site, although in truth you can develop more than one project for a particular site. For example, a site might have one area for shopping, one area for database searches, and another area for customer home pages. Although they all could be stored together in one huge root web or organized in folders, it's more practical to keep these projects separate from one another.

Again, if you want to follow along in this discussion, double-click the FrontPage icon on your desktop, or choose Start | Programs | Microsoft FrontPage.

Webs, Subwebs & Cobwebs

Each web (project) is stored in its own folder, or subweb. There is also a special folder called the root web that is the master container for all the subwebs (also called child webs) that you may choose to create.

You can ignore subwebs and create all your content in the root web, but this limits you to designing only one project and makes it difficult to keep the content for various projects or versions of a web separated. Instead, you should always start any new web project as a new FrontPage web. When you publish a web (a project created as a subweb) to the Internet, you can at that time put it in the root web of the Internet web server, or better, upload it as a subweb so that you can use the same site for more than one project. The root web need only contain a single master home page with links to the pages stored in subwebs.

To help you better understand the relationship between the root web and subwebs, consider Figure 1-6. The root web and every child web are isolated entities, and in normal circumstances, none of them can "see" each other in FrontPage Explorer, although you can still create links between the subwebs if you like, as long as you know the appropriate path. (For example, a link from the root web to a child web might be in the form of /gusweb/home.htm, and a link from that page back to the root web's home page would be /index.htm.) These issues are explored more deeply in other chapters in this book, particularly in Chapter 5 and Chapter 6.

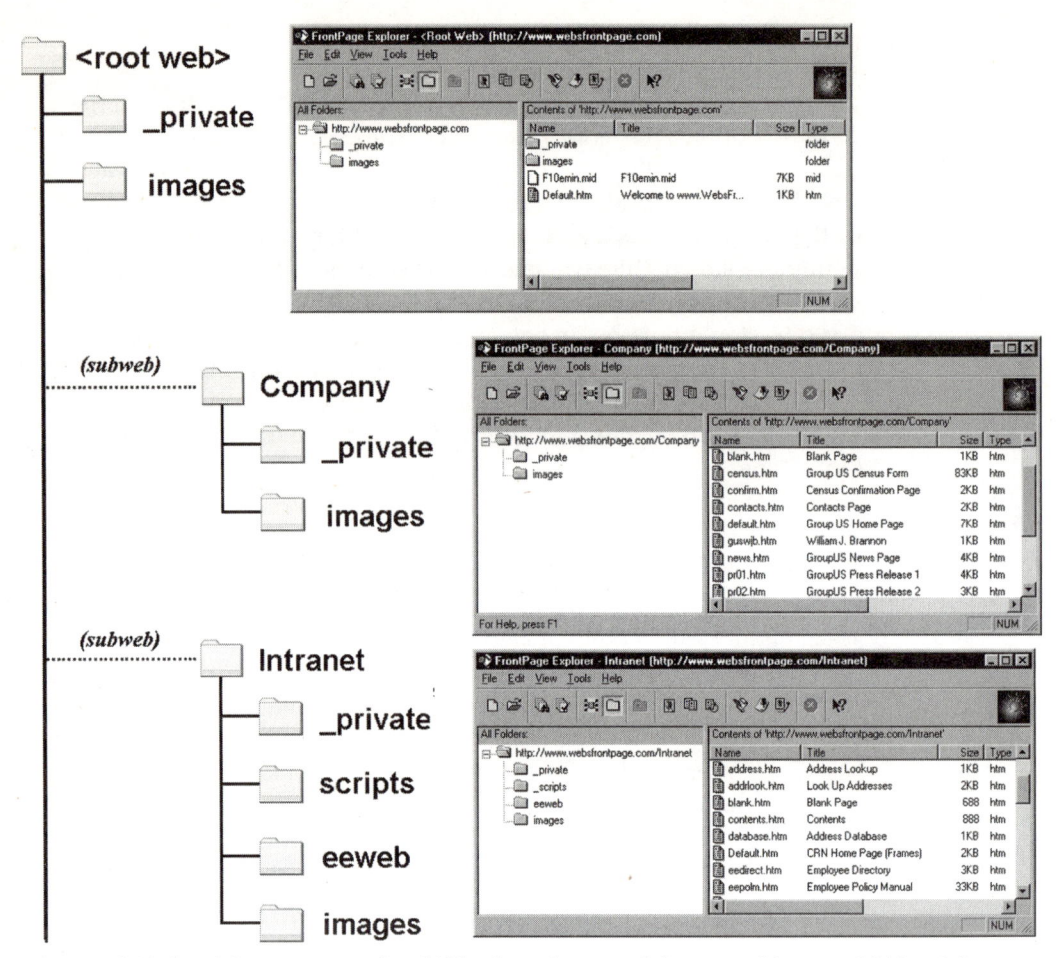

Figure 1-6: Each web is a separate project, hidden from the root web but accessible as a subfolder of the root web from a web browser.

The only other special relationship between the root web and the child webs comes up when you are publishing to an Internet web server. By publishing the root web and including all child webs, you are uploading in one fell swoop the FrontPage content for all the projects you've developed. Otherwise, you are free to publish any child web individually and store it as either a child web or as the root web on the Internet web server.

On the Internet web server, the only distinction between the root web and a child web is that the root web can be located via an Internet location such as http://www.websfrontpage.com, whereas a child web must be specified by its subfolder name, as in http://www.websfrontpage.com/book.

Also consider that any web, whether it's the root web or a child web, can have its own subfolders. It's common to keep related content together in folders. The main web can store the HTML pages, graphics can go into the images folder, hidden content in a folder called _private, server scripts in a scripts folder, and so forth. Although these are subfolders, they are not considered subwebs or child webs, even if they are subfolders of the root web. The distinction is that a subweb is not visible to the folder "above" it in the hierarchy of folders, at least from FrontPage Explorer, whereas a subfolder is an integral part of a web.

However, although you can create subfolders for a web to store related content, you can't create a web that is a child web of an existing web. (Only the root web can, in effect, host child webs.) If you choose to create a new web and add it to the current web, the new web may overwrite existing files within your web, but it won't be created as a third-level subweb. That would only confuse things even more.

Tip

If you insist on developing subprojects within projects, just put the subproject in its own subfolder in the web currently opened by FrontPage Explorer. It won't be a true subweb, and neither will any projects you put in subfolders of the root web.

Don't be dismayed if all this just doesn't click yet. All this talk about webs and subwebs may make you feel like you've got cobwebs between your ears. This is one of those things that can only be mastered with experience and long musing—it took me several weeks to get it clear in my mind, I'm afraid to admit. You don't really have to get a handle on this root web/subweb nonsense to use FrontPage. Just follow a simple rule: Keep every project in its own web. Don't use the root web for any content unless the site or web server will only be used for one project. Instead, keep only a master home page in the root web, with links to home pages in each web.

FrontPage Explorer Toolbar

See Chapter 10 for a complete reference to FrontPage Explorer. Here, let's do a low flyby and check out the scenery.

The FrontPage Explorer (shown in several figures in this section, including Figure 1-7) includes the following toolbar commands, from left to right: New Web, Open, Cross File Find, Cross File Spelling, Hyperlink View, Folder View, Up One Level, Hyperlinks to Images, Repeated Hyperlinks, Hyperlinks Inside Pages, Show FrontPage Editor, Show To Do List, Show Image Editor, Stop (pending action), and Help.

Again, you don't have to memorize these tools; just let the mouse hover over any button (without clicking) and a tool tip appears with the name of the button. You can also access most of these functions from one of the FrontPage menus, which drop down from the menu bar just above the toolbar. And you can click the Help button at the far right of the toolbar; then for quick help on any feature, use the Help pointer to click on any toolbar or use it to choose any menu command.

Link View

FrontPage Explorer makes it really easy to understand what you're doing and where you're going. It will only show you the content of the current web, whether it's a subweb or the root web, so you can focus on the project at hand.

You already saw how FrontPage Explorer lets you view the link relationships between the pages in your web in Figure 1-1, and I include another example as Figure 1-7.

There are a few variations of the Link view, which you can choose from the View menu or from the toolbar. Use View | Hyperlinks to Images if you want to add images to relationships shown in the Link view. If some pages contain more than one link to the same page and you want to see them all, turn on View | Repeated Hyperlinks. Otherwise, it's an unnecessary distraction.

Web pages can also include links to themselves; you bookmark some text and create a link to that bookmark. This is commonly used in a table of contents, product listing, glossary, or other reference material.

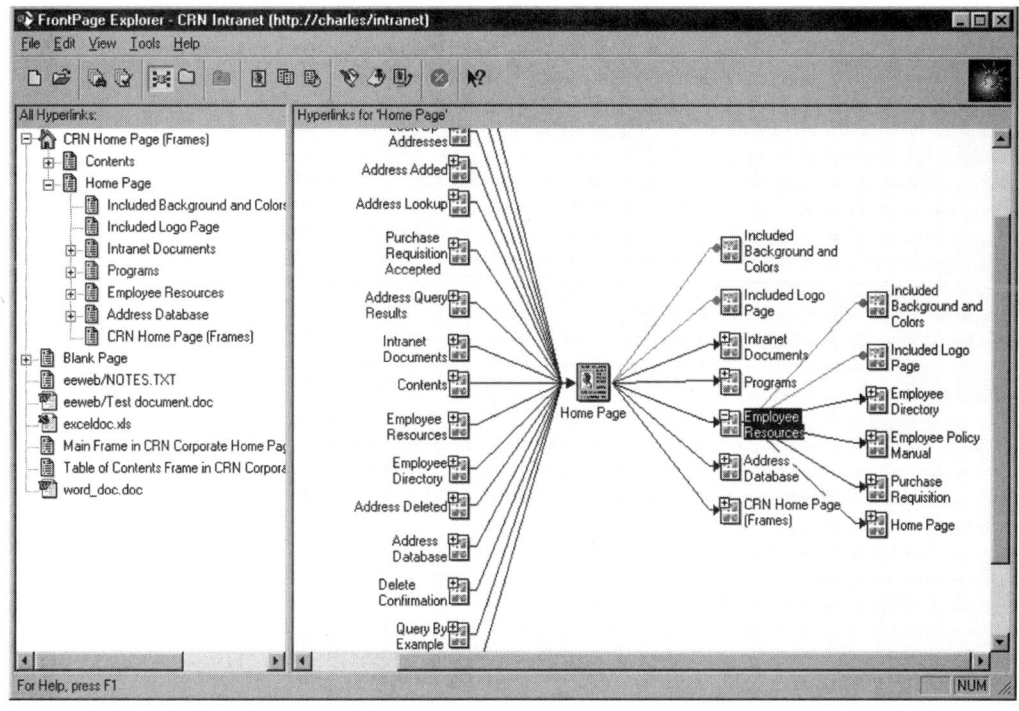

Figure 1-7: Link view is crucial for visualization and link troubleshooting, but it can drive you batty, too.

While in Link view, you can also avail yourself of the left-hand pane of FrontPage Explorer, which lists each page that links to other pages. To reveal these links, just double-click on one of the pages or click the plus symbol to the left of the page. When you click on a page in the left-hand pane, that page becomes the central page in the right-hand pane of FrontPage Explorer, so that you can visualize which pages link to it or which pages it links to. (From the Link view, you can also right-click on a page and choose Move to Center to accomplish the same thing.)

Folder View

Link view is fine for visualization, but it's too complicated for routine web management. If you're at all familiar with the Windows 95/NT4 user interface, you've probably gotten the hang of using Windows Explorer to navigate the folders on your hard drive or network. Folder view, new in FrontPage 97, gives you the same blessedly simple view of the files and folders on your web. See Figure 1-8 to see what I mean.

Web Publishing With FrontPage 97

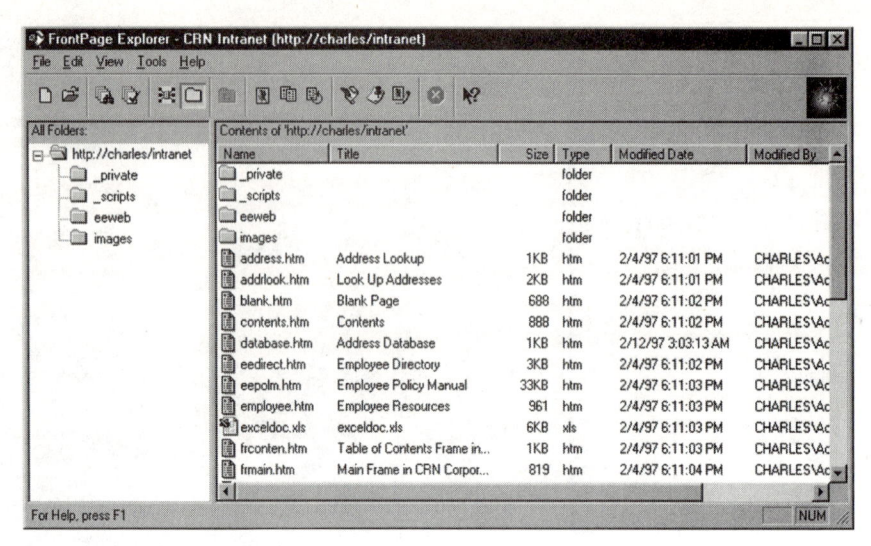

Figure 1-8: Folder view is the author's favorite way to manage a web, and it will be your best friend, too.

You can switch to Folder view by choosing View | Folder View, or by clicking the button on the toolbar. You get a traditional Explorer-style layout with folders on the left side and folders and files in the right-hand pane. If you already know how to use Windows Explorer, you pretty much know how to use Folder view.

You can double-click on any page shown in FrontPage Explorer to open it with the FrontPage Editor, or right-click on it to get other options, including Open, Open With, Cut, Copy, Rename, Delete, and Properties (you only get Open, Open With, Delete, and Properties in Link view).

You can drag and drop pages and files between folders, and if you want to copy files from a Windows Explorer window to your current web, just drag the files from Windows Explorer to a folder (or into the right-hand pane) of FrontPage Explorer, as long as it's in Folder view. This practically eliminates the need to use the File | Import command, which lets you set up a list of files and folders to import into the web, and after all the files and folders have been chosen, you can then import them all at once.

To make a copy of a page, just drag and drop it within the right-hand pane. If you want a shortcut to it on your desktop (ready to browse or edit with FrontPage Editor), drag it to the desktop.

Drag and drop goes one step further: You can drag a page from FrontPage Explorer into a page open within the FrontPage Editor, and a hyperlink is inserted to that page automatically.

Since FrontPage Explorer always creates links as relative URLs to locations within the same web, you don't have to worry about the network location of the various files unless you want to force a link to point to an absolute location on the World Wide Web or on a different web server.

Furthermore, if you use FrontPage Explorer to rename a page or move it to a subfolder, all pages that link to that page will be adjusted automatically. What a terrific feature! That one alone will save you hours of work trying to track down why certain links seem to fail.

Note: For the remainder of this book, I'm assuming that you are operating FrontPage Explorer in Folder view. While you're free at any time to switch to Link view to visualize how the pages interrelate, you'll need to switch to Folder view any time you are working through the tutorials or examining the example webs on the Companion CD-ROM.

Tools

Another FrontPage Explorer feature lets you verify all the links on your web, including links to pages in other webs or on the Internet. Use Tools | Verify Links. (Use this after deleting a page to detect if any pages were linked to it.)

You can use Tools | Search to locate pages by searching for some text you think may be found within them. Use search and replace (Tools | Replace) to globally alter some word or phrase in the selected web page or in all web pages. Run a spell check on the currently selected page or in all files in the current web with Tools | Spelling.

I describe how to use the To Do List (Tools | Show To Do List) in Chapter 2. This feature lets you keep track of work that you are planning to do but have postponed. It's the procrastinator's best friend since it helps you remember these pending tasks, and it lets you create or edit missing pages with just a double-click. You can use the To Do List to delegate and track tasks and pages if you're working as part of a team to develop a web site.

Templates

As if all this power and flexibility weren't enough, FrontPage also saves your valuable time with a collection of almost-ready-to-use web page templates. The templates are designed to cover the most common types of documents needed for web sites and intranet webs. Frankly, I won't discuss the templates much in this book since they are little more than boilerplate text, but it's good to know you have them at your fingertips. You can also use FrontPage Editor to create your own templates simply by choosing File | Save As and choosing the Save As Template option.

For a reference to the templates provided with FrontPage 97, consult your user's manual or look to Chapter 10 in this book.

Wizards

While the templates are pretty boring stuff, the wizards are a different matter. Several FrontPage Web wizards are at your beck and call to automate the creation of an entire web site or to quickly build a custom page. In Chapter 2, I'll show you how to start with the Corporate Presence Wizard to prototype a company home page (a common misnomer, actually a company site); then in Chapters 3 and 4, I'll show you how to completely customize and personalize the site with page textures, graphics, an animated toolbar, and custom web-based electronic forms.

Other web wizards available from the FrontPage Explorer File | New Web command include: Customer Support Web, Discussion Web Wizard, Personal Web, and Project Web. These wizards walk you step-by-step through the process, allowing you to make choices about how the web will develop and letting you enter specific information to tailor the site to your needs.

You can choose additional wizards from FrontPage Explorer, although they are usually specialized. Where necessary, I explain how to use some of these wizards, such as the Database Connector Wizard (Chapter 8).

Nevertheless, except for the Corporate Presence Wizard (Chapter 2), I've chosen not to focus on the wizards in this book, either. First of all, they are largely self-tutorial and obvious. Also, they are rather limited in terms of flexibility and layout. I would prefer to ration the words in this book to teach you the techniques you need to know to create your own web pages and sites from scratch. One of my favorite aphorisms goes something like this: "Give a man a fish and you feed him for a day. Teach a man to fish and you feed him for life." Ahem.

WebBots

WebBots are components of FrontPage that provide some of the "magic" in the product. Some WebBots are prosaic. One of them, called the Substitution 'bot, allows you to define a special word and store a piece of information associated with that word. For example, you can define CompanyTelephone as 910-555-1515. Wherever you want to place the telephone number in your pages, insert the Substitution WebBot for CompanyTelephone instead. That way, if the phone number ever changes, you can change the original text in the Substitution WebBot, and every page is automatically updated.

The Include WebBot works similarly. You can create a master page in FrontPage Editor with text or graphics and then include that page in other pages you design. For example, create a page with your company logo, and insert that page as an element on every page in your site with the Include WebBot. If you ever want to revise your logo or change its size or colors, change the master page, and every other page gets updated automatically.

Another simple WebBot inserts the date and time a page was last edited, a recommended addition to every page in your site to help yourself and visitors determine when information has been updated. There are also 'bots to provide site search services, 'bots to register users for access to a restricted web, 'bots that generate or update a table of contents, and specialized WebBots for forms processing and database access.

Nowhere in this book do I treat WebBots separately—there is not a WebBot chapter. Instead, several WebBots are introduced in the course of a tutorial or discussion. Other WebBots are so self-explanatory or easily generated by wizards or templates that I leave them as an exercise to the reader. Again, I would rather spend time teaching you custom techniques than rehashing the FrontPage manual or covering the same tired old ground that the other FrontPage books tread upon.

The Art of Webtop Publishing

Before moving on to the practical examples, techniques, and tutorials in this book, it's worthwhile to review a few aspects of webtop publishing as it relates to issues of style and standards. At all costs, try to bypass the excesses of the desktop publishing craze, where anyone with a computer and a laser printer could create the most garish documents, riddled with graphics and staggering under the weight of dozens of different typefaces.

The Seven Elements of a Web Page

When designing a web page, you only really need to focus on a few simple elements, each of which are readily accessible via the FrontPage Editor.

Headings

Generally avoid the Heading 1 style. It is the largest and most garish of the type treatments available in FrontPage. With some web browsers that are based on the original Mosaic, the level 1 head is outrageously large and uses up most of the width of the browser window.

Try to use the heading styles in a manner consistent with an outline and not just as a way to draw attention to your text. (If you want larger bold text, use the Increase Font Size and Bold buttons on the toolbar.) Nevertheless, you'll break this rule sometimes for the sake of convenience, as I do in several of the examples in this book.

If you have a Heading 2 section followed by a Heading 3 section, you should use at least two Heading 3 sections before adding another Heading 2 section. This balances the outline. Similarly, avoid numbered lists with only one numbered item in a section or odd mixtures of numbered and bulleted text. Many of the principles of desktop publishing and page design apply equally well to web page design.

Body Text & Text Formatting

Keep most of your text in the Normal paragraph style and in the default size. If the text looks too small to you and you try to enlarge it, it may look too large for your visitors. Many web browsers, including Internet Explorer, allow the user to choose from various font sizes, so you really don't have any control over this anyway.

Also try to stick with standard text formatting. Don't underline; underlined text is too easily mistaken for a hyperlink. Use italics sparingly as it can be hard to read on some monitors. Boldface also looks tacky if overused, and you should never use all caps letters unless you're trying to SHOUT AT THE READER.

You may be tempted to use boldface if the text doesn't show up well against the background color or background graphic (texture). A better solution is to use a different text color that shows up better or a different background color. You can use File | Page Properties from the FrontPage Editor to set these preferences, or you can override them for individual sections of text with the Text Color icon on the formatting toolbar.

Try to stick with black text on a light background as much as possible. This conforms with Windows and Macintosh graphical user interface standards, which are based on research that shows eye strain is lessened by this color combination, especially when the eye moves between the computer screen and printed material.

Please be sure your choice of colors contrasts well with the background color. Far too many sites are nearly impossible to read comfortably due to wild overuse and misuse of colored text that probably looked "cool" to the budding web artist who put the page together.

As far as colored text goes, avoid the colors of the default hyperlinks, which are blue for unvisited hyperlinks and purple for visited links. You should also have very good reason to change these default link colors (available via File | Page Properties), since most web visitors have come to expect some standards. Again, this is something you may have no control over anyway, as many web browsers (including Netscape Navigator) allow users to override your preferences with their preferences.

TIP

Don't forget that the most popular desktop resolution is still 640 X 480 pixels; design your pages to be completely visible and readable at this size unless you want to restrict your web site to viewers with more expensive computers (or visitors that have the basic computer knowledge to figure out how to increase their desktop resolution). FrontPage Explorer's File | Preview in Browser command lets you choose the browser size when previewing your pages. Also be sure to preview your pages in 16-color, 256-color, and TrueColor display modes.

True, the 16-color mode will always look horrible, but you would be dismayed to find out just how many people are stuck with it. Even if their computer can do better (many older laptops can't), the visitor may not know this or know how to change the desktop settings. Fortunately, Windows 95 sets the default desktop color depth to 256 colors for new users and for computers with Windows 95 preinstalled. Now if we could only get people to switch to 16-bit or 24-bit TrueColor, supported by most video cards, we could take advantage of this to design some really beautiful pages without distracting dithering. More on this issue in Chapter 2.

Rules

By rules I don't mean the persnickety guidelines I'm trying to suggest for you, but rather, horizontal lines. Rules are a good way to divide a page into logical regions. The FrontPage Editor Insert | Horizontal Line command inserts a simple one-pixel line, usually given a 3D appearance by modern web browsers. By double-clicking on the line, you can choose other appearances as well.

As with any design element, the effectiveness of horizontal rules diminishes with overuse. Again, it should have some meaning and not exist on your page just because it pleases your eye.

The horizontal rule was introduced in Netscape 2.0 and is not supported by earlier browsers, including the pure-text interface used by some terminals in university settings. You can always use a line of dashes, equal signs, or underlines to accomplish the same purpose.

Graphics

Graphics are what makes the World Wide Web appealing, but they have nothing to do with the real meat and potatoes of providing information—or do they? Keep in mind that many web visitors have the graphics display option disabled to speed up web browsing. Don't forget that there are millions of users still browsing with 14.4 kilobit per second modems, and no amount of wishful thinking on the part of overambitious graphic artists is going to change that overnight. Furthermore, by relying too much on graphics, you've excluded your site from the blind, who have text-to-speech translators to help them navigate a world otherwise off-limits to them.

Of course, a picture is worth a thousands words, but it's also worth a thousand bytes or more. There are some tricks you can do to minimize the time it takes to display graphics. The GIF format is the most efficient for simple drawings, icons, and logos, whereas JPEG is more efficient and visually pleasing for photographic and other continuous tone images, such as 3D computer graphics. You can also insert a tiny graphic and scale it up to a larger size by dragging its handles in FrontPage Editor or by right-clicking on it and setting a custom height and width property.

TIP

Because a browser keeps frequently accessed files on the hard disk in the browser cache, you can repeat the same graphic anywhere on a page or on a site without the penalty of reloading the graphic, as long as you always use the same URL (path and filename) for the graphic.

When you right-click on a graphic and choose Properties from the shortcut menu, you can use the Low-Res box to specify a low-resolution (small file size) version that displays while the larger graphic is loading, and you should always type a description of the graphic in the Alternate Representations text box. See Figure 1-9. The Alternate Representations text is the only thing that is visible if graphics are disabled in the browser. Also, Microsoft Internet Explorer pops up a tool tip showing this text when the user moves the mouse over the graphic, which is kind of cool.

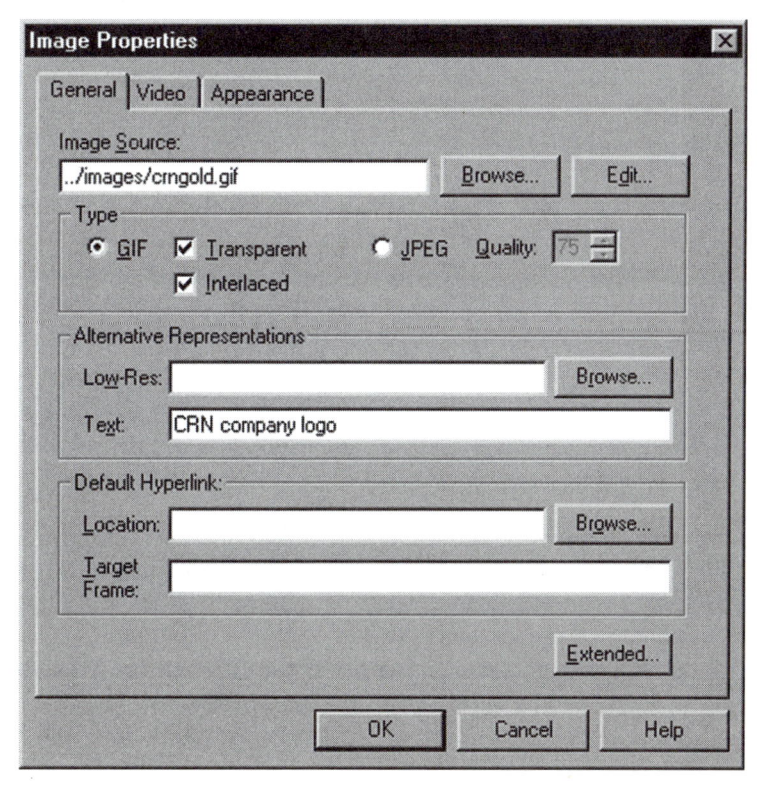

Figure 1-9: Be sure to fill out a description of your graphic in the Alternate Representations text box.

The type of GIF or JPEG you use for a page can make a psychological difference to the visitors to your page. An interleaved GIF displays in stages as it loads, filling in alternate rows with each pass. That way, a user can see what the graphic will look like in as little as one-fourth the time and have something to watch in the meantime. The new progressive JPEG version of the JPEG/JPG graphics standard does the same thing for TrueColor images, but is supported only by the newest web browsers.

Before we leave this subject, don't forget to consider copyright implications. Although the legal status of intellectual property has not yet been formalized for the Internet, by and large the same principles that apply in other media, such a print, radio, or television, should apply equally to an Internet site. That means using only graphics and other content that you have rights for, either because you are the artist or because you've received written permission, have a contractual right to use the material, or the image is clearly in the public domain.

TIP

Any work that is more than 50 years old is automatically in the public domain, as is any work whose copyright owner has failed to adequately enforce his copyright or trademark rights. That's why so many "big companies" will seek to prevent any misuse of their trademark or copyrights; they really have no choice if they want to protect their intellectual property.

This enforcement can take the form of a warning letter or a lawsuit, and the law is on the side of the copyright owner. All the copyright owner has to do is prove that the work is original and attributed to the owner; no formal copyright registration or even copyright notice is required. Civil liability (worldwide) for copyright infringement is up to $100,000 per violation— that's for every time any reader or visitor encounters the copyright image on your page, which can potentially run into a fine of millions of dollars. Better safe than very, very, sorry.

Don't make the mistake other web authors make by assuming that any image you find on other people's web pages if fair game. Over time, some of these images may end up in the public domain, but for now, avail yourself of the numerous clip-art collections, many of which are fully customizable using programs such as the CorelDraw! Graphics Suite. There are also dozens of Internet clip-art sites, which I've included in Appendix B.

Note: One particularly hazy area of copyright law is whether you can embed on your page a link to an image located on another web server. You aren't copying the image because it is not stored on your web server; you're merely including it on your page by way of reference. Copyright aside, the administrator of the "borrowed" web server may try to ban your server access to the resource because it increases web traffic on the server without providing any benefit to the operators of that server.

Links

I discussed links earlier in this chapter, but they are the most important element of a web page. Without links, you're not taking advantage of the hypertextual nature of the World Wide Web. You also need links as a way to break up your material into smaller, more easily digested chunks. Keep the home page or start page as simple as possible and add links to your real content. Carefully organizing your site is the key to successful webtop publishing.

Do some research to find out other sites with related information and provide inline links to this material, or create a link page or section of a page with useful links. Use text links whenever possible because if graphics are unsupported or disabled, the user won't be able to tell if a graphic even has a link. (Use the Alternate Representations property mentioned above if you would rather have graphical links, making it clear that the graphic does link to another location on the Internet.)

Note: Whenever you have links to outside sites, frequently use the FrontPage Explorer's Tools | Verify Hyperlinks command to make sure that none of them have become outdated. Few WWW experiences are more frustrating than clicking on an obsolete link and receiving an error message or other "page unavailable" message.

It's also preferable to use client-side image maps or navigation bars constructed as separate images aligned within a table than to use an image map that is decoded by the server. This allows the visitor to preview on the status bar where the image link will take her when she clicks on it instead of blindly ending up at some mysterious or forbidden site. (Client-side image maps and adding hot spot links to graphics are discussed in Chapter 3.)

Although links are crucial to good web site design, some of the worst web sites offer little more than someone's favorite links to other sites on the Internet. Always try to offer original content; otherwise, you need to question why you're publishing on the Internet in the first place. Link pages can be a useful reference, but since link pages often connect to other link pages, it can turn the Internet from a window onto the world into a house of mirrors. (Thanks to the InterNIC Newsletter for introducing me to that apt metaphor.)

Tables

Tables allow you to align text and graphics precisely on the screen, or at least ensure that they will end up in neat columns. You can use a table to offset a page from a border element (discussed in Chapter 3), or to format a multicolumn newsletter layout, or to align form elements neatly. Of course, tables are good for displaying tables, too, or any type of columnar information.

Tables have become so essential to the webmaster's bag of tricks that many designers have forgotten (or chosen to ignore) that millions of web browsers still don't support tables. This has an impact on hundreds of thousands of America Online users who haven't upgraded to the America Online 3.0 software, users of CompuServe's early Mosaic browser, visitors from educational institutions using outdated computers, and anyone who is too lazy to upgrade to a new browser.

Fortunately, you can probably ignore most of these people on the principle that if a web user hasn't upgraded, he is already missing out on a lot of good web content and is probably not an active web user anyway.

TIP

Of the most popular web browsing activities, over 7 percent of the time people are using their browser to upgrade to a new version. It generally takes less than 3 months for the majority of active users to upgrade to the latest version of a browser. This rapid turnover has helped Microsoft take away a huge slice of Netscape's browser business. Users of Microsoft Internet Explorer now account for over 20 percent of all active web users, partly because MSIE is either preinstalled or free, and partly because it's technically superior and easier to use than Netscape Navigator.

Forms & Controls

As discussed in Chapter 4, no web site is truly complete without some element of interactivity, a way for the visitor to give back to you rather than passively consuming the information you're shoveling out. Many web sites encourage participation via feature request forms, surveys, guest books, and other feedback forms. Even if you don't really need this feedback, it makes the visitors happy to be able to participate and keeps 'em coming back for more.

More practically, web forms permit you to implement web-based electronic forms. Almost any form you're now having filled out by hand can be put up on a web site and automated. This can save your company some serious dollars and cents and grow your business by taking advantage of the easy access the WWW gives to your customers and clients. Sites with online service and forms rank among the most popular of all types of company web sites. Few people are interested in merely browsing your corporate literature or sitting still for an extended advertisement. If you want people to visit your site, you need to provide a useful service or easy access to products.

Web forms contain the familiar graphical user interface elements known as *controls*: text boxes, multiline scrolling text boxes, radio buttons, check boxes, drop-down menus, lists, and push buttons. Anyone who knows how to use Windows or the Macintosh already knows how to use your forms.

Try to provide both a Submit button and a Reset button so that users can clear the form and start over if they make too many mistakes. While many webmasters suggest using the standard buttons, I would instead suggest you change the default caption for the buttons to make it clear what will happen when the button is pressed. Instead of a generic Submit button, you can have it read Send Quote Request Now or something similar. Reset is also confusing; Clear Form or Start Over is clearer to the user.

When possible, use validation rules to enforce correct data entry. You can require information entered into certain fields to be provided and/or formatted correctly. For example, you might require that a date be entered in mm-dd-yy format. This helps to avoid wasting the visitor's time by submitting an erroneous form with data that you can't use. Validation rules are a new feature of FrontPage 97 that you can attach to any form field. The rules are built from JavaScript or VBScript and automatically inserted into your page by the FrontPage Validation WebBot.

Chapter 4 includes a tutorial on designing a custom, complex form with validation rules, and Chapters 7 and 8 include information on building forms that store and retrieve information from a corporate database management system (DBMS). In Chapter 9, you'll learn how to script your own custom validation routines.

Other Page Elements

Okay, I lied; there are more than seven elements, but the first seven are the most important and the only elements necessary for most pages. You can also use Java applets, ActiveX controls, scripting, and multimedia files such as music, sound, and motion video to add pizzazz to your sites. Scripting, Java, and ActiveX are discussed in Chapter 9.

However, since multimedia is difficult to communicate in print, I've shied away from it in this book, but I think a few tips on taking advantage of Web-based multimedia will be useful to you.

Beware of Multimedia Content

Even a fast and costly ISDN connection tops out at 128,000 kilobits per second, roughly equivalent to the speed of an early 1X CD-ROM. In today's market, anything slower than a 4X CD-ROM is considered obsolete and unsuitable for multimedia. Yet most Internet users have less than one-fourth the speed of a 1X CD-ROM available for their Internet connection, and that assumes that the Internet itself can deliver at the top speed, something you'll only experience if you surf during the wee hours of the morning.

You can play back motion video in a window using formats such as Motion Picture Experts Group (MPEG), QuickTime, and Windows Audio Video Interleave (AVI) movies. The latest advance in "video in a window" is streaming movies that play back as they are downloaded, thanks to technologies such as VivoActive, Microsoft NetShow, and VideoLive.

Don't get too excited about Internet video, though. The state of the art is still limited to a "postage stamp" video window with halting, jerky playback and lots of noise. This won't improve for years as we wait for the Internet infrastructure to be improved and for end-user delivery technologies to increase the speed of the pipelines. (The new 56 kilobits per second modems, such as the USR X2 modem standard, and the K56Flex standard are a step in the right direction, but are not a phenomenal advance.)

Although the bandwidth (network capacity) of an intranet is near ideal for multimedia playback, too much of a good thing will drag down the speed of your local area network (LAN), which is probably already kept busy enough serving routine file requests. Like sugar or spice, multimedia should be used sparingly for added zest.

Background Sound & Music

One easy way to exploit multimedia is to insert a background sound into your pages. You can choose a Windows WAV file or MIDI music file as the background music for a page by choosing File | Page Properties from the FrontPage Editor and clicking the Browse button on the General tab. This method only works with Internet Explorer 3.0 (or higher) and possibly with the 4.0 or higher release of Netscape Navigator/Communicator (which was still in the early beta stage as this book went to print).

A shortcut to this method is to choose Background Sound from the Insert menu. Or put a link to a sound file format stored on your web (Windows .WAV, Macintosh AIFF, or UNIX AU or SND formats). When the user clicks the link, the helper application for playing sound takes over the job of audio playback. (There are many good commercial and shareware tools for processing and converting sounds between various formats. One of the best for Windows PCs is Cool Edit, found at http://www.syntrillium.com.)

A good way to save valuable download time is to compress the audio signal. You can save a WAV file using the Microsoft ADPCM format if you know it's going to be played back on a modern Windows PC, which usually has this audio codec (encoder/decoder) preinstalled.

An even better choice is the RealAudio format. You can download the free RealAudio encoder from http://www.realaudio.com and use it to convert an audio file you've recorded or sampled from another source (be sure the copyright allows you to use the sound on your page—if in doubt, get written permission). Put a link to the RAM file on your page, and voila, instant Internet radio.

Some FrontPage web servers also give you access to the RealAudio server, which lets you send the same audio file simultaneously to your visitors without opening a separate connection on the server for each file. The audio streamed by the RealAudio server plays back in real-time as the sound is retrieved instead of first requiring the sound to be downloaded. You may also have the ability to set up live audio feeds.

Inserting a Video Clip

Adding motion video to your site is as simple as inserting a graphic. Start with a new page in the FrontPage Editor, or open an existing page from your web. Choose Insert | Video, and choose a video file from your hard disk, a CD-ROM, or another location (even a location on the Internet). The video is inserted on your page and appears to be a graphic. You can click on the image and resize it by dragging the tiny black handles that appear at the corners of the image. Beware though; enlarging a small efficient video may make it play back less smoothly. But it's better to scale up a small-sized video than to try to use a larger video.

> **TIP**
>
> *When creating video for Internet playback, use the most efficient compression settings available to your target audience. Apple QuickTime movies can play back on both Windows PCs and the Macintosh, whereas the Microsoft AVI format is optimized only for Windows. (However, Microsoft's ActiveMovie support for Macintosh Internet Explorer 3.0 allows playback of all common media types.) If you can use MPEG-1 compression for your videos, you'll minimize the download time considerably, although you'll need access to MPEG compression hardware or a software MPEG encoder such as the Xing MPEG Encoder or Ulead's MPEG Encoder. Any computer running Internet Explorer 3.0 with ActiveMovie can play back MPEG video at full screen size if the computer uses a Pentium or PowerPC processor.*

As shown in Figure 1-10, you can change the settings for the video by right-clicking on its icon and choosing Image Properties from the pop-up menu. By default, a video will download and play back after the page is loaded, which can take a long time. Instead, you can choose to play the video only when the user moves the mouse over the video. More practically, enable the Show Controls in Browser check box so that the user can manually press the Play, Rewind, and Stop buttons to control playback. (The actual controls available will depend on the type of video playback software supported by the end user's web browser.)

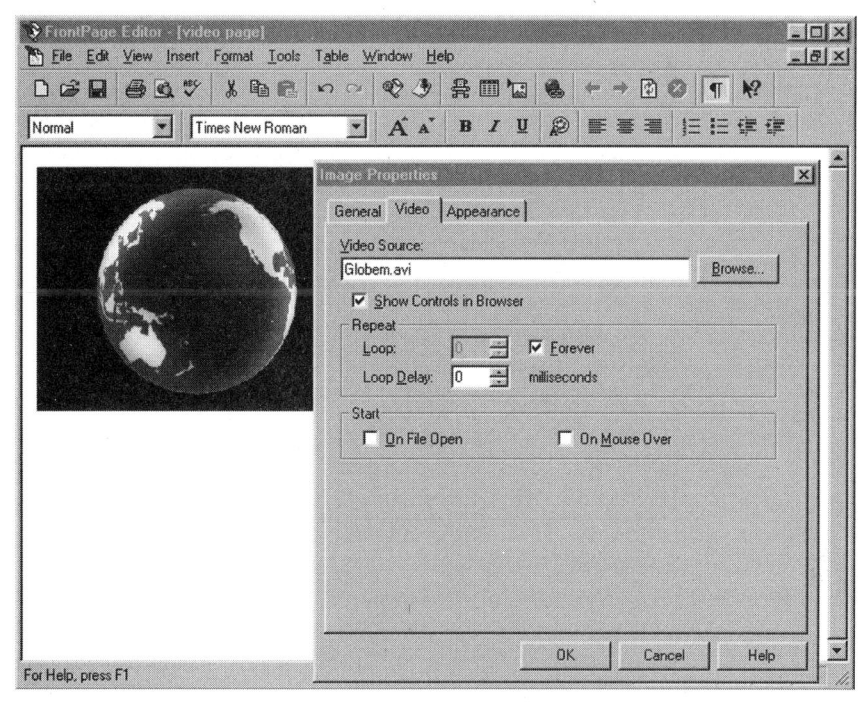

Figure 1-10: Video can be an expensive waste of a slow connection, but it's frighteningly cool.

If you choose one of the automatic playback options, your video will probably benefit from the Loop option, which lets you choose how many times to repeat the playback (or you can let it run indefinitely by clicking the Forever check box). You can enforce a delay between repetitions by entering a value into the Loop Delay text box, which is a duration expressed in thousands of a second (milliseconds). In other words, for a delay of a half-second, use a value of 500.

This type of embedded video is really intended only for tiny inline videos commonly used as an alternative to GIF animation (which is typically not as fluid as inline videos). Animated GIFs are more popular since they can be viewed with just about any web browser. I'll show you how to build animated GIFs in Chapter 3. Also look on the Companion CD-ROM for trial/shareware versions of two excellent GIF animation tools: GIF*GIF*GIF and VideoCraft GIF Animator.

For larger videos, it's best to simply create a hyperlink to the video stored in your web. That way, the video gets downloaded to the client's computer and played back using the video software already installed on that computer. This makes video playback optional, a vital consideration for many people who suffer with slow modems.

Inserting PowerPoint Animations

Microsoft PowerPoint, available separately or as part of Microsoft Office, is a fast and easy way to put together slide show presentations. The Internet Assistant for PowerPoint 7.0 (available for free download from http://www.microsoft.com/office) lets you convert a PowerPoint slide show into a series of linked standard HTML documents. (This feature is built into PowerPoint 8.0, part of Office 97, and you can also publish a PowerPoint presentation as a streaming video in the ActiveMovie Stream format so that the presentation plays back as it is downloaded.)

An even better way is to insert the original PowerPoint presentation as is. You can embed it either as an ActiveX Control (which only works so far on Internet Explorer 3.0 or later, but is promised for Netscape's 4.0 release of Communicator/Navigator) or as a Netscape plug-in that is also compatible with Internet Explorer. The ActiveX version includes a self-contained playback engine for PowerPoint. The plug-in version requires the installation on the client machine of the Microsoft PowerPoint plug-in for Netscape.

Inserting Netscape Plug-Ins

Other multimedia content, like Shockwave content, requires an authoring tool such as Macromedia Director and the insertion of a Netscape plug-in. A *plug-in* is a program that the web browser downloads and the user installs to extend the capabilities of a web browser. Most plug-ins were designed for Netscape Navigator, but now Internet Explorer 3.0 (or higher) can also take advantage of Netscape plug-ins.

You can insert a plug-in on your web page by choosing Insert | Other Component | Plug-In and filling out the Plug-In Properties dialog box, shown as Figure 1-11.

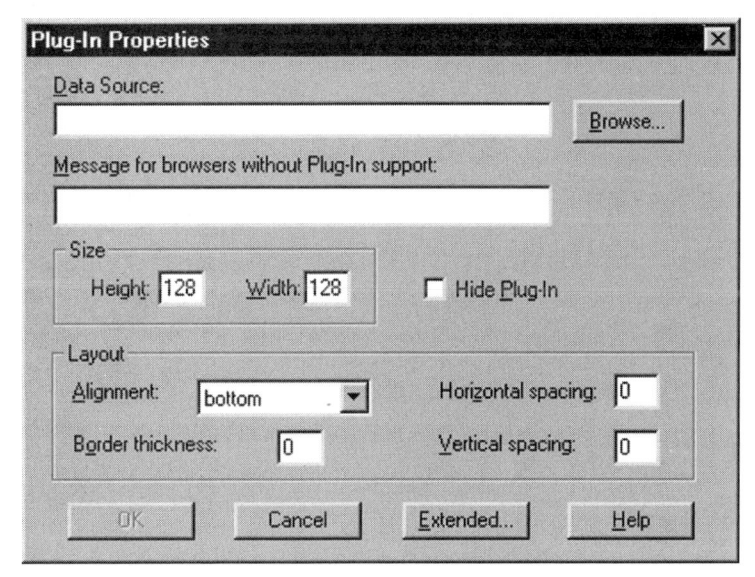

Figure 1-11: After choosing Insert | Other Component | Plug-In, you can set up the specifications for the plug-in using the convenient Plug-In Properties dialog box.

Most of the settings on the Plug-In Properties dialog box are provided to you by the developer of the plug-in. The dialog box simply helps you avoid inserting manual HTML code.

The Microsoft ActiveX Control is a vast improvement over Netscape plug-ins. For one thing, they install themselves automatically and transparently without requiring a restart of the browser. (This feature is promised for the new Netscape 4.0 plug-in specification.) See Chapter 9 for more about ActiveX Controls.

Inserting Special HTML Coding & Extended Tags

As I've emphasized in this chapter, HTML coding is a dying art, and FrontPage saves you from virtually ever needing to tinker with HTML. To accomplish this, the FrontPage Editor (in conjunction with the FrontPage Explorer, which manages authoring-time WebBots such as the Include WebBot) continuously analyzes the page you're editing and generates HTML automatically. Because FrontPage is always rewriting the HTML for the page, you may find it stubborn about the way it reworks any HTML you've manually edited (with View | HTML) or inserted using another tool. (You can edit a page with Notepad or another text editor by right-clicking on the page in FrontPage Explorer and choosing Open With from the pop-up menu.)

In fact, it's impossible to get away with some kinds of manual HTML edits or insertions. To overcome this "feature" of FrontPage, you can insert an HTML Markup WebBot with Insert | HTML Markup. This 'bot wraps itself around the HTML and hides it from the FrontPage Editor so that the HTML will be left alone. FrontPage can't check the contents of the Markup 'bot for validity, so be sure to test your insertions with several web browsers to make sure it works as you anticipated.

Even if you don't know much or care much about HTML (and who can blame you), there are times you'll want to cut and paste HTML from one site to another, as when configuring a Java applet or taking advantage of boilerplate HTML. First try inserting it using the HTML Editor (View | HTML) to see if FrontPage can understand the HTML and present it as part of the graphical user interface. If not, or if by using View | HTML you see that the coding has been altered, delete the bad code and recreate it as an HTML Markup WebBot.

While FrontPage supports most of the newest HTML 3.2 specifications, it may be ignorant of some special variations. These are usually specified by adding extended tags to the basic tag specification. That's why nearly every FrontPage dialog box includes an Extended button, so that you can add these tags if necessary.

Another tricky HTML technique is the use of the META tag, part of the <head></head> section at the top of an HTML file. FrontPage will always insist on adding META tags to specify that the content of the page is standard HTML that uses the International Standards Organization (ISO) character set. FrontPage also adds a <!doctype> tag to the beginning of the HTML document to make it clear which version of HTML should be used to interpret the document.

These extra tags aren't really necessary, but it is part of the HMTL specification for web pages. FrontPage also inserts a META tag of GENERATOR to indicate that the page was created with FrontPage 2.0 (the actual version number of FrontPage 97). If you try to delete these with the View | HTML editor, FrontPage simply adds them back in. You can edit the page with a text editor if you insist on removing or altering these elements, but if you ever edit the page with the FrontPage Editor, it will add them back. Before you get too frustrated, ask yourself if it really matters. After all, you aren't ashamed to let the world know you've used

FrontPage to design your web, are you? On the contrary, it shows that you've got better things to do with your time than tinker with HTML.

In Chapter 5, I show you how to add some other META tags that help your document get noticed by search engines. I also show you a cool trick that, after a delay, lets one page automatically open another page without the user having to click anywhere. This client-pull technology will be the basis for many new interesting web developments in the next few years, including live updated news, stock tickers, and favorites links right on your desktop.

Moving On

FrontPage is both a simple entry-level web editor and a sophisticated, feature-rich, professional-level tool. In this book I have strived to serve the needs of both entry-level and professional-level users by providing detailed tutorials and gradually working up to the more complex topics. This chapter alone has presented a lot of varied information, but in subsequent chapters, I'll focus on separate aspects of FrontPage. In Chapter 2, you'll learn how to get started by building a company home page with the Corporate Presence Wizard and going beyond the generic look of the wizard to customize the web for your needs. The company home page you'll create is based on an actual project that led to a commercial web site.

chapter 2

Your First FrontPage Project

Now that we've got our introduction to the features of FrontPage out of the way, it's time to get real. In this chapter, we'll design a web site for a company's home page, based on an actual commercial web site for Group US, Inc., a wholesale insurance services company.

As we've discussed in Chapter 1, the templates and wizards included with FrontPage make it easy to get a site up and running quickly. Although sites created from templates have a generic look, you can start with a web created from a template and then customize it as much as you like. This is the approach we'll take with our first FrontPage project as we design a company home page. (The term *home page* usually refers to a single HTML document that is the starting point for a WWW site, but many also use it to generically describe an entire site.)

Getting Started

Naturally, we'll start with the Corporate Presence Wizard. Whereas a template can only contain preformatted individual pages, a wizard is a computer program, launched from within the program you're working with, that designs a complete web. (As you know, a *web* is the FrontPage term that describes a site of linked pages on the World Wide Web or on a private intranet.) The Corporate Presence Wizard walks you through the creation of a web design to promote and advertise a company's products and services by letting you specify the company-specific information (such as company name, address, phone number, etc.) and make certain decisions (such as whether you want to include a What's New page).

To get started with our project, we'll create a new subweb using the Corporate Presence Wizard. As we've already mentioned in Chapter 1, it's easier to manage multiple web sites by creating a single root web that contains entry points to the home pages for each subweb. Each project in this book is designed as a subweb so that you can work on many FrontPage projects without worrying about overwriting one project with another. In practice, many readers will be responsible for the creation and/or maintenance of a single site, so the root web would be used to store the final version of the web when published to the production server. (See Chapter 6 for more on server issues.)

Note: To create a new web using the Corporate Presence Wizard, you must have already installed and started the Personal Web Server (if using Windows 95 or NT 4 Workstation) on your personal computer. As an alternative, you can create the new web by accessing a different computer running an HTTP server with FrontPage Server Extensions installed, such as Internet Information Server running on Windows NT Server, a third-party server such as Netscape Commerce Server, or a UNIX server provided for your use by a web hosting service. (Refer to Chapter 6 for more on server issues.)

Wizards at Work

If you want to follow along with the FrontPage software while reading this text, go ahead and start the FrontPage Explorer now. In the Getting Started With Microsoft FrontPage dialog box (see Figure 2-1), the first choice you are asked to make is whether to open the current web, open an existing web, or create a new web. (Notice the Show Getting Started Dialog check box at the bottom. If this box has been turned off, you won't get the dialog box shown in Figure 2-1 when you first start FrontPage Explorer. Instead, you'll have to choose New Web from the File menu to proceed.)

To begin developing the Corporate web project, choose New Web from the Getting Started dialog box.

Note: If you're trying out the steps in this chapter with the FrontPage software (as opposed to simply reading the text and examining the figures, which is equally valid), be sure you follow the instructions fairly literally. You may be tempted to vary from the steps shown to more closely match the kind of web you have in mind, but you can always create your own customized sites later. For now, it's important that what you see on your screen matches the figures in this book, and the only way to ensure this is if you follow the steps closely. Also, while you can click Finish at any time to force the wizard to make the rest of the decisions for you, don't do it until I tell you. I want you to be able to see all the pages of the wizard. Instead, click Next after filling out each page.

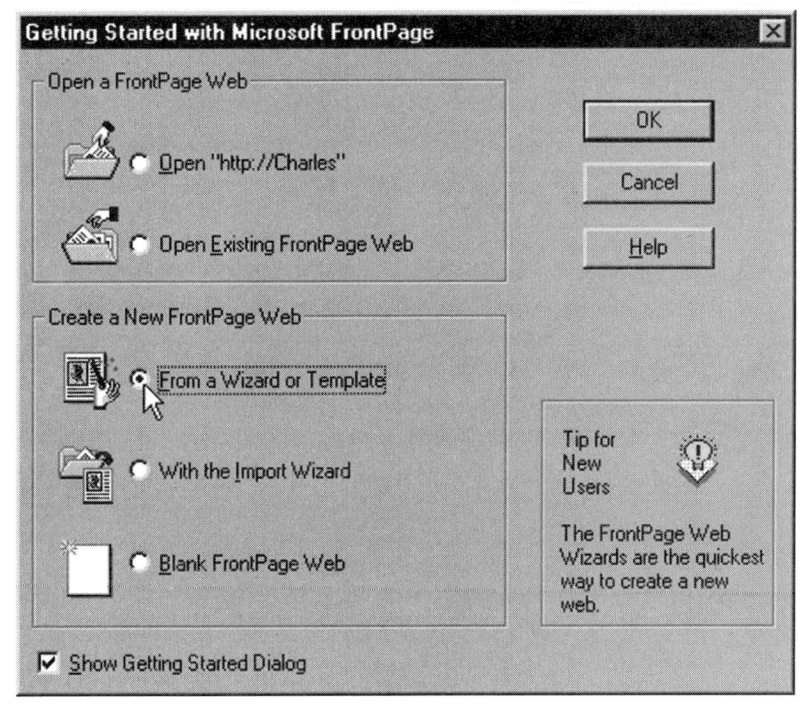

Figure 2-1: When you first start FrontPage, you can open a web or create a new one. To create a company home page using the Corporate Presence Wizard, choose the From a Wizard or Template option before clicking OK.

Choosing a Wizard or Template

After you choose to create a new web, you're asked to choose a template or wizard to use when creating the web, as shown in Figure 2-2.

In the New FrontPage Web dialog box, click on the Corporate Presence Wizard choice in the Template or Wizard list, and then click OK.

(When creating a new web from scratch, you can choose the Normal Web template, but for the sake of this discussion, we'll use the Corporate Presence Wizard to quickly prototype our first web project.)

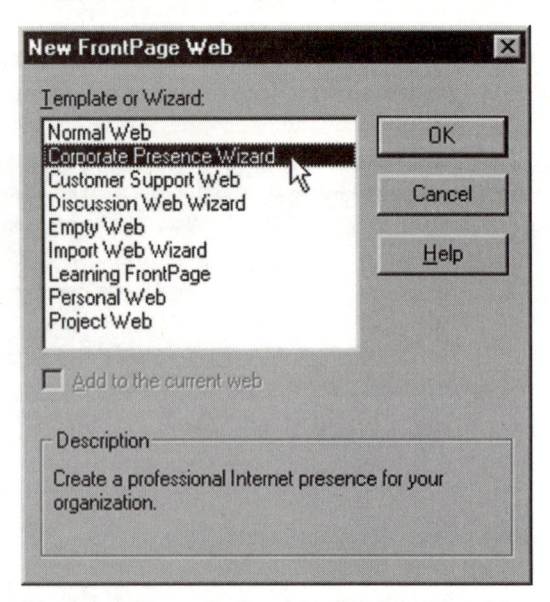

Figure 2-2: Choose the Corporate Presence Wizard from the New FrontPage Web dialog box.

Once you've chosen the Corporate Presence Wizard, the wizard starts running to collect information from you and allow you to make some decisions. We'll walk through this wizard step by step in the remainder of this section.

If you're following along with the FrontPage software, fill out each page of the wizard as shown in the figures in the rest of this section.

Choosing a Server & Naming the Web

Before you can create a new web (or even a single web page) with FrontPage, you have to choose a server to host the web. Thus, the first dialog box for the Corporate Presence Wizard prompts you to specify a server location for your new web (Figure 2-3). When prototyping your web, it's best to use a server that is local to your own computer for the sake of speed. If you are running Windows 95, I recommend installing the Microsoft Personal Web Server for Windows 95, which is included with FrontPage 97. (If you are using the FrontPage Personal Server that came with FrontPage 1.1, you can continue to use it with FrontPage 97, although you may want to upgrade it to the version that comes with FrontPage 97 to take advantage of the new server extensions and improved performance.)

If you're using Windows NT, you're probably running Internet Information Server on NT Server or the Peer Web Services that run with NT 4 Workstation. You can also use any WWW server that can run the FrontPage server extensions.

To find out how to set up and configure your personal server, consult Chapter 6 or your FrontPage user manual. In most cases, FrontPage 97 automatically configures the server when you install the software.

Figure 2-3: Enter the name of the web server (or accept the default name) and the name of the subweb you're creating.

In any case, for now you only need to know the name or IP address of the web server that is ready to host your pages. You'll enter this information into the text box labeled Web Server or File Location, as shown in Figure 2-3. (Click the down arrow next to this text box if you want to recall a name you've previously entered.)

If you're running the web server on the same machine as FrontPage, you can use the name http://localhost or simply localhost as the name of the server. (You can also use your computer's machine name as the server name, as in http://Charles.)

When accessing a server running on another computer, enter that computer's name (accessible via the World Wide Web or your local TCP/IP intranet) or IP address. For example, if you're storing your pages on a WWW server managed by a web hosting service, you would use the FTP or WWW location of that server, such as http://www.companyname.com. Or the server might only be known by its IP address, such as 192.168.0.5.

If your web server supports the Secure Sockets Layer interface, you can turn on the check box for Connect Using SSL. This will ensure that changes to your web are protected from unauthorized monitoring. If you're authoring pages hosted by your local computer, leave this check box alone (unchecked) for the sake of speed—security issues aren't very important at this stage of development.

To complete this page of the wizard, enter a name for the web into the text box labeled Name of New FrontPage Web. You should choose a name without spaces—this will become the name of a subfolder within the root web that will store your pages. If you leave this entry blank, the new web will be created in the root folder of the web server, which is fine if you only plan to develop a single web site on that server. Since we want to develop many sites in this book, I recommend using a subweb for each new web that you create. So for now, enter Company as the name of the web.

Pages & Topics to Include

After filling out the entries in the screen shown in Figure 2-3, click the Next button to proceed to the next page of the wizard, shown in Figure 2-4. Since this is simply an introductory page, click Next to move on to the next page.

On the third page of the wizard (Figure 2-5) you can choose which component pages to include in addition to the home page. In the figure, the check boxes for What's New and Products/Services are enabled; these are the choices you should click, as well. You may wish to use the Table of Contents, Feedback Form, and Search Form for your own project, but we've skipped these to make our examples more concise.

After checking What's New and Products/Services, click Next to move on to the next page of the wizard.

Chapter 2: Your First FrontPage Project   59

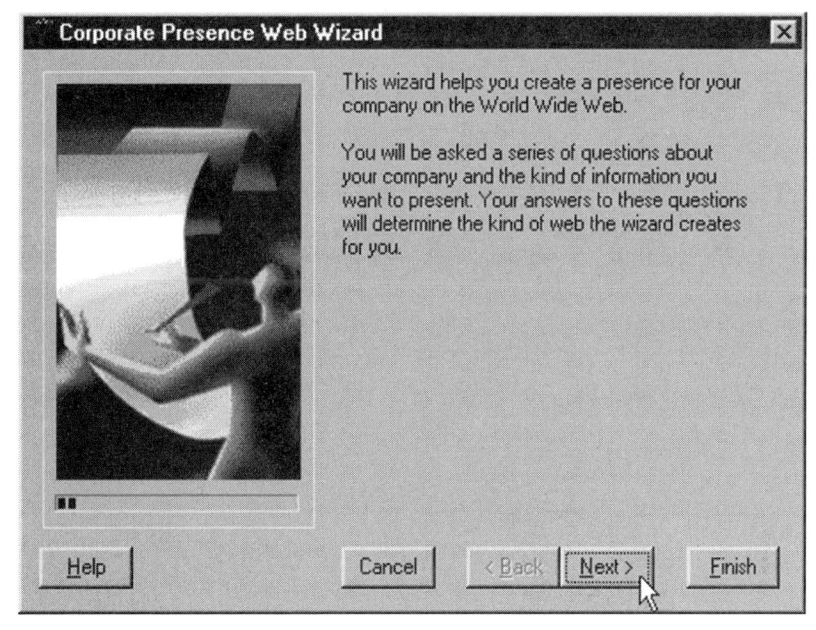

Figure 2-4: Just click Next to continue after you've read the introduction.

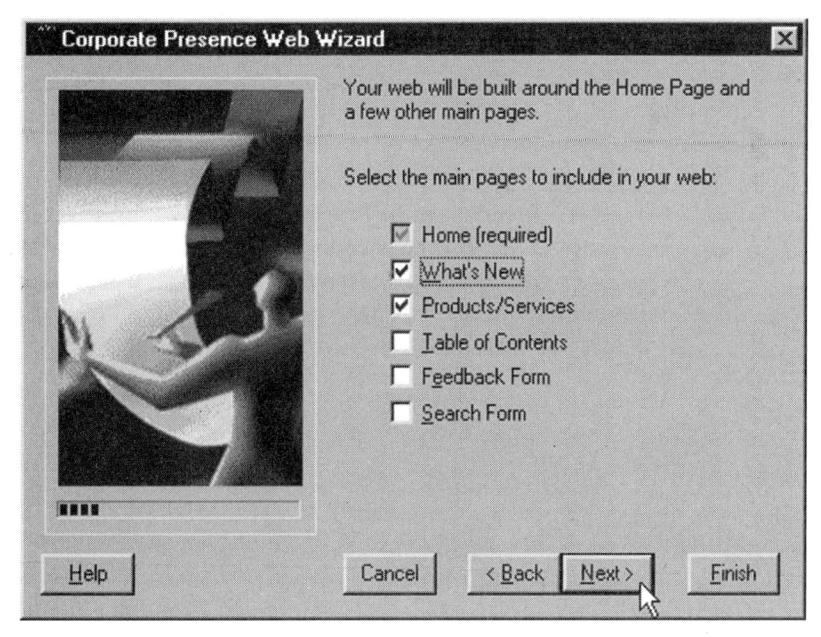

Figure 2-5: Check the What's New and Products/Services check boxes and clear the others; then click Next.

On the fourth page of the wizard (Figure 2-6), check the topics that you want to include on the home page, the entry point of your web. These topics become headings that you can use as guidelines when customizing your company home page.

Enable all four check boxes, and then click Next.

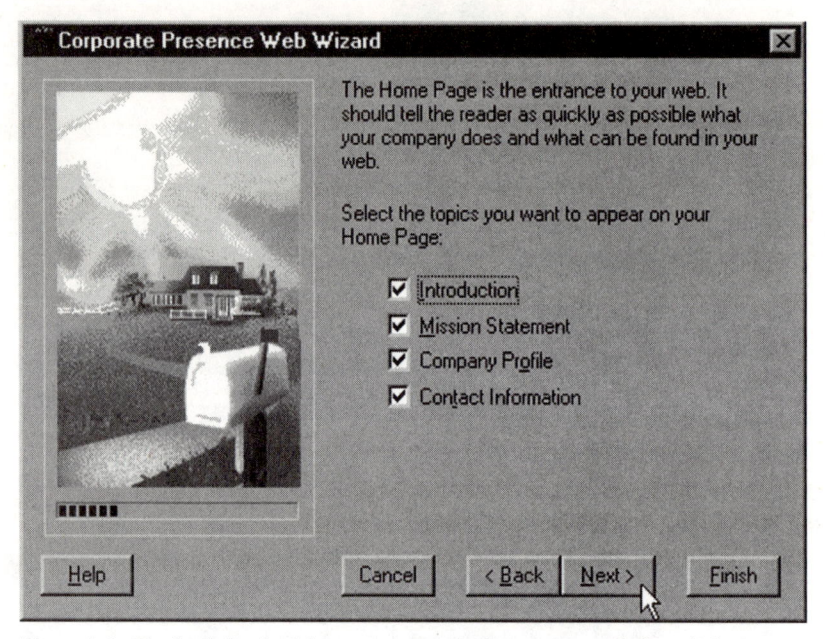

Figure 2-6: Check all the check boxes to set up the home page, and then click Next.

Figure 2-7 shows the fifth page of the wizard. As you did for the home page, check the topics that you want to include on the What's New page. These topics are used as headings that you can use as guidelines when customizing your What's New page.

Enable all three check boxes and click Next.

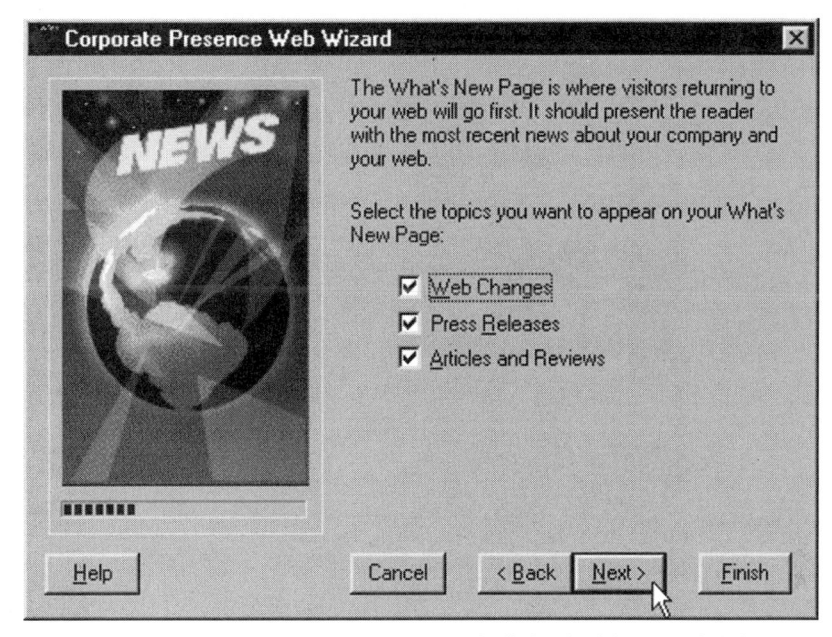

Figure 2-7: To set up the What's New page, check all the check boxes and click Next.

Since you chose to include Products/Services as part of the Company web, you're now asked to tell the wizard how many entries to create for products and services. If you choose 0 for either products or services, that part will be skipped.

The company this web was designed for chose to include only its services, so enter 0 products and 2 services as shown in Figure 2-8; then click Next.

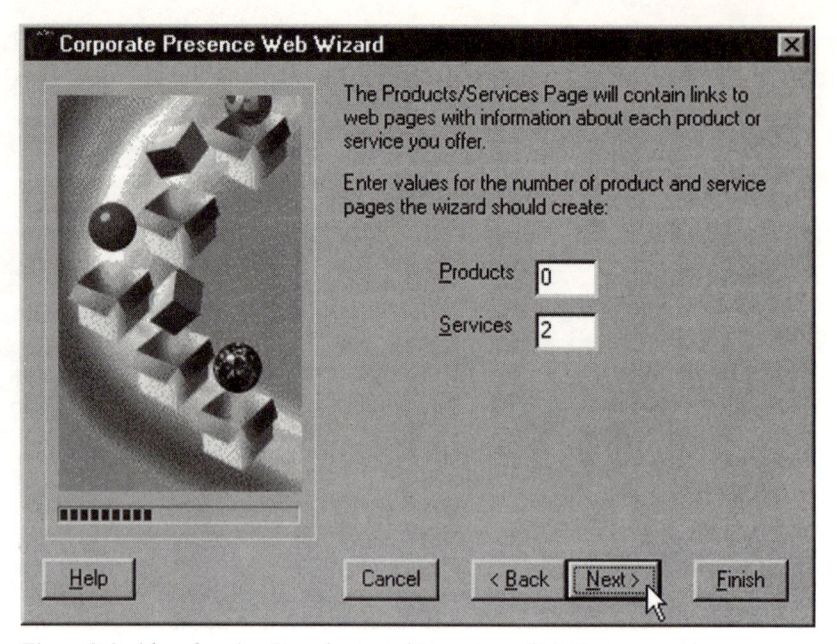

Figure 2-8: After choosing 0 products and 2 services, click Next.

The next wizard page (Figure 2-9), lets you further refine the look of the Products and Services pages. Since we chose 0 products earlier, the Product Image, Pricing Information, and Information Request options at the top of this page are disabled (grayed out).

We'll choose only the Information Request Form check box at the bottom of the page before clicking Next.

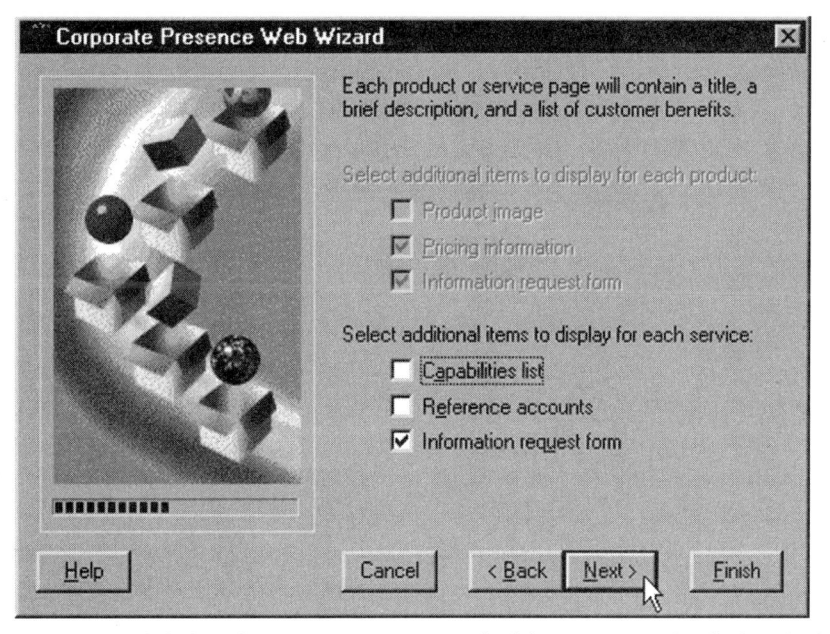

Figure 2-9: Click the Information Request Form check box to turn on the checkmark; then click Next.

Consistency Considerations

Now you get your first chance to customize the elements that make up your pages. All pages in a web should have a consistent design and consistent methods for moving between pages. For example, links to each web page can be made available from any other web page, and each page can contain a copyright notice.

The screen in Figure 2-10 appears after you select the Information Request Form page and click Next. Turn on all the check boxes under the heading "What should appear at the top of each page?" and all but the first under "What should appear at the bottom of each page?" (This avoids having the same links at the top and the bottom of the page, although this can be desirable if the page is lengthy.) Click Next to proceed.

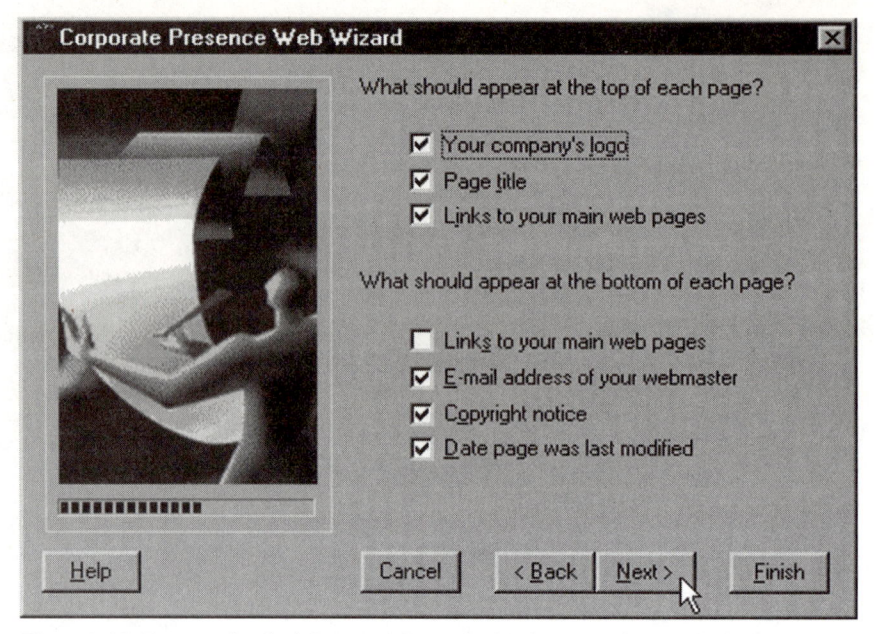

Figure 2-10: Turn on the check boxes as shown in this figure to choose which elements to include on each page; then click Next.

Now it's time to start having some fun with the look of your pages. In Figure 2-11, you'll see two examples of how you can choose between different styles of the template. Choosing a style specifies a set of graphics, backgrounds, and colors for your page. Otherwise, the pages created by the wizard would be identical. If you want full control over these choices, choose Plain, which creates the pages and links but avoids custom graphics, backgrounds, and colors. Click each alternative to preview it at the left side of the dialog box. In Figure 2-11, we've chosen first the conservative look, then the cool look.

If you're following along, choose the Cool option before clicking Next so that your screen will continue to match the figures in this chapter.

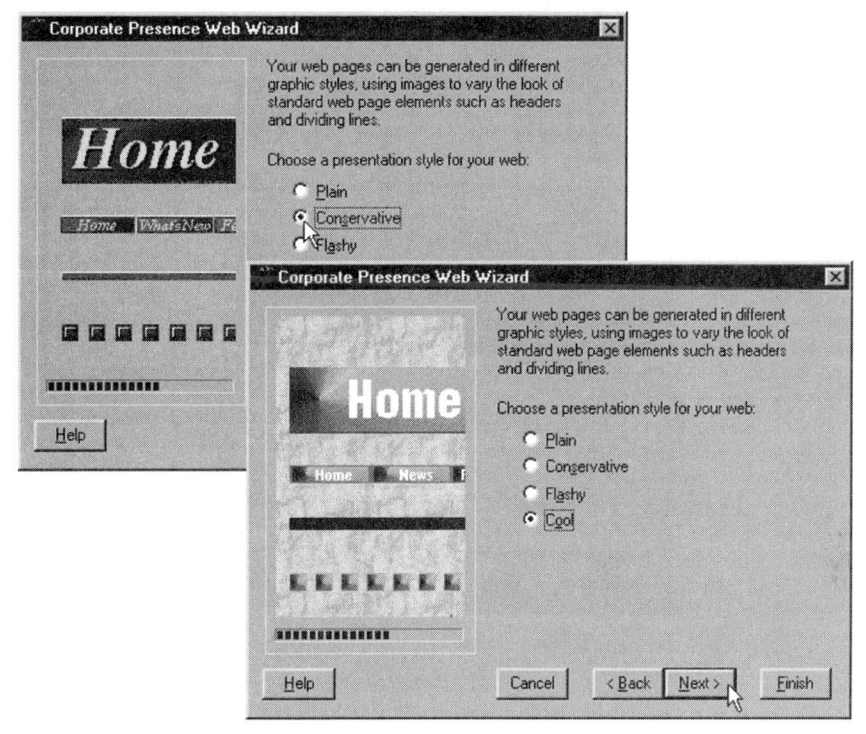

Figure 2-11: Audition each "look" offered by the wizard to see which best fits your style, and then click Next.

In the next page of the wizard, shown in Figure 2-12, change the default background graphic, or texture, to White Texture 2. For the best readability, light-colored textures are best with the default colors. Dark backgrounds can also be used if you change the default colors. For example, white is preferable for Normal text if you use a dark background. In any case, the results of your choices are previewed at the far left of the wizard so you can judge for yourself how your colors work with the background texture.

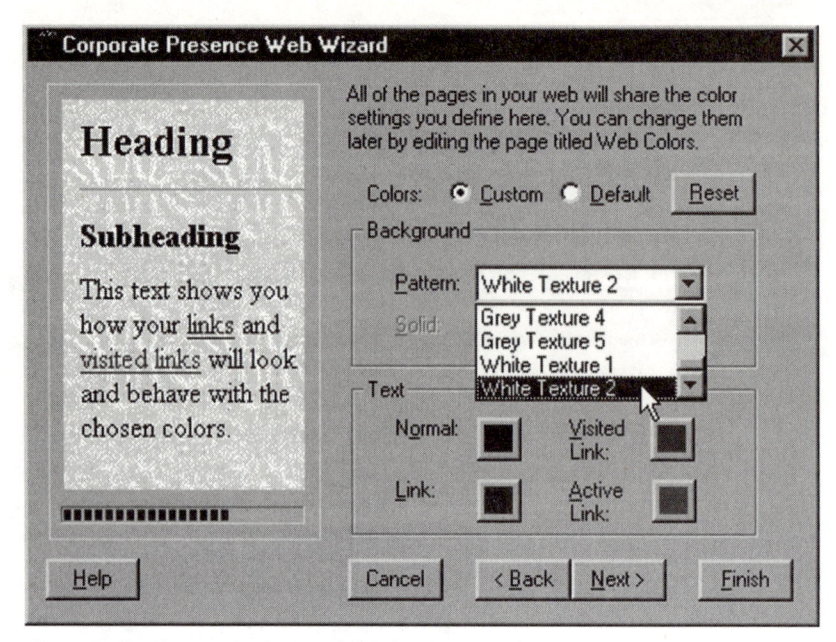

Figure 2-12: Choose a background graphic (texture) from the Pattern drop-down list box, and customize the colors if you like.

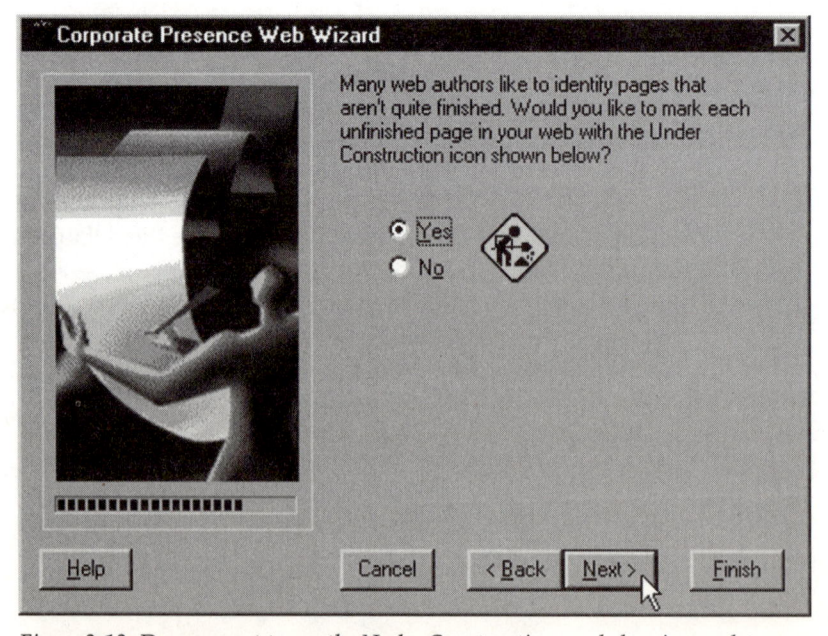

Figure 2-13: Do you want to use the Under Construction symbol on incomplete or uncustomized pages? After deciding, click Next.

Click Next to move on to the wizard page shown as Figure 2-13. On this page, you're simply asked if you'd like to identify incomplete pages with the Under Construction web graphic. If you publish the web before it has been completed, it can be helpful to those browsing your web; visitors to your site won't have to wonder why the page looks unfinished. When you customize each page, you can remove this graphic symbol easily, so I recommend including it. (Some WWW purists detest the Under Construction convention on the principle that all web pages are under construction at all times, since the World Wide Web is a set of living documents rather than a stack of static pages.)

After you make that momentous decision (choose Yes to use the construction symbols), click Next to begin entering the company-specific information.

Substitution Settings

While the pages created by the Corporate Presence Wizard are indeed generic, here is your opportunity to at least personalize the name of the company and other stats such as address and phone number. FrontPage also wants a one-word phrase to identify the company. This word is used whenever a computed value based on the company name can't contain a space.

The Corporate Presence web includes "slots" for these personalized items. With the wizard, you'll fill in the company name and address as well as telephone and FAX numbers and two e-mail addresses. These items will be inserted onto the finished pages automatically. The e-mail addresses will become hyperlinks on each page. When the client who is browsing your pages clicks on one of the Mailto links, the web browser launches the e-mail software and lets the client send a message to that e-mail address. It's an easy way to solicit feedback and stir up business.

The values for name, address, telephone number, and so on will be used by the Corporate Presence Wizard to create Substitution WebBots on several pages. Each Substitution WebBot has a simple job: take a setting, like CompanyName, and substitute the value for that setting, such as Group US, Inc. If you later need to change any of the settings, such as a phone number, you can use the Tools | Web Settings menu choice from FrontPage Explorer. Any pages that include the phone number will be instantly updated.

Web Publishing With FrontPage 97

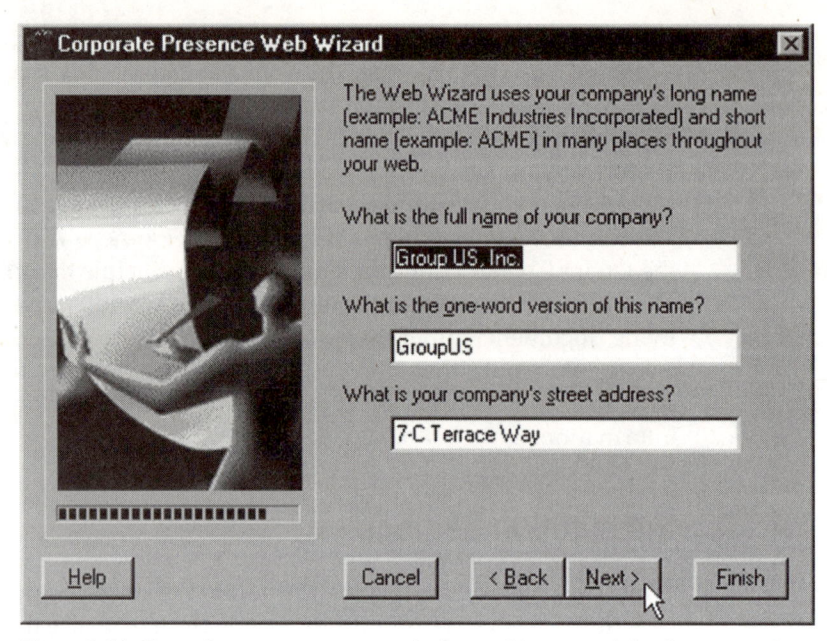

Figure 2-14: Enter the company name, a single word (no spaces) for the company name, and address; then click Next.

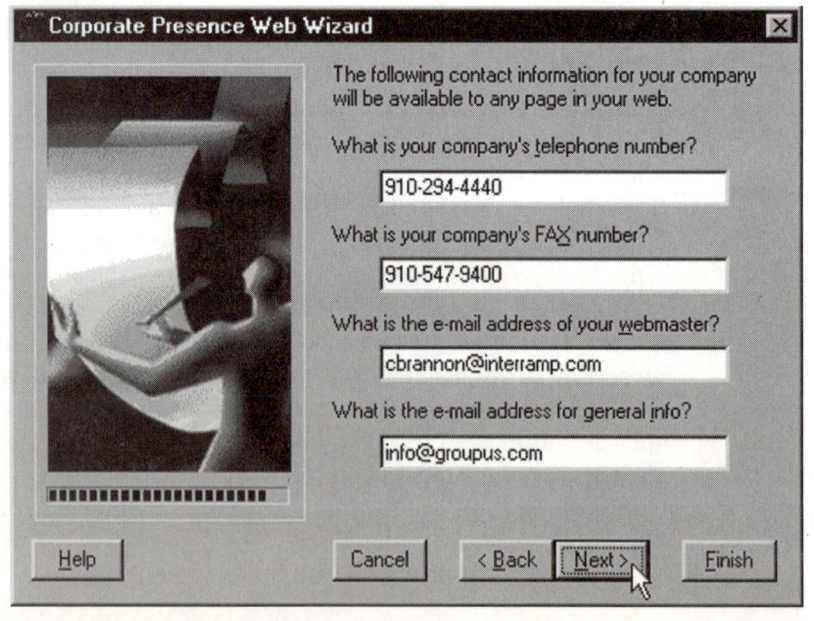

Figure 2-15: Here's where you fill in the telephone and FAX numbers, the e-mail address of the webmaster (that's you), and an e-mail address that clients can use to send a general e-mail request.

After filling out each page as shown in Figures 2-14 and 2-15, click Next. (If you're following along, you should use the actual information for Group US if you want your pages to match the ones we demonstrate later in this chapter.)

The last page of the Corporate Presence Wizard, shown in Figure 2-16, lets you know that FrontPage is now about to upload to your web server a set of pages that it creates based on your input. (When you create your own pages, if you don't want to be bothered with a list of tasks to be completed, you can turn off the Show To Do List check box so the To Do List won't appear after the web has been created. For now, leave the box enabled.)

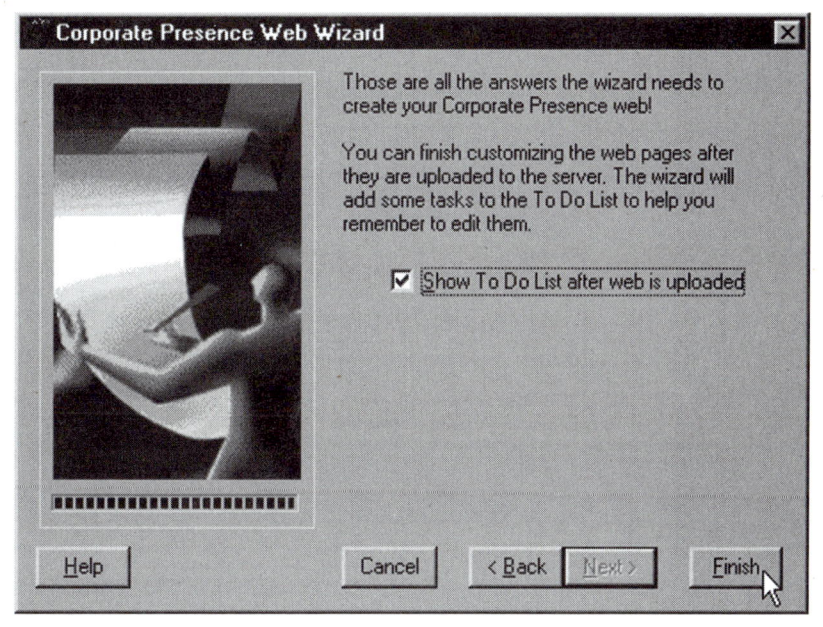

Figure 2-16: That's it. You're finished, so click the Finish button.

Click Finish to start the upload of the web created by the wizard. If you're running a local server, this will happen quickly. Depending on how fast your Internet or network connection runs, uploading to a web hosting service or other server may take several minutes.

It's Alive

After the upload completes, you're returned to FrontPage Explorer, which should resemble the screen in Figure 2-17. (If necessary, click on the FrontPage Explorer toolbar to return to folder view, which is what we'll use for most of the examples in this book.)

You've created a skeleton for a web site almost effortlessly. This site can be quickly customized if you're in a hurry to publish your web or extensively customized if you want a more professional, personalized site. We'll take a look at the first option in the next three sections of this chapter and more challenging customization tasks in the subsequent two sections of the chapter.

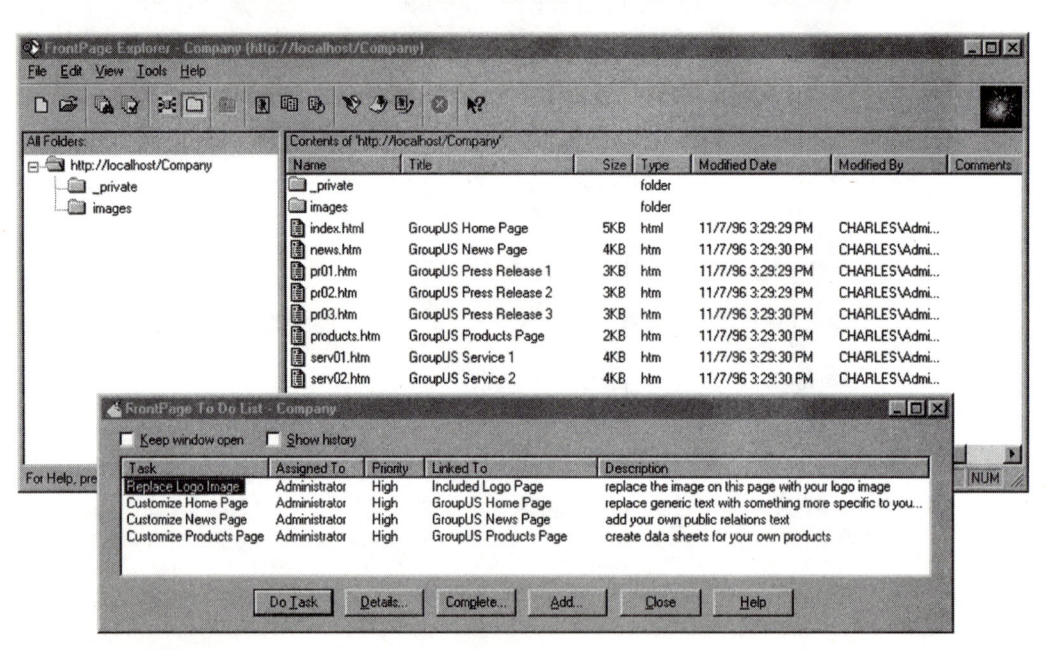

Figure 2-17: The output of the Corporate Presence wizard appears in the FrontPage Explorer ready for you to personalize it.

Planning & Delegating Web Work

Before you rush to publish the web created by the Corporate Presence Wizard, consider that you haven't yet actually created any content for your site. Graphics, colors, formatting, and fancy HTML all have to take a back seat to the most important aspect of your site: the content. Adding content usually boils down to writing some text and perhaps adding a few graphics. If you're not comfortable with writing, this task can often be delegated to the marketing or public relations staff of your company, but then again, your web site is not exactly the Great American Novel, so relax. (Don't forget that FrontPage includes a full-featured spelling checker, which you can apply to the entire site using the FrontPage Explorer Tools I Spelling menu option.)

The Corporate Presence Wizard has created for you the structure of the web—a set of pages that link to each other, with headings that guide you when typing in your content, graphics, and icons for a toolbar and placeholder graphics for things like your company logo.

If you're in a hurry to get published, the "quick-and-dirty" way to complete your site is to simply complete each task in the To Do List conveniently set up for you by the wizard. The To Do List is shown in Figure 2-17 and includes the following tasks:

- **Replace Logo Image.** Replace the image on this page with your logo image.
- **Customize Home Page.** Replace generic text with something more specific to your company.
- **Customize News Page.** Add your own public relations text.
- **Customize Products Page.** Create data sheets for your own products.

To complete a task, click on it in the To Do List and then click the Do Task button (you can't simply double-click on a task). If you want to manually mark a task as completed and/or remove it from the list, click the Complete button. You can use the Add button, which pops up the dialog box shown in Figure 2-18, to add a new task to the list.

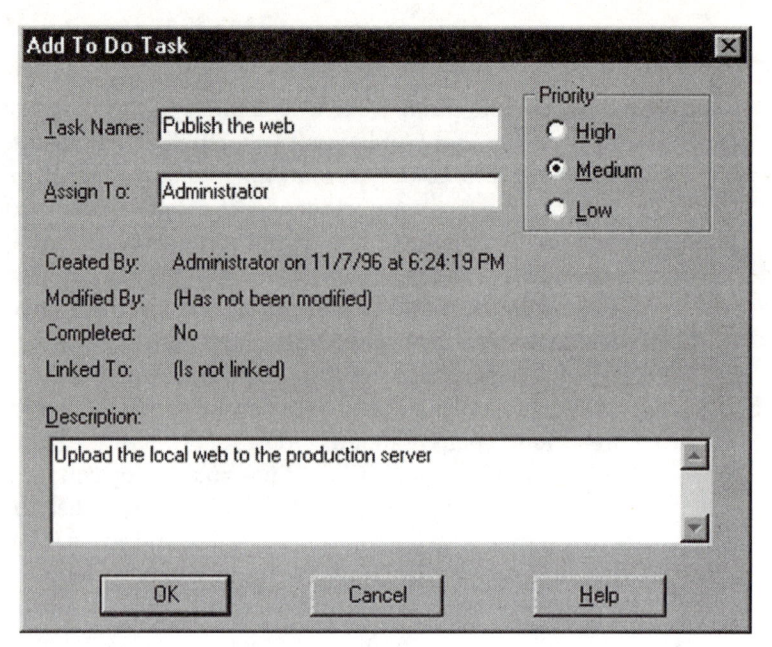

Figure 2-18: Fill in a short name for the task, the name of the author you want to assign it to (which defaults to your login name), and add a longer meaningful description of the task. Finally, choose a priority (High, Medium, Low).

Clicking the Add button only allows you to enter general tasks. If you want to link a task to a specific page, first click on the page in the list in the right pane of the FrontPage Explorer window and choose Edit | Add To Do Task. You can also link the task to the page that's currently open in the FrontPage Editor by choosing Add To Do Task from the FrontPage Editor's Edit menu. When you add a task from the FrontPage Editor, the page linked to that task is automatically opened when an author clicks the Do Task button.

Since many users (authors) can work on the same web, you can delegate a task to an individual author. When a task is completed, the name of the user who completed the task is added to the task. Normally, completed tasks are left on the list as history (if the Show History check box at the top of the To Do List window is turned on). If you prefer to delete a task permanently (such as when a task is never completed and is dropped), manually delete it by clicking the Complete button and choosing Delete.

> **TIP**
>
> *To sort the To Do List by the name of the tasks, click the heading labeled Task. Each heading is clickable; you can arrange the list according to the categories specified by the headings. You might also want to click on the Assigned To heading to arrange the list by the author assigned to each task.*

Creating a Custom Logo

Let's quickly complete each To Do Task to finish the Company web. First click on Replace Logo Image in the To Do List, and then click the Do Task button. This causes FrontPage Editor to start, automatically opening a page named Included Logo Page.

To complete this page, you only need to replace the generic graphic (which appears as the text "Company Logo" rendered as a graphic image) with a graphic image for your company logo. We'll see how to do this in a moment, but first let's step back and examine exactly what we're doing here.

The Included Logo Page is like a "master" web page because its contents will be included on every page of your web. This is accomplished with the use of an Include WebBot. An Include WebBot is already positioned at the top of each page created by the wizard. For example, when the home page is opened with a web browser, the Included Logo Page is displayed first; then the rest of the page appears.

The WWW server with FrontPage Server Extensions is responsible for merging the Included Logo Page with the rest of the page—the pages themselves, when viewed with the FrontPage Editor, appear to contain the logo, but they really only contain a reference to the page containing the logo. The merger of the main page and the logo is implemented by an Include WebBot. Later in this chapter and this book, we'll see how to manually add WebBots, but for now you can take them for granted.

The beauty of this scheme is that if the company logo ever changes, you need only update the one Included Logo Page, and instantly every other page in the web is also updated, since the other pages are designed to include the contents of the Included Logo Page.

How It Works

The Corporate Presence Wizard creates the Included Logo Page and adds the Include WebBots automatically to every other page. The Included Logo Page is stored in the _private subfolder of your web. Since the

Company web is a subweb, the actual location of the file is http://server/Company/_private/logo.htm. (Substitute for server the actual name or IP address of your WWW server. This would be localhost if you are running the Personal Web Server, Peer Web Services, or another web server on your local machine.)

When you clicked on Replace Logo Image and then clicked Do Task, the logo.htm file was automatically opened by the FrontPage Editor. At this point, you're ready to replace the default logo with the actual company logo graphic.

Whither the Logo?

The logo you use can be generated by an artist using a graphics package like CorelDRAW! or scanned from existing corporate literature. It should be resized using a graphics utility like Paint Shop Pro or Microsoft Image Composer to a modest size to avoid consuming too much screen space and download time. Save the image as a Graphics Interchange Format (GIF) or Joint Photographic Experts Group (JPG/JPEG) file anywhere on your hard drive. If the image already exists as a different type of file, such as a bitmap (BMP) graphic, you can import it into FrontPage and FrontPage will convert it to either a GIF or JPEG, depending on how many colors are contained within the graphic.

> **TIP**
>
> *Paint Shop Pro is one of the best graphics tools available as shareware. I encourage you to download a trial version from http://www.jasc.com/psp.*

We'll go into more detail on graphics formats in Chapter 3, but for now, take a look at the next subsection, "Graphics Formats: GIF or JPEG?" for a quick overview.

Graphics Formats: GIF or JPEG?

We recommend using GIF images for most web graphics because they download quickly (if the images are small) and preserve the full quality of the original graphic. As a bonus, GIF images can have a transparent background color, which allows the background texture of the web page to "show through." (If you want to support more primitive browsers without transparent GIF support, be sure to fill the background of your image with a color that closely matches the background color or texture of the page. That color can be marked as transparent—more on this in a moment—and that background color will disappear and blend into the background texture when viewed using most browsers.)

The disadvantage of GIF is that it can only display images containing 256 colors. Each pixel of the image is assigned a number from 0 to 255. This number is used as an index to look up the actual color in a table containing 256 entries. Each entry in the table, or palette, is a triplet of numbers. Each triplet contains three bytes, and each byte is a value of 0 to 255, representing the darkness or brightness of the red, green, and blue components of the color. For example, bright blue would have a value of 0,0,255. Dark red would be 64,0,0. A shade of purple might be 64,0,255.

While in principle a GIF image can be saved using a custom palette that picks from the image the 256 colors most often used in the image (an optimized palette), web browsers such as Netscape Navigator and Microsoft Internet Explorer always use the same, or fixed, palette of colors, which contains a variety of brightness levels for each of the primary colors. The 216 basic colors in the fixed palette remain the same whether the browser is running on a Windows computer or a Macintosh computer (or on any other platform). The remaining colors in the 256 color palette are reserved for the system colors used by the computer running the browser.

So when saving an image as a GIF, it's best to convert the image to the common browser palette. With Paint Shop Pro, you can use the menu option Colors | Load Palette (Shift+O) to force a graphic to convert its colors to match the colors in the palette. Where do you get this palette? One way is to save an image from a browser while running in 256-color mode. Open the image with Paint Shop Pro and use Colors | Save Palette to save the palette as a .PAL file, as in browser.pal.

We've also provided two palettes on the Companion CD-ROM that accompanies this book. In the folder \Palettes on the CD-ROM, ie3.pal is a custom palette designed for use with Internet Explorer running on the Windows platform, and safe.pal is a palette that contains only the 216 "safe" colors that will work with any web browser on any computer platform, including the Macintosh.

With Microsoft Image Composer (MIC), you can apply a custom palette to a graphics composition by choosing that palette from the drop-down list box at the top of the MIC window. To import a palette, click on the color selection box on the left side of the MIC toolbar, and then click the Custom Palette tab heading. Click the Load button, and open the palette ie3.pal from the \Palettes folder on the Companion CD-ROM or use safe.pal to apply the 216-color safe palette. Once the palette has been loaded, you can preview how the current image will look when using that palette by choosing the palette from the drop-down list box at the top of the MIC window.

Another way to use the safe palette is to apply the Balanced Ramp palette already included with MIC. When you save a GIF image from MIC, you can choose which palette to use from the Save As dialog box.

JPEG is a good alternative to GIF, ideal for photographic or realistic images such as raytraced 3D graphics. It's best for images that contain more than 256 colors; in fact, any image must be converted to TrueColor (24-bit color) before it can be made into a JPEG file. (These files are saved with an extension of JPG, as in flowers.jpg, so they will be compatible with earlier file systems that only allow 3-character filename extensions.) Because JPG uses a form of compression that can degrade the original image (lossy compression), it's best to maintain the original image in a form that isn't degraded, such as compressed tagged image file format (TIFF). You can import the TIFF version into FrontPage and let FrontPage convert it to a JPEG graphic.

Since JPEG images always use TrueColor, which supports over 16 million color combinations, these pictures can't be faithfully rendered if the browser is running in a 256-color graphics environment, which is all too common. Instead, the browser will dither the original colors as necessary.

For example, a pink flower can be represented as a true shade of pink on a computer running in a TrueColor display mode. In 256-color mode, the browser generates a close match to that shade of pink by combining bright red and white pixels in a checkerboard pattern. (This is somewhat of an oversimplification; the dithering process actually uses a method called error diffusion that randomly distributes red and white pixels to avoid a crude crosshatch effect.)

Error diffusion more closely approximates the way color photographs are printed in magazines and books using halftoning. Whereas halftoning uses various sizes of colored dots, error diffusion uses varying, though randomized, clusters of pixels. See Figure 2-19 to see how dithering works.

Figure 2-19: From left to right, the same image in TrueColor, dithered using 216 colors, and with error diffusion using 216 colors.

The choice of whether to use GIF or JPEG images boils down to image quality and file size. Many graphics can be saved as a GIF file with no loss of quality. Photographic images will look best as JPEG, and the file size of JPEG images can be as small or smaller than the equivalent GIF. If you want to ensure that no dithering will be used to display the graphic image, convert it to a GIF using the browser-safe palette.

Ready to Use

We've included the logo for Group US on the Companion CD-ROM in the Webs/Groupus/Images folder as Guslogo.gif. It is already in GIF format, with its background color marked as transparent. Let's import the Windows bitmap version of the same graphic (Guslogo.bmp), however, so that you can see how FrontPage converts images and lets you mark the background color as transparent.

With the _private/logo.htm (Included Logo Page) document opened in FrontPage Editor, click on the default graphic (Company Logo), and then press the Del key to delete it from the page. This leaves you with just the "purple text" Comment WebBot that reminds you to replace the generic logo with your company logo. Delete this, too, by clicking on it and pressing Del. (Notice that the mouse pointer changes to a "robot" symbol as you move to the embedded WebBot; this is to show you where the 'bot is located.)

Inserting Graphics

Now click the Insert menu, and choose Image. The dialog box shown in Figure 2-20 appears, allowing you to choose the location where the image is stored. This dialog box has three tab headings: Current FrontPage Web, Other Location, and Clip Art. In Figure 2-20, we show all three variations, but you'll have to click on the appropriate tab heading to see each dialog box.

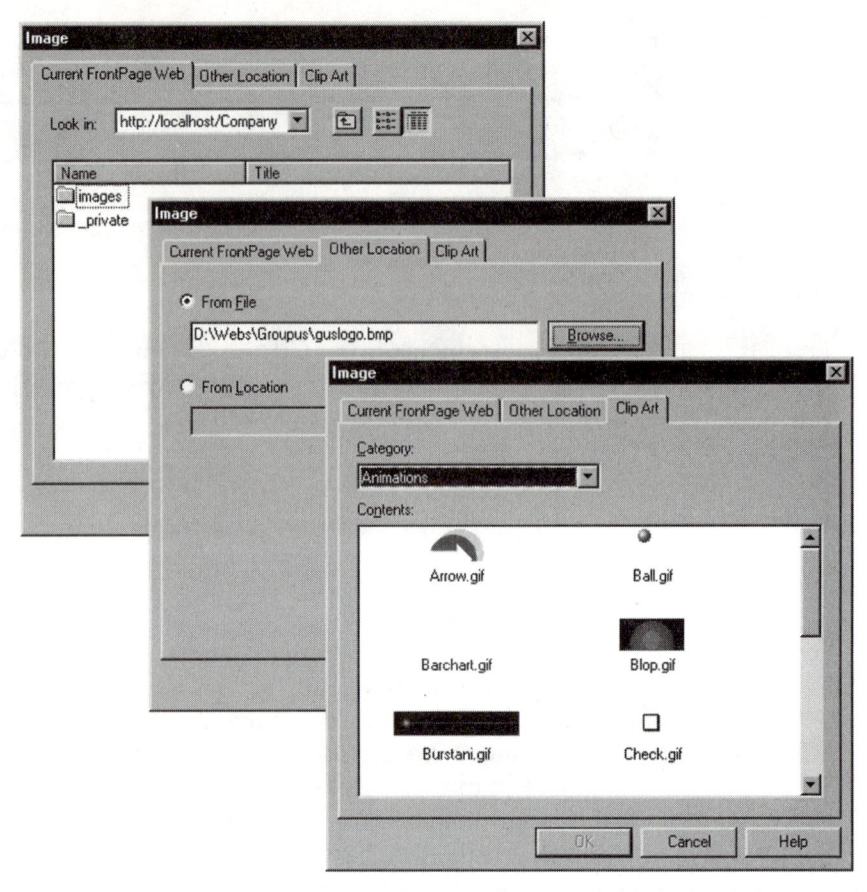

Figure 2-20: Use Current FrontPage Web to insert graphics that have already been copied to your web, Other Location to insert graphics from your hard disk, or the Clip Art tab heading to choose from the sample clip art included on the FrontPage 97 compact disc.

From the Current Web

You can use the Current FrontPage Web tab to insert an image that has already been imported into your web. These graphics are normally stored in the Images subfolder of the web. However, whenever you import a graphic (using the Other Location or Clip Art dialog boxes), you can choose where to store it after you save the page.

> **TIP**
>
> *Another way to add graphics to your web is to open a Windows 95 or NT Explorer or folder window and drag and drop graphics files from the Explorer or folder window into the FrontPage Explorer window. To prepare the FrontPage Explorer to receive the graphics, click the Folder toolbar button or choose View | Folder View and double-click on the Images folder to open it. Now you can drag files from your hard drive (using Explorer) into the Images folder of the web. If you attempt to use Explorer to copy files directly to the actual hard disk location of your web—the folder used by the WWW server—the FrontPage Explorer won't know about it unless you close FrontPage Explorer and restart it, or use View | Refresh (F5).*

Using Clip Art

Right now, we'll use the Group US logo, but when you create your own web pages, you can use the Clip Art tab to browse through various categories of artwork included on the FrontPage 97 CD-ROM. (During setup, you were given the option to copy these files to your hard drive. If you chose to keep the images on the CD-ROM to save space, you'll need to insert the CD into the CD-ROM drive before you can actually insert any graphics.)

From Other Location

The Other Location tab lets you import graphics from your hard drive, network, or from any location on the Internet. To open a graphic from the hard drive, enter the location of the graphic file in the text box labeled From File. If you don't know the exact path to the file, click the Browse button to bring up a standard Open dialog box that lets you navigate to the drive and folder (or network location) containing the image.

Since we're importing a graphic from the Companion CD-ROM, insert that CD and enter the path of the logo image, which if your CD-ROM uses drive D:, would be D:\Webs\Groupus\Images\guslogo.bmp. (If you use the Browse button to locate this file, note that by default, only GIF and JPG graphics are shown. Click the down arrow next to Files of Type and choose either All Files or Bitmap so that the guslogo.bmp graphic will be shown.)

If the graphic you want to use is stored on the Internet, enter the URL of the graphic using the From Location text box. For example, you might use http://www.microsoft.com/gallery/files/images/bullet1.gif to insert a graphic of a three-dimensional red ball. (Visit the gallery using your web browser to examine all the free graphics you can pick and choose from.)

The Eraser Tool

After you choose the graphic, it appears at the top of the page. As you can see, the background color of the logo graphic is similar to the graphics texture of the page, but ideally, we'd like the graphic to blend seamlessly with the page no matter what background graphics are used. To do this, we'll take advantage of the transparency feature of GIF graphics.

Click on the graphic image to select it. This reveals the Image toolbar, which appears within the FrontPage editor. On the toolbar, click the Eraser icon. This causes the mouse pointer to become a pencil eraser symbol. Use the tip of the eraser to click anywhere within the gray background color of the logo. Instantly, the background graphic of the page "shows through" the logo.

Save the Logo

When a graphic is first placed on a web page, it is a temporary graphic. The only place the graphic exists is as a clipboard object (if you pasted it) or as a link to a file on your hard disk. Since these graphics won't be available when the web is browsed, FrontPage needs to save the graphics files to the web, in a form compatible with web browsers. This happens automatically when you save the page. (This only works if you save the page to the web. If you save the page as a file on your hard disk—not recommended—the graphics will have to also be saved as files on the hard disk.)

Furthermore, unless the graphic is already a GIF or JPEG/JPG graphic, FrontPage converts the graphic to a GIF if the original image uses 256 colors or fewer, or to a JPEG in order to preserve the colors of an image that uses more than 256 colors, such as a TrueColor photograph.

With that explanation out of the way, let's see what happens when you save the current page with the custom logo.

1. To save the page with the customized logo, click the Save button on the toolbar or choose File I Save. As soon as you do this, a message pops up asking you if you want to mark the To Do task as completed. Click Yes.

2. Next, FrontPage asks you where you want to store the graphic (logo) that you just imported (Figure 2-21). It has already converted the graphic to a transparent GIF, and if you click Yes, it will be stored in the main (root) folder of your web. Some authors prefer to keep the HTML pages, graphics, and components all in the same folder at the "top" of the web, but let's store the graphic in the Images subfolder with the other graphics.

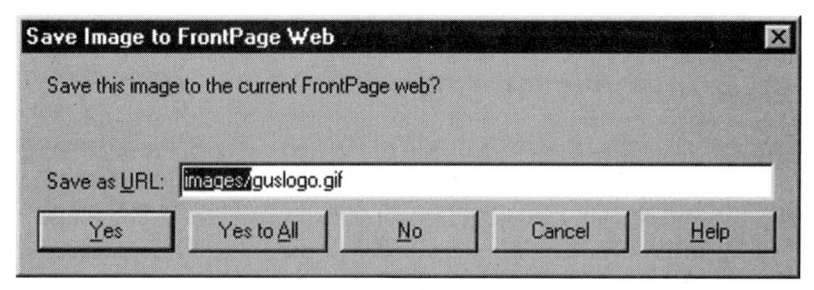

Figure 2-21: Choose the location within your web that you want to use to store the graphic.

To store the graphic in the Images subfolder with the other graphics, simply edit the path, changing it from guslogo.gif to images/guslogo.gif. Click Yes to save the image.

TIP

It's a good idea to use all lowercase when saving files to your web. Although it makes no difference when browsing a web stored on a Windows web server, Unix web servers make a distinction between uppercase and lowercase in filenames. Should you save the graphic using uppercase, but create the link as lowercase, the graphic will fail to appear when browsed.

Now that you've saved the logo page, you can close the FrontPage Editor. However, since we'll continue to work with pages, you may prefer to simply close the document by choosing File | Close. (Don't choose File | Exit if you want to keep the FrontPage Editor running.) The FrontPage Editor uses a Multiple Document Interface (MDI) to allow you to work on many documents at the same time. By closing documents that you've finished, you free up some memory and reduce clutter.

> **TIP**
>
> *If you are using the FrontPage Editor to work with many documents, press the Ctrl+F6 keyboard shortcut to move from one document to another. You can also use the Window menu to manage and move between document windows.*

Race to the Finish

Let's see how to quickly finish up this web. From either the FrontPage Explorer or FrontPage Editor, choose Tools | Show To Do List. Choose the next task on the To Do List (Customize Home Page) and click the Do Task button. (Notice that the Replace Logo Image task has been removed from the To Do List. Click the Show History check box if you want to see tasks that have been completed.)

As shown in Figure 2-22, the home page for your web is opened by the FrontPage Editor. The actual name of this page in your web will be index.htm, index.html, or _default.htm (or some other variation), depending on the default page set by your web server. (See Chapter 6 to see how to customize your server settings.)

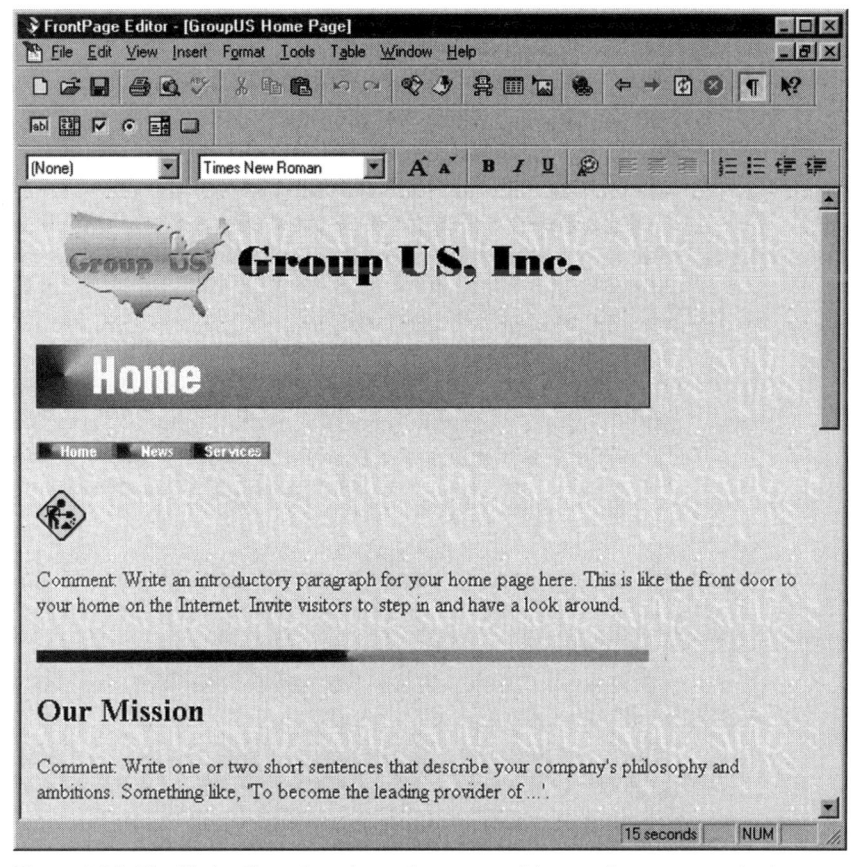

Figure 2-22: The "before" version of your home page. It's now time to customize it.

First Impressions

The first thing you may notice is that the home page already shows the custom logo. This is due to the Include WebBot at the top of the page, which merges the _private/logo.htm document with the home page. You can't directly change the contents of an Include WebBot, even though it appears to be part of the page. To edit an included page, you can right-click on the WebBot and choose Open from the pop-up context menu. (Don't do this now—we've already customized that page.)

Web Page Properties

You'll also notice that the home page already has a background texture. This was set up automatically by the Corporate Presence Wizard. Choose File | Page Properties (or right-click on the page and choose Page Properties from the context menu) to see how it's done.

For a FrontPage document, the General tab of the Page Properties dialog box, shown in Figure 2-23, is where you can name your page. This title is shown within the title bar of the web browser when your page is viewed and is used as the name of the page within FrontPage Explorer. If you don't title your pages, the filenames of the pages are used instead, and that's not very pretty. FrontPage prompts you for both a filename and title for a page when you save it to the web. The title shown for the home page was generated by the FrontPage Corporate Presence Wizard using the ShortCompanyName setting, the one-word version of the company name that you defined during the wizard setup. Edit the Title text box entry to read Group US Company Home Page to improve on the default title.

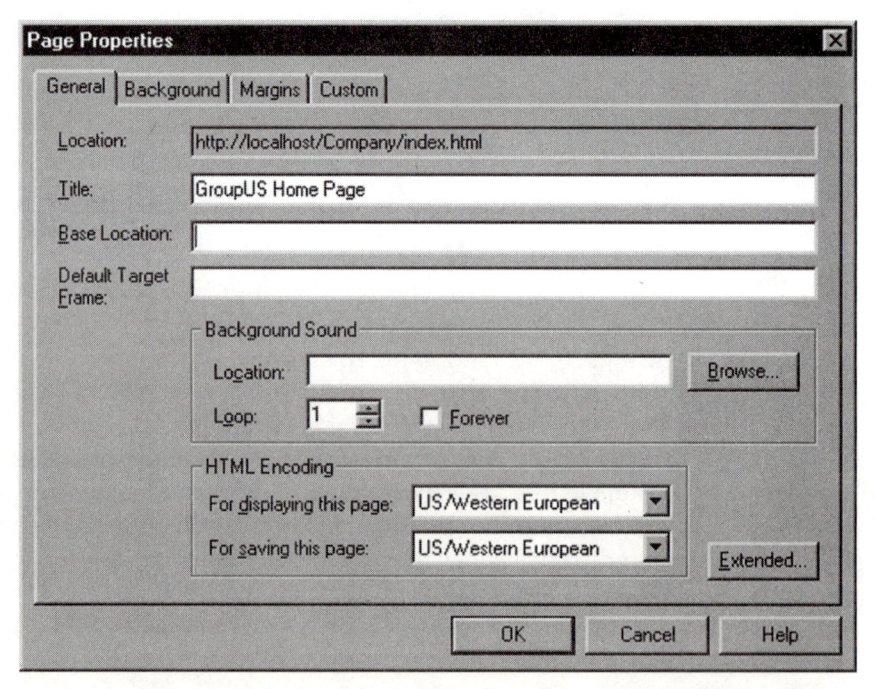

Figure 2-23: You can use the General tab of Page Properties to name your page and choose a background sound.

You can safely ignore most of the other settings on this page for now, such as HTML Encoding, Base Location, and Default Target Frame.

Background Sound & Music

Note, however, the Background Sound section (see Figure 2-23). This lets you choose a Windows waveform (WAV) audio clip or a Musical Instruments Digital Interface (MID or MIDI) music clip.

When you choose to insert music onto the page, you can browse on your local hard drive, floppy disk, or CD-ROM using the Other Location tab of the Browse dialog box. Choose From File, and click Browse again to find the file.

When you save the page, you'll be prompted to resave the MIDI or WAV file to the web. Just click OK to accept the default location, or edit the suggested name and path.

Later, when the page is browsed using Internet Explorer 2.0 or later, the music is automatically played as an accompaniment. Click the Forever box if you want the sound or music to play again and again (not recommended) or choose how many times to loop (repeat) the sound. You may wish to restrict the sound effect or music to the home page or a few key pages, since otherwise it can be too distracting to your audience. (Future versions of Netscape Navigator may also support background music, but users of Navigator version 3.0 or earlier, or clients using computers incapable of playing WAV or MIDI clips, won't hear anything.)

Paper Textures

Click the Background tab of the Page Properties dialog box to switch to the Background property sheet (Figure 2-24). Here's where you can customize the background image (texture) and text colors for the page. Many users expect a web page to use the standard colors (such as blue for a hyperlink or purple for a visited hyperlink), but you may need to change these colors if you're using a distinctive color scheme or custom background. For example, if your background texture is dark, you'll want to use a light shade (such as white) for the text instead of the default black color.

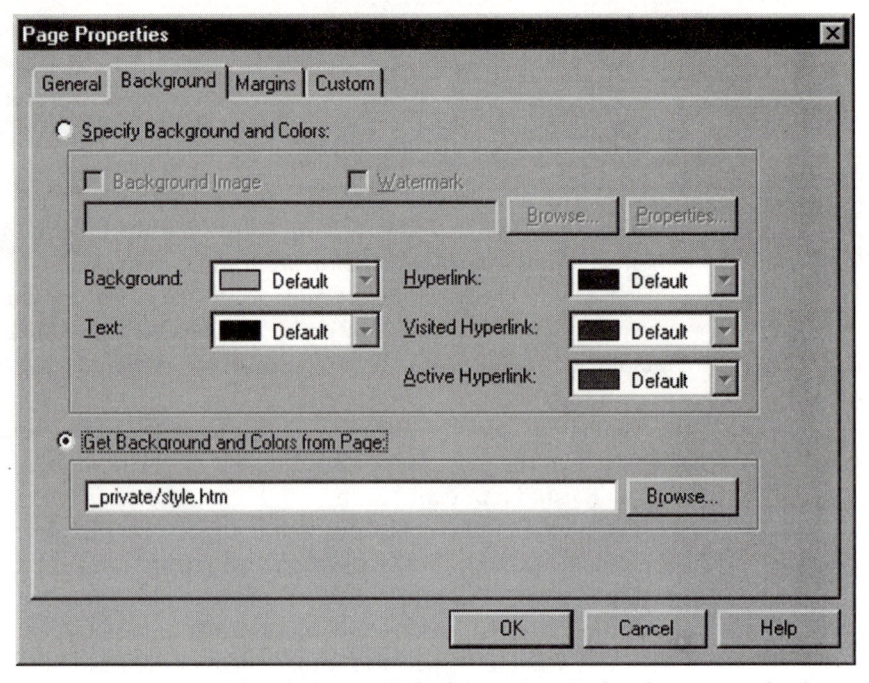

Figure 2-24: You can either choose specific backgrounds and colors for a page or let the page assume the settings of another page.

> **TIP**
>
> It's best to use extremely light-colored backgrounds with the standard black text color. You can convert virtually any image to a suitable background image by using a graphics tool to lighten the image and reduce its contrast. With Paint Shop Pro, use the Colors | Adjust | Gamma Correction dialog box to choose a high gamma (greater than 2). With Microsoft Image Composer, use the Warps and Filters tool, choose Color Enhancement, then Wash, and choose a value of 50% or less; then click Apply. This "washes out" the image, muting it. You can experiment with other filters and art effects as well.

Watermarks

The Watermark check box (see Figure 2-24) can be clicked to convert a standard page background image to a Watermark background. What's the difference? Normally, the background image is part of the page, and if the page is scrolled, the background image scrolls along with the page. When viewed with Internet Explorer 2.0 or later, a watermarked background won't scroll; it's as if it were on a separate layer "behind" the page. Unfortunately, the page tends to flicker rather noticeably when scrolling with watermark enabled, and watermarks are not supported by Netscape Navigator 3.0 or earlier, so you'll want to avoid watermarks for most purposes.

Consistency Revisited

We already mentioned that it's highly desirable to enforce some consistency between your pages. This helps communicate a "branded" identity for your site that makes it clear that all the pages are related. We've discussed how the Include WebBot makes it easy to include standard elements such as logos on each page. Another way to standardize your pages is to use the Background property sheet (Figure 2-24) to let each page get its custom colors and background image from another page, a style page. You can specify the style page using the Get Background and Colors From Page text box.

The FrontPage Corporate Presence Wizard has already set this up for you. Each page in your web looks at the style.htm document stored in the _private subfolder of your web to get its background image and colors. As with the Include WebBot, the advantage this offers is undeniable: Should you decide to change the background texture or colors, you only need to change the _private/style.htm page, and all the other pages in your web are instantly updated.

We'll take advantage of this technique in Chapter 3 when we further customize the Group US Company web. For now, you can close the Page Properties property sheets by clicking the Cancel button.

> **TIP**
>
> *When you create new pages from scratch, you'll have to manually use Page Properties to get the background and colors from _private/style.htm. You'll also use the Insert | WebBot Component menu command to insert an Include 'bot that includes the _private/logo.htm page to merge the standard logo with the page. To save time in the future, create such a page and save it to your web as Blank Page so that you can reuse it for other pages. When opening the blank page to create a new page, be sure to save it immediately using a different name so that you don't accidentally overwrite the blank page when you save your changes. Another way to get a blank page is to start with one of the template pages, such as the home page, delete everything on it except for the Include WebBot, and save it to the web as Blank Page.*
>
> *The Save As dialog box includes an option for As Template, which lets you store this page in your FrontPage template folder for future use. However, custom pages may refer to subfolders such as _private, which aren't copied to the template folder. When you create a new page with the custom template, the template will fail, because it can't find the _private/logo.htm or _private/style.htm files within the template folder—these files are stored within your web and aren't copied to the template folder.*
>
> *One way to work around this is to ignore the errors that appear when you choose File | New to apply the template. Next, save the page to your web, and then use the View | Refresh command to reload the page. When the page is reloaded, it can then find the _private/logo.htm and _private/style.htm, since the page is now part of your web, and the custom page elements will show up just fine.*

Importing Text & Word Processing Documents

To complete the home page, you'll have to do some typing. Replace each of the "purple text" Comment sections with text as suggested by the comments. If you can find suitable information in your company's standard literature, you can use Insert | File to locate a word processing document or text file that you want to insert. You can then edit the text you've inserted to suit the contents of your page. FrontPage will automatically convert the formatting used by word processors to HTML, with varying degrees of success.

If you want to delegate content development, authors and typists can use familiar tools such as Microsoft Word, and you'll be able to import the material directly into the FrontPage Editor. With the new features of Office 97 (supported in Office 95 with Office Assistants, which can be downloaded from http://www.microsoft.com/office), authors can save their documents as HTML and use HTML-specific features in the documents, without requiring a license for or training with FrontPage.

If you're following our examples using the FrontPage software, you can save some typing by choosing Insert | File from the FrontPage Editor menu bar and choosing one of the following documents from the Webs/Groupus/Text subfolder on the Companion CD-ROM: intro.txt, mission.txt, profile.txt, and contact.txt. Insert each text file to replace the suggested purple comment text. (Note that you'll have to click on Files of Type and change from HTML, the default, to either All Files or Text Files in order to see these filenames in the Insert File dialog box.)

When you insert a text file, FrontPage pops up a dialog box (Figure 2-25) asking you how you want it to convert the text into HTML. Most of the time, you'll choose Normal paragraphs before clicking OK.

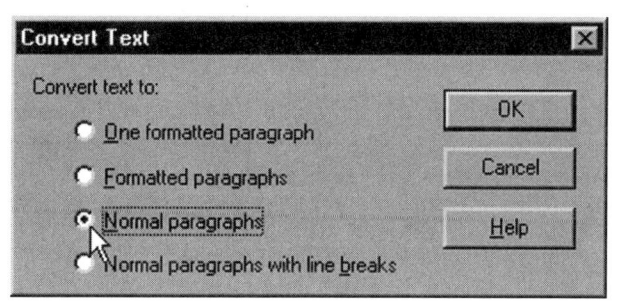

Figure 2-25: When you insert a text file, FrontPage needs to know how it should be converted.

The option One Formatted Paragraph strips out all the carriage returns (line endings) in the text file, which is useful if the text contains unwanted manual line endings. (Text files are often formatted typewriter style, with a carriage return at the end of each line rather than just at the end of each paragraph, which is the standard for HTML and most word processors.)

Since some text files (such as tables) are formatted with spaces and a fixed-width typeface (such as used by Notepad), the default option is One Formatted Paragraph. This marks the text in the FrontPage Editor as formatted text, which displays in the web browser (and in FrontPage Editor) as a fixed-width typeface such as Courier or Courier New. A single formatted paragraph is shown in the browser as a long continuous line of text. Formatted text is not wrapped to fit the browser window.

If you want to preserve the line breaks in the text file and import it as formatted (Courier) text, use the Formatted Paragraphs option. The Formatted Paragraphs option preserves existing line breaks, while Normal strips out the extra line endings.

Since our text files are intended as normal body text, click the Normal Paragraphs choice and then click OK to import the text. For some types of text files, you may wish to use Normal Paragraphs With Line Breaks to preserve any manual paragraph formatting.

No matter which option you choose, you can always reformat the text once it's in place within the FrontPage Editor by choosing a paragraph format from the drop-down list at the left of the FrontPage toolbar. You can also spiff up the text by changing words or phrases to boldface or italics or custom colors; to do so, select part of the text and click the appropriate buttons on the formatting toolbar (such as the B symbol for boldface).

Once you've finished customizing the text, you may wish to delete the Under Construction graphic from the page. Just click on the yellow diamond symbol and press the Del key. Finally, save the page back out to the web. As soon as you do this, you're asked if you want to mark the task on the To Do List as completed. Click Yes.

Mission (Almost) Accomplished

You've now completed the company's home page, or at least your first draft of it. (Your page should now resemble Figure 2-26.) By completing the remaining two tasks on the To Do List, you will have completed your "quick-and-dirty" customization of the Company web, and you're ready for publication.

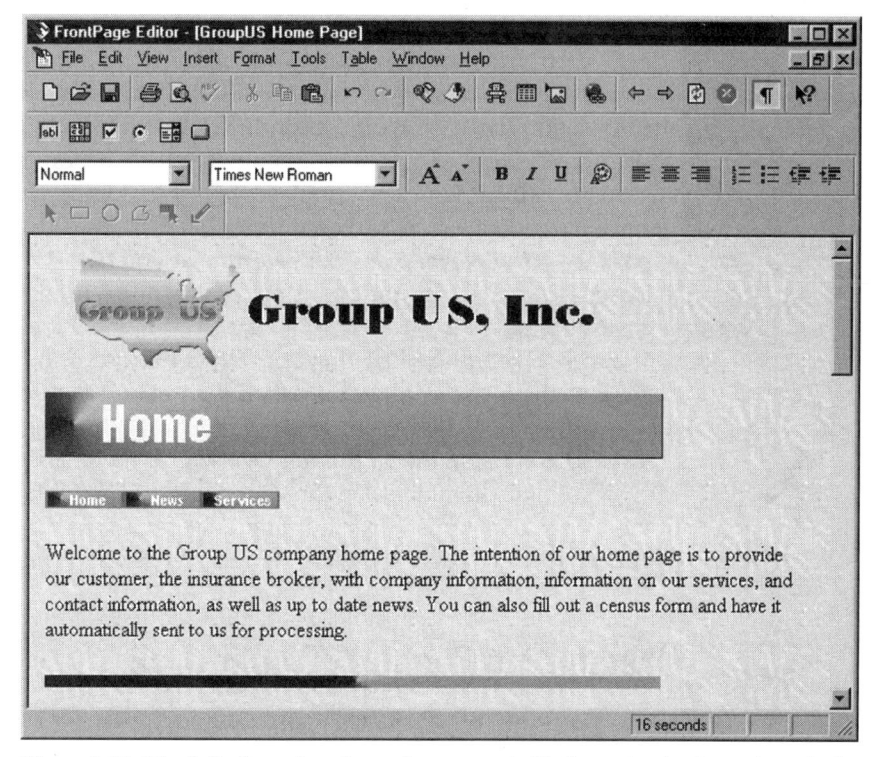

Figure 2-26: The "after" version of your home page, with the customized text, is ready for publication.

Customizing the What's New page (news.htm) involves a little more work, and since it's called "What's New," the News page will never truly be finished. You'll need to routinely update this page to tell your visitors how the site has changed recently. You can create press releases and add information on media coverage.

Keep in mind that the pages created by the wizard offer only guidelines, with some of the text formatting already prepared for you, but you have to add the content. You may also wish to simply delete some of the suggested text. For example, for the Group US company site, we chose not to include the Media Coverage section.

When you open the News page into the FrontPage Editor (using File | Open from FrontPage Editor or double-clicking the News document in FrontPage Explorer), you'll notice that there are some hyperlinks already set up (notice the blue underlined text). These hyperlinks (or simply, links) point to other documents that the Corporate Presence Wizard created for you. The simplest way to customize these documents (such as Press Release 1) is to hold down the Ctrl key while clicking the hyperlink on the News page. For example, if you Ctrl+Click upon Press Release 1, FrontPage Editor opens the pr01.htm document, ready for you to customize it.

When you've finished editing both Press Release 1 and the News page, save them both, and when asked if you want to mark the To Do task as completed, click Yes.

To help you finish the Company web, we've included pr1.doc, a Microsoft Word document, on the Companion CD-ROM; it can be found in the \Webs\Groupus\Text subfolder. Insert this file directly into the pr01.htm document using the FrontPage Editor Insert | File command.

Customizing Pages: A Closer Look

Just as you did with the News page, you will add text to customize the Products/Services page (in our example, we only have services on this page). Let's take a closer look.

Use the FrontPage Editor or FrontPage Explorer to show the To Do List (using the Tools menu). Click on Customize Products Page, and then click Do Task. The Group US Products page opens within the FrontPage Editor. The first thing you'll want to do is to use File | Page Properties to change the title of this page—there are no products on this page, so change the title to Group US Services Page.

First, delete the Comment ("Write a brief overview . . .") and replace it with some text describing the services in general, such as:

```
We offer Quick Quote and in-house proposal services for groups of
one to fifty employees and a sophisticated Market Search shopping
service for larger groups. We are a living "Who Writes What" and a
source of technical information and expertise.
```

You can use Insert | File to save typing, importing the Word document from \Webs\Groupus\Text\services.doc, found on the Companion CD-ROM.

Editing & Creating Links

Next, select the wording of the first hyperlink by dragging over it with the mouse, and type over it, changing it from Name of Service 1 to Small Group Services. When you change the wording, the hyperlink may change back to standard text. To fix the hyperlink, use the mouse to select the line "Small Group Services" and then click the toolbar button or choose the Edit | Hyperlink menu item. (The shortcut key is Ctrl+K.)

The Create Hyperlink dialog box (Figure 2-27) appears, prompting you to type in the name of the page you want to link to. By default, it shows a middle tab, Current FrontPage Web. From here, you can click the Browse button to look within your web for a page you want to link to.

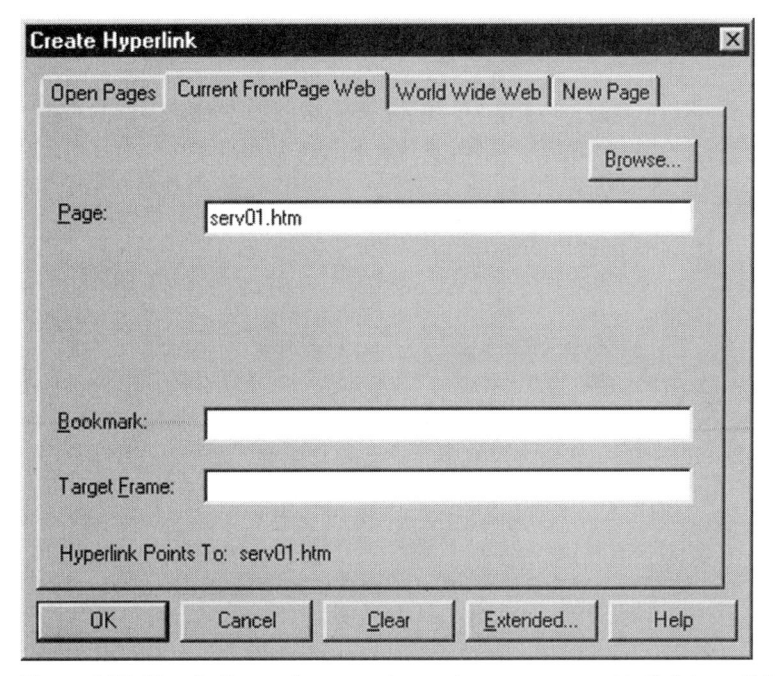

Figure 2-27: Use the Browse button to locate the page you want to link to, or if the page is already open in the FrontPage editor, try the Open Pages tab.

To complete the link from the Services page to the first service, type serv01.htm in the Page text box and click OK. Before we move on, let's see what other options you have for creating links.

If the page you want to link to is already open within the FrontPage editor (which may be the case if you've been editing many pages without closing them), use the Open Pages tab to choose among them.

> **TIP**
>
> *When you are forming Internet URLs (network addresses), remember to use the forward slash (/) with Internet locations instead of the backslash (\), which is the DOS/Windows file standard. The forward slash symbol is used by UNIX servers and has become the standard on the Internet.*

Links & URLs

The *Uniform Resource Locator (URL)* makes it easy to link to any Internet resource, regardless of its type. URLs are most often used with a web browser hyperlink when accessing (opening) a web page from the World Wide Web. The URL is like a post office address, uniquely specifying the location of a file or folder on the Internet. You can also use URLs to download files from an FTP server, send and receive electronic mail, or take part in discussions in newsgroups.

A World Wide Web URL is usually preceded by the characters http:// and is usually followed by the name of a server, such as www for World Wide Web. (The http is an acronym for HyperText Transfer Protocol. Since this is the most common type of URL, you can usually leave off the http:// part when specifying locations on the World Wide Web.)

After the www, there is a period, then the name of the location on the Internet (often the name of a company followed by .com). The URL can include additional / characters to specify a particular folder (directory) on the Internet computer. If the URL only includes folder names, the WWW server usually opens the default page, such as index.htm.

Another type of URL is used with FTP (File Transfer Protocol) servers, which let you easily download files from a computer attached to the Internet. For example, the URL ftp://ftp.winsite.com lets you access a huge library of Windows software. A URL such as mailto://support@groupus.com causes a web browser to open a new e-mail message, whereas a URL like news://comp.os.ms.windows would open the newsreader utility installed on your computer to browse a newsgroup, which contains a list of messages on a particular topic.

When accessing files stored locally on your hard drive or network, the file: URL comes in handy, such as file:\\c:\graphics\turtle.gif, which would display (or open) the Turtle GIF image stored in the Graphics folder on the C:\ hard disk drive.

Whereas URLs are most often used with the Internet, they can also be applied to access files stored on a TCP/IP local area network, or intranet.

Most web pages include blue underlined words or phrases that, when clicked on, take the user to another location within the same site or to a different Internet site altogether. These hyperlinks (or simply links) contain a reference to a URL that lets the web browser look up the site. Graphics within a web page can also be linked to a URL, which is handy for constructing toolbars and other site navigation aids.

The URLs we've described so far are absolute URLs, because they completely specify the location of a file. Yet when linking to pages within your own web, you'll leave off the details such as http:// and any folder (directory) names. These are called *relative URLs*.

Relative URLs are preferable because they allow you to move all the pages from one location to another without having to redo all the URLs. Let's say your home page is located on your local web server, at http://localhost/index.htm. The home page may have a link to the What's New page, at http://localhost/news.htm.

What happens when you upload the web to the Internet? If you have uploaded the page to an America Online web account (more on this in Chapter 5), the page is now stored at an Internet location, such as http://members.aol.com/ceemeister.

When a user clicks on the link from the home page to the What's New page, the link will fail if it is hard coded as http://localhost/news.htm, which can not be found on the World Wide Web. (Localhost is restricted for local web authoring.)

Relative URLs

Instead, you would simply link to news.htm, and leave off the name of the server and any other information specific to the exact location of the page. When the web browser looks up this URL, it assumes that the page is found in the same folder as the home page. (This is similar to the "current directory" concept you may be familiar with from DOS.)

Relative URLs can also reference subfolders without sacrificing relativity; a link to images/toolbar.gif looks for the graphic in the folder Images, which is assumed to be a subfolder of the default folder.

What if a page is itself stored in a subfolder, but you want it to link to a page stored in the parent folder? The trick is to use a link such as ../index.htm, which points to the home page, relative to the current folder. The first part, the .., refers to the folder "above" the current folder.

Choosing either of the first two tabs on the Create Hyperlink dialog box (which you display by selecting the link text and choosing Edit|Hyperlink) inserts an HTML hyperlink (HREF) using a relative URL. A relative URL is most often the name of the page you're linking to. The page to which you're linking is found within the same folder as the page you're linking from, so you don't need to specify a fully qualified URL (such as http://yoursite.com/page.htm).

Absolute URLs

The third tab in the Create Link dialog box, World Wide Web (Figure 2-28), lets you insert an *absolute URL*, which you can use to link to a page on someone else's WWW site. By default, you can leave off the http:// part of the URL. If you want to compose a URL to an e-mail address, click the arrow next to Hyperlink Type, and choose from the list of URL types, including http:, https:, mailto:, news:, telnet:, and wais:.

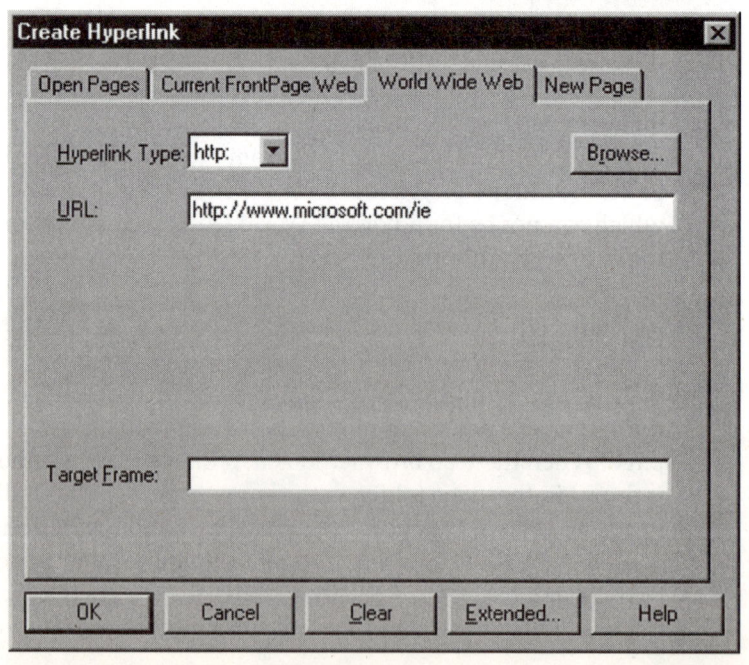

Figure 2-28: Use the World Wide Web tab to insert a link to a page stored on the World Wide Web or to insert an absolute URL.

TIP

You don't have to choose from the Hyperlink Type box. Just type the prefix before the address, as in mailto:cbrannon@vmedia.com.

Now or Later

When creating your own web, you'll sometimes want to go ahead and create a link to a page you're planning to develop, even before that page is created. To do so, use the New Page tab of the Create Link dialog box, shown here as Figure 2-29.

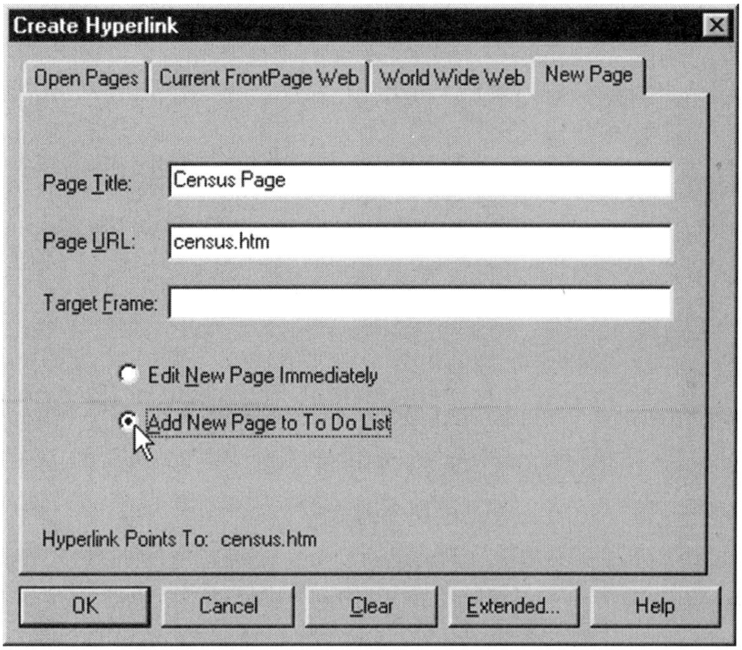

Figure 2-29: You can anticipate pages you are planning to develop and add the task to your To Do List.

Let's say we want to add a link from the Services page to a page we're planning to develop that lets the visitor fill out a census form requesting an insurance quote.

Rather than wait until that page is complete, we can go ahead and prototype the Services page to include the link. Type the hyperlink text Census Form on the Services page in the FrontPage Editor, select (highlight) the phrase, and press Ctrl+K. Then, use the New Page tab of the Create Hyperlink dialog box to enter the proposed name of the page (Census Page). FrontPage creates the filename (page URL) of the proposed page automatically, usually based on the first eight characters of the page title. (Although most WWW servers permit long filenames, it's best to avoid spaces in the name and keep it short, in case the web is moved to a server with limited features.)

By default, FrontPage assumes that you want to create the new page immediately, but procrastination is all too human, so you can choose the Add New Page to To Do List option button on the New Page tab before clicking OK if you want to postpone working on that page. In general, this is not a good strategy, since it leaves broken links on your site, which you may forget to fix. (The Tools | Verify Links menu command from the FrontPage Explorer can help you locate bad links within your web and fix them.)

Nevertheless, since we're not yet ready to create the Census page, be sure to use the option to Add New Page to To Do List if you're following along with the FrontPage software. We'll create the Census page in Chapter 4.

Tip

Perhaps an even easier way to insert an absolute URL is to simply type the URL as plain text using the FrontPage Editor. When the FrontPage Editor examines what you've typed and sees a likely Internet address (the http:// is usually a pretty good clue), it instantly converts the text you've typed into a hyperlink to that URL. (If you don't want this to happen, choose Edit | Undo or press Ctrl+Z to reverse the automatic conversion.) The only disadvantage here is that the text shown on the screen for the hyperlink is the URL itself instead of a meaningful phrase such as "download now."

Are We There Yet?

So far, you've customized the name of the first link from Name of Service 1 to Small Group Services. Go ahead and change the Name of Service 2 link to read Large Group Services and make sure it links to serv02.htm. Replace the phrases "Description of Service 1" and "Description of Service 2" with "(One to 25 Employees)" and "Quick Quote and Market Search Services," respectively. The finished page should resemble Figure 2-30.

Figure 2-30: Once you've customized the Services page, don't forget to edit the pages pointed to by the two links.

At this point, you might be tempted to call it a day, but you're not finished yet. All you have to do to complete the web is edit the pages that the services links point to, serv01.htm and serv02.htm. To do so, Ctrl+click on each link (or right-click and choose Follow Link from the pop-up menu) to open the corresponding page, and customize the text on those pages.

The Services pages created by the Corporate Presence Wizard contain suggestions for the content you should insert. You'll edit the Level 1 heading, which by default reads "GroupUS Service 1" and add a description of the service, followed by the key benefits of the service. Again, this is just a suggestion. You should feel free to format the text as you wish. To start with, where it says "GroupUS Service 1," type Small Group Services. Under this, you can type (One to 25 Employees). (You may wish to set this line as a Heading 2 paragraph using the drop-down list box at the left of the FrontPage toolbar.)

If you're following along with the FrontPage software, you may wish to save some typing and replace the suggested text by using Insert | File and inserting the file Smallgrp.doc from the \Webs\Groupus\Text folder on the Companion CD-ROM. When editing the Serv02.htm page, insert the file Largegrp.doc.

Introducing Forms

When you scroll down toward the bottom of either of the Services pages, you'll notice that the Corporate Presence Wizard has created an Information Request form on the page (Figure 2-31). We'll discuss how to create your own forms in Chapter 4, but now let's take a quick look at how forms work.

A form is made up of elements called form fields, or sometimes controls. Form controls include text fields (text boxes), radio buttons (sometimes called option buttons), check boxes, drop-down menus, push buttons, and images. Notice that the entire form is enclosed by dashed-lines—any fields positioned within the dashed-line box are part of the same form.

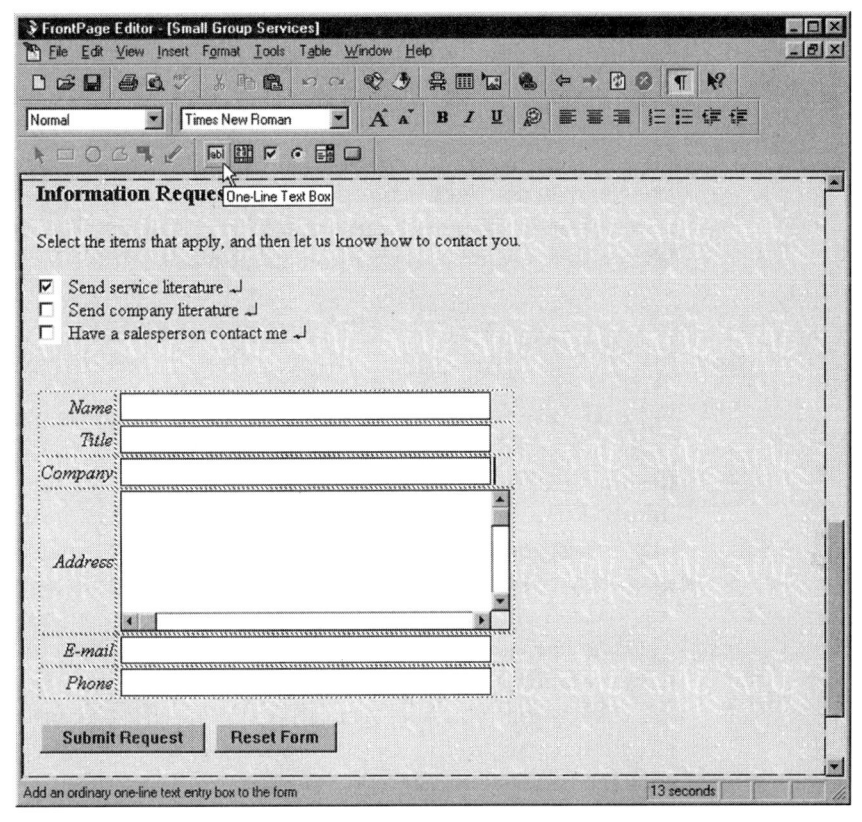

Figure 2-31: The Information Request form, built from standard form fields and a Save Results WebBot, was created on the Services pages by the Corporate Presence Wizard.

Forming Fields

Most fields (controls) on a form have a name and a value. The name is like a labeled shoebox, whereas the value is like the shoe that's stored in the shoebox. The form fields store information entered or clicked upon by the user. A text field can store an arbitrary line of text (the scrolling text box can store multiple lines of text). A check box or option button can store a value of checked/unchecked or on/off, which boils down to a numeric value of 1 or 0. A drop-down menu stores which menu item was chosen.

There are two types of push buttons: Submit and Reset. The Reset button simply clears out all entries and resets all controls to their default state. The Submit push button is special; it links all the form controls on a form to a form handler. The form handler collects all the data and does something with it. By default, FrontPage forms are handled by a Save Results WebBot. The Save Results WebBot collects all the information and stores it in an output page, which is usually an HTML page that can be viewed using a web browser. The page consists of name/value pairs and lets you discover what information was stored in the form. You can also choose to store the results in a form usable by other programs, like Microsoft Excel, or directly into a database accessible by the web server.

How It Works

When the user enters information into the Information Request form and clicks Submit, the FrontPage Server Extensions (which support the Save Results WebBot) add the information to an HTML document named inforeq.htm, and titled Results From Form 1 of Page Serv01.htm. The idea is that you can access the page from any web browser (which can be a security risk if the name of the output file is known to the outside world) to "harvest" the data collected by the form.

Once you've completed editing serv01.htm and serv02.htm (don't forget to update the page titles using File | Page Properties), use File | Save All. If you like, you can first remove the pesky Under Construction icon from the Services page, now that it's complete. When you save the pages, you'll be asked if you want to mark the task as completed in the To Do List. Click Yes.

Mission Accomplished

Believe it or not, at this point, you've completed a fully functional web site. If it's "quick and dirty," then so be it. To try out the site, use your web browser to access your web. If you're using the Personal Web Server or a local WWW server, you can open the default page from Internet Explorer or Netscape Navigator by typing http://localhost into the Address box or Open dialog box.

Note: The completed version of the Company web developed in this chapter can be found on this book's Companion CD-ROM in the \Webs\Company folder. If you want to work with this web with FrontPage, copy the Company folder to the root directory used by your web server; then run FrontPage Explorer and open your root web. Use the File | Import menu command and choose Add Folder to import the folder into FrontPage 97. You can now close your root web and open the Company subweb. This technique is the fastest way to import an entire existing web site as a FrontPage web.

Taking a Peek

Another way to try out your web is to open the home page using FrontPage Editor and then choose Preview in Browser from the File menu. Even though the FrontPage Editor closely matches the appearance of the actual web page, you'll find yourself previewing your pages often while working on your web. Just click the (Preview in Browser) icon on the toolbar.

TIP

One way to make the FrontPage Editor more closely resemble an actual web page is to hide the marks that FrontPage uses to show normally hidden material such as line breaks and form outlines. To switch between these views, click the Show/Hide Marks button.

If you have more than one WWW browser installed on your computer, the Preview in Browser window (Figure 2-32) lets you choose which browser to use and also lets you choose the default size of the browser window. This is great for anticipating how your pages will look at various screen resolutions. It's a good idea to install both Internet Explorer 3.0 and Netscape Navigator 3.0 or later so that you can make sure your pages "look right" when viewed by either popular browser. It's also a good idea to set your screen's color depth to 256 colors and preview the pages, especially if you normally work in TrueColor mode, so that you aren't surprised about how some of your graphics turn out.

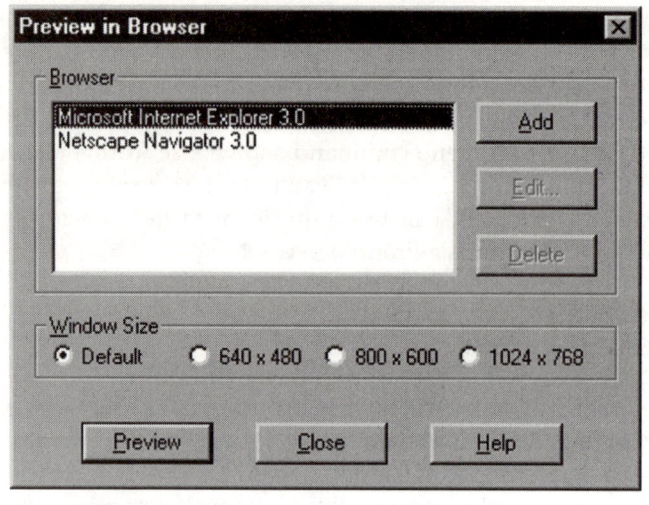

Figure 2-32: Try viewing your pages with both popular web browsers to avoid surprises.

Why Worry?

Why should you preview your pages, and why should you do so with more than one web browser? I alluded to this in Chapter 1. HTML is intentionally vague in the way it specifies formatting so that HTML documents can be displayed on a variety of computers with varying capabilities. A line of text using a Level 1 head should display in a larger typeface than normal text and in boldface. But there's no way (with standard HTML) to specify an exact point size or font for the text. So the same pages will look slightly different when viewed in one browser when compared to the same pages viewed with another browser.

Moving On

You've now completed your first "real-world" FrontPage web—or have you? Quick and dirty may be good enough for one's first effort, but for a really professional web site, you'll need to spiff things up. In the next two chapters, we'll learn how to take advantage of FrontPage techniques to add a custom background texture and use tables and the layout tools to produce typeset-quality pages. We'll also invent a custom animated toolbar, craft a complex data entry form from scratch, and demonstrate some of FrontPage Explorer's site management abilities.

chapter 3

Enhancing Your Site: FrontPage Techniques

As we saw in Chapter 2, the quickest way to get a site up and running is to prototype it with a template or wizard provided with FrontPage. The Company web we put together with the Corporate Presence Wizard is now ready for further enhancement—the spit and polish that will transform a generic web into a professional one.

As you work to enhance the Company web in this chapter, you'll incorporate custom graphics and design elements and see how to use tables for formatting text in columns. You'll take a closer look at how you can use the Include WebBot to easily update the look of related pages and use the Microsoft GIF Animator with FrontPage to create an animated navigation bar (toolbar) for convenient site navigation.

Creating a Custom Page Background

The first enhancement you'll make seems trivial, but it can have a great impact on the fit and finish of your web. You'll design a custom graphic to use as the page background (sometimes called a texture) for the pages in your web. The page background is one of the consistent design elements that can communicate a unique identity for your web site. In the previous chapter, you already customized the logo that's used on all pages. The page background graphic personalizes what would otherwise be a generic-looking site created from a template. After all, you don't want your company home page to resemble everyone else's.

Company Literature Suggests a Design

The page background we'll design is loosely based on the actual company literature used by Group US, the company we used for our example web in Chapter 2. The company letterhead is designed with a blue strip running down the left margin. *Group US Newsletter*, another company publication, uses this design element, which is also commonly employed in web page design. Figure 3-1 shows how the newsletter looks. You'll want to take into account the look of your company's (or your client's) existing literature when designing the site, again to establish a branded identity. Because the clients of Group US are familiar with the letterhead and newsletter, the look of the company's home page immediately communicates a continuity between what's on paper and what's on the Internet.

How do you create custom graphics? Although FrontPage has no graphical drawing features built into it, the FrontPage with Bonus Pack CD-ROM includes a powerful graphics manipulation tool called Microsoft Image Composer, along with a slew of ready-to-use clip art. (Be sure to install this software if you want to follow along with this chapter's examples.)

Chapter 3: Enhancing Your Site: FrontPage Techniques

Figure 3-1: The page design shown here in the Group US Newletter is one that's commonly employed in web page design.

Introducing Microsoft Image Composer

Image Composer lets you arrange clip art or imported graphics and apply various tools and special effects to the artwork. All the while, the independent clip-art elements (*sprites*) can be repositioned, since each sprite is a separate layer.

A more traditional tool like Adobe Photoshop can also work with artwork arranged in layers, but the focus is on pixels, the dark and light colored "dots" that an image comprises. Photoshop has tools for editing pictures by changing the values of these dots. For example, you can lighten an area of an image by choosing the dodge tool and dragging the mouse across the part of the image you want to lighten. Other popular graphics tools include Corel PhotoPaint (available separately or as part of the Corel Draw graphics suite), Ulead PhotoStudio, and Jasc Paint Shop Pro.

Image Composer also lets you darken or lighten, but the effect is applied to the entire sprite, not to a subregion. The only way to affect a region is to create a new shape, superimpose it over the original sprite, and use the Sprite-to-Sprite Copy tool to fill the new shape with a region from the original sprite. The new region can then be manipulated separately from the original image.

With some experience, you can accomplish virtually any image manipulation technique with Microsoft Image Composer, but a more traditional pixel-pushing program can be more productive, especially if that's the type of painting program you're accustomed to.

A Worthy Addition to Your Toolbox

In addition to Microsoft Image Composer, I highly recommend Paint Shop Pro 4.12 for image manipulation. Paint Shop Pro 4.12 is available for download from http://www.jasc.com/psp as shareware. In other words, if you decide to keep using the software, you are expected to pay a license/registration fee. (Paint Shop Pro is also available as a retail product.)

Paint Shop Pro offers virtually every feature of Adobe Photoshop and includes many specialized features that make it an ideal companion for working with graphics for publication on the World Wide Web or company intranet. It is also much less expensive than Photoshop or similar tools, and being a smaller program, starts up more quickly and makes more efficient use of your computer's memory.

Using Image Composer to Create the Background

Let's start working with Image Composer, assuming you already have it installed. As with the previous chapter, you can choose to follow along with the actual software, or just refer to the figures as you follow the text of this chapter.

After launching Microsoft Image Composer (by default, choose Start | Programs | Microsoft Image Composer), the first thing you need to do is to change the size of the composition guide. The composition guide in Image Composer is like a canvas used by a traditional artist. When you save your image as a GIF or JPG graphic, only the artwork positioned within the composition guide is created as a graphic. Since only the artwork within the composition guide is saved, the picture is cropped at the edges of the guide.

You can also save your images as MIC files, native to Microsoft Image Composer, in which case all the sprites are saved, even those that lie outside the boundaries of the composition guide. MIC files also preserve the independent nature of each sprite. Saving to another file format "flattens" your picture, merging all the sprites into a single graphic. For this reason, it's a good idea to always save your original compositions as MIC files so you can easily redesign them if needed. When you're ready to publish the graphic on your web, you can save a copy as a GIF or JPG. (FrontPage automatically converts an MIC file to a GIF or JPG when the page is saved. GIF graphics are created for pictures with less than 256 colors, otherwise JPG is used.)

Taking Advantage of Tiling

Use File | Composition Properties, which displays the Composition Properties dialog box (Figure 3-2), to change the size of the composition guide. Choose a width of 1024 and a height of 64, and then click OK. This will be the size of the strip that runs the width of the browser display. With a width of 1024, the background graphic will be wide enough to fit within the full size of a browser. Page backgrounds are automatically repeated horizontally and vertically using a method called tiling. Imagine you had to completely cover a surface with postage stamps. You'd use tiling to arrange the stamps across the page and along the length of the page.

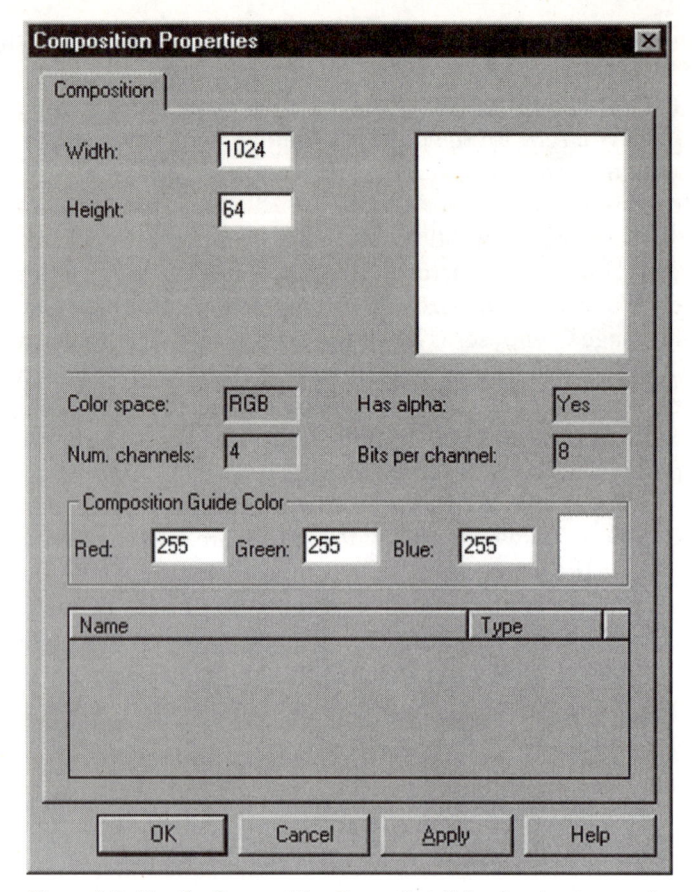

Figure 3-2: Use the Composition Properties dialog box to view or change the settings for the composition guide.

If the tile is wide enough, it appears to cover the entire page without repeating horizontally. Actually, if your computer's display was set to a resolution of 1600 X 1200 or so, the browser window could be made large enough to show the pattern repeating from left to right—there would be more than one blue border. The typical browser is operated in a graphics mode of 1024 X 768, 800 X 600, or 640 X 480, so only the leftmost part of the 1024-pixel-wide strip will show up.

On the other hand, by choosing a small height for the image, we can take advantage of tiling to completely fill the page background from top to bottom and keep the size of the graphic to a minimum, which saves download time for your visitors. We could have used a height even less than 64 for the image, but it can be tricky to manipulate the image if it's too tiny.

Chapter 3: Enhancing Your Site: FrontPage Techniques

> **TIP**
>
> *Another way to save download time is to save the image as a GIF with a reduced palette. Many graphics don't need the full range of 256 colors supported by the GIF format (actually 216 colors as implemented by most web browsers). By creating a custom palette that contains only the colors within the composition, the resulting GIF is smaller. You'll still want to use colors from the Balanced Ramp palette to avoid dithering when the image is viewed in 256-color mode. Let's say you've created an image using only 8 colors from the Balanced Ramp palette.*
>
> *To create a reduced palette with Microsoft Image Composer, choose Tools | Color Palette (or click the color box on the left side of the Image Composer window) and on the Custom Palette tab, click the New button. When prompted for a palette name, enter something like 8 color custom palette and choose a palette size of 8. Next, click the Generate Colors button, and then click the arrow next to the Generate From drop-down list and choose Composition.*
>
> *You can preview how your graphic looks with the custom palette simply by choosing the 8-color palette from the drop-down list box at the top of the Image Composer window. When saving the final graphic as a GIF file, make sure that the 8-color palette is chosen from the Save As dialog box.*
>
> *If you missed the discussion on GIF palettes, you may want to refer back to the section "Graphics Formats: GIF or JPEG?" in Chapter 2.*

The Image Composer window now shows the resized composition guide, but it's probably too wide to fully fit within the window. Choose the magnify tool (which looks like a magnifying glass), and to zoom out, hold down the Ctrl key while clicking on the composition guide. You can then use the scroll bars on the window to center the composition guide within the window. Your screen should resemble Figure 3-3.

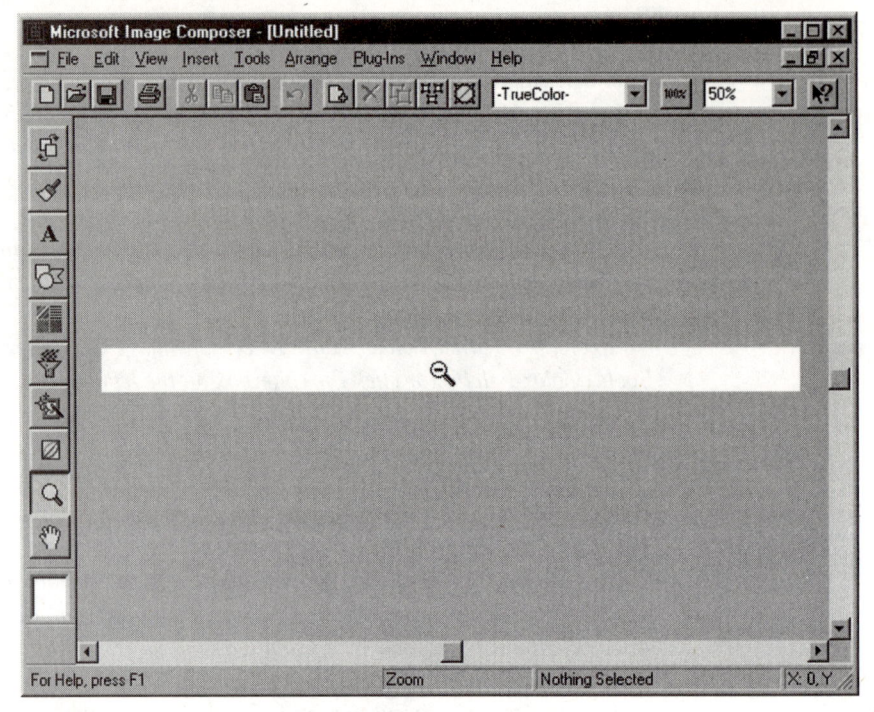

Figure 3-3: Once you've resized the composition guide, zoom out and center the guide within the window using the scroll bars.

Sketching It Out

Image Composer has no way to paint directly onto the composition guide, so we'll draw a rectangle just within the guide. This rectangle will form the body of the strip. Whereas the Group US letterhead and newsletter use a plain paper background, we want to have a little more texture, so we'll create a plain white rectangle and then add a touch of color.

To choose white as the default color for shapes, click the color box (found on the left side of the Image Composer window). When the Color Picker dialog box appears, choose the Balanced Ramp palette (from the Custom Palette tab), and choose white, the last color in the palette. Then click OK.

Once you've set the default color, use these steps to add the white background to the background tile:

1. First choose Tools | Shapes (Alt+4) or click the shapes icon (the fourth one on the toolbar at the left of the Image Composer window).

2. Click on the rectangle (box) shape at the top of the Shapes-Geometry tool palette. Each tool displays its options in a floating dialog box called a tool palette, not to be confused with the color palette used by an image. Figure 3-4 shows the Shapes-Geometry palette.

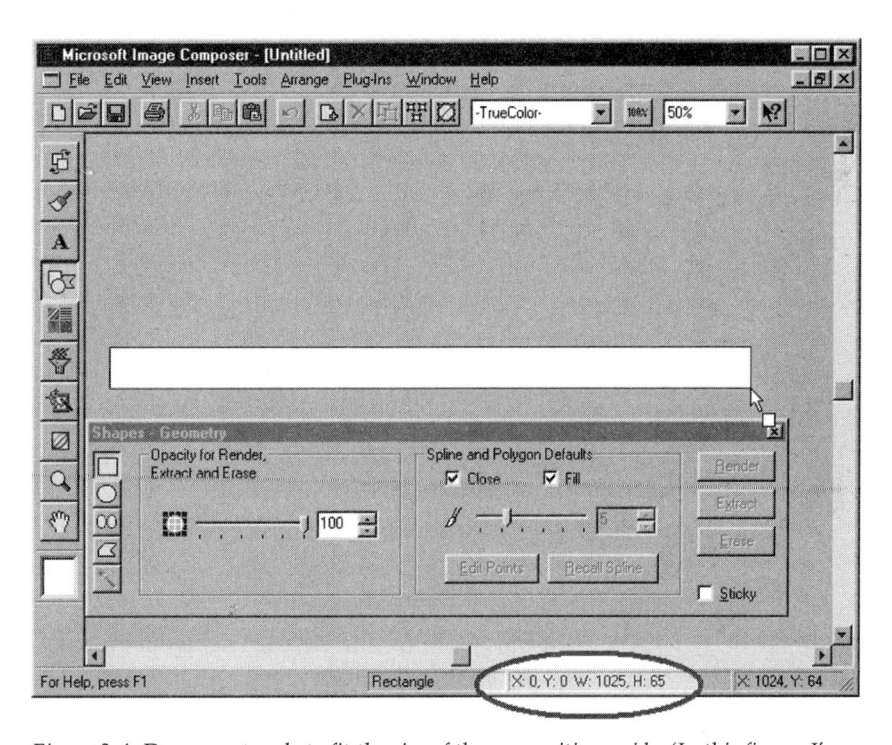

Figure 3-4: Drag a rectangle to fit the size of the composition guide. (In this figure, I've highlighted the region of the status bar that shows the height and width of the shape you're drawing.)

3. You'll use the mouse to drag out a box that fits within the composition guide. Pay attention to the right-hand side of the status bar: it reports the X, Y (across, down) position of the pointer, and when you drag the mouse (as when drawing the rectangle), the status bar also shows the height and width of the shape. (This region of the status bar is highlighted in Figure 3-4.) Position the pointer in the upper left corner of the guide (X=0, Y=0) and drag down and to the right until the shape has a width of 1024 and a height of 64 (see Figure 3-4). Because you're zoomed out, you may find that only odd-numbered coordinates appear, so you can set the width to 1025 and the height to 65, keeping in mind that the extra pixels will be cropped when the image is saved, to fit within the composition guide.

4. Draw another box from X=0, Y=0 with a width of about 116 and height of 64 (or W:115 H:65 if you can only get odd-numbered coordinates). This box is placed at the left of the first box you've drawn. This is the one that will be colored blue. (Note that the boxes appear to have a border, but this is only to delineate the shape on the screen—when the image is saved, only the interior of the shape is used.)

Adding Color & Texture

Now we can add some color. We'll use the Patterns and Fills feature of Image Composer to create a patterned texture and then adjust it to allow for more readable text:

1. Choose the Patterns and Fills tool palette by clicking the fifth icon on the toolbar at the left of Image Composer or by choosing Tools | Patterns and Fills (Alt+5).

2. Click the color box and set the current color to a shade of blue (I used the sixth color from the left on the sixth row of the palette). Click the smaller box (you can press the Tab key to move from shape to shape) and choose Current Color Fill from the Patterns and Fills tool palette; then click Apply. The smaller box is now blue.

3. Now select the larger rectangle, and choose Patterns from the Patterns and Fills tool palette. Using the Patterns drop-down list box, choose Color Noise. Next, drag the slider at the bottom to 15 percent. Click Apply.

A washed-out grainy color background appears within the larger rectangle. (Setting the slider to more than 15 percent creates a more dramatic effect, but we need to use a washed-out, light background so that the text will show up clearly.) This is demonstrated in Figure 3-5.

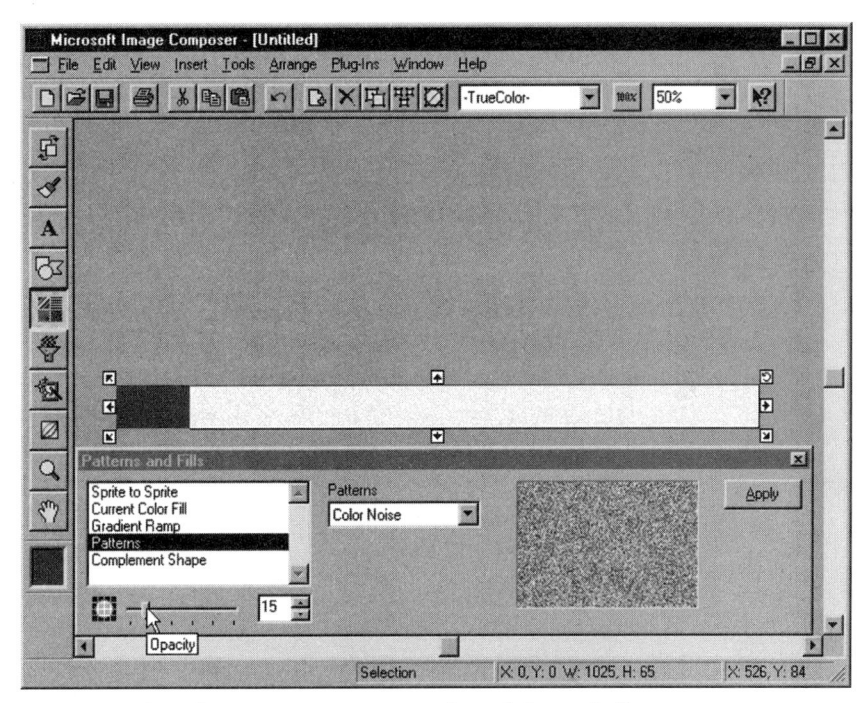

Figure 3-5: The Color Noise pattern creates a "recycled paper" effect.

You can play around with some of the other Image Composer tools, such as the Art Effects palette, to vary the appearance of the background and apply special effects, but for now, let's go ahead and save the completed background texture.

First, use File | Save (or the toolbar button) to save the image as a Microsoft Image Composer file, using a filename like gusbkgd (for Group US Background). Save it to a folder on your hard drive. It's a good idea to create a dedicated folder on your hard drive to hold the components of your web. You can then easily import these graphics into a page with Insert | File in the FrontPage Editor. The originals remain available on your hard drive for future use and modification.

Use File | Save As to also save the image as a JPG graphic (ignore the warnings that tell you the sprites will be flattened—the sprite layout is preserved in the MIC version of the file you saved). JPG is the file type that best preserves the color range of the graphic—to see how the graphic would look when saved as a GIF, choose the Balanced Ramp palette from the top of the Image Composer window. You can try saving the background both as a GIF and a JPG and use the one that has the smallest file size. (The completed graphic, gusbkgd.jpg, can be found in the \Webs\Groupus\Images folder on this book's Companion CD-ROM.)

Applying the Custom Background

Now we're ready to try out the custom background. You can close the Image Composer program to free up memory and then start the FrontPage Explorer, if it's not already running. From the Getting Started dialog, open the Company web that we created in Chapter 2. (If the Company web is not shown on this dialog, use File | Open from FrontPage Explorer and click List Webs so that you can choose it.)

Here's how to apply the custom background to all the pages in the web:

1. Using the FrontPage Explorer, switch to folder view and open the Web Colors (style.htm) page from the _private folder.

2. Next choose File | Page Properties (Figure 3-6). From here, click the Background tab heading and click Browse.

3. From the Select Background Image dialog box, click the Other Location tab, and again click the Browse button. Navigate to the folder in which you saved the gusbkgd.jpg file, and select that image.

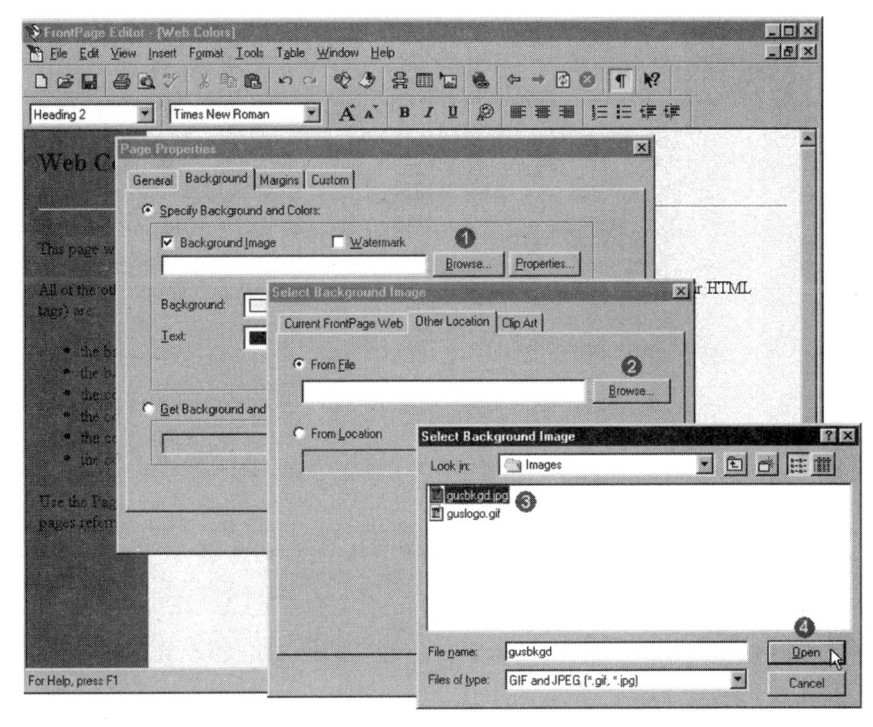

Chapter 3: Enhancing Your Site: FrontPage Techniques 117

Figure 3-6: Use File | Page Properties to reveal the Background property sheet, which lets you change the background graphic. (a) Click Browse to open the Select Background Image dialog box, and then (b) click Browse from the Other Location tab. You can then (c) locate the image on your hard drive and (d) click Open to import it.

At this point, you've placed the graphic on the Web Colors page, but the graphic file is still located on your hard drive. This isn't acceptable for web publishing, where all files should be located in the web folder (or one of its subfolders). To fix this, save the Web Colors page. You'll be prompted for a folder to store the background graphic. Edit the default URL, gusbkgd.jpg, to read images/gusbkgd.jpg, so that the graphic will be stored with the other images. FrontPage Explorer copies the file from the hard drive to the web.

Now that you've created a custom page background, you're ready to see how the rest of the Company web looks. Switch to the FrontPage Explorer and open the home page (index.htm or index.html). It should resemble Figure 3-7.

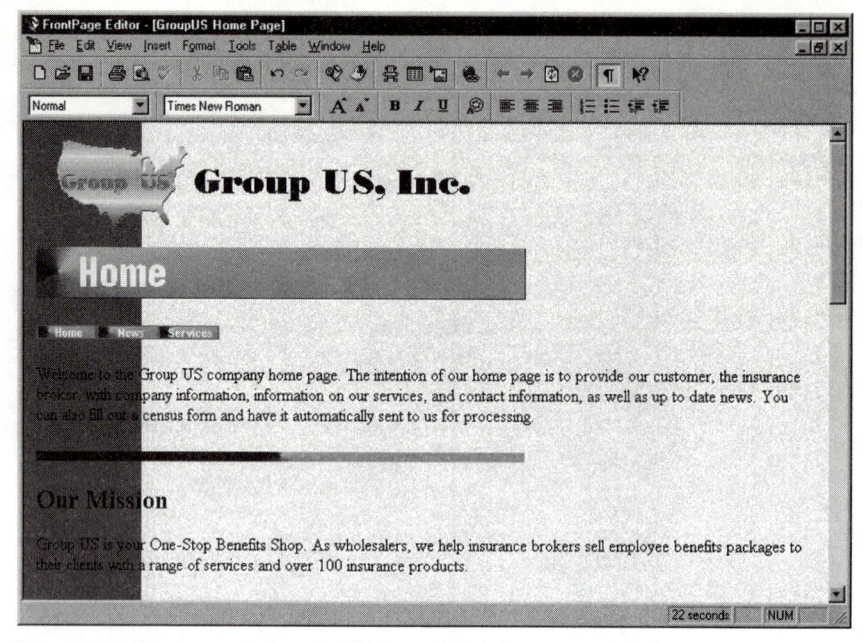

Figure 3-7: The custom background looks cool, but the text needs to be moved out of the way of the blue strip.

Don't Cross the Border

When you examine the home page (or Figure 3-7), a problem is immediately apparent. The text on the page starts at the left margin, which is occupied by the blue border. Since the text is black, it doesn't show up clearly on a dark blue background. What we need is a way to shove the text over to the right, so that it avoids the blue strip.

Easy Over

The easiest way to move the text is to indent it. Click the mouse pointer anywhere within the first paragraph ("Welcome to the Group US company home page . . ."), and then click the Increase Indent toolbar button. Click it two more times. After applying the indent to several other paragraphs and graphics, your screen should resemble Figure 3-8.

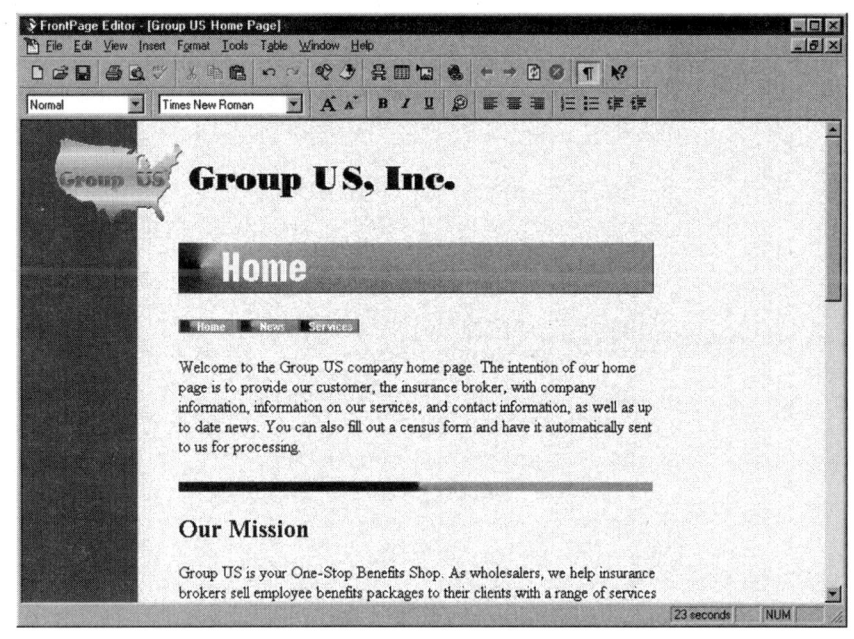

Figure 3-8: With the page content indented to the right, it no longer overlaps the border element.

Technically speaking, the indent command inserts a <BLOCKQUOTE> HTML tag prior to the paragraph or item and a </BLOCKQUOTE> tag after. Although originally designed for the formatting of quoted material, which is traditionally indented, BLOCKQUOTE is handy any time you want to arbitrarily indent text. (The amount of indentation may vary depending on which browser is used to view the page and the settings used by that browser, such as font size.) Of course, you don't need to know which HTML tags are used, since FrontPage generates the code automatically, but if you'd like to see how the BLOCKQUOTE tags work, use the View | HTML menu command.

Indentation Limitations

Problem solved? Not quite. While you can indent most items, including graphics and embedded Include WebBots (our logo doesn't need to be indented—refer to Figure 3-1), HTML doesn't permit text using certain tags to be indented. You'll run into this new problem when you try to indent the contact information at the bottom of the page. This text is formatted as pairs of Defined Term/Definition HTML tags, which automatically boldface the Defined Term and indents the Definition. Since indentation is built into this HTML style pair, the BLOCKQUOTE is ignored when applied to the Defined Term text.

You could work around this problem by changing the contact information to Normal text. The indentation does appear to solve the original problem: how to get the text off the blue strip.

Aligning Text With Tables

There's a better way, however, to align text, a method vastly preferred by webmasters. We'll create a two-column table. The leftmost column will occupy the area reserved for the blue strip, and the remaining column will hold the content (text and graphics) on the page. By using a border width of zero, the outlines of the table will be invisible when the page is browsed—all you get is the alignment of the text into columns.

You can use tables any time you want to overcome the inherent limitations of HTML formatting. Whether you want a three-column newsletter format, a way to line up labels and text boxes, or a catalog format with pictures and descriptions, use a table.

Note: Some people have not upgraded to modern browsers with table support, or are browsing the web with a text-only browser. While tables are now considered essential for web page layout, keep in mind that a few of the visitors to your page won't be happy with the way the text is formatted. The only alternative to tables for formatted text is the simple HTML formatting tags, such as the BLOCKQUOTE (indent) method discussed earlier.

I recommend that you use tables, and if for some reason your visitors complain, design another simpler version of your site for the browser-impaired. Put a link to this version ("No Tables") on the home page, and you might as well also leave off the graphics on that version of the site. Or don't bother—anyone who hasn't upgraded to a newer browser isn't going to be a very active Internet user in any case.

Let's see how this works. First, remove the indentation you applied earlier by selecting each paragraph and clicking the Decrease Indent toolbar button.

Next, position the text insertion point at the bottom of the document, press Enter to insert a blank line, and insert a table by choosing Table | Insert Table.

TIP

Instead of manually reversing each indentation, you may simply wish to revert to the previous version of the home page. Choose View | Refresh, and when prompted to save the page, click No. This reloads the version of the page currently stored in the web.

When you use Table | Insert Table, the Insert Table dialog box appears (see Figure 3-9). With this dialog box, you can choose the number of rows and columns in the table and specify other table settings, such as the alignment of the table on the page (default, left, right, center). You can also choose a border size, which sets the number of pixels to use for the lines that divide the table into rows and columns. *Cell padding* is the amount of space that's inserted "around" the text inside a cell to separate it from the table's borders. *Cell spacing* is the amount of space that's inserted between cells. (A *cell* is an individual area, at the intersection of a given row and column, that holds an item in a table.)

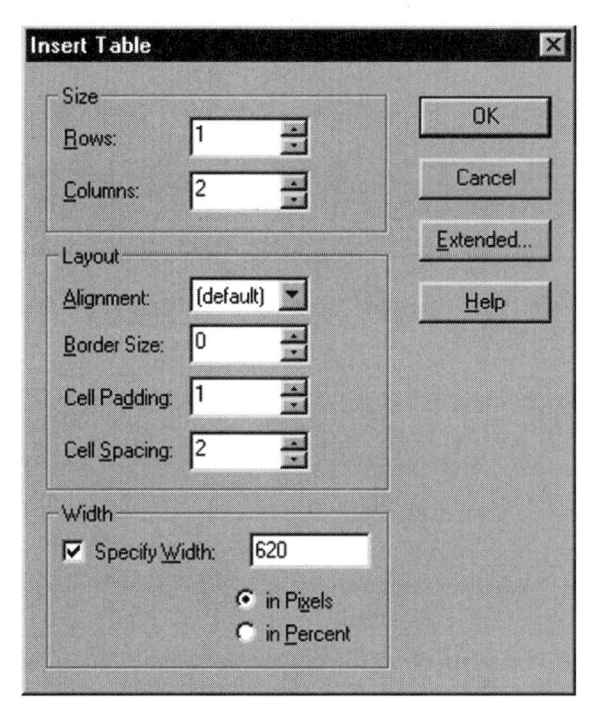

Figure 3-9: Fill out the dialog box as shown here to create a two-column table with one row.

> **TIP**
>
> *Rather than using Table | Insert table, you may prefer to click the Insert Table toolbar button. A grid appears beneath the button, representing rows and columns. Just drag within the grid to choose the number of rows and columns you'd like for your table. To change other table properties, right-click inside the table and choose Table Properties from the context menu.*

Fill out the Insert Table choices as shown in Figure 3-9. We're creating a table with a single row and two columns, default alignment, and no border, with a cell padding of 1 and cell spacing of 2.

Also note the Width section. If you click the check box or enter a value into the Specify Width box, you can set a fixed width for the table in pixels or as a percentage of the width of the browser. Many times, you'll leave the check box turned off so that the table can grow or shrink to fit the full width of the browser, but a narrow table can be created by choosing a percentage width.

By choosing a particular width in pixels, you gain greater control over the layout of the table. We'll use a width of 620 pixels so that the table will fit within the browser window when running at desktop resolutions as low as 640 X 480.

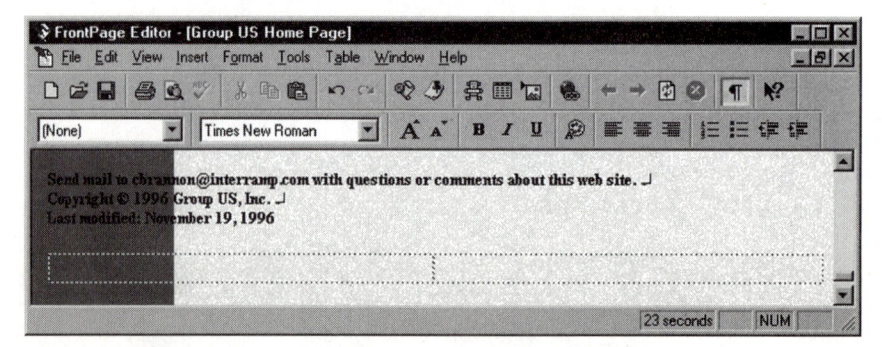

Figure 3-10: We've created a table with one row and two columns, but we haven't set the width of the columns yet.

Click OK to insert the table on the page. It will initially resemble Figure 3-10. After inserting the table, you're ready to type into the first cell of the table.

Cell Properties

But don't type anything yet. Instead, use Table | Cell Properties (or right-click on the first cell and choose Cell Properties from the pop-up context menu). This pops up the Cell Properties dialog box (Figure 3-11).

Note: The table has only one row, so you can set the properties of each cell to change the width of the columns. If the table has more than one row (which is typical), you first need to select the entire column or row before choosing Cell Properties. To do so, position the mouse pointer just above the first cell in the column. Look for the pointer to change to a thick arrow pointing down. Click. This selects the entire column. You can also set the cell properties for an entire row. Again, first position the pointer just to the left of the first cell, and when the pointer changes to a right-pointing arrow, click to select the entire row and then choose Table | Cell Properties.

If you don't select the column before setting cell properties, you may end up changing only the properties of a single cell. This can result in a table with varying widths for each cell, which is rarely desirable.

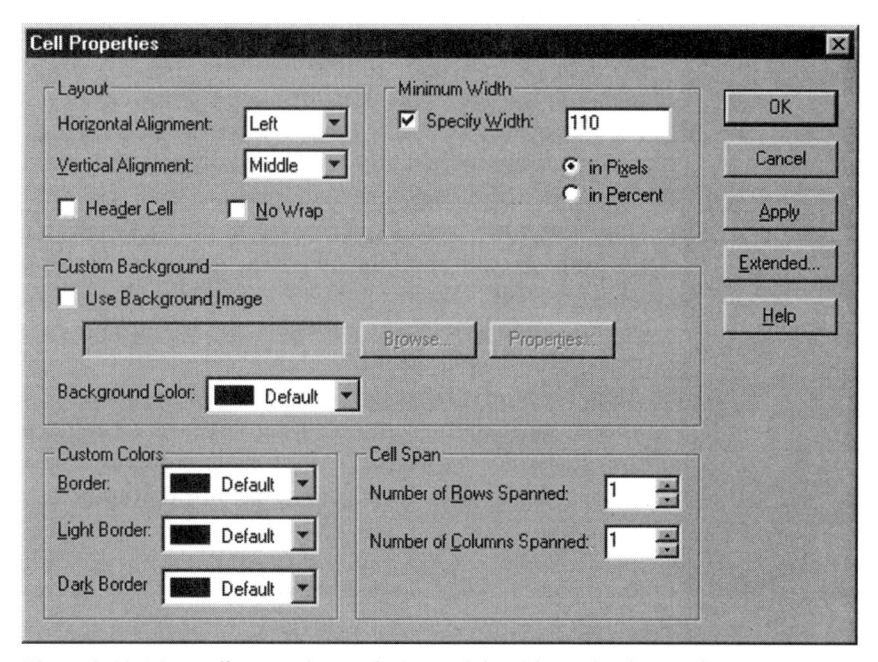

Figure 3-11: Most cell properties can be ignored, but it's good to know what options you have at your fingertips.

The Cell Properties dialog box (Figure 3-11) is a busy place. You can choose from a dozen different properties (settings) to customize the cell (or row/column if that's what you selected). The most important are the layout options, which let you choose how text in a column is lined up. Horizontal alignment is obvious enough—you can use it to left-justify, center, or right-justify the text within a cell.

Vertical alignment only makes sense if you realize that a cell can span several rows. This can happen if you've used Table | Merge Cells to join two cells together or if the text in the cell can't fit on a single line and is wrapped to the next line. (You can prevent this by checking No Wrap.) When a cell is taller than one line of text, you may want to choose how the text is aligned vertically within the cell. Choose Middle to center the text vertically, Top to align the text starting at the top of the cell, or Bottom to line up the text against the bottom of the cell.

Another option in the Alignment section, Header Cell, can be checked to tell FrontPage to format the cell (or row or column of cells) as a header cell, which tells most browsers to simply boldface the text.

Taking Control of Column Width

Note the section labeled Minimum Width. This is an important part of our scheme to align the text using a table. Normally, no minimum width is set, so that the full width of the cell is available for text. This width can vary depending on the length of text in the cell, the width of the table, and the width of the browser window.

You want more control over formatting, so specify an exact width in pixels for each column in the table. The leftmost column will be set to 110 pixels, and the remainder of the table's 620-pixel width, which is 510, will be assigned to the rightmost column. Using 110 pixels for the leftmost column enlarges that column sufficiently to "push over" the rightmost column far enough to avoid the blue strip.

Note: If you set one column's minimum width in pixels, be sure to set all the other columns, too, so that all the column widths add up to the table's width in pixels. If you fail to do this, there's no telling how the table will look; that will depend on how the browser decides to deal with the problem. There's no way to set a maximum width, but as long as you allow the text to wrap, it will fit within the minimum width. Some items, like large graphics, can override the minimum width, so be careful if you want to preserve your layout.

Colored Tables & Table Backgrounds

As long as we're examining the Cell Properties dialog box, let's take a quick look at the other options, most of which are unnecessary for most tables. You can use the Custom Background section to insert a graphic as the background of the cell. You can use the Background Color choice to choose a color for the cell. We could have used this technique to create the blue strip simply by setting the leftmost column to blue. But table background colors are not supported by all browsers, so to reach the largest audience, it's best to avoid advanced features. However, both Internet Explorer 3.0 and Netscape Navigator 3.0 (or higher versions) do support table backgrounds.

If your audience uses one of the advanced browsers, you may wish to choose custom colors for the table borders. Leave all the settings to default if you want the browser to choose these colors. Otherwise, you can set the color of the border itself, the light border color, which is the "highlight" color of the 3D border, and the dark border color, which is the "shadow" color of the 3D border.

Merging Cells

The Cell Span section lets you see if the cell is merged with other cells. You can use this feature to make a cell span (or occupy) more than one physical row or column. An easier way to merge cells is to use the FrontPage Editor. Select more than one cell by dragging the pointer between cells, and choose Table | Merge Cells. Cells already joined can be broken apart with Table | Split Cells.

Changing the Column Widths

To create columns that reserve space for the border and allow space for the page content, we only need to set the minimum width for each column, using these steps:

1. If the Cell Properties dialog box isn't shown, click within the first (leftmost) cell of the table and choose Table | Table Properties.
2. Click the Specify Width check box, choose the option In Pixels, and enter a width of 110.
3. Click OK.

4. Click within the second column and choose Table | Cell Properties.

5. Click Specify Width, set Minimum Width to 510 pixels, and click OK. The table should now resemble Figure 3-12.

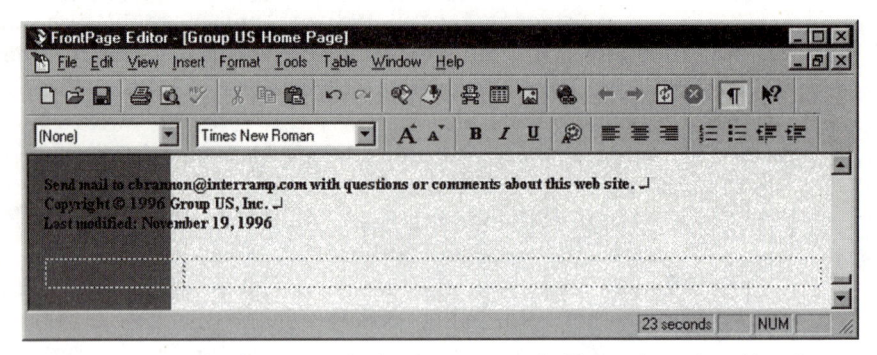

Figure 3-12: Now there's a reserved column to occupy the blue strip, and a wide column to hold the rest of the page.

Moving the Content Into the Table

Now the table is ready to use to transform the page. To accomplish this, you have to move all the content from above the table into the rightmost column of the table.

1. First move to the top of the document by pressing the Ctrl+Home key combination.

2. Press the Down arrow key once to move past the logo, which won't be placed inside the table.

3. Next, select the rest of the document, all the way down to the text just above the table, by holding down the Shift key while pressing the Down arrow key. (If you go too far and select the table by mistake, keep holding down Shift and press the Up arrow key until the table is no longer part of the selection. You can also select text by dragging across it with the mouse pointer, but the keyboard method is somewhat more reliable and precise.)

4. Now that all the text is highlighted, press Ctrl+X or choose Edit | Cut. The text disappears from the page, having been moved into the Windows clipboard.
5. Click inside the second cell of the table we created earlier, and press Ctrl+V or choose Edit | Paste. The text flows into the second cell, which expands vertically to fit all the content within it.

After you remove a few blank lines left over, the FrontPage Editor should now resemble Figure 3-13. Save your work. You can click the Preview in Browser button to make sure it all checks out in the actual browser.

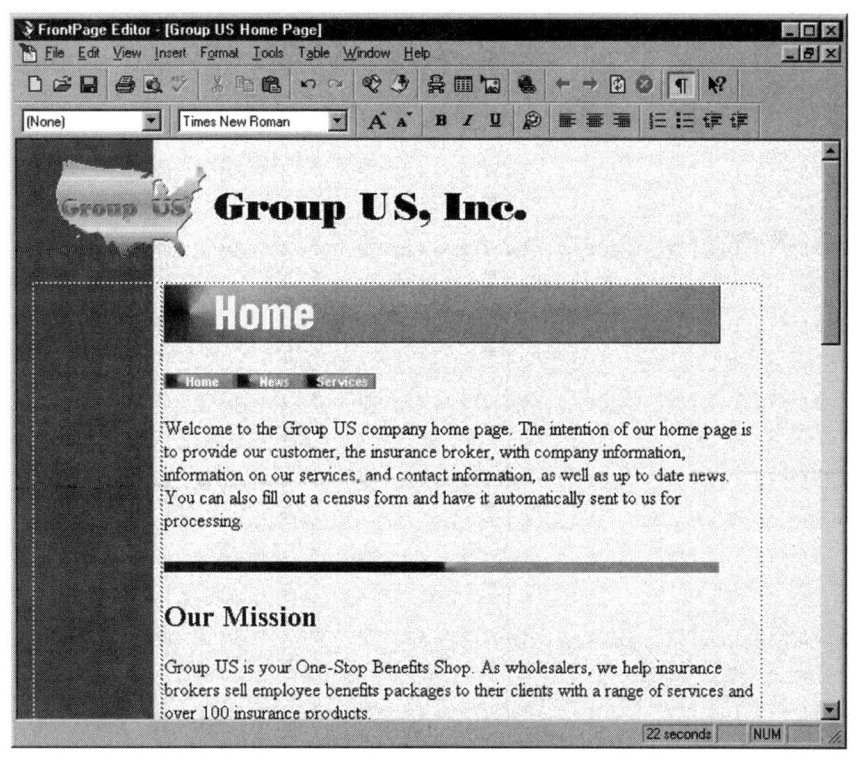

Figure 3-13: The table takes care of aligning the content so that it avoids the blue strip.

Whew! All that trouble just to use a simple design element like a blue border? It looks cool, though, and you've now learned the fundamentals of using tables for aligning text.

Update the Other Pages, Too

At this stage, you need to apply the same technique (inserting a table and moving the content into the second column) to all the other pages in your web, since they all use the new background with the blue strip. We won't belabor the point with all the details, just come back to this point in the chapter when you're finished. You may also wish to create a blank page to use as a template for future pages. Just customize a page like we did with the home page, delete all the content (but leave the table behind), and save it to your web as Blank Page.

If you followed along with Chapter 2, you may have already created such a page. Just update it by adding the table, and it's ready for any new pages you wish to add to your web. Just open the page titled Blank Page, and immediately use File | Save As to save a copy with a new name (so you don't accidentally wipe out Blank Page), and start working with the new page.

Creating a Blank Page

Whenever we add a new page to the web, we'll start by opening the Blank Page. If you don't have such a page, create one now. It will be very useful when creating new pages for your web:

1. From the FrontPage Editor, click the New Page button.
2. Choose File | Page Properties, and change the title of the page to Blank Page.
3. Click the Background tab, and click the option button for Get Background and Colors From Page.
4. Click the Browse button and select Web Colors (style.htm) from the _private folder. (The custom page background should now appear on the new page.)
5. Click Insert | WebBot Component. Choose the Include WebBot.
6. When asked for the page URL to include, type **_private/logo.htm**, and click OK. The Group US logo will appear at the top of the page.
7. Press the Down arrow key to move to the line beneath the logo.
8. Choose Table | Insert Table. File out the Table dialog box to specify a table with one row, two columns, and a width of 620 pixels.

9. Right-click within the first (leftmost) cell of the table and choose Cell Properties. Change the minimum width to 110 pixels.
10. Right-click within the second (rightmost) cell of the table and choose Cell Properties. Change the minimum width to 510 pixels.
11. Left-click within the rightmost column, and choose Insert | Comment. Type the comment **Place web content here.** Click OK.
12. Use File | Save and save the page as Blank Page. (You may wish to change the default URL from blankpag.htm to blank.htm for simplicity.)

Because templates don't support WebBots (but wizards can), you may have problems saving the blank page as a template. If you do save the page as a template, you'll be able to call it up using File | New, but the logo will be missing until you save the page and use View | Refresh to reload the page.

In any case, you can use Blank Page as a template by simply opening the page and then using File | Save As to make a copy of it with the name of the new page you're creating. This avoids accidental replacement of the original Blank Page web page.

When you update your web design (later in this chapter, we'll add a custom navigation bar), be sure to update Blank Page, so that it will always be ready for creating a new page in your web.

Creating a Contacts Page

Another use for tables is to support, well, tables. Tables with the gridlines showing are handy for storing lists of information, including data imported from databases (such as tables created with the Internet Assistants for Access 95 or Excel 95 or those saved as HTML from Office 97). You'll use tables to create a Contacts page with links to pages for each employee of Group US.

Open the blank page you created earlier (and named Blank Page), and use File | Save As to save it as Contacts Page, with a URL of contacts.htm. (Be sure to change both the title and the URL, or you'll overwrite the blank.htm page.) We'll now add a table for the staff of Group US.

Since we want the new table to also avoid the blue border, place the new table inside the table that's already on the page. That's right—you can place tables inside of tables. The inner table is called a *nested table*. (If an empty table doesn't already exist, refer to "Creating a Blank Page" earlier in the chapter.)

Here's how to create the nested table:

1. First click within the rightmost cell, delete the comment (if present), and type **The Staff of Group US**.

2. Use the drop-down list at the top of the FrontPage Editor to change this line to Heading 1. Press the Enter key to move to the next line.

3. Click on the Insert Table button and drag down five rows and across three columns (a 5 X 3 table). After creating the table, use Table | Table Properties to set the width of the table to 500 pixels and the border size to 1. Or use Table | Insert Table and specify 5 rows and 3 columns, with a width of 500 pixels and border size of 1. The table will resemble Figure 3-14.

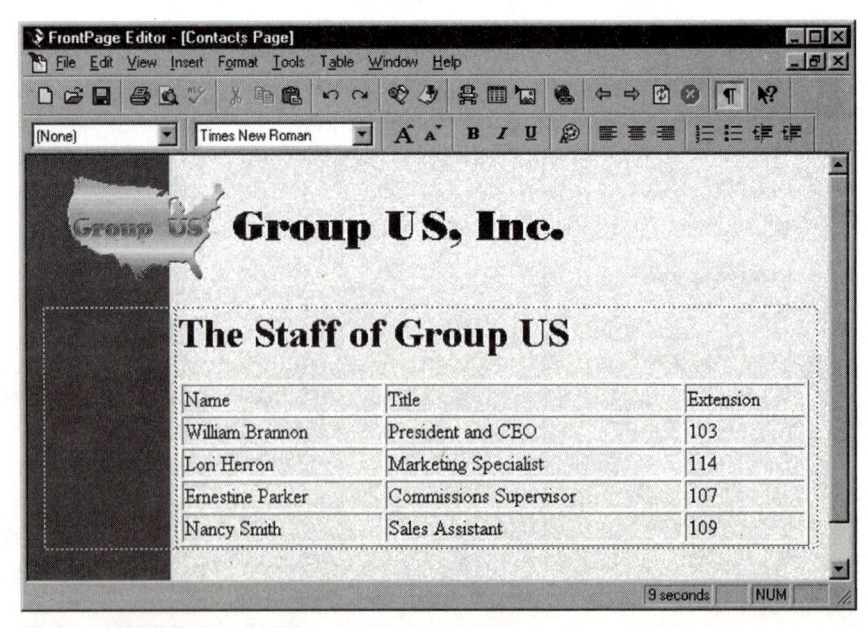

Figure 3-14: The Staff table is inserted inside the layout table.

4. Fill out the entries in the table to match the figure. Note that you don't have to size the columns individually (unless you want more control over column widths). The columns resize automatically as you type to balance the available space with the width of the text in each column.

Let's spiff up the table a bit:

1. First, position the pointer just to the left of the first row (containing the headings), and when the pointer changes to a right-pointing arrow, click to select the entire row. Right-click on the selection and choose Cell Properties from the pop-up context menu.

Since you've selected a row, the Cell Properties will be applied to all cells on that row.

2. Click the Header Cell check box, then click OK. (You may wish to first choose a custom background color for the heading before clicking OK, but that's optional.) By choosing the Header Cell check box, you've turned the first row bold. You could have just clicked the Bold button on the toolbar to make the text bold, but by using the standard HTML Header Cell format, you'll allow the browser to choose whatever formatting is appropriate for table headings.

Next, improve the layout of the table by centering the second and third columns:

1. First select both columns: position the pointer just above the second column until it changes to a downward-pointing arrow. Click and drag across to the third column. Both the second and third columns are now selected (highlighted in black).

2. Click the Center button on the formatting toolbar. This has the same effect as choosing Cell Properties and changing the Horizontal Alignment to Center.

Let's say you now want to add a link to return to the home page. The link needs to be inserted underneath the table. Try as you may, you probably won't be able to move the text insertion point beneath the table. As you move the arrow down, the insertion point moves down from the nested table directly to the area beneath the outer table. There seems to be no way to position the text insertion point beneath the Staff table yet within the outer table.

Here's the tricky workaround. While the text insertion point is within the inner Staff table, press Ctrl+Enter (hold down the Ctrl key while pressing the Enter key). This inserts a new line beneath the table. You can use this trick any time you need to add a new line between objects on a page.

3. Now you can type: **Return to Home Page.**

4. Use the drop-down list on the formatting toolbar to change the text to Heading 3, which makes it large and bold enough to stand out without being too distracting.

5. Select the text with the mouse, and press Ctrl+K or click the Edit Hyperlink button. Choose Home Page from the Current FrontPage Web tab (or from the Open Pages tab if the home page is still open within FrontPage Editor).

The home page of a web normally has a URL of index.htm. (Depending on the settings of your web server, the home page may be stored as index.html or _default.htm.)

The Contacts page should now resemble Figure 3-15. Not bad for a few minute's work.

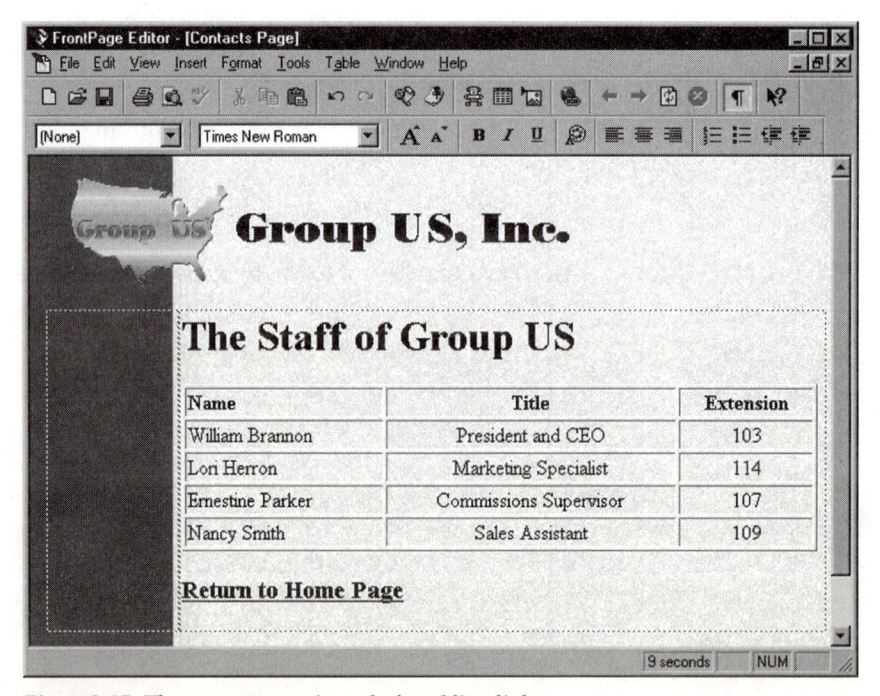

Figure 3-15: The contacts page is ready for adding links.

6. Now click File | Save to save the (nearly) complete Contacts page to the web. Leave this page open; we're not quite finished yet.

To make the Contacts page even more useful, we can create a page for each employee and link the person's name in the table directly to that page. Let's create a page for the first entry, William Brannon.

7. From the FrontPage Editor, click File | Open and open the blank page you created earlier (see "Creating a Blank Page" earlier in the chapter).

8. Immediately use File | Save As and save it with the title William J. Brannon with a URL of guswjb.htm.

9. Click within the second column of the table, delete the comment (if present), and type **William J. Brannon**. Click the Center button on the formatting toolbar, and using the drop-down list at the left of the FrontPage Editor's toolbar, set the paragraph style to Heading 1. Press Enter.

10. On the next line, type **President and Chief Executive Officer**. Set this paragraph to Heading 2. Beneath that line, enter the text Extension 103 and set that paragraph to Heading 3.

11. Beneath the extension text, add another line that reads Email: WilliamBrannon@groupus.com; then press Enter. As soon as you press Enter, FrontPage automatically converts the e-mail address to a Mailto hyperlink.

When the visitor to this page clicks on the e-mail address, the e-mail program (installed on the client's computer) appears with the address already filled in, ready to send a message. Set the paragraph style of this line also to Heading 3.

Now we'll add an employee "mug shot."

12. Click within the first column of the table, then choose Insert | Image. We've included a scanned photograph of the Group US president, scaled to a width of 128 pixels, and saved as a grayscale GIF. Look for it on the CD-ROM accompanying this book in the \Webs\Groupus\Images folder as wjb.gif.

Don't forget to add a link to the previous page. Links are the most important way to make your site convenient for your visitors.

13. Beneath the text "Extension 103," add the text Return to Contacts Page, and set it to the Heading 4 style.

14. Select the text, press Ctrl+K, and use the Open Pages tab to set the link to the Contacts page (contacts.htm).

If for some reason the Contacts page is no longer open within the FrontPage editor, use the Current FrontPage Web tab and browse to the Contacts page.

When you've completed the steps above, the William J. Brannon employee page is essentially complete. It should resemble Figure 3-16. Depending on the nature of your company's business, you can add additional information here such as job responsibilities, biographical information, awards won and designations earned, and so on.

15. Choose File | Save to update the page on the web. You'll be asked to approve the location of the GIF (the photograph) you inserted. Make sure it goes into images/wjb.gif.

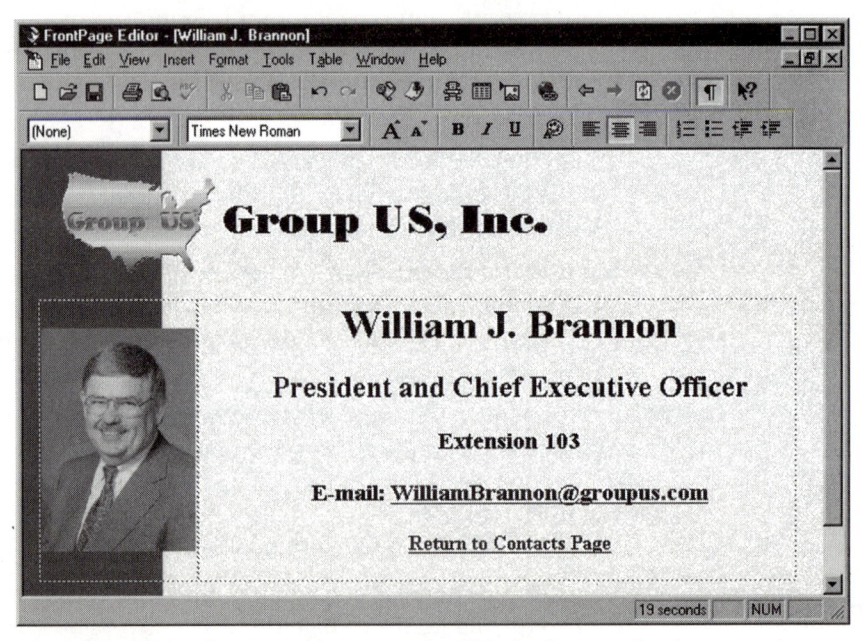

Figure 3-16: This is how an employee page should look when completed.

As with the blank page, you may also want to reuse this page whenever you add additional employees. Start by erasing the information specific to William Brannon, replacing his name with Employee Name, his extension with Extension XXX, and remove the picture (or insert a placeholder picture, such as the one provided on the Companion CD-

ROM as \Webs\Groupus\Images\placehold.gif). You can then save the page as Blank Employee Page with a URL of eeblank.htm. Whenever you create a new employee page, start by opening Blank Employee Page, save it with a new name and URL, and start typing.

Linking the Web Together

Now that you've created an employee page and a Contacts page, you need to link these to the rest of your web. (As it stands now, these are "orphaned" pages, since no other pages link to them.)

Right-click on the Return to Contacts Page link and choose Follow Link from the pop-up menu (or just Ctrl+Click on the link). This opens Contacts Page into the FrontPage Editor, a convenient way to verify that the link is correct.

To link the Contacts page to the William J. Brannon page, follow these steps:

1. Select the text "William Brannon" in the table, and press Ctrl+K.
2. From the Open Pages tab, choose the William J. Brannon page.

The Contacts page contains a link back to the home page.

3. Follow that link (by using Ctrl+Click upon the link) back to the home page. Now the home page is open within the FrontPage Editor.

Although the Contacts page points back to the home page, there is no link from the home page to the Contacts page. Let's add one:

4. Scroll toward the bottom of the Home Page document, and insert a blank line above the text "Telephone" by pressing Enter. On this line, type **Additional Contact Information**, and set its paragraph style to Heading 3.
5. Select the text, press Ctrl+K, and link it to the Contacts page using the Open Pages tab. (Figure 3-17 shows you how this looks.)

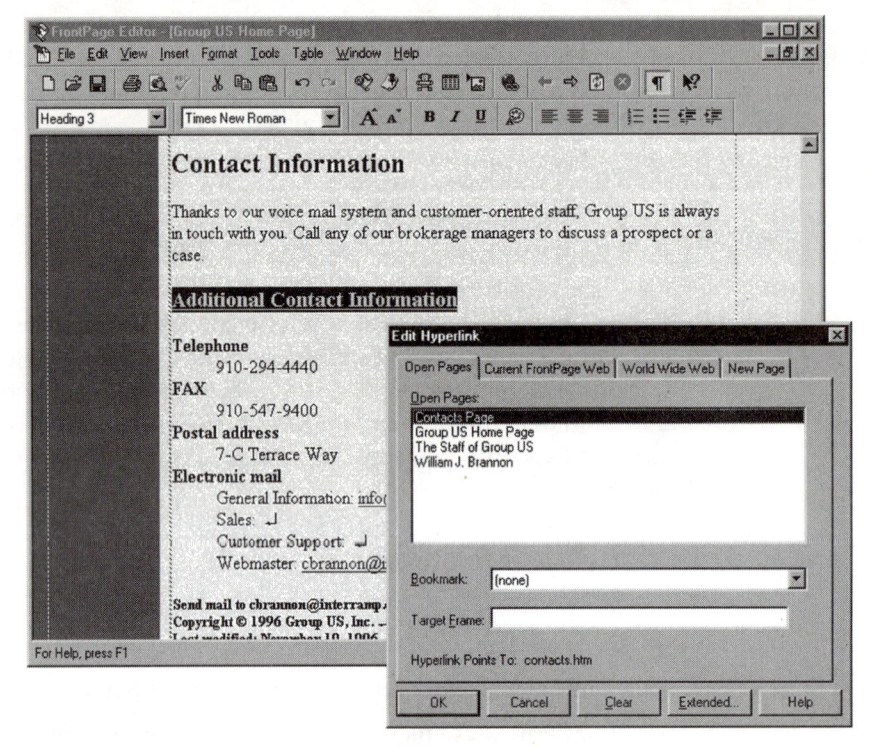

Figure 3-17: Add a link to the home page so that the Contacts page is no longer an orphan.

Building an Animated Graphic for Use as a Navigation Bar

The next enhancement you'll add to your web is an animated navigation bar (similar to a toolbar) to replace the rather lame graphics inserted by the Corporate Presence Wizard. We'll place our navigation bar inside the blue border, so the space isn't completely wasted.

To begin, you'll create an animated GIF image. Later in this chapter, you'll insert the animation onto the Included Navigation Bar page (replacing the one created by the Corporate Presence Wizard) and turn the animation into a working navigation bar by adding links to it.

To download the Microsoft GIF Animator, visit http://www.microsoft.com/sitebuilder and register for Guest Access to the Site Builder Network. (Originally, this tool was to be included with the *Microsoft FrontPage 97 With Bonus Pack CD-ROM*, but was not included on the shipping version.)

MS GIF Animator makes it easy to link together a series of graphics to create an animated GIF. Web browsers that support the animated GIF format, such as versions 3.0 or greater of Microsoft Internet Explorer and versions 2.0 or greater of Netscape Navigator, automatically display each frame in the animation in succession, and can loop the animation so that it appears to move continuously.

To get started, you need to create several graphic images. Each image is one frame of the animation. To create your graphics, you can combine clip art sprites in Microsoft Image Composer or use Microsoft Paint (the standard Windows accessory) or another graphics program to draw your frames from scratch.

Five GIF images are included on the CD-ROM that accompanies this book, in the Webs\Groupus\Images folder. These images (and their filenames) are shown in Figure 3-18.

Figure 3-18: When these five images are drawn at the same position in sequence, you get an illusion of a moving highlight.

How GIF Animator Works

We'll use GIF Animator to create a single animated GIF that combines the five images found on the Companion CD-ROM. Figure 3-19 shows you Microsoft GIF Animator's user interface.

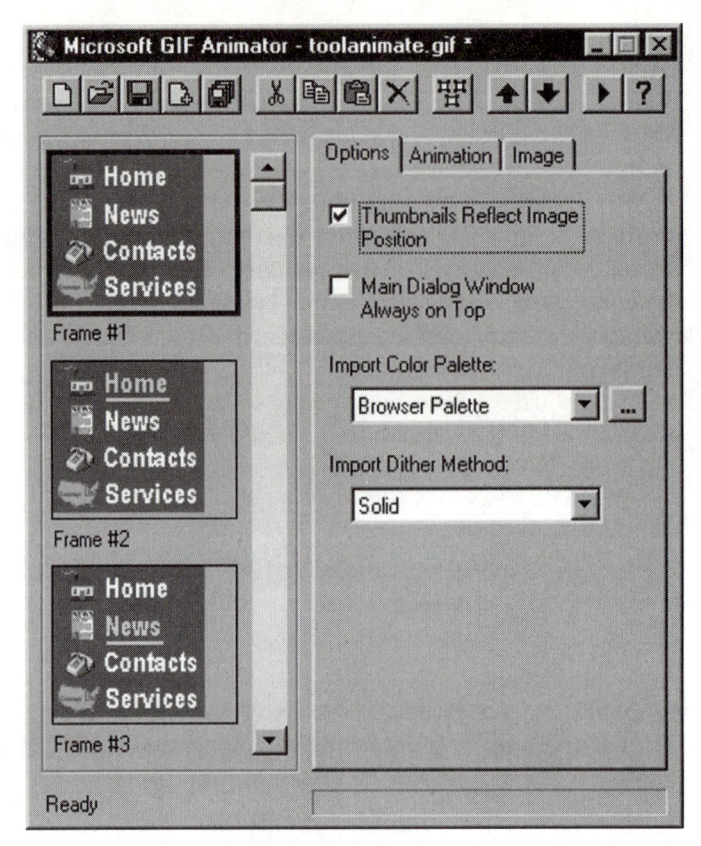

Figure 3-19: The GIF Animator user interface: The thumbnails run from top to bottom on the left; the properties are in tabbed dialogs on the right. The toolbar at the top of the GIF Animator contains commands for New, Open, Save, Insert, Save As, Cut, Copy, Paste, Delete, Select All, Move Up, Move Down, Play, and Help.

On the left-hand side of GIF Animator is a series of frames. Each frame holds a thumbnail representation (shrunk to fit if necessary) for each image in the animation.

Note: The term frame is used to describe each GIF graphic that is part of the complete GIF animation; the GIF animation is saved as a single file automatically by GIF Animator. This term should not be confused with the HTML term frame, which refers to a way to display two pages side-by-side or in other arrangements. (HTML frames are discussed in Chapter 7.)

The right-hand half of GIF Animator is divided into three property sheets, each with a tab heading: Options, Animation, and Image. Options sets the way images are imported and displayed. Animation contains settings for the entire animation. Image is used to set properties for an individual image in the sequence.

Open the GIF Animator from the Start menu (Start | Programs | Microsoft GIF Animator). When GIF Animator starts up, only the Options property sheet is shown, since you haven't inserted any thumbnails yet. We'll examine each property sheet in the following paragraphs, but first, you need to add some images to the animation so that it matches Figure 3-19.

GIF Animator has one glaring omission: there's no way to create a new animation and directly insert frames. Instead, you have to first open one of the GIFs and then insert additional GIF frames. If you click the Save button, the original GIF (the one you started with) is replaced by the animated GIF. This isn't desirable if you want to maintain each GIF separately in case you ever want to edit the frames and rebuild the animation. So after opening the first frame, click the Save As button and save the animation with a new name.

TIP

Look on the CD-ROM that accompanies this book to try out VideoCraft GIF Animator and GIF*GIF*GIF, which are powerful GIF tools that offer features lacking in Microsoft GIF Animator. I'm focusing on the MS tool because it was widely available during the beta version of FrontPage 97, and can still be obtained for free download. Also check out Ulead's web site at http://www.ulead.com to try out evaluation versions of their wide array of GIF tools.

We'll use the Open toolbar button to open the last image in the animation, then insert the other frames above it in GIF Animator:

1. Click the Open button and open \Webs\Groupus\Images\toolservices.gif from the Companion CD-ROM.

2. Click the Save As button and save the animation to a working folder on your hard drive as ToolAnimate. The GIF extension is added automatically. (You have to save the animation to your hard drive since the CD-ROM is read-only.)

3. To add the other frames of the animation, use the Insert button.

4. Repeat the Insert operation until you've added all the images, in this order: toolcontacts.gif, toolnews.gif, toolhome.gif, and toolbuttons.gif. Since images are inserted above existing frames in the animation, we insert each image starting from the last and ending with the first.

5. You can reorder the sequence if necessary by clicking an image thumbnail and pressing the up and down arrows on the toolbar. You can also move a thumbnail by holding down Shift while dragging the thumbnail within the list (if you don't hold down Shift, the thumbnail you're dragging is copied to the position where you drop it).

There are several other ways to add frames to the animation. You can copy a graphic from another application and use the Paste button or simply drag and drop the graphic from one program (such as Paint Shop Pro or Microsoft Image Composer) into the GIF Animator. If you want to convert a Windows AVI movie into an animated GIF, click the Open button. GIF Animator automatically converts the frames in the movie to frames in the animation. (Ideally you'll use a short video with a modest window size, else the animation will take forever to load over a typical modem connection.)

Once all the images are inserted into GIF Animator as thumbnails, you can set the properties for the animation. Let's take a look at each property sheet of GIF Animator.

Options Tab

The first check box on the Options sheet (shown in Figure 3-19), Thumbnails Reflect Image Position, is a tricky one. In the animation we're creating, this check box is not an issue since each graphic occupies the full space of the animation region—this region is defined by the size of the individual frames. Another way to animate something (like a ball) is to simply change its position within the animation region (whose size is determined on the Animation tab). Using the Image tab (described in "Image Tab" later in the chapter), you can choose a different position for the ball in each frame. When played back, the ball appears to bounce around within the animation region. For now, leave the check box as is.

The second check box, Main Dialog Window Always on Top, allows the GIF Animator window to remain on top of all other windows on your desktop. It's not clear what advantage this offers, especially since it prevents you from dragging and dropping graphics into place from another application.

Import Color Palette

Take a close look at the options Import Color Palette and Import Dither Method. Since each GIF in the animation might have its own palette, GIF Animator has to decide how to build a palette for the animation as a whole. If the animation is going to be played back on a computer with 256 colors, you might as well choose Browser Palette from the Import Color Palette drop-down list box. If you use Optimized Palette, a new palette is created that best supports the colors in every image in the animation.

You can also click the button labeled ". . ." to choose a PAL file from your hard drive. PAL files can be created with Microsoft Image Composer when a palette is exported. Paint Shop Pro also lets you save the palette of an image to a PAL file.

Import Dither Method

Since a 256-color palette can't contain every color that may exist in the individual frames, GIF Animator has to find a way to deal with colors that either aren't in the browser palette or couldn't be included in the optimized palette. By default, error diffusion is used, which arranges various colored pixels in a "cloud" of pixels to approximate the original color. Let's say you had a purple square, but the exact shade of purple isn't in the palette. Error diffusion colors that box with a cluster of red and blue pixels that when viewed at high enough resolution, appear to merge to the human eye to give the illusion of a purple color.

You may prefer, however, for GIF Animator to choose the closest shade of purple in the palette and avoid dithering. Choose Solid from the Import Dither Method drop-down list to force GIF Animator to substitute the color in the palette that most closely matches the original color in the GIF. You can also choose Pattern to use traditional checkerboard-style dithering instead of error diffusion, or you can choose Random, which is a cross between standard dithering and error diffusion. If in doubt, try various options and import the component graphics to see the effect.

For the sake of our example animation, set the Import Color Palette to Browser palette and the Import Dither Method to Solid. Since each GIF in the example animation was saved with the same palette (the browser-safe palette we discussed in Chapter 2), no dithering will be necessary.

Animation Tab

You can use the Animation property sheet (shown in Figure 3-20) to change the size of the animation region. Normally, this is set automatically to fit the size of the largest GIF in the animation sequence. If you "spoof" the width and height by changing these settings, you don't change the size of the animated GIF (this can be achieved once you've inserted the animated GIF on a page by changing the image properties using the FrontPage Editor). Instead, you can increase the height and width if you want to enlarge the "stage" on which the animation plays, a rectangle that encloses the animation.

More useful is the Looping option, which tells the browser that's displaying the animated GIF to repeat the animation. Most animated GIFs are designed to loop over and over again, but you can also choose a specific number of repeats. (Once the animation is complete, the last image in the animation is left on the screen.)

For our example animation, click both the Looping and Repeat Forever check boxes. You can enter a description of the animation, which won't appear on the web page, in the Trailing Comment text box.

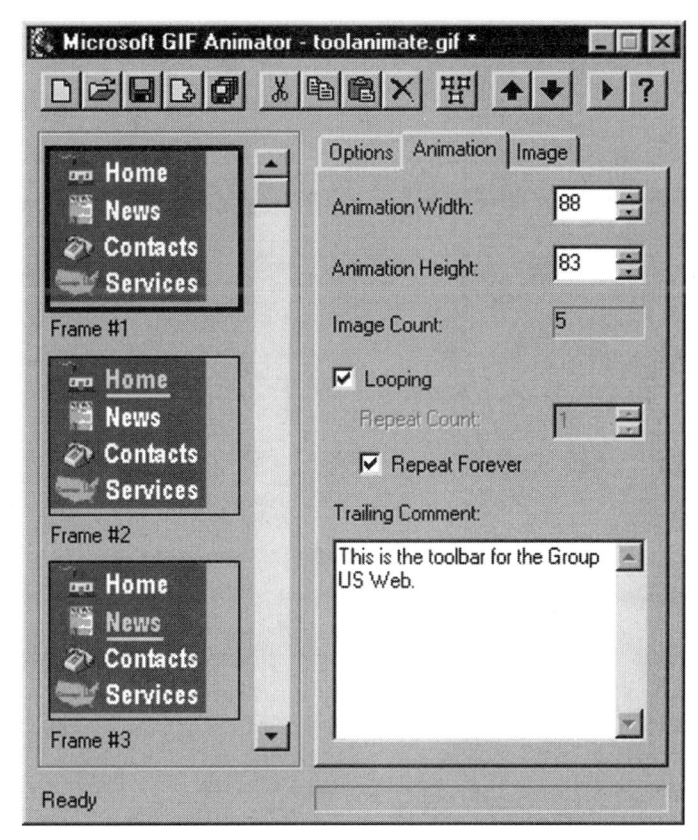

Figure 3-20: Check Looping and Repeat Forever if you want your animation to cycle continuously.

Image Tab

The first two property sheets, Options and Animation, control settings that affect the entire animation. The Image property sheet, on the other hand, contains settings for each individual image (thumbnail). The Image property sheet is shown in Figure 3-21. The most important setting on the Image tab is Duration. This specifies how long the current image will remain on the screen before being replaced by the next image in the animation. To allow fine control, the duration is specified in hundredths of a second. So to delay for a full second, use a duration of 100.

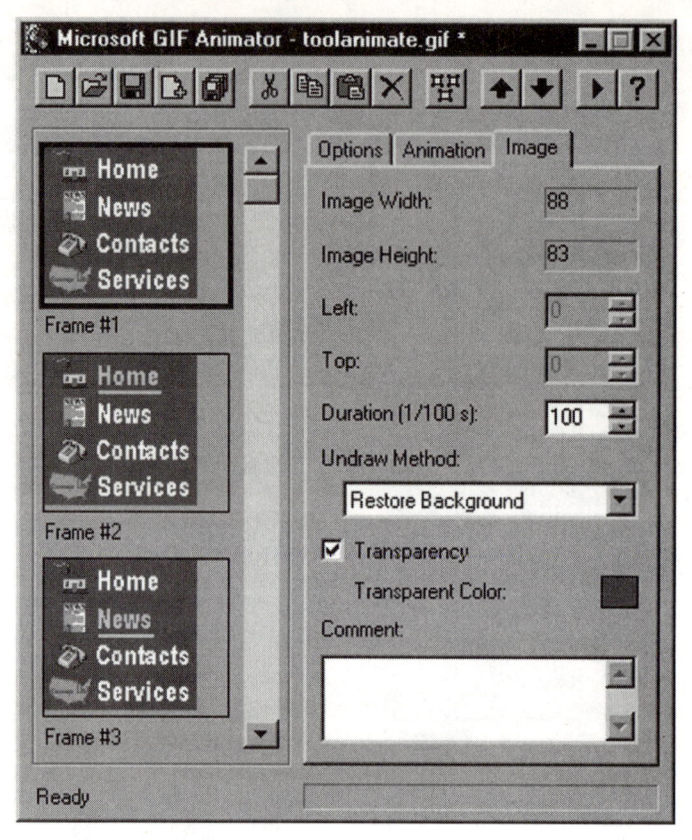

Figure 3-21: From the Image property sheet, use the Duration setting to specify how long the thumbnail is displayed before moving on to the next image. You can also choose how the background behind the animation is treated and whether to set a transparent color.

Height, Width, Left, Top

You can also view, but not change, the height and width of the current frame. If you've chosen an animation region larger than the images in the animation (using the Animation tab), you can set the Left and Top values to offset the image within the animation region. You also must turn on the Thumbnails Reflect Image Position check box on the Options page before you're allowed to set the Left and Top values. (With our example animation, these boxes are disabled because the size of the images matches the size of the animation region.)

Undraw Method

Another important setting is the Undraw method. This lets you control how each frame is updated within the animation region. The default choice, Undefined, tells the browser to do nothing to the background of the animation before displaying the frame. This usually gives the same effect as the Leave option, which leaves the previous frame in the animation region while drawing the current frame. It merges the pixels of the current frame with the pixels of the previous frame. You can also choose Restore Background, which redisplays the browser's background within the animation region while the current frame is drawn. Finally, you can use Restore Previous, which redraws the previous image as the current frame is being drawn.

How do you know which Undraw method to use? Restore Background is a good choice, since it lets each frame appear as is, without merging with the previous frame. You may need the other undraw methods to achieve special effects. If you were animating a bouncing ball, Restore Background would remove the previous ball when drawing the current ball, as you would normally expect. If you used Leave, the previous image of each ball would remain on the screen, so you'd see a trail of balls.

Transparency

The Transparency check box lets you choose one of the colors in the image, usually the background color, as the transparent color. As we mentioned in Chapter 2, transparent GIFs allow the background color or texture of the web page to "show through" the transparent parts of the GIF. This seamlessly merges a graphic with the background.

If you import a GIF that is already saved as transparent (as were all the GIFs you've already inserted), the color you used for the transparent color is shown in the Transparent Color box. Otherwise, you can click on this box to choose which color in the palette to treat as transparent. To verify that you've chosen the correct color, you can press the Play button. The transparent parts will be colored gray to match the background of the preview window.

Remember, the Image properties apply to each image individually. Since we want to set all the Image properties for a range of frames, first select a range of frames. You can click the Select All toolbar button or click on the first frame and then Shift+Click on another frame. The first and last frames and all the frames in between are selected. (Selected frames have a heavy outline.) You can then apply the same image properties (except for transparency) to all the images you've selected.

To complete the animation, click the Image tab (if it's not already displayed) and then click the Select All toolbar button. You can now assign the same duration (try values between 50 and 200) to all the frames, which effectively sets the speed of the animation. (After setting the duration for all frames, you can override the duration for individual frames if you like.)

Also set the Undraw method for all the frames to Restore Background. Click the Play toolbar button to try out the animation.

The last option on the Image page lets you add a comment that can be used to describe each image. Normally, you'll leave it blank since it has no effect on the animation.

The animation is now complete. Press the Play button on the toolbar to try it out. When you're satisfied with your work, click the Save button to store the ToolAnimate GIF on your hard drive. Close the GIF Animator program. The animation is now ready for use in FrontPage.

Converting the Animation to a Navigation Bar With Hot Spots

The Corporate Presence Wizard created a navigation bar (similar to a toolbar) automatically. The navigation bar is stored as the page _private/navbar.htm with the name Included Navigation Links. This page is inserted as an Include 'bot on every page in the web, allowing the visitor one-click access to any page. To customize the navigation bar, open the Included Navigation Links page from FrontPage Explorer to load it into the FrontPage Editor.

The Old Way

Before we kill the old navigation bar, let's see how it works. The FrontPage Corporate Presence Wizard creates a series of individual GIF images (bhome.gif, bnews.gif, bservs.gif). These images are stored in the web's Images folder. Each GIF is assigned a link.

To see the link for the home page, click the Home graphic and then press Ctrl+K to open the Edit Hyperlink dialog box. As shown in Figure 3-22, the link points to ..\index.html, which is the relative URL of the home page. (Since the navbar.htm page is in the _private folder, which is a subfolder of the web's main folder, the two periods tell the browser to back up to the parent folder to retrieve the home page.)

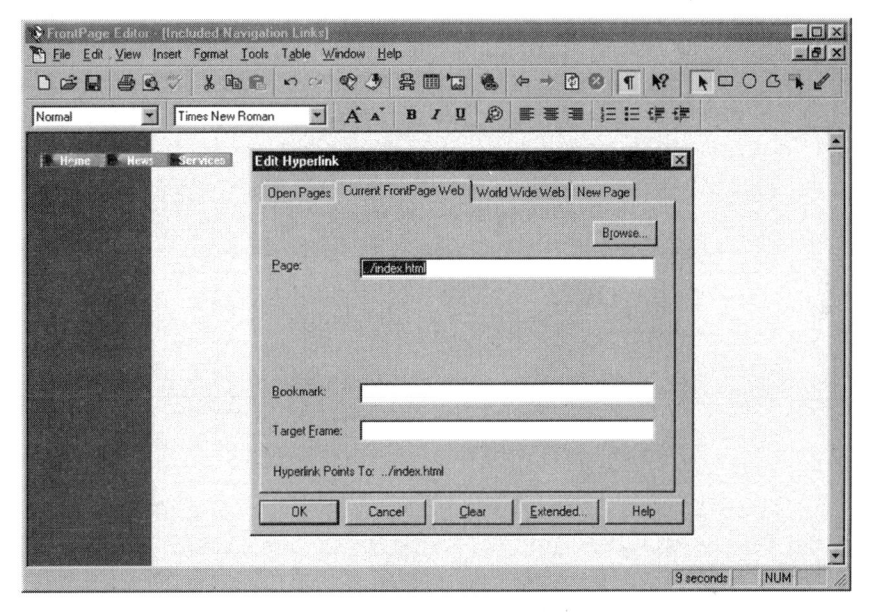

Figure 3-22: The bhome.gif graphic is linked to the home page.

Likewise, the other two graphics link to the News and Services pages, respectively.

A Better Way

This is a pretty straightforward way to create a toolbar, but it can be inelegant, especially if you want to set up a vertical orientation like we planned for the animated toolbar. Instead, we'll use a method known as image mapping to define special regions, or hot spots, within a single image. Each hot spot in turn links to a page in the web.

Note: Image maps are usually driven by the server, which is the most compatible way to use image maps with the widest variety of browsers. Each time the visitor clicks on a hot spot, the coordinates of the mouse pointer are sent to the server. The server decides which hot spot contains that point and retrieves the page linked to that hot spot. If the server is busy, clicking on a hot spot can sometimes be slow.

Another way to drive image maps is to let the browser look up the coordinates and load the page that the hot spot points to. This method is fast and efficient, but only the newest browsers (version 3.0 or greater of Internet Explorer or version 2.0 or greater of Netscape Navigator) support client-side image mapping.

FrontPage Explorer lets you choose which image mapping method to employ for your web. Click Tools | Web Settings, and choose the Advanced property sheet. If the server hosting your web supports FrontPage server extensions, leave the Style set to FrontPage. (You can also choose from NCSA, CERN, Netscape, or <none>.) To also generate client-side image maps (the default), click the Generate Client-Side Image Maps check box. This offers the best of both worlds—if the browser supports client-side image mapping, the server isn't burdened. Otherwise, the click on the hot spot is passed to the server. (If you only want to support client-side image maps, use the <none> option from the Style list.)

TIP

Look on the CD-ROM accompanying this book for the MapEdit utility, which lets you track the coordinates necessary for custom image mapping, an enhancement over the basic features included with FrontPage 97.

Inserting the Animation

First we need to remove the old navigation bar. Just click on each graphic and press the Del key. Next, we'll insert the animated navigation bar we created in the previous section. From the FrontPage Editor, use Insert | Image, click the Other Location tab heading, and click the Browse button to locate the ToolAnimate graphic where you stored it on your hard drive. Click the ToolAnimate graphic, then click OK to bring it onto the Included Navigation Links page. Your screen should resemble Figure 3-23. (The FrontPage Editor window shown in the figure has been reduced in size to save space. Your window can be any size you like.)

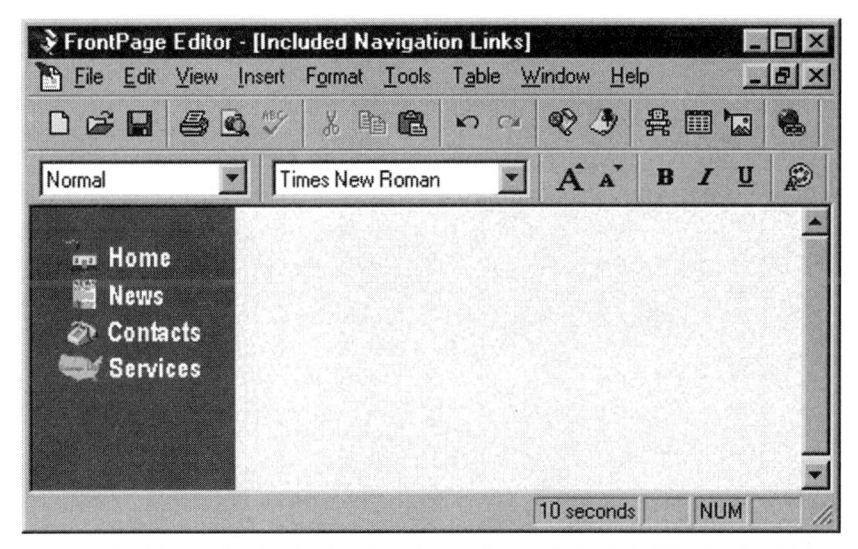

Figure 3-23: The navigation bar has been inserted onto the Included Navigation Links page, but no hot spots have been created yet.

Don't be dismayed that the graphic isn't animated. The FrontPage Editor only shows the first frame in the animation. You can click the Preview in Browser toolbar button if you want to see it animate.

Mapping Hot Spots

The new navigation bar looks cool, but it doesn't do anything yet. To add functionality, you'll create hot spots within the image. A hot spot is a rectangular, circular, or arbitrary (polygonal) region that defines an area within a graphic. Any pixels enclosed by the outline of the hot spot are part of the hot spot, and if your web visitor clicks within the boundary of the hot spot, the page pointed to by the hot spot is opened by the browser.

Image Toolbar Commands

Click the navigation bar graphic to select it. FrontPage displays the Image toolbar automatically when you click on a graphic. (This toolbar can be floating, like that shown in Figure 3-24, or docked along with the other toolbars. You can drag and drop toolbars to arrange them on your screen.)

Figure 3-24: From left to right, the commands on the Image toolbar are Select, Rectangle, Circle, Polygon, Highlight Hot Spots, and Make Transparent.

The commands available on the toolbar (Figure 3-24), from left to right, are Select, Rectangle, Circle, Polygon, Highlight Hot Spots, and Make Transparent. (We used the Make Transparent button in Chapter 2 when we created the custom logo. This button is unavailable with animated GIFs, but you can set transparency using the GIF Animator as described in the previous section.)

Each tool on the Image toolbar changes the default arrow mouse pointer to one resembling the tool. Use the Select tool to get back the normal arrow when you simply want to click on a hot spot to edit its link, delete it, or reposition it. Click the Rectangle or Circle tool if you want to "draw" a rectangle or circle on top of the image to define a hot spot. To use the Polygon tool, click once to set the first point of the polygon, then click where you want to set each additional vertex. To close the polygon, double-click or click upon the first vertex.

Most of the time you'll use the Rectangle tool to define hot spots. Circular hot spots can be handy if your toolbar buttons are round instead of square. You can use the Polygon tool to define arbitrary regions. For example, if the image was a family photograph, you can outline each family member. When a visitor to your page clicks on a family member, it can link to that person's home page.

The Highlight Hot Spots button lets you see the regions occupied by the hot spots on the image. This blanks out the image and shows only the position of the hot spots (the currently selected hot spot is black, the others are outlined). This can be handy to make sure that none of your hot spots overlap, which is a no-no.

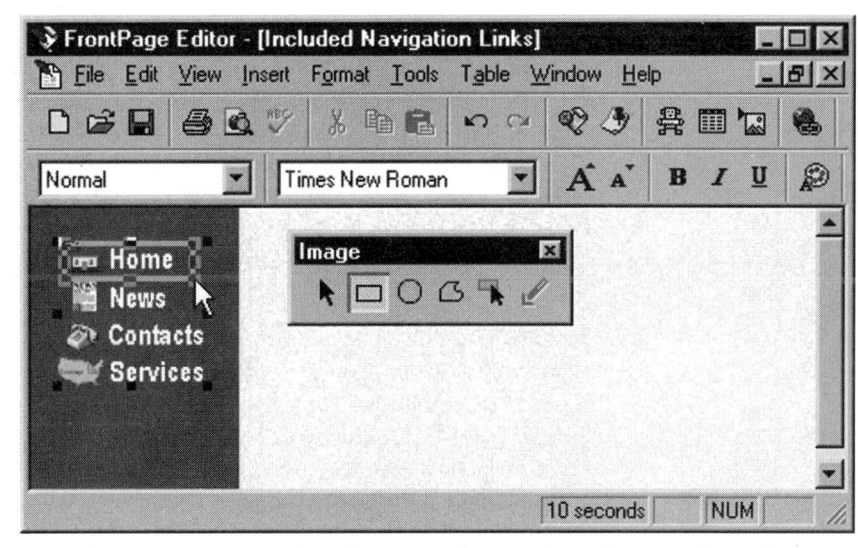

Figure 3-25: Use the Rectangle tool to create a hot spot for each item on the toolbar.

Follow these steps to add hot spots to the animated graphic:

1. Use the Rectangle button to draw a rectangle around the first item in the toolbar, Home. You should draw the rectangle around the button and the text, since the visitor may click anywhere within that region. Make the hot spot only as large as necessary to surround the text and the graphic. (See Figure 3-25.)

    As soon as you release the mouse button to complete the hot spot, the Edit Link dialog box appears. From here, you can set the link to a page within your web or to a location on the World Wide Web. (We discussed how to create links and URLs in Chapter 2. See the sidebar "What's a URL?" in Chapter 2.)

2. For the Home hot spot, set the link to the Group US home page (..\index.htm or ..\index.html).

3. As you did with the Home hot spot, draw rectangles around the News, Contacts, and Services items in the graphic. Link these hot spots, respectively, to ..\news.htm, ..\contacts.htm, and ..\products.htm. (Don't forget the ../, it's necessary because the Included Navigation Links page, navbar.htm, is stored in the _private folder, which is a subfolder of the main web folder. The two dots mean "back up to the parent folder." If in doubt, use the Browse button on the Current FrontPage Web tab to locate the exact page you want to link to.)

4. To make sure none of the hot spots overlap, click the Highlight Hot Spots button. If necessary, use the Select tool to drag the handles (the little squares) at the corners and sides of each boundary to resize a hot spot rectangle, and click inside the boundary to move the entire hot spot.

Updating the Navigation Links

Use File | Save or the Save button on the FrontPage Editor toolbar to write the customized navigation bar page back out to the web. (When prompted for a location to save the navigation bar, use images/navbar.gif.) You can now load one of the pages on the web to see how the navigation bar looks.

Open Home Page from the FrontPage Explorer (this page may already be open in the FrontPage Editor. If so, use View | Refresh to reload the page and update the navbar.htm Include bot.) It will resemble Figure 3-26. It's hard to read the text of the navigation bar because as a transparent GIF, the white text of the graphic blends in with the light page background. This won't be a problem when it's moved to the infamous blue strip.

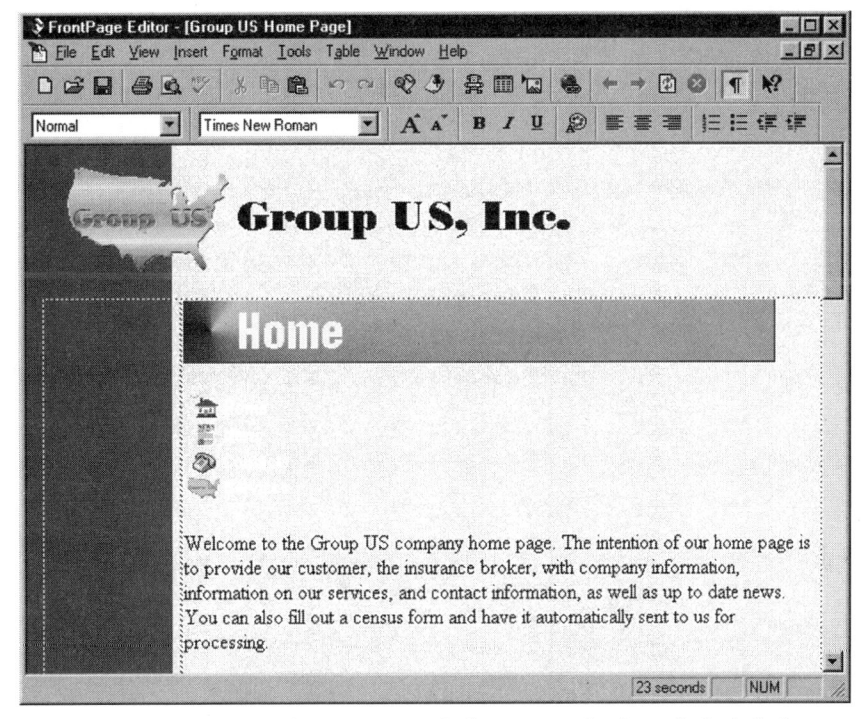

Figure 3-26: The navigation bar appears on the home page, thanks to the Include 'bot.

You may be wondering how the navigation bar graphic made it onto the home page. After all, you only updated the Included Navigation Links page, not the Home Page. Recall that Home Page already contained an Include WebBot that included _private/navbar.htm. This was set up by the Corporate Presence Wizard. By changing the original navbar.htm to a custom one, the appearance of the navigation bar on every page changes automatically.

To move the graphic, you have to move the Include WebBot. You could use Edit | Cut and Edit | Paste, but there's an easier way. First click on the navigation bar graphic. A region of the page will turn black to highlight the WebBot. Now drag the highlighted region and drop it inside the leftmost cell of the table (where the blue strip exists). This drag-and-drop method moves the selected item, in this case a WebBot, to a new location. You can use drag and drop to move any text or content within your page to a different place on the page. (If you use one of the Window Arrange options like Tile Vertically, you can even drag material from one page to another.)

Right at Home

Once you've moved the Include WebBot, the navigation bar appears in its rightful place within the blue border (see Figure 3-27). Save the home page to complete the change. You'll then need to perform the same operation on every other page in your web to move the navigation bar to its proper place. (If you want the navigation bar to appear toward the top of the page instead of the middle, set the cell properties for the first column, choosing Top for Vertical Alignment.)

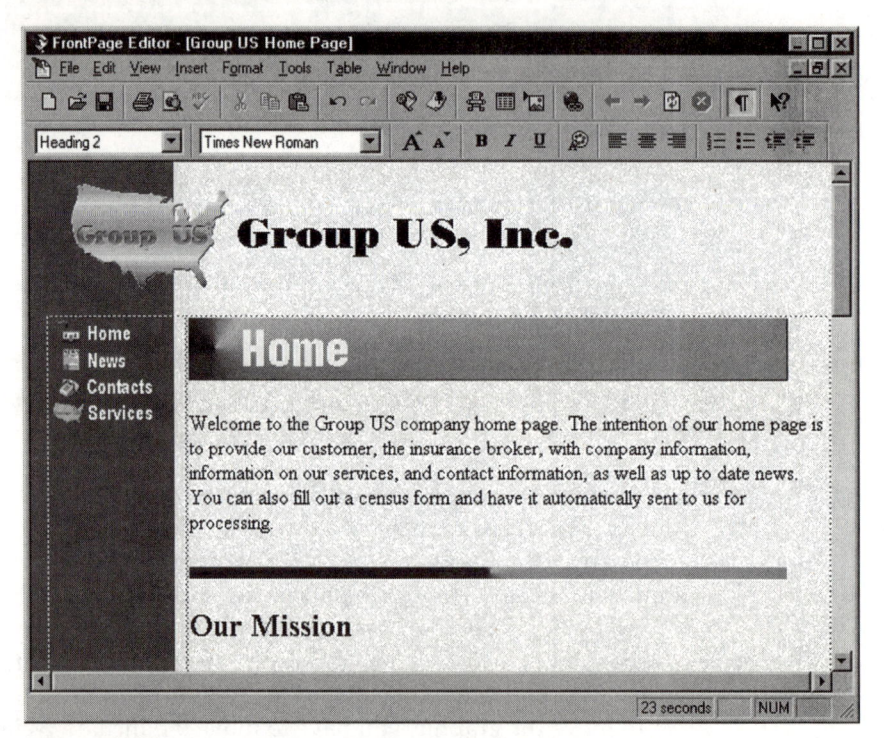

Figure 3-27: The navigation bar is in place on the home page.

Try out the new navigation bar by pressing the Preview in Browser button from the FrontPage toolbar. Click on each link and verify that it takes you to the proper page.

Moving On

We've come a long way from the simple pages created by the Corporate Presence Wizard. You've learned how to use Microsoft Image Composer with FrontPage to create a custom background, how to exploit tables for formatting (and for creating tables), and how to create an animated GIF that acts as a toolbar, complete with hot spots.

In the next chapter, we'll add a data collection form to the Group US web, taking advantage of the built-in form elements and the Save Results WebBot. You'll see how to use Validation Rules to include business logic directly to your page. We'll examine some other possible uses for forms and work around some of the known limitations.

chapter 4

Building an Interactive Web Site: Forms & Form Handlers

If you've been following along in Chapter 2 and Chapter 3, you've seen how to quickly prototype a company home page using the FrontPage Corporate Presence Wizard and how to enhance that site using custom graphics and navigation aids. The Group US Company web we've created so far looks good and serves a basic purpose: providing information for the clients and feedback for the company. Yet the site lacks interactivity: a way to actually accomplish a practical task related to the business goals.

Actually, there is some interactivity, supported by the Information Request forms on the Services pages. Together, we quickly dissected this form, generated automatically by the Corporate Presence Wizard, in Chapter 2. In this chapter, we'll create a custom form from scratch for collecting census information.

A *form* is a reserved area of a web page that contains form fields (often called controls) and a Submit button. You've doubtless seen forms on pages while browsing the World Wide Web, such as a registration page to gain access to a download area.

Form fields, such as text boxes, collect information from the visitor. When the user clicks the Submit button, the *form handler*, a special program running on the web server, collects the data from each form field and processes it, usually storing it on the web server. FrontPage makes form design interactive, and the Save Results WebBot automates form processing.

After completing this chapter, you will be able to design and implement your own data collection forms. Another resource for quickly prototyping forms is the Forms Wizard. To try it out, create a new page with the FrontPage Editor by choosing File | New, and choose the Forms Wizard. This wizard prompts you to supply questions that you wish to ask of the visitor to your page, and lets you choose which type of form field (text boxes, radio buttons) to use to collect the information. The wizard also walks you through setup of the Save Results WebBot, which stores form results on a special page stored in your web.

As mentioned in Chapter 1 and in the introduction, the focus on this book is mastery of fundamental and advanced FrontPage skills. This wizard, like many other wizards and templates, is fine for getting started or to save you some typing or mousing around, but is no substitute for learning how the software really works.

Using the Forms Wizard doesn't really teach you how to create your own data collection forms, so I won't get into any more detail on how to use it.

Planning a Form

In the group insurance business, a census form is used by insurance brokers to collect key information about the employees of a company. The information is then used to generate a proposal (or quotation) illustrating the coverage and costs for employee benefits products, such as life insurance, health insurance, disability insurance, and so on.

Many insurance brokers can now run their own proposals for smaller groups of employees using software provided by the insurance companies. This can be time consuming and limits the broker to insurance products that he or she is already familiar with. Agents are better served to work with a service such as Group US, which can shop the group with a wide variety of insurance carriers (with access to wholesale pricing), collect the various proposals, make recommendations, and help with enrollment and employee education. (Like a travel agency, Group US doesn't charge the agents for these services, instead collecting an overwrite commission directly from the insurance companies.)

The whole ball game gets kicked off with the submission of a census table: a list of employees, their ages (or date of birth), whether or not they smoke, salary information, and information on employee spouses and children. (Basic privacy is protected by simply numbering the employees rather than using their names and by keeping census information confidential.)

Traditionally, a paper census form is filled out by the agent and mailed or faxed to Group US. A Group US employee types the census information into software designed to produce proposals, which are then mailed or faxed back to the agent.

To make the most of the Group US web, we'll modernize this process by creating an electronic form, a page that can be used to enter census information. When the user submits the form, the FrontPage Submit Results WebBot stores the information in a special results page on the Company web. Since the results page is a standard HTML file, it can be easily viewed and printed from any web browser.

Likewise, the broker has the advantage of access to the census form anywhere a web browser is available (many agents travel with notebook computers with modems, capable of accessing the Internet on demand).

Modeling the Form

To build the census form, start by examining the paper form to decide how to best convert it to an electronic one. The paper-based Group US Census form is shown as Figure 4-1. Let's take a look at how it can be supported in the web browser using FrontPage.

Census Information

Ee #	Sex M/F	S/N	☐ Age ☐ YOB	☐ Life ☐ Sal. Amount	Dependents Sp.Age	S/N	#Children	Ee #	Sex M/F	S/N	☐ Age ☐ YOB	☐ Life ☐ Sal. Amount	Dependents Sp.Age	S/N	#Children
1								16							
2								17							
3								18							
4								19							
5								20							
6								21							
7								22							
8								23							
9								24							
10								25							
11								26							
12								27							
13								28							
14								29							
15								30							

Figure 4-1: Many paper forms can be converted into web-based "electronic" forms.

At first glance, the form doesn't look too tricky. All we have to do is set up a table with eight columns (the right half of the census form is just a continuation of the left half) and insert a text box into each table cell to create data entry "zones."

Formatting the header of the table is the tricky part. Census data can exist in several forms. Sometimes the employee information includes the current age of each employee. Other times the equivalent data is in the form of date of birth.

Life insurance quotes require either the salary of the employee or the current amount of life insurance. So this data can be formatted either as life or salary amounts.

With the paper form, the agent simply shades either the Age or YOB check box on the form and fills in the square for Life or Salary in the Amount column. (This is repeated for the spouse, if any.)

Choosing Form Fields

When designing a form, you have several tools at your disposal, illustrated by the Form Fields toolbar in Figure 4-2. These tools are the various form fields (sometimes called controls) for entering different types of data.

A check box field can hold one of two values, depending on whether the box is checked or not checked. A group of radio buttons holds one of several values, depending on which button was clicked. A drop-down displays a list of items, from which the user can choose by clicking with the mouse (or typing the first letter of a choice). The result of this selection is temporarily stored by the drop-down menu field.

As the visitor enters information into each form field, the web browser temporarily tracks the data entered into each form field. This storage is transient, however, and the data won't be permanently copied from the user's computer and stored in the web until the visitor clicks the Submit button.

For free-form entry, you can use a single-line text box, which lets the user enter a word or phrase, or a scrolling (multiline) text box, which lets the user enter several lines of text within a larger text box that can be scrolled up and down to view all the data contained within it.

Rounding out the field controls is the push button, which links to either the Submit or Reset functions. (Although a push button is considered a field, it doesn't really store any useful information itself.) Submit usually sends the form data to the FrontPage Save Results WebBot, but you can also assign custom form handlers such as a CGI script, a program that runs on the web server. If the user clicks Reset, the data already entered on the form is erased, so that new data can be entered.

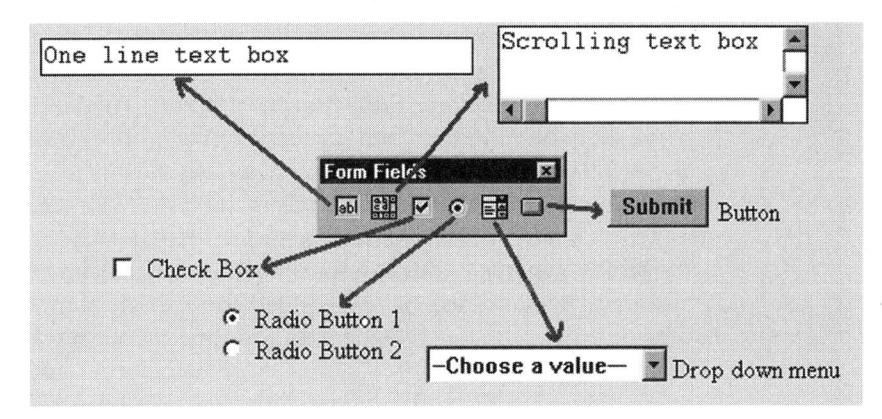

Figure 4-2: The buttons on the Forms toolbar let you insert form fields, also called controls, on a FrontPage form.

You can also place an Image field on a form, which works like a standard Submit button, allowing a custom graphical appearance for your buttons. Like the push button, an Image field has a name, but doesn't store a value. When clicked, it acts like a Submit button.

A form can contain hidden fields as well. Hidden fields don't accept entries by the user, but can be useful for storing additional information. For example, you could have two forms, a detailed form and a quick form. The detailed form might contain name and address information. The quick form might be used to update information stored earlier using the detailed form. Hidden fields on the quick form would contain the name and address entered earlier so that the results saved by either form are consistent.

A hidden field can also be employed to carry data from one form to the next, propagating a value like a username so that it's remembered from one page to the next. (This requires scripting or the Internet Database Connector, covered in Chapter 8.)

Designing the Census Form

Since we're trying to duplicate a form that the agent is already familiar with, we'll implement the Age, YOB, Life, and Salary Amount check boxes as radio button (option button) fields. That way, the agent can click Life or Salary, but not both. A radio button is designed to let you choose one of several options. (Using a check box field would work, but it would be possible to choose both Age and YOB, for example, and it might be difficult to make sense of the data; does the entry 33 mean the employee is 33 years old, or was the employee born in 1933?)

The data stored by the FrontPage Save Results WebBot will be the name of the radio button group and the value of the button clicked. You can also choose the default value of the button, so that the button is already chosen for the most common type of data entry: YOB and Life amounts.

To track the census data, we'll also need to collect information such as the broker's name, address, telephone number, fax number, and e-mail address. The FrontPage Save Results WebBot can automatically collect other information, too, like the date and time the form was submitted.

When laying out a form like this, it can be helpful to sketch out a list of the data entry fields. Each field you place on a form has a name and a value. The name is a word that describes the data item, and the value is the information associated with that item. For example, the text box for entering the broker's name will have a name of Broker, and the value will be whatever is typed by the user (the visitor to the web). On the other hand, the Life/Salary option buttons take the form of a Group name (such as EmployeeAgeYOB) and a value of either Age or YOB, depending on which radio button was selected.

Text fields can be limited to a fixed number of characters, which also sets the width of the text box. The limit helps to both keep the total data set to a reasonable size and match the limits already specified by a database. (Group US transfers new agents and their addresses to a mailing list database.)

Table 4-1 summarizes the data storage requirements for the census form. Each of the 30 rows uses the same name for the fields (EENum, for EmployEE number), with an underscore and a number added to the name, such as EENum_01 for the first row, EENum_02 for the second row, and so on.

These field names are the names of the text boxes on the form, and are also output, along with the form data, on the results page generated by the Save Results WebBot. For example, this is an excerpt of what the results file might look like (data not entered is not stored):

```
EENum_01: 01
EESex_01: F
EESmoke_01: S
EEAgeYOB_01: 32
LifeSalary_01: 30000
SpouseAgeYOB_01: 33
SpouseSmoke_01: N
Children_01:
```

Since the Save Results 'bot can't store data directly into a database file, these field names need have no relation to the field names in an existing database. (To learn how to store data into a database file, you'll have to wait until Chapter 8.)

The field names also have no relation to the labels you type onto the form that describe each data entry field. In Table 4-1, these labels are found in the Description column. You might place the text "Enter your name here" on a form next to a text box, but the text box itself would have a name like "Broker" which isn't visible to the user.

Form Field Name	Type	Size	Description
Case	Text	30	Case Name
Broker	Text	30	Broker Name
Address1	Text	30	Address Line 1
Address2	Text	30	Address Line 2
CityStateZip	Text	30	City, State, Zip Code
Telephone	Text	15	Telephone number
Fax	Text	15	FAX Number
Email	Text	30	E-mail address
EEAgeYOB	Radio	n/a	Choose Age or YOB
LifeSalary	Radio	n/a	Choose Life or Salary
SpouseAgeYOB	Radio	n/a	Choose Age or YOB
——For each row of the table:——			
EENum_01	Text	2	Employee number
EESex_01	Menu	1	Sex (M or F)
EESmoke_01	Menu	1	Smoker/Non-smoker (S or N)
AgeYob_01	Text	3	Either age or year of birth
LifeSalary_01	Text	8	Either life or salary amount
SpouseAgeYob_01	Text	n/a	Either age or year of birth
SpouseSmoke_01	Menu	1	Either S or N
Children_01	Text	2	Number of children

Table 4-1: Data storage requirements determine the field properties for each field (text box or other) on the form.

When you examine Table 4-1, notice that several of the field types are Text. This refers to the field itself, a text box, not the type of data you intend to store. A text box doesn't care whether it holds a number, a word, a phrase, or whatever. Later, we'll see how to add validation rules to make sure that only numbers can be used for numeric values (such as the life/salary amount), and that only valid choices (such as S or N for Smoker/Nonsmoker) can be entered for other fields.

Another way to limit data entry is by choosing the appropriate type of field. There is no way to enter a value other than Age or YOB in the AgeYOB field, because the radio button only allows one or the other to be clicked on, and it automatically returns Age if the Age radio button is selected, or YOB if the YOB radio button is selected. (Don't get carried away with this idea, though. While you could implement data entry for AgeYOB using a drop-down list of values from 1 to 99, it's more convenient for the user to simply type a number into a text box rather than picking from such a long list.)

We'll use a drop-down menu for the Male/Female and Smoker/Nonsmoker choices, so that only M or F can be picked from the list. (Using the mouse to click on this control can slow down data entry, but fortunately, the user can also simply type M or F to choose the appropriate item in the list.) If you implemented a text box for these choices, you'd have to deal with mistakes and invalid entries, such as Y for the EESex field. While validation rules can force the user to reenter incorrect data, it's far easier for everyone concerned to limit the choices to valid ones in the first place.

Laying Out the Census Form

Now that the planning is complete, crack your knuckles, grab the mouse, and get ready to lay out the form using the FrontPage Editor.

1. Start by opening the Blank Page web page from the FrontPage Explorer. (You created this page in Chapter 3. Refer back to the section "Creating a Blank Page" in Chapter 3.)

2. Immediately use File | Save As to save the blank page as Census Form using the URL census.htm.

Notice the empty table on the page. As I discussed in Chapter 3, this table is used to align text on the page, mostly to avoid the blue border, which is reserved as a design element and to host the animated toolbar you designed in Chapter 3.

The first occurrence of the table will remain useful for aligning the introductory content of the page (the title of the page and instructions for using the census form).

Chapter 4: Building an Interactive Web Site: Forms & Form Handlers

You'll create two more tables on this page, too. The second table will hold the contact information for the insurance agent (name, address, telephone, etc.). The third table will hold the rows of the census table itself.

3. Begin designing this page by replacing the comment ("Insert web content here") with the title of the page: Group US Census Form. Set the title to the Heading 1 paragraph style using the drop-down list to the left of the FrontPage Editor toolbar.

4. Next, type in the instructions to the user. (If you want to avoid typing, use Insert | File and insert the file \Webs\Groupus\Text\Census.doc from the Companion CD-ROM.) Beneath the title, type the following:

```
Fill out the table below with your employee census
information. You can enter up to 30 entries at a time. To
enter the first 30 entries, just fill out the table below;
then scroll to the bottom of this page and click the Send to
Group US button. To enter the next 30 entries, click New Form
to clear the form, and change the entries in the EE# column
(31, 32,33, etc.).
```

Now you will create a table for the contact information part of the form.

5. Press the Down arrow key on the keyboard until the text insertion point is positioned beneath the first table on the page. Press Enter to insert a blank line; then Choose Table | Insert Table, and choose 8 rows and 3 columns, using a table width of 620 pixels. Click OK.

You now need to set the widths of the three columns. For the following steps, make sure you are working with the second table on the page, not the first one, which simply holds the page heading.

6. Position the mouse pointer just above the border of the first column of the table you just created. When the mouse pointer changes to a down arrow, click to select the entire column.

7. Choose Cell Properties from the Table menu, and set the minimum width to 110 pixels. Use the same technique to set the minimum width of the second column to 130 pixels, and assign the remaining 380 pixels to the third column. The column widths now add up to 620 pixels (110+130+380=620).

Note: If you intend to resize the entire column, always select the entire column before choosing Table | Cell Properties. If you change the width of a single cell, the table may become unbalanced since each cell of a table can have a different width, whether intended or unintended.

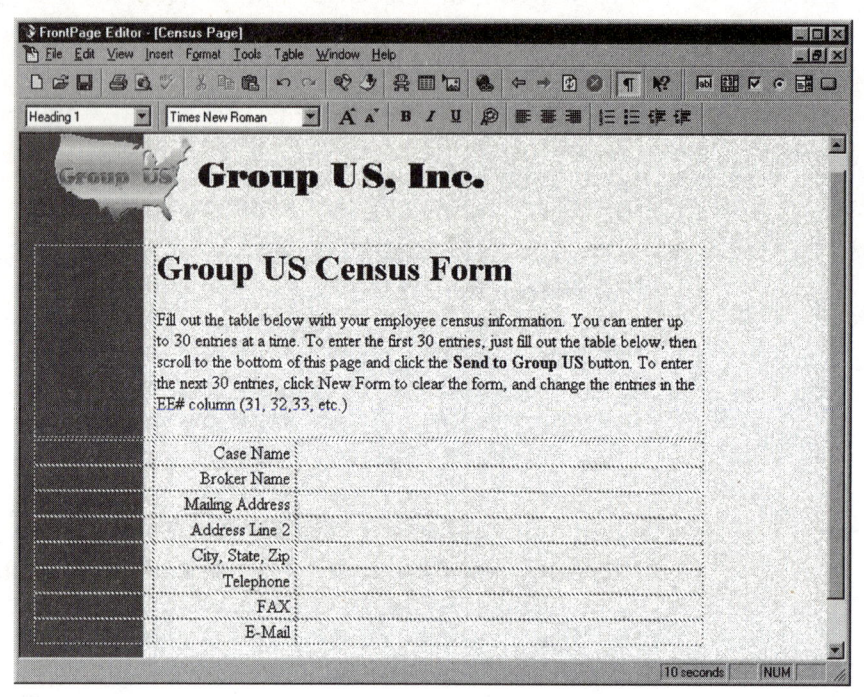

Figure 4-3: Fill in the second column with labels as shown here (using the Normal paragraph style), and align right.

8. Using Figure 4-3 as a guide, type the labels for the text fields into the second column. Each label occupies a different row—don't press Enter to move to the next line, press the Down arrow key instead. (Enter inserts a blank line; the arrow keys move from cell to cell.)

9. Once all the labels are in place, align the text in the second column so that it's right justified. You might think you could simply click the toolbar button (Align Right), but if you try this, it will have unusual results. For technical reasons (vagaries in HTML), aligning text this way in a table is unreliable—it changes the cell height for no good reason.

10. Instead, highlight the column (using the mouse method or Table | Select Column) and choose Table | Cell Properties. Choose Right from the Horizontal Alignment list box (in the Layout section of the dialog box). When you click OK, the table entries are right justified to abut with the third column, which will hold the text fields.

Inserting Text Fields

Now you can start inserting the actual text fields that are required by the form. There are two ways to do so: use the Forms toolbar (refer to Figure 4-2) or the Insert | Form Field submenu choices of One Line Text Box, Scrolling Text Box, Check Box, Radio Button, Drop Down Menu, Push Button, and Image. (If the forms toolbar is missing, choose View | Forms Toolbar.)

Again, while following these steps, make sure you are working with the second table on the page, used to request the broker contact information.

Click within the topmost cell of the *third* column of the (second) table to move the insertion point there, and click the One Line Text Box button on the Forms toolbar, or choose Insert | Form Field | One Line Text Box (if you prefer menus over toolbars).

When you insert a text field, the text box appears, wrapped in dashed lines representing the area of the page occupied by the form. Immediately, you may discern a problem—the entire form occupies only the cell you inserted the text box into. If you insert additional text fields into the other cells, each will be contained within its own form.

This is going to be a problem, since all the fields (controls) in our table need to be part of the same form. Only then can the Save Results WebBot store all the related fields together. (If you have multiple forms on a page, a different form handler manages each form, creating a separate results file for each form. Some pages you create might benefit from more than one form, but not this page.)

You'll need to trick FrontPage to accomplish your goal. While tables can contain forms, forms can also contain tables. The way to straighten out this mess is to first create the form, then move the table into the form. You can then insert fields that are part of the same form into the table. (Most of the time, you can create the form first, then create the table, but for alignment purposes, I instructed you to create the table first. It won't be a problem, because once the form is prepared, you'll simply relocate the table to the interior of the form.)

Follow these steps to create a form, and move the table into the form region.

1. First, use Edit | Undo or press Ctrl+Z to undo the insertion of the text box on the table. (If this doesn't work, click on the text box and press Delete twice.)
2. Next, click on the blank line that exists between the two tables.

If you didn't insert that line earlier, you'll find it impossible to move the insertion point between the two tables and insert a line. The secret, which I first mentioned in Chapter 3, is to move the insertion point to the end of the text in the first table and press Ctrl+Enter to open up a blank line beneath the first table.

3. Once you've positioned the insertion point between the two tables, click any form field button. This creates a form, a dashed outline, to hold the form field automatically. Press Enter to insert another blank line.

As you can see in Figure 4-4, the form occupies only the region between the two tables. We now need to move the second table into that region.

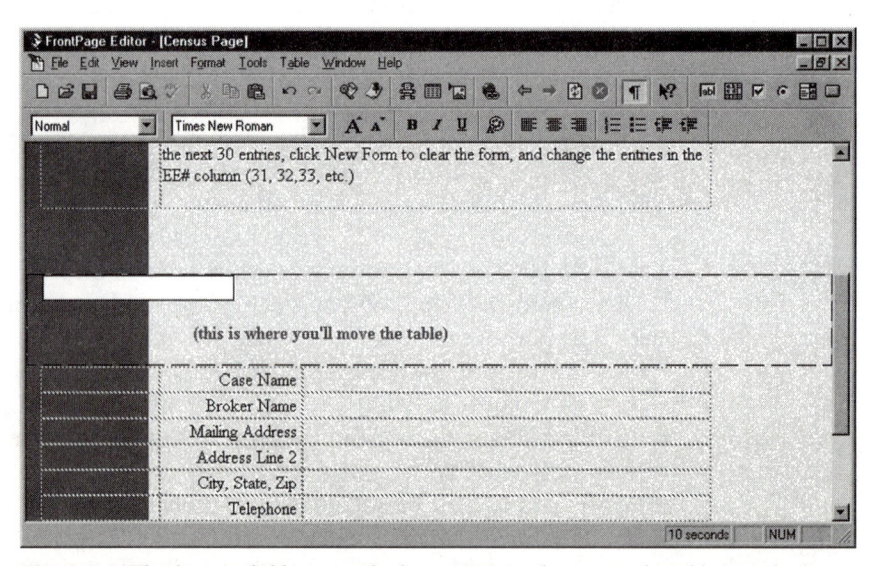

Figure 4-4: The dummy field creates the form. You can then move the table into the form boundaries. (Don't type the instruction "this is where you'll move the table." It was added to this figure for clarity.)

4. Position the mouse pointer at the top-left corner of the second (data entry) table, just outside of the border region. The pointer should change to a right-pointing arrowhead (the reverse of the normal pointer shape). Double-click to select the table. If this mouse technique proves to be too cumbersome, just use Table | Select Table.

5. With the table selected, choose Edit | Cut (Ctrl+X) to cut the table out of the page (don't worry, it's stored in the clipboard).

6. Now move the insertion point into the form, just below the dummy field you inserted earlier. Choose Edit | Paste (Ctrl+V) to paste the table into its new position.

> **TIP**
>
> *Instead of using Cut and Paste to move items on a page, you may instead wish to try the drag-and-drop method of moving the table. Once the table is selected (highlighted), simply drag the table upward with the mouse. The pointer changes to an arrow with a box attached to it. Without releasing, drag the arrow until it points to the location within the form. Release the mouse button to drop the table into place.*

7. You can now click on the dummy field and press Del to remove it. The form remains on the page.

8. You can also remove any extraneous blank lines to tidy things up.

You've now placed the table inside the form boundaries. When you insert fields, they will occupy the table without creating a separate form for each field.

Now that the second (data entry) table exists within the form, click in the cell next to each label and insert a single-line text box. After inserting the text fields, the page will resemble Figure 4-5.

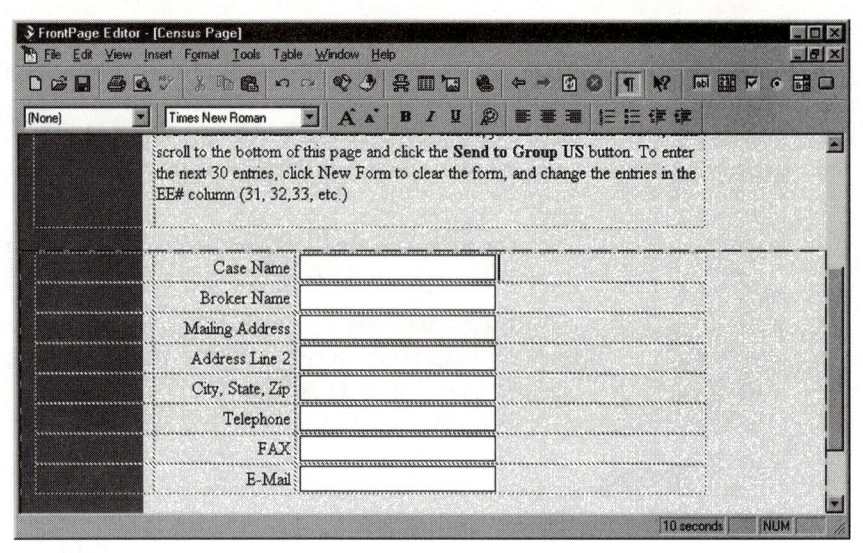

Figure 4-5: By default, all text boxes have the same size, a width of 20 characters.

You now need to change the widths of the various text boxes and assign a unique name to each one. (Recall that the names will be used to store the value of each field.)

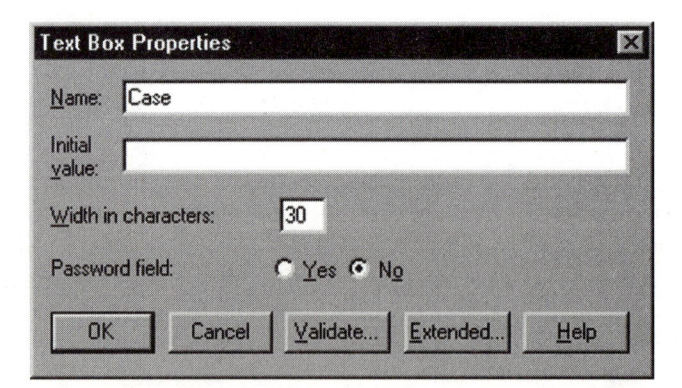

Figure 4-6: Each text field is named and has a width. You can also assign a default (initial) value.

1. Double-click upon the first text box, the one next to Case Name. The Text Box Properties dialog box appears, as shown in Figure 4-6.

2. For the first text box, replace the default name of the text field (something like T2) by typing Case in the Name box, and leave the Initial Value box blank. Set the Width in Characters value to 30. Leave Password Field set to No.

TIP

If you're creating a field that lets the user enter a password or other secret information, setting the Password Field to Yes causes asterisks to appear while the user types in the box, protecting the security of the password from over-the-shoulder snoops.

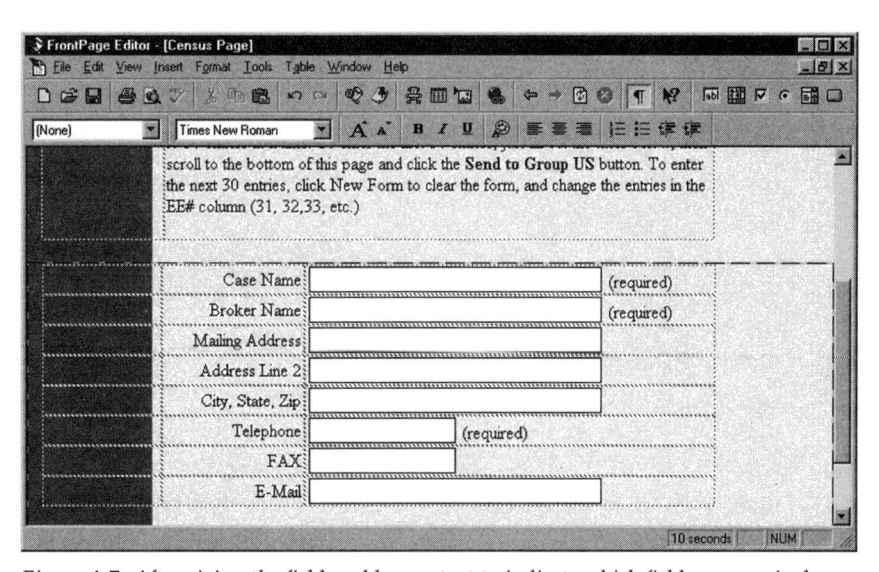

Figure 4-7: After sizing the fields, add some text to indicate which fields are required.

3. Using the Field Name column in Table 4-1 as a guide, set the names and widths of the other text boxes.

4. As shown in Figure 4-7, type some additional text to the right of each text box as a guideline for the user, to show which fields are optional and which are required.

You've now prepared the first row of the census table. You can now set some validation rules for the required entries.

Enforcing Data Entry With Validation Rules

Validation rules, a new feature introduced in FrontPage 97, allow you to enforce the type of data that can be entered into a form field. In addition to marking a field as required (meaning the user must enter information into that field to be able to submit the form), you can also set limits on the types of characters that can be entered. Not only can this help the user avoid mistakes, it ensures that the data entered is formatted correctly, which is important if you plan to import the data into another program like a database management system or spreadsheet.

Validation rules are also essential for implementing business logic. Business logic uses validation rules to enforce company standards for information. It can also take the form of custom scripts that perform computation and deliver live feedback to the user as he or she works. (I won't cover custom scripts here. For an introduction to the easy way to learn the VBScript language, refer to Chapter 9.)

How It Works

How do validation rules work? Traditionally, form validation requires the web server to examine the data entered in a form, check the rules for valid entry, and prompt the user to back up and reenter missing or incorrect data. Not only does this tax the server, it also results in slow feedback for the user.

To accomplish the same results without burdening the server, FrontPage 97 builds custom JavaScript (also called LiveScript in Navigator or JScript in Internet Explorer) or Visual Basic script (VBScript) program code for each form field with validation rules. You don't have to know how to program in JavaScript or VBScript—FrontPage creates the code automatically.

Note: These scripts are embedded within a WebBot, and are updated whenever you edit the page from FrontPage Explorer. This explains why you won't see any language code if you use View | HTML to look at the raw HTML code of the page. Because WebBots are used to insert the script, the web server you're publishing to must support the latest FrontPage 97 server extensions. For more on this topic, consult Chapter 5.

Validation Limitations

The only caveat is that JavaScript is supported only with Netscape Navigator version 2.0 or later or Internet Explorer 3.0 or later. (VBScript is supported by IE 3.0 or later and is promised for the version 4.0 Communicator release of Netscape Navigator.) What this means is that your rules will be ignored if the user has JavaScript/VBScript disabled in their browser or is using an unsupported browser.

TIP

By default, FrontPage uses JavaScript to build the validation rules, since it is supported by both Internet Explorer (3.0 or later) and Netscape Navigator (3.0 or later). If you prefer VBScript (perhaps you know the Visual Basic language and wish to study the generated scripts), you can tell FrontPage to use VBScript instead of JavaScript. VBScript also tends to be more compact than JavaScript.

Using FrontPage Explorer, open your web (if it's not already open) and choose Tools | Web Settings. Switch to the Advanced tab, and use the Language drop-down menu (in the Validation Scripts section, not on the Language property sheet) to choose between JavaScript or VBScript. Or you can choose <none>, which prevents any validation features from being used. (You might use this feature if your web server doesn't yet support the FrontPage 97 server extensions.)

When you change the language type, FrontPage recalculates the web, and any existing scripts are converted to the chosen language—you don't have to worry that your pages might end up with a mix of both JavaScript and VBScript.

Making the Validation Entries

Fortunately, you don't have to know anything about how to program in JavaScript or VBScript to take advantage of validation rules. It's really quite easy, as shown next.

Double-click on the first text box field (Case). In the Text Box Properties dialog box (illustrated in Figure 4-6), click the Validate button. You'll get another dialog box, shown in Figure 4-8.

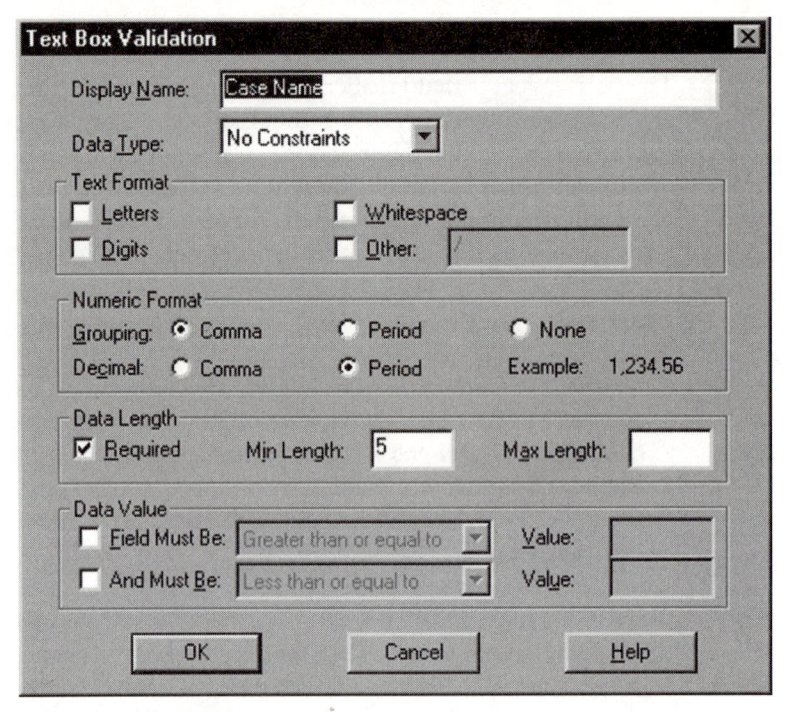

Figure 4-8: By choosing various combinations of options and check boxes, you can create a wide variety of possible validation rules for data entry.

Figure 4-8 shows you how you'll fill out the Text Box Validation dialog box for the Case text field. Let's examine these options further.

Use the Display Name box to enter an alternate name for the field. Since the validation code only knows the name of the field (it can't "see" the labels you typed), you should fill out the Display Name with a meaningful description of the field. If the validation code has to display an error message prompting the user to reenter the data in a field, it uses the Display Name for the error message, as in "Please enter a value for the 'Case Name' field."

Filling in a meaningful Display Name is especially important if the field names are cryptic, such as EEAgeYOB. Otherwise, the user won't be able to figure out which field has the error. In general, you should use the label or description of the field here, not the name of the form field control.

Data Type

For the Data Type drop-down menu (in the Text Box Validation dialog box), you can choose from the following: No Constraints, Text, Integer, or Number. The default is No Constraints, which means that any characters can be entered. This disables the Text Format and Numeric Format sections, so if you want to choose any limits on text or numeric formatting, don't use No Constraints. (I rigged the figure to show all the options clearly, even though No Constraints is chosen in Figure 4-8.)

Text Format

Choose Text (from the Data Type drop-down list in the Text Box Validation dialog box) if you want to choose which characters are allowable ("legal") in the field for text entry. Normally, you'd leave all the check boxes in the Text Format section unchecked, so that any characters can be typed.

Sometimes, however, there are strict rules about the type of text that can be entered. For example, if you had a text field that should store dates in the form MM/DD/YY, you only want to allow digits and the slash character. You would enable the Digits check box and type a / character into the Other box (also checking the other box to enable it). Although this doesn't prevent some mistakes, such as entering 01/004// 2168 when only two digit dates are desired, it does catch the majority of errors. (You can enable the Whitespace check box if you want to allow arbitrary usage of space and tab characters within a field, which is necessary if you want to allow more than one word to be entered. Leave this check box unchecked to prevent leading or trailing spaces from being entered into a field.)

Numeric Format

If you choose the Number data type from the Data Type drop-down list, the Numeric Format section of the dialog box allows you to choose the grouping character and decimal character. In the United States and many other countries, the comma is the grouping character, and the period is used as the decimal point. The number 1,436,232.33 contains these characters. In some European countries, this usage is curiously reversed; the same number would read 1.436.232,33. Consider your intended audience when choosing between these options. If you don't want to allow any commas in the numbers, choose None as the grouping character.

If the numbers to be entered are whole numbers (without decimal fractions), you should use the Integer data type. You can still choose the grouping character for this data type, but since the number is an integer, you don't need to set the decimal character (and you won't be given that choice—the Decimal choices will be grayed out to show that they are disabled).

Data Length

Under the Data Length section, click the Required check box to enforce data entry; the user won't be allowed to submit the form unless every required field has been filled out. You can also set a minimum and maximum length for the entry. Choosing a modest minimum entry is a good way to enforce a valid entry and bypass an attempt to type just a few characters to get around the restriction. After all, few people have a name less than five characters long.

For a one-line text box, you might think that you don't need to set the maximum length since the text box itself has a specified width, but this only sets the viewable width of the text box. The user is free to type any number of characters into the box, which scrolls when the insertion point reached the limit of the box.

For this reason, you'll still need to set a validation rule if you want to limit entries to the width of the text box.

Sometimes you'll want to assign a width to a text box for aesthetic reasons, such as sizing a group of text boxes to the same width.

Even for narrow text boxes that you want to limit to one character of input, you'll want to use a width of at least two characters so that the text box doesn't look too anemic. Since the text box font will vary from one browser to the next, or vary depending on the font choices the user has chosen for the browser, you should always allow a generous width for text boxes, even if you decide to limit the number of characters that can be accepted.

Keep in mind that the limit on the length of a text field isn't checked until the form is submitted; you can't prevent the user from *trying* to type too many characters.

Data Value

You can use the Data Value section to finesse the rules further. To limit entry to a range of values, use the Field Must Be check box and/or the And Must Be check box. For each, choose from Less Than, Greater Than,

Less Than or Equal To, Greater Than or Equal To, Equal To, or Not Equal To. Then fill in a value. Combining these can yield an expression such as "Field data value must be greater than or equal to 1 and less than or equal to 10," which is how you'd describe a text field that asks you to enter a number from 1 to 10.

Ideally, the validation rules would check the input as you type so that the user wouldn't even be able to type anything into the box other than the legal characters, thereby avoiding an error message unnecessarily. We'll have to put it on the wish list for the next version of FrontPage. (This kind of validation-as-you-type could also be implemented by writing your own VBScript or JavaScript code, which is discussed in Chapter 8.)

For tracking purposes, this form requires the Case Name, Broker Name, and Telephone fields, since otherwise it might be difficult to match a census sheet with the broker who submitted it. As long as we require some entry for Case Name and Broker Name, we might as well require at least five characters to ensure complete data entry, so in the Data Length section of the dialog box, the Min Length field is set to 5 and the Max Length field is left alone, since the width of the text box will limit input to 30 characters or less.

Validating the Case Name Field

Let's return to our project and see how to set the validation options for each field.

1. After double-clicking on the Case text box on the Census page and clicking the Validate button in the Text Box Properties dialog box, fill out the Text Box Validation dialog box by typing **Case Name** as the Display Name, and choosing No Constraints for Data Type.

2. Click the Required check box, and set the Min Length field to 5. Click OK.

3. Repeat the same validation steps for the Broker text field, using Broker Name as the Display Name.

4. To validate the telephone number, double-click on the Telephone text box. From the Text Box Properties dialog box, click the Validate button. In the Text Box Validation dialog box, type **Telephone Number** as the display name, click Required in the Data Length section, and set the Min Length field to 7. Don't click OK yet.

5. To continue setting up the validation rules for the telephone number, click the Data Type drop-down menu and choose Text (since telephone numbers contain non-numeric characters). For the Text Format section, click to enable the check boxes for Digits and Whitespace. Click the Other check box, and type +()- into the box.
6. Compare the settings to Figure 4-9, and then click OK.
7. Apply the same validation rules for the FAX field, except that Required should not be enabled, since FAX isn't a required field for this form.

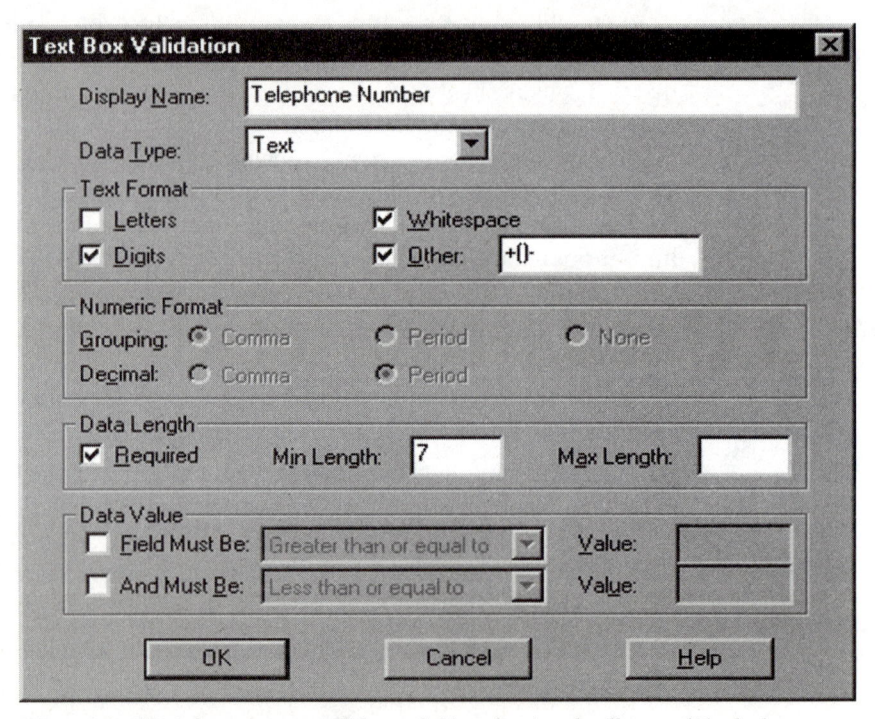

Figure 4-9: This is how you can validate a field so that it only allows valid telephone numbers, such as +1 (910) 555-1212.

If you wish, you can set some other validation rules, such as permitting only characters, digits, and @ characters for the E-mail field, but don't get carried away. Too many rules can make the page slow to retrieve from the server, and the Internet is slow enough as it is!

Validating Other Types of Input

Note that only the text box (either One Line or Scrolling) offers the full range of validation settings. There are no validation settings for the check box; after all, it can only be on or off. For radio buttons, you can require an entry; in other words, at least one radio button must be clicked in a group of radio buttons.

For drop-down menus, you can set a validation rule to require data entry, and you can prohibit the selection of the first item in the list. This unusual rule is to support a common convention with drop-down menus—the first item in the list is an instruction such as "—Click to select your country—." This is entirely optional, though.

Image fields have no validation options.

Building the Census Table

The first half of the census form is complete. Now we can put together a third table to hold the actual census data. Let's get this straight: The first table on the page aligns the heading. The second table collects contact information. The third table, which you'll create next, is the "meat" of this form, collecting detailed census statistics. Both the second and third tables must exist within the dashed boundaries of the form.

Here's how you put together the census table:

1. Begin by moving the insertion point beneath the second table on the page (the contact information), yet still within the boundaries of the form.

If you forgot to leave a blank line after the table (always a good practice; you can always remove blank lines later), position the insertion point at the end of the table next to the E-mail text box and press Ctrl+Enter to insert a blank line.

2. From the line beneath the second table, use Table | Insert Table to insert a third table. Choose 31 rows and 8 columns, and set the table width to 620 pixels. Unlike the other tables, this one should have visible gridlines (borders), so choose a border width of 2 to make it good and heavy.

Make sure the new (third) table is placed within the boundaries of the form; otherwise the data will be ignored. If necessary, use cut and paste to move the table where it belongs, beneath the second table, and within the form boundaries.

The first row will hold the table headings, which will also contain radio buttons that let the agent specify the type of data that he or she is entering. The remaining 30 rows are reserved for the census entries, as in the paper form.

Note: A table this large uses lots of memory when displayed by the browser and may display slowly with some browsers. In particular, I've noticed that Netscape Navigator displays the table much more slowly than Internet Explorer, probably because Microsoft's programmers knew a few programming tricks to take advantage of the Windows graphical user interface.

Although we chose 30 rows to better match the paper form, in practice you may need to use smaller tables for best results. The instructions on the page tell the user what to do if the data exceeds 30 employees: After submitting the first 30 employees, use the New Form (Reset) button to start a new table and manually renumber the employee number fields as needed. If you are conversant in JavaScript or VBScript, you could add a Continue button to the form to fill in the numbers automatically for subsequent entries beyond 30.

You don't really need to set the widths of the columns, since they will resize automatically to fit the size of the fields you insert. You don't use a dummy column to skip over the border for this table because you need the full width of the table for all the columns. This won't be illegible, since the text boxes for the Employee Number fields have a white background.

To continue with the table layout:

3. Place the column headings left to right across the first row of the table: EE#, Sex (M/F), Smoker (S/N), Employee Age YOB, Amount Life Salary, Spouse Age YOB, Smoker (S/N), # Children.

As you type, don't be disconcerted by the way the column widths change size; the column widths will be (approximately) correct once you've typed in all the headings.

To make the headings line up more neatly, you can insert a line break for the headings that span more than one line.

4. Move the insertion point (using the arrow keys or by clicking) to a position just to the left of Age in the Employee Age YOB box. Press Shift+Enter to insert a line break (shown onscreen as a crooked arrow). Also insert a line break just prior to YOB. This will make it easier to insert the radio buttons.

5. Repeat the same technique to break the Amount Life Salary and Spouse Age YOB into three lines. Refer to Figure 4-10 to see how this should appear onscreen.

Chapter 4: Building an Interactive Web Site: Forms & Form Handlers

6. Next, select the entire row with Table | Insert Row, then choose Table | Cell Properties. (By now, you already know the mouse shortcuts for these methods: Left-click just to the left of the row to select it, and right-click on the selection to display the pop-up menu and choose Cell Properties.)

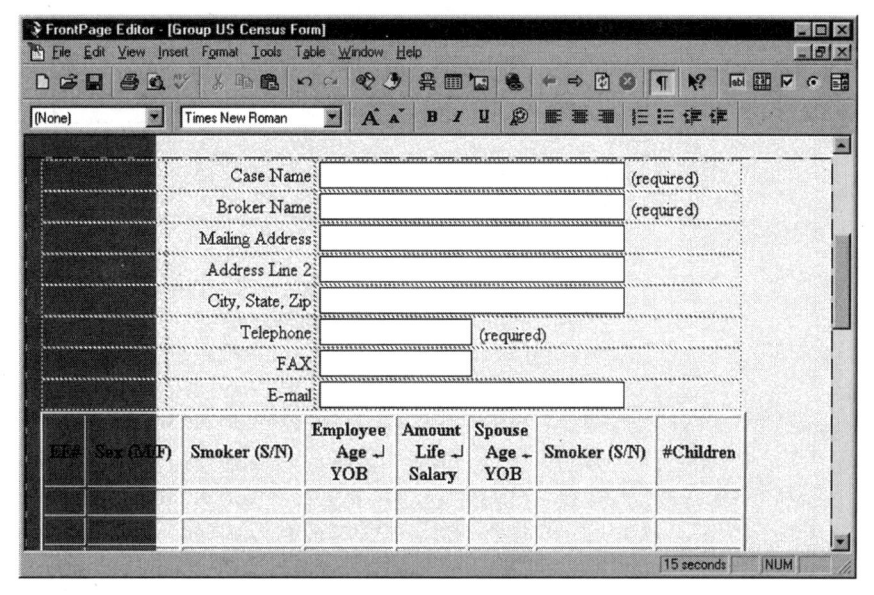

Figure 4-10: The text of the headings is now formatted and centered.

7. From the Cell Properties dialog box, choose a Horizontal Alignment of Center and turn on the Header Cell check box.

Compare your results with Figure 4-10. If you like, save the page and take a break before moving on.

To complete the heading of the table, you'll insert three groups of radio buttons. Each group will contain two radio buttons to choose between either Age/YOB or Life/Salary.

1. Use the arrow keys on the keyboard to position the insertion point just to the left of Age in the cell containing the text "Employee Age YOB." Click the Radio Button button on the Forms toolbar or choose Insert | Form Field | Radio Button. Insert another radio button just to the left of the text "YOB."

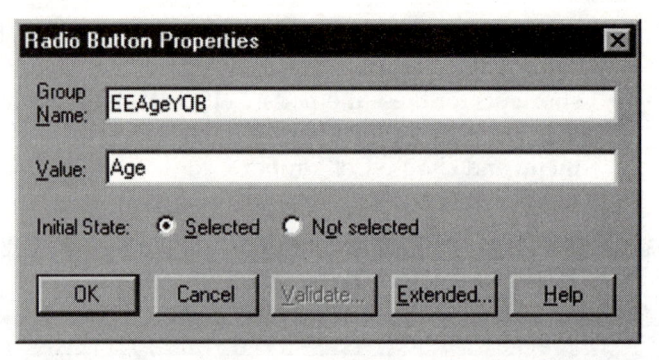

Figure 4-11: For each radio button in a group, use the same group name and a unique value.

2. Double-click upon the first radio button. This pops up the Radio Buttons Properties dialog box (Figure 4-11). Change the group name to EEAgeYOB and the value to Age. Double-click the second radio button and set its group name to the same as the first button, EEAgeYOB, but set the value to YOB.

When you type the same group name for two or more radio buttons, the buttons are part of a set that only allows one of the radio buttons to be chosen. The term comes from the old-style push-button radios found in vintage automobiles. Pushing a station button caused the previously selected station's button to pop out. Buttons on cassette tape recorders also work this way.

Furthermore, the Save Results WebBot includes on the results page an entry for the name you entered in the Group Name text box. The value associated with that name is the value of the chosen radio button. This can be any arbitrary value, really. If the option buttons are in a long list, you might simply assign a number to each radio button as its value.

We use Age and YOB as the value for these radio buttons, so if Age is clicked, you'll see the EEAgeYOB="Age" when you examine the page output by the Save Results WebBot. This fact is what tells the person reading the census results that the values in the EEAgeYOB column are Age values rather than Year of Birth information.

The initial state of a radio button can be either Selected or Not Selected. You can set all buttons in a group to Not Selected, but only one radio button in a group can be set as Selected by default. That is consistent with the way radio buttons are supposed to work.

Let's continue inserting and setting the properties for the radio buttons on the heading of the table.

3. As you did with Employee Age YOB, insert two radio buttons for Spouse Age YOB. Double-click on each radio button, and type **SpouseAgeYOB** into the Group Name text box. Set the value of the first button to Age and the value of the second radio button to YOB. Set the initial state for the Age button to Selected.

Notice that the Group Name text box defaults to that of the last button you inserted. This lets you set the group name for the first button you insert and conveniently pick it up for each additional button, assuming you want all the radio buttons in the same group. In this case, you don't, so be sure to change the group name for each heading that uses a radio button.

4. Also insert radio buttons for Amount Life Salary, setting the group name for these buttons to LifeSalary and the button values to Life and Salary. Set the Life button's initial setting to Selected.

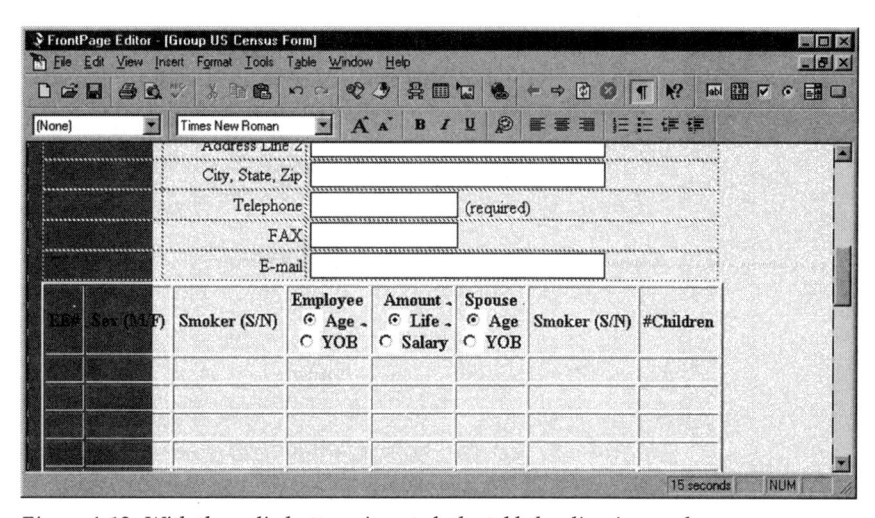

Figure 4-12: With the radio buttons inserted, the table heading is complete.

Now the table heading should look like Figure 4-12. We're ready for the last step, creating the entries for the 30 rows of the table.

Laying Out the Census Entries

You've already created the heading for the census data entry table, now you'll design the first row of the census table. Follow these steps:

1. Use the arrow keys (or click) to move the text insertion point to the first column of the second row of the census table.
2. Click the One-Line Text Box) toolbar button on the Forms toolbar.
3. Double-click on the resulting text box, and set its name to EENum_01, its initial value to 01, and the width to 3.

Although you might think you only need two characters for this field to allow up to 99 entries, it doesn't hurt to use the extra space, both to allow larger numbers and to puff up the text box a bit.

When you finish the table, you'll name successive entries in this column EENum_02, EENum_03, EENum_04, and so on.

TIP

You can usually name a field (control) arbitrarily, but if you intend to apply validation rules, the name of the field has to be legal in the JavaScript and VBScript languages. This means that the name of the field should only contain upper- or lowercase letters from A to Z, digits from 0 to 9, and optionally, the underscore character (_). Avoid spaces and punctuation.

To proceed with laying out the census table:

4. Insert a drop-down menu in the next cell. Double-click on it to get the Drop-Down Menu Properties dialog box shown in Figure 4-13.

A *drop-down menu* (also called a drop-down list box) contains a list of values from which the visitor to your web page can choose. You use the Drop-Down Menu Properties dialog box to build your menu. Click Add to enter a value to add to the list, Modify to change a value, Remove to delete a value, and use the Move Up and Move Down buttons to rearrange the list.

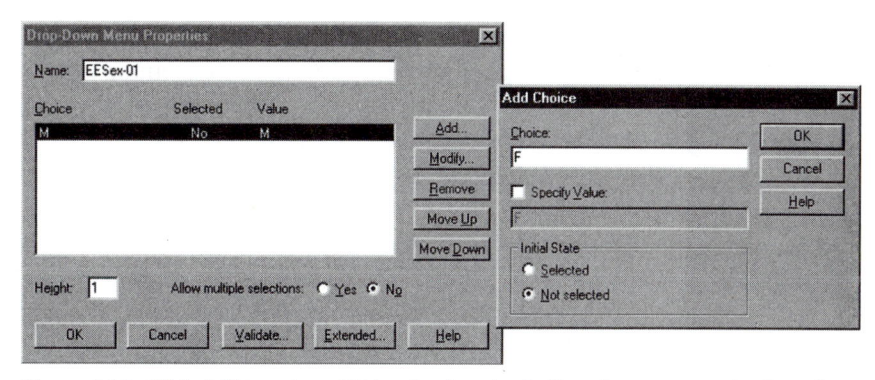

Figure 4-13: Click Add to enter additional values in the list, choose a name for the value, and optionally, enter the actual value to store, if different than the name.

Should you need to allow the user to choose more than one value at a time, click Yes for Allow Multiple Selections. This usually isn't necessary nor good practice, but it may be necessary for some applications. (The user makes additional selections with Ctrl+Click, Shift+Click, and other mouse selection techniques.)

In Figure 4-13, you'll see that M has been added to the drop-down menu. Here's how:

5. Click the Add button, and enter M in the Choice text box, then click OK. Set the Initial State to Selected. Don't change any other settings.

6. Click Add again, and add F as the Choice. Leave the other settings blank; the Initial State should be Not Selected. Click OK.

I could have used Male and Female for Choice, and specified M and F for Value. That way, the user sees the Male and Female choices, but the more compact M or F is what gets stored in the results page. I decided to show (and store) only M and F on this form so that the columns wouldn't use up too much space on the page.

7. After adding the choices, type **EESex_01** into the Name box of the Drop-Down Menu dialog box. (The fields in this column on subsequent rows will be named EESex_02, EESex_03, etc.)

8. Click OK to complete the definition of the drop-down menu.

Since the nature of a drop-down menu forces the user to choose either M or F, the only validation rule that may apply is whether or not the value is required.

If none of the entries in a drop-down box are set to Selected, and if the user doesn't explicitly choose a value by clicking on the menu, no value will be stored in the results page for that menu item. In other words, since neither M nor F will be selected in the browser by default, the user will still have to type M or F, or click the menu, to choose an appropriate value. Without validation, it's possible for the value of this menu field to be empty (null). That can foul up the data, since the gender is usually necessary for a valid census.

That's why you set the Initial State of the M choice to Selected. This corresponds to what the user sees on the screen—that M is apparently selected by default. (Another way to make the choice clear without choosing a default selection would be to add an entry to the top of the list that reads "Choose M or F." A validation rule could be added to ignore the first line. But we don't have enough room in the table to display an instruction that large.)

While you could use the Validate button to force the value to be required, we've already taken care of a default selection by modifying the M value in the list. Adding too many validation rules can slow down processing of the page, so we'll avoid them where possible.

In Figure 4-13, note the property labeled Height. It lets you choose how many lines appear for the menu. If you choose as many lines as there are entries, you have what's called a list box—it doesn't need to drop down. As in our table, however, it's preferable to save screen space and use only one line for most menus. (A greater Height value is desirable for longer menus, nevertheless.)

Completing the First Row of the Census Table

To complete the first row of the census table, you'll add additional fields for each column.

1. As you did with EESex_01 (Sex M/F), insert a drop-down menu into the cell beneath the Smoker (S/N) heading. Name the menu EESmoke_01, and insert values for S and N. Set the S value to be initially selected.

2. Insert a one-line text box in the cell beneath Employee Age YOB. Double-click on it, and set its name to EEAgeYOB_01 and its width to 3.

3. Likewise, insert a text box in the next cell (beneath Amount Life Salary), name it LifeSalary_01, and set its width to 30.

Chapter 4: Building an Interactive Web Site: Forms & Form Handlers 187

4. Continue by inserting a text box in the cell beneath the heading Spouse Age YOB, setting its name to SpouseAgeYOB_01 and its width to 3.

5. For the entry for the Spouse's smoker/non-smoker status, insert a drop-down menu, and add the values S and N as you did with the other Smoker/Non-smoker field. Name this one SpouseSmoke_01, and set the S value to be the one that's initially selected.

6. Finish up the row by inserting a text box in the cell beneath the #Children heading, setting its name to Children_01 and its width to 3.

7. Select the entire row you've just created, and choose Table | Cell Properties. Change the horizontal alignment to Center.

Adjusting Fit & Finish

You may find that the Smoker table headings look too wide compared to the rest of the headings. To make them consistent, insert a line break (Shift+Enter) between Smoker and S/N. The resulting census table is nearly complete.

Compare your table with Figure 4-14. All you have to do now is duplicate the second row of the table on each remaining row, changing the field names to suit. (For the third row, the fields are named EENum_02, EESex_02, EESmoke_02, AgeYob_02, LifeSalary_02, SpouseAgeYob_02, SpouseSmoke_02, Children_02, and so on.)

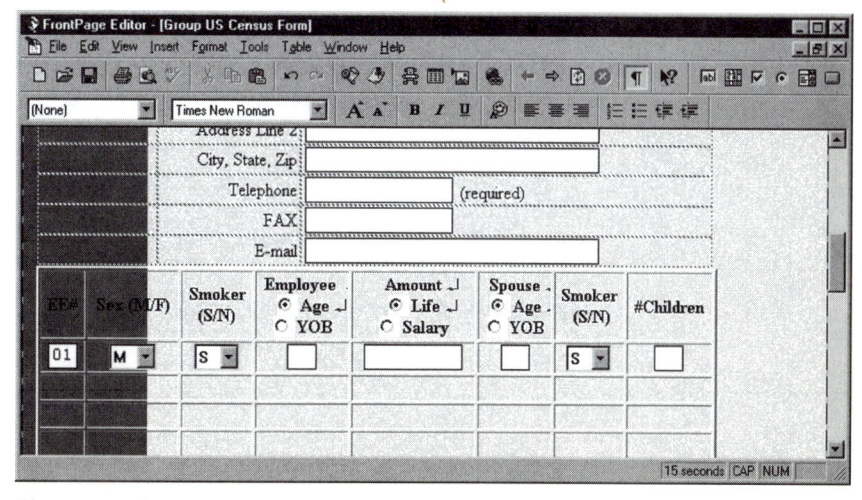

Figure 4-14: Once the first row is completed, we can duplicate it down the page.

Since the remainder of the table will be created by copying the row you just completed (the second row of the table), it's important to make sure that this row is configured just the way you like. Otherwise, if you want to make a change to a cell, you'd have to make the same change to all the other cells in that column.

Setting Validation Rules

This is a good time to add validation rules to the table. Any rules that we create for the cells on the second row of the table (the data entry row) will be copied to the remaining rows of the table. This saves a lot of time: Do you really want to edit the validation rules for each of 240 cells (30 rows multiplied by 8 columns)?

Keeping in mind that too many validation rules can slow down the page, here's how you can set some limits on valid data in the table.

1. Double-click on the text box in the cell beneath Amount Life Salary on the second row of the census table (the text box is named LifeSalary1).

2. In the Text Box Properties dialog box, click the Validate button, which brings up the Text Box Validation dialog box. Set the data type to Number, and leave the grouping and decimal characters set to command and period (the default). In the Display Name text box, type: **Life/Salary Amount**. Don't click OK yet.

This form can also catch some simple mistakes by ensuring a minimum and maximum value for the life/salary amounts. Few people make less than $1,000 per year or have less than $1,000 of life insurance. Likewise, not many earn $10,000,000 or have $10,000,000 of life insurance. So we can catch some simple mistakes, such as dropped or extra characters, by setting a data value rule that reads, "Field must be greater than 1000 and less than 10000000."

3. To set this rule, click the check box next to "Field Must Be" in the Data Value section. Choose Greater Than from the drop-down menu, and enter a Value of 1000. Beneath that entry, click the check box next to "And Must Be," choose Less Than from the drop-down menu, and enter a value of 10000000 (seven zeros). Compare your entries to Figure 4-15.

You could also have clicked the Required check box, since a census entry is often useless without life or salary amounts, but consider what happens if a short census (less than 30 employees) is entered. The Required validation rule sees that there are many blank entries left over, and these are required entries. The user would have to fill up the table with dummy entries to get around the restriction. No way. It's better not to use the Required property for this field.

In principle, you could add some other validation rules for the other cells on the row, such as ensuring that the Age/YOB data is an integer between 1 and 130 (now considered by demographers to be the maximum attainable human life span) or that the number of children is an integer between 0 and 10 (don't make this a required entry, since many employees don't have children—you can interpret a blank entry as zero children).

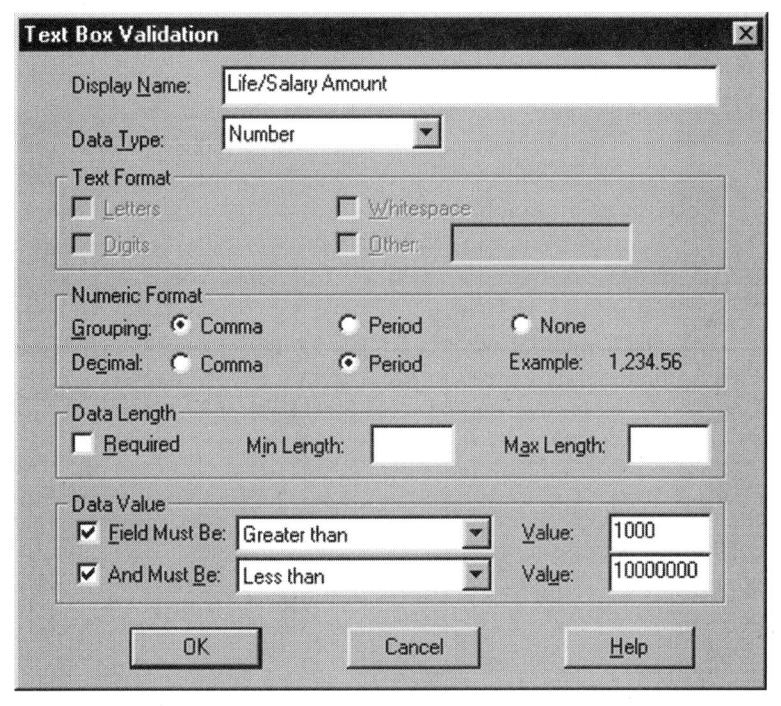

Figure 4-15: This validation rule ensures valid numeric input within a range of 1000-10,000,000.

Filling the Rest of the Census Table

Now that you've "perfected" the second row of the table, you can complete the table by copying the second row of the table to the remaining 29 rows.

To duplicate the second row, use Table | Select Row (or click just to the left of the row), and then use Edit | Copy (Ctrl+C). This places a copy of the row into the clipboard.

Now select the third row of the table. The entire row should be highlighted. Choose Edit | Paste (Ctrl+V) to replace the blank entries of that row with a copy of the second row. There are now two data entry rows on the census.

When pasting the duplicate rows, be sure to always select a blank row first. If you paste a row (or any copied range of cells) into a table cell, a new nested table is created inside the cell you pasted it into. While nested tables can be useful (we took advantage of this technique in Chapter 3), it's usually undesirable.

Another rule is that you can only replace table cells with cells from the clipboard if the original selection and the pasted selection have the same shape (same number of rows and columns). Since you copied a single row, you can't simply highlight the rest of the table and use Paste to fill the rest. If you copied a single cell into the clipboard, you can only paste it on top of a single cell.

Instead, continue to select one blank row at a time, followed by Ctrl+V to paste the copied row into place. Once you have 5 rows created, it is faster to select those 5 rows and copy them to the clipboard; then you can select 5 blank rows at a time when you paste. This lets you complete the table in just 5 more steps. (The first 5 were created one at a time, the next 5 steps insert 5 copies each, for a total of 30 rows.)

Creating Unique Names for Each Row

Although you've now completed the rows of the census table, there is a serious problem to deal with. All the fields in each column have the same name. For the first column, each text box has a Name of EENum_01 and has an initial value of 01. Obviously, you are going to have to edit the names for every cell in the table. Otherwise, the data produced by the Save Results WebBot will be useless. (In addition, the validation rules can't work unless each field has a unique name. If you try to save your page before you solve this problem, FrontPage will warn you: "One or more forms contains validated fields with duplicate names. Validation will not work correctly with duplicate field names on the form.")

Fortunately, changing the names won't be too tedious. Just double-click on each entry in a column, and replace the 01 at the end with the next number in the sequence. When editing the EENum column, the names for each cell will be EENum_01, EENum_02, EENum_03, and so on, and the initial values will range from 01 to 30. (The other cells in the table don't have initial values, so you can change just the names.)

Actually, it is pretty tedious to change all these values this way. Perhaps it would have been better to have built a smaller table! There is another method, though, that may make it easier to change all the values in one place and with a lot fewer clicks.

Editing Raw HTML

If you're feeling bold, you may wish to edit the HTML coding of the table directly. That way, instead of double-clicking on each of 232 cells (you don't need to edit the original row), you can scroll through the HTML and change the numbers directly. This technique is optional; if you feel more comfortable editing each cell using FrontPage Editor (by double-clicking on each field), skip to the next section in this chapter, "Adding a Form Handler."

Web Publishing With FrontPage 97

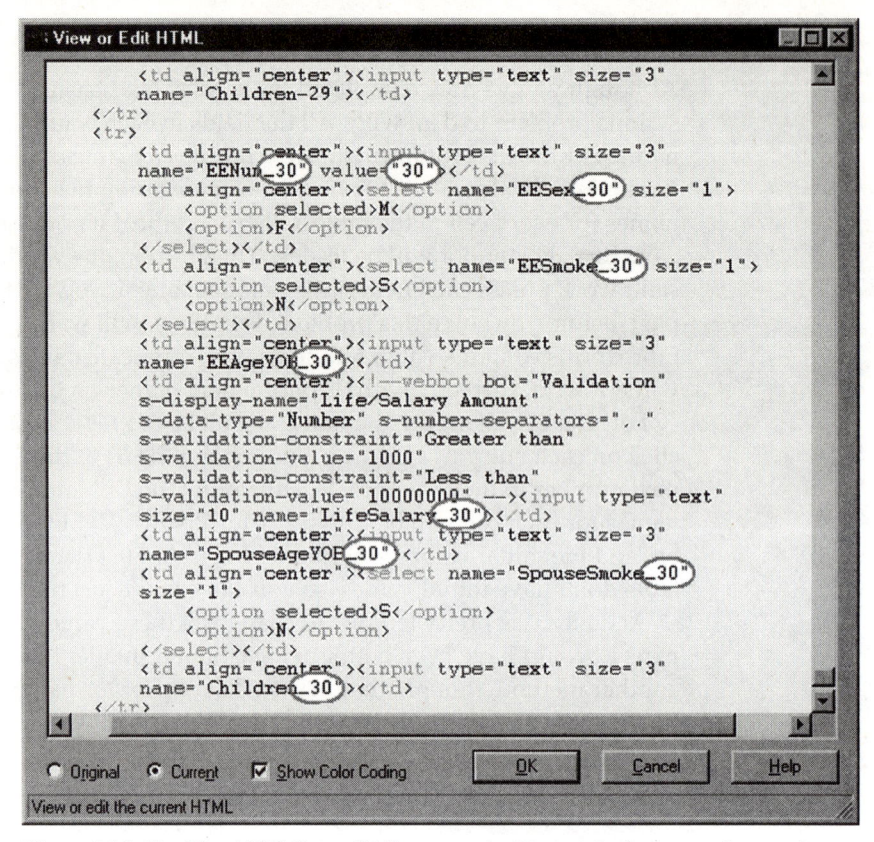

```
View or Edit HTML
            <td align="center"><input type="text" size="3"
name="Children-29"></td>
        </tr>
        <tr>
            <td align="center"><input type="text" size="3"
name="EENum_30" value="30"></td>
            <td align="center"><select name="EESex_30" size="1">
                <option selected>M</option>
                <option>F</option>
            </select></td>
            <td align="center"><select name="EESmoke_30" size="1">
                <option selected>S</option>
                <option>N</option>
            </select></td>
            <td align="center"><input type="text" size="3"
name="EEAgeYOB_30"></td>
            <td align="center"><!--webbot bot="Validation"
s-display-name="Life/Salary Amount"
s-data-type="Number" s-number-separators=",."
s-validation-constraint="Greater than"
s-validation-value="1000"
s-validation-constraint="Less than"
s-validation-value="10000000" --><input type="text"
size="10" name="LifeSalary_30"></td>
            <td align="center"><input type="text" size="3"
name="SpouseAgeYOB_30"></td>
            <td align="center"><select name="SpouseSmoke_30"
size="1">
                <option selected>S</option>
                <option>N</option>
            </select></td>
            <td align="center"><input type="text" size="3"
name="Children_30"></td>
        </tr>
```

○ Original ● Current ☑ Show Color Coding   OK   Cancel   Help

View or edit the current HTML

Figure 4-16: Use View | HTML to edit the raw code. Start at the bottom and renumber the entries. (This figure shows the HTML code for the bottom row of the table. I've highlighted the numbers you need to replace 01 with 30.)

To view and edit the HTML for the Census page, choose View | HTML from the menu bar of FrontPage Editor. Scroll toward the bottom of the list until it resembles Figure 4-16. Although much of the HTML may look like gibberish, you can clearly see where the names of the form fields are specified: Name="EENum_01" or Name="EESex_01."

Chapter 4: Building an Interactive Web Site: Forms & Form Handlers   193

> **TIP**
>
> *The HTML editor can show either the original HTML code (the code that currently resides on the web) or the current HTML code by clicking either the Original or Current radio button at the bottom of the screen. If you save your web page prior to editing the HTML, both views will be the same. Otherwise, the original is the version that is saved to the web (residing in FrontPage Explorer), and current is the version in the FrontPage Editor.*

You can move the insertion point with the arrow keys on the keyboard and edit the HTML document just like any text or word processing document. Note that the HTML for each row is an indented block of statements, starting with <tr> (for table row) and ending with </tr> (end table row).

Start at the bottom of the document, changing the entries such as Name="EENum_01" to Name="EENum_30" within each block. Work your way up to the top until you reach the original Name="EENum_01." (You can also edit the initial value for the EENum fields, where it reads Value="01.")

Make sure the Show Color Coding check box is enabled. That way, the text you need to edit shows up clearly in blue. Take pains not to edit any of the red or purple text—if you make a mistake while editing HTML, you can ruin the entire page.

When editing the HTML, you'll notice that FrontPage doesn't let you increase the size of the HTML coding, perhaps because the large amount of HTML fills the editor to its capacity. (Normally you can insert and delete text in the View HTML dialog box.) In other words, you can overtype characters, but you can't insert new ones. That's why you padded the numbers less than 10 with zeros, so that you can edit the 01 values when you need to change them to two-digit numbers like 10, 11, 12, 13, . . . , 28, 29, 30.

After making the changes to the HTML, click OK to save the changes. You can now save the page without an error message. (If you do get an error, you still have duplicate entries, so go back and double-check your work.)

> **TIP**
>
> *If you prefer to use Notepad or another text/HTML editor to modify the HTML, right-click on the page in FrontPage Explorer and choose Open With. (If the page is open in the FrontPage Editor, save and close it first.) From the Open With Editor dialog box, choose which editor to use. To configure this list, use Tools | Options and modify the Text Editor entry to use your preferred program.*

Adding a Form Handler

A form by itself lets the visitor to your page enter and edit data, but without a form handler, the data isn't going anywhere. The form handler is a special program (or script) that runs on the web server and processes the data returned by the browser. Before you can assign a form handler, though, you have to add a Submit button and a Reset button.

The Submit button sends the data from the form (in this case, the contact information and the fields in the census table) to a form handler that processes it. Usually, you'll assign the FrontPage Save Results WebBot to handle the form. It creates an output page containing name/value pairs for every field on the form.

To add Submit and Reset buttons to the Census page:

1. Move the insertion point to the line beneath the census table, at the end of the page but within the dashed borders of the form. If there isn't a blank line beneath the table already, move the insertion point to the last cell on the table (the lower-right corner) and press Ctrl+Enter to open up a line. Then you can move the insertion point to that line.

2. Click the Push Button button on the Forms toolbar, or choose Insert | Form Field | Push Button. This inserts a Submit button on the form. Insert another button. This inserts another Submit button on the form.

3. To move the buttons toward the right of the page, avoiding the blue border, click the Center toolbar button.

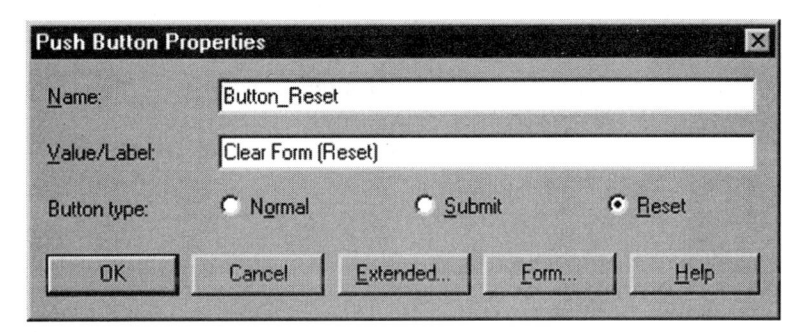

Chapter 4: Building an Interactive Web Site: Forms & Form Handlers

Figure 4-17: You can change the default name and value (label) for a button and set the button type to either Normal, Submit, or Reset.

4. Let's customize these buttons. Double-click on the second Submit button. This pops up the Push Button Properties dialog box. As shown in Figure 4-17, change the Name text box entry from B2 (a generic name for button two) to Button_Reset, and set the Value/Label box to Clear Form (Reset). (The name and value of the button are stored in the data collected by the form handler, but the Value/Label box is really only useful for changing the caption on the button.)

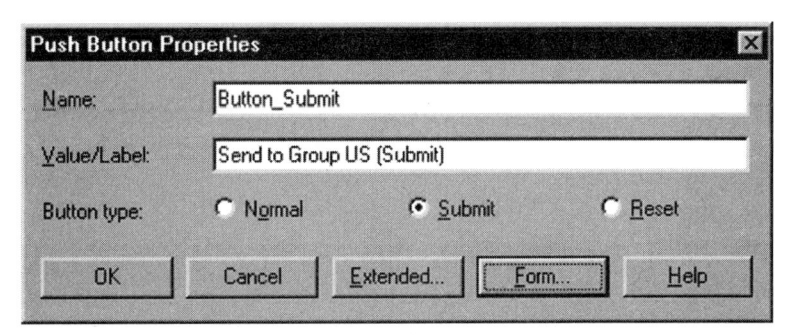

Figure 4-18: The Submit button sends the form to the form handler for processing. You can change the default name to a more descriptive one if you like. If you leave the name blank, it defaults to Submit Query.

5. Now double-click on the second button, the one labeled Submit. Edit its properties as shown in Figure 4-18, changing the name to Button_Submit and the value/label to Send to Group US (Submit). Don't click OK yet.

> **TIP**
>
> *You can also assign a button a type of Normal. This prevents it from submitting or resetting the form. Instead, you can link a script written in JavaScript or VBScript to the button. When the user clicks the button, the script is executed, presumably performing some useful function. Use Insert | Script and the ScriptWizard to build scripts. For more information on scripting, consult Chapter 8.*

6. Click the Form button in the Push Button Properties dialog box. This brings up the Form Properties dialog box for the form (Figure 4-19). You can also edit the form properties by right-clicking anywhere within the form boundaries and choosing Form Properties from the pop-up menu.

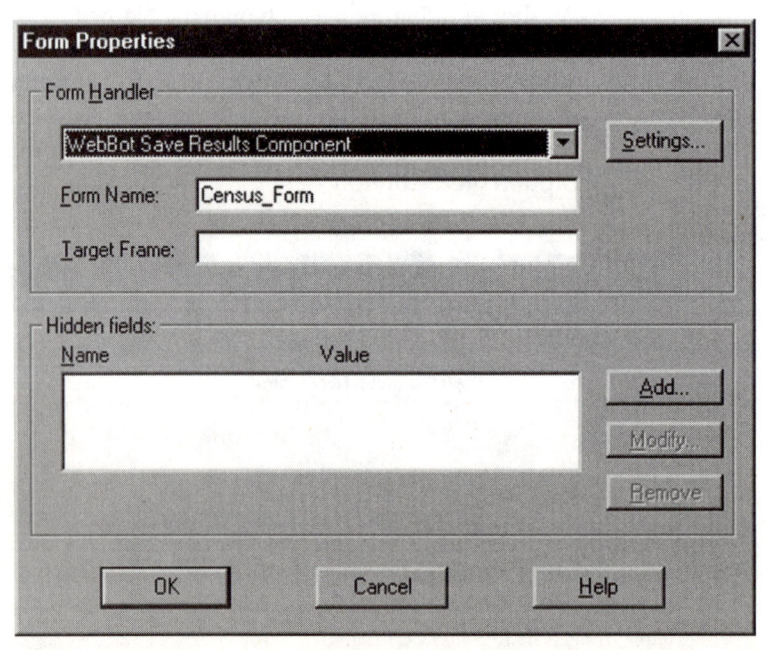

Figure 4-19: The Form Properties dialog box lets you assign a form handler to your form, and set up hidden fields.

Chapter 4: Building an Interactive Web Site: Forms & Form Handlers

As shown in Figure 4-19, the Form Properties dialog box can be used to assign a custom form handler or tell FrontPage to use the Save Results WebBot. You can also name the form and add hidden fields. Hidden fields are stored on the results page generated by the Save Results WebBot, but don't appear on the form itself.

7. Change the Form Name text box entry from the generic FrontPage_Form1 to Census_Form. Choose WebBot Save Results Component from the drop-down list at the top of the dialog box, and click the Settings button. You get the Settings for Saving Results of Form dialog box (Figure 4-20).

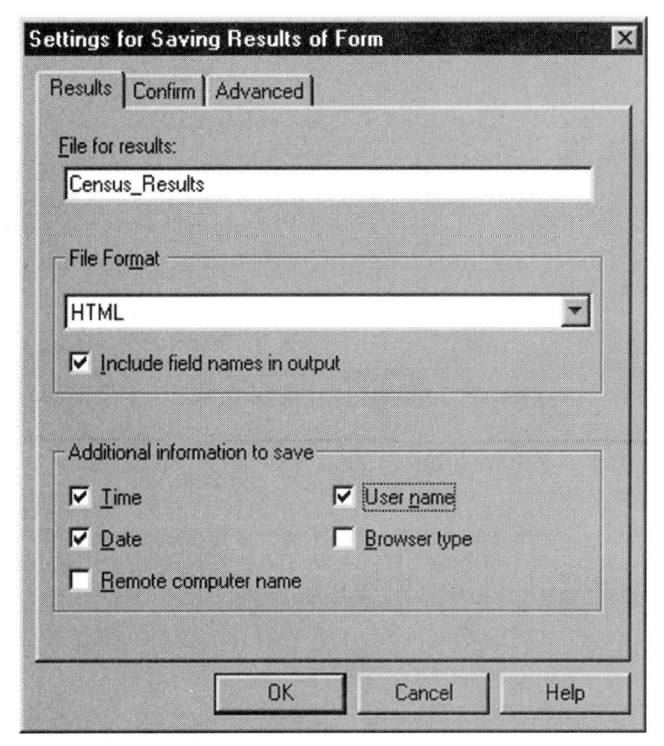

Figure 4-20: The Results tab of the Settings for Saving Results of Form dialog box lets you choose a filename (page URL) for storing the data collected from the form, choose the format for the results (HTML is the default), and choose additional information to save.

The first property sheet of this dialog box, Results, is where you choose the name of the file (page) that is created when the user clicks Submit and the format for the results page.

You can choose whether or not to include the field names with the output. If the Include Field Names in Output check box is not checked, only the values of the fields are saved. You can also turn on check boxes to save additional information as fields, such as date and time, username, browser type, and remote computer name. (It's usually not helpful to use the last three.)

8. In the File for Results text box, enter Census_Results. Don't click OK yet. First, let's examine how the census results are stored on your web site.

As users visit the web and fill out the census form, the information is added to the bottom of the results page. Periodically, you or a delegated employee can access this web site with any web browser and open the results page (e.g., http://*website.com*/Census_Results.htm) to view the census data submitted by the brokers.

So can anyone else, so if you want to preserve the security of the data, make sure your server is set to disable directory/folder browsing. When directory browsing is enabled, the default page in a folder is not displayed. Instead, the filenames of the pages are listed in a manner similar to a DOS directory listing, as you may have seen when browsing FTP sites. This reveals the filenames of all the pages in that folder, making it easy to locate the results page.

By disabling directory browsing, the results file will be effectively hidden. Unless a possible intruder knows the name of the results file, it will be inaccessible. You can also choose to store the file in a hidden directory on your web server (FrontPage automatically considers folders beginning with the underscore character to be hidden).

For example, using _private/Census_Results for the results file causes the file to be stored in the _private folder, which can't be seen by visitors to your page. You might also want to use a nonobvious name for the results page, such as oldjunk.htm, to further obfuscate its purpose.

9. Leave the File Format drop-down list box set to HTML. Let's examine the other alternatives.

The File Format option allows you to choose various ways to format the results page. By choosing HTML, the results file can be opened and read from any web browser. The File Format option also lets you choose some HTML variations, such as HTML Definition List, which formats field names and values pairs using pairs of Defined Term/Definition Paragraph styles; HTML bulleted list, which formats the results as bulleted items; or Formatted Text Within HTML, which stores data using the Formatted Text paragraph style (this displays using the fixed-width Courier font in most browsers).

You can also save the results as a non-HTML file, a text file. If you use Formatted Text, the results will be easy to read using Notepad or a word processor. The other text options, such as Text Database Using Comma as Separator, are for when you plan to import the data into a database program or spreadsheet (see the sidebar, "Analyzing Form Data With Microsoft Excel").

A text database file consists of a header containing the names of each field, followed by a line containing the data for the page. Header names on the first row and data values on subsequent rows are separated in the file by inserting either a comma, a tab character, or a space character between each value, depending on the file format you chose.

Regardless of the file format, keep in mind that the results file is cumulative. Each time a user fills out the form, the results are added to the end of the results form (or appended to it). When you import the data into a database or spreadsheet program, you'll have both old and new data in the file.

You may wish to save both a human-readable version of the data (using one of the HTML variations or Formatted Text) and a version ready to import into a database or spreadsheet program. To do so, click the Advanced tab in the Settings for Saving Results of Form dialog box and specify a different filename for the results. You can also choose the file format for the second file, and on the Advanced tab, you can choose either to send all fields to the form handler or only the fields you name in the Additional Field Selection box.

10. Click OK to close the Submit Results dialog box. The page is now ready for data collection and storage. Save the page.

Analyzing Form Data With Microsoft Excel

Microsoft Excel is popular not only as a way to set up columnar tables and calculations, but as a quick-and-dirty database management system (DBMS). Actually, over the years the database features of Excel have become sophisticated enough to rival the capabilities of advanced DBMS systems.

It's easy to save your form results so that you can open them and analyze the data with Excel. Just choose Text Database Using Comma as Separator from the File Format drop-down list box on the Results tab of the Settings for Saving Results of Form dialog box, and include the suffix .CSV (for Comma Separated Values) as the extension of the results file.

To harvest the data, download the CSV file from your page. The easiest way to do this is to open the web with FrontPage Explorer, click on the CSV file, and use File|Export to copy it to your hard drive.

Once you have the file on your hard drive, use Windows Explorer to browse the folder where you stored the file, and double-click on the CSV file. (Instead of downloading it to your hard drive first, you can also double-click on the CSV file directly from FrontPage Explorer.)

If you have Microsoft Excel installed on your computer, it will automatically open the file. You can then use the features of Excel to restructure the data, format it, and analyze it.

Other programs, such as Microsoft Access, also let you import Text Database (CSV) files, and it's also relatively straightforward to write your own software (using a product like Borland Delphi or Microsoft Visual Basic) to process the database.

It's a good idea to erase the results file from your web whenever you download the results to your hard drive. That way, each time you import the data, you'll only be collecting new results, and you keep the cumulative addition of data to the results file from growing too large.

After exporting the CSV file from your web, use File|Delete, or click on the CSV file in the web and press the Del key. (The deletion can not be reversed, so make sure you've copied the data file before removing it from your web.)

Creating a Custom Confirmation Page

You can use the Confirmation tab of the Settings for Saving Results of Form dialog box (Figure 4-21) to choose a page that is displayed after the form data has been accepted (assuming it passes the validation rules). If you don't specify a page here, FrontPage automatically builds a page that shows the user all the data that has been submitted. It's not a pretty sight, so we'll create our own custom confirmation page. You can also choose a custom validation failure page or just let FrontPage report the validation error automatically.

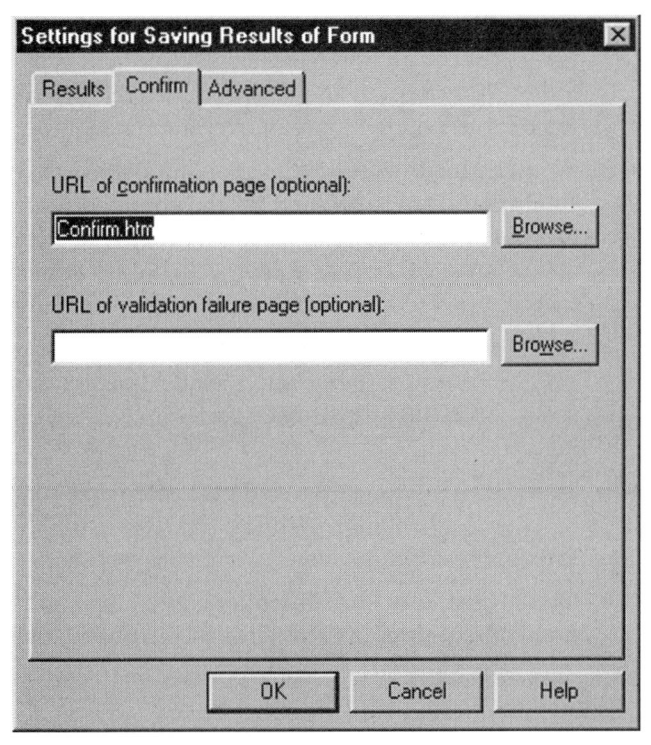

Figure 4-21: If you don't specify a page that you've set up for handling the confirmation and rejection of the form, FrontPage will build them automatically.

Since you'll replace the default confirmation page with your own, fill in the first box on the Confirm tab by typing Confirm.htm. Let FrontPage build the failure page automatically; do so by leaving the second text box blank. Click OK to close the dialog box. (FrontPage warns you that the page doesn't exist—no kidding—but you can ignore this warning for now.)

Building the Page With Confirmation WebBots

To build the custom confirmation page, double-click on the page named Blank Page from FrontPage Explorer or use the File | Open command from the FrontPage Editor to open the Blank Page. Immediately use File | Save As to save it with a title of Census Confirmation Page, using a URL of Confirm.htm.

To build the custom confirmation page:

1. Start by replacing the comment with the text: **Your census has been accepted.** Set this line to the Heading 1 paragraph style using the drop-down menu at the top of the FrontPage Editor window.

2. Press Enter to go down to the next line, and type: **Case Name** followed by a colon and a space. Click the (Insert WebBot) toolbar button, or choose Insert | WebBot Component.

3. From the Insert WebBot Component dialog box, choose the Confirmation WebBot, and when prompted for the name of the form field to confirm, type: **Case**. (Case is the field name of the Case Name text box, as shown in Table 4-1 at the beginning of this chapter.) Click OK to insert the confirmation field on the page.

4. Press Shift+Enter to move to the next line. If you press Enter, there will be too much space between the lines, which is distracting.

5. Type: **Broker Name** followed by a colon and a space, and insert another Confirmation WebBot, this time using the field name Broker. Press Shift+Enter.

6. On the next line, type: **Telephone** and insert another Confirmation WebBot using a field name of Telephone; then press Enter.

You get the idea. If you wish, you can add additional confirmation items to the page. This gives the users feedback without overwhelming them with detail.

Special Confirmation Fields

You can also use some special field names with the Confirmation WebBot. Use Registration-Username to display the name of the user (most web browsers allow customization with name, e-mail address, etc., which is sent from the browser to the web server when the form is submitted).

Chapter 4: Building an Interactive Web Site: Forms & Form Handlers

When designing a validation failure page, you can use the special field name Registration-Error to output the description of the error that occurred. (Another reserved field name, Registration-Password, is used only with the Registration WebBot to display the password entered. This WebBot is discussed in Chapter 5.)

To complete the page, add a link that returns the user to the form to reenter data and a link that returns to the home page.

1. Type: **Return to form**, and set it to Heading 3.

2. Press Enter, type: **Return to home page**, and set it also to Heading 3.

3. Highlight the first prospective link (Return to form), and click the Edit Hyperlink button. Choose the Census.htm page as the destination of the link. Likewise, link the second line to the home page.

4. Your custom confirmation page should resemble Figure 4-22. Save the page and close it.

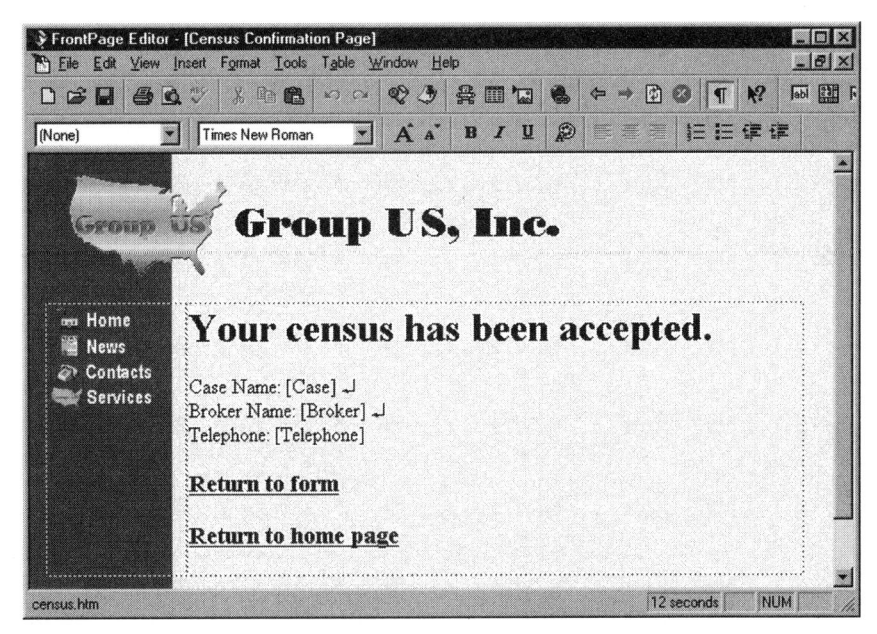

Figure 4-22: The WebBots on the confirmation page appear as bracketed field names, but they display the actual data when the user submits the census form.

To wrap up this project, you need to add a link to the Census Form page from the home page and from the Services page.

1. Open the home page, titled Company Home Page, from the FrontPage Explorer. Look for the text that reads, "You can also fill out a census form and have it automatically sent to us for processing." Drag the mouse to select the two words "census form," then press Ctrl+K to open the Edit Hyperlink dialog box (with which you should be quite familiar by now). Link to the Census page.

2. Also open the Small Group Services page (serv01.htm). This page, describing how to submit a quote request, is also a logical place to link to the Census page. Beneath the bulleted items, insert a blank line, and upon it type:

   ```
   If you prefer, you can also fill out our electronic census
   form for rapid turnaround.
   ```

3. As you did with the home page, highlight "electronic census form," press Ctrl+K, and link it to the Census Form page.

4. Save all pages and close the FrontPage Editor.

You'll now want to fire up your web browser and try out the pages, rigorously testing the Census Form page.

Note: You may encounter minor error messages using Internet Explorer 3.0, since Microsoft hasn't killed all the bugs in the JScript interpreter, at least as of this writing. The problem seems to be related to the excessive amount of validation code generated to support all the data entry fields in the census form. Nevertheless, the pages should still be fully functional.

That's it! Over the course of three chapters, you've learned how to build a full-featured company home page (actually an entire web site), complete with data collection features.

Of course, you're never really finished. Over time, as you create your own sites, you'll come up with more ideas for enhancing the site, and you'll need to routinely maintain the site by updating the What's New page, adding press releases, and expanding the goals of the site.

For example, Group US is planning to add pages describing the various group insurance products it offers. The company would also like to add selected newsletter articles, Internet and mail links to insurance companies and insurance resources on the WWW, and more interactive forms, including (ideally) online insurance quoting. To check out the latest, visit http://www.groupus.com.

Note: The contents of the Group US site are copyrighted by Group US, Inc. I published some of this material on the Companion CD-ROM and in this book by permission of Group US for educational purposes, but you should not use any of the material as is in your own projects. Instead, look to the techniques we've presented as inspiration for developing your own FrontPage webs.

Alternatives to Save Results

The FrontPage Save Results WebBot is flexible and efficient, but by no means is it a complete solution for form handling. Many FrontPage authors would like a way to send the form data via e-mail. Instead of having to visit the company page using a web browser or downloading the data via FTP to retrieve the form data, the form results can be delivered just like any other e-mail message. Another employee can easily forward the e-mail for handling by the appropriate staff member.

There is a relatively simple trick that allows form data to be sent as an e-mail message, but unfortunately, it isn't very practical. Instead of assigning the FrontPage Save Results WebBot as the form handler, you can delegate this function to a Custom ISAPI, NSAPI, or CGI script. (*ISAPI* refers to the Internet Server Application Programming Interface, whereas *NSAPI* is for Netscape Applications Programming Interface. Both are methods to execute program functions directly on the web server instead of indirectly by interpreting a text-based script file.)

Using Mailto to Send Form Results via E-Mail

If you want to see how this technique works, open the Census Form page and right-click within the boundaries of the form. Choose Form Properties from the pop-up menu. From the drop-down menu at the top of the Form Properties dialog box, choose Custom ISAPI, NSAPI, or CGI Script (see Figure 4-23). Then click the Settings button.

Figure 4-23: Instead of using the Save Results 'Bot, assign a custom CGI script.

On the Settings for Custom Form Handler dialog box, fill in the Action text box with mailto: followed by the e-mail address to which you want the form data sent. Leave the Method text box entry as POST, and the Encoding Type text box blank. This is illustrated in Figure 4-24. Click OK to complete the setup of the form handler and close the dialog box.

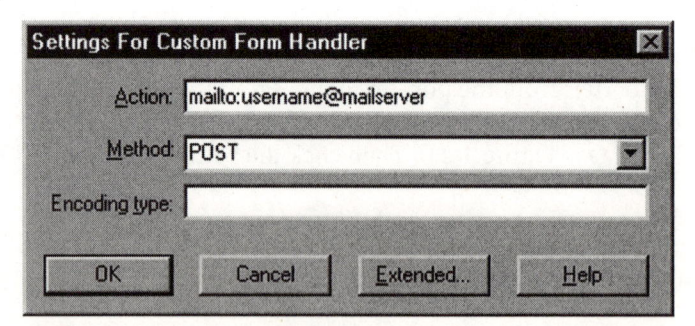

Figure 4-24: Use the mailto URL prefix to e-mail a form to an address.

Save this version of the Census Form page using a title of Census Form (Mailto) and a URL of censmail.htm. Click the Preview in Browser button. Try out the form with both Microsoft Internet Explorer and Netscape Navigator, assuming you have both installed on the same computer (which is a good idea for testing your web), by choosing File | Preview in Browser.

When you fill out the form and click Submit, a new e-mail message is started using your default e-mail client (Microsoft Exchange/Windows Messaging, Microsoft Internet Mail and News, or the built-in Netscape mail client). The e-mail address is filled in automatically, and you should also see the form data as a continuous line of characters in the body of the message.

A Nasty Surprise

Don't be surprised if all you get is a blank e-mail message. When sending form data with mailto using Internet Explorer, the form data never makes it into the mail message. Netscape Navigator should be able to send the form data, however.

Nevertheless, there are a significant number of Internet Explorer users. Microsoft claims an estimated 30 percent of the total web browser market, and this figure is growing at the expense of Netscape's installed base. Unless you can guarantee that the visitor is using Navigator (which is really only possible in a controlled environment like a company intranet), the mailto trick is unfortunately obsolete for sending form data.

CGI E-Mail Alternatives

There are some alternatives, but they require you to install a custom Common Gateway Interface (CGI) program on the web server. Many web hosting providers, including quite a few FrontPage web presence providers, forbid their clients to use CGI scripts. Other providers will allow the script, but only after the administrator checks it out and approves it first, and for an extra charge. Of course, if you run your own server, you have more flexibility, and can use any scripting language you like.

Table 4-2 lists some sources for CGI e-mail scripts on the Internet. Some are designed for UNIX servers, others for the WinCGI interface supported by Windows-based web servers. Of special interest for FrontPage authors without CGI access is http://icg.resnet.upenn.edu/mailto, which offers you access to the CGI e-mail script installed on the icg.resnet.upenn.edu server.

> **TIP**
>
> *Also be on the lookout for Java or ActiveX components that can mail form data. I've not seen any yet, but there's no reason why it wouldn't work as well or better than the CGI method.*

http://home.sol.no/jgaa/cgi-bin.htm	WinCGI
http://websunlimited.com/mailit.htm	CGI (Perl)
http://www.rcsoftware.com/scripts.html	Many CGI scripts
http://icg.resnet.upenn.edu/mailto	Public e-mail script
http://web.mit.edu/wwwdev/cgiemail/	CGI e-mail

Table 4-2: Links to CGI e-mail scripts.

It's also possible to write your own CGI, Java, or VBScript scripts to handle form data. This makes it possible to use a web page as a container for a custom application. You can use form fields, plug-ins, and ActiveX controls as the user interface and the scripting language to process the data and give feedback to the user. Writing CGI scripts is a complex topic that is outside the scope of this book, but in Chapter 9, I'll show you how to use scripting and ActiveX controls to add powerful new form capabilities to your sites.

Moving On

Webs without forms and data storage are missing the point of the World Wide Web. It's not just about publishing information and advertising, it's about engaging the visitor. With forms you can encourage feedback and solicit a customer's business. You can process service requests, take surveys, collect names and addresses, even experiment with Internet commerce.

The tutorial in this chapter was designed to give you the tools and techniques you need to design powerful, interactive forms with practical data storage and retrieval. Mastering forms is a crucial milestone in your quest to becoming a true webmaster.

To complete your excursion, you need to move the site from your local authoring environment to a WWW server accessible from any location on the Internet. Chapter 5 goes into all the details on web site publishing, including choosing a Web Presence Provider, taking advantage of free or low cost web hosting, uploading your webs, and maintaining and securing your site.

chapter 5

Reaching Your Audience: FrontPage Publishing

In this chapter, we'll explore the options available to you when you're ready to put your own webs on the World Wide Web. You'll learn how to use FrontPage with a Web Presence Provider or other third-party commercial web server, take advantage of free web publishing, and learn some techniques for efficient web management.

Up to now, you've no doubt been developing and testing your webs on your local machine. You're also probably using a local web server, either the FrontPage Personal Web Server, the Microsoft (Windows 95) Personal Web Server, NT 4 Workstation's Peer Web Services, or the industrial-strength Internet Information Server (IIS).

While developing your webs, you must use a server, unless you are only interested in creating isolated, static pages with the FrontPage Editor. This is called a disk-based web, and is covered in Chapter 7.

When you installed FrontPage, you chose either to install one of the personal web servers (the Microsoft Personal Web Server is recommended for Windows 95) or let the FrontPage setup program install the FrontPage Server Extensions for Peer Web Services or IIS.

The web server is required for most of the interesting and useful FrontPage features, including most WebBots, and is the only way to use

FrontPage Explorer to manage your web. We'll assume you already have a local web server up and running. If you need help troubleshooting, configuring, or optimizing your local web server, consult Chapter 6.

Of course, these servers need not run on your local machine as long as they are accessible from your network. (Accessing a web server over a local area network requires TCP/IP networking, the basis of an intranet, which is covered in Chapter 7.)

Webs Online

Unless you plan to deploy your webs on an intranet, you're probably wondering how to make your pages accessible from the public Internet. There are really only two ways to do so: lease space on a commercial web server or operate your own web server connected to the Internet.

The latter method is the easiest approach, but as we'll see, it is also the least practical. In fact, you may not realize it, but your web server may already be a true Internet web server.

If your computer is already running a web server (such as the ones mentioned at the beginning of this chapter), all you have to do is connect your computer to the Internet via Dial-Up Networking or Windows NT Remote Access Service.

The web server on a computer uses that computer's TCP/IP address as its "name." Every computer has at least one TCP/IP address: 127.0.0.1 is the address reserved for the local computer, called localhost. If your computer is connected to a TCP/IP network, it is also assigned either a fixed or dynamic IP address, such as 192.168.0.1. (Setting up TCP/IP networking is covered in Chapter 7.)

When you have an active connection to the Internet, your computer is given yet another IP address, this time assigned by the Internet Service Provider (ISP) that you dial in to. All these IP addresses "point" to the web server running on your computer.

For example, you probably already know that you can open a web browser (like Internet Explorer) and type your IP address into the Address box to open the root web. If you type the name http://localhost or http://127.0.0.0 into the Address box, the default page for your web server (default.htm or index.htm) is opened automatically. You can also type your machine name into the Address box, and the web browser will look up the address. (The machine name is configured using the Identity property sheet of Network Setup, run from Control Panel.)

If your computer is part of a TCP/IP network, then it has a TCP/IP address that is specific to your local area network. From your own computer, or from any other computer on the network, you can start a web browser and access the web server running on your computer simply by entering its IP address into the Address box (called Location with Netscape Navigator/Communicator). For example, if the computer running the web server has an IP address of 192.168.0.5, then typing http://192.168.0.5 opens the default page on the root web stored on that server.

When the computer running the web server is logged in to the Internet via Dial-Up Networking, it will have an IP address assigned by the ISP, perhaps something like 38.11.237.25 (a fictional address). If you type that into the Address box, it too will open your web page. In addition, anyone on the Internet can access your web page, as long as they know your current IP address.

I say *current* IP address because most ISPs assign you an IP address dynamically from a pool of IP addresses that have been allocated to them by the InterNIC, an Internet standards organization. A few ISPs still offer a fixed IP address, but usually at a premium price because that IP address will not be available for any other use by the ISP, even when you're not logged in.

To reiterate, publishing your pages on the Internet is as simple as setting up a Dial-Up Networking connection on the computer running the web server and dialing in to the ISP. (We won't cover how to set up dial-up networking in this book since it's a prerequisite for any Internet activity, and surely you have Internet access up and running by now.) Once you're online, you can find out your current IP address, and notify anyone who wants to access your web pages. There are several ways to find out your current IP address:

- From Windows 95, click Start I Run, and type **WINIPCFG**. This pops up the dialog box shown in Figure 5-1. From this dialog, you can see your current Internet IP address. If you use this tool frequently, you can easily create a shortcut to it on your desktop by right-clicking on the desktop, choosing New I Shortcut, and entering WINIPCFG as the command line.

- From Windows NT, open the Dial-Up Networking Monitor (from Control Panel or by double-clicking on the telephone icon in the taskbar's notification area) and click the Details button. See Figure 5-2.

- From Windows NT, open a Command Prompt (from the Start menu) and type the command **IPCONFIG**. You'll see a complete report on the current IP addresses, as shown in Figure 5-3.

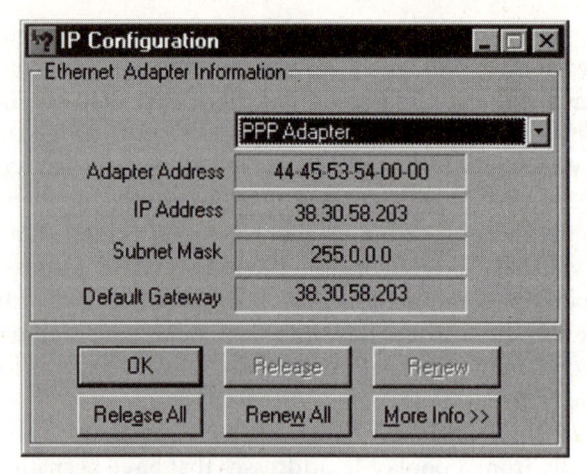

Figure 5-1: Use the WINIPCFG command to determine your current IP address from Windows 95.

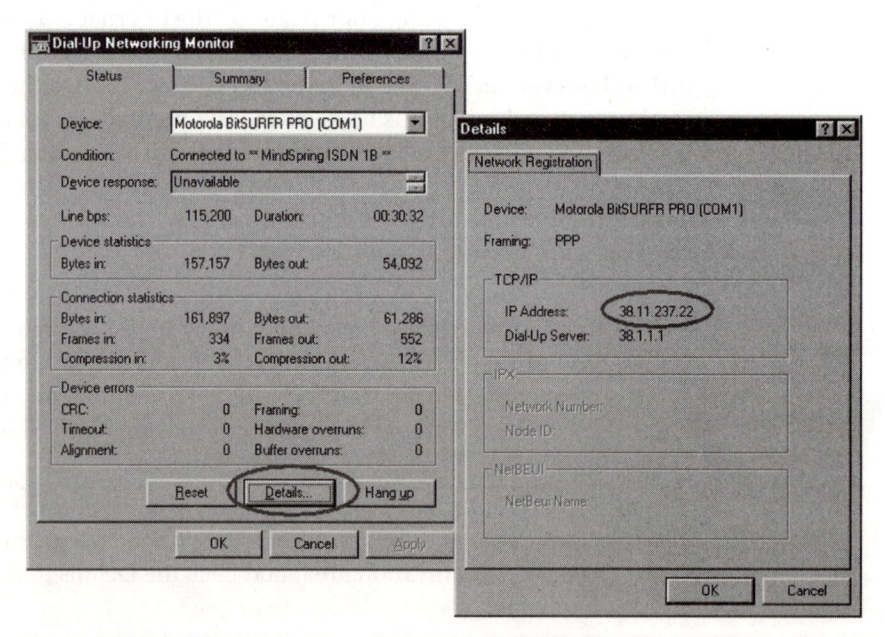

Figure 5-2: From Windows NT 4, open the Dial-Up Monitor and click Details to get your IP address.

```
N:\WINNT\system32>ipconfig

Windows NT IP Configuration

Ethernet adapter NE20001:

        IP Address. . . . . . . . : 192.168.0.1
        Subnet Mask . . . . . . . : 255.255.0.0
        Default Gateway . . . . . :

Ethernet adapter NdisWan7:

        IP Address. . . . . . . . : 0.0.0.0
        Subnet Mask . . . . . . . : 0.0.0.0
        Default Gateway . . . . . :

Ethernet adapter NdisWan6:

        IP Address. . . . . . . . : 38.11.237.22
        Subnet Mask . . . . . . . : 255.0.0.0
        Default Gateway . . . . . : 38.11.237.22
```

Figure 5-3: Windows NT also offers the Command Prompt IPCONFIG command to list your IP addresses.

Once you have your IP address in hand, you can call up your friends or colleagues and tell them the IP address of your server so they can access your pages. You're serving up your pages directly from your computer to the worldwide Internet. Or if your contact is not available by telephone (perhaps because the person is logged in to the Internet using the only telephone line available), you could instead meet on a chat server to swap IP addresses.

TIP

To join ongoing chats on the Internet, try the Internet Relay Chat (IRC) client included on this book's Companion CD-ROM, the popular mIRC utility. See Appendix A for instructions on installing the software included on the Companion CD-ROM.

Clearly, publishing your web via your IP address isn't very practical. Only if you are lucky enough to have a static IP address can you really get much mileage out of running a web server this way. On the other hand, knowing how impractical it is to find a web server via its IP address should allay some fears over security. Even though your web server is exposed to the worldwide Internet, it's not likely that anyone will even know about it since there is no practical way to look up the IP address of a computer. If an "evil hacker" doesn't know your IP address, he or she can't snoop around in your web pages. Nevertheless, you'll want to read Chapter 6 to find out how to improve the security of your web server.

Master of Your Domain

Even if you have a static IP address, there are two problems: (1) An IP address is ugly, hardly a good way to promote your web site, and (2) your modem just isn't fast enough to provide access to more than a handful of active users at any given time.

Problem #1 can be solved by getting yourself a true domain name. In theory, you can do this even if you run your own server, but it will take extensive Internet know-how.

To start the ball rolling, you can go to http://www.internic.net. Here, you can search for an unused domain name (get 'em while they're hot). Should your desired name be unused, you can fill out a few forms to register your request. You'll need to supply the IP addresses of the primary and secondary DNS servers that can look up the IP address of your web page. These DNS servers will also need static IP addresses, and they will need to be online 24 hours a day. That means running the Windows NT DNS service or some other third-party DNS server, a complicated and difficult project at best.

Fortunately, your ISP may allow you to use their DNS servers to host the IP address for the domain you are registering. That way, you only need a single static IP address for your web server, and you don't need to worry about configuring or operating a full-time DNS server.

For the privilege of a "vanity" domain name, you'll pay a $150 setup fee for the first two years and $50 each year thereafter.

Nonprofit, religious, and some other organizations can qualify for a free domain name ending in .org. Likewise, educational institutions can get a free .edu domain, military sites can use .mil, and branches of federal or state government can have .gov. If you want to use your site for any commercial purpose (including a company home page), you'll have to pay for a .com domain. The .net domain suffix is reserved for ISPs and other Internet entities.

Don't bother registering your own domain name unless you insist on running your own web server. If your ISP offers domain name hosting (sometimes called virtual hosting), let them take care of registering your IP address. The InterNIC fee is usually rolled into your web hosting account bills.

In the future, other companies will compete with the InterNIC and offer new domain name suffixes, such as www.yourcompanyname.firm, at reduced cost.

> **TIP**
>
> *In fact, the reorganization of the Internet's domain naming system is moving away from the InterNIC's U.S.-centric monopoly to a distributed arrangement maintained by several companies and organizations worldwide. Under the new plan, there will be seven new top-level domains: .firm, .store, .web, .arts, .rec, .info, and .nom, for companies, online shopping sites, WWW-related activities, cultural, entertainment, publishing, and personal sites, respectively. Registration costs are expected to decline as well.*

Another alternative to the expensive registered domain is the virtual domain, such as www.yourcompany.w1.com. I'll explain what this means in "Finding a Home" later in this chapter.

The Need for Speed

Problem #2, the limited speed of your modem, is more difficult to overcome. You can improve things considerably by using a faster connection such as ISDN, an expensive leased digital line, or some future technology such as cable modems or ADSL (asymmetric digital subscriber loop) modems. A standard modem connection just doesn't have enough bandwidth (input/output capacity) to support potentially hundreds of web page visitors.

The new 57 kilobits per second (Kbps) modems, such as U.S. Robotic's X2, allow you to access your ISP at the enhanced speed, but in only one direction. Data flows from the ISP to your computer at up to 57 Kbps, which is great when you are web browsing, but anyone accessing your computer will still be limited to the old 28.8 Kbps speed (33.6 Kbps over extraordinarily good telephone connections), since that remains the maximum speed that your computer can send information back to the ISP.

> **TIP**
>
> *If you want a rough gauge of how many characters per second can be sent over a connection, divide the bits per second by 8. A 28.8 Kbps modem transfers up to 3,600 characters per second. By contrast, even the slowest type of CD-ROM drive (the 1X speed) transfers data at a rate of 150,000 characters (bytes) per second.*

In other words, don't count on X2 or similar technologies to speed up your web server. If you want to double or quadruple your speed, move from a modem to ISDN or a dedicated digital line. A residential or small business ISDN connection allows speeds of either 64 Kbps for a single-bearer (B) channel or 128 Kbps for two-bearer channels (2B).

A leased T1 line, with speeds of up to 1.5 megabits per second, is equivalent to 32 times the speed of a regular modem. (To keep these speeds in perspective, a T1 line is about as fast as an archaic single-speed CD-ROM drive.)

For a site that's not too busy, a regular modem might be able to keep up with web browsing since the server is typically sending just a few small files per page. After all, even a web server with a T1 line is often burdened by the demands of serving up many web sites, whereas you're probably only trying to publish a single web. However, to be truly practical, consider installing an ISDN router or terminal adapter and subscribing to a 128 Kbps ISDN service if these options are available in your area.

Keep It Up

OK, so let's say you have an ISDN or other higher-speed connection to the Internet, or you don't care how slow your server runs over a standard modem. Do you want your web site to be available 24 hours a day? If so, you'll need a full-time Internet connection. "No problem," you might say, "I have an unlimited access account for just $19.95 a month."

Sorry, but that just won't do the trick. No ISP in their right mind is going to equate unlimited access with full-time or dedicated access. In fact, most ISP servers watch your connection like a hawk and will disconnect you after as little as 15 minutes of inactivity. (Your web server is inactive when no one is accessing it.) This is to free up the line for other callers who are waiting their turn to get online.

There are ways to deal with this disconnection (in an attempt to keep your web server up and running as long as possible) if you're inclined to cheat.

In Windows NT 4, you can configure Dial-Up Networking to automatically reconnect when disconnected. To do so, open the Dial-Up Networking Phonebook (Start | Programs | Accessories | Dial-Up Networking, or right-click on the telephone icon to the right of the taskbar and choose Dial | Open Phonebook). When the DUN Phonebook is open, click More | User Preferences. (The More menu drops down from the button labeled More.) From the Dial tab, turn on the Redial on Link Failure check box. See Figure 5-4.

While you're looking at User Preferences, you'll also want to set the Idle Seconds Before Hanging Up setting to 0, so that even when your web server isn't busy, the computer will keep the connection open. Normally, this is set to a nonzero value to let NT hang up the connection after it's been idle for too long, which saves connect time charges if you have anything other than an unlimited access account.

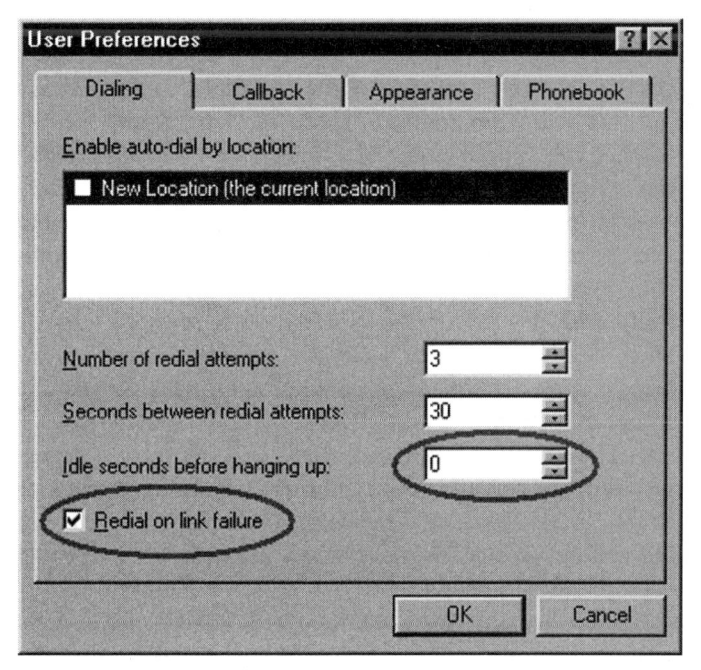

Figure 5-4: Use Redial on Link Failure to tell Windows NT to reconnect whenever the connection fails.

To automatically reconnect when dropped in Windows 95, you'll have to install a third-party utility such as RAS+ (available at http://www.lambsoftware.com), Redial (ftp://ftp.coast.net/Coast/nt/ras/redial12.zip), or RTVReco (ftp://ftp.cdrom.com/pub/simtelnet/win95/inet/rtv_reco.zip). All of these tools have the ability to automatically reconnect whenever the ISP drops your connection.

These tricks may help you maintain a more-or-less continuous connection, but you'll still have a problem. If you've notified others of your IP address so that they can log on to your web server, you'll have to do so again once the connection is broken and reestablished, since you will almost certainly have been assigned a different IP address in the new session.

While you may think you're saving money by not paying for a dedicated connection, there's a hidden cost to trying these methods: Your ISP may cancel your account if it determines you're trying to cheat. Check your ISP's terms of service. Nearly every ISP that offers unlimited access forbids any attempt to abuse this privilege as a full-time connection.

Dedicate Yourself

Is there any other alternative if you want to run your own web server? Yes. You can pay for a true dedicated dial-up connection, which typically starts at over $250 per month for a modem, higher for ISDN. Or if you want to use a high-speed T1 connection (1.5 megabits per second), you can install a T1 router on your network.

A *T1 line* is a leased line, a piece of wire strung between your location and the location of the ISP that connects you to the Internet. The *router* is a piece of hardware that connects to your local area network and routes traffic from the Internet to your network and vice-versa. (Routers of this kind are combined with hardware or software firewall products that protect your network from outside access and can selectively restrict access to the Internet by network users.)

A T1 line offers unlimited access to the Internet, but the price might be prohibitive. Excluding installation and hardware costs, you'll pay between $2,000 and $3,000 per month for the privilege of just over a million bits of Internet per second. Share your T1 line with other businesses by using fractional T1, and you can save some money and get speeds anywhere between 57 Kbps and the full 1.5 Mbps of a dedicated T1 line.

In many areas of the country, ISDN service is either metered or will be moving to metered rates soon. This may make ISDN untenable for a full-time connection, as you're paying not only for the router, maintenance costs, and ISP service, but also for per-minute rates.

Most businesses will find it hard to justify the costs of running an in-house web server, especially when outsourcing with an ISP is such a viable alternative. You'll need one or more powerful web server computers, which typically include 256 megabytes of RAM, 9 gigabyte hard drives, and quad Pentium Pro motherboards. Surely a power-user's dream, but an accountant's nightmare. Yet even this pales in comparison to the salary of one or two seasoned web professionals to keep the site up and running reliably.

Operating your own server gives you full control over the web server environment. If you want to use Windows NT, IIS, and other powerful Microsoft web server tools and do it all yourself, there *is* a way to have your cake and eat it too. Many ISPs permit you to install your own server at their location and connect to their full-bore Internet connection. This lets you take advantage of T3 (45 megabits per second) and even fatter OC3 pipelines.

Cost aside, there's no reason why you can't run your own Internet web server. At the very least, it's not a bad way to get started. Eventually, however, you'll have to bite the bullet and sign up for a web server hosting account with an Internet Service Provider (ISP) or Web Presence Provider (WPP).

Finding a Home

The alternative to running your own web server is to let someone else run the server for you. We mentioned the possibility of installing your own server at your ISP's location, but it's much easier and more practical to let the Internet experts handle all the details for you. As we've already mentioned, it will also cost you less to lease space and capacity on the ISP's servers.

If you are a customer of America Online or CompuServe, you already have a home page waiting for you. America Online provides space at http://members.aol.com (or http://users.aol.com, a synonym), and CompuServe offers space at http://ourworld.compuserve.com. The best way to learn about these free accounts is to go to either of the pages I just mentioned. Later in this chapter, I'll show you how to use the Microsoft Web Publishing Wizard to upload a FrontPage web to either America Online or CompuServe.

Geocities (http://www.geocities.com) and Bigfoot (http://www.bigfoot.com) are among the Internet companies that offer free web pages to anyone, and many ISPs provide a free home page for their users as part of the standard or high-end dial-up account.

These free (or included) web accounts have their limitations; typically, they allow less than 5 megabytes of storage with limits on how many files and folders you can set up. Your site can't become too popular because there are also severe limits on how much data can be transferred from your web per month.

Worst of all, none of the "free" web accounts provide the FrontPage Server Extensions, so most of the enhanced functionality of FrontPage (all WebBots except the Include and Substitution 'bots) will be lost. Without the FrontPage Server Extensions, you can't publish directly to these sites but instead must upload your content using an FTP client or the Microsoft Web Publishing Wizard (included with FrontPage 97 with the Bonus Pack CD-ROM). More on this in "Uploading Your Web With the File Transfer Protocol" later in the chapter.

There's no reason you shouldn't take advantage of these free (or nearly free) web accounts for at least some purpose. You'll just have to use them for disk-based webs, collections of more-or-less static web pages. (You can still provide some interactivity by employing client-side scripting, Java, and ActiveX Controls, which we cover in Chapter 9. Some ISPs also let you use simple preinstalled CGI scripts such as web page counters.)

In "Publishing on a Non-FrontPage Server" later in this chapter, I'll show you how to use the Web Publishing Wizard to upload your site to either America Online or CompuServe.

FrontPage Web Presence Providers

Microsoft has been criticized for alleged unfair business practices. Whatever your take on that argument, it's hard to ignore the fact that, far from stifling the computer industry, Microsoft continues to create new business opportunities for third-party companies.

When Microsoft acquired Vermeer Technologies, the creators of FrontPage, savvy Internet companies quickly recognized an opportunity to provide FrontPage web hosting services. Your choice of companies to host your FrontPage webs has grown from a handful of early adopters to over 150 companies. These providers range from inexpensive startups to established giants such as AT&T and NetCom. FrontPage hosting prices start at as little as $10 per month for a personal account and can cost as much as $500 to $1,000 per month for a commercial account.

Where to Shop

Microsoft's FrontPage site, at http://www.microsoft.com/frontpage, includes a link to http://microsoft.saltmine.com/frontpage/wpp/list, where you can find an index of companies offering FrontPage web hosting.

While there are even more choices available if you don't require the FrontPage Server Extensions, there's no good reason to give up the defining features of FrontPage, such as WebBots. You'll be better served by insisting on a true FrontPage service provider.

One thing to watch out for: FrontPage 97 was introduced in January 1997. At that time, many FrontPage Web Presence Providers (WPPs) had not yet upgraded their servers to support the new features of FrontPage

97. These companies will need time to test and deploy the server extensions to make sure there are no security, usability, or compatibility concerns, especially for the sake of users still running the FrontPage 1.1 software. (Microsoft insists this will not be a problem, but it's best to be cautious when you're an Internet Service Provider.)

> **TIP**
>
> *Most WPPs operate their sites with UNIX web servers or are using Netscape server software. Microsoft Internet Information Server running on Windows NT is also catching on like wildfire. If you want to use the latest Microsoft Internet technology, such as the Internet Database Connector and Active Server Pages, make sure your provider is running IIS and confirm that you will be granted the necessary access permissions to use these features of IIS.*

While FrontPage 97 is compatible with the FrontPage 1.1 Server Extensions (the software on the web server that supports WebBots and other FrontPage bells and whistles), some FrontPage 97 features require the latest server extensions. For example, you can't use the validation 'bots (explained in Chapter 4) successfully without the FrontPage 97 Server Extensions. While your pages will still work overall, the validation code won't work, and you'll see extraneous text on pages using validation (e.g., 'Bot-Validation'). Before signing on the dotted line, make sure the provider fully supports FrontPage 97.

Determine Your Requirements

Not only do you have hundreds of choices for Web Presence Providers, you usually have many packages to choose from for each provider. It boils down to how much power, storage, and speed your site really needs.

For larger businesses, ISPs and WPPs can install and maintain for you a dedicated web server. Since the server machine is all yours (even though you're only leasing the right to use the computer), you're often free to dictate your requirements. You can certainly insist on having the FrontPage 97 Server Extensions installed and tested. The ISP will make sure your preferred domain name is linked to the dedicated server.

Not surprisingly, this is an expensive choice. It's more common to lease space on a virtual server. The ISP or WPP operates one or more physical server computers, which take advantage of multitasking (specifically, multihoming) to let each customer appear to have their own dedicated web server even though the resources of the server computer are shared with other users.

The FrontPage Server Extensions make this process completely transparent to you and simplify the job of the service provider.

If you don't need or can't afford a registered domain name, many companies also offer virtual domain hosting, such as www.yourcompany.w1.com or www.yourcompany.isp.com. Except for the "w1" part (or the name of the WPP/ISP), it looks a lot like a bona fide registered domain name and costs a lot less.

Pricing Plans

Most companies charge an initial setup fee and a monthly charge. You can sometimes save some money by paying for several months in advance (in fact, this is often required).

If you don't need your own domain name (perhaps you're just testing the waters, or don't plan to offer commercial services, or just don't give a hoot about a "vanity name"), you can get started for less than $15 with several companies.

Business or commercial accounts may or may not include InterNIC registration, which will make a difference in the setup fee and monthly account.

Disk Usage

The price you pay will also likely be based on how much disk usage and bandwidth your site requires. Usually you're given anywhere from 5 to 10 megabytes of storage space on the virtual server for your pages and charged an additional amount for each additional megabyte. Other plans may include unlimited disk storage (or at least unrestricted; after all, you have to be reasonable).

Bandwidth Usage

The more popular the site, the more visitors are pulling text, graphics, and so forth from the server. As a site becomes more popular, it will drain capacity from the WPP's network, forcing the company to upgrade and add additional servers or install new leased lines to keep up with the capacity. To keep growth at a manageable rate, it's common to place limits on how much throughput is allowed for your site.

Different pricing plans exist to accommodate varying needs. The price you pay is usually based on megabytes of transfer per month. Let's say your site stores about 1 megabyte of text and graphics, and that each user browses every page on your site. So each user will "use up" 1 megabyte of transfer per visit. You can see that a busy site can rack up high transfer rates. Some plans offer unmetered (although not necessarily unlimited) transfer rates, depending on the pricing structure you choose.

CGI-BIN Access

FrontPage 97 is designed to provide the most popular and useful web functionality, via its WebBots, without requiring custom programming. Without the FrontPage Server Extensions, you would have to develop or purchase custom software and install it onto the web server. These programs are run by the web server on demand via the Common Gateway Interface.

You may find that FrontPage doesn't do everything you need it to do. For example, there is no way to send the results of a data entry form via electronic mail, at least with the basic features of FrontPage 97. However, if you are allowed by the WPP to install custom CGI programs with your account, you can buy CGI scripts to accomplish a wide variety of tasks. If you're inclined to do some programming, you can learn the Perl language (or another server-side language) and copy your scripts to the CGI-BIN folder on your virtual web server. The web administrator examines and tests your scripts before making them live.

> **TIP**
>
> *Appendix B includes a list of links to authoring resources on the WWW, including CGI script providers.*

Unfortunately, CGI-BIN access is usually not included with your account. Because CGI programs run on the server, mistakes on your part, or nefarious hacking by others, can end up crashing the server, using up too much of the server's speed, or leaving the site open to security violations. Since FrontPage does so much without programming, many providers assume you won't need it anyway.

Should you ever need to use CGI, you'll be grateful it's available, so consider access to CGI scripting a valuable component of a web hosting account.

Goodies

Many WPPs offer additional server features to their FrontPage customers. The features include RealAudio server support, which lets you include efficient audio streams that play back in real-time (without the visitor waiting for the file to download first) and even streaming video with VivoActive or Microsoft NetShow. You may find that a "shopping cart" solution for electronic commerce is included, or custom WebBots. For example, AT&T includes a Submit via E-mail WebBot so that form data can be sent to an e-mail address rather than stored locally on the server on a results page.

Another great bonus can only be delivered if the WPP uses Windows NT Server and Internet Information Server. FrontPage accounts on IIS may be able to use the IIS features for database storage (via the Internet Database Connector, discussed in Chapter 8) or the new Active Server Pages method. Other Microsoft IIS technologies are also juicy, including ActiveX live chat windows, web-based newsgroups, and electronic commerce via Microsoft Commerce Server.

Whom Do You Trust?

One concern shared by novices to web publishing is whether or not their site will remain a viable presence and if it will be reliably operated by the ISP/WPP. Unfortunately, no company has a very long track record in this business. These concerns are very real. If your customers have come to expect to find your web page at a certain Internet address, and the provider hosting your account goes belly-up, will you have to change your address when you sign up with a new provider?

That's one good reason to get an account with a virtual domain name. That way, your web site will always be www.yourcompany.com. If your preferred WPP dies on the vine, you can take your business elsewhere by relocating your domain.

With the least expensive web accounts, it's assumed you have already registered your domain name and paid the $150 InterNIC fee. This is actually preferable, since you are shown as the administrative and billing contact when your account is queried with WhoIs, an Internet standard for determining who owns a domain.

Furthermore, you have clear rights to relocate your domain to another DNS server (the DNS server is usually run by the ISP or WPP). If the company providing your web site does the domain registration for you (usually included in the more expensive accounts), make sure you are listed as the administrative contact so that you own the domain name and will have the ability to relocate the domain to another provider when you so desire.

> **TIP**
>
> *Visit the InterNIC at http:/www.internic.net to run their WhoIs tool and find out who owns the popular domains and to check if your desired domain name is available or has already been snapped up. There's no time like the present to secure your own domain.*

Having your own domain name also makes it easy to route Internet mail. Most companies let you use a blind forwarding or aliasing technique to send all mail addressed to anyone at your domain name to a real mailbox that you have already set up.

You may also be able to set up one or more individual aliases so that mail sent to info@yourcompany.com goes to one e-mail address (such as the employee handling those requests) and mail sent to sales@yourcompany.com is sent to a sales manager's existing e-mail account. Everything else sent to the domain, such as Lisa@yourcompany.com, is sent to another e-mail address. An employee can be delegated to get the mail from this box and forward it to whomever its intended recipient by examining the Internet headers on the mail message.

Some web hosting accounts also include Internet mail (POP mail) accounts, so you don't need to already have a dial-up account with a mail address on the Internet. Most web hosting accounts do not include dial-up access; for that you'll need to use your existing ISP or pay extra for a dial-up access account.

There's little doubt that a web hosting service run by an industry giant, such as AT&T's Easy World Wide Web (http://www.ew3.com), will provide good web service for many years to come. There's a bit of prestige connoted by having your account hosted by one of the communications giants. This service comes at a price, however; AT&T's FrontPage hosting services are the most expensive of the companies I've surveyed.

Don't be afraid to give the "other guys" a chance, though, especially if you can check references and test a trial account. For example, Realacom (http:/www.realacom.com) offers a publicly accessible FrontPage test page that you can use to upload subwebs and try out FrontPage hosting on the Internet. Look up http://frontpagesite.com. (You'll need to pay for a real account to accomplish your real goals, however.) Realacom has no setup fee and extremely reasonable FrontPage hosting prices.

I'm also impressed by the services of A1 Terabit (http://www.a1.terabit.net). A1 Terabit sells FrontPage hosting accounts at rock-bottom prices yet gives you full access to Internet Information Server features such as database publishing, ActiveX Server, Microsoft NetShow, RealAudio Server, and VivoActive streaming video.

A1 Terabit does not meter storage space or throughput, so you don't have to worry about exceeding a fixed allowance.

> **TIP**
>
> Check out the author's independent web site at http://www.websFrontPage.com for a special offer on FrontPage hosting services.

The WPP you choose need not be a local company. You are uploading your pages via the Internet, after all, so as long as you can dial in to any ISP from a local phone connection, it doesn't really matter where the server is located. In fact, it's much more important that the server has high-speed connections to the Internet and is located in a geographic area that is near where you expect most of your customers to be. If you're located in Europe, and you want to attract customers from the United States, it makes sense to lease space on a server located in the United States rather than in Europe.

Ordering Your Account

Once you've made up your mind, you can usually order your account online with a credit card; you may have to print out and fax a contract first. Whether you register your own domain or let the ISP/WPP do it for you, it can take anywhere from a few days to a few weeks to get your domain published on the Internet. In the meantime, you can access your site via its IP address or temporary name, such as www.yourcompany.wpp.com. Nondomain accounts are usually ready as soon as the paperwork and billing is complete, sometimes within 24 hours.

You'll receive important information with your account, such as the site URL (web address), IP address, username, and login password. You may also be given an FTP or Telnet account to directly upload files to the site. Keep this information handy for the next section, where we'll explore how to use the FrontPage software to upload your site to the Internet.

Publishing to a Non-FrontPage Server

As long as you have a FrontPage web hosting account, publishing your web to the Internet is easy and relatively trouble free. Just open your web with the FrontPage Explorer, and choose File | Publish Web. You'll be asked a few questions concerning the site name or IP address of the server and prompted to enter your username and password for the site.

Before we take a look at publishing to a FrontPage-enabled server, you probably would like to know how to post your web to a non-FrontPage Internet site, a web server that does not have the FrontPage Server Extensions installed and enabled for your account.

Why bother? For one thing, you may already have an existing non-FrontPage account, either from a previous project or included with your online service account (such as America Online or CompuServe). Seeing how to upload content to a standard web server also helps you to understand how the information in your local web gets moved to the server.

WebBot Limitations on a Non-FrontPage Server

Prior to publishing, you should have already prepared your site (ideally in the form of a subweb, explained in Chapter 1) for the non-FrontPage server. This means avoiding or removing any browse-time (user interactive) WebBots. Here is a list of the WebBots that you can safely use with a non-FrontPage server:

- Annotation (Comments)
- HTML Markup
- Include
- Scheduled Include
- Scheduled Image
- Substitution
- Table of Contents

These 'bots run only while authoring your web locally, such as when you are editing, updating, or saving pages. They will fail if you try to edit pages directly on the hard drive with the FrontPage Editor. Instead, open the web first with the FrontPage Explorer. There is no way to edit pages directly on the non-FrontPage server. In order for the changes to be reflected on the non-FrontPage server, you will have to re-upload any content that has changed.

Unless the web hosting account fully supports FrontPage 97, avoid the following WebBots, and any others not mentioned in the preceding list:

- Confirmation
- Discussion
- Internet Database Connector
- Registration
- Save Results
- Search
- Timestamp
- Validation

You must also avoid server-side image mapping and instead rely on client-side mapping. This is discussed in Chapter 3, where you learned how to build an animated toolbar with clickable hot spots.

Also watch out for differences in the way UNIX servers interpret filenames, especially if you're accustomed to the Windows 95/NT 4 rules. In Windows 95/NT 4, you can have a file named FooBar.gif, yet reference it on in your page as foobar.gif. On UNIX systems, however, the case of a filename is significant. The literal reference to foobar.gif will prevent that graphic (named FooBar.gif) from loading, unless you either change the reference or rename the file on the server. Also avoid using spaces in filenames, which are only permitted on Microsoft web servers and browsers.

To avoid filename discrepancies, use Browse when linking to pages or graphics on your site instead of manually typing in the link locations, or try to use only lowercase in all filenames.

Note: Some low-end or free web accounts restrict you to a single folder. That means storing all pages, graphics, and other files in the same (root) folder instead of using folders such as /_private or /images to organize your files.

You'll also want to be aware of variations concerning extension mapping, which is how the server decides what to do with certain files based on the characters following the final period in a filename. For example, an extension of .htm or .html tells the server to deliver the information using the HTTP protocol without examining the content.

On some servers, you must use .html as the extension for your pages instead of .htm. The default home page may be default.html, _default.htm, index.html, or some other variation. This is the page sent to the browser if the user doesn't specify a specific page when visiting your site, such as when he or she opens www.yourcompany.com. This is usually not a problem with a FrontPage server, which is designed to support both the .htm and .html extensions. If necessary, use the FrontPage Explorer to rename the extensions for your files so that all the links will be fixed automatically. Do this before uploading the web to the Internet.

> **TIP**
>
> *To make your life easier, set the default home page on your personal server (Microsoft PWS, NT Workstation PWS, NT Server IIS) to match the settings employed by your Internet Web Presence Provider. With Windows NT (Server or Workstation), run Internet Service Manager. With Microsoft PWS, use the Personal Web Server icon in Control Panel. See Chapter 6 for more on administering your local web server.*
>
> *No matter what you local settings are for the home page extension, FrontPage Explorer will rename your home page to the name required by the WPP, as long as it's a FrontPage-supported WPP.*
>
> *If the web server doesn't understand pages ending with .htm (actually quite rare), you will have to manually rename the home page and any other pages to use the extension .html. Use the FrontPage Explorer to make this change so that any links will be corrected automatically. Do this before uploading your pages to the ISP/WPP.*
>
> *Also, even if you prefer the .html extension to .htm, the FrontPage templates and wizards will continue to generate files ending with .htm. So if at all possible, configure the web server (or ask the administrator to do so) to support the .htm extension for HTML pages. This may require setting up a new MIME type for .htm.*

Uploading Your Web With the File Transfer Protocol

Uploading the pages in your web involves copying them from your local hard drive to the network hard drive of the service provider. In many cases, you can do this directly with an *FTP client*, software that lets you use the Internet File Transfer Protocol to transfer files. While both Windows 95 and NT include a rudimentary FTP command for use in DOS or the Command Prompt, you'll never want to put yourself through that much trouble.

Instead, download and install an FTP client such as WS_FTP32 or WS_FTP (free for personal or educational use). The former requires a 32-bit Winsock, and is preferred for use with Windows 95 or NT 4 Dial-Up

Networking. If you want to upload while logged in to the 16-bit version of America Online (all versions except for AOL 3.0 for Windows 95), you'll need to use the 16-bit version of the FTP client.

Getting Ready for FTP

When you're ready to upload your site, you'll need to know the location and the account information of the File Transfer Protocol (FTP) server. If your web page is www.yourname.wpp.com or www.wpp.com/~yourname, the FTP site may be something like ftp.wpp.com. You'll need to know the name of the folder on the FTP server that "points" to your web contents, such as /users/~yourname or /pub/www/~yourname, and the login name and password for the FTP server. (Sometimes you don't need to specify the folder/directory names. Simply logging in to the FTP server as the correct user tells the FTP server to automatically make your user directory the root directory.)

For security reasons, you may also be required to dial in to the information service (required for America Online) before uploading in order to authenticate you as the user of the web account. Some Web Presence Providers go an extra step to ensure security. For example, AT&T Easy World Wide Web, which supports FrontPage extensions and FrontPage security, nevertheless requires you to use an AT&T dial-up connection to access your web, which is stored behind a firewall accessible only to the AT&T dial-up service. Most other WPPs rely on the FrontPage username/password security scheme as sufficient security.

> **TIP**
>
> *Use FrontPage Explorer's Tools | Permissions menu to choose which users are allowed to author (edit or save pages). You can assign these privileges for the entire site or restrict access to individuals or groups on a per-subweb basis. That way, the marketing staff can change the press releases but can't accidentally overwrite information in the root web.*

I've included WS_FTP and CuteFTP on this book's Companion CD-ROM. See Appendix A to find out how to install the software included with this book. Whereas WS_FTP is basically freeware, you'll have to pay a license fee to use CuteFTP beyond the evaluation period, but it's ease of use and powerful capabilities will make it worth your while. (You'll also want to check the CuteFTP Web site if you want to obtain the latest version of the software. Check out http://www.cuteftp.com.)

Uploading With CuteFTP

CuteFTP lets you set up many sites, storing them in a kind of phonebook. To prepare to upload your pages, create a new site and fill in the FTP Site Edit dialog box as shown in Figure 5-5. What you enter in the Site Label text box is what's shown in the phonebook. Type the actual FTP server name in the Host Address box. If you need to log in using a name and password, fill those in using the User ID and Password boxes. You may also need to specify the initial remote directory, and you'll want to fill in the entry for Initial Local Directory as the path to your web site on your local computer.

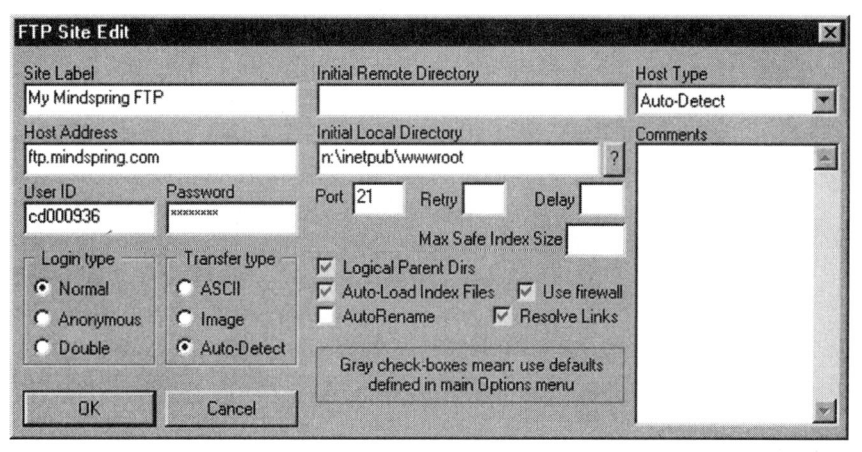

Figure 5-5: Setting up a CuteFTP session for uploading your pages.

Often, you won't have to fill in one or more of the boxes at all. When uploading to America Online, for instance, you should already be logged in to America Online using the AOL software. That's enough to validate your access, so you don't need to specify a username or even a remote directory. Just specify the server name **members.aol.com**. (Don't add the FTP prefix commonly used with FTP sites. You also don't need the ftp:// prefix required by web browsers.)

You log in to AOL's FTP server anonymously, and AOL validates you and takes you to your private folder. That's where you put the content for your web site, and only you can store pages there. (You can create an incoming folder if you want others to be able to store information on your FTP server, but this will eat into your 2 megabyte allowance for web/FTP storage.) If you aren't logged in to AOL with their software, you can view the top level of the FTP server, but you won't be able to store into your private folder.

Note: CompuServe does not allow FTP access to your web pages. I'll show you how to use the Web Publishing Wizard instead in the next section.

Once you have your site profile set up, click it, and then click the Connect button to go online. Pay attention to any login messages that you see; some servers will report your statistics here, such as megabytes of web usage.

In Figure 5-6, you'll see what CuteFTP looks like once you've logged in to the FTP server. On the left are the folders for your local computer's hard drive. On the right is a representation of the FTP server's directories (folders). Sometimes, as shown in Figure 5-6, there is a separate folder for FTP and WWW usage. Any files copied to the WWW folder will be those seen when the web site is browsed.

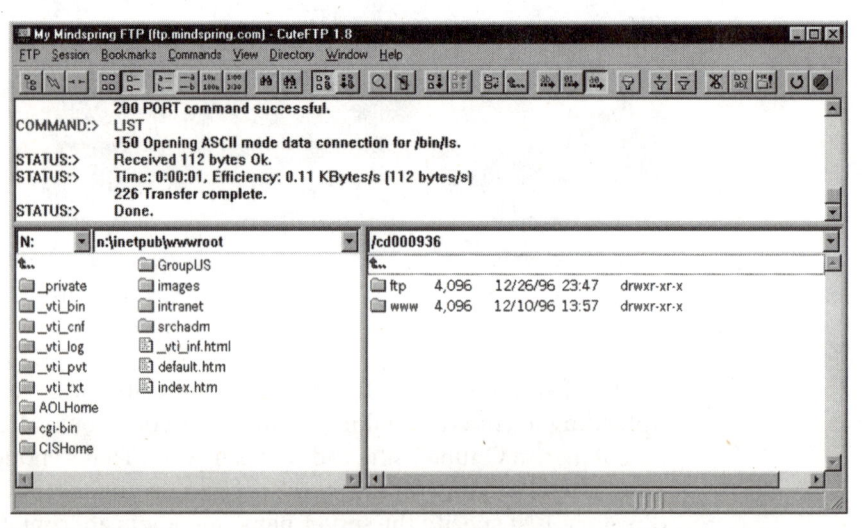

Figure 5-6: Before you upload your files, be sure you've changed to the correct folders on both the local hard drive and on the FTP server.

Before you upload the pages you're interested in, change to the correct directories. On the left, double-click on the folder name that matches the subweb containing the pages you want to upload. On the right, double-click on the folder that will receive your content (WWW in the example).

You can now simply drag and drop files from the left pane to the right pane. To speed things up, hold down the Ctrl key while clicking files on the left so that you can select several files at once; then drag the entire selected group of files into the pane on the right.

Once the files are uploaded, you're ready to test your web. The URL for the site shown in Figure 5-6, would be http://www.mindspring.com/~cd000936. For America Online, your web page would be found at http://members.aol.com/*screenname*, where *screenname* is the screen name of the account you logged in with when you performed the upload. (You have separate web space for each screen name, and a single AOL account can have up to 10 screen names. You only need to be logged in while uploading the files. You can use any dial-up account or web browser to view your finished pages.)

TIP

For more information on using and managing your America Online home pages, use KEYWORD: MYPLACE. You can also use the My Place menus to upload from your hard drive to your site, create folders, and set access rights for folders.

Uploading With the Web Publishing Wizard

As easy as it is to use CuteFTP, many people will appreciate the step-by-step wizard-based approach of the Microsoft Web Publishing Wizard. This software is included on the FrontPage 97 CD-ROM with Bonus Pack, and it can also be downloaded from http://www.microsoft.com/windows/software/webpost/. (If this link has moved, look for a Download Free Software link on the main entry point to the Microsoft Web site, http://www.microsoft.com.)

The Web Publishing Wizard lets you set up sites for your web hosting service providers, and once installed, is integrated with the FrontPage Explorer's File | Publish Web command. Let's step through the process of uploading a site to CompuServe. (For more information on CompuServe web hosting, go to http://ourworld.compuserve.com, where you can also download CompuServe's Home Page and Publishing Wizard, which complements the Microsoft Web Publishing Wizard.)

The Web Publishing Wizard lets you upload your pages to any service provider that gives you FTP access to your web directory. It also has special support for America Online, CompuServe OurWorld, and CompuServe SpryNet. (Ironically, The Microsoft Network does not yet support home pages for its members.)

Using the Web Publishing Wizard with America Online is similar to uploading with CuteFTP. Prior to and during the upload, you will also need to be logged in with the America Online software. The Web Publishing Wizard will automatically detect the screen names in use and ask you which screen name account you'd like to use when uploading.

Publishing to Your CompuServe Home Page

If you want to publish a web on CompuServe's OurWorld, follow these steps. Unlike with America Online, you don't need to be logged in using the CompuServe software during the upload process:

1. Start by running FrontPage Explorer and opening the web that you want to publish.

2. Choose Publish Web from the File menu.

3. Fill in the name of the FTP server as shown in Figure 5-7. Use the name of the FTP server (which doesn't necessary start with "ftp") as the entry for the Destination Web Server box.

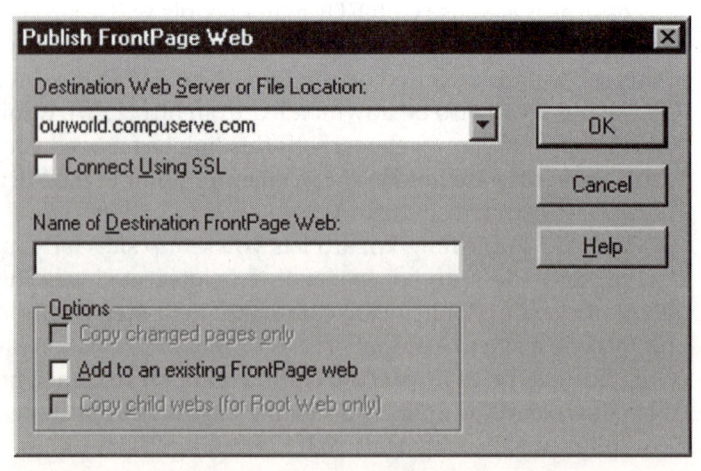

Figure 5-7: FrontPage automatically invokes the Web Publishing Wizard if the destination server does not support the FrontPage server extensions.

4. If the FTP server requires that you specify a folder for your pages, add it to the FTP server's name in the Destination Web Server box. (Most web account FTP sites will put you in the correct folder automatically.) For example: ftp.servername/users/myaccount. Don't worry about any other text boxes or check boxes. These are only for use with FrontPage servers.

5. If you want to upload only pages that have changed since the last time you uploaded the web, leave the Copy Changed Pages Only check box turned on. The first time you run the wizard, and whenever you want to make sure all pages are resent, turn off this check box. (Do not enable Connect Using SSL.)

Note: The Web Publishing Wizard works much like CompuServe's own Publishing Wizard. The CompuServe wizard, however, includes an additional option that lets you erase all pages on your web account. This is useful because you can't directly access the files, so there's no way to eliminate obsolete files other than erasing them all and then uploading only the pages you need.

The Microsoft Web Publishing Wizard will notice if there are files in the CompuServe server that don't exist in your web and will offer to delete the obsolete or redundant files during the upload of the new content. If you used the Copy Changed Pages Only check box, you'll also be prompted if you want to remove the pages on the site that haven't changed, since there's no way to make a distinction between obsolete pages and pages that you simply don't choose to update. Watch out for this.

6. The first time you publish the web, you'll be prompted to enter additional information for the server, such as your name, address, occupation, and hobbies. Fill out this information and click Next.

7. You may also be requested to enter your login name or user ID and your password. The Publishing wizard will store this information and you won't have to enter it the next time you publish. Fill in the necessary information, and click Next to move on to the next screen of the wizard.

8. Prior to uploading the pages, you may also be prompted to choose which file should be used as the default (home) page. Click on the index.htm or default.htm page, and then click Next.

9. You may be asked at this point if you want to remove pages from the server that don't exist in your web. (See the preceding note.) After dealing with this question, click Next.
10. The wizard uploads the pages, graphics, and other files to the web, and the wizard completes.

When the wizard completes, you're ready to browse your web. To find your page on CompuServe's OurWorld, use the URL http://ourworld.compuserve.com/homepages/*username*.

When you first upload your pages, CompuServe also lets you register a meaningful username. This name is used instead of your numeric user ID, and you can use the name to find your pages and as your e-mail address, as in http://ourworld.compuserve.com/homepages/cbrannon or cbrannon@compuserve.com. Use GO REGISTER to register your preferred username. (Actually, if you haven't registered your name yet, the wizard will prompt you for the name you'd like to use and will register the name for you.)

TIP

If you want to upload your pages again, first close FrontPage Explorer and then restart it. This prevents a bug that may occur when the old files in the temporary upload folder are still marked as "in use" by FrontPage as it tries to overwrite them with your new content.

Running the Publishing Wizard Without FrontPage

The Microsoft Web Publishing Wizard can also be run as a stand-alone tool. By default, you can find it on the Start | Programs | Accessories | Internet Tools menu. There's an extra step at the beginning where you choose the folder (or files) on your hard drive that you want to copy. In effect, it acts like an easy-to-use FTP client. There's no obvious reason why you would want to run the wizard outside of the FrontPage Explorer unless you have some content that you've developed directly on the hard drive with the FrontPage Editor, content that has never been imported as a FrontPage web.

Publishing to a FrontPage Server

The complications of using FTP or the Web Publishing Wizard can be avoided by relying on a true FrontPage web hosting account. When you order your web hosting account (discussed earlier), make sure you request a FrontPage account; most WPPs sell both FrontPage and non-FrontPage (standard) web sites.

In fact, it's almost too easy to upload your site. All you'll need is the name of your web server (such as www.yourcompany.com or www.yourcompany.wpp.com), the username for your account, and the password.

Note: To distinguish between your local server (the one you use when authoring pages locally) and the FrontPage server run by the Web Presence Provider, I'll refer to the latter as the Internet web server.

Preparing Your Web for the World Wide Web

I already mentioned this in "Publishing on a Non-FrontPage Server," but it's worth repeating, especially if you skipped that section: Watch out for differences in the way UNIX servers interpret filenames, especially if you're accustomed to the Windows 95/NT 4 rules. In Windows 95/NT 4, you can have a file named FooBar.gif, yet reference it on your page as foobar.gif. On UNIX systems, the case of a filename is significant. The literal reference to foobar.gif will prevent that graphic (named FooBar.gif) from loading unless you either change the reference or rename the file on the Internet web server. Also avoid filenames with spaces in them. To avoid these problems, use Browse when linking to pages or graphics on your site instead of manually typing in the link locations, or try to use only lowercase in all filenames.

Support for FrontPage 97 May Be Lacking

Also, as mentioned earlier, some FrontPage service providers haven't yet upgraded to the FrontPage 97 server extensions. Should this be the case, these are the features of FrontPage 97 that you'll have to avoid until the upgrade is implemented:

- Deploying the Internet Database Connector Wizard (also requires IIS as the server and ODBC setup, usually at extra cost)
- Form Field Validation
- Renaming, copying, moving folders

- Scripting (VBScript or JavaScript, see Chapter 9)
- Support for multiple languages
- Using a Secure Sockets Layer connection to view or change pages
- Using NT Challenge/Response Logon (IIS only)

If some of these features are unfamiliar to you, don't worry; you probably aren't going to need them right away. (The most vexing problem will be trying to manage your site with the FrontPage Editor. When you try to delete a folder, you may be refused access. Renaming or moving files between folders may appear to fail, but try using the View | Refresh command or press F5 to see if the changes were indeed made, but simply not updated.)

Root Web or Subwebs?

There's one more consideration to keep in mind before uploading your web or webs. In Chapter 1, you learned that the FrontPage Explorer not only manages single pages or just one site, but also lets you store and manage many webs. Each web is a self-contained project, stored in a subfolder (subdirectory) on the hard drive attached to the web server. The root web is special because normally it won't show the content of the subwebs, and it can have different security settings than the individual webs.

> **TIP**
>
> *Another term for subweb is* child web, *as if each project were dependent upon or related to the root web. In fact, each subweb is a peer to every other web. The root web is special, because no subdirectory name is needed to access its content, but the root web does not control or manage the content of the child webs.*

It is always best to set up new webs in FrontPage Explorer as subwebs. Avoid storing anything in the root web except perhaps a master home page that can link to any of the subwebs. Likewise, when publishing a subweb, it's best to upload the web to a subweb on the FrontPage server on the Internet. You are allowed to copy (publish) a subweb from your server to the root web of the Internet web server, in case you only plan to use one project on that server, but you may have problems if you try to remove content from the root web. You're allowed to delete subwebs, but you can not delete the root web.

By using subwebs, you can use the same web hosting account for different purposes. You could have www.companyname.com/sales, www.companyname.com/info, and www.companyname.com/support, each with its own home page and content. By placing a master home page in the root web, you don't lose your easy-to-remember domain name, www.companyname.com. Users browsing www.companyname.com will still be able to reach any of the subwebs with just one click. See the sidebar below for another way to take the user from the "greeting" page in the root web to the home page of the content in the subweb.

Automatic Hyperlinks With Client-Side Pull

Using a technique called *client-side pull*, you can set up the home page in the root web to send the user to a subweb automatically.

1. Use the FrontPage Editor to create a simple master home page with a welcome message. It's like the title page of your web site.
2. Store the master page on the root web of the Internet web server.
3. Get the page properties of the master page by right-clicking on it. Switch to the Custom tab of the Page Properties dialog box.
4. Under the System Variables section, click Add. You'll be prompted to enter a name and a value. For the name, use REFRESH. For the value, enter something like the following:

```
5; URL="support/default.htm"
```

The first part tells the browser to wait for five seconds, and the second part tells the browser where to go after the five second delay. You'll want to add some text to the master home page that tells the user what's going to happen and include a hyperlink on the master page so that impatient viewers or users without client-side support can reach the site directly.

You can also use this method when you've moved a site from one location on the Internet to another. Put up an apology page where the site formerly existed, include a link to your new site, and use the META REFRESH tag to send the user there automatically.

Publishing to the Internet Web Server

To publish a web on the Internet web server (the server that hosts your account and that supports FrontPage extensions), first open the web from your local web server using FrontPage Explorer. You should have already created and tested the web locally. All you're doing now is copying it to the World Wide Web.

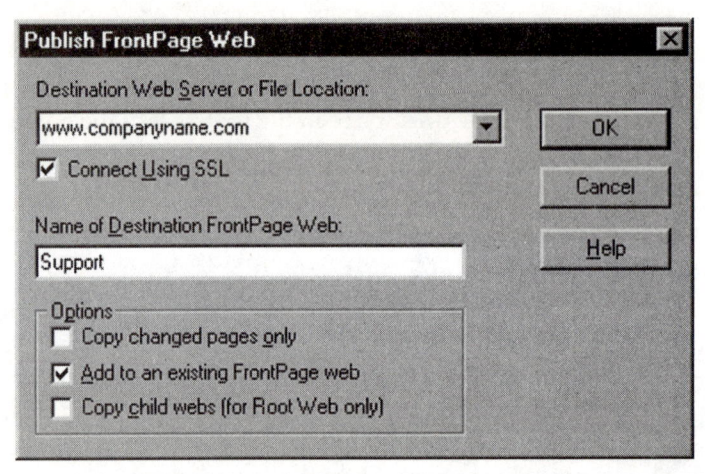

Figure 5-8: This is an example of how to fill out the Publish FrontPage Web dialog box if you're copying the content to an existing subweb and you want to make sure all files are copied. If you haven't yet created the subweb, turn off the Add to an Existing FrontPage Web check box.

Choose Publish Web from the File menu. Fill out the Publish FrontPage Web dialog box as suggested by Figure 5-8. The following sections give a breakdown of the options.

Destination Web Server or File Location

Put the name of the web server here, such as http://www.companyname.com. (The http:// part is optional.) You can also use the IP address if there is no domain name assigned. For virtual domain names, type the web address that you use to browse the page, as in www.companyname.w1.com.

Connect Using SSL

The first time you publish your web, turn on the Connect Using SSL check box. This encrypts the data sent to the server so that it can't possibly be intercepted by a hacker (unlikely in any case). If you get an error message indicating that SSL is not supported, turn off the check box the next time you try and leave it turned off for every subsequent upload. Check with the FrontPage provider to see whether SSL should be allowed, and make sure it has been enabled for your account if it's supported.

Name of Destination FrontPage Web

This text box is normally set to the same name as the subweb you're publishing. If you have the root web open and you want to publish it, leave this box blank if you want it to become the root web on the Internet web server. If you want to copy the local root web to a subweb on the Internet web server, choose a name for the subweb. You don't have to use the same name as the subweb currently open in FrontPage Explorer. The first time you publish the web to the Internet web server as a subweb, make sure to clear the Add to an Existing FrontPage Web check box so that the subfolder and subweb structure can be initialized. Subsequently, leave the check box turned off, since the subweb was created the first time you published.

Copy Changed Pages Only

Turn off the Copy Changed Pages Only check box the first time you copy your web to the Internet web server and whenever you want to make sure that every file in the local web gets copied over. In the future, as you make changes to the master copy of the web on your local computer (the recommended method, as opposed to making changes directly on the Internet web server), turn on this check box so that only the pages you've updated are uploaded, saving you time and connect charges.

Add to an Existing FrontPage Web

Turn on the Add to an Existing FrontPage Web check box only if you are updating pages on a subweb you've already copied over or if for some reason the subweb already exists. (Perhaps you previously created the subweb but manually removed the pages from it.) Turn off this check box the first time you're publishing a web from your local server as a subweb on the Internet web server. This box must be checked if you're copying a web to the root web on the Internet web server.

Copy Child Webs (for Root Web Only)

Should you be copying the root web, you might wish to also publish the content in every subweb hosted on your local computer. This only applies if you are publishing from the root web of your local web server. Child webs, or subwebs, are not the same as subfolders/subdirectories. If your web contains subfolders like _private or images, they will always be copied to the destination web along with FrontPage configuration folders such as vti_cnf.

Proceed to Upload

After you click OK, the publishing process begins. First the pages in your local web are listed; then the pages are streamed to the Internet web server. The time this takes depends on how much content you have, how busy the Internet web server is, and how busy the Internet in general is. During the upload, the FrontPage Explorer displays a percentage of completion message in the status bar.

> **TRAP**
>
> *If the web server is very busy, such as during peak daytime usage hours, it's possible that the upload process will time out. If this occurs, only part of the content may be updated. It's also possible that the root web will be corrupted, requiring administrative work by the staff of the Internet/web service provider. To avoid this, try to schedule your uploads late in the evening or before 9:00 A.M. EST, upload only changed pages, and use subwebs for your content, reserving the root for a master home page, as previously discussed. Another way to avoid this potential problem is to use the File Transfer Protocol or the Web Publishing Wizard to upload your pages (as discussed earlier in this chapter).*

When the upload completes, the web is updated on the server, and FrontPage informs you that the web has been successfully copied to the server. The web is now ready for you or the general public to browse.

Web Site Maintenance

Now that your web is on the World Wide Web, you can relax, right? Hardly. The WWW is by nature dynamic. Likewise, nothing in your life or your business will remain unchanged. You will no doubt need to make changes to your web, perhaps several times a day.

Authors will need to be able to upload changes or make changes directly on the server in some cases. That brings up an important issue: Do you modify the content directly on the Internet web server, or must you make your changes locally and upload the changes manually?

The latter method is highly recommended. By keeping your "master" content on the local hard drive or local web server, you can work on your web even when not connected to the Internet. Local edits and web recalculations are tens to hundreds of times faster than the same procedures over a modem connection. You can easily back up the data to local storage media.

It may seem like an inconvenience to have to update the "real" server on the Internet every time you make a change locally, but by insisting on making changes only locally, you will avoid discrepancies between the local version and the Internet version.

It's your choice whether or not to maintain the site directly over the Internet. Just start FrontPage Explorer, and when prompted for the web server, enter the IP address or web address of the site; then fill in the username and password if prompted. You have the same FrontPage Explorer features at your fingertips as you would when authoring locally. You can double-click on a file to edit it, drag and drop it from one folder to another, switch between hyperlink view and folder view, and so forth.

One reason you may want to edit pages directly on the server is if you can't get to the local machine or local area network web server to edit the content. This is common if you have authors off-site. In this case, it makes sense to keep the "master" content on the web server. You should occasionally publish the web "in reverse" to store a backup copy on the local web server. Just use FrontPage Explorer to open the Internet web on a computer that can access the local web server, and publish to that local web server.

Team Web Development

For large projects, you'll commonly delegate (or be delegated) the responsibility for updating or adding content to a web site. Your site may consist of a number of subwebs, or it may have just one large subweb or root web. For every person that needs to be able to publish to the web, you'll want to assign authoring privileges. These rights can be assigned equally to all authors, or you can restrict some authors to individual subwebs.

Some authors will also need the ability to restructure the site by moving files, deleting files and folders, and changing permissions and passwords for other authors. This administrative access need not be granted to every author.

Finally, you can decide if anonymous users (the world) can browse the web at all, or if it should be restricted to certain users who will have to provide a username and password to enter your site. That's a common requirement for a company intranet hosted on an Internet server or for subscription-based web sites.

Security Issues

The way FrontPage implements security depends on how the web is being served. For a standard web server running the FrontPage Server Extensions, you can specify which users are allowed to browse, author, or administer a FrontPage web. Or you can restrict access to specific computers based on their IP address (assuming each computer has a fixed IP) or to a subnet mask (any IP within a range of IP addresses).

When the web server is running on Windows NT IIS, as is common with an intranet, you can assign which valid NT users or NT groups can browse, author, or administer the content of the web. These users must also have been granted directory access to the folders where the web content resides. We won't get into detail on NT security here, but there is more information on that subject in Chapter 6.

To edit permissions, first use FrontPage Explorer to open the root web or subweb on the Internet web server. (Opening the local web server lets you set permissions that apply only to users accessing or authoring locally.)

Choose Permissions from the Tools menu. As shown in Figure 5-9, you can add, edit, and remove users. You can also choose whether everyone (the world) can browse the web or if the web will be restricted to only users granted browse access.

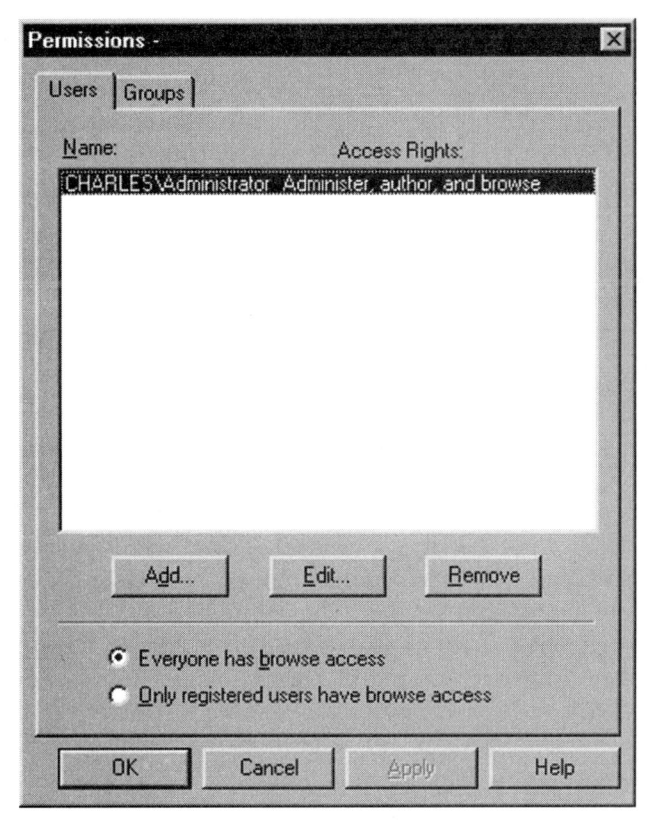

Figure 5-9: You can authorize users and groups for authoring and enable or disable browsing of the web.

When you add users (or groups) to the permissions list, the names of the users you can add are restricted to authorized users for the workgroup or domain if the web is hosted by Internet Information Server or Peer Web Services running on Windows NT. Or the list could come from whatever method the web server uses to restrict access by user. With the Microsoft Personal Web Server for Windows 95, users can be added to the master list with the Web Server Administration page. We'll examine these security issues in Chapter 6.

Each user can be allowed any of the access levels shown in Figure 5-10, which shows what you'll see when you edit a user's settings. You don't need to explicitly assign the browse access to anyone unless you have disabled browsing for all users. Instead, you'll choose whether to grant only authoring (with browsing permitted regardless of the settings for all users) or both authoring and administration (which includes browsing rights regardless).

Figure 5-10: For each user or group, you can set specific access rights.

The Groups tab heading lets you assign these permissions to groups of users instead of or in addition to individual users, which saves time if you are giving access rights to large numbers of users, or if you want to easily change a user from one level of access to another simply by moving them from one group to another. (This tab is only shown if the web server is hosted on Windows NT running IIS or PWS.)

The root web has one set of permissions, and each subweb inherits the same settings by default unless you allow unique permissions for a particular subweb. To allow this, open the subweb with FrontPage Explorer and choose Tools | Permissions. Use the Settings tab to choose this option. See Figure 5-11.

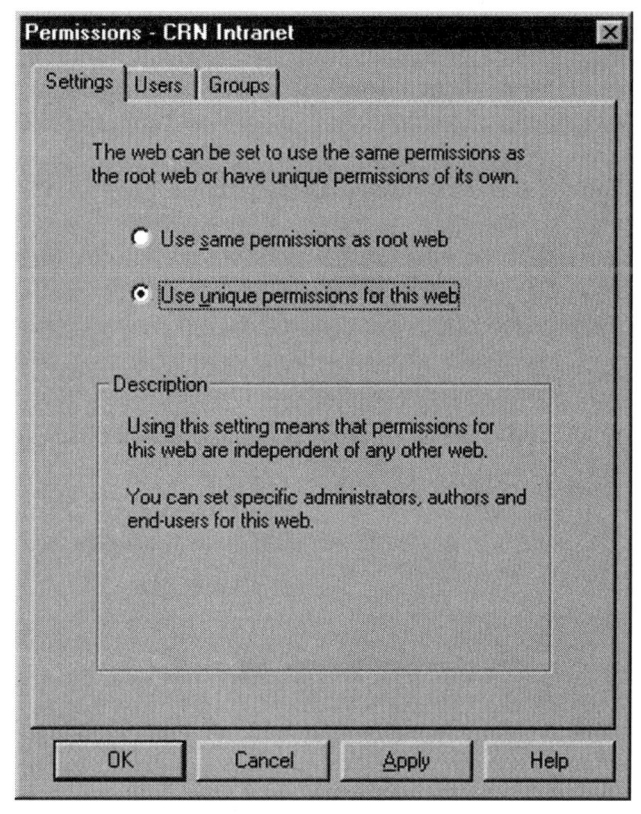

Figure 5-11: If you want to restrict access to a particular subweb or set unique authoring permissions for a subweb, enable it on a per-web basis.

This feature is exploited by the Discussion Web Wizard, which builds a Discussion subweb where either all users or only authorized users can participate in a threaded (topically organized) discussion, similar to the forums in online services or Usenet newsgroups. When you set up the wizard (via File l New from FrontPage Explorer), you can choose whether to allow anyone to participate or require users to register. The registration page is set up in the root web, where there are no restrictions on browse access. The discussion subweb, on the other hand, denies browse access to all users. When users register for the discussion, the Registration WebBot adds each user to the permissions list and gives them browse access.

You can exploit the Registration WebBot in the same way, perhaps to monitor access to an intranet web. Here's how (the following assumes you are familiar with form creation, which was discussed in the preceding chapters):

1. Create a registration page in the root web, with text boxes for name, password, and confirmation password.
2. Right-click on each text box to get its properties, and name the text boxes Name, Password, and Confirm.
3. While editing the names, set the properties for the two password text boxes as password fields to use asterisks during entry (to prevent over-the-shoulder snooping).
4. Also place a Submit button on the form.
5. If you like, add a table with three rows and two columns. Move the fields into the second column and type descriptions in the first column. This keeps things nice and tidy.

An example of how this form might look is shown as Figure 5-12.

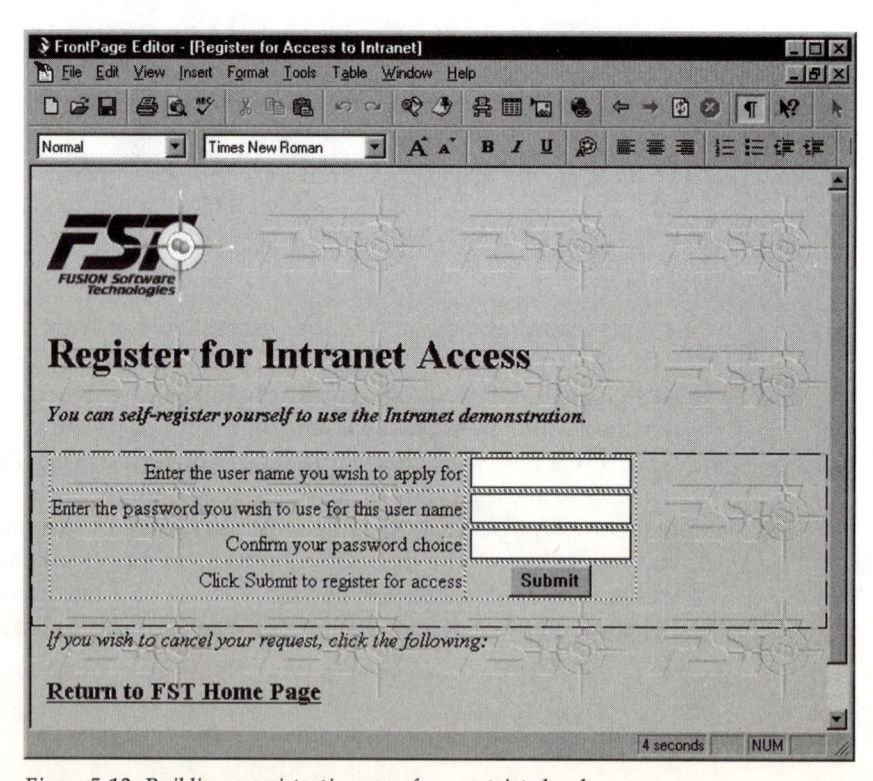

Figure 5-12: Building a registration page for a restricted web.

The form handler activated when the user clicks on Submit will be the Registration WebBot Component. To configure it, get the form properties by right-clicking within the form. From the Form Properties dialog box, assign a name to the form, and choose the WebBot Registration Component as the form handler. Click Settings to set up the Registration WebBot, as shown in Figure 5-13.

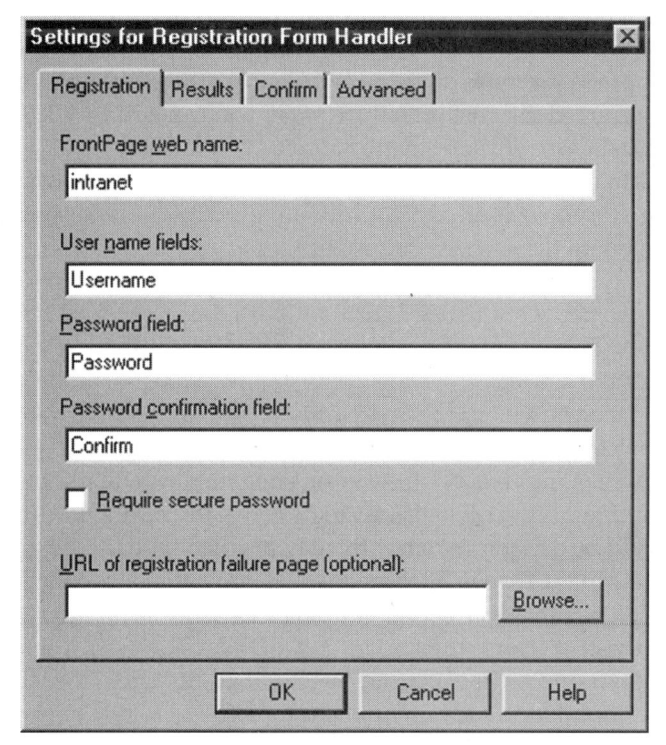

Figure 5-13: The Registration WebBot needs to know which web you want to grant access to and the names of the text fields.

When filling out the settings on the Registration tab, put the name of the subweb you want to grant access to in the FrontPage Web Name text box. Tell the form handler the names of the text boxes by filling in the User Name, Password, and Password Confirmation entries. (If you use more than one text box to form a username, such as one for first name and one for last name, put both field names in the entry, separated by commas. They will be combined to form the username.)

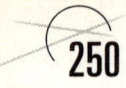

Turn on the Require Secure Password check box to enforce "good" password enforcement: six characters or more, and the password does not match any part of the username. This is not a secure password in the technical sense of being encrypted, however.

Should the registration process fail (because another user has the same username, or the password is not valid), the Registration WebBot automatically displays a warning and prompts the user to try again. You'll probably want to build your own custom page for good looks, using the Confirmation WebBot to display the entries entered by the user. See Chapter 4 for more on using the Confirmation WebBot. Once you've constructed the custom failure page, you can add its URL (filename) to the last entry of the Registration property sheet.

You can also use the Confirmation tab to choose a custom "you're in" page for those users whose validation succeeds. Otherwise, the user is taken into the subweb automatically.

The Registration WebBot can also act like the Submit Results WebBot, in case you want to use a form for both data entry and registration purposes. This lets you log attempts to enter the restricted web in an HTML file, for example.

Once you've built the registration page in the root web, open the subweb and use Tools | Permissions to disable access to all users.

Note: Windows NT (Server or Workstation) will not permit the FrontPage Server Extensions to dynamically create new users. That would be dangerous, since the new users might also be granted remote access to the server. That means that you can not use the Registration WebBot with a web server running Internet Information Server, nor can you restrict users when operating a Discussion web. There is no workaround for this glaring oversight at this time other than using the Microsoft Normandy component for USENET-style newsgroups, an advanced feature offered by some providers running IIS servers.

Is the Registration WebBot Worth the Trouble?

Using the Registration WebBot is a little bit dumb, however, if you really want to restrict access to a page. It's true that by turning off browsing for the protected subweb, there's no way to enter the subweb, even if the "intruder" knows the path to the subweb. Yet the Registration 'bot has no way of restricting who can sign up for access. Once the user has registered, he or she has full access to the protected web. At best, using the Registration WebBot lets you keep track of who has joined.

If you truly want to restrict access, use unique permissions for the subweb and disable browsing by all users. Instead of using a self-registration technique with the Registration WebBot, you'll have to manually add registered users using Tools | Permissions for the subweb.

Versioning & Backup Security

Whether you maintain your content on a local computer and upload it to the Internet web server or make your changes directly to the Internet web server, you are going to want to implement a plan to make backups of the web content on a regular basis.

This is to protect you from your own mistakes and to let you go back to a previous version of webs or files in case you change your mind. For example, if you delete a subweb, there is no way to recover the data. Even the Recycle Bin won't save you in this case.

Typically, the service providers will back up your data as part of their own security protocols, but this is only for recovery from catastrophic data loss. The service provider won't make it easy to recover individual files from the master backup simply because you deleted a file by mistake.

To back up the web site, you might try to use the Export command from the File menu of FrontPage Explorer to send the content to a local hard drive. Export is nearly useless, however, since it can only export one file at a time. You also can't drag and drop files from the FrontPage Explorer to your local hard drive (although the reverse action works; you can copy any file from your computer to the web by dragging and dropping the file into the right-hand pane of FrontPage Explorer).

Instead, to back up the local web, find the directory on the hard drive containing the files, such as \InetPub\wwwroot, \FrontPage Webs\Content, or \Webshare\wwwroot. Copy the files in this folder to a backup medium such as a removable cartridge drive (the Iomega Zip drive is a popular and inexpensive choice), or back up the folder (directory) to tape using the software that comes with any tape drive. (Large capacity tape drives are available for under $100.)

Should you choose to keep your master web pages on the Internet web server, you'll have to publish your web from the Internet to your local web server. Do this from any computer that can open webs from either server. First open the Internet web, and use Publish Web to copy the web to the local web server. To back up the entire Internet site, copy the root web and all child webs. This can be sent to either the root web on the local file server or to a subweb on the local web server if you don't want to risk overwriting any local projects.

You can then back up the information on the local web server, assuming you have access to and backup privileges for the computer running the web server.

It's a good idea to maintain several backups, and rotate the backups so that you never overwrite your most recent backup. The idea is that if something goes catastrophically wrong with the current web site, you can "roll back" to the last known good backup. That's why you don't want to maintain only one backup copy, as you might discover too late that you just overwrote the only good backup with a corrupted version of the site.

To restore from a backup, first delete the files in the subweb that you backed up, and then use the Import Wizard (File | Import from FrontPage Explorer) to pull the pages back in. Don't simply copy the files back to the hard drive folder hosting the webs, since this may overwrite FrontPage security information.

Advanced Recovery

The following procedure is for emergency use only. If the entire web folder becomes corrupted, first try to uninstall the FrontPage Server Extensions using the FrontPage Server Administrator. (A shortcut to this program is in the folder where you installed FrontPage.) Use Windows Explorer to delete the web folder (wwwroot or Content), and then use File | New Folder to recreate the folder. Rerun the FrontPage Server Administrator and reinstall the server extensions. This sets up the configuration information for the web folder.

You can now import your content into the freshly created folder. If you have problems with this, copy the files from your backup to a temporary folder. Open the temporary folder with Windows Explorer, and use Tools | Find to locate all files and folders matching the pattern vti*.*. From the list of files returned by the Find command, delete all the vti files. This leaves behind just the raw content for your webs.

Now you can copy the contents of the temporary folder (but not the temporary folder itself) back to the root folder of the web server (Inetpub/wwwroot, Webshare/wwwroot, or FrontPage Webs/Content).

To complete the recovery, start FrontPage Explorer and create a new subweb for every web that exists in the backup data. The name of the subweb must match the name of the folder containing that web. This lets FrontPage Explorer rebuild the configuration information for every file. Don't open the root web until you've told FrontPage Explorer about every subweb, or they will be listed as subfolders of the root web, which can be confusing, since child webs (subwebs) aren't really treated as subfolders by FrontPage.

Note: By deleting the vti files, some configuration information is lost. For example, you'll have to recreate any substitution variables that should exist on the Parameters tab that you can when choosing Tools | Web Settings, and reestablish security settings and script folder permissions.

Promoting Your Site

Now that the hard work of creating and publishing your site is over and done with, it's time for the fun part, spreading the word. It's not very satisfying to publish a site if nobody ever visits it. On the contrary, you want to shout it from the rooftops.

The latter method won't get you very good results, in fact, you may end up getting a shoe thrown at you. The modern method is to visit the most popular search engines and register your site.

Most people find the web sites they are looking for with one of the popular search engines, such as AltaVista (http://www.altavista.com), Excite (http://www.excite.com), Infoseek (http://www.infoseek.com), HotBot (http://www.hotbot.com), WebCrawler (http://www.webcrawler.com — hmmm... do you see a pattern here?), and others.

If you do nothing, your site will probably end up on many of these search lists eventually. That's because the most powerful search engines don't wait around to be told where to find the new sites. They proactively rummage through the Internet, visiting every possible and reasonable IP address (there are billions of possibilities), and indexing the titles, URLS, keywords, and even the text content of every page encountered.

To help others find your page, you'll want to use a meaningful title for at least the home page and add variables to your page that describe the content and provide keywords. The description is part of what is returned by the search engine, and it is often shown on the list of items returned by the search.

To add a description, follow these steps:

1. Open your home page from FrontPage Explorer.
2. When the page appears in the FrontPage Editor, right-click on the page and choose Page Properties.

3. Switch to the Custom tab, and in the User Variables section, click Add.

4. From the User Meta Variable dialog box (as shown in Figure 5-14), enter the name as **DESCRIPTION**, and in the Value box, type a plain-English description of your site, products, or services.

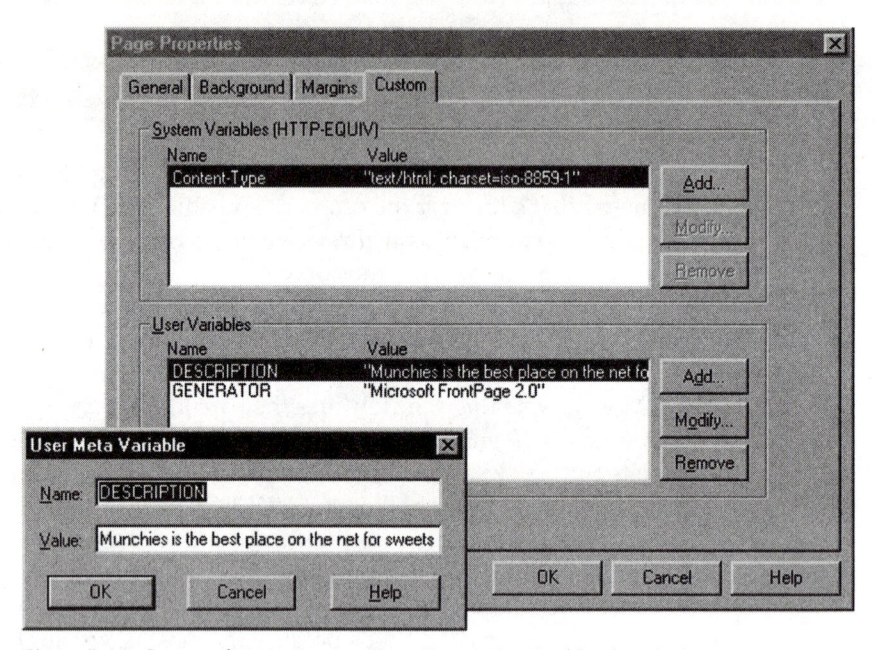

Figure 5-14: On your home page, use Page Properties to add a description meta tag to help searchers know if they've found the right site.

5. Next, create a variable named KEYWORDS, and type a list of words that you think might be tried by others searching for your site, products, or services.

It's common to overstuff this list to help your site reach the top of the list. "Adult" sites include a string of words like "sex sex sex sex sex hot hot" and other unmentionables in hopes of getting to the top of the search list. This rarely helps, as most web indexers now screen out excess keywords.

If you don't want your page indexed, you'll usually have to fill out a form on the search engine to exclude your site or otherwise mark your page as excluded from indexing. (The method varies, so you'll have to research this issue with each major search engine.)

On the other hand, if you want to get noticed right away, you can also visit each major search engine and directory service (Yahoo is an example of a directory service) and manually submit your site.

If you really want to get noticed, you can pay a submission service to post your site to every possible search engine and web directory. To give you an idea of how much work this can be, visit the page http://www.strutyourstuff.com/search.htm, which is supposed to offer over 1,001 places you can visit to promote your site. Or, for "just" $149, they'll do it all for you.

Following is a list of additional sites that you can visit to find out how to promote your site. You can find services that will do the job for less than $50 if you shop around:

Register It!
http://www.register-it.com

100% On Target
http://www.webthemes.com/

AAA Internet Promotions
http://www.websitepromote.com/index.html

Add It!
http://www.liquidimaging.com/submit/

InfoSpace
http://www.infospace.com/submit.html

Easy-Submit
http://www.the-vault.com/easy-submit/

FreeLinks
http://www.freelinks.com/

Go Net-Wide
http://www.gonetwide.com/goguide.html

Promoting Your Page
http://www.orst.edu/aw/stygui/propag.htm

Link Exchange
http://www.linkexchange.com

Web Promote
http://online-biz.com/promote/index.cgi

Promote-It!
   http://www.itools.com/promote-it/promote-it.html

Publishing and Promoting Your Web Site
   http://www.desktoppublishing.com/webpromote.html

Web Top 100
   http://www.mmgco.com/top100.html

Yahoo Announcement Services
   http://www.yahoo.com/Computers_and_Internet/Internet/World_Wide_Web/Announcement_Services/

Not all of these links cost money to take advantage of them. Some of these sites are actually "link referral" services. As long as you put a link to their site on your page, they'll put a link to your site on their page.

Members of Link Exchange embed some HTML on their pages that displays a banner ad. Each time the page is visited or refreshed, a new banner is displayed. The banners display links to other members of Link Exchange. The frequency that your banner appears on other member's sites depends on how often your site is visited on the WWW. In effect, you get free advertising in exchange for providing free advertising.

Don't assume you have to pay big bucks to promote your site, especially if you're willing to do a little legwork on your own.

Moving On

Now that you've mastered the essentials of publishing to an Internet web server, it's time to revisit the local web server. Efficient operation of your local web server is vital for trouble-free authoring. Moreover, if you plan to operate a networked web server for intranet applications or if you plan to put your company on the Internet with IIS, you'll want to learn all you can about how to configure, optimize, and establish security for your web server. Chapter 6 shows you how.

chapter 6

FrontPage Configuration & Server Issues

In this chapter, I'll explain what you need to know to make the most out of FrontPage when running it in a local authoring environment. I'll discuss the two primary servers that are recommended for FrontPage authoring: Microsoft Personal Web Server for Windows 95 and Microsoft Internet Information Server/Peer Web Services for Windows NT 4.0.

A *server* is a computer, or software running on a computer, that provides services to other computers (or sometimes to the same computer). A network *file server* is a common fixture in both small and large businesses, the hub of a local area network (LAN). The LAN ties together employee (client) desktop computers so that the workers can share files and printers. It also extends the capabilities of the personal computer by tapping into the power of sophisticated *application servers* that take over some of the computing jobs formerly delegated to individual PCs. (The ODBC database services, discussed in Chapter 8, are an example of an application server; they perform database lookup and storage for computers on the network.)

A *web server*, then, is software running on a computer that provides World Wide Web services via the HTTP protocol. (The HyperText Transfer Protocol was introduced in Chapter 1, if you want to refresh your memory.) As is convention, the term also refers to the computer running the web server software.

Why Web Servers?

The contents of an HTML file are self-sufficient to describe the layout of a page. I explained the principles of the HyperText Markup Language (HTML) in Chapter 1, and you've been working with it every time you edit a page with the FrontPage Editor, which generates HTML behind the scenes.

If you double-click on an HTML file, your default web browser (such as Internet Explorer or Netscape Navigator) starts, opens the file, and "draws" the web page on your screen by interpreting the HTML layout instructions. For example, the characters <strong> in the HTML file, a plain text file like the kind you edit with Notepad, tell the web browser to display any subsequent text in boldface (or apply some other emphasis if the computer's display technology can't display boldface).

You can build a complete web-based application by creating individual HTML pages, saving them to a folder on your hard drive, and inserting hyperlinks to connect the pages together. This is called a *disk-based web* (DBW) and is explored further in Chapter 7.

Since isolated HTML pages appear to work just fine without a web server, you may have wondered if it is worth all the bother to install, maintain, and troubleshoot a web server. Indeed it is. Let's see why.

Chapter 7 points out the limitations of a disk-based web. A web browser only displays the text and applies the formatting in the HTML file and shows any embedded graphic images. It allows the user to click on links to discard the current page and open the page indicated by the link. Each page just sits there looking pretty (if properly designed), but it doesn't *do* anything.

Worse, the disk-based web can only be opened on the computer that stores the pages on its hard drive. One way around this restriction is to put the pages on a network file server or enable the *peer-to-peer* file sharing services of the computer's operating system. (Windows for Workgroups, Windows 95, Windows NT Workstation, and the Macintosh and OS/2 platforms support peer-to-peer file sharing.)

Why Web Servers? Why Not?

Once you've gone so far as to share the disk-based web pages, you're already using a web server, in effect, but one with woefully limited features, so you might as well deploy a web server and enjoy all the benefits it offers. A true web server, with support for two-way HTTP communication, can not only send web pages to web browsers on the network (either a local area TCP/IP network or the Internet), but can accept requests from the web browsers so users can fill out forms or click on buttons and send the results to the web server, which can process or save the results.

The web server can also dynamically generate web pages instead of sending only static, unchanging pages. A trivial example of this would be an instruction in an HTML page containing a date stamp. Whenever a web server sends that page to a browser, it changes the date stamp to the current date and time. Each time the visitor "hits" (accesses) that web page, the date is always current. (The original web page is never changed; it is modified on the fly by the web server while it is transmitted to the web browser.)

TIP

Thanks to advances in web browser technology, the dichotomy between server functionality and browser stupidity isn't as clear as it once was. Modern web browsers (IE 3 and Navigator) can recognize programming statements embedded within the HTML description of a page and act upon them. As you'll see in Chapter 9, this permits many interactive and "intelligent" applications for even static pages and is often combined with server-side processing.

For example, the web browser can make sure that form data is valid (as described in Chapter 4) before sending the form results to the server.

On-the-fly (dynamic) HTML generation (or customization) is crucial for FrontPage web development and deployment. The most useful features of FrontPage rely on dynamic server features. Any page containing a substitution WebBot, such as one that will replace the text "CompanyWebMaster" with your e-mail address, has to be modified whenever it's edited or saved in case you've changed the substitution definition. The Include WebBot also modifies pages as they're saved (or when the web is recalculated using Tools | Recalculate Hyperlinks) to merge the included pages with the content in the page containing the Include 'bot.

The Substitution and Include 'bots are examples of *authoring-time* WebBots. Other 'bots are required only when the pages are sent over the Internet (or intranet) or to retrieve information sent back by the web browser. These are the *browse-time* WebBots. The Save Results WebBot, which collects form data from the browser and stores it on the web server, only works when the page is browsed from and submitted via a web browser connected to a web server.

Note: To support browse-time 'bots such as Save Results, the web server must be running the FrontPage server extensions. If the web server publishing your content doesn't or can't support these extensions, you'll have to limit yourself to authoring-time WebBots. When you are creating disk-based webs not stored on a web server, no WebBot functionality is available.

If you want to take advantage of these 'bots, you have to create your web and its pages via the FrontPage Explorer, which communicates with the web server using HTTP. Thanks to the FrontPage server extensions, the web server can take over much of the work of the FrontPage Explorer, which is appropriate because only the web server should have direct access to web pages, even in a trusted web authoring environment.

Local Authoring

Local authoring refers to using the FrontPage Explorer to open webs stored on a web server that is running on the same computer as FrontPage. Since FrontPage Explorer requires a web server (although the FrontPage Editor can be run separately to create or edit disk-based web pages), the only way to avoid installing a web server on the same computer as the computer running FrontPage is to access a web server on an intranet or on the Internet.

The advantage of local authoring is speed. No network transfers occur, so FrontPage runs quickly, pages are opened and saved efficiently, and you don't need to be dialed in to the Internet or even to a LAN. The local web server lets you faithfully simulate the way your web would work over the Internet, complete with all WebBot features.

When you're ready, you'll publish your web on the Internet (discussed in Chapter 5) or to a web server on your company intranet (discussed in Chapter 7). FrontPage Explorer can also let you author and edit pages directly on the intranet or Internet web server, ideal for when web development is a distributed team effort.

This brings us to the other advantage of authoring and browsing via a web server, the enhanced security provided by a web server.

> **The Seduction of Speed**
> When developing your local webs, don't get seduced by the incredible speeds you get when authoring or especially when testing your pages with the Preview in Browser command on the FrontPage Editor's File menu. This may tempt you to overuse graphics or multimedia, and you'll be astonished how slow and unusable the web may turn out when browsed via the Internet. Worse, once you've gone to all the trouble to design a graphically rich site (an understandable tendency for graphic designers and other publishing professionals), you may resist suggestions to trim it down. How else can one explain the profusion of Hollywood-inspired, all-graphics, multimedia-engorged sites that so frequently are the calling card of web professionals? These sites may be glorious and flattering both to the artist and to the board of directors, but a constant source of frustration for 14.4 Kbps and even 28.8 Kbps modem users. It's easy for professional designers, who often enjoy dedicated T1 Internet connections, to forget this.
>
> Even over the relatively swift speed of an intranet, too many graphics and "bells and whistles" can overload the server and bring the network to its knees.
>
> As an alternative to graphics, consider the special effects that you can achieve with text and tables (including custom table and table cell background colors and textures), optimized animated GIFs, and other thrifty yet cool web effects. And don't forget that the medium is not the message.
>
> Perhaps my bias as an author is showing here, but I believe that glitz and glamour can't make up for a site that doesn't have any useful content, content in the form of textual information. Where it matters, a picture is not worth a thousand words. After all, you're not reading a comic book right now.

Introduction to Web Security

Since all authors (and web administrators) access the pages via the web server, the web is protected from unauthorized tampering. This may seem excessive when you're authoring pages on the same machine running the web server. After all, you already have direct hard disk access to those pages. (On Windows NT, even this assumption may fail if you're not logged in as the computer's administrator, since the administrator can restrict direct access to certain files and folders by taking advantage of the Windows NT file system, NTFS.)

As long as you are sharing the pages using server software, you might as well implement a true HTTP web server. This offers several advantages right off the bat. HTTP is more secure than a typical peer-to-peer connection because it was designed for anonymous connections where the user doesn't have to log in to see the pages. (This is an advantage even when running on NT Server or NT Workstation, which support a high degree of user-based file and folder security.)

A client computer running a web browser can retrieve and display pages from an HTTP web server (and even this can be restricted should some pages be considered "eyes-only"), but there is no way for a client to make changes to the content on the web server or access any resources on the web server other than allowed web pages. The web browser can send *requests* to the web server for storage, such as when submitting form results, but it has no direct access. See Figure 6-1.

Contrast this with the user-based or password-based security of a file server, which for practical reasons always grants at least some level of unrestricted access directly to the hard drive of the file server. (For example, employees in a workgroup need to be able to list, open, save, rename, and even delete spreadsheet files in order to collaborate properly.)

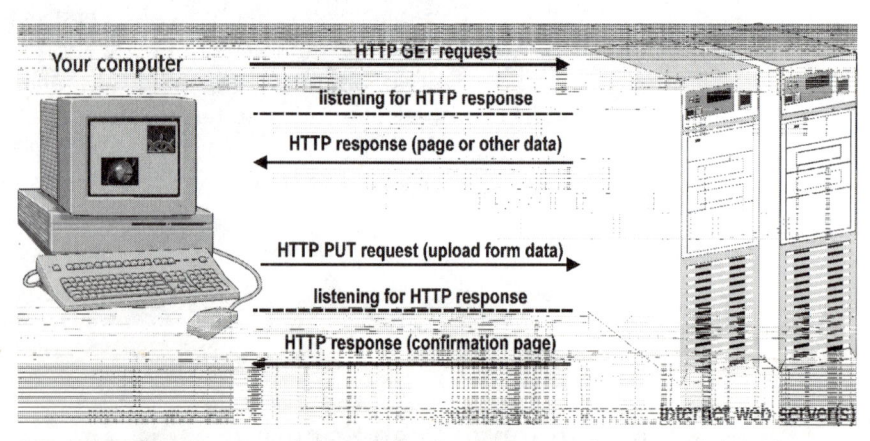

Figure 6-1: This diagram can help you visualize the way a web server and the web browser (or FrontPage itself) communicate with each other.

Since anonymous Internet users have no direct access to network files, a web server is considered safe for worldwide Internet access. While the Internet contains its share of malcontent, overly clever, or perversely ambitious computer experts that view any security measure as a challenge to their hacking skills, true hackers have no wicked intent. The original use of the term referred to clever programmers and harmless types that would never dream of breaking any type of security system.

Of course, no security system is perfect, even with all the limitations of a web server, so many corporations go so far as to entirely isolate any computers attached to a two-way Internet connection via a software or hardware *firewall* product. Only approved traffic, subject to extreme security rules and scrutiny, is allowed through the firewall to users of the network, and many firewalls are designed to prevent any Internet access within the network.

That's why I'll discuss a few security settings relevant for FrontPage in this chapter, although I'd be doing you a disservice if I didn't insist you pursue your own research into this area, armed with the *Windows NT Server Resource Kit* or other advanced Windows NT books. Even Windows 95 web servers need careful attention to security issues, although there aren't many good books available on this subject (you're reading one of them now).

TIP

There is some online documentation for Microsoft Peer Web Services for Windows 95, although it's almost impossible to discover. Double-click on the PWS icon on the taskbar and from the General tab of Personal Web Server Properties, click More Details. (See the Microsoft Peer Web Server section later in this chapter if you need more details on how to find this icon and install PWS.)

For an introduction to networking and network security, I can recommend two books that I cowrote, *The Windows 95 Book* (Ventana) and *Windows NT 4 Workstation Desktop Companion* (Ventana).

Microsoft Web Servers Overview

Microsoft FrontPage was designed to support open industry standards for Internet web servers. Microsoft has never insisted that every Web Presence Provider, ISP, and intranet webmaster dump their perfectly good UNIX or Netscape web server in favor of a Microsoft web server. In fact, the FrontPage developers have gone out of their way to support every popular web server in use today. Since FrontPage relies on features rarely standard on web servers, it has provided the FrontPage server extensions that can be installed to extend the capabilities of almost any web server.

Many readers will have no prior experience with web servers, which is why I've strived to avoid assumptions in this chapter as to your experience level. Since even local web authoring (prior to publishing on a "real" Internet web server) requires a running web server, I chose to focus this chapter on the Microsoft web servers that support FrontPage, especially since the Microsoft Personal Web Server is the only really good choice for Windows 95 and FrontPage.

If you're enamored of another type of server, such as Netscape Commerce Server, by all means continue to use it, for local authoring, intranet authoring/browsing, and for Internet applications. I just can't devote the space in this book to every popular server, and if you're already running a web server, you probably don't need much help with it.

> **TIP**
>
> *For details on deploying the FrontPage server extensions on UNIX, consult http://www.rtr.com/fpsupport. Additional information on FrontPage server extensions is located at http://www.microsoft.com/frontpage/wpp.htm.*
>
> *Also check out the newsgroup microsoft.frontpage.extensions.unix and microsoft.frontpage.extensions.winnt, found on the news server msnews.microsoft.com.*

All in the Family

For FrontPage users authoring pages locally or over an intranet, there are really only two good choices: Microsoft Personal Web Server for Windows 95 and Microsoft Internet Information Server (a.k.a. Peer Web Services) for Windows NT 4.0.

These servers are part of a family of Microsoft servers that support the Internet Server application programming interface (ISAPI). The advantage of ISAPI is that custom web programming (such as programming relied upon by the FrontPage WebBots or generated by expert web developers) can access functions of the server directly instead of going through the HTTP protocol, which is a generic and inefficient technique required for traditional Common Gateway Interface (CGI) web programming.

Of course, you don't have to worry about programming issues with FrontPage, but ISAPI makes webs developed with FrontPage run faster. Further, ISAPI-based applications use server resources, such as memory, more efficiently. ISAPI also supports the Internet Database Connector, discussed in Chapter 8, as a way to store form data in a true relational database or publish live database information on your web pages.

ISAPI is a direct programmer's interface to Microsoft Internet Information Server, which appeared on the scene only a year ago. In its current 3.0 version, IIS is fast, feature rich, and secure. Internet Information Server version 2.0 is included with Windows NT Server 4.0, but you're well advised to install Service Pack 2 for Windows NT 4.0 in order to upgrade to IIS 3.0.

> **TIP**
>
> *ISAPI also supports Common Gateway Interface (CGI) programming. A great way to get started with CGI is to install the Win32 version of the Perl script language from Hip Software. Find their web site at http://www.perl.hip.com/.*

NT Workstation users need not feel left out. Although it is not offered as part of the default installation, I'll show you how to install the Microsoft Peer Web Services for NT Workstation 4.0, which aside from a few missing features and a different name, is otherwise identical to Internet Information Server.

The FrontPage Personal Web Server, a legacy of Microsoft's acquisition of Vermeer Technologies (the inventors of FrontPage, and still at work in Redmond, Washington), was more than capable enough for authoring and testing FrontPage webs and could even be deployed as a small-scale Internet or intranet web server, but it was not compatible with ISAPI, and it overlapped the functionality of IIS and Peer Web Services. Microsoft's own Windows 95 development team had already been at work crafting something even better.

As Microsoft focused its Internet development around Windows NT and IIS, it became obvious that the Windows 95 platform also needed a state-of-the-art, efficient web server, especially for testing and authoring FrontPage webs. Thus was born Microsoft Personal Web Server for Windows 95 (sometimes simply called Microsoft Personal Web Server, although it truly only runs on Windows 95).

Although I'm not privy to any inside information, I can also speculate that a built-in web server is going to be an important element of Microsoft's Active Desktop initiative, a merging of the Windows 95 desktop user interface and Internet Explorer 4.0, due out with the release of the next version of Windows 95 (Windows 97?) in mid-to-late 1997.

Microsoft first released Personal Web Server for Windows 95 in the OEM Service Release 2 of Windows 95 (sometimes called Windows95b), installed on most new computers sold after August 1996. The PWS was updated to version 1.0a to be compatible with standard Windows 95, and is included with FrontPage 97.

Is the original FrontPage Personal Web Server obsolete? In a word, yes. It's not even offered as part of the default installation of FrontPage 97. It remains supported by FrontPage 97 (with certain restrictions mentioned in Chapter 5) only to help ease the transition for users upgrading from FrontPage 1.1, which preferred the FrontPage PWS for local authoring.

The transition from FrontPage 1.1 and the FrontPage Personal Web Server to the Microsoft Personal Web Server is a bit tricky. You can run both web servers at the same time, but the Microsoft Web Server will need to be installed on a port other than port 80. This lets you open your root web with FrontPage Explorer (which opens it from the FrontPage PWS), choose the Publish Web command from the File menu, and choose the Microsoft PWS location to copy the webs to.

I see no reason to duplicate in this chapter Microsoft's excellent and detailed instructions on accomplishing this transition, found at http://www.microsoft.com/frontpage/upgrade/engupgrade.htm.

However, I can describe an alternate and possibly easier technique. First uninstall the FrontPage PWS server extensions (see the relevant section later in this chapter) and uninstall the FrontPage PWS software. Install the Microsoft PWS and its server extensions (also discussed later). You can then use any of the restore techniques discussed at the end of Chapter 5 to transfer your web content from the FrontPage Webs\Content folder to the Webshare\wwwroot folder. After you've verified that the webs imported properly, you can delete the FrontPage Webs folder.

A Fork in the Road

Although both the Windows NT Internet Information Server/Peer Web Services and the Microsoft Personal Web Server for Windows 95 work alike where it matters, they differ drastically in the user interface you use to configure them. What's more, the method for installing and keeping security is also unique between the two platforms. So at this point, this chapter splits off into two largely separate discussions. Continue reading if you're running Windows 95, or skip ahead to "Internet Information Server" if you prefer to author or serve up pages using Windows NT Server or Workstation.

Microsoft Personal Web Server for Windows 95

Using the formal name of the Microsoft Personal Web Server for Windows 95 is becoming onerous, so I'll simply call it Microsoft PWS (or PWS) from now on. I've included this section mainly for reference purposes, since the PWS was most likely installed and configured automatically when you installed FrontPage 97. If not, you've probably been unable to use the FrontPage Explorer at all.

TIP

When browsing an intranet or administering the PWS (which requires web browser access to the Administration pages), you may find that Internet Explorer always attempts to open a Dial-Up Networking connection. The same thing may occur when you use File | Preview in browser or click the (Preview) button on the FrontPage Editor toolbar.

To avoid this frustration, double-click on the Internet icon in Control Panel, and from the Connections tab, turn off Connect to the Internet as Needed. You'll have to manually dial in to the Internet using Dial-Up Networking (via its icon in My Computer) whenever you do want to surf the Net.

Also, if your web browser is configured to use a proxy server on the network for web access, you'll need to disable Connect Through a Proxy Server if you want to be able to preview the pages using the local web server.

Installing Microsoft PWS

Just to cover all bases, let's briefly discuss how to install the PWS. In most cases, you need only insert the FrontPage 97 CD-ROM and let the Windows 95 Autorun feature start the CD-ROM setup program, as shown in Figure 6-2. If this doesn't happen, open the CD-ROM with My Computer and double-click on the Setup icon.

TIP

The floppy disk version of FrontPage 97 does not include the Windows 95 PWS. Download it and other Bonus Pack components from: http://www.microsoft.com/frontpage/documents/bonus.htm.

Figure 6-2: After running Setup from the FrontPage 97 CD-ROM, click the "computer" icon to install Microsoft Personal Web server.

After you reach the main Setup program shown in Figure 6-2, just click the icon for Personal Web Server, and the Personal Web Server is automatically installed, hands-free. After you reboot it, your computer is ready to serve up web pages.

The FrontPage 97 Server Administrator

The FrontPage 97 Setup program both installed the Windows 95 PWS and automatically configured it for use with FrontPage, assuming you chose a typical installation. If you chose a custom installation, you have the PWS installed, but the FrontPage extensions, which let FrontPage communicate with the server, are probably not installed yet. Should you regret this decision, install the PWS and come back to this point in the text.

After installing the PWS, you need to run FrontPage Server Administration and install the server extensions. You can find an icon for the FrontPage Server Administrator program in the same folder that you chose for the installation of FrontPage. (The default folder is in your Program Files folder.) You can browse to this folder with FrontPage Explorer, or better yet, use the right mouse button to drag the Server Administrator icon to your desktop, or you can copy it into the Programs folder of the Start menu. (To open that folder, right-click on the Start button, then double-click on the Programs folder from the Start Menu folder.)

Figure 6-3 shows the user interface for the FrontPage Server Administrator. If the FrontPage extensions are installed, the entry 80 will appear in the Select Port Number list. To verify proper installation, click the Check button.

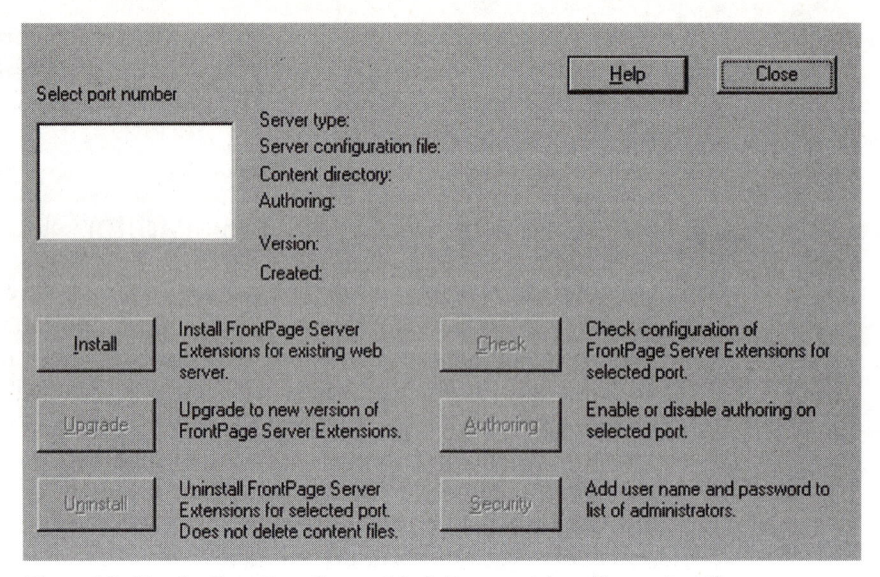

Figure 6-3: Use the FrontPage Server Administrator to install or uninstall server extensions.

To install the server extensions if they don't appear to be installed (as implied by Figure 6-3), click the Install button. From the dialog box that appears next (Figure 6-4), be sure to choose Microsoft Personal Web Server, *not* the FrontPage Personal Web Server.

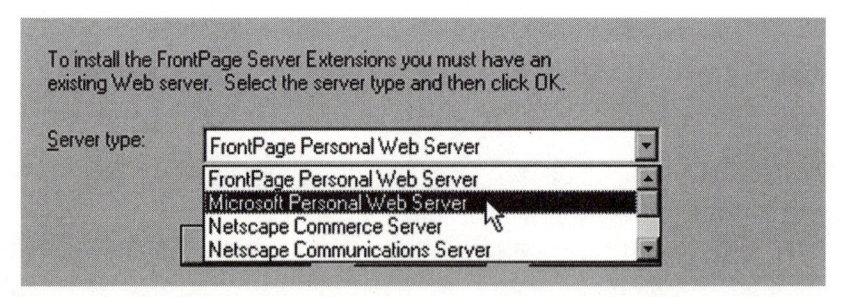

Figure 6-4: For Windows 95, always choose Microsoft Personal Web Server as the type of server for which to install support.

You're then given a rather useless dialog box informing you of the settings that FrontPage will use for the server (Figure 6-5). Write down the information if you like, but otherwise just click OK to close the dialog and move on.

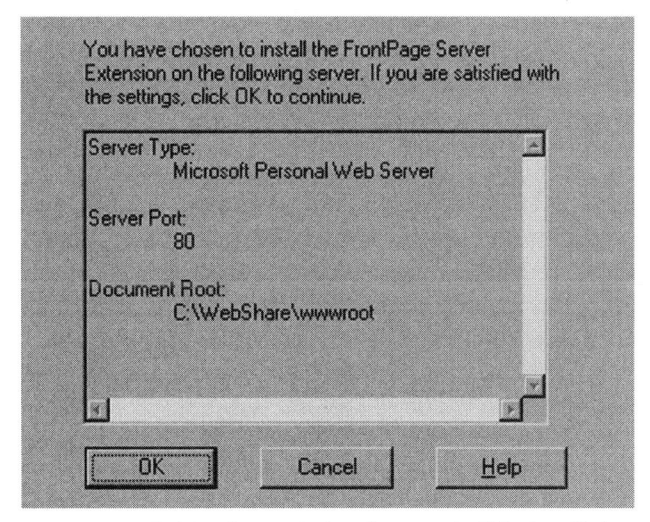

Figure 6-5: All this tells you is that the server will be installed on port 80 and that the web content will be stored on the hard drive at C:\Webshare\wwwroot. Click OK to continue.

As shown in Figure 6-6, you're next asked to provide a name to identify yourself when authoring and administering your webs. This is not important unless you have PWS security enabled (we'll discuss this in "Microsoft PWS Security" later in this chapter), but it's a good idea to choose a name you'll remember, such as the username you use to log in to the computer (if any).

Figure 6-6: Administrator is a good name to use for administering your FrontPage web accounts. Only this user has full control over the web.

> **TIP**
>
> *If you need or add additional administrators, click the Security button in the FrontPage Server Administrator window.*

The FrontPage Server Administrator then warns you that it needs to stop and restart Peer Web Services. (This could possibly disrupt any use of the server if it's being used by the FrontPage Explorer or on an intranet, so I don't recommend running the Server Administrator unless your computer is otherwise idle, just to be safe. Don't worry about this now, you don't yet have any web services running that could be interrupted.) Click Yes to allow it to proceed.

Assuming all goes well, you'll click OK to accept the good news that the installation has completed successfully. Please refer to Figure 6-7 below. You're now ready to use FrontPage Explorer to open and create FrontPage webs and/or test your webs with a web browser.

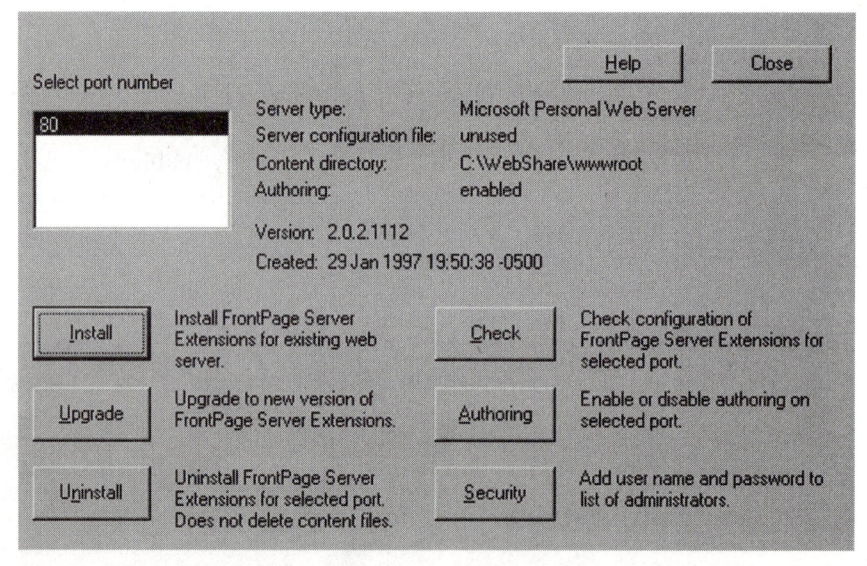

Figure 6-7: Here's how the FrontPage Server Administrator appears when all is well after you've installed the server extensions.

Microsoft PWS Administration

For the purposes of local authoring, you'll find that you never really need to modify the default settings of the Microsoft Personal Web Server. FrontPage Explorer can update most settings automatically. Nevertheless, so that you have all the information you need, I want to show you how to administer your web.

Figure 6-8: Right-click on the PWS icon to open the Administration page or your server's home page or to change the overall properties of the PWS.

The key to controlling the PWS is a tiny icon on the taskbar's notification area (next to the clock). For your reference, it is shown in Figure 6-8. Right-click on this icon to pop open the menu also shown in Figure 6-8, or double-click on it to go straight to the Administration dialog box. Figure 6-9 shows all the tabs (property sheets) of this dialog box.

TIP

You can also access the PWS Properties dialog box by double-clicking the Personal Web Server icon in the Windows 95 Control Panel.

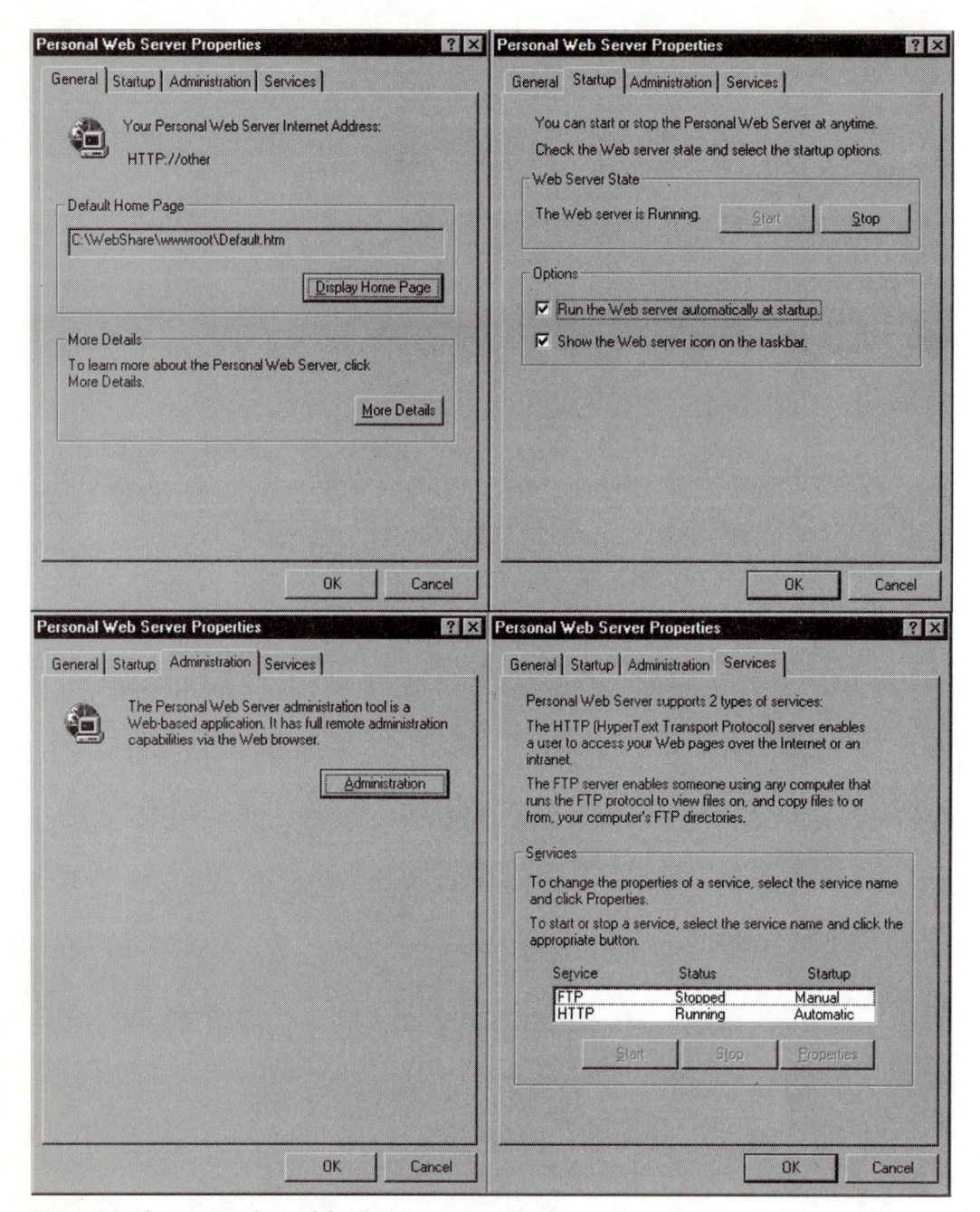

Figure 6-9: The property sheets of the PWS Properties dialog box.

General

The General tab provides basic configuration information for the server, including its Internet address. (Actually its intranet address, since the machine name can not be reached via the public Internet, although you can browse your webs using the current IP address assigned during a Dial-Up Networking session. See Chapter 7.) You can click the Display Home Page button to launch your browser and display the home page shown in the Default Home Page box. Click the More Details button to read the online documentation for Microsoft Peer Web Services.

Startup

Use this tab to manually stop or start the web server. You might need to do this to prevent any intranet users from accessing the server when you take it down to back up or restore files to it. It also slows your computer to run the web server, so you might not want to run the web server except when authoring with FrontPage. If this is the case, you may also want to use this tab to turn off the Run the Web Server Automatically at Startup check box. There's no good reason to turn off the Show the Web Server Icon on the Taskbar check box unless you want to try to hide the fact that your computer is running PWS, for security reasons, or if your taskbar gets too crowded. If you do get rid of the tiny icon, you can access the administration functions from the PWS icon in Control Panel.

Administration

There is only one function on this page. Click the Administration button to launch the web-based PWS Administration page. You can get the same results by right-clicking on the PWS icon on the taskbar and choosing Administer.

Services

You'll use the Startup tab to stop and start the web server, but you can also stop or start the HTTP service, which amounts to the same thing, from the Services page. In addition, you can choose whether to allow (start) the FTP service. The File Transfer Protocol service allows others on your intranet (or on the Internet if you tell others your IP address while online) to view and download files from the \Webshare\ftproot folder or upload files to this folder or another folder.

You can also view and change some of the properties of the FTP and HTTP services by clicking on one of them in the list in the Services area and then clicking the Properties button. As shown in Figure 6-10, on the FTP and HTTP Properties pages, you can only set some pretty basic properties (such as the hard drive directories to serve from). Moreover, you really shouldn't ever need to change these, unless you want to change whether or not a service is started automatically when Windows 95 starts.

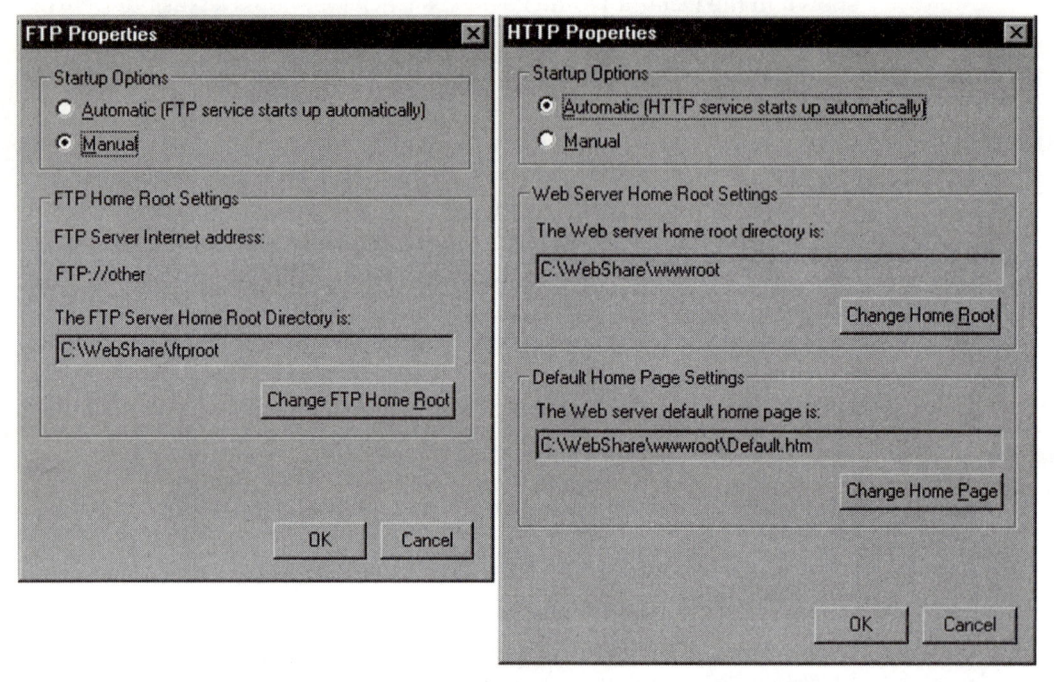

Figure 6-10: Access the properties for the FTP and HTTP services of the Microsoft Personal Web Server from the Services page of Personal Web Server Properties (refer back to Figure 6-9).

Microsoft Personal Web Server Administration

The PWS Properties dialog box doesn't give you any real access to the settings for the PWS. Instead, you must launch the PWS Administration page, which is a seemingly ordinary web page. You can open the administration page by right-clicking on the PWS taskbar icon and choosing Administer, or you can choose the Administration button from the PWS Properties dialog box.

> **TIP**
>
> *One advantage of using a web page for administration: You can administer your web from another computer via an Internet or intranet connection. If you have PWS local security enabled, only the user granted administrative access to the computer is permitted to administer your web from another computer.*
>
> *Permitting remote administration is controlled via the Passwords icon in Control Panel (using the Remote Administrator tab). You can add users to the Remote Administrators list. They must either be validated by a Windows NT Server domain or be a member of the users listed in the local security list.*
>
> *See "Microsoft Personal Web Server Security" later in this chapter for more on local security versus domain security.*
>
> *Assuming you are logged in as an administrator, you can browse and control the Administration page from another computer. Use the address http://computer/htmla/htmla.htm, where* computer *is the machine name or IP address of the computer running the Microsoft PWS that you want to control. You can not view or change local security settings from another computer, however.*

The Microsoft PWS Administration page for your computer will resemble Figure 6-11. Most of the time, you'll go straight to WWW Administration. I'll explain the other two main links in "Microsoft Personal Web Server Security" later in this chapter.

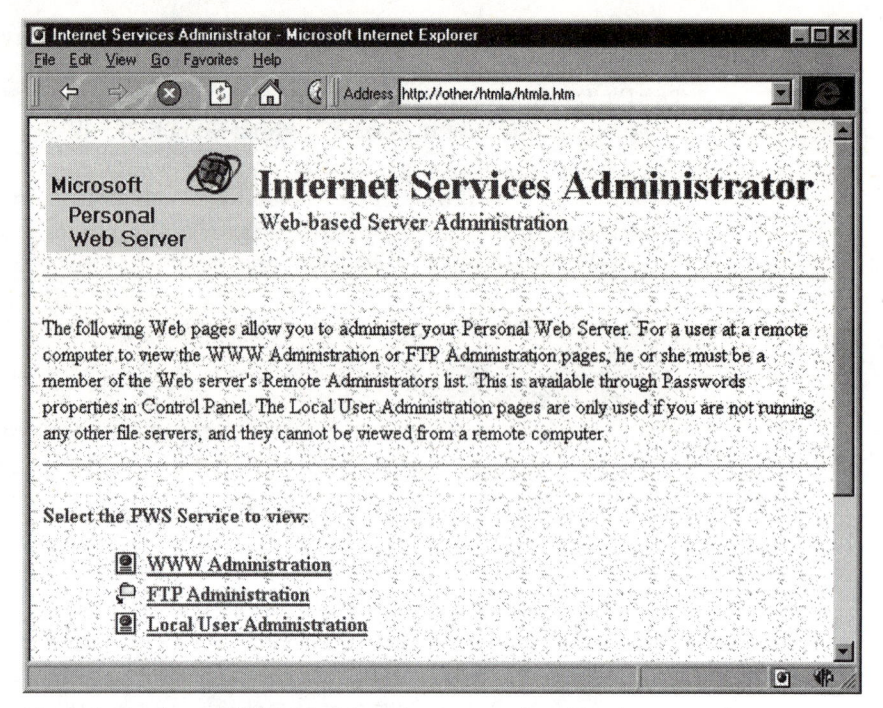

Figure 6-11: Choose WWW Administration to control settings for your web server.

Service

Once you've clicked WWW Administration, you'll be taken to the page shown in Figure 6-12. This web page is actually the first of three separate pages that use the tabbed dialog box approach to switch between them. In other words, click the words Service, Directories, or Logging to switch from page to page of the WWW Administration settings. Since these "dialog boxes" are really somewhat hokey HTML pages, it may not be obvious to you which page you're on; the current page's tab heading is in boldface.

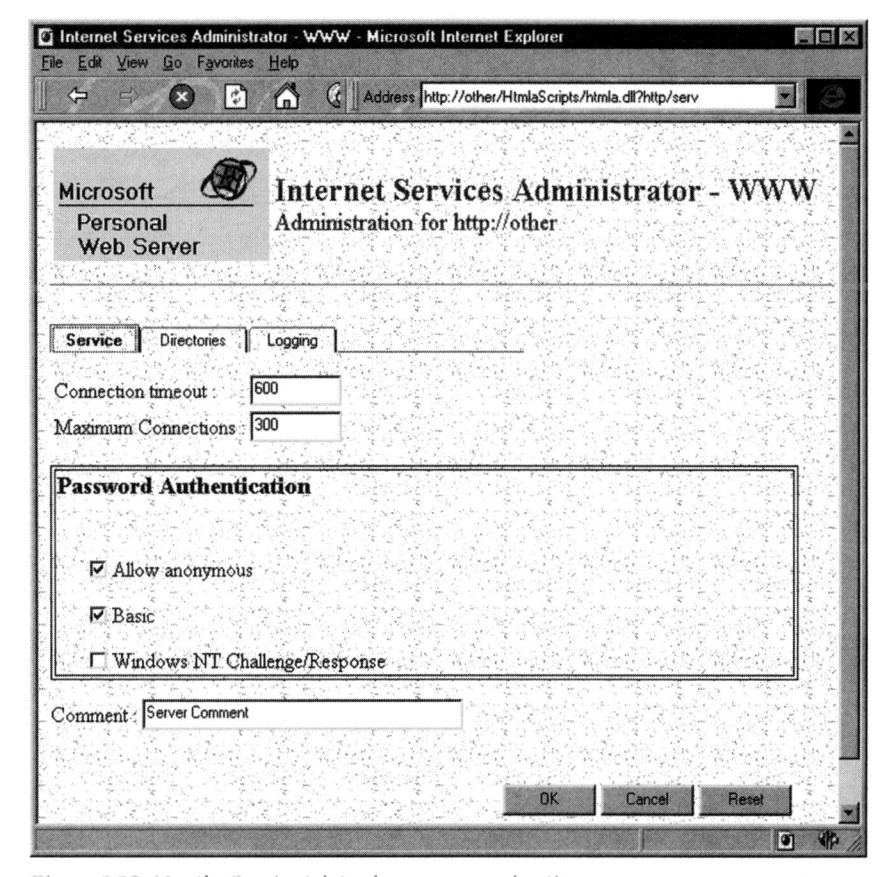

Figure 6-12: Use the Service tab to choose password options.

Use the Connection Timeout and Maximum Connections values to adjust how much of your computer's time will be used up by web surfers. The Maximum Connections value of 300 is just that; about how many connections PWS can handle and still let you use your computer. It's much more reasonable to reduce this value to less than 100 for a small workgroup. (Keep in mind that for even one visitor, every object on a web page may require a simultaneous connection, at least until the page has finished loading.)

If your server gets really busy, you can decrease the Connection Timeout so that new users, idle users, or users with slow connections get disconnected so that your web server can adequately service existing connections. (This is why a long download from a popular site can be canceled for seemingly no good reason.)

I'm going to discuss the other options on the Service tab in the next section in this chapter, "Microsoft Personal Web Server Security." I'll continue the discussion now with the Directories tab.

Directories

The Directories page is shown in Figure 6-13. Since the Directories list can become quite lengthy if you've created some FrontPage webs, I've altered the figure to cut out some of the entries so you can see both the top and the bottom of this page without wasting too much space in this book.

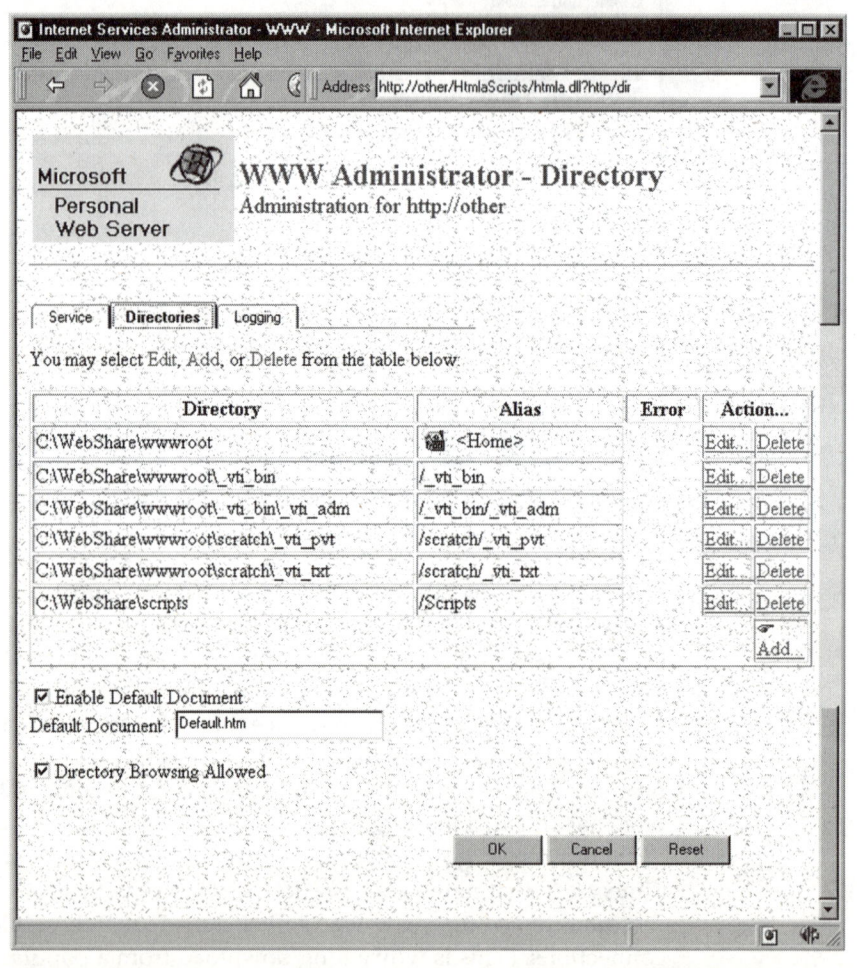

Figure 6-13: Use the Directories page to add, delete, or edit directory permissions and to set the default page and browsing options for the server.

Let me again emphasize that you really don't need to change any of these settings; this discussion is primarily for reference purposes. Let's say you want to change one of the directories to allow scripts to execute. (This type of server script is used for the Internet Database Connector, which I discuss in Chapter 8.) Click on the Edit button next to the /Scripts entry, and you get another web page, shown in Figure 6-14.

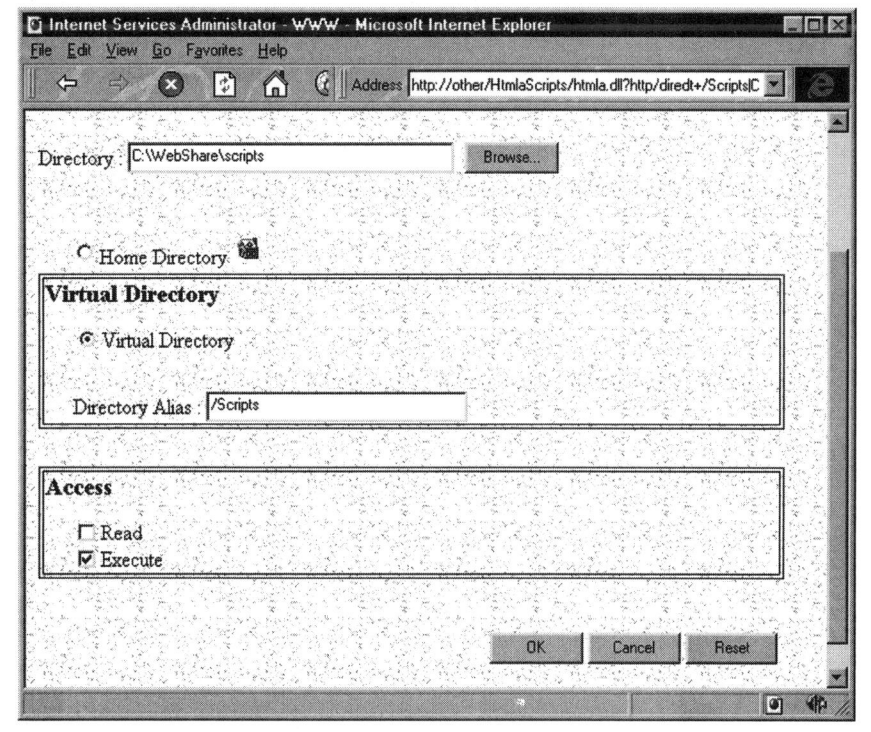

Figure 6-14: Use this page to edit the permissions for a directory or virtual directory. You use the same page when adding a directory.

If you've used Internet Information Server on Windows NT, you've already realized how much this works like the IIS WWW Service properties, and the same type of settings apply. The Directory box is used to name a new directory entry or change the path of a directory entry you wish to modify. Your server should have only one home directory, which is set by clicking the Home Directory radio button.

Perhaps you'd like the directory to be treated as a virtual directory. This lets you reference the web directory as if it were a subdirectory of C:\Webshare\wwwroot (or whatever home directory you've set up), even if the actual directory is on another hard drive or on a network file server.

In Figure 6-14, the actual location of the Scripts directory is C:\Webshare\scripts, which is not normally visible to a web browser; a web browser can only "see" pages in C:\Webshare\wwwroot (or in its subdirectories). When you tell the server to map a virtual directory, /Scripts, a web browser can refer to this page as http://*computer*/Scripts, as if the scripts directory were found at C:\Webshare\wwwroot\scripts.

Why would you do something so wacky? For security reasons. On Figure 6-13, you'll notice a check box labeled Directory Browsing Allowed, which is enabled by default. This means that you or any visitor to your web can get a directory listing of your web site just by browsing any of its folders. The visitor can see inside every web and find the name of web pages that you might rather keep secret, such as the name of a Results page of a Submit Results WebBot. This is why you should always turn off the Directory Browsing Allowed check box.

If Directory Browsing was left enabled, users would be able to see the names of the script files in the Scripts directory even though they would not be able to open or view the scripts themselves, thanks to the Access section at the bottom of Figure 6-14. By enabling the Execute check box and disabling the Read check box, the client's (user's) browser can run server scripts, but can't open the scripts to read them. This not only protects any trade secrets found in your clever scripts, but makes it harder for a determined hacker (oh no, not him again) to trick your server into executing modified scripts. In general, only enable read access for general web pages, and only enable execute access for script directories.

TIP

Microsoft Active Server Pages require both read and execute access to any directories containing .ASP files. Just so you know.

Logging

The Logging options, shown in Figure 6-15, can also be safely left as is, unless you're running low on disk space. As long as you've enabled the Enable Logging check box, the server keeps a record of all transactions (accesses) made, a fascinating way to keep track of site activity. Actually, I'm being sarcastic; the log entries are boring and nonsensical, although you can at least see the IP addresses of every computer that has tried to access your pages.

TIP

*To trace an IP address back to its source, open an MS-DOS prompt and type **tracert** followed by an IP address or domain name. TraceRoute finds the destination address and reports on every "hop" (handoff from server to server) made along the way. The last domain shown is the source of the IP address. TraceRoute is a powerful tool to detect unauthorized attempts to access a site or to track down the true source of junk e-mail where the recipient tries to use a fake e-mail address but fails to spoof the IP address in the e-mail header. To see all the options you can use with TraceRoute, type **tracert** by itself at the command prompt.*

Since the log file grows each time a page is visited, it can get too large to make sense of, so PWS starts a new log once a month by default, using a name like in9702.log for February 1997. The previous logs are not deleted, so if disk space is at a premium, don't choose to log any more frequently. On the other hand, if the server is very busy, you might need to log more frequently just to keep the log files from growing impractically large. Another technique to keep the log files from getting too large is to use the When the File Size Reaches radio button and fill in the MB box with how large the log can get (in megabytes) before it is closed and a new log is created.

It's probably a good idea to change the default logging directory so that you don't clutter up your Windows directory. Create a subfolder matching the name you choose somewhere else on your hard disk. Feel free to delete obsolete logs; they aren't used by PWS once closed out.

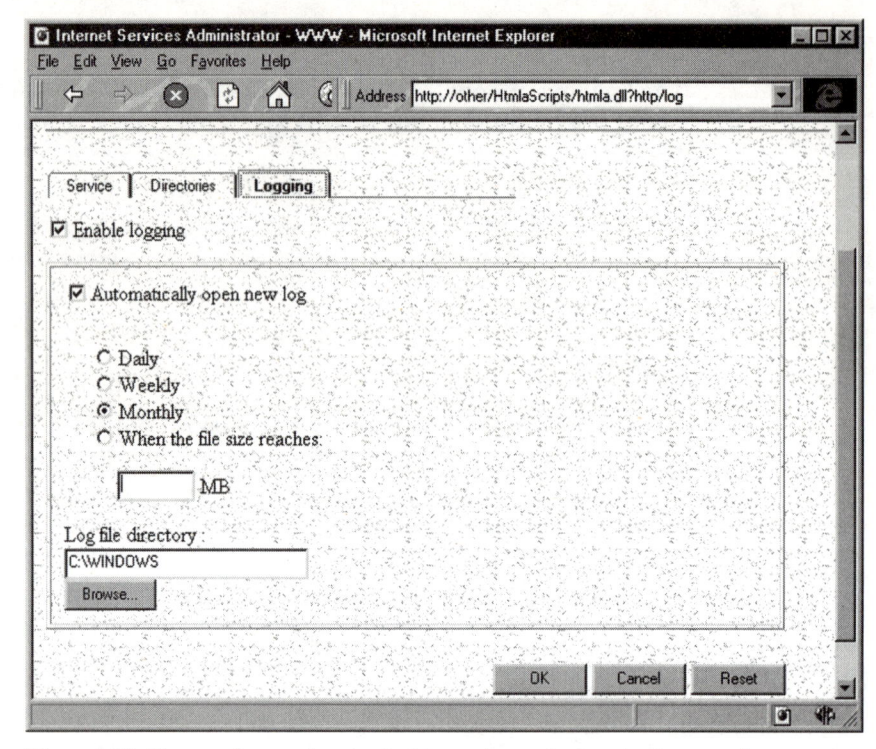

Figure 6-15: You can choose when to start a new log and where to store new logs.

Changes Ignored!

Whenever you make a change on any of the administration pages, be sure to click OK before leaving the browser, clicking on link, or using the back button, or your changes will be ignored. If you do make a change that you don't like, you can use the Reset button to undo any changes you've made since the last time you clicked OK on that page.

Microsoft Personal Web Server Security

Consider the following scenario: You're running FrontPage 97 on your own PC, and you're not part of a network. If that's the case, you really don't need to worry at all about server security. The server isn't being used to let others browse your webs; you're only using it to author the webs with FrontPage.

Even if you're not on a LAN, you still need to be somewhat concerned about security if your computer uses Dial-Up Networking to connect to the Internet (the only way with Windows 95). This is because whenever you are online with the Internet, your web server is also accessible to anyone on the Internet. This is both good and potentially bad. If you want to be extra cautious, stop the WWW (or HTTP) service whenever you dial in to the Internet.

If you want to publish your pages on the Internet, all you need to give to others is your current IP address. Click Start | Run, and enter the command **WINIPCG** to find out the current IP address of the Dial-Up Adapter. You can give out this IP address to friends and colleagues who want to try logging in to your web server. For example, the address http://206.68.137.16 opens the Microsoft home page, but it could just as easily open your home page if your IP address was substituted. (Every active user on the Internet has his or her own IP address, but it's usually a different IP address each time a new connection is established.)

Of course, this just isn't a very practical way to operate a web site, as I emphasize in Chapter 5 and Chapter 7. More practically, you may choose to deploy Microsoft PWS as a small-scale intranet web server. See Chapter 7 to find out how to add your computer's permanent IP address (configured for the network card, also detailed in Chapter 7) to the list of hosts on every other computer on your network. (You really should read Chapter 7 to learn how to do this, since you'll also need to set up the TCP/IP protocol on your LAN.)

Security Paranoia

The Internet seems to have made so many of us paranoid about security. Consider credit card transactions. There's been a lot of press about the "danger" of ordering products over the Internet unless the server has a secure sockets layer (SSL) connection or employs some other form of secret-code encryption to prevent interception of your credit card number.

What a bunch of hogwash. You run a greater risk by giving out your credit card to some anonymous order-taker at a mail-order firm, allowing a waiter to walk off with your card to process a meal transaction, or failing to destroy the carbons or customer receipts you accumulate in your wallet. The odds are slim to none that your credit card information, as it *flashes* to the site where it's stored, will be intercepted by top-notch hackers with expensive TCP/IP protocol analyzers. There is too much traffic on the Internet for any hacker to monitor all of it.

Besides, you know very well that legally you are only liable for as much as $50 of a fraudulent credit card transaction, and that's assuming you don't promptly report suspicious activity or fail to dispute a charge you don't recognize.

No, it's the banks and merchants that have to worry about credit card fraud, and they too are always at greater risk from conventional and mundane credit card rip-off schemes. Exaggerated concerns over Internet security (and related issues of no real concern, such as the worry that a web site can violate your privacy by reading your browser cookies) only serve to slow progress.

Since it's no trivial matter for a hacker to identify your IP address out of billions of possible addresses, you're really not exposing anything to the Internet by going online, security or no security, web server or no web server. Unless you work for a Fortune 1000 corporation and operate a confidential intranet using the Microsoft Personal Web Server for Windows 95 don't flatter yourself by thinking that hackers are even interested in breaching your computer's security.

Security Precautions

Okay, so perhaps I'm making too much light of this issue. There are always some valid security concerns for any nontrivial web site.

On an intranet, there are some good reasons to be concerned about access levels to information, which is related to security. You might have a database query for the human resources department to let them view employee records; you wouldn't want it to fall into the wrong hands. This means that you need to be able to limit access to some webs based on a valid username and password.

You also need a way to limit authoring and web administration to protect your web content from the mistakes of naïve users or meddlers. (You know the type—the self-styled computer expert who has learned everything about computers in the last year, and who prefers to waste time messing around with Control Panel and RegEdit instead of playing Solitaire.)

The techniques for protecting and restricting your webs by choosing Tools | Permissions from FrontPage Explorer were discussed in Chapter 5. This only works, however, if the web server validates users.

It would take too much space in this book to go into the details of Windows 95 networking methods, so the following discussion assumes that you are familiar with them. To view or change the settings for Windows 95 networking, double-click the Network icon in Control Panel.

Valid Users & Groups

Microsoft Internet Explorer 2.0 and higher allows you to restrict access to sites based on the NTLM security model. Basically, this means that the same security used to restrict access to a Windows NT server is used to authorize web users. Most web access is permitted anonymously, with no login prompt. If your site is 100 percent confidential, you might not want to allow any anonymous users. Refer back to Figure 6-12. By default, the Allow Anonymous check box is turned on so that it is possible for any user to access your web. This means no usernames and passwords are transmitted unless you set a particular directory as restricted.

To set a directory as restricted, you need to use FrontPage Explorer. By default, subwebs inherit their security settings from the root web. If you want to enforce passwords for the entire site, open the root web. Otherwise, open a subweb. Choose Tools | Permissions. For a subweb, you can enable the check box for Use Unique Permissions for This Web on the Settings tab.

Figure 6-16 shows the Permissions dialog box for the Groups tab. Here you can choose which user groups can access the web. You can use the Users tab instead to restrict access to a particular set of users, although it's more efficient just to add those users to a group and give the group access rights. Notice that the group Everyone is given Browse access. This is what makes the web unrestricted for anonymous users. By removing the Everyone group, only users and groups explicitly added to the list and given Browse access can open pages on a subweb. (Further, you can restrict which users or groups of users can author and/or administer a web.)

To change the access rights of a user or group you've added to the list, double-click on a user. To add a new user to the list, click the Add button.

> **TIP**
>
> *You can also set the permissions for a folder by browsing the hard drive with Windows Explorer. Locate the folder containing the web you want to restrict, and right-click on it to get the properties. From the Security tab, you can add or remove users and groups and set the access level for each. This technique is specific to Microsoft PWS for Windows 95 and is not recommended for FrontPage webs.*

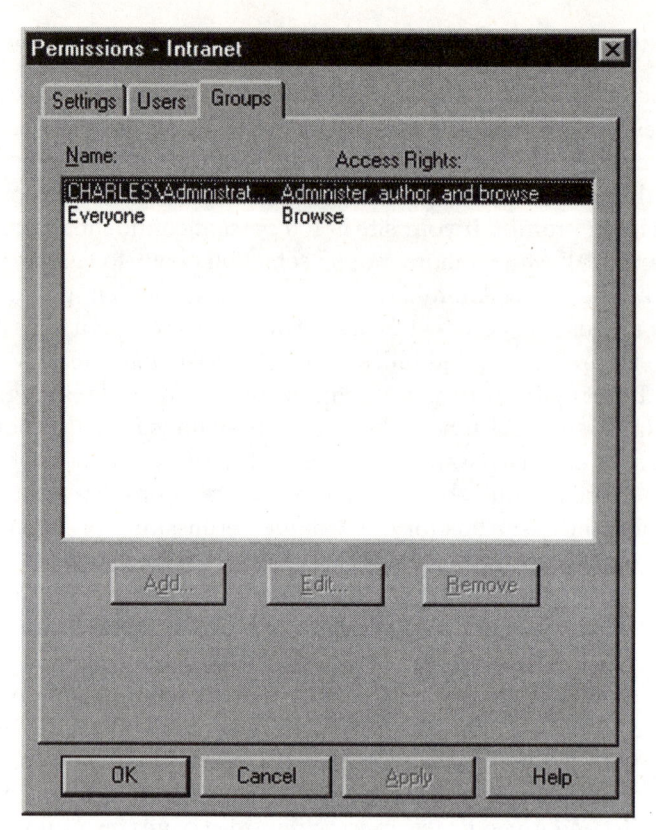

Figure 6-16: Remove the Everyone group if you want to prevent anonymous access, but for the elite users who are permitted access, add one or more users or groups with Browse access.

When you click the Add button, the Add Group or Add User button appears. Add Groups is shown in Figure 6-17. You can add any valid user/group from a Windows NT domain, or from the list of local users/groups for that computer, by clicking on a name and then clicking the Add button. You then choose the access level at the bottom of the dialog.

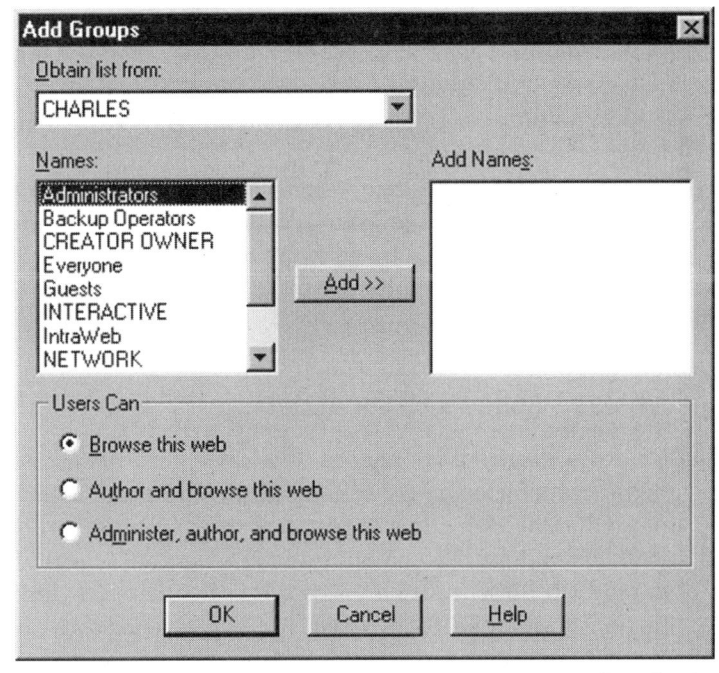

Figure 6-17: Here's where you add groups to the list of users allowed to browse the web.

Keep in mind that even if you have Everyone on the list of users allowed to browse, this right can be revoked by turning off the Allow Anonymous check box shown in Figure 6-12.

Password Security

Should you choose to restrict a subweb (or the entire web), you have another concern. When a visitor or legitimate client of the protected web tries to open a page on that web, Internet Explorer pops up a dialog box requesting a login name and password. How is the name and password transmitted to the server for verification?

If you use Basic security (see Figure 6-12), the name and password are sent with the unencrypted Base64 encoding system commonly used to send binary information, such as electronic mail attachments, as plain text files made up of special symbols. If a hacker has "wiretapped" into your network or somehow tapped into the TCP/IP packet stream on the Internet, *in principle* the passwords and usernames could be captured and later used to break into your system or gain unauthorized access to your web.

The only way to avoid this is to turn off the Basic check box and turn on the Windows NT Challenge/Response check box. Unfortunately, this only works if the list of users is obtained and kept on a Windows NT Server computer running as a domain server. NT Challenge/Response does not work with local security.

Note: Keep in mind that Basic security is the standard method employed by web servers to grant access to restricted resources and is the only method supported by all web browsers. Should you choose to keep Basic authentication in place, avoid assigning usernames or passwords that are already in use on your network.

What Is Windows 95 Local Security?

Windows 95 normally only has two ways to restrict access to a folder made accessible on a network. Windows 95 supports peer-to-peer sharing so that the files or printers on one computer can be accessed by another Windows 95 (or Windows NT) user that is part of the same workgroup. To set restrictions on who can access the directory, Windows 95 can use either share-level security or user-level security.

Most Windows 95 peer networks use share-level security so that a password is required to access a particular shared directory (or *share*) for reading, writing, or reading and writing. The same password is always used for a particular share no matter who is trying to access the shared resource. This is not a big problem on a small trusted workgroup, but should the password leak out, others in the organization or outside the organization (if the computer is connected to the Internet, for example) could in theory use the common password to have free rein over the shared folders.

Another way to restrict access is to enable user-level security so that the Windows 95 administrator can allow only certain users or groups of users to access files and folders. This only works if the network is part of a Windows NT Server domain, which maintains a list of users.

To make web sharing more secure, Microsoft added another facet to Windows 95 security. As long as File and Printer Sharing is not enabled on a Windows 95 computer, the PWS can maintain its own list of valid groups and users, mimicking the abilities of a Windows NT computer. (This works like the workgroup mode of NT Workstation.)

The reason you have to disable the File and Printer Sharing service in order to use local security is that PWS can't override the security model of peer-to-peer File and Printer sharing. If the computer running the web server must also share some folders on a network, then you just can't set any security restrictions for webs running on the computer. You can still use the computer as a casual web server, but there will be no restrictions.

> **TIP**
>
> *Another reason to disable File and Printer Sharing is that, in principle, your peer-to-peer network extends its reach across the world if File and Printer Sharing is bound to the TCP/IP protocol used for Dial-Up Networking. While you are connected to the Internet, your IP address is the gateway for other users who might like to log in to your computer. In fact, this can be advantageous for you as long as you are confident in your security method. Share-level security is pretty easy to crack, so user-level security is preferred. To learn more about sharing files over the Internet without a web server, consult the* Windows 95 Power Toolkit *(Ventana) by Evangelos Petroutsos and Richard Mansfield.*
>
> *Microsoft Internet Explorer will detect this configuration and offer to disable File and Printer sharing on the Internet connection. However, this only prevents File and Printer Sharing over the Dial-Up Adapter's TCP/IP connection. If you want to use local security (see "Local Security and Adding Local Users" later in this chapter), you'll have to remove the File and Printer Sharing service altogether.*

The only way to have the best of both worlds, peer file sharing with File and Printer Sharing, and restrict access to the web is if the network is part of a Windows NT Server domain. In that case, the properties for File and Printer Sharing must be set to user-level security, as shown in Figure 6-18, and a valid NT domain name must be included. (This box is blank if File and Printer Sharing is disabled since the user list is obtained locally from the PWS.)

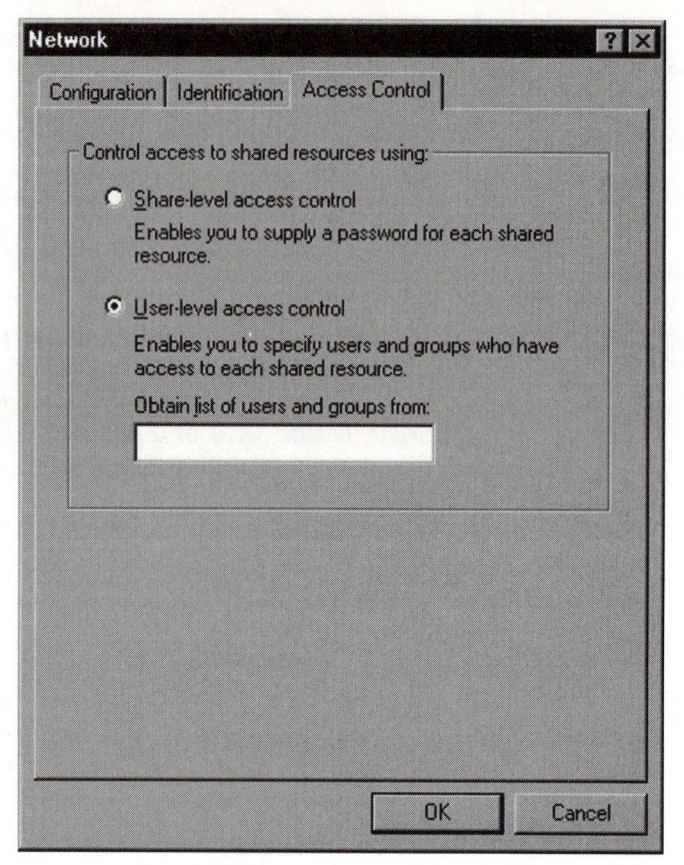

Figure 6-18: User-level security is the only choice if you want to restrict access to your webs. If you are using File and Printer sharing, this list must be obtained from a Windows NT domain. If you want to use local security, you must remove File and Printer Sharing.

Enabling Local Security & Adding Local Users

If you were using File and Printer Sharing before you installed the personal web server, then local security was not enabled. Otherwise, it was added automatically to your network properties as part of the Personal Web Server. If you want to start using local security (perhaps your company can't justify deploying NT Server), you'll have to remove File and Printer Sharing from the Network Properties dialog box, accessed via the Network icon in Control Panel.

You also need to change a property for Peer Web Services. From the Configuration tab of Network Properties, double-click on the Personal Web Services entry, and set Use Local Security to TRUE.

Once you've done this (and restarted the computer), you can choose Local User Administration from the WWW Administration page to add or maintain users and groups for your local computer (see Figure 6-19). The user list and passwords are verified by PWS, but anyone whose name is on the list, and who has a matching password, can be granted access to a restricted web as long as your server is set for Basic security (see Figure 6-12).

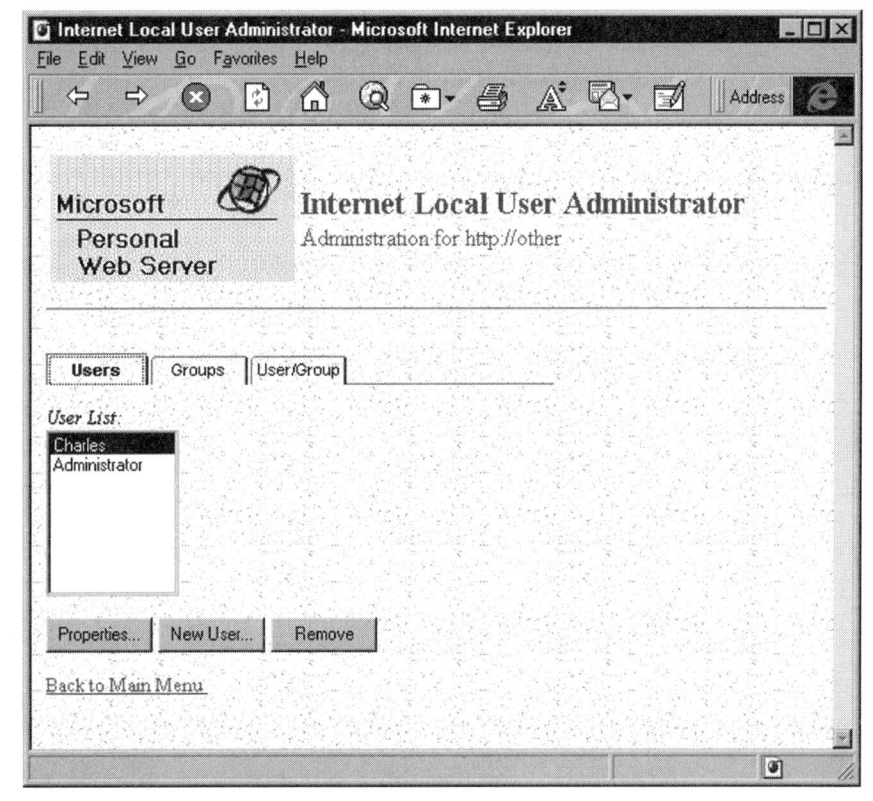

Figure 6-19: Click Properties to change a password, New User (or New Group) to add a group, or Remove to delete a user or group.

Enabling & Maintaining the FTP Server

For security reasons, the FTP server is disabled by default because it's the only way that anonymous users can access part of your hard drive directly. (It's also not necessary for FrontPage, so you might not want to bother with the FTP server in the first place.)

Don't worry, though; anonymous users can only read from the FTP directory (\Webshare\ftproot by default), and even if you enable write access, you can limit it to a particular folder and to authorized users. What's more, only Internet users that know your current IP address (which is likely to be unique every time you dial in to the Internet) can find the FTP server on your computer. For utmost security (short of never enabling the FTP service), you can restrict all access to only authorized users.

Once you've started the FTP service, you can use the FTP Administration icon from the web-based administration page to set access restrictions (see Figure 6-20).

Service

The Service tab of the FTP Administration page lets you choose a connection timeout value and a maximum connections limit. File transfers typically tend to use up much more of your available network/Internet bandwidth, and for a longer period of time, than does web browsing, so you'll want to severely limit how many users can connect simultaneously. By reducing the timeout value, you can drop idle users like a hot potato. (It's not uncommon for FTP clients to leave the connection open long after a file transfer has been completed.)

By enabling Allow Anonymous Connections, you can let any Internet guest download files from the FTP directory. Since you can choose which files you place in \Webshare\ftproot, you have full control over which files are available.

Turn on the Allow Only Anonymous Connections check box if you want to prevent usernames and passwords from being transmitted over the network, since Basic authentication is the only way to log in to a secured FTP server. Naturally, this means that you can't restrict access based on usernames.

The Comment text box is for your record keeping, in case you want to remind yourself why you've made a change; it's not shown to the users.

Messages

On the other hand, you can display a message to users prior to logon, as soon as their FTP client has attempted access. You can explain the purpose of your server, provide login instructions, and issue legal warnings if your system is not intended as a public server (see Figure 6-21). Failure to issue legal warnings may be construed as an open invitation to gain access to the FTP files. You can also enter a custom message to display when the user closes the FTP connection (Exit Message), or an error message to display when the FTP server is full (Maximum Connections Message). Be sure to click OK to make the change "stick."

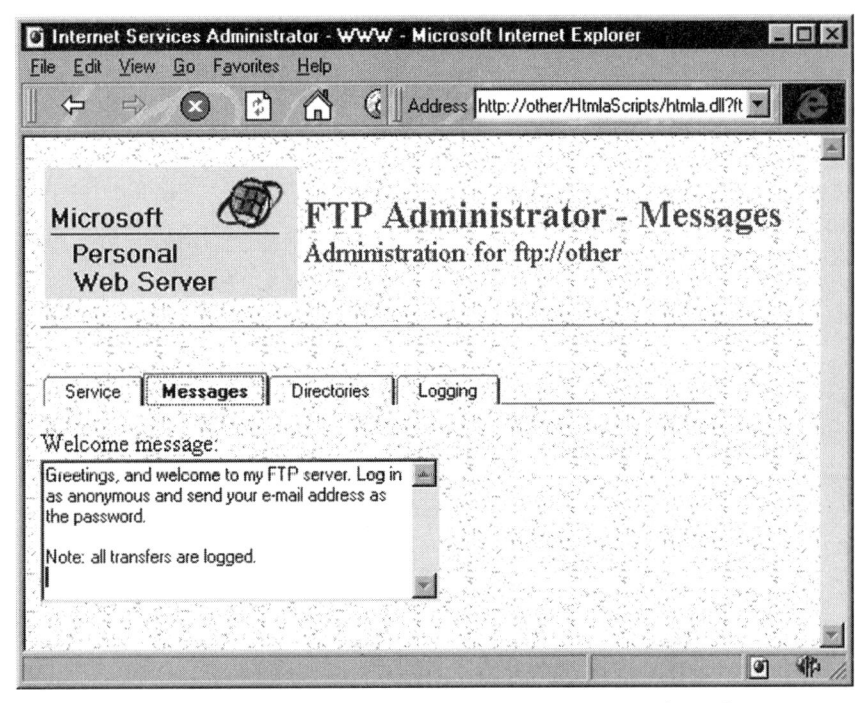

Figure 6-21: Enter a welcome message to greet users to your site. Or leave the entry blank if you'd rather.

Directories

You use the Directories tab (Figure 6-22) to choose which directories to make available for FTP users. By default, the \Webshare\ftproot folder is set as the home directory. When an FTP client requests a directory listing, the entries in the ftproot folder are the only ones shown—the user can not "back up" to previous directories and can not access any other folders on your hard drive.

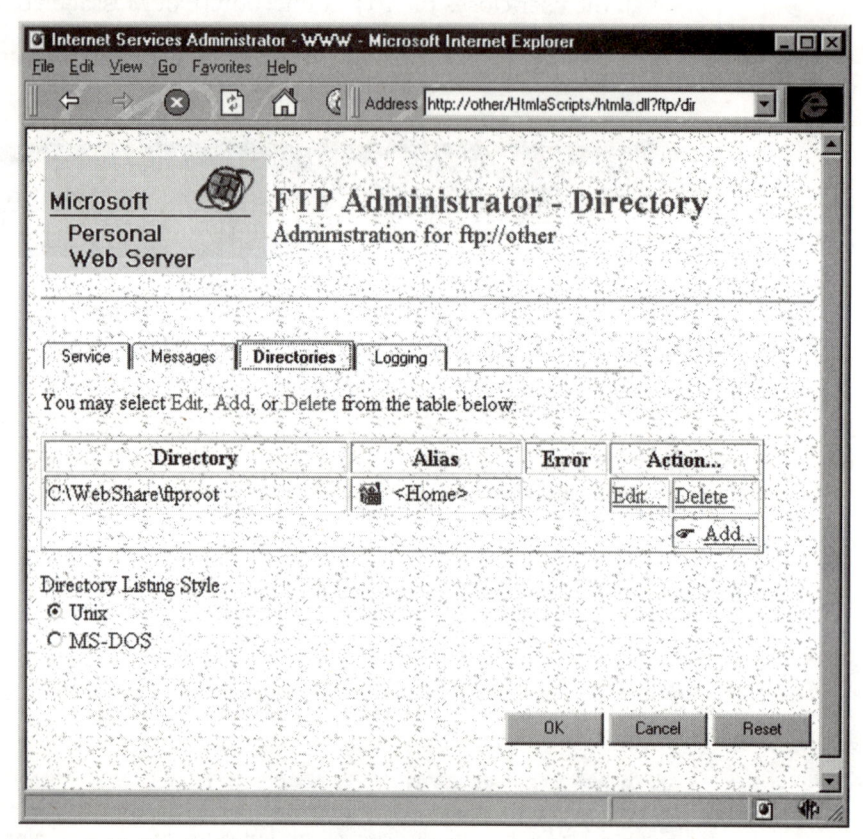

Figure 6-22: Use the Directories tab to modify basic FTP directory permissions.

Always use the UNIX directory listing style; it's required for the FTP client built into most web browsers.

You can click the Edit button next to any directory on the list to change its rights. The page shown in Figure 6-23 will appear. This is the same page you'll see when you add a directory. Specify a hard drive folder in the Directory box, and unless you want it to be mapped as the root of the FTP server, enter an alias and turn on the Virtual Directory option. (Don't choose the Home Directory option unless you are changing the location of the FTP root directory.) You don't have to use a subfolder of \Webshare\ftproot when adding a directory or virtual directory, but if you do, it will be visible when the root directory is listed.

TIP

> *Users can view the files on your server and click on them to download them by typing something like ftp://198.105.232.1 in the Address or Location box of the web browser. (This is the IP of ftp.microsoft.com, but you can substitute your IP address.) This always logs the user in with anonymous credentials. To log in with a username and password, use the format: ftp://username:password@server, as in ftp://anonymous:ceemeister@ftp.microsoft.com. This syntax prevents sending a true e-mail address as the password, however.*

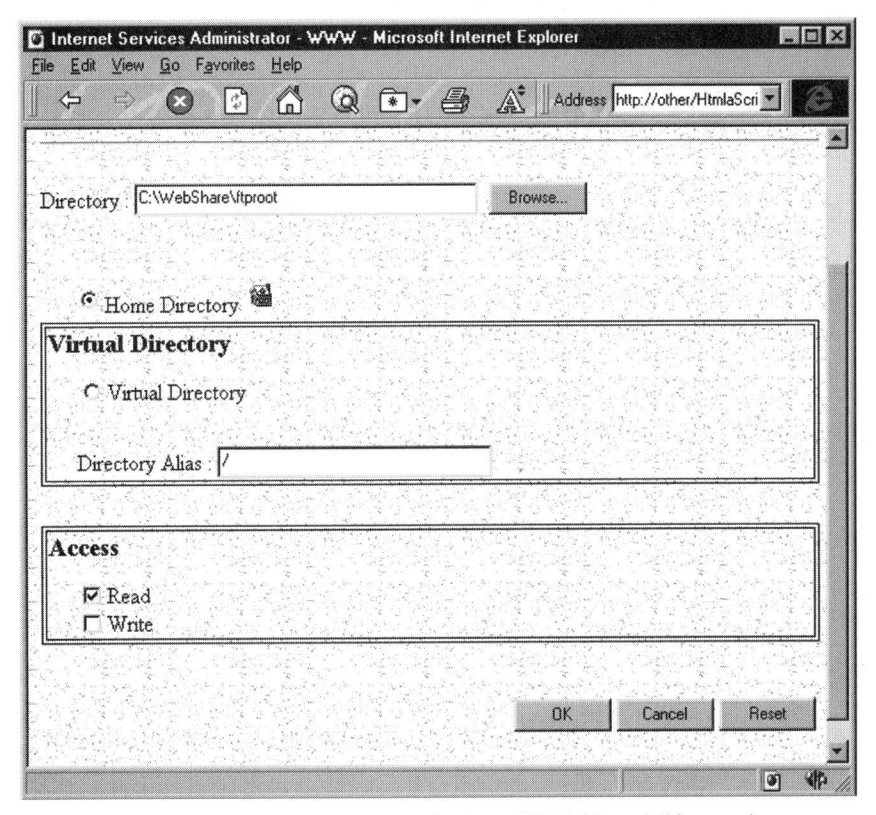

Figure 6-23: Here's where you add, edit, and remove FTP folders visible to end users.

By choosing either Read, Write, or both check boxes, you can decide whether the user can view and download files and/or send files. It's common to list public files in the root of the server or in a folder named Public and also to create a virtual directory alias called Incoming to point to a folder that will receive files sent by FTP clients.

A download directory should be set to Read Only (to prohibit tampering or unwanted uploads), and an upload directory should be set to Write Only. These settings ensure that the client won't be able to list or retrieve material sent by other users to the upload directory. (This may seem paranoid, but it protects you from liability should a user upload illegal or pornographic material to you. You can review submissions before moving them to the Public or Download folder should you decide to share the file with others. Naturally, also watch out for copyright restrictions on material you make available for download.)

Logging

The logging page works the same as the one you use for the WWW service, although the name of the log file is unique. See Figure 6-15.

MS PWS Intranet FTP Applications

Microsoft Office 97 allows users to save documents as HTML directly to an FTP server. The administrator can then move the content to the web server. However, you can also permit the employees to upload their pages directly to a live web server.

First, establish a subweb or a subfolder of a web that can be modified by staff members. You could have a separate one for each department, team, or project group. This web or subfolder is managed entirely by the staff, and it's their own fault if someone screws it up by deleting or overwriting pages (such as the default "home" page).

Second, you need to create a virtual FTP directory that points to the *web server* directory holding the intranet content. Use the Directory tab of the FTP Administration page to create a virtual directory and permit both read and write access. In the next section, "Restricting FTP Access on a Per-User Basis," you'll see how to add valid users for the web and prevent anonymous access.

Don't create an FTP virtual directory to point to \Webshare\wwwroot, for heaven's sake; that would allow access to all your web content. Instead, point the virtual directory to a specific folder that you want to reserve for an employee-operated web or subdirectory.

The virtual directory eeweb, for example, can point to the directory c:\Webshare\wwwroot\Intranet\eeweb, and be accessed via ftp://*machine_name*/eeweb. You might as well also use the Directories tab of WWW Administration to enable the virtual directory so that the web can be conveniently browsed with http://*machine_name*/ eeweb instead of http://*machine_name*/intranet/eeweb. When you add the directory, it will resemble Figure 6-24.

Note: If the other employees aren't using FrontPage, there is no distinction between a subweb and a subdirectory. You may still want to be able to use FrontPage Explorer to manage the employee web, so you can create it as a subweb, but to employees, it will just be the "web folder."

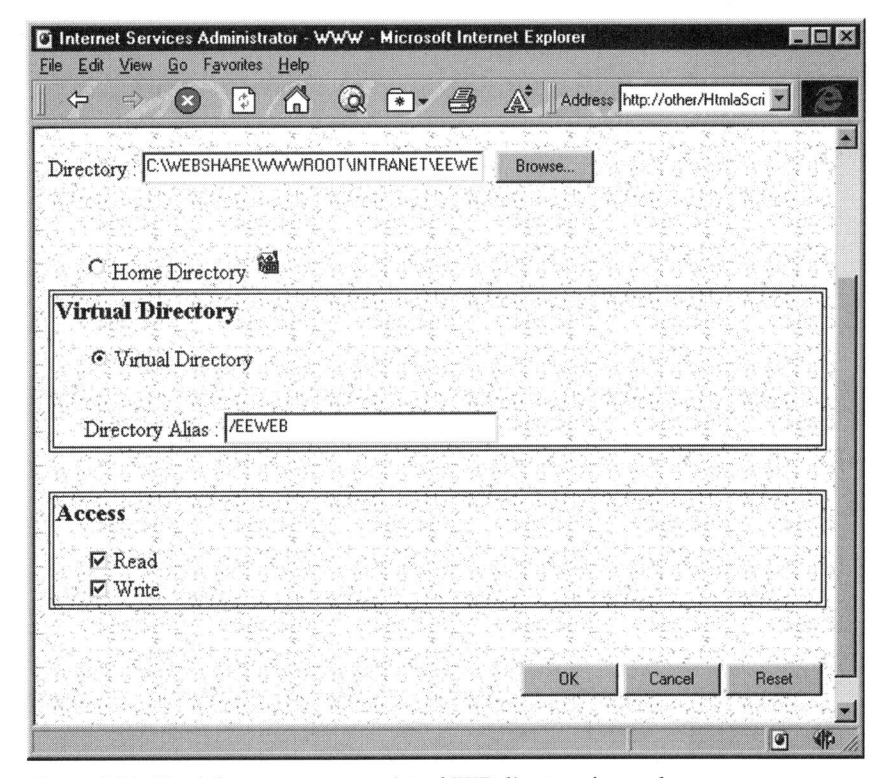

Figure 6-24: Here's how you set up a virtual FTP directory for employee access.

When a user wants to save a new web page to the employee web, tell him or her to choose Save as HTML from the File menu or Save As to store the file in the web in the native format of the program. (On an intranet, users can browse and view Word documents, for example, as easily as HTML documents, and Word documents can contain links between themselves and other files, so you have the best of both worlds.)

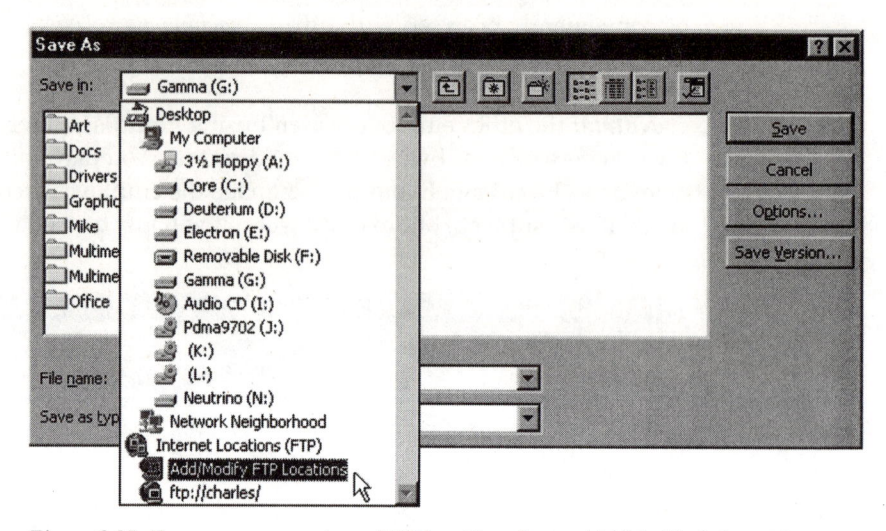

Figure 6-25: To prepare or save to an FTP location, choose Add/Modify Internet Locations from the Save In drop-down menu.

To set up the FTP client, tell the users to choose Add/Modify FTP Locations or choose an FTP location that's already been defined (Figure 6-25). When a user sets up an FTP location, he or she fills out the dialog box shown in Figure 6-26. (The Add button is only enabled if Office can verify that the FTP location is valid. This requires a TCP/IP intranet connection to the server machine, or for Internet FTP servers, that the user is dialed in to the Internet.)

The name of the FTP site takes the form of the server name and directory on that server. The server name is usually the machine name of the computer running the FTP server, or you can tell the users to type in the IP address of the server. (See Chapter 7 to find out how to register IP addresses as plain-English names in the HOSTS file on every computer.) After the server name comes the name of the virtual directory that points to the web content folder.

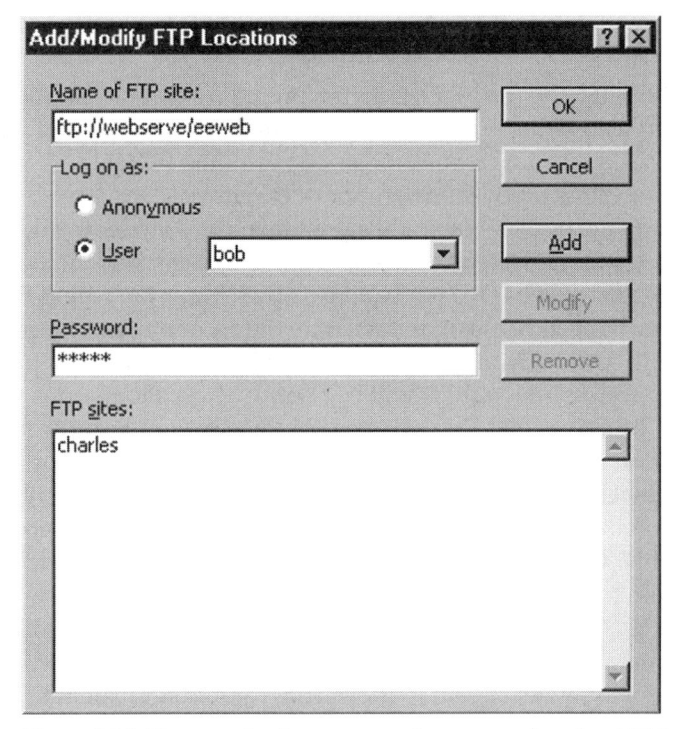

Figure 6-26: Users can log in anonymously, as a member of an NT domain, or as a member defined by local security running on the FTP server computer.

As shown in Figure 6-26, a user can log in anonymously or with a username. Anonymous login is recommended only for nonsensitive subwebs on an intranet. Instead, you can require users to log in with a username or password. These usernames are either authenticated from a Windows NT domain or validated by local security (if enabled) on the computer running the FTP service of Microsoft PWS.

Once the FTP location has been set up, users can open and save documents directly to the FTP folder, and hence, to the employee web. It's exciting for the end users to be able to publish to a web (you can even set up personal home pages for every interested user), and you avoid having to pay for additional FrontPage licenses—just let everyone use Office 97, which they probably need anyway.

Note: I'm not endorsing Microsoft Office 97 as the only solution for intranet applications; it's just the only one I've had a chance to work with. Corel's WordPerfect 7 and Office Suite 7 also feature direct-to-web publishing features.

Restricting FTP Access on a Per-User Basis

Although the instructions in the preceding section are appropriate for the end users when logging in to open and save files on an FTP server, you have to set some security restrictions on the FTP folders to restrict them to certain employees or groups of employees.

By default, all web publishing directories are set to allow anonymous access for all web browsers so that anyone can surf the pages in the employee web. This is a bad idea if the employee web is of a confidential nature, such as one maintained by the accounting or human resources staff. Although an anonymous web browser client can't make changes to the web subfolder, this will be permitted via anonymous FTP.

To secure a folder against web browsing, use FrontPage Explorer's Tools | Permissions command if the folder is a subweb or a subfolder of a subweb (or a subfolder of the root web). Otherwise, use Windows Explorer on the computer running the FTP server and right-click on the folder that contains the web content you want to restrict. Choose Sharing from the pop-up menu.

You'll find that the folder has already been shared as EEWEB and that certain users have been granted access by default, including the user named *, which means "The World," and is equivalent to the Everyone group in Windows NT.

The first thing you want to do is click on the * user and then click the Remove button. Removing the * user deprives anonymous users the right to do anything, including browsing the web or uploading files via FTP. If the web permits public browsing but restricts writing privileges, you can allow the * user to retain Read Only permission.

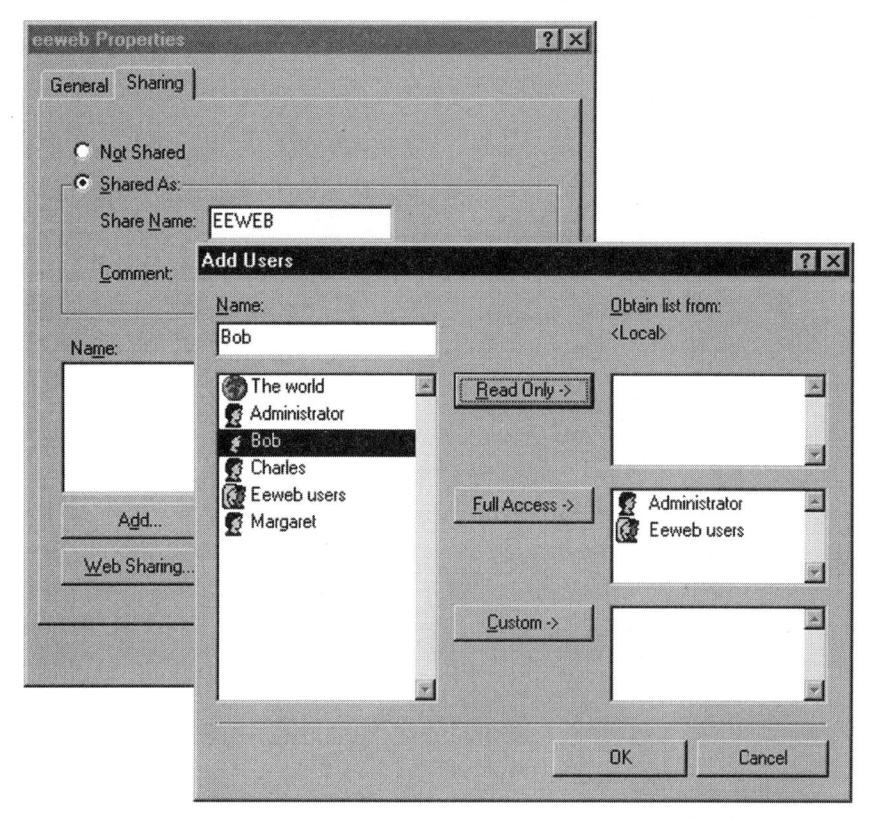

Figure 6-27: On the left, choose the users you want to add, and click the appropriate button to choose the level of access granted.

As shown in Figure 6-27, the folder is already prepared for HTTP and FTP sharing by the steps you followed earlier with the WWW and FTP Administration pages. You now can modify the user access rights, which by default allow read access to everyone (the world) unless you've already permitted both read and write access. Click Add to choose which users are given read-only access, full access, or custom access. (I won't discuss the custom option, but it gives you control to configure specific rights to list directories, update files, delete files, change access rights, etc.) The Web Sharing button (see Figure 6-28) duplicates the functions of the WWW and FTP Directory Administration pages, allowing you to enable read and/or write access for the authorized users.

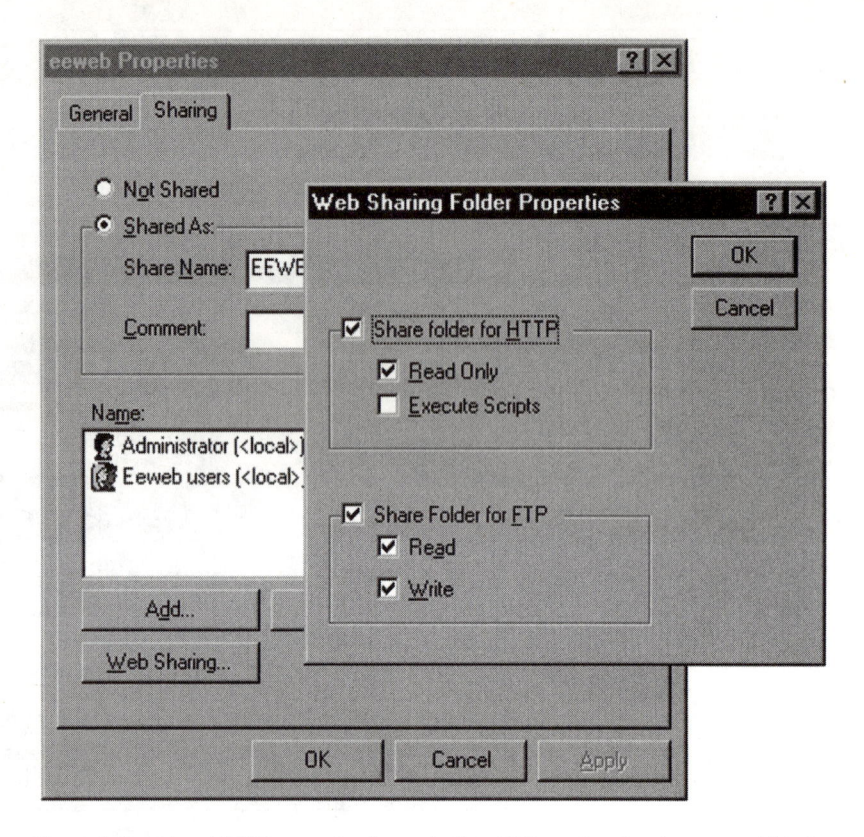

Figure 6-28: Leave HTTP as read-only, and allow FTP read and write access. This is nonetheless limited to authorized users.

The Little Server That Could

This chapter includes some of the most detailed information you'll find anywhere on how to set up and configure the Microsoft Personal Web Server for Windows 95. Although it's primarily intended as a nonsecure local tool for use with FrontPage 97, PWS is "the little server that could," and features a surprising amount of functionality and security.

From the point of view of a web developer, Microsoft PWS supports virtually every capability of Microsoft Internet Information Server but uses much less memory and processing power, making it the ideal web server for Windows 95. You can take advantage of ActiveX server applets and server-side scripting with CGI or ISAPI and exploit the Internet Database Connector for database access.

Some users have even reported success using it for Active Server Pages, a feature only recently added to IIS 3.0. (You need Microsoft Visual InterDev or strong experience with scripting to write ASP applications, so it's not covered in this book. The IDC provides many similar features, however, and is covered in Chapter 8.)

If you're strictly a Windows 95 user, you need not read the rest of this chapter. Instead, proceed along to Chapter 7, where you'll learn how to set up a corporate intranet and craft useful intranet applications with FrontPage.

Microsoft Internet Information Server for Windows NT

This section of the chapter is intended for Windows NT users. Both Windows NT Server and Workstation use the Internet Information Server as a high-performance, reliable web server with full support for every advanced Microsoft web technology, including ISAPI applications, the Internet Database Connector, Active Server Pages (requires IIS 3.0), server-side scripting and ActiveX, and support for extensions such as Microsoft Index Server and Microsoft Merchant Server.

The Windows NT Workstation version of IIS is called Peer Web Services, and it works exactly the same as IIS. In fact, I'll focus on Peer Web Services in this chapter since most FrontPage users working with NT will be using NT Workstation. Only the name on the title bars and in the web documentation reveal which flavor of IIS you're running.

Note: There are security issues with IIS and a Windows NT Server-based network that are beyond the scope of this chapter. That's another reason I'm focusing on Peer Web Services, where security is less of a concern. While this chapter is enough to acquaint you with managing IIS and user-level security, anyone responsible for operating a Windows NT Server machine with IIS should do his or her homework and study the professional-level documentation.

If you've followed along by reading the Windows 95 section of this chapter, you'll be struck by déjà vu as you read the following. Most of the same material is repeated here, although it's been completely revised for NT Workstation. Although it would have been possible to combine both operating systems into the same discussion, it would have been a nightmare of confusion for most readers, who really only need to read one half or the other of this chapter.

Installing NT Peer Web Services

The setup procedure for Windows NT Server offers (no, practically insists) to install Internet Information Server, so it's most likely already running if you operate a Windows NT Server machine. I'm focusing here on NT Workstation, so let's briefly discuss how to install Peer Web Services, although the same method applies to installing IIS.

If you haven't yet upgraded to NT Service Pack 2, now is the time to do so. You'll get access to the latest and most reliable 3.0 version of IIS/PWS, with support for all the latest Microsoft server technologies. You can install the service pack either before or after installing PWS, but it's probably best to install it first, just to get off on the right foot.

> **TIP**
>
> *You can download the Windows NT Service Pack 2 from the following location: http://www.microsoft.com/ntwkssupport/. There are a few known problems with the upgrade that can be fixed with Post Service Pack 2 hot fixes, available at ftp://ftp.microsoft.com/bussys/winnt/winnt-public/fixes/usa/nt40/hotfixes-postSP2.*
>
> *I recommend installing the RAS fix if you have problems dialing in to your ISP and the kernel fix if you get blue-screen errors when accessing a floppy disk (only a problem if antivirus software is installed).*

Installing Peer Web Services

Follow these steps to install Peer Web Services:

1. Double-click the Network icon in Control Panel.
2. On the Services tab of the Network dialog box (Figure 6-29), click the Add button.
3. Choose Microsoft Peer Web Services from the Network Service list in the Select Network Service dialog box, also shown in Figure 6-29.

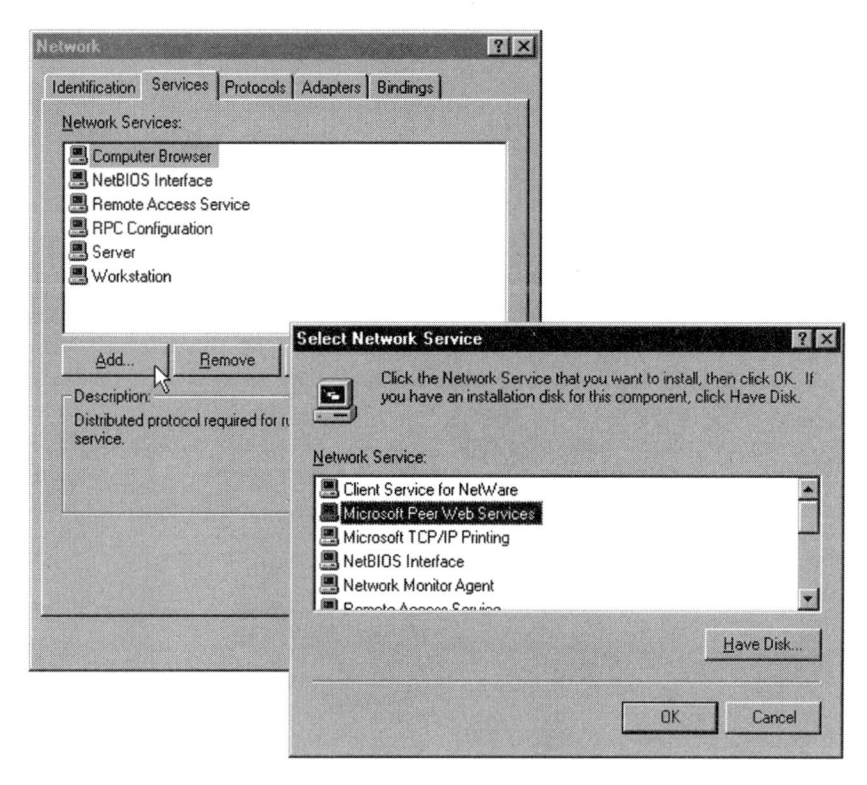

Chapter 6: FrontPage Configuration & Server Issues 307

Figure 6-29: Click Add and then choose Microsoft Peer Web Services.

4. After the Microsoft Peer Web Services Setup program starts, click OK to begin installation (Figure 6-30).

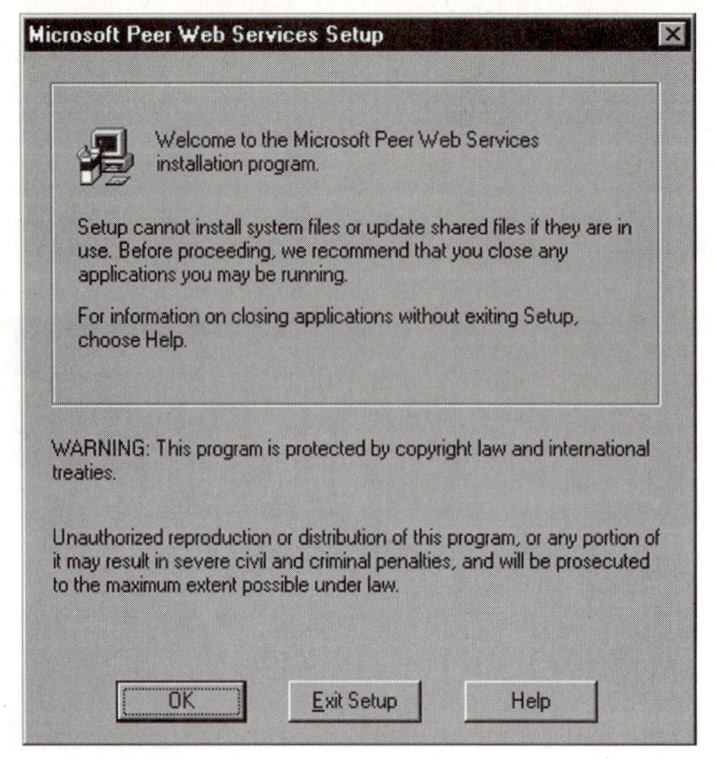

Figure 6-30: Click OK to begin installation of Peer Web Services.

5. The next setup page (not shown here) lets you choose which components of Peer Web Services to install. Normally you would accept the default configuration and click OK. If you know you don't need one of the components, such as the useless Gopher service, you can clear the check box to save a little bit of disk space and server resources.

6. Turn on the Internet Service Manager (HTML) check box if you want to install a series of HTML pages on the hard drive that let you configure PWS using a web browser, even from another computer. Otherwise you'll have to use the Internet Service Manager program on the computer running PWS to configure its settings.

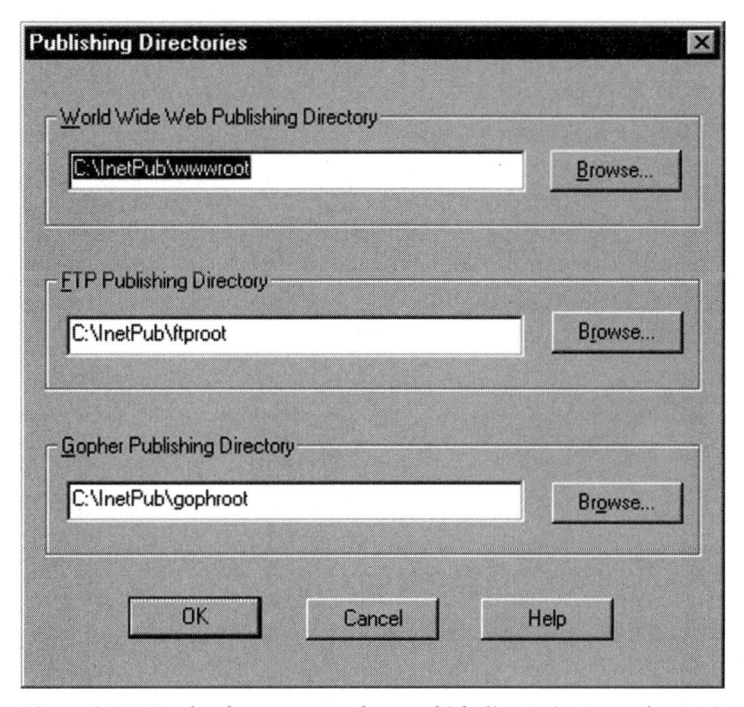

Figure 6-31: Here's where you can choose which directories to use for storing WWW and FTP content.

7. Next, as shown in Figure 6-31, you can choose the default directories (folders) for the World Wide Web publishing directory.

   This is the directory where the HTML files and attachments (such as graphics) are stored. If you already have a directory with existing HTML content, you may want to enter the name of that directory instead of using the default directory. Or you may wish to store the actual content on a different hard drive or even a different computer. Otherwise, just accept the default entries and click Yes when you're asked if you wish to create them.

8. Now Windows NT sets up and configures the PWS software. The last step is to choose which ODBC (Open Database Connectivity) drivers you want to install, such as the SQL server that can be used to link database files to your Web pages via the Internet Database Connector (IDC) that is included with PWS.

When PWS Setup is finished, you can start using PWS right away—just create or copy HTML files into the wwwroot directory (\InetPub\wwwroot). Try opening your default HTML page (index.htm) by opening your preferred web browser and typing in the address **localhost**.

Other computers on your TCP/IP network can connect to your machine by using your computer's IP address or machine name. For example, if your computer's name is BIGTIME, others on your network can access the Web pages by entering http://bigtime, or simply bigtime, into the Address box of the web browser.

> **TIP**
>
> If the other computers on your TCP/IP network can't find your server's name (which may be the case if there is no DNS server or you don't have Microsoft Networking installed), open or create a file named HOSTS (no extension) in the Windows directory (or Winnt\System32 directory for NT) of each client machine. You can add IP address lookups to this file in the form of a server (host) name followed by a space or tab character, which is then followed by the IP address of the host machine. For example, you could add this line to the HOSTS file to let the client workstations look up the fixed IP address of the server:
>
> 192.168.0.1 bigtime
>
> If you don't have any Web content yet, opening the address of your server will display the Peer Web Services home page, which contains lots of additional information on how to take advantage of Peer Web Services. You may wish to make a copy of this page so that it doesn't get overwritten when you add a web to the root web with FrontPage.

The FrontPage 97 Server Administrator

After installing Peer Web Services, you need to run FrontPage Server Administration and install the server extensions. You can find an icon for the FrontPage Server Administration program in the same folder that you chose for the installation of FrontPage. (The default folder is in your Program Files folder.) You can browse to this folder with FrontPage Explorer, or better yet, use the right mouse button to drag the Server Administrator icon to your desktop or copy it into the Programs folder of the Start menu. (To open that folder, right-click on the Start button and then double-click on the Programs folder from the Start Menu folder.)

Figure 6-32 shows the user interface for the FrontPage Server Administrator. If the FrontPage extensions are installed, the entry 80 will appear in the ports list, as it does in Figure 6-34. To verify proper installation, click the Check button.

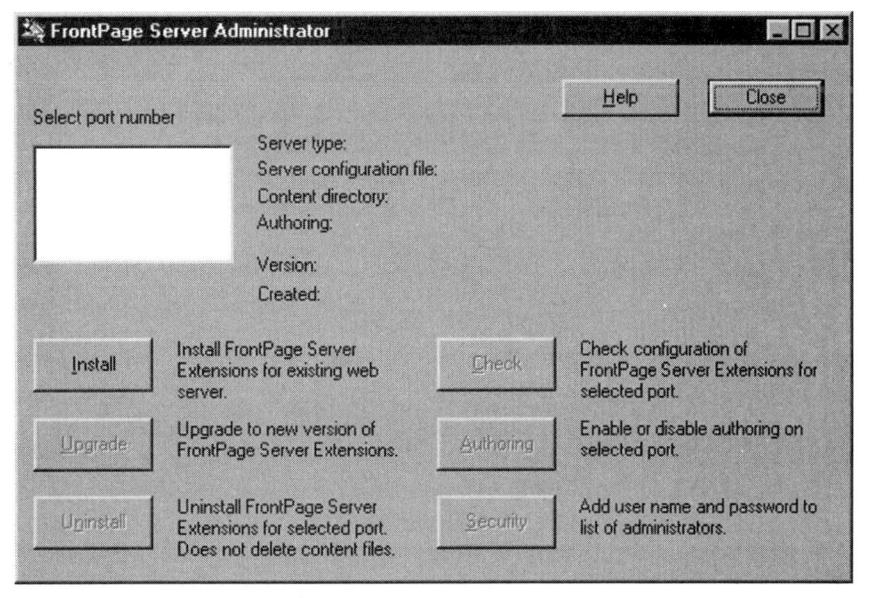

Figure 6-32: Use the FrontPage Server Administrator to install or uninstall server extensions.

To install the server extensions if they don't appear to be installed (as implied by Figure 6-32), click the Install button. From the dialog box that appears next (Figure 6-33), be sure to choose Microsoft Internet Information Server, *not* the default FrontPage Personal Web Server. (There is no separate choice for Peer Web Services, which is the same thing as IIS.)

TIP

If you've upgraded to Service Pack 2 or experience any difficulty using FrontPage with IIS or PWS, it's a good idea to uninstall the current extensions and reinstall them. You can save some time by just clicking Upgrade instead, but it may not remove any outdated references as thoroughly.

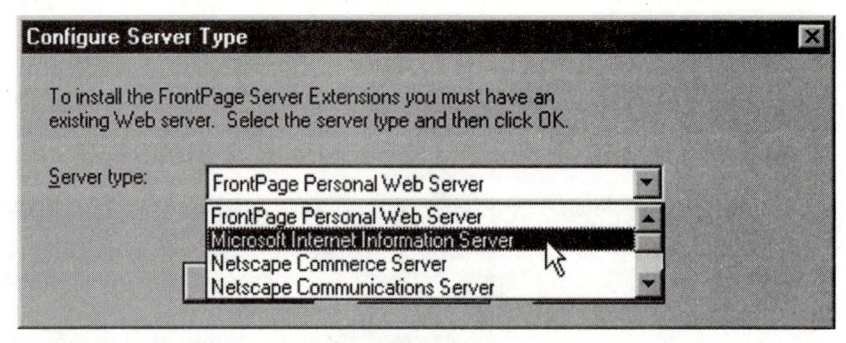

Figure 6-33: For Windows NT, always choose Microsoft Internet Information Server as the type of server for which to install support.

You're then given a rather useless dialog box informing you of the settings that FrontPage will use for the server (Figure 6-34). Click OK.

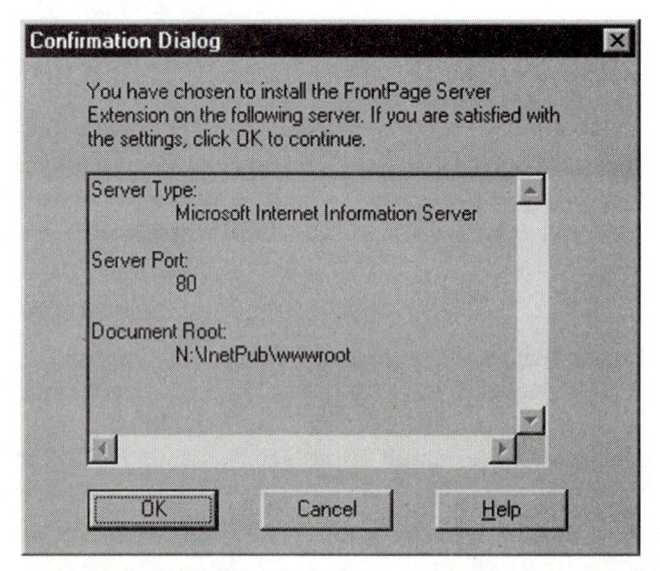

Figure 6-34: All this dialog box tells you is that the server will be installed on port 80 and that the web content will be stored on the hard drive at C:\Inetpub\wwwroot. Click OK to continue.

As shown in Figure 6-35, you're next asked to provide a name to identify yourself when authoring and administering your webs. Use the same name you use to log in to the computer. By default, all administrators are allowed full access to FrontPage webs. If you aren't allowed to log in to your computer as Administrator, you'll need to request the necessary security permissions from your network supervisor. Refer the network guru to http://www.microsoft.com/kb/articles/q162/1/45.htm.

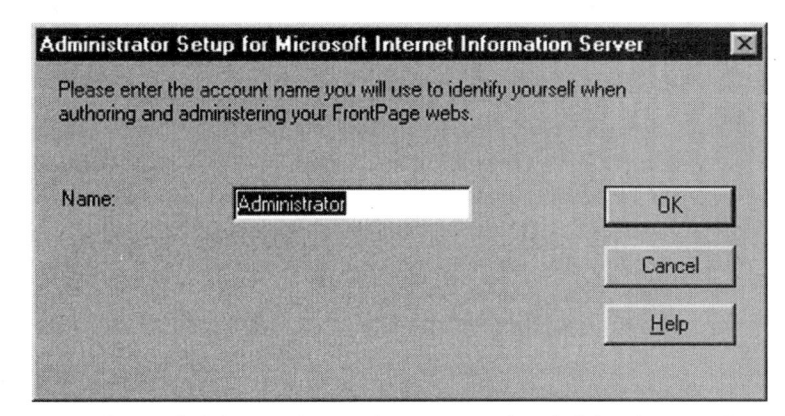

Figure 6-35: Administrator is a good name to use for administering your FrontPage web accounts.

The server extensions are installed, and the necessary changes are made to the configuration of Peer Web Services. (This can take several minutes if you already have a lot of content on the web server.)

Next, the FrontPage Server Administrator warns you that it needs to stop and restart Peer Web Services. (This could possibly disrupt any use of the server if it's being used by the FrontPage Explorer or on an intranet, so I don't recommend running the Server Administrator unless your computer is otherwise idle, just to be safe.) Click Yes to allow it to proceed.

Just prior to the completion of the installation, you may be given the warning shown in Figure 6-36. This is a reminder about how Windows NT authorizes access to restricted web content. For basic authentication, which is the default for IIS, this means that you must include the right to log in locally in the rights for any users you want to have access to restricted material, even if those users will never step foot into the building where your server resides. It's premature to discuss security at this point in the chapter, but we'll return to that topic.

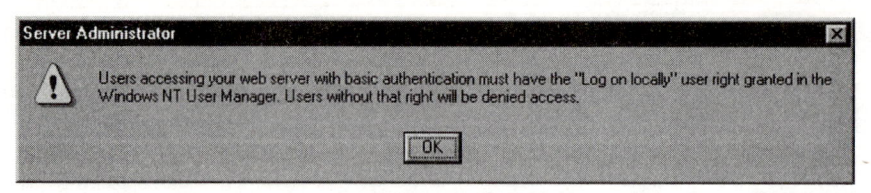

Figure 6-36: Just click OK to accede that you've been warned.

Assuming all goes well, you'll click OK to accept the good news that the install has completed successfully. The Server Administrator should now resemble Figure 6-37.

Click Close to exit the Server Administrator. You're now ready to use FrontPage Explorer to open and create FrontPage webs and/or to test your webs with a web browser.

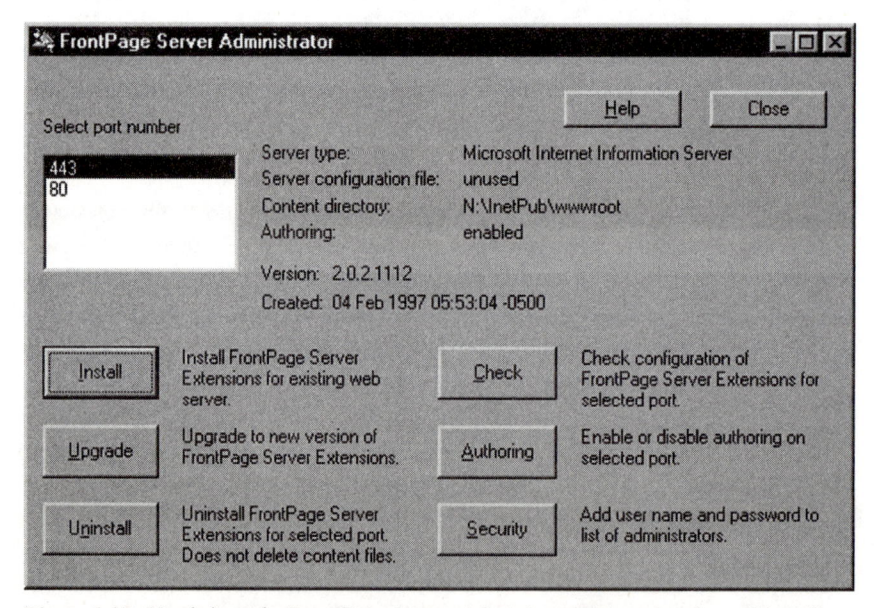

Figure 6-37: Here's how the FrontPage Server Administrator appears when all is well and after you've installed the server extensions.

NT Workstation PWS Administration

For the purposes of local authoring, you'll find that you never really need to modify the default settings of the Microsoft Personal Web Server. FrontPage Explorer can update most settings automatically. Nevertheless, I want to show you how to administer your web, so that you have all the information you need.

Click Start | Programs | Microsoft Peer Web Services | Internet Service Manager to start the program running. You'll see the first page of the tool, shown in Figure 6-38.

TIP

You can also use the HTML version of the Internet Service Manager, although it's pitiful compared to the program version. The only real advantage is that you can access the HTML version from any other computer on an intranet (or via the Internet) as long as you have an administrator account for that computer. The shortcut on the Start menu for the HTML version is outdated and will open the page with Internet Explorer 2.0. (You simply must upgrade to IE 3.0 or higher if you want to take advantage of every feature of FrontPage 97, although Netscape Navigator will do in a pinch.)

*To replace this shortcut, right-click on the Start menu and choose Explore All Users. Double-click on the Programs folder and then on the Microsoft Peer Web Services folder. Delete the obsolete folder, and use File | New | Shortcut to type the following Internet shortcut: **http://localhost/iisadmin/default.htm**. Name it Internet Service Manager (HTML).*

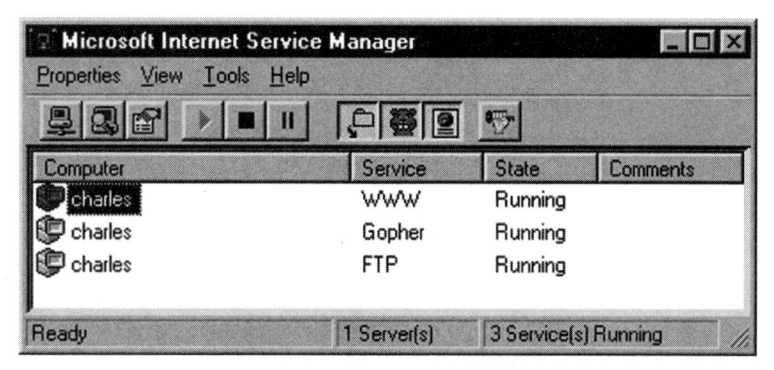

Figure 6-38: The Internet Service Manager lets you change the properties for the various Internet services and stop, start, or pause those services.

The Internet Service Manager lets you administer your local web server and other Windows NT IIS servers. In this chapter, I'll focus on local administration.

I'll explain how to configure the FTP service in "Enabling & Maintaining the FTP Server" later in this chapter, but I'll ignore the useless Gopher server, if you don't mind. Inquiring minds can turn to the online documentation for Peer Web Services, at \WINNT\system32\inetsrv\iisadmin\htmldocs\inetdocs.htm, also available on the Peer Web Service menu of the Start menu.

To work with a service, double-click on it, or click once on it to select it and then click one of the buttons on the toolbar. As usual, you can find out what any toolbar button does by pointing to it without clicking and waiting about a half second.

Let's see how to work with the WWW service. Double-click the computer name shown at the top of the list. You'll get a set of property sheets, which I've combined into a single figure (Figure 6-39). Each is discussed in the following sections.

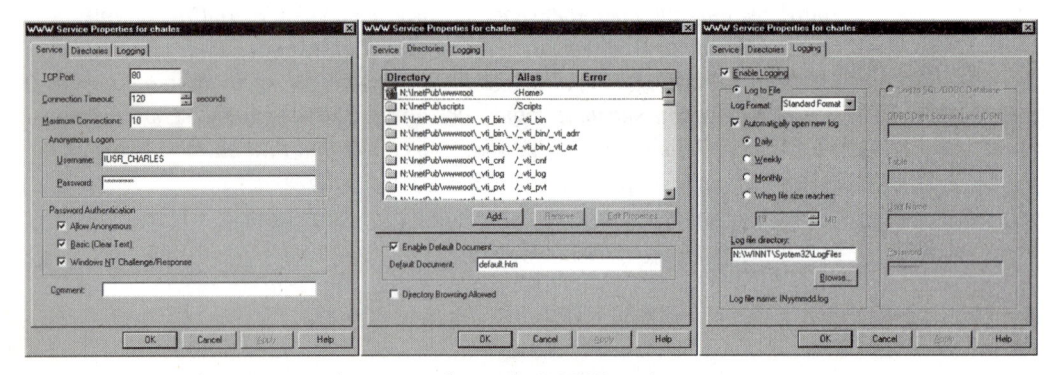

Figure 6-39: Use these property sheets to configure the WWW service.

Service

As shown in the Service tab in Figure 6-39, you can change which port (normally 80) that PWS "listens to" for HTTP requests, which is useful if you want to run more than one web server or both a web server and a proxy server on the same machine.

Use the Connection Timeout and Maximum Connections values to adjust how much of your computer's time will be used up by web surfers. The Maximum Connections value specifies how many connections PWS can handle before it starts refusing connections. It's reasonable to reduce this value to less than 100 for a small workgroup, or even as few as 10 if you're the only user of the server (when you're authoring with FrontPage). Keep in mind that for even one visitor, every object on a web page may require a simultaneous connection, at least until the page has finished loading.

If your server gets really busy, you can decrease the Connection Timeout so that new users, idle users, or users with slow connections get disconnected so your web server can adequately service existing connections. (This is why a long download from a popular site can be canceled for seemingly no good reason.)

I'm going to wait until the next section in this chapter, "Peer Web Services Security," to discuss the other options on the Service tab. I'll continue now with a discussion of the Directories tab.

Directories

Let me emphasize that you really don't need to change any of the settings on the Directories tab. The FrontPage Explorer takes care of the details for you automatically; the following discussion is for reference purposes. Let's say you want to change one of the directories to allow scripts to execute. (This type of server script is used for the Internet Database Connector, which I discuss in Chapter 8.)

To change a directory setting, double-click on it or select it and click the Edit Properties button (see Figure 6-40). This is the same type of dialog box you use when adding a new directory.

The Directory Properties dialog box is used to name a new directory entry or change the path of a directory entry you wish to modify. Your server should have only one home directory, which is set by clicking the Home Directory radio button.

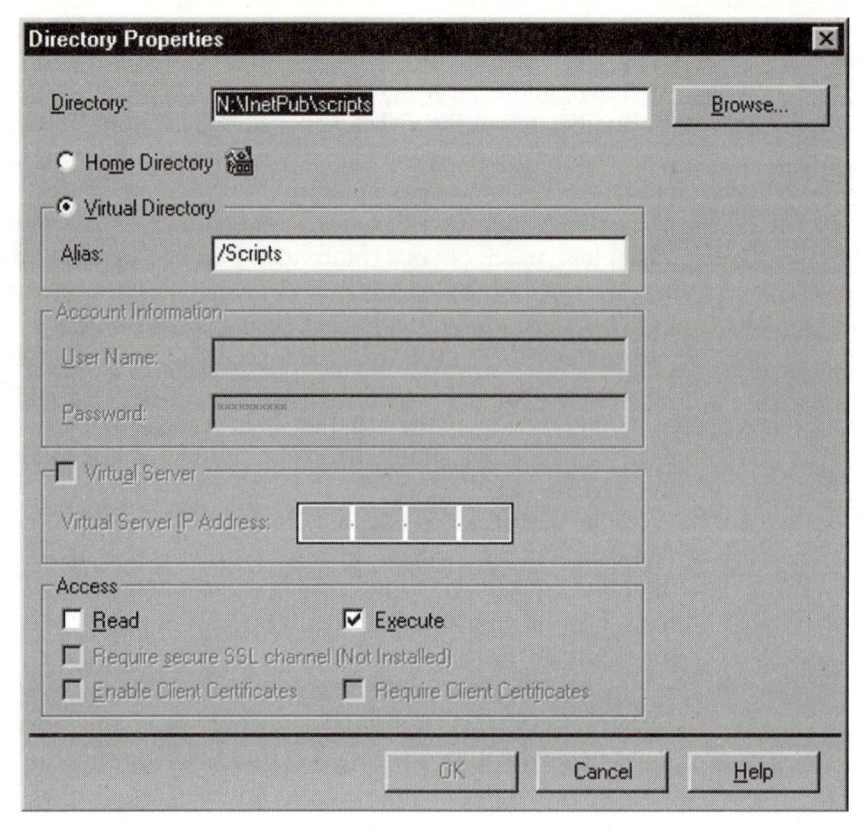

Figure 6-40: Use this dialog box to edit the permissions for a directory or virtual directory.

Perhaps you'd like the directory to be treated as a virtual directory. This lets you reference the web directory as if it were a subdirectory of \Inetpub\wwwroot (or whatever home directory you've set up) even if the actual directory is on another hard drive or on a network file server.

In Figure 6-40, the actual location of the Scripts directory is N:\Inetpub\scripts, which is not normally visible to a web browser; a web browser can only "see" pages in \Inetpub\wwroot (or in its subdirectories). When you tell the server to map a virtual directory, /Scripts, a web browser can refer to this page as http://computer/Scripts, as if the scripts directory were found at N:\Inetpub\wwwroot\scripts.

Why would you do something so wacky? For security reasons. On the Directories tab shown in Figure 6-39, you'll notice a check box labeled

Directory Browsing Allowed, which is enabled by default. This means that you or any visitor to your web can get a directory listing of your web site just by browsing any of its folders. The visitor can see inside every web and find the name of web pages that you might rather keep secret, such as the Results page of a Submit Results WebBot. This is why you should always turn off the Directory Browsing Allowed check box.

If Directory Browsing was left enabled, users would be able to see the names of the script files in the Scripts directory even though they would not be able to open or view the scripts themselves, thanks to the Access section at the bottom of Figure 6-40. By enabling the Execute check box and disabling the Read check box, the client's (user's) browser can run server scripts but can't open the scripts to read them. This not only protects any trade secrets found in your clever scripts, it makes it harder for a determined hacker (oh no, not him again) to trick your server into executing modified scripts. In general, only enable read access for general web pages, and only enable execute access for script directories.

There are several options grayed out (disabled) in Figure 6-40. The three at the bottom are relevant only if you've installed a security certificate for Secure Sockets Layer. This is an involved procedure that is beyond the scope of this book, but it is covered in the online documentation.

Also, on Peer Web Services, the Virtual Server check box is disabled. In Internet Information Server, you can assign a unique IP address to a virtual directory. This is called multihoming, and it allows a single web server to provide simultaneous access to several separate home directories, perhaps for different clients. This is usually needed only for Internet Service Providers, so you probably won't miss it anyway.

TIP

Microsoft Active Server Pages require both read and execute access to any directories containing .ASP files. Just so you know.

Logging

The Logging options, the dialog box to the far right of Figure 6-39, can also be safely left as is unless you're running low on disk space. As long as you've enabled the Enable Logging check box, the server keeps a record of all transactions (accesses) made, a fascinating way to keep track of site activity. Actually, I'm being sarcastic; the log entries are boring and nonsensical, although you can at least see the IP addresses of every computer that has tried to access your pages.

> **TIP**
>
> *To trace an IP address back to its source, open an MS-DOS prompt and type **tracert** followed by an IP address or domain name. TraceRoute finds the destination address and reports on every "hop" (handoff from server to server) made along the way. The last domain shown is the source of the IP address. TraceRoute is a powerful tool to detect unauthorized attempts to access a site. You can also use it to track down the true source of junk e-mail where the recipient tries to use a fake e-mail address but fails to spoof the IP address in the e-mail header. To see all the options you can use with TraceRoute, type **tracert** by itself at the command prompt.*

Since the log file grows each time a page is visited, it can get too large to make sense of, so by default PWS starts a new log once a day using a name like in970214.log for February 14, 1997. The previous logs are not deleted, so if disk space is at a premium, don't choose to log any more frequently. On the other hand, if the server is very busy, you might need to log more frequently just to keep the log files from growing impractically large.

Another technique to keep the log files from getting too large is to use the When the File Size Reaches radio button and fill in the MB box with how large the log can get (in megabytes) before it is closed and a new log is created. Feel free to delete obsolete logs; they aren't used by PWS once closed out.

Peer Web Services Security

Consider the following scenario: You're running FrontPage 97 on your own PC, and you're not part of a network. If that's the case, you really don't need to worry at all about server security. The server isn't being used to let others browse your webs; you're only using it to author the webs with FrontPage.

Even if you're not on a LAN, you still need to be somewhat concerned about security if your computer uses Dial-Up Networking to connect to the Internet. This is because whenever you are online with the Internet, your web server is also accessible to anyone on the Internet. This is both good and potentially bad. If you want to be extra cautious, stop the WWW (or HTTP) service whenever you dial in to the Internet.

If you want to publish your pages on the Internet, all you need to give to others is your current IP address. Open a Command prompt and type the command **IPCONFIG** to find out the current IP address of the Dial-Up

Adapter. You can give out this IP address to friends and colleagues who want to try logging in to your web server. For example, the address http://206.68.137.16 opens the Microsoft home page, but it could just as easily open your home page if your IP address were substituted. (Every active user on the Internet has his or her own IP address, but it's usually a different IP address each time a new connection is established.)

> **TIP**
>
> *Double-click on the telephone icon on the taskbar notification area (next to the clock) and choose Details to display your IP address without opening a command prompt.*

Of course, this just isn't a very practical way to operate a web site, as I emphasize in Chapters 5 and 7. More practically, you may choose to deploy NT Workstation PWS as a small-scale intranet web server.

Security Precautions

On an intranet, there are some good reasons to be concerned about access levels to information, which is related to security. You might have a database query for the human resources department to let them view employee records; you wouldn't want to let them fall into the wrong hands. This means that you need to be able to limit access to some webs based on a valid username and password.

You also need a way to limit authoring and web administration to protect your web content from the mistakes of naïve users or meddlers. (You know the type—the self-styled computer expert who's learned everything about computers in the last year, and who prefers to waste time messing around with Control Panel and RegEdit instead of playing Solitaire.)

The techniques for protecting and restricting your webs by choosing Tools | Permissions from FrontPage Explorer were discussed in Chapter 5. This only works, however, if the web server validates users.

It would take too much space in this book to go into the details of Windows 95 networking methods, so the following discussion assumes that you are familiar with them. To view or change several of the settings for Windows NT networking, double-click the Network icon in Control Panel. You'll also need to be familiar with the User Manager, found at Start | Programs | Administrative Tools.

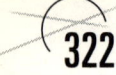

Valid Users & Groups

Microsoft Internet Explorer 2.0 and higher allows you to restrict access to sites based on the NTLM security model. Basically, this means that the same security used to restrict access to a Windows NT server is used to authorize web users.

Internet Information Server and Peer Web Services need to be able to access the hard drive on the server. This is accomplished by the IUSR_*computername* account. By limiting the access of this user, you can control which folders can be "seen" by IIS/PWS and what access rights are required. For use with FrontPage, you should leave these rights as is since FrontPage Explorer needs full control over the web content, which it can only obtain via IIS/PWS and the IUSR_*computername* account.

You can also restrict access to subwebs or subdirectories (from the point of view of IIS/PWS, there is no distinction) to specific users. By default, these users are accessing the web server as if they were local users (which is why any new users you create for the webs must have the Log On Locally right granted). To restrict access to a folder, it must be stored on an NTFS partition, since NT has no way to restrict local access to a folder on a FAT partition.

Most web access is permitted anonymously, with no login prompt. If your site is 100 percent confidential, you might not want to allow any anonymous users. Refer back to the Service tab of Figure 6-39. By default, the Allow Anonymous check box is turned on, so it is possible for any user to access your web. This means no usernames and passwords are transmitted unless you set a particular directory as restricted.

The easiest way to set a directory (subweb or subfolder) as restricted is to use FrontPage Explorer. By default, subwebs inherit their security settings from the root web. If you want to enforce passwords for the entire site, open the root web. Otherwise, open a subweb. Choose Tools | Permissions. For a subweb, you can enable the Use Unique Permissions for This Web check box on the Settings tab.

Figure 6-41 shows the Permissions dialog box for the Groups tab. Here, you can choose which user groups can access the web. You can use the Users tab instead to restrict access to a particular set of users, although it's more efficient just to add those users to a group and give the group access rights. Notice that the group Everyone is given browse access. This is what makes the web unrestricted for anonymous users. By removing the Everyone group, only users and groups explicitly added to the list and given browse access can open pages on a subweb. (Further, you can restrict which users or groups of users can author and/or administer a web.)

Chapter 6: FrontPage Configuration & Server Issues

To change the access rights of a user or group you've added to the list, double-click on a user. To add a new user to the list, click the Add button.

TIP

You can also set the permissions for a folder by browsing the hard drive with Windows Explorer. Locate the folder containing the web you want to restrict and right-click on it to get the properties. From the Security tab, you can add or remove users and groups and set the access level for each. You can only restrict access to webs if they are located on an NTFS partition because IIS/PWS accesses them as a local user.

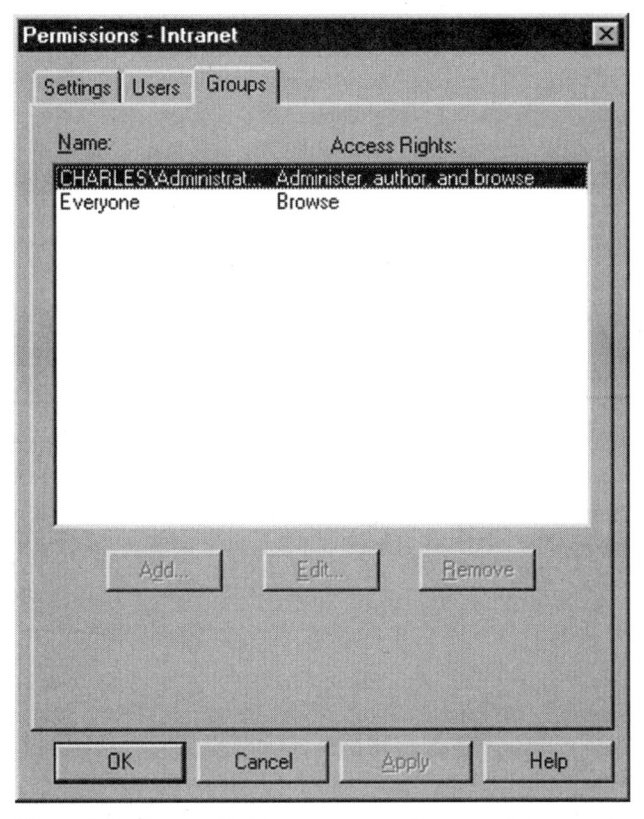

Figure 6-41: Remove the Everyone group if you want to prevent anonymous access, but for the elite users who are permitted access, add one or more users or groups with Browse access.

When you click the Add button, the Add Group or Add User button appears. The Add Groups dialog box is shown in Figure 6-42. You can add any valid user/group from a Windows NT domain, or from the list of local users/groups for that computer, by clicking on a name and then clicking the Add button. You then choose the access level at the bottom of the dialog (in the Users Can section).

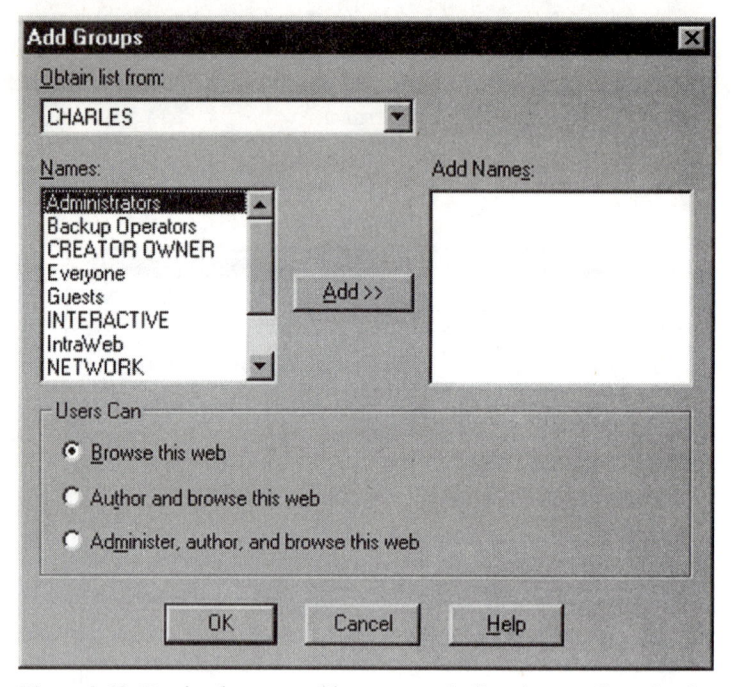

Figure 6-42: Here's where you add groups to the list of users allowed to browse the web.

Keep in mind that even if you have Everyone on the list of users allowed to browse, this right can be revoked by turning off the Allow Anonymous check box in the Service tab shown in Figure 6-39.

Password Security

Should you choose to restrict a subweb (or the entire web), you have another concern. When a visitor or legitimate client of the protected web tries to open a page on that web, Internet Explorer pops up a dialog box requesting a login name and password. How is the name and password transmitted to the server for verification?

If you use Basic security (see the Service tab in Figure 6-39), the name and password is sent with the unencrypted Base64 encoding system commonly used to send binary information, such as electronic mail attachments, as plain text files made up of special symbols. If a hacker has "wiretapped" into your network or somehow tapped into the TCP/IP packet stream on the Internet, *in principle* the passwords and usernames could be captured and later used to break into your system or gain unauthorized access to your web.

The only way to avoid this is to turn off the Basic check box and turn on the Windows NT Challenge/Response check box. Unfortunately, this only works if the list of users is obtained and kept on a Windows NT Server computer running as a domain server. If the web server is running on an NT Workstation computer, the user list for that computer can be used to validate users. (This assumes that NT Workstation is running in workgroup mode; in domain mode, usernames are kept on the server except for local users.)

Note: Keep in mind that basic security is the standard method employed by web servers to grant access to restricted resources and is the only method supported by all web browsers. Should you choose to keep basic authentication in place, avoid assigning usernames or passwords that are already in use on your network.

One way to improve the security of basic authentication is to send all traffic requiring passwords over a Secure Sockets Layer (SSL) connection, usually by using https:// instead of http:/ in the link that takes the visitor to the site. By default, SSL is not enabled with IIS/PWS, as it requires certification with Verisign or another digital certificate vendor.

Enabling & Maintaining the FTP Server

The FTP service is administered from the Internet Service Manager. Double-click the computer name associated with the FTP server to view or change its properties. I'll discuss each property sheet used by the FTP service in the following sections.

Service

The Service tab of the FTP Administration page (Figure 6-43) lets you choose a connection timeout value and a maximum connections limit. File transfers typically tend to use up much more of your available network/Internet bandwidth, and for a longer period of time, than does web browsing, so you'll want to severely limit how many users can connect simultaneously. By reducing the timeout value, you can drop idle users like a hot potato. (It's not uncommon for FTP clients to leave the connection open long after a file transfer has been completed.)

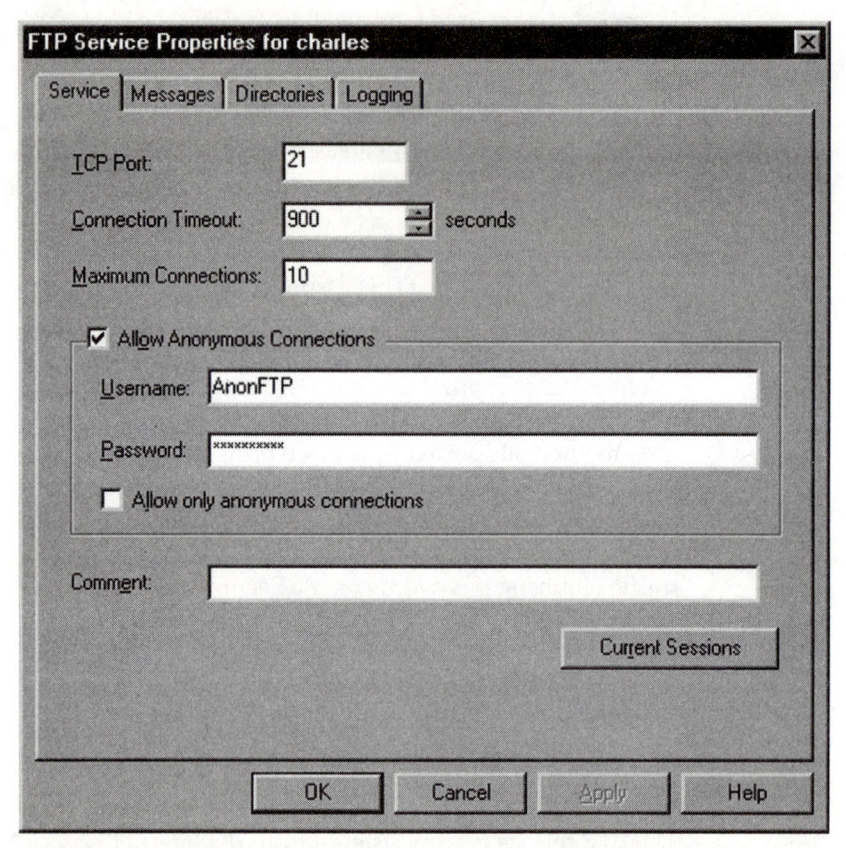

Figure 6-43: Use the Service tab primarily to permit or deny anonymous access.

By enabling Allow Anonymous Connections, you can let any Internet guest download files from the FTP directory. Since you can choose which files you place in \Inetpub\ftproot, you have full control over which files are available for download.

The Username and Password text boxes are filled in automatically after you run the setup for PWS/IIS. In order to control file access rights, the anonymous users in effect log in to Windows NT using the username and password shown. Normally, this defaults to IISUSR_*computername*, but you can also set up a separate user (AnonFTP in Figure 6-43) to keep the access rights of anonymous FTP users and web browsing users distinct. If you use the default username and password, you need not change this setting. If you want to specify a different account for the login, create that user in User Manager and fill in the username and password so that the FTP service can log in to that account.

Although by default the anonymous user can only see what's in the Inetpub/ftproot folder, you may end up creating virtual directories that point to other locations on your hard drive or network. You can restrict the type of access granted to these folders by removing Everyone and Interactive from the permissions list and adding the FTP username to the access list, choosing which rights (read, write, full control, etc.) you want to restrict for that folder.

Turn on the Allow Only Anonymous Connections check box if you want to prevent usernames and passwords from being transmitted over the network, since basic authentication is the only way to log in to a secured FTP server. Naturally this means that you can't restrict access based on usernames.

The Comment text box is for your record keeping in case you want to remind yourself why you've made a change; it's not shown to the users.

Messages

Use the Welcome box to choose what text to display to users prior to logon, as soon as their FTP client has attempted access. You can explain the purpose of your server, provide login instructions, and issue legal warnings if your system is not intended as a public server (see Figure 6-44). (Failure to issue legal warnings may be construed as an open invitation to gain access to the FTP files.) You can also enter a custom message to display when the user closes the FTP connection (Exit Message) or an error message to display when the FTP server is full (Maximum Connections Message). Be sure to click OK to make the change "stick."

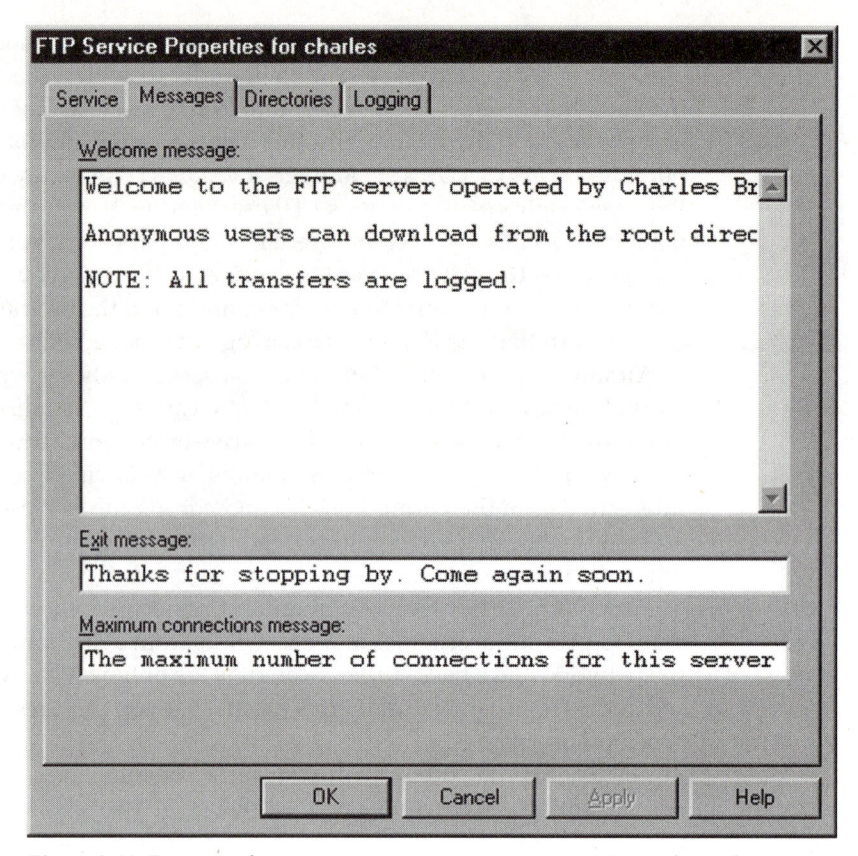

Figure 6-44: Enter a welcome message to greet users to your site. Or leave the entry blank if you'd rather.

Directories

You use the Directories tab (Figure 6-45) to choose which directories to make available for FTP users. By default, the \Inetpub\ftproot folder is set as the home directory. When an FTP client requests a directory listing, the entries in the ftproot folder are the only ones shown—the user can not "back up" to previous directories and can not access any other folders on your hard drive.

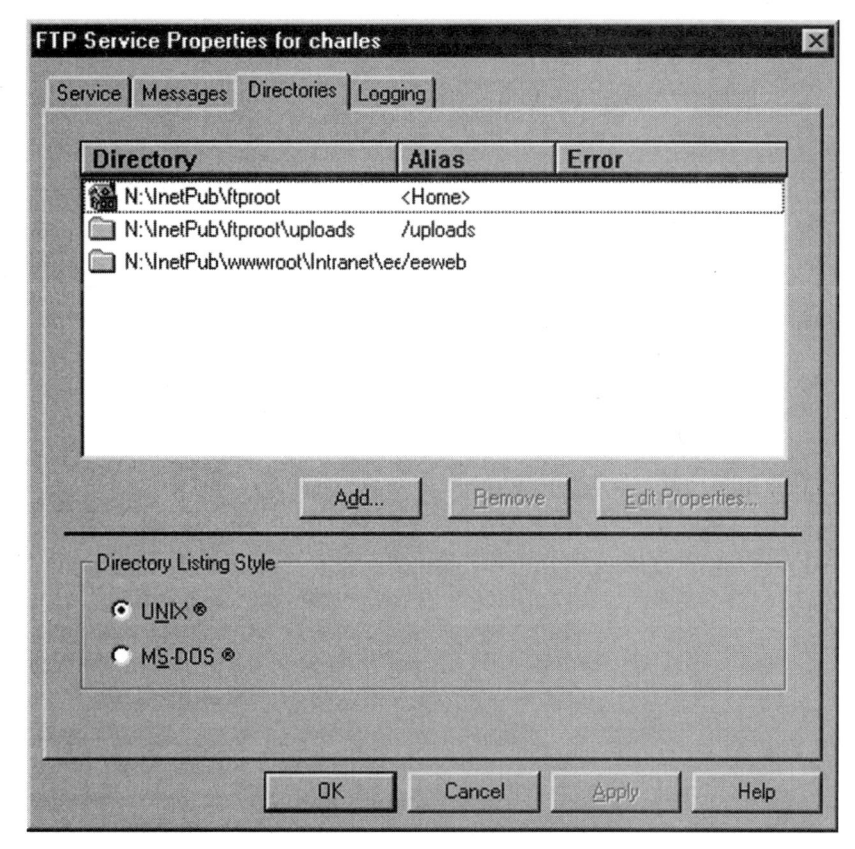

Figure 6-45: Use the Directories tab to modify basic FTP directory permissions.

Always use the UNIX directory listing style; it's required for the FTP client built into most web browsers.

TIP

Users can view the files on your server and click on them to download them by typing something like ftp://198.105.232.1 in the Address or Location box of the web browser. (This is the IP of ftp.microsoft.com, but you can substitute your IP address.) This always logs the user in with anonymous credentials. To log in with a username and password, use the format: ftp://username:password@server, as in ftp://anonymous:ceemeister@ftp.microsoft.com. This syntax prevents sending a true e-mail address as the password, however.

You can click the Edit button next to any directory on the list to change its rights; the page shown in Figure 6-46 will appear. This is the same page you'll see when you add a directory. Choose a hard drive folder from the Directory box, and unless you want it to be mapped as the root (home) of the FTP server, enter an alias and turn on the Virtual Directory option. You don't have to use a subfolder of \Inetpub\ftproot when adding a directory or virtual directory, but if you do, it will be visible when the root directory is listed.

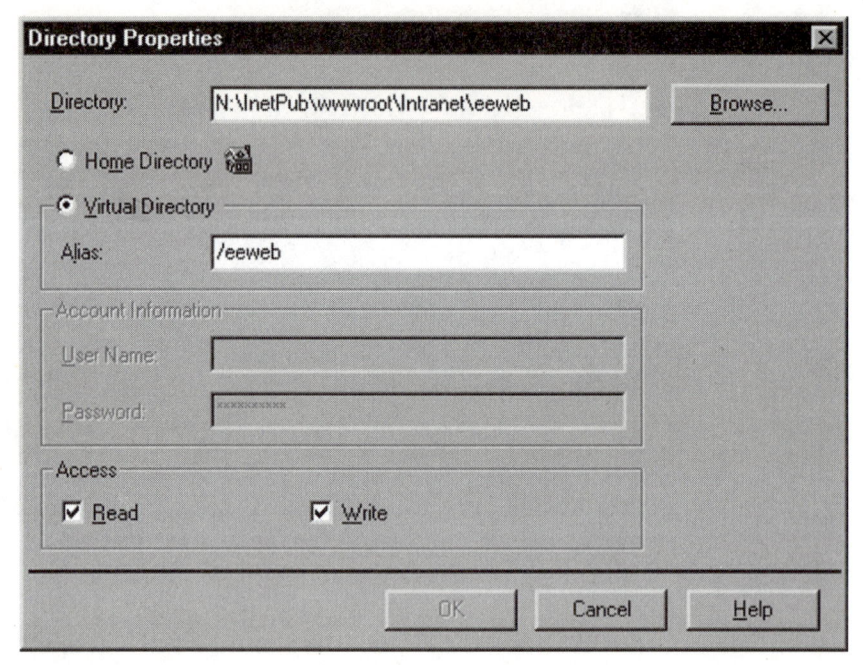

Figure 6-46: Use this property sheet when adding, editing, or removing FTP folders visible to end users.

By choosing either Read, Write, or both check boxes, you can decide whether the user can view and download files and/or send files. It's common to list public files in the root of the server or in a folder named public and to create a virtual directory alias called Incoming to point to a folder that will receive files sent by FTP clients.

A download directory should be set to Read Only (to prohibit tampering or unwanted uploads), and an upload directory should be set to Write Only. These settings ensure that the client won't be able to list or retrieve material sent by other users to the upload directory. (This may seem paranoid, but it protects you from liability should a user upload illegal or pornographic material to you. You can review submissions before moving them to the Public or Download folder should you decide to share the file with others. Naturally, also watch out for copyright restrictions on material you make available for download.)

Logging

The Logging page works the same as the one you use for the WWW service, although the name of the log file is unique.

IIS & Peer Web Services Intranet FTP Applications

Microsoft Office 97 allows users to save documents as HTML directly to an FTP server. The administrator can then move the content to the web server. However, you can also permit the employees to upload their pages directly to a live web server.

First, establish a subweb or a subfolder of a web that can be modified by staff members. You could have a separate one for each department, team, or project group. This web or subfolder is managed entirely by the staff, and it's their responsibility to make sure someone doesn't delete or overwrite pages (such as the default "home" page).

Second, you need to create a virtual FTP directory that points to the *web server* directory holding the intranet content. Use the Directory tab of the FTP Administration page to create a virtual directory and permit both read and write access. In the next section, "Restricting FTP Access on a Per-User Basis," you'll see how to add valid users for the web and prevent anonymous access.

Don't create an FTP virtual directory to point to \Inetpub\wwwroot, for heaven's sake; that would allow access to all your web content. Instead, point the virtual directory to a specific folder that you want to reserve for an employee-operated web or subdirectory.

The virtual directory eeweb, for example, can point to the directory c:\Inetpub\wwwroot\Intranet\eeweb and be accessed via ftp://*machine_name*/eeweb. You might as well also use the Directories tab of WWW Administration to enable the virtual directory so that the web can be conveniently browsed with http://*machine_name*/eeweb instead of http://*machine_name*/intranet/eeweb. When you add the directory, it will resemble the one shown in Figure 6-46.

Note: If the other employees aren't using FrontPage, there is no distinction between a subweb and a subdirectory. You may still want to be able to use FrontPage Explorer to manage the employee web, so you can create it as a subweb, but to employees, it will just be the "web folder."

When the user wants to save a new web page to the employee web, tell him or her to choose Save as HTML from the File menu, or Save As to store the file in the web in the native format of the program. (On an intranet, users can browse and view Word documents, for example, as easily as HTML documents, and Word documents can contain links between themselves and other files, so you have the best of both worlds.)

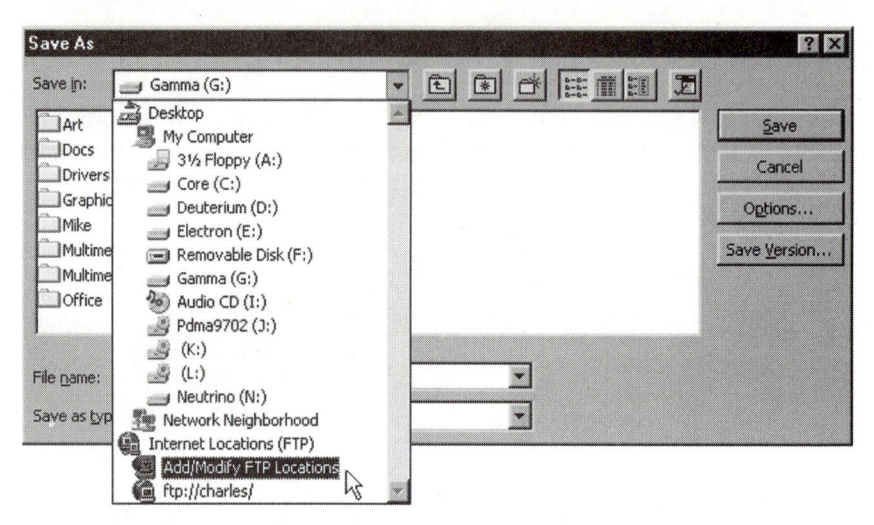

Figure 6-47: To prepare or save to an FTP location, choose Add/Modify Internet Locations from the Save In drop-down menu.

To set up the FTP client, tell the users to choose Add/Modify FTP locations or choose an FTP location that's already been defined (Figure 6-47). When a user sets up an FTP location, he or she fills out the dialog box shown in Figure 6-48. (The Add button is only enabled if Office can verify that the FTP location is valid. This requires a TCP/IP intranet connection to the server machine, or for Internet FTP servers, that the user is dialed in to the Internet.)

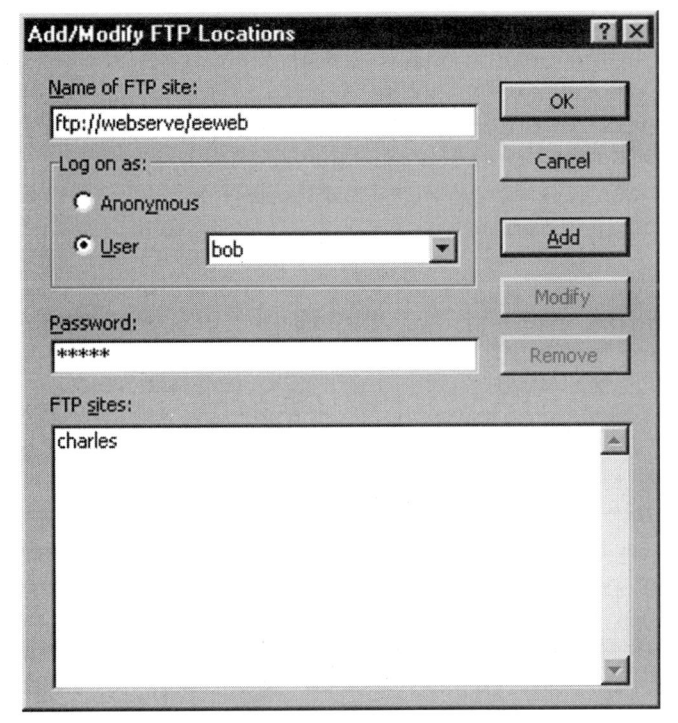

Figure 6-48: Users can log in anonymously, as a member of an NT domain, or as a member defined by local security running on the FTP server computer.

The name of the FTP site takes the form of the server name and the directory on that server. The server name is usually the machine name of the computer running the FTP server, or you can tell the users to type in the IP address of the server. (See Chapter 7 to find out how to register IP addresses as plain-English names in the HOSTS file on every computer.) The name of the virtual directory that points to the web content folder comes after the server name.

As shown in Figure 6-48, a user can log in anonymously or with a username. Anonymous login is recommended only for nonsensitive subwebs on an intranet. Instead, you can require users to log in with a username or password. The usernames are either authenticated from a Windows NT domain or validated by local security (if enabled) on the computer running the FTP service of NT Workstation PWS.

Once the FTP location has been set up, users can open and save documents directly to the FTP folder, and hence, to the employee web. It's exciting for the end users to be able to publish to a web (you can even set up personal home pages for every interested user), and you avoid having to pay for additional FrontPage licenses—just let everyone use Office 97, which they probably need anyway.

Note: I'm not endorsing Microsoft Office 97 as the only solution for intranet applications; it's just the only one I've had a chance to work with. Corel's WordPerfect 7 and Office Suite 7 also feature direct-to-web publishing features.

Restricting FTP Access on a Per-User Basis

Although the instructions in the preceding section are appropriate for the end users when logging in to open and save files on an FTP server, you have to set some security restrictions on the FTP folders to restrict them to certain employees or groups of employees.

By default, all web publishing directories are set to allow anonymous access for all web browsers so that anyone can surf the pages in the employee web. This is a bad idea if the employee web is of a confidential nature, such as one maintained by the accounting or human resources staff. Although an anonymous web browser client can't make changes to the web subfolder, this will be permitted via anonymous FTP.

On the other hand, if you want to restrict access to the FTP server for the web folder, you'll have to change the default FTP user from IUSR_*computername* to another user you create with NT User Manager. The IUSR account is what IIS/PWS uses to log in to the computer for anonymous web access. If you granted FTP write access to a web folder, you would also be granting write access to users browsing the web. That's why I recommend creating a new user called AnonFTP to keep these access rights unique. Of course, you can also restrict access on the basis of usernames or group names just as you would for any network access.

Moving On

Now that you've completed the first six chapters of this book, you've got a pretty good handle on what it takes to put together FrontPage webs, publish them on the Internet, and configure your web server for local FrontPage authoring or intranet web publishing. This is a good basis for moving into the next chapter, where you'll learn specifically how to set up a TCP/IP intranet and explore several intranet applications you can develop with FrontPage.

chapter 7

Private Webs: Deploying a Corporate Intranet

In the previous chapter, I discussed the pros and cons of operating your own web server. You'll almost always run a local web server when developing your webs, either the FrontPage personal web server, the Personal Web Server for Windows 95, or when running on Windows NT, the Internet Information Server (IIS) or its sibling, Peer Web Services for NT Workstation. (You can also use a non-Microsoft server running the FrontPage Server Extensions.) Having a web server run on your own computer is essential to support all the features of FrontPage 97 while you develop the web.

However, when it comes to deploying your web for public consumption, running your own server isn't always practical. As I discussed in Chapter 6, it is costly to provide high-speed links between the server and the Internet that are sufficient for practical applications. Most sites on the Internet, then, run on powerful servers run by Web Presence Providers (WPP) or Internet Service Providers (ISPs), who are connected directly to the Internet backbone via "wide pipes" (T1, T3, or other leased lines).

There is another situation, however, where running your own web server is an ideal solution: the deployment of a corporate or private intranet. *Intranet* is a generic term for a network made of multiple networks. A wide area network (WAN), which links together local area networks (LANs), is a type of intranet.

In this chapter, I'll show you how to put together a basic corporate intranet. Although every company's needs for intranet applications vary, I'll show you how to get started with the most popular and easiest-to-implement applications for an intranet, including: access to network documents, employee web publishing, one-click program launching, employee resources, and online forms. The latter leads into the following chapter, Chapter 8, where I'll show you how to integrate your intranet with corporate databases, using FrontPage HTML as the front end.

Intranet Fundamentals

Intranet is a term that is more properly applied to any network that runs the TCP/IP protocol and takes advantage of Internet protocols such as HyperText Transfer Protocol (HTTP) or File Transfer Protocol (FTP). In your own private corner of the world, you can solve business problems by the clever application of WWW technology. In essence, you can grab a piece of the WWW for yourself and create a private Internet.

> **TIP**
>
> *A* protocol *is an agreed-upon standard for performing a task. Most protocols were established by industry consortium committees or standards organizations. Without standardized protocols, there would be no way to ensure that any computer could communicate with any other computer.*

In the intranet, the web server runs on a centralized server computer, most likely already set up as a network file or application server, and serves up HTML documents for employees running a web browser (or other Internet applications such as electronic mail). This is called client-server computing. The client (the individual employee's computer) makes requests from the server and is fully capable of running programs (such as those written in Java, JavaScript, or VBScript) and downloading software on its own, helping to ease the burden of the server.

The client-server model applies perfectly to intranet applications, allowing corporate information resources to be centralized in one place, with information and updates flowing to the client workstations on demand.

However, this picture is clouded a bit, because individual client workstations can also run intranet server applications, such as the Personal Web Server or Peer Web Services. This allows departments and workgroups to autonomously establish and maintain their own private webs.

Regardless of the scheme, intranet applications are powerful and efficient. For one thing, crafting useful HTML pages (with the FrontPage Editor) is far faster and easier than writing a computer program with a language like Microsoft Visual Basic. Designing good-looking HTML with a WYSIWYG (what you see is what you get) system like FrontPage is more like word processing or desktop publishing than programming, which opens up authoring to a wider audience.

As the features of HTML and Internet applications become ever more sophisticated, intranet designers can reap this harvest to upgrade their intranets. With the upcoming introduction of the Active Desktop for Windows 95 and NT (based on Internet Explorer 4.0, which should also support other platforms, including the Apple Macintosh), HTML and web technologies are fully integrated into the client operating system. It makes sense to take advantage of all this power.

Another fantastic advantage of the intranet is that authors can take advantage of the greater bandwidth of the local area network. While modems are limited to at most 33.6 kilobits per second (at least until the new 57 Kbps modems arrive sometime in 1997), a typical Ethernet network runs at 10 megabits (millions of bits) per second, and Fast Ethernet pumps this up to 100 Mbps.

This means that you can take full advantage of graphics, sound, video, and other multimedia features, like Shockwave applets, in your web pages. Of course, keep in mind the adage, "All good things in moderation." The 10 Mbps speed of a typical network is shared by all the network's users, so overuse of large multimedia content can bring even a powerful file server to its knees.

With that said, many companies are nevertheless uncertain as to how to take advantage of Internet technologies for a private intranet. In this chapter, I'll present some intranet applications that you can design with FrontPage and show you how it's done. Although the examples are necessarily simplified for presentation in this book, they can provide a launching pad for your imagination—even the sky is no limit.

Getting Started With a Disk-Based Web

The simplest way to distribute HTML doesn't even require setting up a company web server. Just use FrontPage Editor directly (without starting the FrontPage Explorer) to design individual web pages, and save them to a folder that is shared on the network. You can link the pages together using the FILE:// protocol. Since all web browsers can open HTML pages directly (from a local hard drive or shared network location), the web server isn't necessary.

Note: You don't have to explicitly add the FILE:// prefix to link pages together on a hard drive or network. Any filename in a URL with a drive name and local path is assumed to be a local file. If the web is not hosted on a web server, but exists only as a set of linked files, it will use the FILE:// protocol in any case.

This method has an obvious limitation. Without a web server, you can only create static pages, similar to word processing documents. For example, you can't create pages with forms since there is no web server to process and store the data from the forms. (Actually, with clever use of Java, JavaScript, or VBScript, even "static" web pages can offer many interactive features, but I won't discuss programming until the next chapter.)

You also can't take advantage of all the FrontPage WebBots, many of which require a connection to the server. (Some WebBots, such as the Include WebBot, don't require the FrontPage Explorer when the page is loaded by the web browser, but while authoring, you can't use the Include WebBot to merge one page with another unless FrontPage Explorer and a server running the FrontPage Extensions are operating. See Chapter 5 for more about what WebBots you should avoid when not running on a FrontPage server.)

Creating a Hypertext FAQ

One good use for a disk-based web (DBW) is implementing a hypertext FAQ (Frequently Asked Questions) document. Traditionally, hypertext documents, which contain links between related information, are created for use with Windows Help. Creating Help files is a tricky and rather tedious technique that requires specialized knowledge. HTML pages, on the other hand, are a snap to create with the FrontPage Editor and offer even more potential capabilities than Windows Help, especially since the pages can be viewed by any user running any computer with a web browser, not just Windows machines.

To try the disk-based web (DBW) concept, close the FrontPage Explorer (if it's currently running) and run the FrontPage Editor from the Start menu. Start your FAQ with some Heading 1 and Heading 2 text describing its purpose; then type each frequently asked question in a list using the Number List paragraph style. The questions will become links to either other pages containing the answers or marked locations within the same document (bookmarks) so that the user can jump directly to the answer to a question.

After typing all the questions, copy and paste them back into the end of the document, and under each question, type the answers. Use Heading 4 for the questions and italicized normal text for the answers.

Finally, to link each question at the top of the page to its counterpart in the answers part of the document, create a bookmark for each location you want to jump to. In the answers part of the document, select each question and use Edit | Bookmark to assign a bookmark name to it.

You can then go back to the top of the document, select each question, and use Edit | Hyperlink (Ctrl+K). Choose the Open Pages tab, and choose the bookmark you want to link to from the BookMark drop-down list. Click OK to close the Edit Hyperlink dialog box.

Save the FAQ to a folder on a hard drive. After you click Save or Save As, click the As File button and choose a folder on the hard drive or a network location. You can even save the HTML page to a floppy disk, since HTML pages (at least those without excessive graphics) have small file sizes.

TIP

To save all the work of creating an index and bookmarking all the entries, you may wish to rely on several FrontPage Editor templates that use bookmarks, including Employee Directory, Glossary of Terms, Product Directory, and Table of Contents, to quickly prototype such a page. Just choose File | New from the FrontPage Editor to try these out.

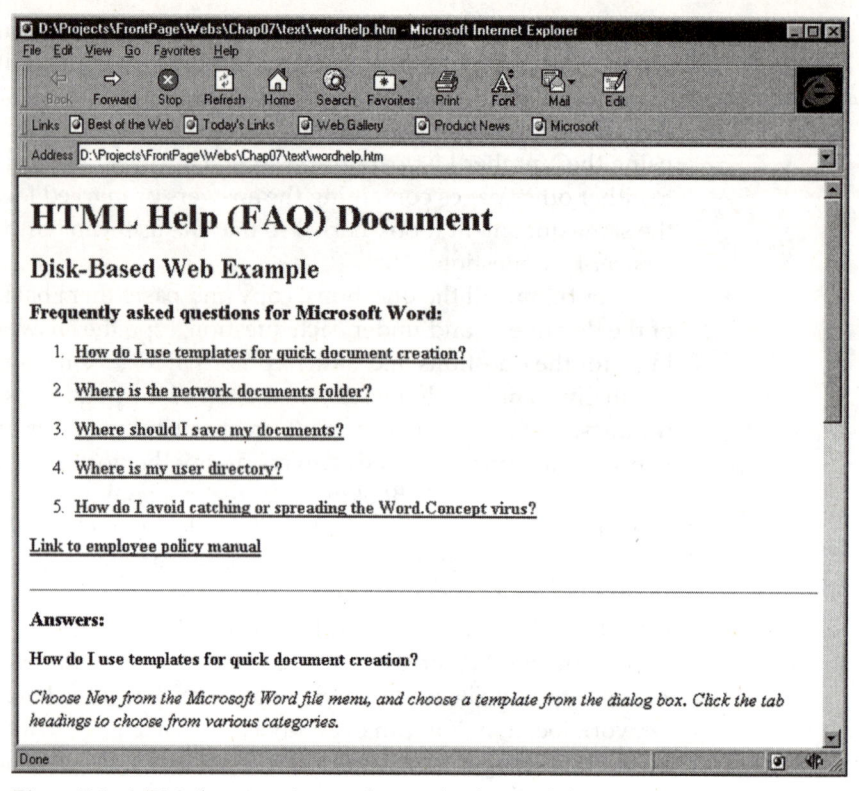

Figure 7-1: A FAQ document is a good example of a simple hypertext file.

To help you see how this works, use the FrontPage Editor to open the file Wordhelp.htm from the \Webs\Chap07\Text folder on this book's Companion CD-ROM. As you can see in the example page (shown in Figure 7-1), you can also create links between FrontPage documents. To create a link, choose the FILE:// protocol from the Hyperlink Type drop-down list on the World Wide Web tab, and in the URL text box, type the location of the document you want to link to. This is demonstrated by Figure 7-2.

TIP

Notice that the hyperlinks point to network folders, in this case, fictional locations on a corporate file server. FrontPage transformed the text into a hyperlink automatically as it was typed. That way, the user can open that folder simply by clicking on the link in the web browser.

If you want to take advantage of automatic link conversion, keep in mind that pressing the spacebar tells FrontPage that you have finished typing the link. If the directory name contains spaces, type it without spaces so that the entire path will become part of the same link, then go back and insert spaces. If you don't want paths to be turned into hyperlinks, just press Ctrl+Z (Edit | Undo) immediately after the path turns into a hyperlink to revert back to normal text.

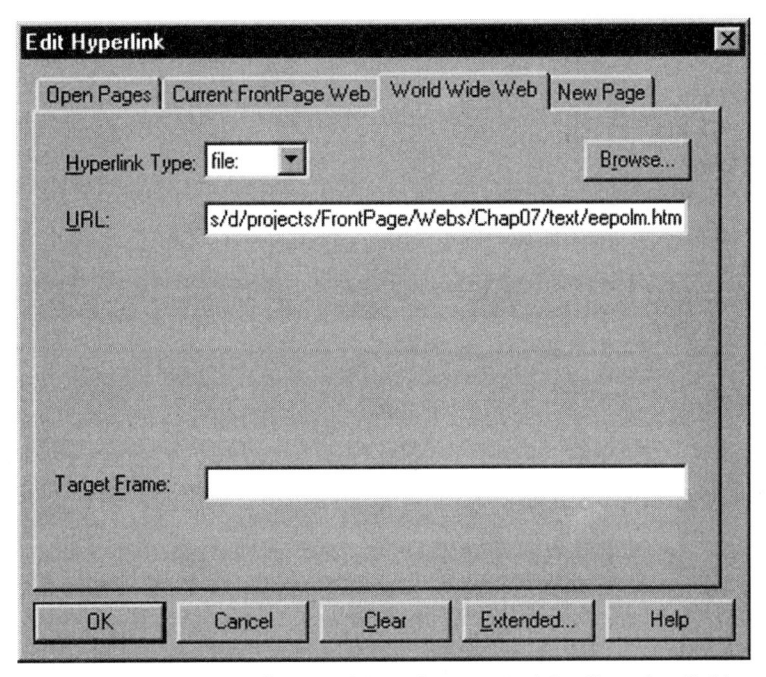

Figure 7-2: Use the FILE:// protocol from the WWW tab heading when linking one document to another in a disk-based web.

Testing the Disk-Based Web

You can use Internet Explorer, Netscape Navigator, or any other web browser to view the pages in a DBW. Just type the path to the file you want to view, such as d:\projects\frontpage\example.htm, into the Address or Location box. (Some browsers may insist you add file:// to the path and use UNIX-style slashes, as in file://d:/projects/frontpage/example.htm.) Keep in mind that there is no web server, so there is no default document—if you type in just the path but not the name of the HTML file, the browser will simply list the directory of the folder.

To access a DBW page from a network file server, use file://servername/sharename/optional_folder_name/page.htm, where servername is the machine name of the file server, sharename is the name of the shared drive or folder, optional_folder_name is the folder containing the page (optional because the sharename may already point to that folder), and page.htm is the filename of the page. For example, you could access a page on the NTSERV server using a path like file://NTSERV/Pages/home.htm, assuming a shared folder called Pages is accessible by the client on the NTSERV server.

> **TIP**
>
> *The easiest way to launch a disk-based web is to navigate to its folder using Windows Explorer. You can then double-click on any of the .HTM file (shown as Internet Document if Details view is enabled) to open them with Internet Explorer or Netscape Navigator, depending on which one is currently set to handle Internet shortcuts. (Both programs will ask you if you want them to take over this function whenever you run them, unless you've already enabled the Don't Ask in Future checkbox that accompanies this prompt.)*
>
> *To create a shortcut to the .HTM files, use the right mouse button to drag the Internet document to the desktop and choose Create Shortcut Here from the pop-up menu. From the web browser, you can also drag any hypertext link to the desktop to create a shortcut to it, or right-click on the link to choose Create Shortcut (wording may vary).*
>
> *As with any Windows shortcut, you can move these shortcuts to program folders in the Start menu, so that your users can easily find the link to your DBW intranet whenever they need it.*

Standard file server security determines who has access to the pages on a disk-based web. Select authorized users can even use simple HTML tools like Word Internet Assistant (built into Office 97) to modify the content. This allows end users to use the HTML-generating features of their existing software to author static content that can be posted on a network file server (as opposed to a web server), and you don't have to grant authoring permissions or buy FrontPage licenses for those users.

If users frequently access the DBW, they may wish to set the first page of the web as the home page of their browser for convenient access to it.

Limitations of Disk-Based Webs

I already mentioned the most obvious limitations of a DBW. The pages you create are static; that is, they don't contain any dynamic content (beyond hyperlinks within and between files), and they don't support interactivity. The only way to update them is to edit the HTML manually, and resave the page as a file to the DBW.

By creating pages directly with the FrontPage Editor, you don't have the services of FrontPage Explorer, which supports authoring-time WebBots such as the Include and Substitution 'bots. If you wish to use WebBots with a disk-based web, create the web within FrontPage Explorer by choosing File | New Web. You can then copy the pages from the web to a folder on the hard drive or to a network folder using File | Export, or by copying the web's folder from the hard drive that hosts the web server's files. (Such as \InetPub\wwwroot on Windows NT, or \Webshare\wwwroot with Windows 95.)

By using the FrontPage Explorer to edit a disk-based web, you can take advantage of its features, such as the ability to automatically fix links when you move or rename pages. Even though you may use the FrontPage Explorer to edit a disk-based web, if you don't put your pages on a web server, they can't tap into the other WebBots, like the Save results 'bot used with forms. Nevertheless, it can be convenient to set up a quick-and-dirty disk-based web—it can always be imported into FrontPage Explorer if and when you decide to implement it as a full-fledged intranet site.

The DBW method (using FrontPage Editor as a stand-alone HTML editor) is also convenient if you want to edit existing HTML pages without resorting to Notepad or bothering to import the pages into FrontPage Explorer.

Setting Up Intranetworking

There's no reason to limit yourself to a disk-based web when you can set up a true TCP/IP intranet running a web server. The previous chapter discussed how to set up the web server, which normally runs on your own machine while you develop content. The same web server can also be used to provide access to your pages from other computers on your network. Just as the Internet uses the Transmission Control Protocol/Internet Protocol (TCP/IP) to communicate between the web host and the browser client, your company LAN can be configured as an intranet to communicate, using TCP/IP, between the host machine running a web server and client workstations running web browsers. (No connection to the Internet is required; your existing network connections will suffice.)

Before you can deploy an intranet, you need to prepare the infrastructure by setting up the TCP/IP protocol on your company network. This alone is a book-length topic, but I'll present some basic techniques on how to configure TCP/IP for your current network setup. If you don't have a local area network already in place, you're not ready for an intranet yet—you'll want to consult another book on setting up and configuring the network. (The network chapters in *The Windows 95 Book* and *Windows NT 4 Workstation Desktop Companion*, both published by Ventana and coauthored by myself, are a good place to start.)

Note: It's possible to set up an intranet without configuring TCP/IP on each workstation. For this, you need a proxy server that translates IPX requests from the client computers to TCP/IP running on the server. You can download Microsoft Proxy Server from http://www.microsoft.com if you want to explore this alternative, but this chapter will focus on the most straightforward method, setting up a true TCP/IP network.

On the other hand, if you know that your company's LAN is already configured for TCP/IP and that the web server (with FrontPage extensions) is up and running, you may want to skip to "Planning a Corporate Intranet" later in this chapter.

Installing TCP/IP Support

You probably already have a file server installed, or some form of peer-to-peer networking. If you're using a Novell NetWare file server, you can install web server software, but at the time of this writing, there is no FrontPage support for NetWare. So I'll assume that you are using either Microsoft Windows NT Server (3.51 or greater running Internet Information Server 2.0 or greater) or peer-to-peer networking (workgroup networking) with Windows NT Workstation 4.0 and/or Windows 95. (Computers running Windows for Workgroups 3.11 can also participate in the intranet, but I won't discuss it here.)

Details on setting up the web server are provided in Chapter 6. Right now, let's see how to set up TCP/IP connectivity between workstations on the network. Before going any further, make sure you are authorized to set up TCP/IP for your workgroup or company. You should always get approval from the data processing or MIS department before setting up or changing the settings of the TCP/IP protocol. Better yet, let them do it for you.

TCP/IP Addressing

Each computer on the network will need to be assigned a unique TCP/IP address, just as every house or office has its own post office mailing address. When a computer is connecting to the Internet, the IP address is usually assigned automatically by the Internet Service Provider. IP addresses can also be assigned dynamically on a network, but only if you have a DHCP server running on Windows NT Server (some UNIX servers also support DHCP, which stands for Dynamic Host Configuration Protocol). Configuring DHCP is a complex topic that is beyond the scope of this book, but I'll present a simpler method here, manually assigning IP addresses to each workstation.

TCP/IP addresses (usually called just IP addresses) consist of four numbers (*octets*) separated by periods. For most small networks, the first three numbers are identical on all workstations, and the last number is unique for each workstation. You can't arbitrarily make up IP addresses, but you can use a Class C network address, reserved for internal networks. This takes the form of 192.168.0.x, where x is a number from 1 to 254. You also need to assign a subnet mask, which is 255.255.255.0.

So the IP address of the server might be 192.168.0.1, and each client machine can be given the next sequential address, as in 192.168.0.2, 192.168.0.3, and so on. You will want to prepare a text file or spreadsheet to help you keep track of the IP addresses of each computer on the network so that you are sure that each computer has a unique address.

When a client computer requests a file from a file server (from either a dedicated file server or a shared folder on a peer server), the file is broken up into small packets. The server sends the packets over the network cabling. Each packet is stamped with the IP address of the destination computer. The packet is actually sent to every computer on the network.

When a packet arrives, each client computer examines it to determine if the packet has in fact reached its intended destination. If not, the client computer simply passes the packet down the line.

When the packet is received on the destination computer, it is combined with other packets to reconstitute the file. If for some reason a packet is missed (perhaps one of the other computers failed to relay it), the client computer asks the server to resend the missed packet. Packets can therefore arrive out of order, but the TCP/IP protocol running on the client computer arranges them in the proper order automatically.

Windows 95 TCP/IP Setup

If the Windows 95 workstation is configured to dial into the Internet, then TCP/IP is already installed. However, TCP/IP is usually only bound to the Dial-Up Adapter, a software network card used to dial into the Internet with a modem. The network card in the computer is probably set up only for NetBEUI or IPX/SPX, the most common and efficient protocols for standard networking.

Follow these steps to install TCP/IP for networking on each workstation or to confirm whether the computer is already set up properly:

1. From the Windows 95 desktop, right-click on Network Neighborhood and choose Properties from the pop-up menu. (You can also double-click the Network icon in Control Panel if you prefer or if there is no Network Neighborhood icon on the desktop.)

    As shown in Figure 7-3, the Network Properties dialog box shows the network components installed on the computer. These include adapters (such as a network card), protocols (such as TCP/IP, NetBEUI, or IPX/SPX), clients (such as Microsoft Networking), and services (such as File and Printer Sharing or Microsoft Personal Web Server).

2. If there are no installed components, click the Add button and choose Adapter. Pick your network card from the list. (If the network card is a Plug and Play card, Windows 95 has probably installed network support automatically. You can also run the Windows 95 setup program on the diskette that came with the network card.) After the network card is installed, double-click it to view or change its resource settings, the IRQ and I/O address the computer uses to communicate with the card.

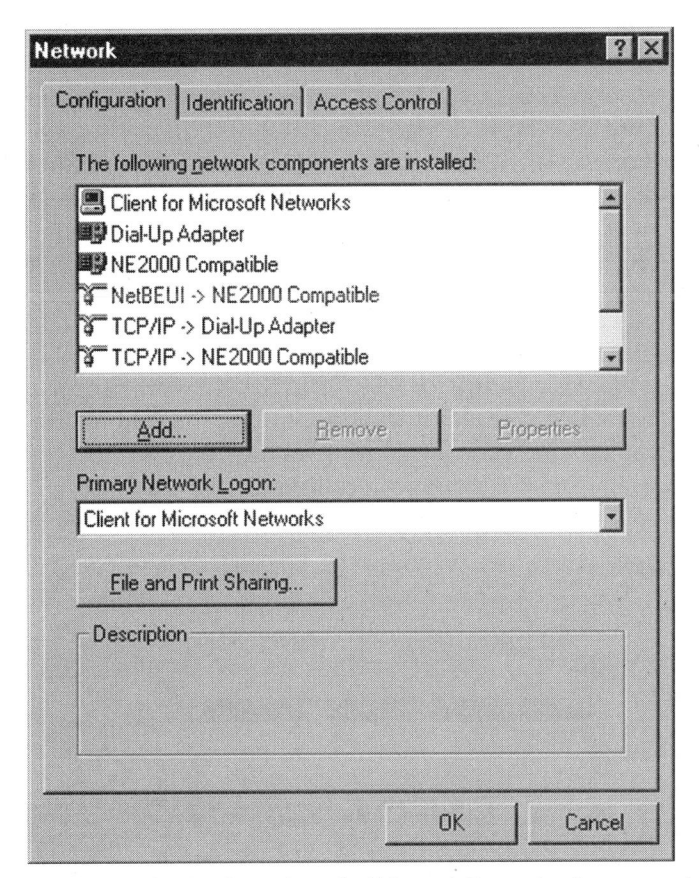

Figure 7-3: The Configuration tab of Network Properties shows you which adapters, protocols, clients, and services are installed.

3. After you install the network adapter (or if it's already set up), Windows 95 automatically installs the Client for Microsoft Networking, and if the card is NetWare-compatible, also installs the Client for Novell NetWare. If you don't use a Novell network, you can click on that client and click Remove to delete it.

4. Windows 95 also normally installs the NetBEUI and IPX/SPX protocols. These are good protocols for general purpose networking, but you also need the TCP/IP protocol for an intranet.

TIP

Should you use only TCP/IP on your network? Too many network protocols make the network run more slowly, and TCP/IP is fully supported on Windows 95 and Windows NT. On the other hand, IPX/SPX is required to connect to a Novell NetWare server, and your existing network may be running fine with its existing protocols, so you don't want to tamper with a good thing. I recommend adding TCP/IP to the existing protocols, at least while you're implementing the intranet for the first time.

If there is an entry for TCP/IP in the Network Properties dialog box, you don't need to add it. Otherwise, click the Add button, choose to add a protocol, and choose Microsoft on the list of vendors on the left and TCP/IP from the list of protocols on the right, as shown in Figure 7-4.

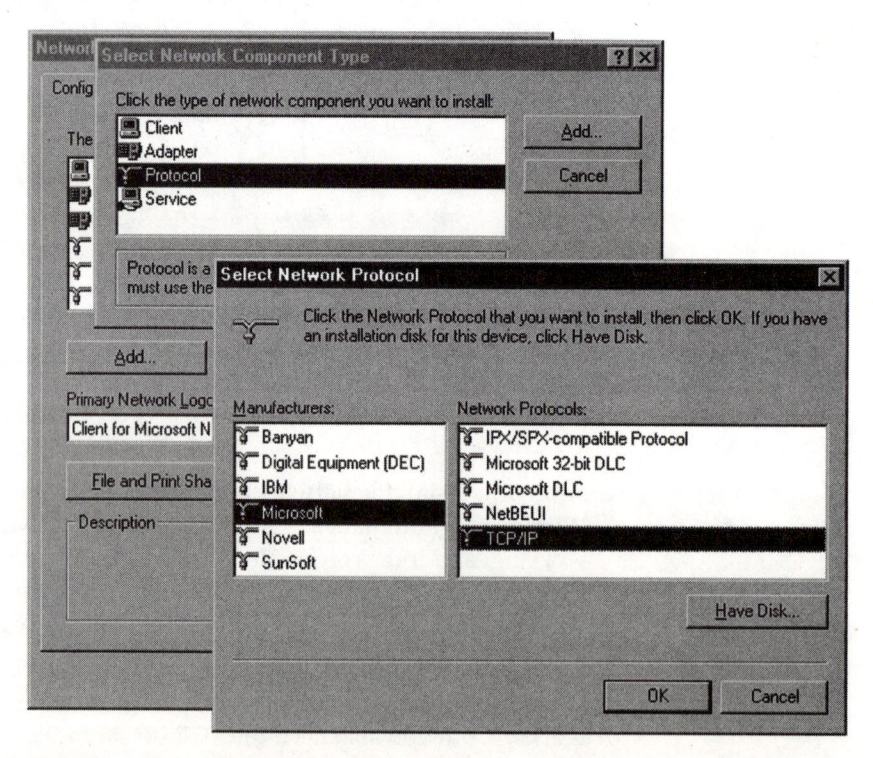

Figure 7-4: After clicking Add from the Network Properties dialog box, choose Protocol and then pick Microsoft TCP/IP.

Once you add a protocol, it is automatically bound (attached) to each network card. If the TCP/IP protocol was only bound to the dial-up adapter, adding TCP/IP again will bind it to the network card also. Another way is to double-click on the network card and on its bindings tab and check the TCP/IP check box.

You'll now have an entry for TCP/IP on the list. If the computer is configured for Dial-Up Networking, it will have two TCP/IP entries: one for the network card and one for the Dial-Up Adapter. You can configure each independently. The TCP/IP properties for the Dial-Up Adapter are only applied when connecting to the Internet. The TCP/IP properties for the network card are used only for intranetworking.

To configure TCP/IP, follow these steps:

1. Double-click on the TCP/IP protocol bound to the network card. You'll see the first property sheet of the TCP/IP Properties dialog box, shown in Figure 7-5.

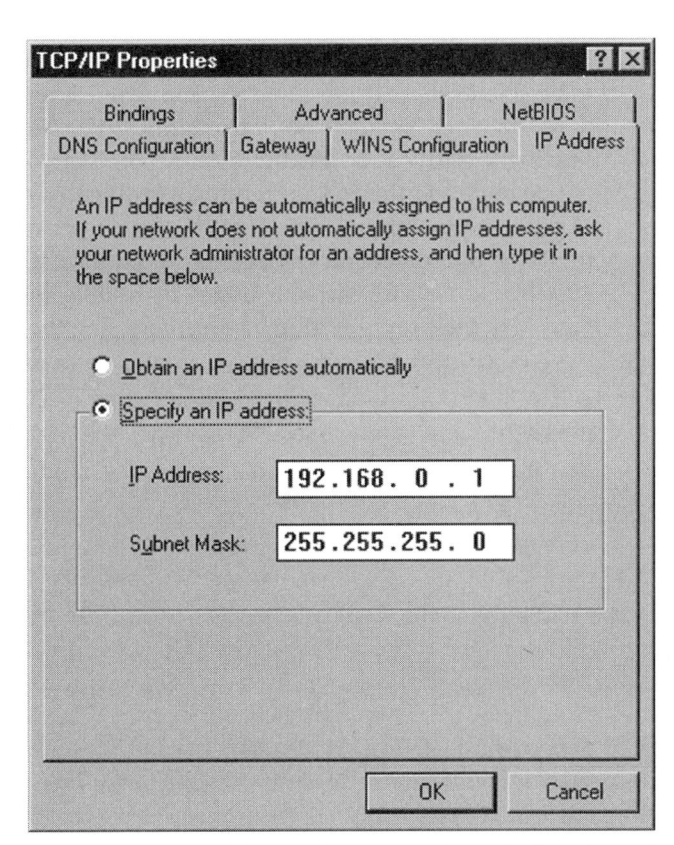

Figure 7-5: The IP Address tab lets you configure the IP address of the card.

2. As shown in Figure 7-5, click on Specify an IP Address, and then assign a unique IP address to the workstation. The first three numbers should be 192.168.0, and the fourth number is a number from 1 to 254. Every computer on the network must be assigned one of these numbers, and no other computer should use the same IP address.

The only way to avoid assigning IP addresses manually is to run a DHCP server on Windows NT. Dynamic Host Configuration Protocol hands out IP addresses to workstations as required from a pool (or range) of assigned IP addresses. Check with your network administrator to see if this is the preferred method.

3. If your network is running a DNS server, you can set it up using the DNS Configuration tab. Similarly, configure the WINS section if your network has a Windows Internet Naming Scheme server. Neither of these is required for an entry-level intranet.

4. You don't need to install the File and Printer Sharing service to let a workstation run a web server; you need it only if you want to be able to share drives, folders, and printers using the standard Network Neighborhood techniques. The File and Printer Sharing service can be bound to Microsoft Networking, but need not be bound to the TCP/IP protocol for the network card (and to prevent possible outside intrusion, should never be bound to the TCP/IP protocol for the Dial-Up Adapter). Bindings for File and Printer Sharing can be changed by double-clicking on the service in the Configuration tab and choosing the Bindings tab.

5. Click OK in all open dialog boxes to close them. You will be prompted to insert the Windows 95 CD-ROM (you can also enter the location of the Windows 95 files on a network file server) so that the necessary drivers and support files can be installed.

You're then asked to restart the computer. After restarting, log in, and you're ready to browse the intranet, assuming at least one web server has already been set up. If you've installed the Windows 95 Personal Web Server, it will publish the web content at its IP address. For example, if a Windows 95 machine running PWS has a TCP/IP address of 192.168.0.5, you can browse the webs it serves from any workstation by opening the address from the web browser, in the form http://192.168.0.5. (The http:// part is optional; you can also just use the raw numbers.)

It's advantageous to make sure that the Microsoft Networking client is installed. It will automatically publish the name of the computer in a network directory service called the *master browse list*. That way, if that computer hosts a web server, other employees can access the home page simply by typing the name of the workstation into the Address box of the browser. You should set up a unique name for each computer on the Identification tab of the Network Properties dialog box. (The workgroup name should be the same for all computers that need to be able to "see" each other in Network Neighborhood, but it's not a requirement for intranetworking.)

Microsoft Networking is also required to validate a computer that logs in to a Windows NT Server machine directly. However, if a web server is running on the server machine, anonymous access to the pages it provides does not require a login or a client license. You only need to log in to the NT Server if you want to use it for traditional networking or if you want to restrict access to some or all web content. (Details on server security are included in Chapter 6.)

TIP

On the other hand, the license for NT Workstation permits only 10 simultaneous TCP/IP connections, a clause widely ridiculed in the Internet community. This means that you can only deploy Peer Web Services for use in workgroups of 10 computers or less, and that you must deploy the much more costly NT Server as a "real" intranet server. I can't recommend that you ignore this legal requirement, but I will tell you that NT Workstation does not enforce this silly rule. There is no such limit in the licensing agreement for the Microsoft Personal Web Server for Windows 95.

If you don't use Microsoft Networking with the client, there is another method to let one computer find another computer's IP address. This involves editing the HOSTS file (no file extension) in the Windows folder on each computer. The HOSTS file contains a list of computer names and IP addresses so the computer can quickly look up each computer on the network. You can create the HOSTS file once (and use it as your master list of computers and IP addresses) and simply copy it to the Windows folder of each computer on the network. Here is an example of how to set up the HOSTS file. Each computer name is followed by a space (or tab character) and its IP address:

```
Customer_Support    192.168.0.5
<ComSales           192.168.0.2
Marketing           192.168.0.3
```

So if the server running the Marketing web has an IP address of 192.168.0.3, then typing the name Marketing into the Address box of the web browser tells the TCP/IP protocol to automatically look up the address 192.168.0.3 in the HOSTS file. (You don't need to add the http:// prefix, just type the machine name into the Address or Location box of the web server. This assumes that there is a default document like index.htm or default.htm in the root directory of the web server. To access a subweb, you'd use a URL like Sales\products\prodinfo.htm.)

There is another benefit to using HOSTS: accessing a page on your intranet from a server that is referenced in the HOSTS file prevents Internet Explorer (or whatever browser you use) from dialing the modem to reach the page. This is a good reason to set the home page of the browser to point to the home page of your intranet, so that a dial-up connection isn't attempted when the web browser is started. The modem should only be dialed if the workstation is configured for Dial-Up Networking and the user is trying to access a site not listed in the HOSTS file.

TIP

If Windows 95 insists on dialing the modem when trying to reach a page on the intranet, you will have to disable the check box for Connect as Needed on the Connection page of the Internet Explorer Properties dialog box. To open this property sheet, use View | Options from within Internet Explorer, or double-click on the Internet icon in Control Panel. Once Connect as Needed is disabled, the user will need to manually start an Internet connection by double-clicking on an icon in the Dial-Up Networking folder (available in the My Computer folder) before browsing the World Wide Web. This is a good policy in any case, as it can save your company hundreds of dollars in connection fees by preventing accidental dial-ups.

Windows NT 4.0 Workstation TCP/IP Setup

I won't discuss how to set up TCP/IP on an NT Server computer; this is a task best left to experienced NT Server administrators. However, you will need to set up TCP/IP for each computer running NT Workstation if you want it to participate on the intranet. If DHCP is running on the Windows NT Server that the NT Workstation logs in to, TCP/IP support for NT Workstation was probably already installed during the setup of NT Workstation on that computer, and the TCP/IP address will be configured automatically. In other words, you don't need to do anything else, so skip ahead to the next section, "Planning a Corporate Intranet."

Even without DHCP, your task should be easy. TCP/IP is installed by default, so all you really have to do is set a unique IP address for each computer. If TCP/IP is missing from the network configuration, you'll have to add it. Here's how:

1. Open Control Panel and double-click on the Network icon.

2. The Network Properties dialog box is divided into five property sheets, each with a tabbed heading. The Identification tab is displayed by default. From here, confirm that the computer is assigned a unique computer name (no other computer on the network should use the same name). The Workgroup box, if shown, should show the name of the workgroup that the computer is part of. If the computer logs in to an NT Server, the server domain is shown instead. You can click Change if necessary to set up the Workgroup or Domain name, but it shouldn't be necessary.

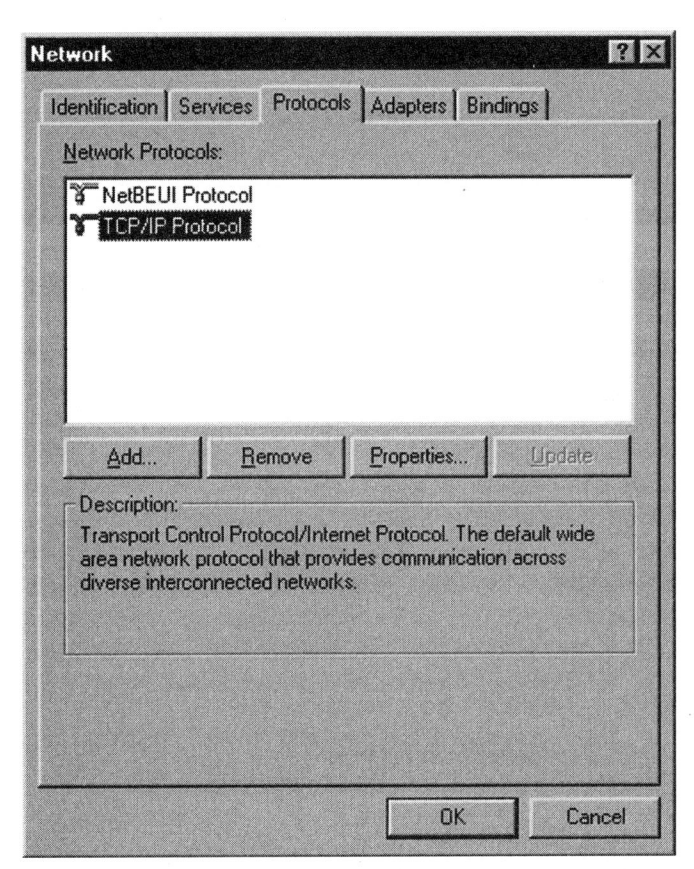

Figure 7-6: Click the Add button if TCP/IP is not already installed.

3. Click the Protocols tab. You should see an entry for NetBEUI, IPX/SPX, and/or TCP/IP (Figure 7-6). If TCP/IP is not shown, click the Add button, and choose the TCP/IP Protocol from the Select Network Protocol dialog box.

4. If you just added the TCP/IP protocol, the property sheet for TCP/IP appears (Figure 7-7). If TCP/IP was already installed, double-click on the TCP/IP protocol (in the list shown in Figure 7-6) to get the property sheets shown in Figure 7-7.

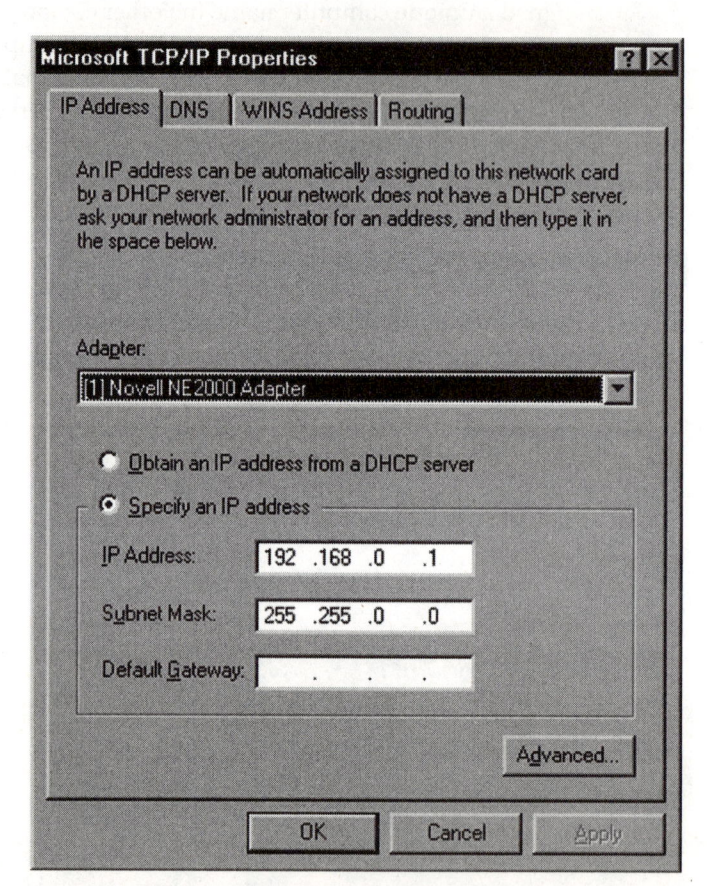

Figure 7-7: Assign a unique IP address to the computer.

5. The IP Address tab is the only one that you need to be concerned with. Assuming your network doesn't deploy DHCP, here's where you set a unique IP address for the computer. In Figure 7-7, the IP address is 192.168.0.1, but you'll substitute a unique address (changing the last number from 1 to a number from 1 to 254). If you have more than 254 computers on your intranet, you probably need to use DHCP, and such a large network is likely already administered by an expert that can take care of this. (If you're the expert, and you don't know how to set up DHCP, you better get a copy of the *Microsoft Windows NT Server Resource Kit* from Microsoft Press and do your homework!)

6. You also need to set the subnet mask. For the Class C IP address range 192.168.0.*, use 255.255.255.0. (If there is more than one network adapter installed and configured for TCP/IP, each card will need a unique IP address. Use the Network Adapter drop-down list to choose settings for each card.)

7. If your network has a DNS server installed, you can configure the name of the server on the DNS property sheet. DNS (Domain Name Service) is used to look up the name of the workstation and find its IP address.

If you don't have a DNS server, you can edit the file HOSTS (no file extension) in the Windows NT folder of each workstation. The HOSTS file contains a list of computer names and IP addresses so the computer can quickly look up each computer on the network. You can create the HOSTS file once (and use it as your master list of computers and IP addresses), and simply copy it to the Windows folder of each computer on the network. Here is an example of how to set up the HOSTS file. Each computer name is followed by a space (or tab character) and its IP address:

```
Customer_Support    192.168.0.5
Sales               192.168.0.2
Marketing           192.168.0.3
```

So if the server running the Marketing web has an IP address of 192.168.0.3, then typing the name Marketing into the Address box of the web browser tells the TCP/IP protocol to automatically look up the address 192.168.0.3 in the HOSTS file.

(You don't need to add the http:// prefix, just type the machine name into the Address or Location box of the web server. This assumes that there is a default document like index.htm or default.htm in the root directory of the web server. To access a subweb, you'd use a URL like Sales\products\prodinfo.htm.)

By using the HOSTS list, you can make sure that NT Workstation doesn't attempt to dial the modem when reaching a site on your intranet. Even without a HOSTS file, as long as the computer is logged in to a valid account on the network, it can find the machine name of other computers, as long as they are also logged in.

8. Click OK to close the TCP/IP properties sheet. You may be asked to insert the NT Workstation CD-ROM to let NT copy any necessary files to complete the installation of the protocol. You can then close the Network Properties dialog box.

Each computer on the intranet can now be accessed via its TCP/IP address. If an NT Workstation computer is running Peer Web Services, then the pages it serves can be opened simply by typing the workstation's IP address into the Address box of the browser. You can also use the machine name or the name in the HOSTS file.

Now that TCP/IP connectivity is in place and the servers are up and running (see Chapter 6 if necessary), you're ready to deploy intranet applications.

Planning a Corporate Intranet

The first step in designing a corporate intranet is to set some goals. You can start with known business challenges and design an HTML-based solution or use HTML to redesign an existing business solution. For example, you may currently use Microsoft Access to allow employees to look up names and addresses in a phone book. This means that each end user must have a license for the privilege of using a huge memory-bloating program (Microsoft Access, in this case), perhaps overkill for most purposes.

One workaround is to design a simple Visual Basic front end to the database, which saves memory and speeds program loading. Another solution is to deploy web pages that link directly to the database, using a supported web server such as Windows 95 Personal Web Server, Internet Information Server, or Peer Web Services.

It's a good idea to start with modest goals and add new capabilities over time. In this chapter, you're going to see how to put together a useful corporate intranet, with the following goals in mind:

- Employees will use the web browser as the primary user interface. It's something that many users are already familiar with, and it's easy to teach new employees how to navigate within a browser. Even the My Computer or Network Neighborhood features of the Windows 95/NT 4 user interface aren't as easy to use as a web browser. (As Bill Gates was said to quip, "When I turn on my computer I don't want to be looking at a bunch of folders.")

- Employees will still want to be able to use their powerful desktop applications, such as Microsoft Office, Corel WordPerfect, or Lotus Smartsuite, so there must be a way to access documents stored on the local workstation or network file server, ideally without leaving the web browser environment.

- Some employees will want to be able to publish their own HTML content, created with the Office Internet Assistants or the new features of Office 97, and have it available for other employees or team members to view.

- Employees will benefit from an online employee directory to look up extension numbers and e-mail addresses and convenient access to the employee policy manual.

- The MIS department will want to be able to set up a page with icons for programs installed on the local hard drive or network file server. This makes it easy to centralize the software interface instead of having to update Program Manager folders or implement a corporate Start menu with all the complications that come with it (such as reading through a 900-page Resource Kit to figure out how to do it!).

- Employees will demand easy access to the mailing address database (address book) for convenient lookup, update, and maintenance features. (This is indeed a modest goal; a more ambitious intranet project would allow full access to all corporate databases, including report generation.)

- The purchasing department will want employees to have access to a web-based requisition form. Soon every department will want all their forms on the corporate intranet.

- Management will want the first version of the intranet completed within a week, to show off at an upcoming board meeting.

Implementing the Corporate Intranet

All these goals can be accomplished with FrontPage and a web server capable of running the Internet Database Connector (IDC), which is how we'll link web content to Access or SQL Server databases. This means you can use Internet Information Server (IIS) 2.0 or later running on a Windows NT Server computer, Peer Web Services running on NT Workstation, or even the Windows 95 Personal Web Server running on a Windows 95 client computer. While UNIX servers with FrontPage Server Extensions can be used to develop corporate intranets, they don't yet support IDC, so I'll focus on the Wintel club for now.

In previous chapters, I showed you how to build sample webs from the ground up. That level of detail is necessary for a tutorial, but because there are so many topics to discuss in this chapter, I need to take a different approach. Instead, I'll start with a completed web and dissect it, showing you how it was put together.

For clarity, some of the instructions will explain step-by-step how to put together a particular element of the intranet web, but this won't be enough to create the entire project. Sometimes you will have to refer to the completed web, by importing it from this book's Companion CD-ROM.

If you want to follow along with the FrontPage software instead of merely reading the text and examining the screen shots and other figures (which is a perfectly valid approach), you'll need to import the Chapter 7 intranet web into FrontPage Explorer. Details on importing the sample webs from the Companion CD-ROM are included in Appendix A. In a nutshell, you simply use the Import Wizard (File | Import from FrontPage Explorer) to import the \Webs\Chap07\Intranet folder as a new web.

You'll apply the FrontPage techniques you've already learned, so I won't delve into too much detail. For example, instead of telling you to type some text, select it, press Ctrl+K, switch to the Open Pages tab, and choose the index.htm page, I'll simply instruct you to type some text and link it to the home page.

Deploying the Browser

Not to put the cart before the horse, but after the intranet web is up and running, you need to prepare the client workstations. First install TCP/IP, as described earlier, and be sure to install the custom HOSTS file in the Windows (or Windows NT) folder of each computer.

Next, decide on a web browser. While Netscape Navigator has enjoyed undisputed mindshare for the last few years, the new 3.0 release of Microsoft Internet Explorer compares well in terms of enhanced browser capabilities, plus IE offers several unique features, such as support for ActiveX Controls, Style Sheets, and dual Jscript/VBScript programmability, not to mention another great benefit—it's free. Netscape Navigator, on the other hand, requires the purchase of a license for each workstation (or an expensive site license for your entire company).

Your choice of browser will likely come down to the type of features you want to exploit on your intranet. If you want to use features supported only by Netscape Navigator or only by Internet Explorer, those particular features will dictate which browser resides on the client desktop. For the examples in this chapter, you can use whichever browser you wish.

TIP

By the time this book is published, the new Netscape browser suite, Netscape Communicator, will have replaced Navigator 3.0. You can download the beta or release version (when ready) from http://www.netscape.com. In the discussion that follows, I'll continue to refer to the traditional Navigator, but the same techniques will apply to Netscape Communicator. Netscape has pledged to support nearly every Internet Explorer 3.0 capability, including ActiveX Controls and VBScript, with the final release of Communicator. (At the time of this writing, much of this support requires the installation of the ScriptActive plug-in from NCompass, which must be purchased separately. Yet another reason to switch to Internet Explorer, in my opinion.)

Both browsers allow you to customize their features for your company. You may wish to download the Internet Explorer Administration Kit from http://www.microsoft.com/ie/ieak/. It lets you add your corporate logo to the browser, set up the button bar with shortcuts to your intranet resources, and obtain a license to freely redistribute Internet Explorer within your enterprise. You can also deploy a "kiosk" version that hides the navigation and toolbar controls. The kiosk mode also prevents the browser from being closed or switched away from. The IE Admin Kit is free of charge.

While the Netscape Navigator Administration Kit is expensive ($1,995), it's the best way to configure and deploy Navigator within your company. Look to http://www.netscape.com/comprod/products/navigator/version_3.0/management/admin/index.html for more information. (If this link has moved, just start browsing at www.netscape.com.)

You'll want to deploy the latest version of your chosen browser and keep all workstations updated as newer versions are released and proven stable. For example, earlier versions of Windows 95 and the first release of Windows NT 4.0 (Server and Workstation) have Internet Explorer 2.0 preinstalled, which is severely limited compared to its 3.0 sibling. Both Windows 95 and NT can be upgraded to the latest 3.0 (actually 3.01) version of Internet Explorer.

It is not recommended, however, to deploy beta versions, despite possible increased functionality, since you risk the bugs and suffer the lack of support typical for beta programs.

Once a browser is installed on each computer, you can add the URL of your company home page as a shortcut to the Startup folder so that the browser starts up and loads the home page automatically when the computer is turned on. This way, the employee is ready to work with intranet resources right away. Alternately, install a shortcut on the desktop for quick access.

Designing the Home Page

For this book, I created a fictional corporate intranet for Carolina Resource Network (a nonfictional company). It is found in the Webs\Chap07\Intranet folder on the Companion CD-ROM. Refer to Appendix A to find out how to import this web into FrontPage Explorer if you want to work with the examples (recommended).

To begin dissecting this web, take a look at the home page in Figure 7-8. The home page includes links that give employees quick access to the intranet resources you offer. In this chapter, I'll show you how to implement each of these resources. Access Intranet Documents lets employees browse and open documents as well as employee or departmental HTML pages. Run Software links to a page containing icons for programs installed on the local computer or on the network. Employee Resources is a page containing an employee directory and other employee-related resources (such as an HTML version of the Employee Policy Manual), and Work With Address Book lets employees look up, add, delete, or update addresses in the Address Book database.

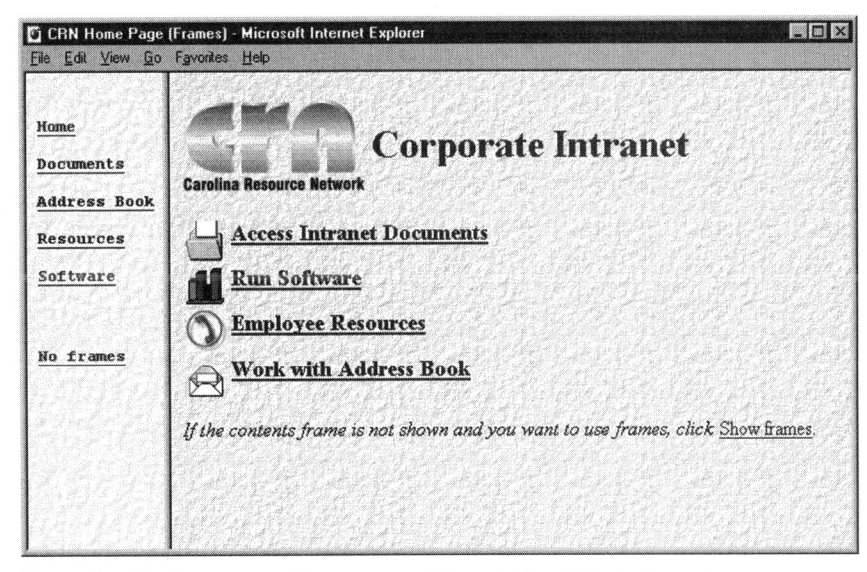

Figure 7-8: The home page of the company intranet offers links to the various resources and a durable "contents" frame that provides these links no matter what page you're viewing.

These links were created by setting up a two-column table with no borders. The icon for each link, placed in the first column of each row, was chosen from the FrontPage clip-art library by choosing Insert | Graphic and choosing from the Animations category on the Clip Art tab. The text for each link was typed as Heading 2. Both the icons and the text were then linked to their respective pages with the Edit | Hyperlink command (Ctrl+K).

Since this home page was created after all the other pages were completed, it was relatively easy to figure out where to point each link. I'll show you how these pages (and the pages they link to) were created in the remainder of this chapter.

Access Intranet Documents	links to	intradocs.htm
Run Software	links to	programs.htm
Employee Resources	links to	employee.htm
Work With Address Book	links to	database.htm

Establishing a Common Theme

Every web should establish a graphical look and feel that is consistent between pages. In Chapter 2, you learned how to customize the page background and logo created by the Corporate Presence Wizard. The same technique is used here.

You'll need to create two HTML documents: One called style.htm, stored in the _private folder, is the master page containing the custom background; the other, called logo.htm, also stored in the _private folder, contains the company logo. On all other pages in the intranet web, use the Include WebBot to incorporate the logo, and set the page properties to use the colors and backgrounds specified in the style.htm page. (These pages have already been created and can be found in the _private folder of the web.)

To add these features to the home page, insert an Include WebBot at the top of the page, using _private/logo.htm as the source. Use File | Page Properties and click the Background tab, assigning _private/style.htm to the text box beneath Get Background and Colors From Page.

You may also wish to create a blank page with these elements so that you can quickly create new pages by opening the Blank Page, using Save As to give it a new name and title, and then adding the rest of the page's content. (If you save the Blank Page as a template, you can retrieve it by using File | New, but the included material won't appear until you save the page and reload it with View | Refresh.)

Frame-Based Navigation

You will no doubt notice the *frames* in Figure 7-8. Frames divide the web browser window into two or more regions. The main frame holds the content, and the frame on the left is a navigation aid, a kind of table of contents for the intranet site. When the user clicks on a link in the contents frame on the left, the page pointed to by that link appears in the main frame, without replacing the contents frame. That way, the navigation links are available no matter what page is being viewed.

We accomplished the same purpose in Chapter 3 with an animated toolbar. The disadvantage of using the toolbar (apart from the time it took to create it) is that it has to be inserted on every page of the web using the Include WebBot. The toolbar can also scroll with the page, perhaps out of sight, whereas the document in each frame can scroll independently of documents in the other frames.

Running the Frames Wizard

A *frameset* is a special HTML document that describes the layout of the frames, the name of each frame, and the default content for each frame. Creating framesets manually is ugly and tedious, but fortunately FrontPage automates this with the Frames Wizard.

To set up the frames for the intranet, run the FrontPage Editor and use File | New to choose the Frames Wizard. The first question asked by the wizard is whether you want to pick a frames template or create a custom grid. Since most common frame types (including the Simple Table of Contents frameset) are already available as templates, you'll rarely need to use the custom grid option, which lets you define the layout of the frames as if it were a table.

As shown in Figure 7-9, frames can get quite complicated. The Navigation Bars frameset consists of four separate frames. This lets you put a table of contents on the left, the main page on the right, and navigation bars at the top and bottom. Clicking a link or icon in any frame can potentially update the contents of any other frame. To help you understand how all this works, pick the Simple Table of Contents template, which consists of only two frames.

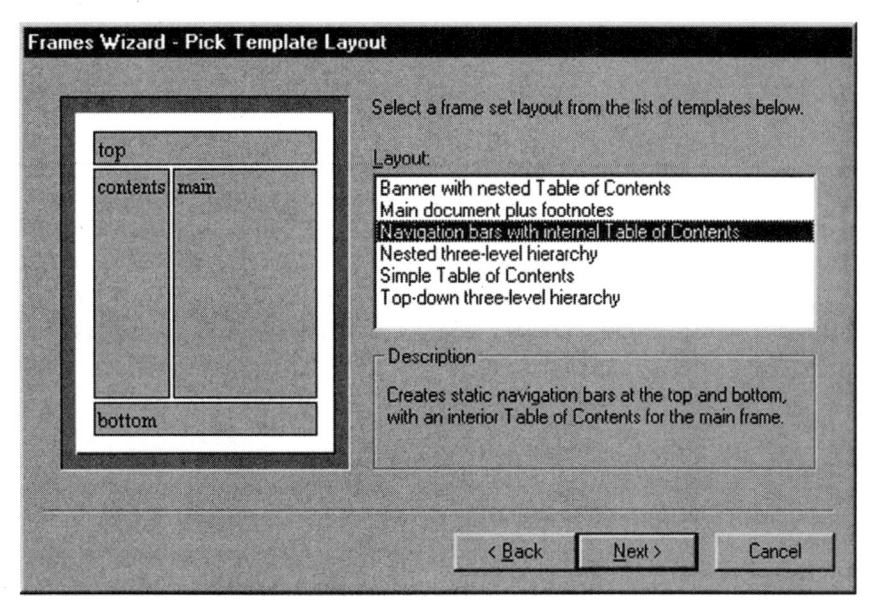

Figure 7-9: Choose a type of frameset from the list of templates.

After you click Next, you can specify the name of a page that is displayed if the browser doesn't support frames. Internet Explorer 2.0 is an example of a web browser that can't display frames. To allow your site to degrade gracefully, you provide an alternate page that is loaded instead of the frameset when a browser can't use frames.

Note: Most experienced webmasters try to avoid frames for two reasons: First, many Internet users, including the huge base of America Online users with the 2.0 AOL software, can't view pages with frames. (AOL 3.0 improves the browser considerably, but it hasn't caught on yet, perhaps because it won't fit on a single diskette!) Secondly, frames can be ugly and ungainly, confusing to users, and somewhat of a gimmick. You should never feel you need to use frames just to prove your competence at web design, or because they fascinate you. Instead, your site must depend on the frames as a crucial element of the site's navigation techniques. This book wouldn't be complete without a discussion of frames and a suitable example, but if I had my druthers, I'd leave it out all together.

In our intranet web, the main frame holds the home page (more correctly, start page) of the intranet, named home.htm. (The actual home page, or default page, is index.htm, but this is the URL of the frameset, which in turn loads the home page into the main frame.) So you can use home.htm as the alternate page. If the frames can't load, the home page displays without the frames. Couldn't be simpler. Click Browse to locate this page within the web, and then click Next.

> **TIP**
>
> *If you use this web as is, make sure your web server is set to use index.htm as the default document instead of default.htm. Both IIS, PWS, and MS PWS for Windows 95 use default.htm when installed, but I prefer index.htm, since it's the most commonly supported default page on Internet web servers. Or, rather than change the default document (discussed in Chapter 6), you can rename index.htm in the FrontPage Explorer, which will automatically fix any links to that page.*

The next page of the Frames Wizard prompts you to give the frameset a title and a URL. Remember that a frameset is treated like any other HTML page. When opened, it creates the framework and inserts the default HTML pages into each frame. Since you want the frames to be displayed as soon as the page is opened, name it Corporate Home Page and give it a name of index.htm. (If you're adding frames to an existing site, use FrontPage Explorer to rename the current index.htm to home.htm, which will automatically update all links to the home page.

Then you can run the Frames Wizard to create the frameset and specify home.htm as the default page for the main frame.)

Click Finish to save the frameset to the web. Now you need to customize it. Locate the frameset in FrontPage Explorer (it should have been saved as index.htm) and double-click it.

Customizing Framesets

When you open a frameset from FrontPage Explorer, the Frames Wizard starts again to let you customize it. This is the same view you would have seen if you had chosen the Custom Grid option earlier while viewing the frameset choices. When creating a custom frameset, you can use the Split and Merge buttons to divide a frame into subframes or merge two subframes into a single frame. You can also use the Rows and Columns boxes to set up the overall frame layout for the page. Since you already used the template to set up the grid, we'll ignore these options.

The first thing you'll want to do is adjust the relative size of the two frames by dragging the border between the frames with the mouse. Trial and error is the best way to adjust the size of the contents frame so that it's just large enough to contain the table of contents frame without stealing too much space from the main frame. (You can also edit the frameset with Notepad and modify the HTML tags, such as <frameset cols="20%,80%">, by right-clicking on the frameset in FrontPage Explorer and choosing Open With from the pop-up menu.)

After you click Next, your next step is to name the frames. Each frame is assigned a name, which is not the same thing as the URL of the page that is loaded into the frame. The frame name is used with hyperlinks to specify which linked page should appear within the frame. Click on each frame and enter a name that is meaningful to you, and then specify the URL of the page that will appear there by default (when the frameset is first opened by the browser).

> **TIP**
>
> *Keep in mind the distinction between the* name *of a frame, and* contents *of a frame. The name of a frame never changes, and is used to choose which frame a target URL should be loaded into. While some frames are designed to always show the same page (like the TOC frame), there really is no one-to-one correspondence between the name of a frame and the page that it shows. Any named frame can display any page. The secret to choosing which frame holds which page is in the hyperlink properties for the links in a particular frame, which you'll find out more about in "Creating Frame Content."*

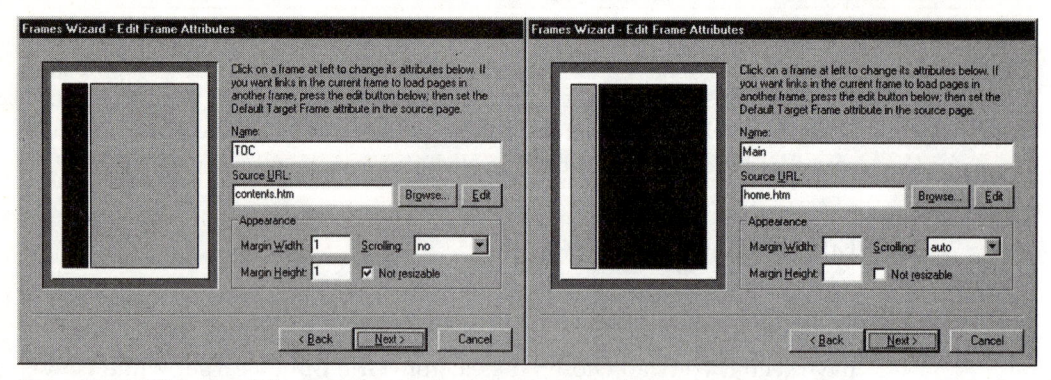

Figure 7-10: Click on each frame and assign it a name and default URL (page).

As shown in Figure 7-10, I used TOC for the name of the leftmost frame and Main as the name of the rightmost frame. The TOC frame loads contents.htm by default, and the Main frame opens with home.htm. At this time, you can click Edit to create or edit the page, but you can postpone this until later.

Also notice the section labeled Appearance in the Edit Frame Attributes window. Here you can choose the width and/or height of the margin (the border between the frames), whether the contents of the frame can be scrolled (if the page exceeds the dimensions of the frame), and whether the user is allowed to resize the frames by dragging the border. Since this can throw off the formatting of the page, most authors make at least one frame Not Resizable. (Since there are only two frames in this frameset, you don't need to use Not Resizable for the rightmost frame; if the leftmost frame can't be resized, the rightmost one can't be resized either.)

> **TIP**
>
> *Internet Explorer supports seamless frames, which display side by side without a distracting border (margin). This is accomplished by adding frameborder="0" to the <frameset> tag. Ideally, you should only need to set the margin width to 0 in the Frames Wizard, but it doesn't work that way.*
>
> *Instead, right-click on the index.htm page in FrontPage Explorer and choose Open Width from the pop-up menu. Choose Text Editor to open the page with Notepad. Find the <frameset> tag, and prior to the closing bracket, type frameborder="0", as in:*
>
> ```
> <frameset cols="18%,82%" frameborder="0">
> ```
>
> *Save the changes with Notepad, and switch back to FrontPage Explorer so that it can import the changes.*

After you click Next, you're asked to specify an alternate page for nonframes browsers. Since you already set this up, click Next again. The last page prompts you for the title and URL of the frameset. Accept the current title and URL (already set for the home page as home.htm), and click Finish. You'll be asked if you want to overwrite a page with the same name in the web. Since this is the page you've edited, the prompt seems unnecessary, but go ahead and click OK anyway.

Creating Frame Content

The page loaded into the TOC frame will be the table of contents for the site. You create this page (saves as contents.htm and titled Contents) with the FrontPage Editor, just as with any other web page document.

From the FrontPage Editor, choose File | New Page, and pick the Normal Page (you can also simply click the toolbar button). Type the contents list using the Formatted paragraph style, as follows (insert a space in front of each entry to separate it from the frame border, and skip a line between Software and No frames):

```
Home
Documents
Address Book
Resources
Software

No frames
```

You're now ready to link each item to its corresponding page. You do this the same way you create any hyperlink, by selecting the text with the mouse and pressing Ctrl+K (or click the toolbar button). Since you're using frames, you need to follow just one more step: specifying the target frame. The target frame specifies which frame a page appears in when you click the link to that page inthe TOC frame. See Figure 7-11.

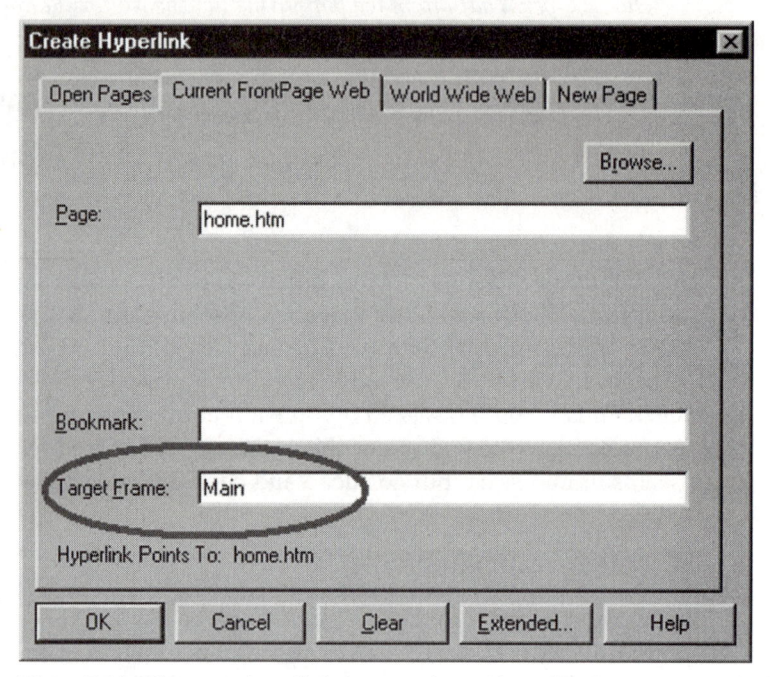

Figure 7-11: When creating a link from one frame to another, be sure to specify the target frame.

Home	links to	home.htm	target frame:	Main
Documents	links to	intradocs.htm	target frame:	Main
Address Book	links to	database.htm	target frame:	Main
Resources	links to	employee.htm	target frame:	Main
Software	links to	programs.htm	target frame:	Main
No frames	links to	home.htm	target frame:	_top

As shown in Figure 7-11, fill out the Page box as you normally do. You can click Browse to locate the page you want to link to from the current web and then fill in the Target Frame box with Main, the name of the rightmost frame. (The Target Frame box is also available from the other tabs, such as Open Pages.) Each link on the Contents page points to one of the other pages in the web. In the example intranet web, all these pages were created before I set up frames. If you're starting with frames and adding the pages later, you can link using the New Page tab and either edit the page immediately or add it to the To Do List.

If you don't choose a target frame, the linked page will appear within the same frame as the link that points to it. In other words, if you leave the Target Frame text box blank, the page will load into the TOC frame on the left. This is not desirable. The links on the home page, however, don't need a target frame, since you want them to appear within the same frame as the home page itself. This makes it easy to add frames to an existing site. All the existing content will continue to display within the main frame as long as at least one of those pages (such as the home page) has been opened within that frame.

Special Target Frames

Leaving the Target Frame text box blank is the same as using a reserved frame name, _self. Two other Target Frame options are worthy of discussion: _top and _parent. (Be sure to start with the underscore character and type using lowercase.) Use _top if you want the page to open within a new web browser window without frames. (This is the target frame of the No Frames link, which points to the home.htm page.)

The _parent target frame is used with multilevel frames. For example, consider a frameset made of three stacked frames. The top frame is used to choose the contents of the middle frame, which in turn updates the contents of the bottom frame. If a link on the middle frame uses a target frame of _parent, that page is loaded into the parent of that page, which is the topmost frame. If used with the bottom frame, the _parent target frame would load the page into the middle frame. In practice, you won't use _parent very often.

Once all the links on the TOC (contents.htm) page have been set up, the frameset is fully functional. Before saving the contents page, you may want to customize it with its own background color or background texture by choosing File | Page Properties. I chose a pleasing background from the clip-art library that comes with the FrontPage CD-ROM.

Testing the Frameset

You can test your frameset by opening your preferred web browser and opening the frameset page. Since the frameset is named index.htm, you can open it with the web browser by using an address like: http://localhost/Intranet/, assuming you are running the web server locally and have created it as a web named Intranet. Click on each link to verify that it replaces the contents of the Main frame with the chosen page. If any pages appear within the TOC frame, edit the link to use Main as the target frame.

Because the user may have clicked the No Frames hyperlink (which points to home.htm using a target frame of _self), there also needs to be a way for the home page to reload the frameset when necessary. This link simply points to the frameset itself, which on this web is index.htm, using a target frame of _top. (If _top was left off, the frames would display inside the existing frameset, if it is currently displayed. Nested frames like this are fully supported and potentially quite powerful, but we don't need them here.)

Designing Intranet Content

Let's see how to set up the other pages in the intranet. We'll take a tour of each completed page and then show you how it was created.

Access Intranet Documents

The Access Intranet Documents page (saved as introdocs.htm and shown in Figure 7-12) contains links to folders on the network. When the employee clicks a link, the folder is opened within the browser. The user can then choose a file or folder within that folder to open. The idea is that there are already network directories (folders) on a file server containing documents, such as Word or Excel files, that the user wants to open.

The links on this page are accessed directly using the FILE:// protocol; the documents do not reside on the web server. As long as the documents are opened directly with the browser, they appear within the container of the web browser. The user never seems to leave the browser environment entirely.

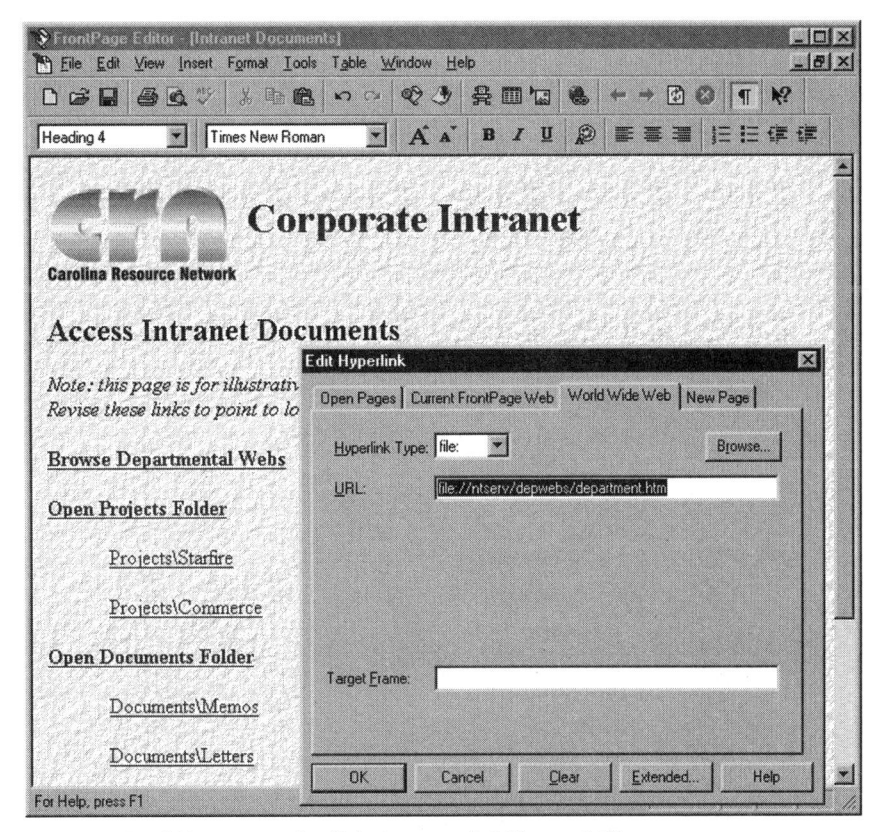

Figure 7-12: This page contains links to network folders and files.

If you examine the links on the page, you'll see that they use the FILE:// protocol to specify a specific folder on the file server, named NTSERV. For example, the Projects folder links to file://ntserv/d/projects, which means, "Open the project folder from the d share on the ntserv file server." Keep in mind that the links on this page are fictional; you would substitute descriptions and paths specific to your installation.

TIP

If you are using Netscape Navigator, you may have to configure a helper application for some of the file types on your intranet. For example, the DOC extension used by Word documents causes Netscape to display the file as text. You can configure DOC files to open with Word by using the Helpers tab of Options | General Preferences.

The first link, Browse Departmental Webs, deserves closer inspection (see the Edit Hyperlink dialog box in Figure 7-12). In the example page, it links to an HTML file on the network file server using a share name of Depwebs (this would be a shared folder on the file server). This is not a true web server. Instead, the page is a static HTML page created with a simple tool like Word Internet Assistant or saved as HTML from Word 97. This page in turn contains FILE:// links to the other folders and pages created and maintained by employees or department heads. The advantage of this method is that you don't need to open up authoring permissions for everyone in your company, and employees can take advantage of the HTML-generation features of their own software.

See the sidebar, "Direct-to-Web Publishing," for an even better way to implement an employee-driven corporate web.

Direct-to-Web Publishing

Microsoft Office 97 includes powerful and practical tools for saving pages or exporting information as HTML documents as simply as choosing Save as HTML from the File Menu.

The new Online Layout view of Word 97 is nearly as effective as the FrontPage Editor for creating web pages, and all applications let you easily create links between Office documents.

Furthermore, users can configure their applications to publish documents directly to the web server, as long as they have an account on an FTP server that includes a virtual directory pointing to the web content. The webmaster or FTP administrator can set security and access rights so that only certain subwebs can be updated by employees, protecting the intranet from accidental erasure or malicious intrusion. Since this is such a powerful capability, I've included some information on how to set it up in Chapter 6.

Of course, Microsoft Office isn't the only choice for workgroup intranet projects. Corel's *WordPerfect Suite 7* and *Corel Office Professional 7* can also boast direct-to-web publishing, and better supports the native capabilities of its products (such as text wrapping around graphics) by automatically generating Java programming that extends the limited abilities of HTML. In my opinion, Corel's Publish-to-Java feature is one of the few true innovations in web publishing. (However, I think that FrontPage, with its WebBots and server extensions, merits first bragging rights for this type of innovation.)

If the departmental webs start getting "serious," demanding interactive capabilities, you can import them into FrontPage Explorer and add them to the intranet web or set up another web server on another machine and let it host the departmental web. Once the pages have been moved to a web server, you will either need to import the latest versions of the pages as needed or give authoring permissions to the department head or other employees.

TIP

If you install the Microsoft Word Viewer, Excel Viewer, or PowerPoint Viewer utilities (available at http://www.microsoft.com/office), employees can view intranet documents even if these applications aren't installed on their computer. The documents even appear within the web browser window.

Run Software

Another way to exploit the FILE:// protocol is to create links to program files (called applications) on the local hard drive or network file server. For example, if Microsoft Word is installed as the program file c:\msoffice\winword\winword.exe, you can create a link to file:\\c\msoffice\winword\msoffice.exe. When the users click that link, they are asked if the want to open the "document" or save it (see Figure 7-13). While saving it would be useless and a waste of time, opening a program file is the same as running it.

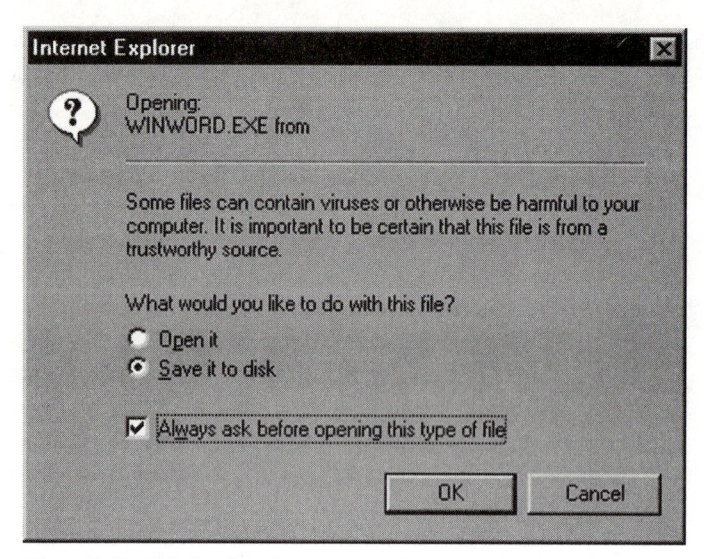

[Dialog box screenshot: Internet Explorer prompt for opening WINWORD.EXE with Open it / Save it to disk options]

Figure 7-13: This is what the user sees when he or she tries to open a program (EXE) file from the browser.

After getting this message a few times, the user is likely to disable the prompt so that the program starts immediately after the EXE link is clicked. (In Internet Explorer, the user can turn off the check box labeled Always Ask Before Opening This Type of File, as shown in Figure 7-13.)

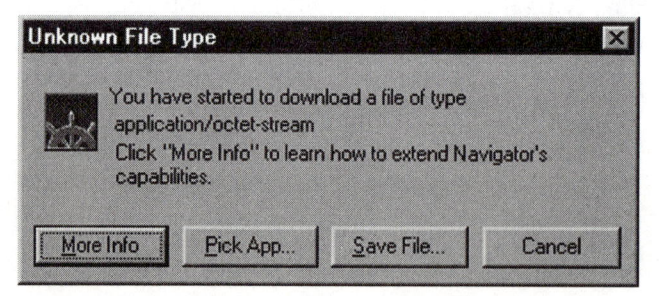

[Dialog box screenshot: Unknown File Type dialog in Netscape Navigator with More Info, Pick App, Save File, Cancel buttons]

Figure 7-14: The user can use Pick App to configure EXE files to be opened automatically with the Start command.

When a user clicks on a link to a program file with Netscape Navigator, the dialog box shown in Figure 7-14 is displayed. This isn't very helpful to the user. The user can use Pick App to choose which type of program to run or use Save File to copy it to the hard disk. Since the program file is already on the hard disk (or on a network drive), using Save File is a waste of time, especially since it doesn't start the program (the user has to find the program on the hard drive and double-click it to run it).

If the user clicks Pick App, he is then prompted to configure an external viewer by supplying the name of the program used to open the file. The question is, in effect, "What program do you use to run a program file?" The answer is to use the Start command, an internal command of the Windows 95/Windows NT command processor that can launch other applications. After the user enters "Start" as the name of the application, from then on, executable (application/octet-stream) files are downloaded to the local hard drive and then run with the Start command.

This works, but it's far from ideal. First, the program is copied to the hard drive before it's run. This wastes hard disk space, network bandwidth, and the user's time. (Internet Explorer doesn't download files that already exist when you choose Open.)

Also, many program files when downloaded won't run as stand-alone EXE files; they also have to be able to find their DLL support files. Further, once configured to open EXE files automatically, the user can't click on EXE files to download them to the hard disk, as is common when downloading updates and so forth from the World Wide Web. Instead, the program is launched, which brings up the most serious problem of all: Some EXE files (programs) on the Internet can contain viruses, so you don't want your employees having one-click access to them, even though your only intention is for them to be able to open programs locally or from the network, which is presumed safe.

Shortcuts to the Rescue

There is a workaround. Instead of pointing to EXE files somewhere on the hard drive or network file server, set your link to point to a Windows 95/NT 4 shortcut. A shortcut is like a hyperlink; it points to a program or document on the hard drive or network. But whereas hyperlinks exist within web pages, shortcuts are stored on the Windows 95/NT4 desktop or in a program folder on the Start menu. Shortcuts can actually be stored anywhere in the file system. When a shortcut, which has the extension LNK, is clicked on, the actual program or document pointed to by the shortcut is opened instead.

To allow running programs from a web page, create shortcuts on the desktop and then drag and drop them into the righthand pane of FrontPage Explorer to import them. (If you import them using File | Import, you'll pull in the file pointed to by the shortcut, not the shortcut itself.) You can then create hyperlinks to the LNK files.

When the user clicks on a hyperlink pointing to a shortcut, the same type of prompt appears as with program files, at least with Internet Explorer. The user is asked whether to save the file or open it. The user should click Open.

In this case, it's much safer to let the employees turn off the check box for Always Ask Before Opening This Type of File, since you control where the shortcut points. You can only edit the properties of a shortcut within your web by going to the location of the web on the hard drive running the server, right-clicking on the shortcut, and choosing Properties. From the Programs tab of the Shortcut Properties dialog box (see Figure 7-15), you can view or change the location and name of the program file.

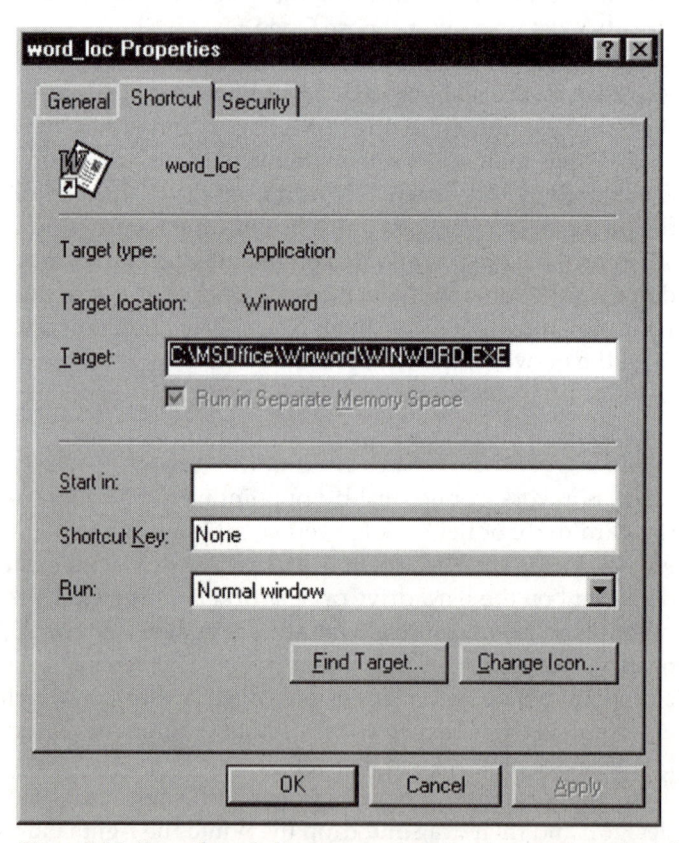

Figure 7-15: From the web directory on the server hosting the web, right-click on the shortcut and choose Properties to edit the shortcut's target. You can also do this before copying the shortcut to your web.

By linking to shortcut (LNK) files, you can avoid the consequences of running EXE files directly. While it's possible to run shortcuts from the Internet, they have to point to files installed locally or on your network; this method is extremely difficult for a nefarious virus author to exploit. Difficult, but not impossible, so if security is a top priority, you'll have to either disable Internet access on your client machines or avoid running programs directly from the web browser.

> **TIP**
>
> *Larger companies use a firewall product or proxy server to limit employees' access to the Internet and the World Wide Web. The firewall or proxy can be set up to prevent downloading EXE files, or restrict this to known safe IP addresses or Internet locations.*

Netscape Navigator makes it more difficult to run shortcuts from a page in the first place. Unrecognized extensions are ignored; if the user clicks on a LNK file, the contents of the file (a few bytes of "garbage") are displayed. You will have to configure Navigator to open LNK files using the Start command, the method for opening EXE files (as I discussed at the beginning of this section). One advantage to shortcuts is that since Navigator downloads files before they can be run, the small size of the LNK file, less than 200K, saves time.

With the Internet Explorer Admin Kit or the Netscape Administration tool, you can configure the web browsers on all your computers to use these settings by default. Nevertheless, it can be more complicated than it's worth to run programs directly from your intranet web. Hopefully, this will become easier with the upcoming release of Internet Explorer 4.0, which is poised to become the primary desktop graphical user interface (GUI) of upcoming versions of Windows 95 and NT 4.

> **TIP**
>
> *Perhaps an easier way of launching programs is to copy empty documents or templates to the web server and link to them. Since users can't save the changes back to the web server (due to server security), opening a blank document has the same effect as running the program that is associated with the document. For example, if you link to a spreadsheet such as sheet.xls, Excel starts and opens the sheet.xls file from the web browser. The user can then create a spreadsheet and save it to the local hard disk or to a network folder.*
>
> *The shortcut technique presented in "Shortcuts to the Rescue" is generally a more useful approach, especially if you want to run programs that don't have a file extension associated with them on the user's computer.*

Designing the Programs Page

Now that you know how program files are run from a web browser, you'll be able to understand how the Run Software (programs.htm) page works. Examine Figure 7-16. This page was built by using Insert | Table to create a table with two rows and five columns. The cells in the leftmost column were set as header cells with a right horizontal alignment using Table | Cell Properties. The remaining cells in the table were set to use a horizontal alignment of center.

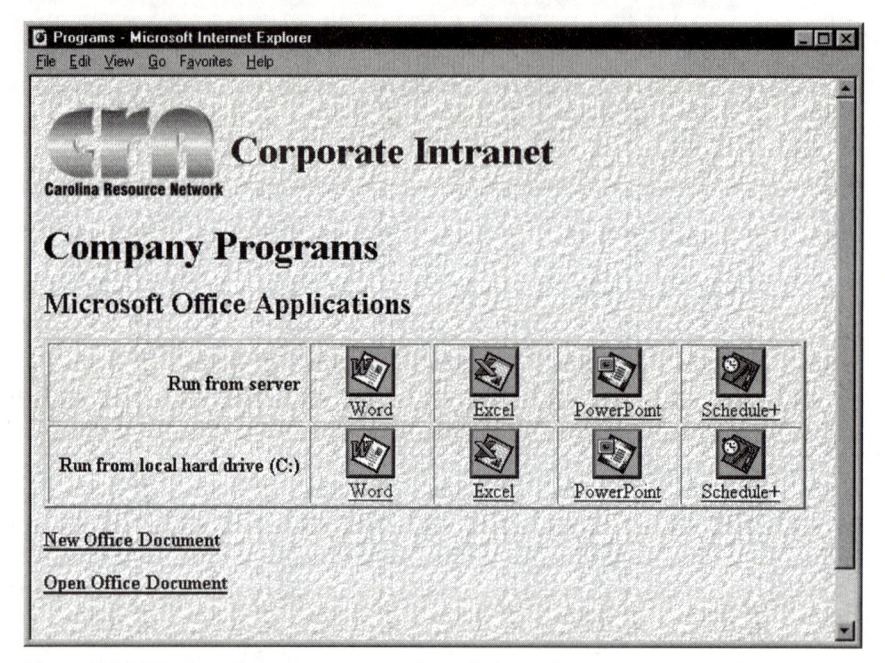

Figure 7-16: The Run Software page uses hyperlinks to shortcuts stored on the web server to run applications (programs) directly.

To create each program link, the name of the program was typed and the text selected. Pressing Ctrl+K brings up the Edit Hyperlink dialog box, where the path to the shortcut is entered. See Figure 7-17.

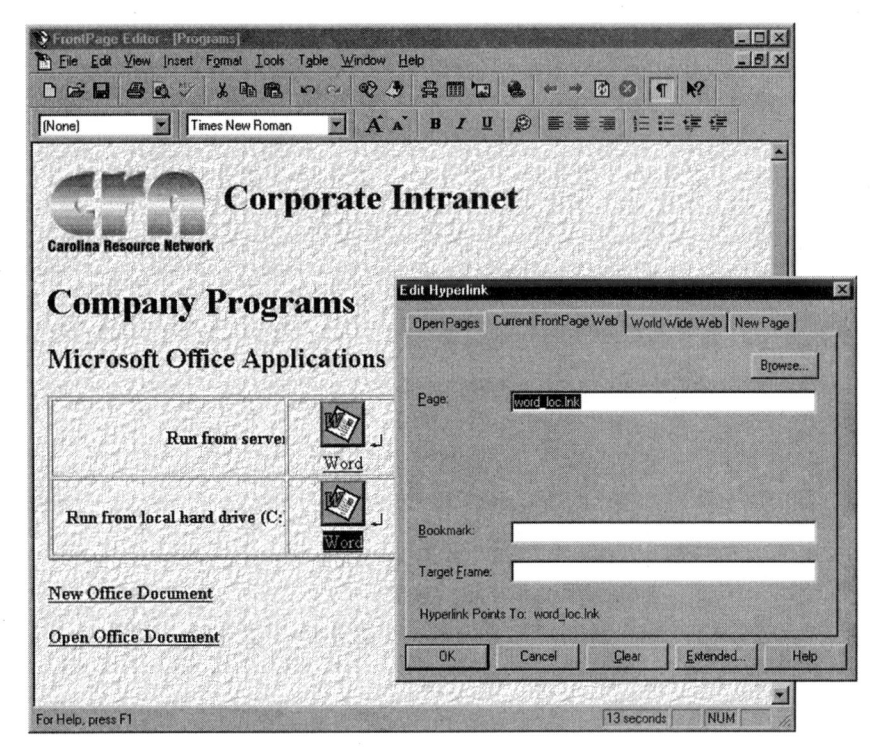

Figure 7-17: The hyperlink points to the shortcut file within the web.

These shortcuts were previously copied to the web folder. There are two versions of each shortcut: one that runs the program from the local hard drive and one that runs the program from its network location. (These links will not work in the example web unless the software is installed in the same locations on your computer/network as it was on mine. This also implies that you need some consistency in the way programs are installed on every workstation's hard disk: If a shortcut points to c:\programs\xfer.exe, it won't work if the program is installed on the D:\ drive on some computers or in a different folder.)

Coming up with the icon for each program was a little more difficult. Icons for programs are stored within the program file itself using the ICO file format. To extract the icons from the programs, you need a utility such as Microangelo Studio, which lets you view or edit icons and animated cursors. (You can download Microangelo from http://www.impactsoft.com.)

Once you have the icon open with the Microangelo Editor, it can be copied and pasted into Paint, or whatever graphics program you choose, and saved as a bitmap or GIF. You can import this graphic into your web by using Insert | Graphic. The graphic can then be linked to the shortcut file it corresponds to.

This page is meant only as a starting point for your own intranet. You'll want to add more rows to the table for all the programs you want to make available to your employees. Of course, they can always use the Start menu as usual, but many will find one-click access to programs more convenient, at least once they've configured their browser properly to run shortcuts.

> **TIP**
>
> *With judicious use of scripting, you can set up even more sophisticated program launching pages, including the drop-down menus that work like the Start menu, and embedded ActiveX Controls that run custom software within the web page itself. I chose to keep things simple in this chapter, especially since scripting and ActiveX aren't even discussed until Chapter 9.*

Employee Resources

The Employee Resources page (employee.htm, shown in Figure 7-18) contains links to three other pages: the Employee Directory (eedirect.htm), the Employee Policy Manual (eepolm.htm), and the Purchase Requisition Form (purchreq.htm). There is also a link back to the home page; it's always good practice to include a link back to the home page, even though you know users can simply press the Backspace key or Back button on the browser to return to where they came from. (The TOC frame also contains a link to the home page, but it's possible that frames have been disabled by the user or are unsupported by the browser.)

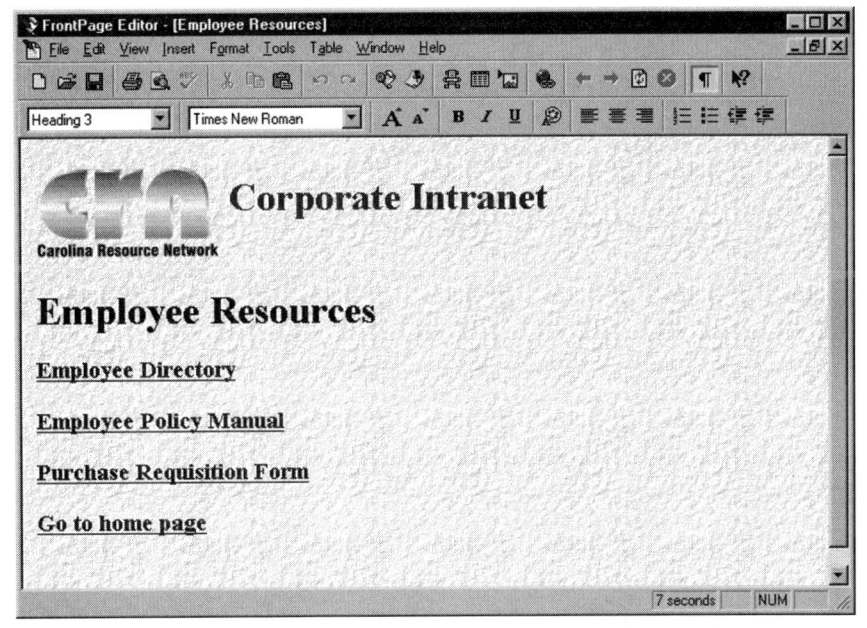

Figure 7-18: Employees will use the Employee Resources page to look up names in the employee directory, read the policy manual, or fill out a purchase requisition form.

Employee Directory

All three pages are straightforward and can be built using standard FrontPage techniques. Consider the Employee Directory page shown in Figure 7-19. It is simply a table with the first column reserved for employee "mug shots," a second column for the employee names, a third column with links to internal e-mail addresses, a fourth column for Internet e-mail addresses, and a fifth column containing the employee telephone extension numbers.

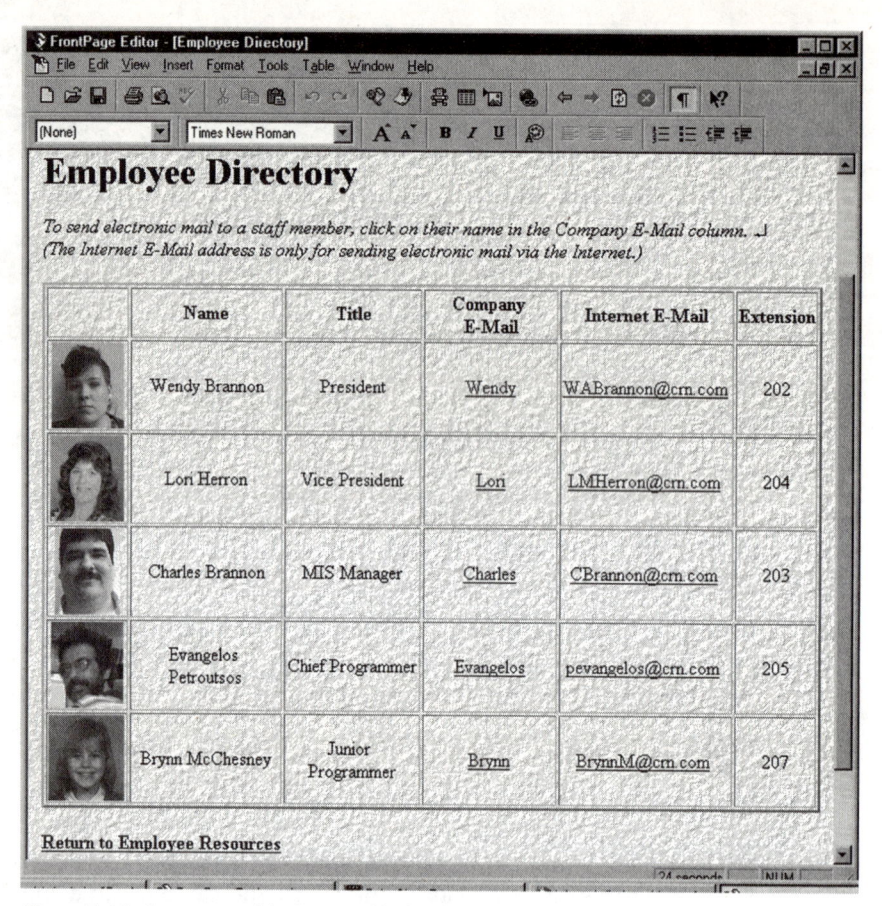

Figure 7-19: Create a multicolumn table for the employee directory.

The photographs for each employee were scanned from photographs using a desktop scanner, and the resulting files were reduced in size using Paint Shop Pro's Image | Resample command. Paint Shop Pro is the web author's best friend; it can be downloaded from http://www.jasc.com/psp. You can also resize images in Image Composer by dragging the handles of the image. (Be sure to reduce the composition guide to match the size of the image before you save it.)

Although you can also resize images within FrontPage by dragging the handles attached to the image (which appear when you click on the image), this does not actually reduce the file size of the image on the web; it only instructs the browser to scale the image to fit the new size. If the original pictures are large graphics, the entire large graphic is downloaded by the browser, then scaled to fit into a smaller region, which can be unacceptably slow. So it's best to manually scale the image before you place it on the page.

> **TIP**
>
> *The best use for image scaling in FrontPage is when you have a small graphic that you want to display in a larger size. You can even create and save a single pixel as a GIF file, with the pixel set as the transparent color, and stretch the single-pixel image to create as much "white space" as you need on a page, which is useful for indenting paragraphs. Notice the column labeled Internet E-Mail. These addresses were created automatically by typing the e-mail address in the FrontPage Editor. After typing the e-mail address (to coin a phrase: edress), press the spacebar, and the FrontPage Editor automatically converts it to a URL using the MAILTO: protocol. When an employee clicks on one of these names, an e-mail message appears with the address already pasted into place, ready to type and send a message.*

Your company probably has an internal e-mail system, such as Lotus Notes or Microsoft Mail, to deliver messages in-house. You can use the same trick used with Internet e-mail addresses to pop up the e-mail editor with the address already typed in. To create these links with the FrontPage Editor, just type the e-mail name, select it with the mouse, and press Ctrl+K. You can then choose MAILTO: as the URL type on the World Wide Web tab and fill in the name of the e-mail box. (Leave off the @ suffix unless your message needs to be routed outside of your company.)

Employee Policy Manual

The employee policy manual started out life as a document in Lotus Ami Pro 2.0. It was then converted to Microsoft Word. The Word Internet Assistant was used to save it as HTML. (Alternately, you could have simply opened the Word document with the FrontPage Editor to convert it to HTML.) With the FrontPage Editor, bookmarks were created for each section in the manual. The table of contents in the manual became a series of links to these bookmarks.

Note: This employee policy manual is based on copyrighted material, courtesy of Group US, Inc., from which I've obtained permission to use in modified form. I regret that I am not able to grant the readers of this book permission to adapt this manual for their own purposes. The sample policy manual is intended solely as an example, for educational purposes.

To create the bookmarks, you can select a line of text, such as the heading for a section, and use Edit | Bookmark to get the dialog box shown in Figure 7-20. This causes a dotted underline to appear beneath the text you bookmarked, as a reminder to you that the text is a bookmark. (If you use Edit | Bookmark without selecting text, or add a bookmark to a graphic or other nontext page element, a flag symbol appears in the text as the bookmark's anchor.)

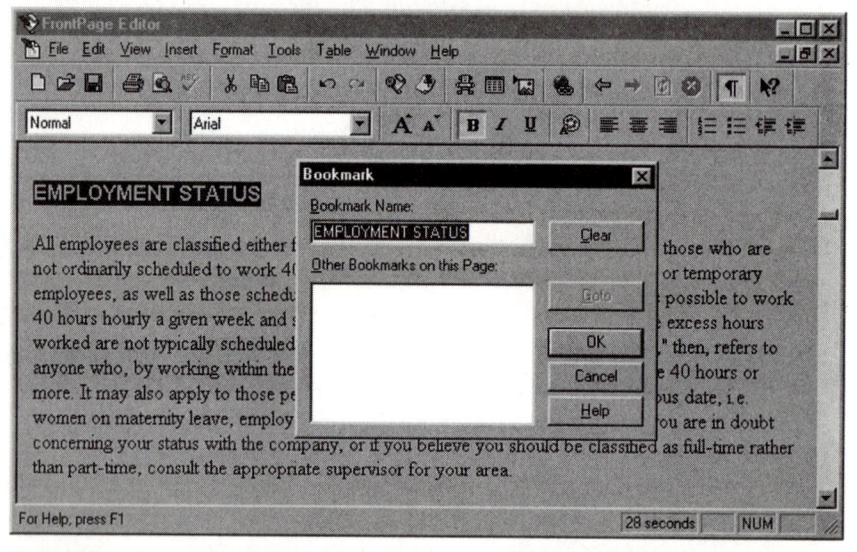

Figure 7-20: Give each location in the document a bookmark so the user can quickly jump to that topic.

You can then move to the table of contents or index and select each line of the contents and link it to the bookmark, as shown in Figure 7-21. Use the Open Pages tab and link to the same page. Click the Bookmark drop-down list to choose the bookmark you assigned earlier.

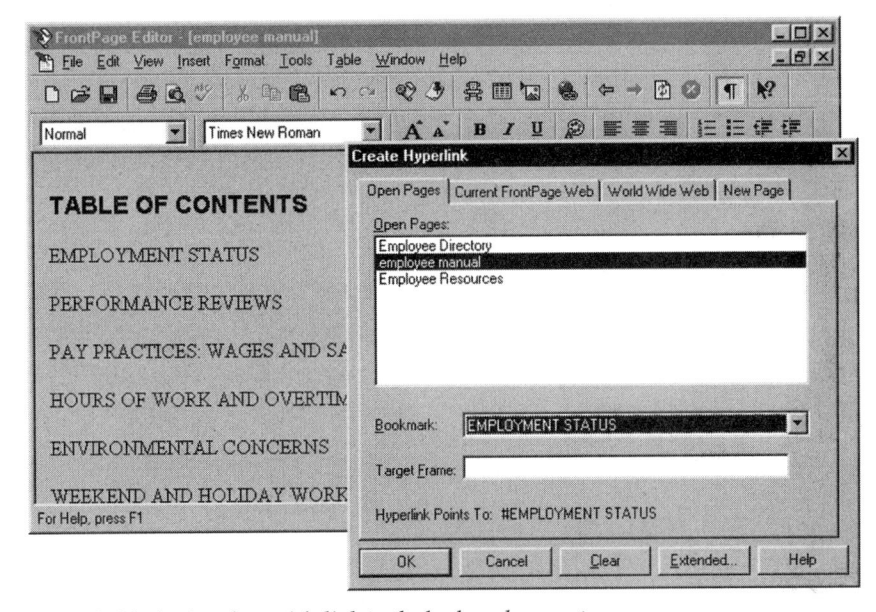

Figure 7-21: Assign the topic's link to the bookmark you set up.

After cleaning up the document by changing a few paragraph styles and adding the logo and page background, the resulting Employee Policy Manual page resembles Figure 7-22.

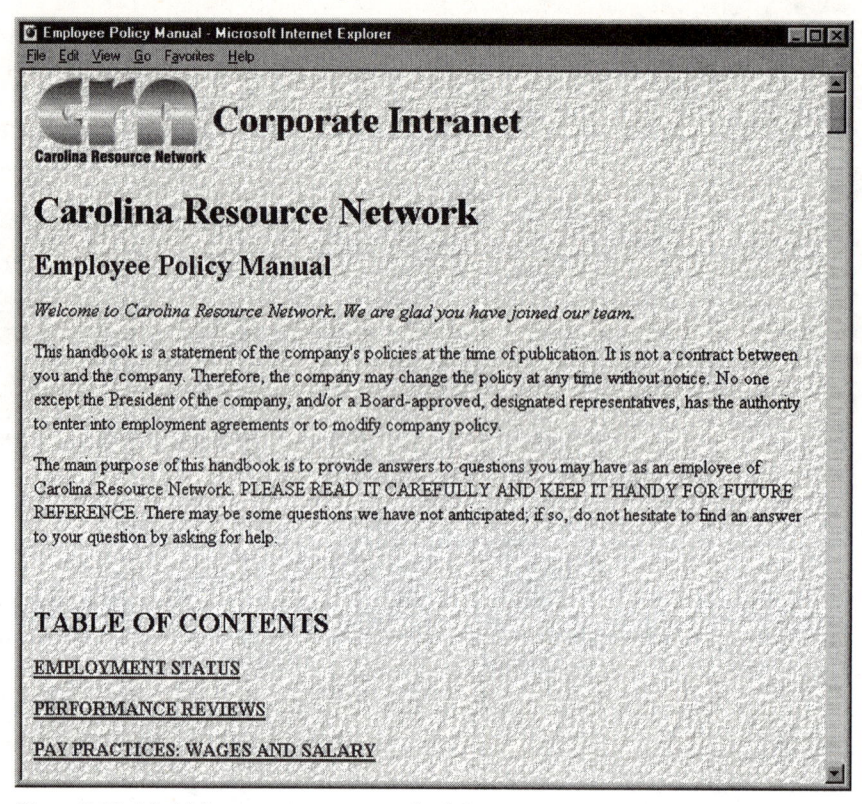

Figure 7-22: It's fairly easy to convert standard documents to great-looking HTML pages.

Requisition Form

CRN company policy states that all purchases in excess of $25 require an approval from the purchasing department. Until now, this has been the domain of the paper form, filled out by hand and sent as a company memo. Forms automation is one of the most powerful intranet applications, so I'll show you how to set up such a form and arrange for the delivery of the information to the appropriate staff member.

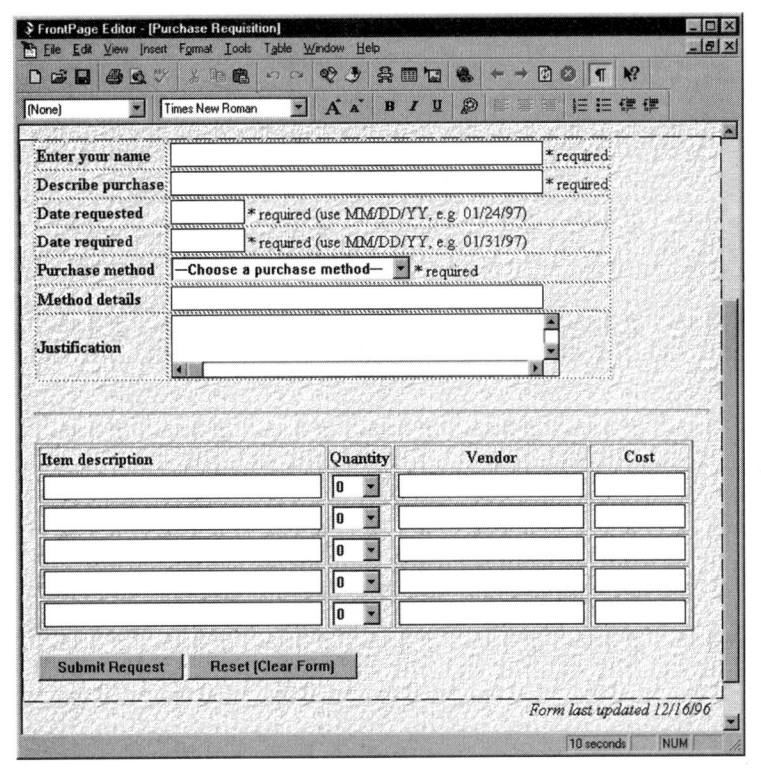

Figure 7-23: The data collected from this form will be stored in a database file, which will be examined by the purchasing department to arrange for approvals.

Figure 7-23 shows the form used for the Purchase Requisition page (purchreq.htm). There isn't enough room in this chapter to provide a step-by-step tutorial that shows you how to reproduce this form. Instead, we'll take a look at how it works. To analyze this form, you'll rely on the skills you learned in Chapter 4, such as inserting a table into a form, placing form fields, and assigning a form handler. Normally, you'd store the data from the form using the Save Results WebBot, but I'll show you in Chapter 8 how to store the form data into a database table.

To get started, I chose Insert | Form Field | Text Box. This places a text box on the page, surrounded by the outlines of the form. I then deleted the text box, which leaves the form on the page. (Don't you wish there was just a way to insert a blank form?)

The table was made up of 7 rows and 2 columns, and no border was then inserted within the form. In the first column, I typed the labels as shown in the Figure 7-23. The form fields were inserted into the second column. For example, a text box was inserted in the second column for the employee name. This text box is named txt_Name and is assigned a width of 40 characters. To make this field required, I double-clicked on the text box and clicked the Validate button. The validation rule for this field requires data entry, with a minimum length of 5 and a maximum length of 40 characters.

Most of the fields are simple text boxes, with the exception of Purchase Method, which is a drop-down menu containing entries for the various purchase methods, such as Company Credit Card, COD, Purchase Order, and Reimbursement. Actually, the first entry is an instruction to the user, —Choose a Purchase Method—. The validation rule for this field was set to disallow selection of the first item, so the user is required to make a valid choice.

The Justification text box was inserted as a scrolling text box to allow for free-form text input. Finally, some text was typed after required field entries to remind the user that these fields must be completed.

Beneath the first table, separated by a horizontal line, is another table, this one with a border and consisting of 6 rows of 4 columns each. Headings were typed into the first row, and were centered and emboldened by selecting the entire row and using Table | Cell Properties to set the horizontal alignment to center and by turning on the Header Cell check box.

I created the second row of the table with text boxes and a drop-down menu containing the numbers 0 to 10. This row was then copied and pasted to the remaining rows of the table; then each of the remaining 4 rows was edited to give each field a unique numbered name. For further details on form field names and corresponding database fields, see Chapter 8, where I begin my discussion of intranet database applications. Beneath the second table, I inserted buttons for Submit and Reset and double-clicked on the buttons to change their names to Submit Request and Reset (Clear Form), respectively.

Since the form data will be stored in a database file, I'll postpone discussing the details of how the form is processed until after we've discussed database applications in the following chapter, Chapter 8, "Database Publishing With the Internet Database Connector."

Moving On

At this point, you should be ready to implement a TCP/IP intranetwork, create a custom intranet home page (with a frames-based navigation system), publish corporate documents in their native format and as HTML, set up custom application links, and prepare paper-saving electronic forms.

The chapter you have just completed lays the foundation for the next chapter, where I'll discuss how to store the electronic forms in an Access database table, and go one step further: integrating "live" database information on any web page, opening a window into your corporate data accessible from any web browser on the intranet.

chapter 8

Database Publishing With the Internet Database Connector

In this chapter, I'll discuss how to exploit the Internet Database Connector (IDC), a feature of Windows NT Internet Information Server and also implemented by NT Workstation Peer Web Services and the Windows 95 Personal Web Server. The IDC is a scheme that lets you create scripts that both query (look up information within) a database table to extract or modify records in it and display the results of a query using a results web page as a template.

The Internet Database Connector is a capability built into Microsoft Internet Information Server. It is also implemented by Windows NT Workstation Peer Web Services (almost identical to IIS), and the Microsoft Personal Web Server for Windows 95. You don't have to install any additional software beyond the web server to take advantage of IIS and IDC, although you will need to run a database engine on the server computer. More on this in the next section.

Note: The FrontPage Personal Web Server, included with FrontPage 97 as an easy upgrade path for FrontPage 1.1 users, does not support ISAPI (Internet Server Application Programming Interface) applications such as the Internet Database Connector. It's strictly provided for compatibility.

You will have to upgrade from the original FrontPage Personal Web Server to one of the Microsoft web servers mentioned previously before you can apply the techniques in this chapter.

You can only write IDC applications on a web server running IIS, or one that transparently supports IDC via FrontPage 97 server extensions. At the time of this writing, I am not familiar with any UNIX- or Netscape-based web server with support for IDC. Since most Web Presence Providers (WPPs, see Chapter 5) operate UNIX web servers, this may seem to severely restrict the usefulness of the IDC features built into FrontPage.

Not so fast. For one thing, more and more FrontPage WPPs and other web hosting services are switching to Windows NT Server and IIS, thanks to its high performance and scaleability (the ability to easily add more capacity and speed by adding more servers or processors). A WPP running FrontPage extensions on IIS can easily support IDC. That is why in Chapter 5, I suggest that you give a WPP high marks if it is running IIS, not because I'm interested in endorsing Microsoft standards.

Intranet Database Applications

You may or may not have access to an Internet web server running IIS. If you do, you may need special approval or may need to work closely with the web administrators to set up a database connection, and you'll probably pay an extra monthly fee above the standard rates to hook into a database stored on the server.

However, a corporate intranet is a near-ideal application of IIS and IDC server technologies. As long as your corporate web server supports IDC (such as the Microsoft web servers for NT Server, NT Workstation, or Windows 95), you're free to design forms that store information into a database table, and provide live database lookup, retrieval, updates, and record management. Furthermore, the overhead on the client computer is minimal. Even a low-end 486 with 8 megabytes (MB) of RAM can run a web browser to connect to a corporate database via a FrontPage-designed HTML form. Furthermore, it doesn't matter what operating system the client computers use, Windows 3.1, Windows 95, Macintosh, or Windows NT Workstation, as long as the computers are internetworked with TCP/IP (see Chapter 7) and have a web browser installed.

Although I'll focus on intranet database examples in this chapter, picking up where Chapter 7 left off, you will nevertheless be able to apply the same techniques to Internet database publishing, as long as your WPP supports the Internet Database Connector and is willing to set up an ODBC data source. (More on ODBC below, "Getting Ready for IDC.")

The Internet Database Connector works in tandem with an SQL database engine, such as SQL Server or the Microsoft Access Jet Engine. This is the key to the client-server performance of an Internet. You can operate just a few very powerful server computers to run network applications, such as database queries, and take advantage of low-cost *thin clients* for each employee's workstation. Whether these thin clients will be the mythical Network Computer (NC), or more powerful personal computers with the ability to do their own work independent of the network (highly recommended), you still benefit from the low overhead of running your database applications within the web browser.

All the database processing occurs on the web server, which is also a database server running SQL Server or another SQL engine such as Microsoft Access. Since the database processing occurs on the server, you don't need to purchase or install database applications on the client computers. This strategy may also enable you to avoid paying for database client licenses, as long as all connections are made anonymously, and you have a web server license for the database engine. Be sure to check your licensing agreement and licensing options before operating on this assumption, however.

Many of the readers will not have access to SQL Server (it's part of Microsoft BackOffice for Windows NT Server), or other powerful database servers such as products from Oracle or Informix. Instead, I'll focus here on connecting web pages to an Access 7.0 (or higher) database. To use these examples, you must have Access 7.0 (or higher version) and/or the Access ODBC32 drivers installed on your computer (see the Note in the following section). Don't worry if you don't know much about Access or anything about ODBC (Open Database Connectivity)—I'll explain everything you need to get started with database publishing with your FrontPage webs.

Overview: Using the Internet Database Connector With FrontPage

FrontPage supports IDC as a form handler, and includes special support for IDC that makes it easy to take advantage of Internet database publishing, without writing a single line of HTML code. I'll show you how to use the IDC Wizard to set up script files for storing or retrieving records from a database table and how to build a results page to display the information retrieved by a database lookup.

An *IDC script* is a few lines of text that specifies a data source, a results template, and an SQL query. *SQL* stands for Structured Query Language and is a computer language for looking up or processing information in a database file. SQL is supported by many database engines, including SQL Server (running on NT Server), Microsoft Access, Borland Paradox, and the Ashton-Tate dBase format. The web server interprets the IDC script, runs the query, and returns the fields matching the query criteria as output on a results template page that you've designed.

The *results template* is an HTML page like any other you create with the FrontPage Editor except that it is saved with an extension of .HTX instead of .HTM. Since the FrontPage Editor won't let you choose the extension when saving files, there is a special template (Database Results) that creates an empty page for you that is already named with the .HTX extension. To display fields from a database table, you simply insert the fields onto the page using the Edit | Database menu within a special region of the page called a *detail section*.

The detail section of an HTX results template contains the fields you want to display. When the page is shown to the user in the web browser, the fields named in the detail section are automatically fetched and displayed for every matching record. The body of the results template is built using standard FrontPage methods.

What About Active Server Pages?

At the time this book was developed, Microsoft had begun to phase out the Internet Database Connector in favor of the more flexible and powerful Active Server Pages technology, supported by Internet Information Server 3.0. IIS 3.0 is included in the Windows NT Service Pack 2 upgrade.

Unfortunately, there is virtually no built-in support for Active Server Pages (ASP) in FrontPage 97, yet IDC is fully integrated into FrontPage via the FrontPage Editor's Insert | Database menu, and the IDC Wizard. Developing ASP applications really requires the much more expensive and sophisticated Microsoft Visual InterDev system, which uses an enhanced version of FrontPage and includes built-in support for ASP prototyping and layout.

It is possible to use ASP with FrontPage, although there are a few known problems. If this is something you would like to pursue, consult the Microsoft Knowledge Base article Q161779, *Using FrontPage 97 to Edit, Manage Active Server Pages*, which can be found at http://www.microsoft.com/kb/articles/q161/7/79.htm.

Although IDC is an earlier IIS technology, you shouldn't feel slighted or left out. IDC is fully supported by both IIS 2.0 and IIS 3.0, NT Workstation Peer Web Services, and the Microsoft Personal Web Server for Windows 95. IDC is a full-featured and robust technology, and is more than capable enough to support both basic and advanced database publishing. Because IDC is the preferred method for FrontPage database publishing, IDC is where we'll focus our attention in this chapter.

IDC Intranet Examples

Now that the fundamentals are out of the way, it's time to turn our attention to some practical examples. The example database applications in this chapter are intentionally simplistic, so that you can focus on the mechanics of web database integration, rather than on the complexities of relational database design. Nevertheless, you'll be pleased with how well FrontPage supports live database publishing and storage, and with the experience you acquire in understanding this material, you'll be ready to tackle more sophisticated intranet and Internet database applications.

Note: This chapter uses the same example web as Chapter 7, found in the \Webs\Chap07\Intranet folder on the Companion CD-ROM. Therefore, there is no separate folder for Chapter 8. Refer to Chapter 7 or Appendix A for instructions on importing this web (if you haven't done so already), so that you can follow along with the tutorial in this chapter.

Getting Ready for IDC

In the next section, I'll explain how to set up IDC scripts and HTX result templates for two intranet applications: address book lookup and filing electronic forms such as the Purchase Requisition form we put together in Chapter 7.

As mentioned in the introduction to this chapter, the Internet Database Connector is a built-in feature of the Microsoft web servers: NT Server's Internet Information Server, NT Workstation Peer Web Services, or Windows 95 Personal Web Server. IDC, in turn, relies on the Open Database Connectivity (ODBC) software.

Note: Microsoft Access is part of Microsoft Office Professional 95 (or Office Pro 97). It is also available as a stand-alone application. During the installation of Access, you were given the opportunity to install the ODBC32 drivers. If you missed this opportunity, you can rerun the Office setup program and choose to install additional components. Another way to install the ODBC support for Access is to install Visual Basic 4.0 or higher. It's possible that these drivers were also installed if you previously installed a Visual Basic program that requires the Access Jet Engine. End users (those who are browsing the database with their web browser) do not need these drivers; they only need to be installed on the computer running the web server.

One more note: IDC will only work with 32-bit ODBC data sources, such as Access 95/97. You may have 16-bit ODBC sources installed if you use 16-bit database programs, such as earlier versions of Access or Paradox, but you must upgrade to 32-bit ODBC before you can use the databases with IDC. (The databases themselves will also have to be converted to the format used by the 32-bit version of the database management system.)

Before you can publish database information on your web pages, you need to prepare the databases themselves, using Access 95 or Access 97, and set up an ODBC system data source. Two sample databases have already been prepared for you, included on the Companion CD-ROM. Copy the files Addrbook.mdb and Purchreq.mdb from the \SampleDB folder of the Companion CD-ROM to a folder on your hard drive. Next, you need to turn off the read-only attributes of these files; they were marked read-only for inclusion on the CD-ROM, which is itself a read-only medium.

In the rest of this chapter, I'll assume you've copied these files to a folder on your hard disk named C:\SampleDB. If you choose a different folder or folder name, substitute that folder for the SampleDB folder in the instructions that follow.

Here's how you copy the sample databases from the Companion CD-ROM and set them up on the computer running the web server.

1. Use Windows Explorer to drag the \SampleDB folder from the CD-ROM to a hard drive on the computer running the web server. I'll assume you copied to drive C: for the remainder of this discussion. If not, make the appropriate adjustments to the steps as you go along.

2. Open the C:\SampleDB folder from Windows Explorer, select both database files (click on the first one; Shift+click on the second one), and choose File | Properties. Turn off the check box for read-only, then click OK. The databases can now be read from and written to.

Chapter 8: Database Publishing With the Internet Database Connector

3. Now you can set up an ODBC system data source. Start the Windows Control Panel (Start | Settings | Control Panel) and double-click the ODBC icon. (If you don't see this icon, ODBC is not installed. See the Note at the end of the previous section.)

4. You'll see the Data Sources dialog box shown in Figure 8-1. It should contain a driver for Access 7.0 or higher. (If not, you will need to install Microsoft Access on the computer hosting the web server.)

Note: The user interface of the ODBC tool will not match the figures if you've installed Office 97 on the web server computer, and the steps you have to follow may vary slightly. However, the same methods still apply, you'll just have to carefully follow the intent of the steps, and figure out how it works with the new ODBC tool. It's actually pretty obvious what to do.

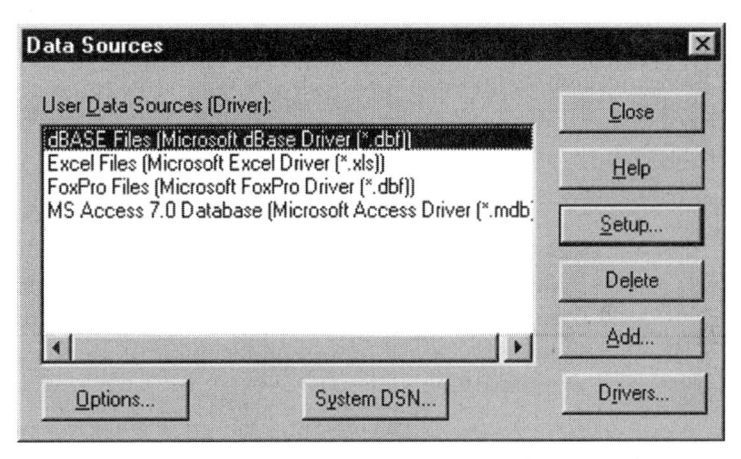

Figure 8-1: Click the System DSN button to set up a data source for IDC.

5. Click the System DSN button in the Data Sources dialog box. IDC only works with System DSNs, because IIS and IDC run as a system-level process. In the System Data Sources dialog box, click Add. You're next asked to choose an ODBC driver. Click the Microsoft Access driver (*.mdb), then click OK.

6. Fill out the ODBC Microsoft Access 7.0 Setup dialog box as shown in Figure 8-2.

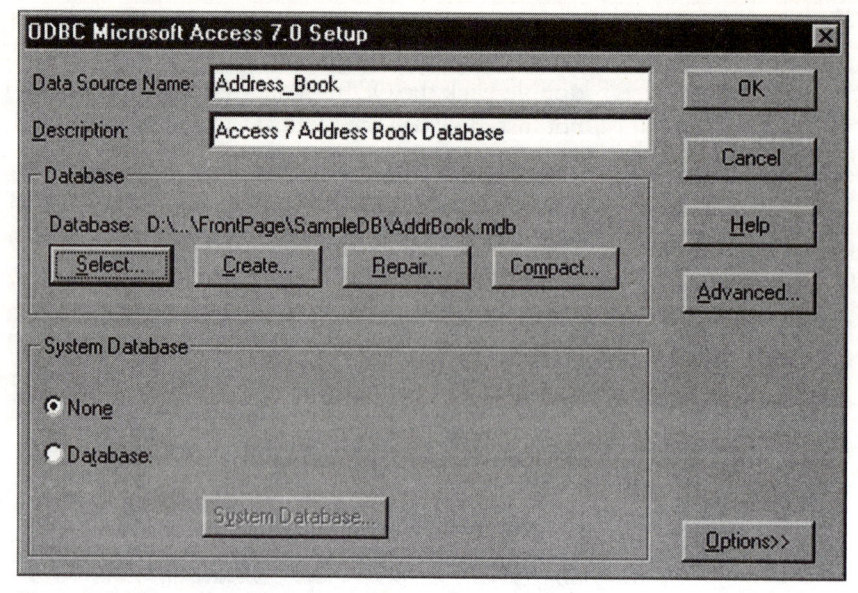

Figure 8-2: To set up a system data source, make up a data source name and description and use Select to specify the location and filename of the database.

The data source name (DSN) is a plain-English (or whatever language you prefer) word that you'll use with the IDC script. Instead of referring to the exact location and filename of a database, you use the data source name. The ODBC driver takes care of the details. The description is not important, but it's a useful aid to documentation.

7. To link the DSN to the database, click the Select button. (The Create button can be used to set up a blank database, but it won't have any fields defined, hence, it's useless. You need to use Microsoft Access to create your databases. The Repair button is more useful if you suspect database or index corruption. Use Compact routinely to weed out records that have been deleted—deleted records are only marked as such, and the disk space they occupy is not freed up until you compact the database. You can also repair and compact databases from within Access.)

Chapter 8: Database Publishing With the Internet Database Connector

8. After clicking Select (which works like the Browse button in other dialog boxes), choose the drive, folder, and database filename that you want to link to the data source. For the Address_Book DSN, you'll link it to C:\SampleDB\AddrBook.mdb.
9. Click OK to close the dialog box you're working with.
10. From the System Data Sources dialog box, click Add again, and this time set up a data source name of Purchases, linking it to C:\SampleDB\purchreq.mdb.

> **TIP**
>
> *To enhance security, you can use the built-in features of Access to restrict database operations based on username and passwords. You would set up the Administrator account to allow full database access (the default), and one or more users with more limited rights. You can then use the Advanced button (shown in Figure 8-2) to specify the username and password of the user that you want IDC to impersonate when working with the database. Only assign the rights that the IDC scripts will need. For example, if you are only providing database lookup services, you don't need to allow the "IDC user" to update, append, or delete records.*

You now have system data source names set up for the AddrBook database (Address_Book) and PurchReq database (Purchases). Now you're ready to work with the IDC features of FrontPage 97.

Work With Address Book

The Address Database page (database.htm) is simply a list of links to the examples that we'll explore in the remainder of this chapter (see Figure 8-3). For your reference, the URLs of each link are included on this page. If this was a real intranet, this page would probably be refined somewhat.

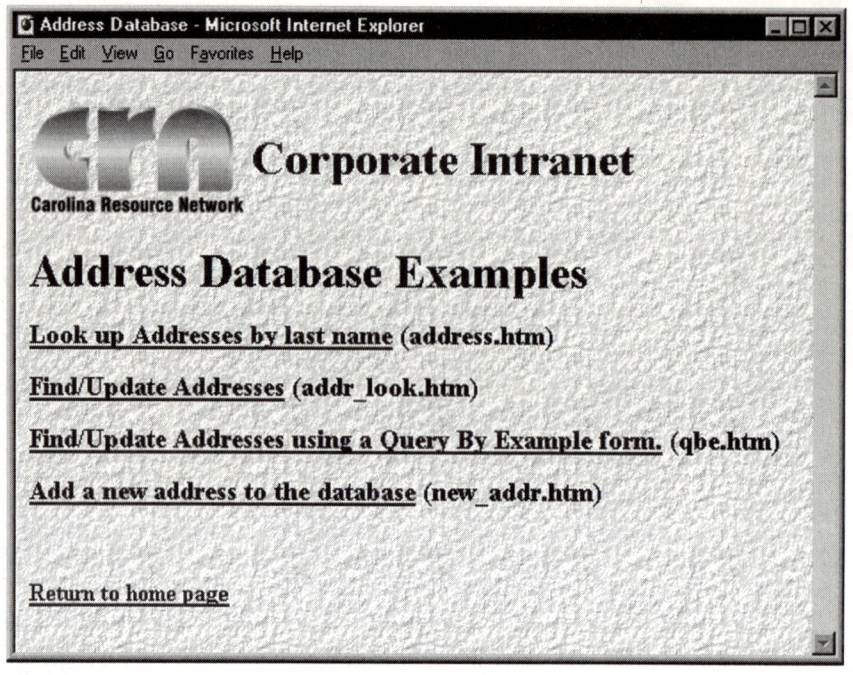

Figure 8-3: From the Address Database page (database.htm), you can try the example database applications.

Look Up Addresses by Last Name

I'll start with the simplest example. Figure 8-4 shows a web page (address.htm) that lets a user look up a record in the database based on the entry in the text box placed next to the Last Name label. This example is a simple form with a single text box. Give the text box control a name of Lname (not Last Name, that's just the text typed on the page) by double-clicking on the text box and typing Lname into the Name box of the Text Box Properties dialog box.

If you open this page (address.htm) with the FrontPage Editor, you can see how the user's entry in the Lname text box is sent to the Internet Database Connector. Right-click within the form region and choose Form Properties.

TIP

The names you use for text fields and other controls should not be identical to the field names in the database file you're storing into. While using the same names for both form fields and database fields is not prohibited outright (the fields on the form have special characters added to them by IDC to make sure this conflict never happens), it certainly helps avoid confusion when you're writing or analyzing the IDC. It's best to keep straight what fields are on the form and what fields are in the database.

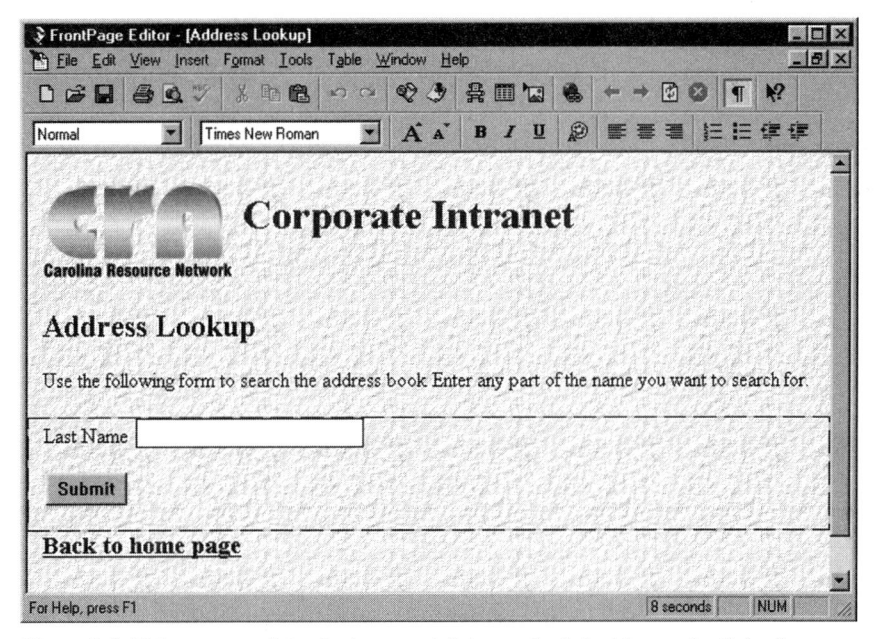

Figure 8-4: This page consists of a form containing a single text box and a Submit button.

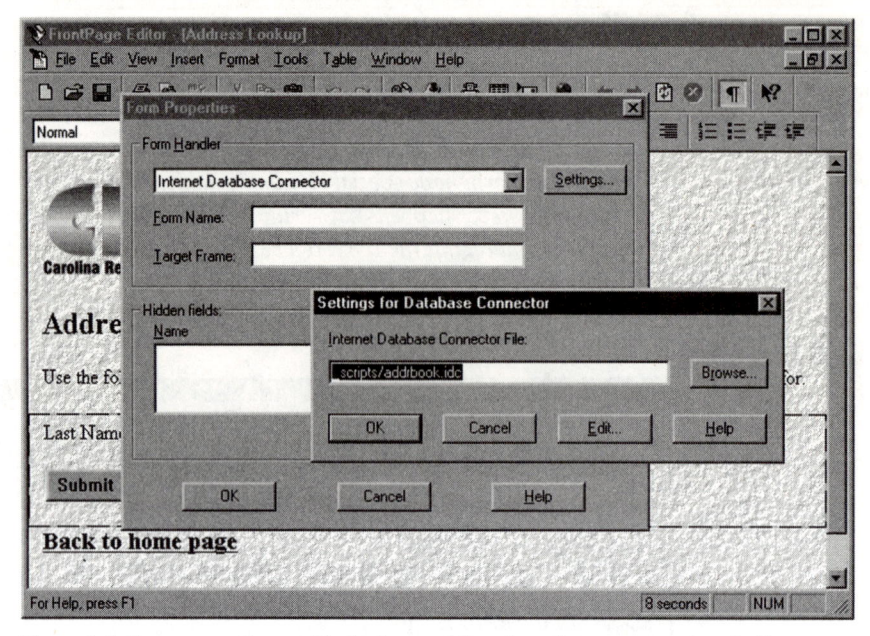

Figure 8-5: To process a form with the Internet Database Connector, assign the Internet Database Connector form handler and click Settings to choose the script file.

As shown in the Form Handler area of the Form Properties dialog box in Figure 8-5, the Internet Database Connector form handler is assigned instead of the familiar Save Results WebBot (discussed in Chapter 4). When you click the Settings button beside the form handler choice, you'll see that there is only one setting for IDC, which is the name of the IDC script to use. In this case, the script is a file named Addrbook.idc, stored in the _scripts folder of the intranet web site.

Establishing a Scripts Directory

Before you can create IDC scripts, you need to set up a subfolder (subdirectory) for them in the intranet web. From FrontPage Explorer, choose New | Folder and rename the folder _scripts. By using the underscore character at the beginning of the folder name, it will be hidden, even if folder browsing is permitted by the web server. Although you can now put your scripts in this folder, they won't run unless you give the folder permission to run programs. You can configure this permission from the web server's configuration utility (e.g., turn on the Execute check box for that folder in Internet Service Manager), but there's a better way built into FrontPage Explorer.

From FrontPage Explorer, right-click on the _scripts folder you just created and choose Properties. Turn on the check box labeled Allow Scripts or Programs to Be Run. That's all there is to it. One ramification of this change is that the folder can only be used to execute scripts and display results templates. Pages within the folder can not be opened directly by the web browser. This is a good thing; it protects your IDC files from inspection.

This is why you need to create a separate folder for the scripts. Although you could place your scripts in the same folder as the rest of your web content, they can't be executed there. If you change the properties of your web folder to allow programs to be run, scripts will work, but the other pages can't be browsed. While some web servers (including IIS/PWS) let you set a folder to both allow reading and executing files, it's not a good idea for security reasons.

> **TRAP**
>
> *Never set the properties for the root web to allow scripts or programs to run. Once enabled, the entire site, including the root web and all subwebs, can no longer be browsed. You may also be unable to open any of the webs with FrontPage Explorer, particularly if the web is stored on an Internet web server. Should you make this mistake, you can run Internet Service Manager and turn off the Execute check box in the Directories tab of the WWW service. This is only possible if you run you own web server. To correct this mistake on an Internet web server, such as a FrontPage hosting account, you'll need to contact the web administrator.*

One consequence of putting the scripts in a hidden folder (denoted by the underscore in the folder name _scripts) is that you won't be able to view the contents of the folder in FrontPage Explorer. This is easily solved, however. Choose Web Settings from the Tools menu, and on the Advanced tab of the FrontPage Web Settings dialog box, enable the checkbox for Show Documents in Hidden Directories.

Inside an IDC Script

An IDC script is an ordinary plain text file with an extension of .IDC. When Internet Information Server (or an IIS-compatible server) is asked for an IDC file by the web client, it examines the IDC file for instructions. Here is the IDC file used by the Address Lookup example:

```
Datasource: Address_Book
Template: addrbook.htx
SQLStatement: SELECT * FROM Addresses WHERE Last LIKE '%%%Lname%%%'
```

The first statement, Datasource, is followed by a colon, a space, and the name of the System DSN you want to use (you should have set this up in the previous section). The second statement, Template, is also followed by a colon and space and then the URL of a special HTML file (web page) that contains embedded field names. These fields are retrieved from the database using the SQLStatement line. The SQLStatement keyword is followed by a colon and a space, then one or more lines of Structured Query Language instructions. In the example above, the SQL statement selects all (*) records from the database table named Addresses wherever the Last field is "like" the contents of the text box Lname.

Preposterous Percent Procedures

The % characters deserve special attention, and believe me, this is as hard to explain as it is to understand. In fact, it may drive you slowly mad.

Normally, an IDC script uses the % characters to indicate a field name, or parameter. Using %Lname% causes IDC to substitute the contents of the Lname text box when it runs the script. Let's assume the user entered Son as the last name on the search form. The IDC statement:

```
SELECT * FROM Addresses WHERE Last LIKE '%Lname%'
```

is sent to and evaluated by the SQL engine as:

```
SELECT * FROM Addresses WHERE Last LIKE 'Son'
```

This is fine for finding last names, assuming the user is only searching for names beginning with the search phrase. LIKE 'Son' would return records with last names of 'Sonnet' or 'Sondheimer', but not 'Simpson' or 'Johnson'. The lookup form is more useful if the user can type *any part* of a last name, and offer as the results every record that has a last name containing the search text.

To accomplish this kind of search, this is what needs to be sent to the SQL engine:

```
SELECT * FROM Addresses WHERE Last LIKE '%Son%'
```

In SQL, the % is a special character when it's used with the LIKE comparison operator. In SQL, LIKE is used to match one field with a part of another field. For example, LIKE 'Out' would match fields containing any of the following: Out, Outrageous, Outcast, but not Route or South. By adding a wildcard character, %, to the definition, you could use LIKE to match '%Out%' with any phrase containing the characters OUT (upper- or lowercase), including Mouth, Outer, outré, and so on.

So what about the extra two % symbols at the beginning and end of the comparison, as implemented in the address lookup IDC script?

To use LIKE to match a database field with a form field entry (the Lname text box in our example), you need to use the % symbol redundantly, to say the least. In order for IDC to send a % symbol to the SQL engine, and not try to interpret that symbol as preceding a field name reference, the % symbol needs to be doubled. So in the statement,

```
SELECT * FROM Addresses WHERE Last LIKE '%%%Lname%%%'
```

the outer two %% symbols send a single % symbol to the SQL engine. The inner % symbols cause the value of the Lname field to be substituted.

To reiterate, both the Internet Database connector and SQL treat % as a special symbol, depending on the content. IDC insists that you wrap % symbols around field names, so that it can substitute the actual content of the field before sending it to the SQL query engine.

The SQL engine, on the other hand, uses the % symbol as the wildcard character. IDC will think this symbol is part of a field name. However, IDC is designed to ignore a pair of % symbols, and pass them to the SQL engine as a single % symbol.

In order to send a single "%" character from the IDC to the SQL engine, you have to use the symbol twice, as in:
<ComWHERE Last LIKE '%%Out%%'

If Lname contains the text Son (the quote marks aren't part of the field contents), then '%Lname%' is the same as 'Son'. To get the equivalent of the SQL comparison '%Son%', then, you end up with '%%%Lname%%%'.

How to Create an IDC Query

Although crafting IDC files is as simple as writing a few lines with Notepad and saving it as an IDC file (to be imported into your web), FrontPage 97 provides an even easier way. From the FrontPage Editor, choose File | New, and from the New Page dialog box, choose Database Connector Wizard. This starts the wizard, the first page of which is shown as Figure 8-6.

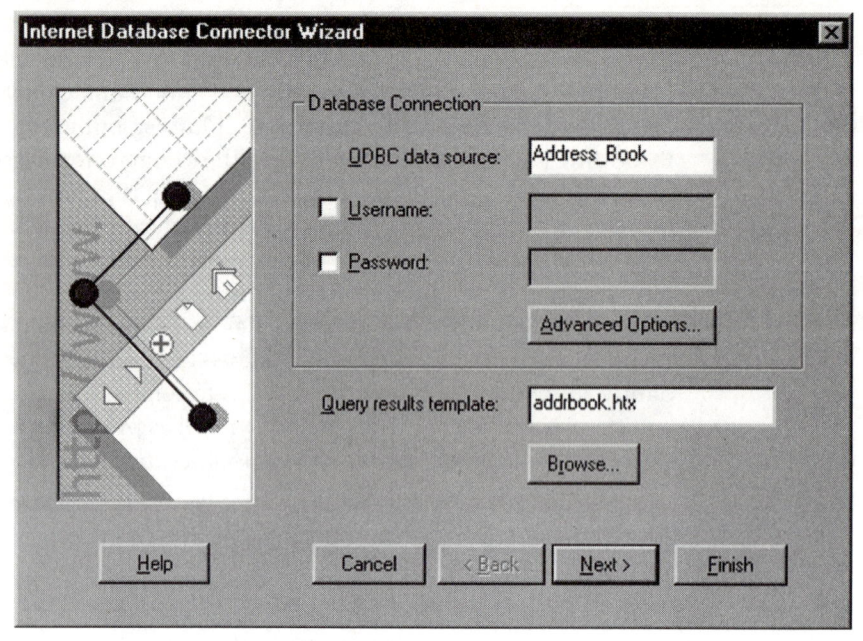

Figure 8-6: Fill in the name of the ODBC system data source, optionally specify a username and password, and choose a query results template (HTX) file.

The Internet Database Connector Wizard creates an IDC file for you; all you have to do is fill in the blanks, so to speak.

In order to look up records in the Addr_Book database file, you must have already used the ODBC icon in Control Panel to create a data source name of Address_Book that "points to" the AddrBook.mdb file, which is the actual Access database. The DSN is a synonym for the database.

If you were to manually create the Addrbook.idc file with Notepad, you would specify Address_Book as the ODBC data source name with the statement:

```
Datasource: Address_Book
```

With the IDC Wizard, you simply enter Address_Book into the ODBC Data Source text box, as shown in Figure 8-6. You'll also need to provide the filename (relative URL of the web page), in the Query Results Template text box shown in Figure 8-6.

We haven't discussed how to create the query results page yet, but even if it doesn't exist, you should come up with a name for it and enter it on the dialog box. (If the query results HTX file does exist already, you

Chapter 8: Database Publishing With the Internet Database Connector 407

can use the Browse button to locate it and save a bit of typing.) The convention for the filename of the query results template is to use the same name as the name you intend to use for the IDC file, but with an .HTX extension. Since the IDC query you're creating is called addrbook.idc, the results template page is named addrbook.htx.

If your Access database has security set up, you can use the Username and Password entries of the IDC Wizard to allow IDC to log in to the database. You can also set up a default user when creating the ODBC System DSN, but the entries here, if used, take precedence.

Structured Query Language Statements

After you click Next, you can enter an SQL query, as shown in Figure 8-7. Unfortunately, this is the most difficult part of using IDC—you have to understand how SQL works and know the SQL language. The most common type of SQL query retrieves selected records from a table based on some criteria, in the form:

```
SELECT [fields] FROM [table] WHERE [dbfield] = [criteria]
```

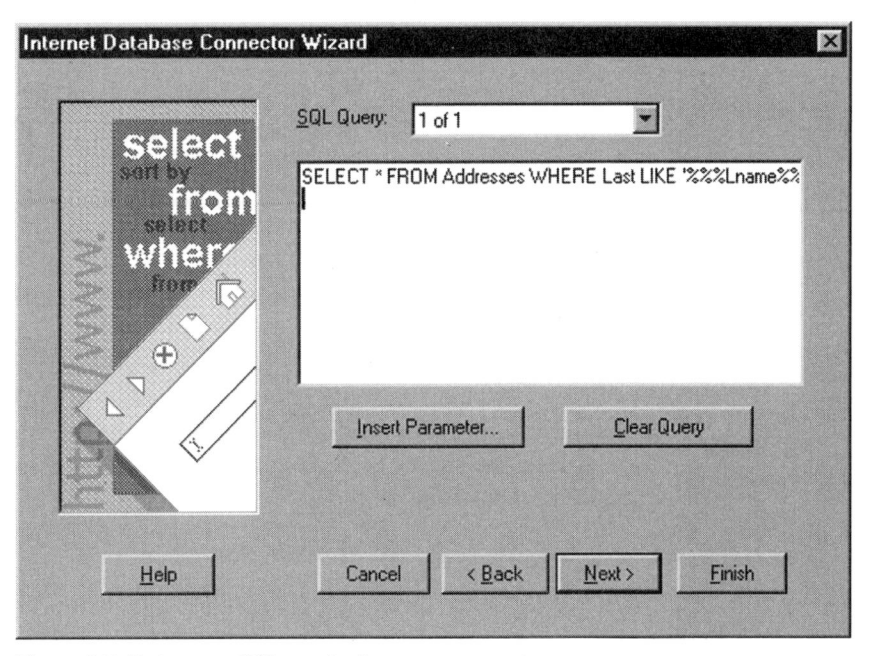

Figure 8-7: Enter your SQL queries here.

Substitute for [fields] the names of the fields you want to return for each matching record. This could be something like First;Last;Telephone, or you can use the * character to retrieve all fields. Substitute the actual database table name (a single Access database can contain many tables) for [table]. In my example, I use the Addresses table in the Addr_Book.mdb database.

If you have queries in the database, you can use a query definition instead of a table name for [table]. For [dbfield], use one of the fields in the table, and for [criteria], substitute either a text phrase that you want to match or a form field name. The = operator requires an exact match; the statement SELECT * FROM Addresses WHERE [Name]='Bob' will not find records where the first name is Bobby, nor will it find a name of BOB. The LIKE operator is more forgiving; it will match any field that matches the first part of the phrase, upper- or lowercase, so SELECT * FROM Addresses WHERE [Name] LIKE 'Bob' would find records where the Name field is either Bob, Bobby, BOB, or Bobbit.

SQL statements can be as simple or as complex as your requirements dictate. In addition to SELECT, you can use UPDATE to update fields within a record, DELETE to delete records, INSERT INTO to add records, and you can include complex criteria by adding AND, OR, NOT, and so on, as in WHERE [First] LIKE 'Bob' AND [Last] LIKE '%R%', which would return records where the first name starts with Bob and the last name contains the letter R.

While typing your SQL query using the IDC Wizard, you can click the Insert Parameter button to add a field to the query. If you click Insert Parameter and enter the name of the text box, Lname, it is inserted as %Lname%. All it does is add the % characters for you, so you may just want to type the fields manually and save a few clicks.

Unless you're conversant in SQL, the structured query language will be a major stumbling block on your path to mastering the Internet Database Connector. Fortunately, you have some resources. First, use Windows Explorer to look for a file called Msjetsql.hlp in the Windows System or System32 folder. Double-click this file to get a brief but fairly complete reference to the SQL language employed by the Microsoft Access Jet database engine.

Using Access to Build SQL Queries

Another way to create an SQL query is to use Microsoft Access itself. I can't begin to teach you the features of Access in this chapter, but the following exercise will at least demonstrate a method for generating SQL queries without having to learn SQL itself. To follow this example, you will need to have either Access 95 or Access 97 installed on your computer.

Open the Addresses database with Microsoft Access by double-clicking the Addr_Book.mdb file in the C:\SampleDB folder (or wherever you copied it to). Choose Insert | Query, and choose Design View as the type of query. (In your own work, you can use the Query wizards if you like, but let's first examine a fairly simple query by using Design View.)

After you choose Design View, you're given the opportunity to add tables to the query. From the Show Table dialog box, choose the Addresses table, click Add, then click Close. The raw query-by-example (QBE) form should resemble Figure 8-8.

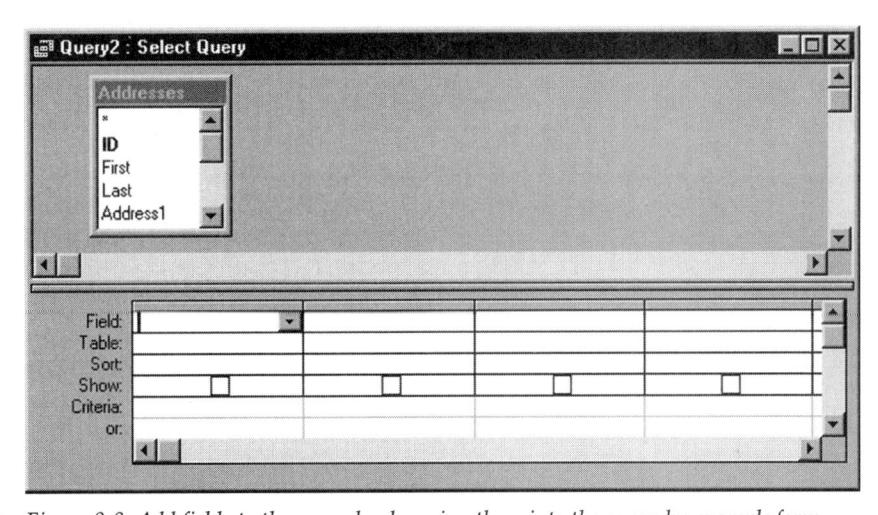

Figure 8-8: Add fields to the query by dragging them into the query-by-example form.

From the Addresses table, drag and drop the * symbol (which stands for "all fields") into the first column of the QBE grid. This will display all the fields in the query results table. To add criteria, drag one or more fields from the table into adjacent columns. For this exercise, drag the First field into the second column. Turn off the Show check box for that column, since the First field is already included in the first column, which shows all fields. In the Criteria row of the second column, enter the text Joe.

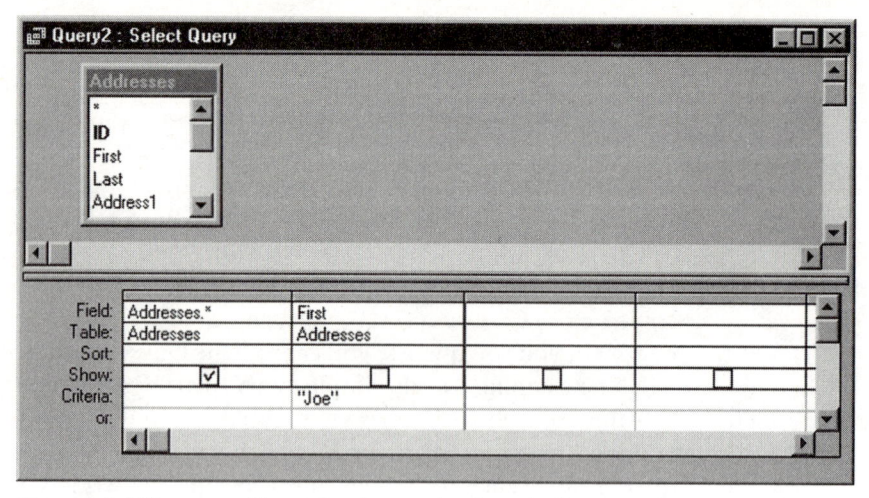

Figure 8-9: This query will match only records where the first name is Joe.

The finished query, shown as Figure 8-9, returns all records from the database where the first name is Joe. Try it by clicking the table button in the upper left corner, or choose View | Datasheet. Now you can see how the query looks as SQL by choosing View | SQL. The SQL version of the query should read like the following:
<ComSELECT DISTINCTROW Addresses.*

```
FROM Addresses
WHERE (((Addresses.First)="Joe"));
```

You can select this text, copy it to the clipboard, and paste it into the SQL window of the IDC Wizard as is. You can then customize it a bit. For example, instead of matching the literal text "Joe", you could rewrite the last line to read:

```
WHERE (((Addresses.First)="%First_Name%"));
```

This assumes that you have a text box named First_Name on the form that is handled by the IDC script. Notice that the quote marks were left intact. IDC always treats parameters (text wrapped with % symbols) literally. Let's say the user entered Margaret as the first name. IDC does not pass the form fields to the SQL engine, only the contents of the fields. Without the quotes, the SQL engine would balk at the statement WHERE [First] = Margaret, since Margaret is not a field name in the database, and that is the only place SQL can look up field names. (Field names can either be inside [] symbols or not.)

Since IDC converts the parameter (the field name on the form wrapped with % symbols) to the contents of the parameter before it's sent to the SQL engine, make sure your parameters are in quotes. (You can use either single or double quote marks.) That way, the phrase:

```
WHERE (((Addresses.First)="%First_Name%"));
```

is seen by the SQL engine as:

```
WHERE (((Addresses.First)="Margaret"));
```

which is what is intended.

SQL generated by Access is a bit redundant. It always includes the table name with the field name, which is optional if there is only one table in the query. It wraps expressions in parentheses characters and includes the DISTINCTROW keyword, which is only necessary with multiple table queries to ensure that duplicates are not returned. You can clean up the SQL by hand if you like, but in most cases, it will work as is.

TIP

Avoid using spaces in the names of the fields you set up in the design view when creating a table in Access. Spaces are illegal in field names in SQL queries unless you enclose the entire field name in bracket symbols, as in WHERE [Last Name] = "Baker". Since even this convention is illegal with some SQL engines, instead of spaces, consider using the underscore character, as in Last_Name.

Finishing the IDC Wizard

After you've entered your SQL query, you can optionally form additional queries by choosing Create Additional Query from the drop-down list labeled SQL Query. The first query you wrote becomes Query 1 of 2, and the second query becomes Query 2 of 2. On the results page, you'll add additional detail sections for each query that you want to perform. This lets you specify multiple types of query actions involving different tables while using a single results page. (If this isn't clear, it may be more obvious once you've worked with the results (HTX) pages. It's a chicken-vs.-egg quandary trying to explain IDC before HTX, since they work in tandem.)

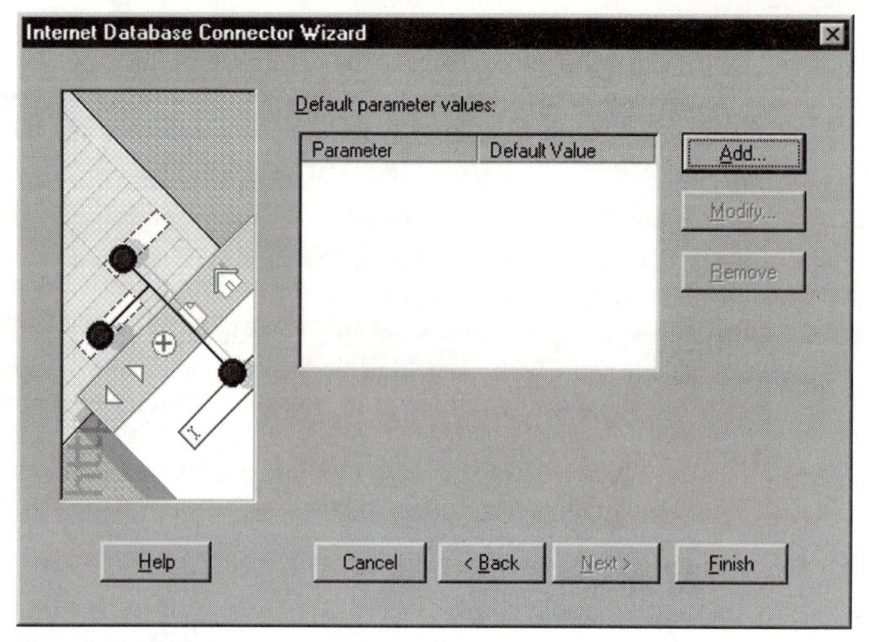

Figure 8-10: You'll almost never need to use this page of the wizard, unless your IDC file needs some predefined parameters.

When all the queries are ready, click Next to proceed to the last page of the IDC Wizard, shown in Figure 8-10. Here, you can add predefined parameters. Recall that a parameter is something like a form field; actually, it's the name of the form field enclosed in % symbols. When IDC runs the script, it substitutes the contents of the field for its name. If you want to create a stand-alone IDC script (as opposed to an IDC script used as a form handler), you can set up predefined parameters for it. That way, if the IDC file is used alone, it will have values for the parameters already set up. If the same IDC file is used with form fields having the same name, those values will override the default parameters. In any case, this is something that you rarely, if ever, need to use. So feel free to click Finish on the previous page of the wizard to bypass this page.

When you click Finish, you're asked to choose a folder and a filename for the script. Double-click the _scripts folder to store it there, and give the script a name ending with .IDC. (If you leave off the .IDC extension, FrontPage adds it for you.) The filename for this sample script is addrbook.idc.

Building a Results Page

After the IDC script runs the SQL query and retrieves the matching records, it needs a place to put them. To create a results page, switch to the FrontPage Editor and choose File | New. Choose Database Results from the New Page dialog box. The Database Results page is a blank page with the required .HTX extension. It contains only a comment that tells you to use the Edit | Database commands to insert table fields on the page. You can delete this comment, of course.

The results page is an HTML file containing special instructions for IDC telling it where to put the field results. Most of the page is like any other HTML page you create with FrontPage. However, there are special instructions embedded on the page, instructions understood only by the IDC and used to insert the fields that matched the query in the IDC file.

Each of these instructions is simply the name of the field returned by the query, surrounded by % symbols. You can't type these directly on the page, however. Instead, use the Edit | Database commands.

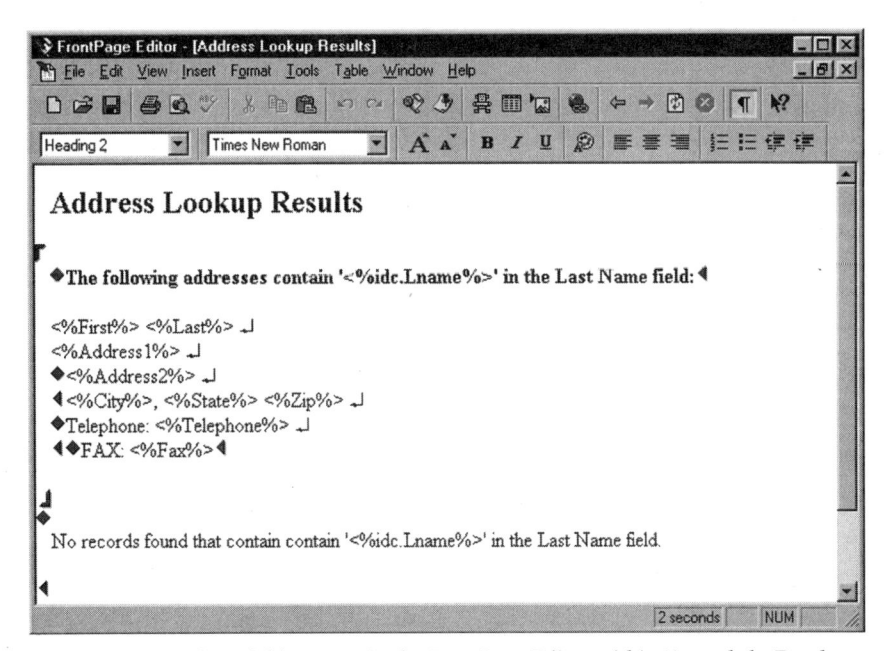

Figure 8-11: Database fields appear in the FrontPage Editor within % symbols. Database directives, such as the tiny brackets defining a detail section, are colored in red on your screen.

You can see these embedded database fields in Figure 8-11. Each one was inserted by using the Edit | Database | Database Column Value command. After choosing the command, you enter the name of the database field (column value) that you want to include on the page. These are the same field names that you used when creating the table in Access. For reference, consult Table 8-1, which defines the Access field names for the Addresses database and the form field names used by the more advanced examples I'll discuss at the end of the chapter. The table fields are wrapped in angle brackets and % symbols to indicate that the actual value of the field will be substituted when the user views the page.

Access DB Field	Type	Length	Web Form Field	Form Field	Type	Width
First	Text	20	txt_Fname	1-line	text box	20
Last	Text	30	txt_Lname	1-line	text box	30
Address1	Text	40	txt_Addr1	1-line	text box	40
Address2	Text	40	txt_Addr2	1-line	text box	40
City	Text	30	txt_City	1-line	text box	30
State	Text	2	txt_State	1-line	text box	3
Zip	Text	15	txt_Zip	1-line	text box	15
Telephone	Text	15	txt_Phone	1-line	text box	15
Fax	Text	15	txt_Fax	1-line	text box	15
Comments	Memo	n/a	txt_Comments	Scrolling	text	50

Table 8-1: Use this table as a reference to the form field names on the results page and the corresponding field names in the Access database.

You can also insert IDC parameters onto the results page. Any form field (such as the Lname text box) sent to the IDC script is available for inclusion on the results page. Just choose Edit | Database | IDC Parameter Value. These become the name of the parameter (e.g., Lname), with idc. added to the beginning. As with the Database Column Values, the whole thing is wrapped in angle brackets and % symbols, as in <%idc.Lname%>.

Let's back up a few steps. When the user enters a value in the Lname text box on the addrlook.htm page (Figure 8-4), the form is sent to the _scripts/addrlook.idc script for handling by IDC. IDC substitutes the characters typed in the Lname box for the %Lname% parameter in the SQL query, which returns the records from the table that contain those characters in the Last Name field. Those fields are then displayed on the results page, _scripts/addrlook.htx (Figure 8-11), so that wherever a placeholder like <%First%> exists, the actual contents of that field get substituted.

You can format the database parameters, the placeholders, like any text. If you make the <%First%> parameter boldface, then when Joe (or whatever the First field contains in the matching record) is displayed, it too will be in bold. If you're familiar with the mail merge capabilities of a word processor, you'll realize that IDC works quite similarly.

Defining a Detail Section

It's possible for a query to return more than one record. There could be many addresses in the address book that have a first name of Joe. You can't anticipate every record returned, and you don't want to have to repeat all the field definitions. The solution is to create a *detail section*. A detail section marks a section of HTML on your page that will be repeated for each record returned by the query. (If you know that the query will return only one record, or if you only want to display the first matching record, you don't need a detail section; just insert the fields where you want them on the page.)

The easiest way to add a detail section is to first design the way you want the page to look and then select the portion of the page that should be repeated for each record. Once you've made the selection (by dragging across the page with the mouse), use Edit | Database | Detail Section.

FrontPage inserts a tiny red bracket on either side of the material you've marked. You can also insert a detail section at the current cursor position, then insert a few blank lines between the starting and ending brackets, and then add the fields in between. Be careful not to accidentally delete either of the red brackets while typing or the detail section will be removed (the information you typed will remain, but it won't be a detail section).

TIP

If you want to set up multiple queries in the IDC file, you'll need a separate detail section for the results of each query. That way, you can include information from more than one database table on the same page. (Multiple queries require IIS or PWS 2.0 or later.)

Conditional Inclusion

Another powerful feature of the results page lets you conditionally include information. For example, the Address Line 2 may be empty for some of the records, but you don't necessarily want to display a blank line. By adding an IF control to the page, you can include that field in the detail section only if it isn't blank. If you view the original HTML, it might look like:

```
<%if Address2 GT ""%>
    <%Address2%>
<%endif%>
```

This is interpreted by IDC to mean "If the contents of the Address2 field are greater than nothing, include the contents of Address2." This works because Address2 is being compared to "", which is a special notation for a null, or empty piece of text (there's nothing between the quotes). If Address2 is empty, it can't be greater than null. If Address2 contains anything, then by definition it is greater than null.

The testing statement <%IF> is always paired with <%ENDIF%>. Anything between IF and ENDIF is only displayed on the web page should the IF condition work out as true. ENDIF marks the end of the conditional statement; anything after ENDIF does not depend on the test anymore, and will be displayed regardless.

For the IF statement, you can compare two fields, compare a field to a parameter value, and compare a field or parameter value with a constant, all by using the operators EQ (equals), GT (greater than), LT (less than), and combinations using AND, OR, NOT, and so on. If you're familiar with the Visual Basic programming language or other scripting languages, IF/THEN will immediately make sense to you.

If not, a diagram might be helpful. Programmers routinely use flowcharts to illustrate conditional logic. IF statements are drawn as diamonds, with arrows leading to each possible outcome. Figure 8-12 diagrams the conditional statement "If the contents of the Address2 field are greater than nothing, include the contents of Address2."

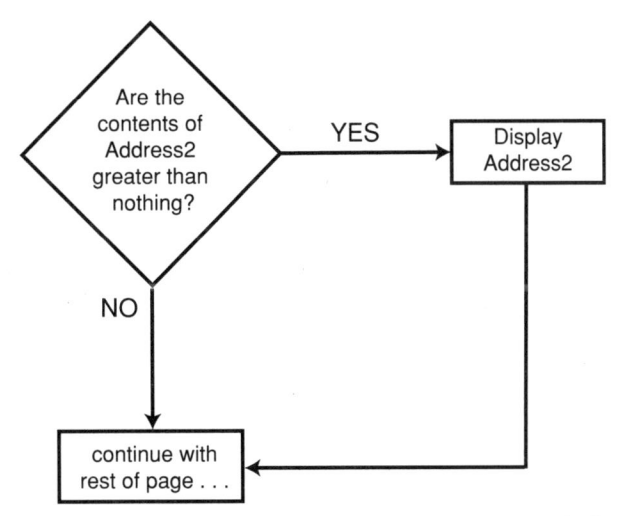

```
                Are the
              contents of        YES      ┌──────────┐
              Address2         ────────▶  │ Display  │
             greater than                 │ Address2 │
               nothing?                   └──────────┘
                   │                            │
                   │ NO                         │
                   ▼                            │
           ┌──────────────┐                     │
           │ continue with│  ◀──────────────────┘
           │ rest of page │
           └──────────────┘
```

Figure 8-12: A Venn diagram (a flowchart) graphically illustrates the flow of information based on conditions.

As usual, FrontPage makes it unnecessary to work directly with HTML. Although programmers might prefer straightforward IF-ENDIF statements visible on the screen, FrontPage uses tiny flowchart symbols instead. An IF condition embedded on a page appears as a little red diamond. Anything after the diamond is only included on the results page when the IF statement is true. To mark the end of this conditional material, the ENDIF statement is shown as a little left-pointing triangle. Everything after the ENDIF marker is not part of the conditional statement and will be included regardless. You can have many IF-ENDIF blocks on a page; you can even have IF-ENDIF statements embedded within other IF-ENDIF statements. (Most of the time, you'll use IF-ENDIF only within a detail section.)

Here's how you insert something on the page based on a condition. First, type the text or insert the database field on the page that you want to include if the condition is true. Select this text. Next, use Edit | Database | If-Then Conditional Section. This pops up the If-Then Conditional Section dialog box, as shown in Figure 8-13.

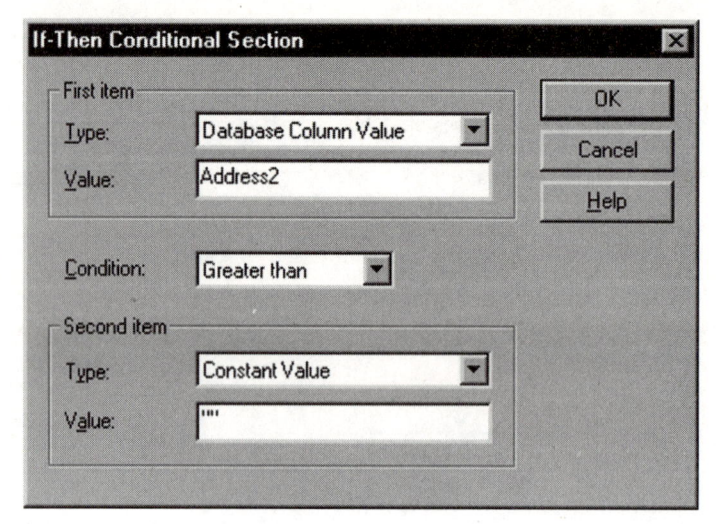

Figure 8-13: Describe the conditional statement by choosing the item you want to compare to another item, the comparison operator (equals, greater than, less than, contains), and the item you want to compare to the first item.

Figure 8-13 shows how you would describe the statement "If Address2 is greater than nothing then...." FrontPage will take the Address2 field (the Database Column Value whose name is Address2) and use the Greater Than operator to compare it with a Constant Value of "" (nothing).

When constructing IF-THEN statements, you are comparing one item (the first item) to another (the second item). To make the comparison, you can choose between Equals, Greater Than, Less Than, or Contains. Either item can be one of the following: Database Column Value (fill in Value with the name of the field), IDC Parameter Value (put the name of the IDC parameter in the Value box), Constant Value (i.e., a literal piece of text that you put in the Value box), CurrentRecord MaxRecords, or HTTP Variable.

When you click OK, the text you previously selected is bracketed by a diamond and a left-pointing triangle. If you want to view or change the IF condition, just double-click on the diamond symbol.

To extend the abilities of IF-THEN, you can add an ELSE clause. Instead of displaying nothing when Address2 is blank, you might want to display another indication, such as the text "[empty]." To do this, you would create the following IF/THEN/ELSE statement: "If Address2 is greater than nothing, include Address2, else include the text [empty]." In HTML, this would appear as:

```
<%if Address2 GT ""%>
    <%Address2%>
<%else%>
    [empty]
<%endif%>
```

To use ELSE, first construct the IF-THEN block as described above. After the ENDIF symbol (the left-pointing triangle), type the text and/or insert the database fields that you want to make part of the ELSE clause and choose Edit | Database | Else Conditional Statement. This inserts a right-pointing triangle after the IF diamond and before the ENDIF triangle. Anything between the IF symbol (the diamond) and before the ELSE symbol (the right-pointing triangle) is only included if the conditional statement is true. Anything between the ELSE symbol (the right-pointing triangle) and the ENDIF symbol (the left-pointing triangle) is only included if the conditional statement is false. Anything after the ENDIF symbol is not part of the conditional statement and will be included regardless of whether the IF statement was true or false.

What a Load of Bull

At this point, you're probably scratching your head, even throwing up your hands in despair, unless you're experienced with programming. If it's any comfort, I also had a lot of trouble making sense of all the little diamonds and triangles. Trying to integrate programming features into the friendly GUI of FrontPage is probably stretching the capabilities of the user interface beyond reason. After all, FrontPage was intended to free designers from the necessity of programming.

If in doubt about the kind of conditional statements you've ended up with, you can always use View | HTML to see what you've coded. In fact, once you've figured out how the conditional statements are represented in HTML, you may wish to simply edit the HTML directly.

Before we leave the topic of conditional statements, there is a special IF-THEN trick you'll want to figure out. You can use the special CurrentRecord item with IF-THEN to test for whether or not any records were returned by the IDC query. Within a detail section, CurrentRecord should be non-zero, since at least one record was returned. Outside of the detail section, CurrentRecord will be zero if there were no records returned. You can take advantage of this to display a message prior to the start of the first record or display a message if no records are found.

> **TIP**
>
> *If you try to display the value of CurrentRecord by including it on the page, as in "Record number <%CurrentRecord%>," it won't work. CurrentRecord can be tested in an IF statement, but it is not available as a value to display on the page. What if you wanted to test for a particular record number? The only workaround is to include the record number as a field in the table, which will then be available as part of the results, assuming you write the SQL query to return all fields. This can be an AutoNumber field, such as used by the Primary Key field.*
>
> *A possible workaround for this is to add a counter field to the database, but the values in counter fields for successive records will not always be sequential, since counter values are not renumbered when a record is deleted. Later, I'll show you how to use the primary key (a counter variable) to keep track of any particular record returned by a detail section, so that record can be deleted or updated.*

I used the CurrentRecord test in the Address Lookup page (addrlook.htm) to display the header "The following addresses contain <search phrase> in the Last Name field," but only for the first record. To substitute the search phrase, I inserted the IDC Parameter Value of Lname, which is the value of the text box on the search form. The IF statement attached to this line of text is equivalent to "If CurrentRecord Equals 0 then..." (see Figure 8-14). Since this line is within a detail section, it won't be displayed at all if no records are returned. Before the first record is displayed, CurrentRecord is 0, but after the first record is displayed, CurrentRecord has a value of 1. So the heading will only be displayed prior to the first record.

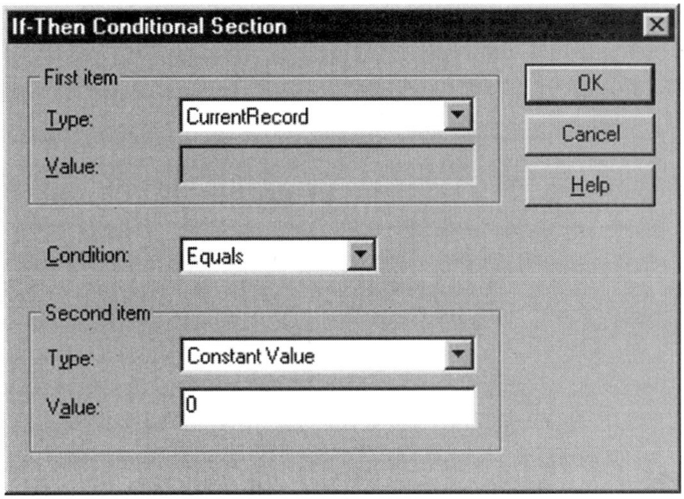

Figure 8-14: Here's how you test whether the current record is zero.

After the detail section, just after the ending bracket, I inserted another line that reports "No records found that contain <%idc.Lname%> in the Last Name field." This is attached to an IF statement that reads "If CurrentRecord Equals 0." Here's how this works: If any records are returned, then by the time the detail section is complete, CurrentRecord will no longer be zero, since at least one record has been displayed and CurrentRecord increases by one for each record. Therefore the "No records" message won't be displayed. On the other hand, if no records were returned, the detail section is empty and CurrentRecord remains zero, so the "No records" message will be displayed.

HTTP Variables

In addition to the form field parameters and the IDC parameter values, you can also insert HTTP variables on a page or use HTTP variables with IF-THEN comparisons. For example, you could record the user's IP address in a database. You could use a test such as <%IF HTTP_USER_AGENT CONTAINS "Mozilla"%> to determine the type of browser accessing the pages in case you need to design a different version of a page to support that browser. You can test for or display any HTTP variable by adding the characters HTTP_ to the beginning of the

HTTP variable and converting any dashes in the variable name to underscores. Here are a few of the most useful HTTP variables for inclusion or comparison on an HTX results page:

HTTP_USER_AGENT	Text containing a description of the web browser
HTTP_REMOTE_ADDR	The user's IP address
HTTP_REMOTE_HOST	The user's hostname
HTTP_REMOTE_USER	The user's name
HTTP_SERVER_NAME	The name of the web server
HTTP_SERVER_PORT	The IP address of the web server
HTTP_SERVER_SOFTWARE	The name of the web server software
HTTP_URL	The URL sent to the IDC
HTTP_QUERY_STRING	The information sent to the URL (following the ? mark)

For complete technical information on IDC and database publishing, consult Chapter 8 of the online manual for Internet Information Server or Peer Web Services (found on the Start menu at Start | Programs | Peer Web Services | Product Documentation or Start | Programs | Internet Information Server | Product Documentation).

Completing the Purchase Requisition Form

Now that you've learned how IDC works, you can anticipate how I set up the IDC (query) and HTX (results) files for the purchase requisition form developed at the end of Chapter 7 (in the section, "Requisition Form"). Consult Table 8-1 to refer to the names of the Access database fields and the names of the text boxes and other form fields on the purchase requisition form.

Access DB Field	Field Type	Size	Web Form Field	Form Field Type	Width
Name	Text	40	txt_Name	Text box	40
Description	Text	40	txt_Describe	Text box	40
Request_Date	Date/Time	n/a	txt_Requested	Text box	8
Required_Date	Date/Time	n/a	txt_Required	Text box	8
Purchase_Method	Text	25	menu_Method	Drop-down menu	25
Purchase_Details	Text	40	txt_Details	Text box	40
Justification	Memo	n/a	txt_Justify	Scrolling text	40
Item1	Text	30	txt_Item1	Text box	30
Qty1	Number	byte	menu_Qty1	Drop-down menu	auto
Vendor1	Text	20	txt_Vendor1	Text box	20
Cost1	Currency	n/a	txt_Cost1	Text box	10
Item2	Text	30	txt_Item2	Text box	30
Qty2	Number	byte	menu_Qty2	Drop-down menu	auto
Vendor2	Text	20	txt_Vendor2	Text box	20
Cost2	Currency	n/a	txt_Cost2	Text box	10
Item3	Text	30	txt_Item3	Text box	30
Qty3	Number	byte	menu_Qty3	Drop-down menu	auto
Vendor3	Text	20	txt_Vendor3	Text box	20
Cost3	Currency	n/a	txt_Cost3	Text box	10
Item4	Text	30	txt_Item4	Text box	30
Qty4	Number	byte	menu_Qty4	Drop-down menu	auto
Vendor4	Text	20	txt_Vendor4	Text box	20
Cost4	Currency	n/a	txt_Cost4	Text box	10
Item5	Text	30	txt_Item5	Text box	30
Qty5	Number	byte	menu_Qty5	Drop-down menu	auto
Vendor5	Text	20	txt_Vendor5	Text box	20
Cost5	Currency	n/a	txt_Cost5	Text box	10
=== not shown on form ===					
Approved By	Text	40	NA	NA	NA
Approved	Yes/No	1	NA	NA	NA

Table 8-2: Field information for purchase requisition form and Access database.

While referring to Table 8-2, take a look at the IDC file (_scripts/purchreq.idc) that adds the purchase requisition to the Requistions table (in the Purch_Req.mdb Access database):

```
Datasource: Purchases
Template: purch_req.htx
SQLStatement: INSERT INTO Requisitions
+(Name,Description,Request_Date,Required_Date,
+ Purchase_Method,Purchase_Details,Justification,
+ Item1,Qty1,Vendor1,Cost1,
+ Item2,Qty2,Vendor2,Cost2,
+ Item3,Qty3,Vendor3,Cost3,
+ Item4,Qty4,Vendor4,Cost4,
+ Item5,Qty5,Vendor5,Cost5)
+VALUES
('%txt_Name%','%txt_Describe%','%txt_Requested%','%txt_Required%',
+ '%menu_Method%','%txt_Details%','%txt_Justify%',
+ '%txt_Item1%','%menu_Qty1%','%txt_Vendor1%','0%txt_Cost1%',
+ '%txt_Item2%','%menu_Qty2%','%txt_Vendor2%','0%txt_Cost2%',
+ '%txt_Item3%','%menu_Qty3%','%txt_Vendor3%','0%txt_Cost3%',
+ '%txt_Item4%','%menu_Qty4%','%txt_Vendor4%','0%txt_Cost4%',
+ '%txt_Item5%','%menu_Qty5%','%txt_Vendor5%','0%txt_Cost5%') ;
```

This IDC file looks more intimidating than it really is. It's lengthy because there are a lot of form fields on the form, which correspond to over 25 database fields in the requisitions table. The meat of the IDC script is an INSERT INTO statement. In SQL, INSERT INTO is used to add records to a database table. You name the table and the fields you want to create and then specify the values to go into each of those fields.

The + symbols are used whenever your SQL statement won't fit on one line or where you want to break a line for readability. You don't need to use the + symbols when you enter your SQL statement using the IDC wizard, only if you edit the IDC file with a text editor like Notepad.

One of the most difficult parts of crafting this SQL statement was finding all the typos. Leaving out a single % symbol can wreck the whole query, and IDC doesn't give you much feedback to help you track down your errors. You may get anything from an ERROR 501 to some vague message reported by the Access Jet Engine.

Another problem is what to do if the user fails to make an entry for one of the text boxes or other form fields. While you can use validation rules to enforce entry, sometimes you want to allow optional entry. For the purchase requisition form, the employee need not fill in all five rows of the table if he or she is only requesting a single item.

Chapter 8: Database Publishing With the Internet Database Connector

Yet by default, text fields in Microsoft Access can not store a null value. This will cause an error when IDC tries to store an empty form field in a table field. To solve this problem, you need to use Access to open the table in Design View, and for each text field, set the Allow Zero Length property to Yes.

A similar problem occurs when you try to assign a null value to a Currency field. To work around this, you could use a regular Number field. I chose to fix the problem by appending the character '0' (zero) to the beginning of each number. If '%txt_Cost1%' is null, then the value '0' is assigned to the Cost1 field. If '%txt_Cost1%' contains the number 150, then '0150' is assigned. Since leading zeros are ignored in Number and Currency field types, the extra zero is harmless. You'll often have to resort to this type of *hack*, as it's called in the programming trade, to work around stubborn limitations.

Every IDC script needs a results page, even if no records are returned by the query. An UPDATE query doesn't return any records (only SELECT statements do that), but you'll still want at least a confirmation message that tells the user that the form has been accepted.

Figure 8-15: The results page for an UPDATE query only needs to provide basic feedback to the user.

The page purch_req.htx in the _scripts folder is the results page for the purch_req.idc file. As shown in Figure 8-15, it simply reports that the requisition has been filed and includes two fields from the form (not from the table, since no field values are returned by the INSERT INTO SQL statement) as confirmation. As is always good practice, there are also hyperlinks to take the user back to the database page or to the intranet's home page.

Advanced Database Examples

The intranet examples included on the Companion CD-ROM include several other powerful database demonstrations, with attractively designed and easy to use forms. You can search for records by last name, first name, telephone number, or zip code, or use the query-by-example form to search using any combination of fields. Once a record is found, it can be updated by typing directly over the record and clicking an Update button, or it can be removed from the database by clicking a Delete button. There's also a page for adding new records to the database.

While these IDC/SQL queries, forms, and results pages are more sophisticated than the examples presented in this chapter, they rely on the same techniques. I encourage you to explore them further by opening the pages from FrontPage Explorer and then dissecting them to examine the properties of the elements on the pages. A complete explanation of every feature of these database pages could easily fill another chapter, but it's time we move on to even more advanced topics. But before we do so, I'll offer a few tips on how these pages were put together.

Query by Example

Figure 8-16 illustrates the Query by Example form. The idea is that the employee can enter text into any of the fields to look up records containing that information. For example, entering C into the First Name field and B into the Last Name field would return records for Charles Brannon, Chuckee Bee, Jackie McBrown, and so on. (Because a wildcard is used with the LIKE statements in the IDC/SQL query, it will find any occurrence of the search phrase within a field, not just those that match the start of the field. You can remove the extra % symbols from the LIKE statement in the _scripts/qbe.idc file if you would prefer to find only addresses that start with the search characters.)

Chapter 8: Database Publishing With the Internet Database Connector

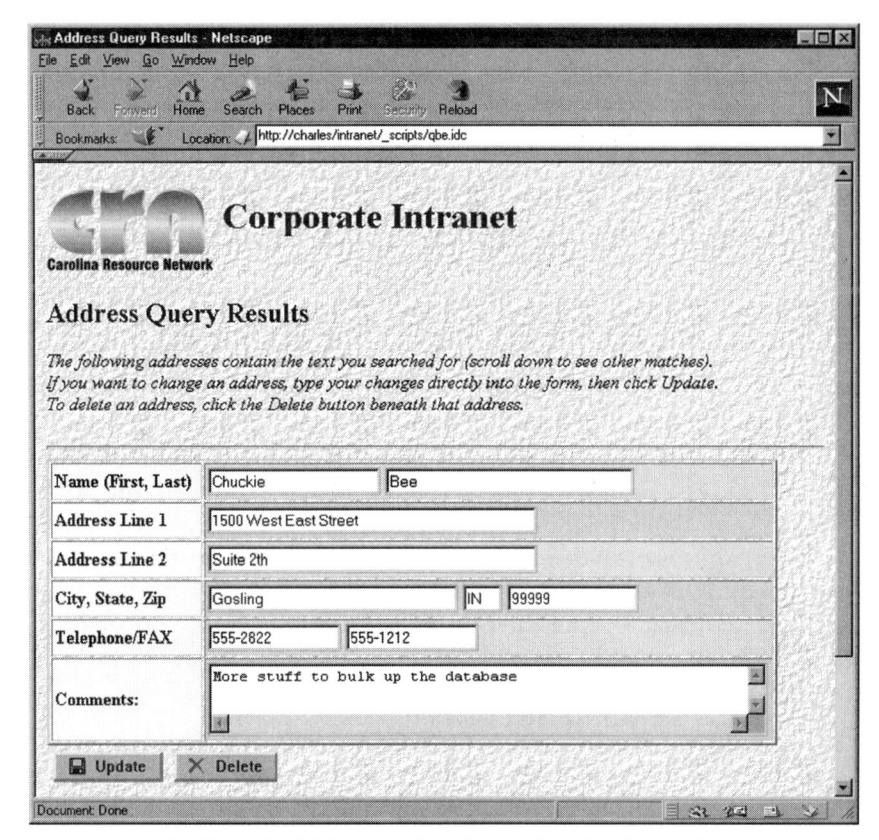

Figure 8-17: This form (the fields are explained in Table 8-1) collects information for the IDC query.

The Find button is an Image form field that acts exactly like a Submit button. It sends the form data to the Internet Database Connector script called _scripts/qbe.idc. This IDC file takes all the input and sends it to a complex SELECT query, which uses LIKE to match all the fields that contain text. Since some fields may be null (empty), the IDC file employs another clever hack to test for either a match with LIKE or a match with a null value. Take a look at the IDC file to see how this works.

Once the form was created, I copied it into the clipboard and pasted it into several other pages to save typing. The results page for the Query by Example form (_scripts/addr_query.htx) uses a copy of the original form to display the results. The secret here was to set the default value of each text box to an IDC parameter value. For example, the %txt_Fname% text box has a default value of <%idc.First%>, so when the results page is built by IDC, it fills in each text box with the field data returned by the query. Since the form is already filled out, it's easy for the user to change any fields that need to be updated and then click the Update button to submit the form.

Updating Records

The Update button is an Image form field, so it works just like the Submit button would. It sends the page to the _scripts/update.idc script. How does this script know which record to update in the database? The key is to pass along the value of the primary key, the ID field included in the Access database table. Since this value is not present on the form, it was added to the Hidden Fields section of the Form Properties with a value of <%ID%>. When the form is submitted, this ID is sent along to the next IDC. So this is a case where a normal page triggers an IDC results page, which in turn triggers another IDC page. The results page for update.idc is update.htx, which simply reports that the record has been updated and includes the original form for confirmation.

Deleting Records

The Delete button on the Address Query results page (addr_query.htx) is an image, but it's not a form field image since the Update button already fulfills that role (remember that image fields can only be used as a substitute for the Submit button). Instead, the image is hyperlinked to the following URL: delete1.idc?ID=<%ID%>. This causes the delete1.idc script to be executed and passes the value of the record's ID (primary key field) to the IDC script so that it knows which record to delete (the ID is the only parameter "seen" by the script since only the form handler has access to the fields on the form). The delete1.idc script doesn't actually delete the record; it uses a SELECT statement to find that record and displays it on the delete1.htx page so that the user can confirm the deletion. After the user clicks Delete again, this time executing delete2.idc, the record is permanently deleted, and the delete2.htx results page confirms this for the user.

Adding Records

Once the Update form was completed, it was relatively simple to resave it as a normal web page (new_addr.htm) in the main web folder and rework it into an Add Address form. Here, the Submit button (another image form field) sends the form data to _scripts/new_addr.idc, which uses an INSERT INTO statement (as used by the Purchase Requisition script) to add that record to the database. I also added a Clear button, using a standard button control, so that the user could reset the form and start over if desired. Unfortunately, there is no way to link a custom image to the form Reset action, so a plain button is used. This is one of the limitations of HTML, something that even IIS and IDC can't overcome.

On the other hand, the Reset button could have been a graphic linked to a VBScript program or JavaScript program on the web page. The program would need to do little more than execute the form reset action. But I haven't covered programming yet; that's a topic for the next chapter.

Moving On

We covered a lot of territory in the last two chapters—all the basics that you need to implement a corporate intranet with database access, or at least a solid starting point for one. If you thought database publishing was a complex subject, just wait until the next chapter. In one fell swoop, I'll discuss the advanced features of FrontPage 97 that let you insert powerful interactive elements on a page by taking advantage of ActiveX Controls, Java applets, and scripting. These features are the cutting edge of web design and will soon be a requirement for any truly immersive and interactive web site.

chapter 9

Advanced FrontPage Techniques

In the previous chapters, you've learned how to build and customize web pages with images, sounds, tables, frames, and image maps. And in Chapter 7, you learned how to go beyond static pages to implement live database access, the first step toward truly interactive sites.

To achieve the goal of true interactivity, it's time to turn our attention to *active* pages. An active page is more than HTML code. It contains a computer program, or script that lets the user interact with the contents of the page. HTML is a document formatting language, but it's not a common programming language with control flow structures. It can't perform simple operations like addition and multiplication to calculate a percentage or even display the current date. It's no surprise, therefore, that the latest extensions to HTML are indeed a new breed of programming languages.

One of them is Microsoft's VBScript, short for Visual Basic, Scripting Edition. *VBScript* is a simple scripting language that allows the web author to access the contents of a page and manipulate them from within the page. The script is a small program attached to the page that is executed on the computer where the document is viewed. To understand what VBScript can do for you, let's look at a couple of examples.

Note: The examples for the other chapters of this book require that you first import them as a FrontPage web, since they rely on FrontPage Explorer and server features. For your convenience, however, the examples in the \Webs\Chap09 folder on this book's Companion CD-ROM can be opened directly from the CD-ROM with either Internet Explorer or the FrontPage Editor. If you want to work with the pages using FrontPage Explorer, you can import each subfolder in the \Webs\Chap09 folder as a separate web or import the entire Chap09 folder as a web.

A Few Active Pages

Look at the page shown in Figure 9-1. This web page is saved as index.htm and named VBScript; you will find it on the Companion CD-ROM (\Webs\Chap09\VBScript\). VBScript is a typical user registration page with a peculiar requirement. The user must supply an e-mail address, or a fax number, or both. As long as at least one of the two fields has a value, the form is valid and can be processed. This type of validation isn't possible with FrontPage techniques. FrontPage allows you to define mandatory fields, but it can't handle even slightly complicated situations like this one, where some of the fields are optional, but a certain combination of them is mandatory.

This page would have to be validated at the server if it weren't for VBScript. To validate this page on the client (the web browser), you write a short program to access the values of the various controls (fields) on the client, such as text boxes or option buttons. This is exactly what VBScript can do for you. It lets you write short programs, or scripts, that access and manipulate the values of the various controls at the client's side.

Before web browsers (such as Internet Explorer and Netscape Navigator) added client-side scripting, all programmatic logic had to be stored in scripts that ran on the web server. Server scripts are powerful, but they add to the burden of the web server and can be inefficient for the very kinds of tasks that client-side scripting is ideal for.

Chapter 9: Advanced FrontPage Techniques

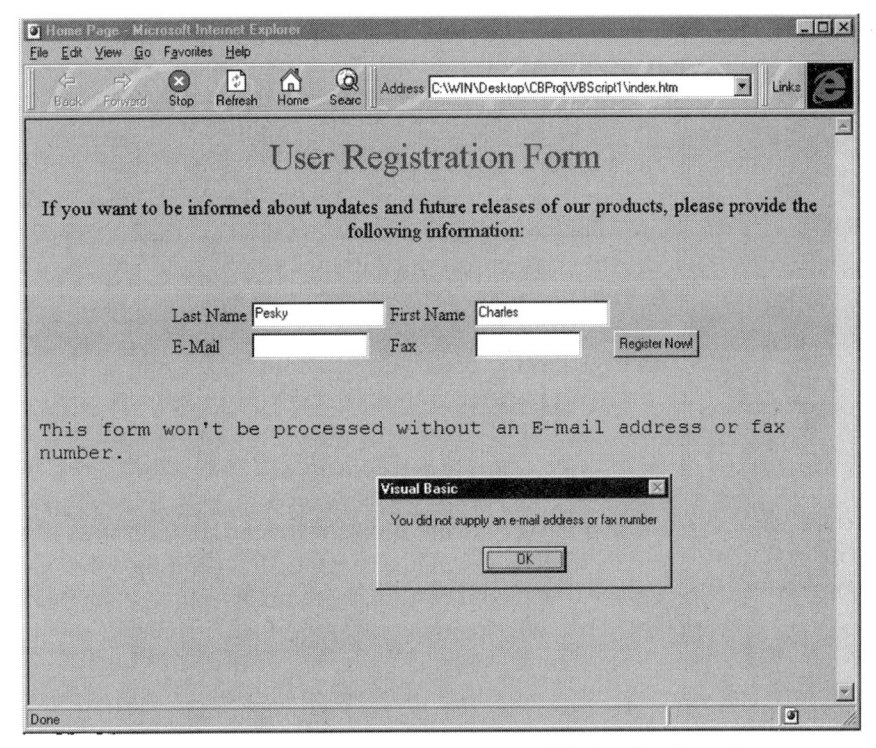

Figure 9-1: This user registration page requires more validation than FrontPage can handle.

Recall our discussion of image maps in Chapter 3. An image map is a way of looking up coordinate points in an image in order to send the web browser to one of several links, depending on what part of the image was clicked on. If the image map is supported only by the web server, the location of the mouse pointer over the image is transmitted to the web server, which looks up the location and then returns the page the link pointed to.

This is inefficient. Since the web browser already has the coordinates of the mouse, why not let the web browser do the image-map processing? FrontPage supports both client-side and server-side image mapping, but you can see that the client-side option is much more efficient since it performs the task on the user's own computer.

The most common use of client-side scripting is data validation. FrontPage can generate JavaScript or VBScript code automatically to make sure that data entries in text boxes conform to your requirements;

so that only numeric characters are allowed in a number field, for example. I'll show you how this works so that you will be able to write your own custom data validation routines.

If you were to validate the data on the server, you would still have to write a program that would read the values of the controls, do the validation, and accept or reject the data. This program wouldn't require any more information than what is available on the client already (which is where the user enters the data), so why should you have to submit the values to the server and wait for a response?

Figure 9-2 is another typical example of the usefulness of scripting. This page lets the user specify a computer configuration by checking the desired components. You know how to design a page like the one of Figure 9-2, but how would you go about updating the total cost of the selected configuration on demand? Without a scripting language, you would have to provide a Submit button, which would transmit all the values to the server, invoke a special program on the server to process the data (that is, calculate the total), and send the total back to the browser. If you could add a little intelligence to your Web page, simple tasks like validating the data, or performing simple calculations, would take place on the client.

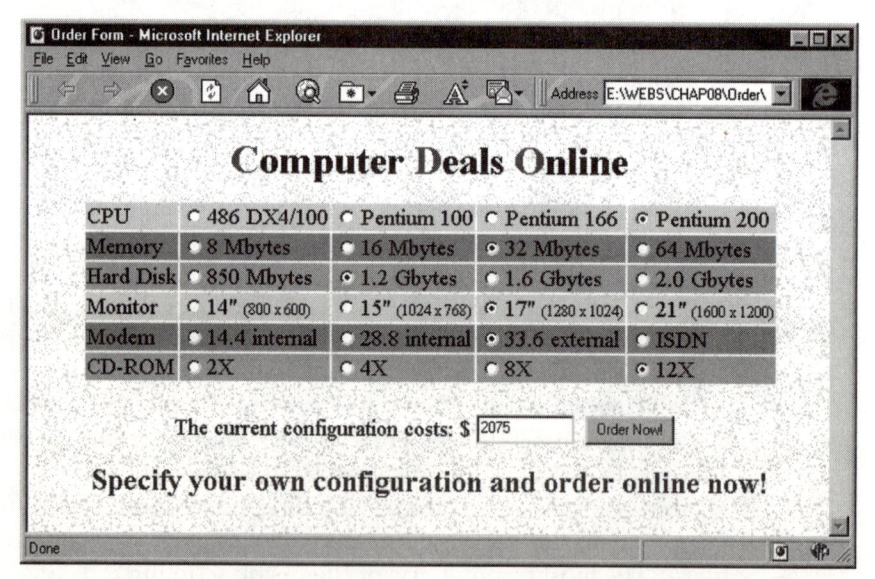

Figure 9-2: The script on this page displays the total cost of the configuration each time the viewer selects a different component.

As you work with FrontPage, you'll run into the limitations of using only HTML to design your pages. HTML can't even display the current date, or calculate a simple sum, or pop up a message box. With a scripting language like VBScript, the landscape is changing drastically. Now you can examine the contents of a form, and design pages that interact with the user without requiring the server's involvement.

VBScript is an example of *client-side scripting*, that is, executing a program on the web browser running on the user's computer. JavaScript, which is loosely based on the Java language, is another popular scripting language, although VBScript is easier to program and easier to understand, which is why we focus on it in this chapter. Netscape Navigator only supports JavaScript, whereas Internet Explorer 3.0 supports both JavaScript (called JScript), and VBScript. The new 4.0 release of Netscape Navigator (Communicator) web browser will support VBScript in its final release.

TIP

Current versions of Netscape Navigator will also support VBScript and ActiveX Controls, as long as the NCompass ScriptActive plug-in has been installed. Go to http://www.ncompasslabs.com/products/scriptactive.htm for more information.

In the following sections you will find a number of VBScript examples for carrying out common tasks such as the ones I just presented. Note that this chapter is only a quick introduction to VBScript; it would be difficult to present an in-depth discussion of VBScript in a single chapter. The goal is to show you how VBScript works and how to develop simple scripts. If you have never programmed in the past, you may find that the information in this chapter is a bit advanced for you.

Nevertheless, you should have no problem following the examples and developing a few simple scripts for your pages. If your pages will benefit from the presence of a script, then you should consult some books on using VBScript. I recommend *The Comprehensive Guide to VBScript* by Richard Mansfield (Ventana).

Programming Concepts
It's a tall order to teach both programming and VBScript techniques in a single chapter. Many of you will already be familiar with Visual Basic for Windows and will be mainly interested in how VBScript is inserted on a web page. Others of you will have no prior experience with programming (other than the database scripting covered in Chapter 8).

It isn't easy to serve both audiences equally well in an advanced chapter. Whatever your experience, you'll find the examples offered here easy to implement, and you'll learn how to use VBScript for various purposes.

If you have no prior experience with programming, what follows is a quick overview of some concepts that you should be familiar with before proceeding with the chapter.

A *script* is a text file, like the kind you create or edit with Notepad. Each line of the script is a line of text ending in a carriage return. The line of text can be blank, a descriptive comment, or a scripting language statement.

When a script is encountered on a web page, the scripting-type tag tells the web browser which scripting language to use. The "*engine*," or interpreter, for that language scans the script, examining each line in the order it appears in the script. It interprets the command words and arithmetic functions and acts upon, or *executes,* the instructions.

Not all lines of the script are necessarily executed. One of the most powerful features of a programming language involves conditional statements, so that a line of code is only executed if a condition is met. For example, a script could use the time of day to decide whether to output Good Morning, Good Afternoon, or Good Evening.

A script is usually divided into a number of *procedures*. A procedure is a self-contained snippet of code that accomplishes a distinct task, or *function*. A true function returns a value (such as a computation), and can be provided with information. In our greeting example, you would pass the time of day to the script procedure, and it would return a piece of text (a string) containing the proper greeting.

While some procedures can be started simply by opening a web page, most procedures are only executed if the user causes some event to occur, such as clicking on a button. When the button is clicked, the event procedure associated with that button is executed. When designing an active web page, you'll have to get used to this kind of event-oriented programming.

To aid you in programming, you can use any of a number of reserved keywords and commands that are part of the BASIC (Beginner's All Purpose Symbolic Instruction Code) language specification, or more specifically, a subset of the Microsoft Visual Basic programming language called VBScript (Visual Basic, Scripting Edition).

You can also use any word (except for reserved BASIC words) as a variable. A variable on the left of an equal sign, such as COST=30, is assigned a value. (The word COST is now synonymous with the value 30.) A variable to the right of an equal sign or used in a mathematical expression (such as TOTAL=COST+TAX), substitutes the value it holds.

There are many arithmetic functions available to you, such as the operators + (addition), - (subtraction), * (multiplication), / (division), and many built-in functions, such as COS(x) for Cosine, or RND for generating random numbers.

Variables in VBScript can also store groups of characters (text) that are called strings. The statement Fname="Charles" lets a variable called Fname store the characters C h a r l e s.

As you read this chapter, you'll pick up some additional tips that help explain the programming, but since VBScript resembles plain English, many of the programming statement you encounter in this chapter should be self-explanatory.

Getting Input & Displaying Output

Let's start with two of the most basic VBScript functions. The InputBox function, which lets you get user input, and the MsgBox function, which lets you display output to the user. The syntax (wording) of the InputBox function is shown in this example:

```
Name = InputBox("Please enter your name")
```

When this line is executed, the script causes the web browser to display a dialog box like the one shown in Figure 9-3, which prompts the user to enter his or her name. When the user clicks on the OK button, the text entered by the user in the dialog box is stored in a variable called Name. (A *variable* is a labeled location within the computer's memory that can store a value.) You can access the user's name from within your script by referring to the name variable. For instance, you can display a message to the user with the MsgBox function:

```
MsgBox("Thank you for visiting our site " & Name)
```

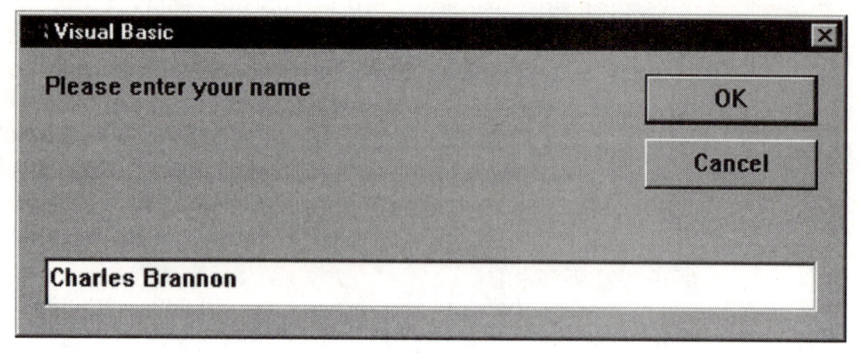

Figure 9-3: Getting input from the user with InputBox.

The symbol & is a special operator, which *concatenates* (sticks together) two strings of text. (A *string* is a programming term for a sequence of characters, such as a piece of text.) The & operator takes the string "Thank you for visiting our site" (without the quotes, of course), tacks the value stored in the Name variable (presumably the user's name), and generates a message like:

```
Thank you for visiting our site Amy
```

This string of text will be displayed by the MsgBox function in a window like the one shown in Figure 9-4.

Figure 9-4: Displaying messages with MsgBox.

InputBox and MsgBox are VBScript commands. Actually, they are called functions, but for all practical purposes, they behave like commands: They cause certain actions to take place. The InputBox function displays a window in which the user can enter information. The MsgBox function displays another window with a message. You may have noticed how different the two windows look. They don't even use the same font. This is a quirk in the language and will be fixed in a future version of VBScript.

The difference between the two is that the InputBox function returns a value, which is whatever the user has typed in the dialog box.

Let's put these two commands to work. With my assistance, you are going to develop a web page that contains two push buttons, which convert inches to centimeters and vice versa. Every time the user clicks on one of them, the script will prompt him to enter the number of inches (or centimeters) to be converted and will display the result in a message box. The page you are going to create will resemble the one shown in Figure 9-5.

Note: In previous chapters, I've referred to items like push buttons, text boxes, and radio buttons as form fields, or field types. This is correct. It is also correct to refer to them as *controls*, which is what they're called in most programming languages, including Visual Basic. A control is an element of the Windows user interface, or an embedded program, that you can get input from and, or take control of to perform a useful task.

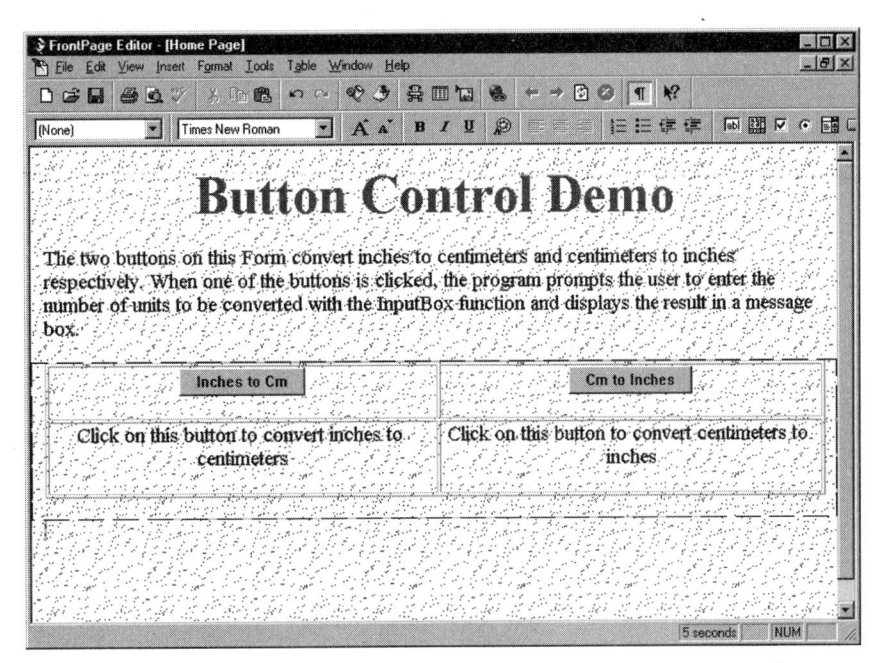

Figure 9-5: This page is actually a utility that converts inches to centimeters and vice versa.

Use FrontPage Explorer to create a new web with a single page. Edit the home page (index.htm) with the FrontPage Editor, and add a form by inserting two push button fields onto the page, using either the Insert | Form Field | Push Button command or by clicking the (Push Button) icon on the forms toolbar. (If the forms toolbar is not shown, use View | Forms Toolbar.)

The first button's caption (value/label) should be Inches to CM and the second button's caption should be CM to Inches. To change the captions, right-click on each push button and from the pop-up menu, choose Form Field Properties (you can also simply double-click on the push button in the FrontPage Editor). Use the Value/Label text box to enter the caption of the button that is displayed on the screen (see Figure 9-6). Also type a name for each button (Inches for the first, CM for the second) in the Name text box. Turn on the Normal check box. By default, FrontPage inserts a Submit button and you must manually change its type to Normal.

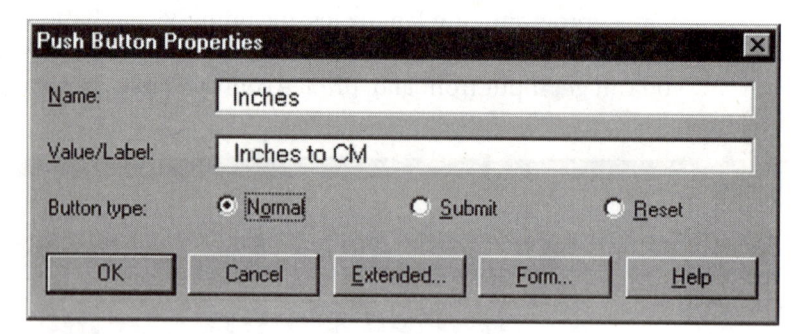

Figure 9-6: To change the settings of a push button, open this window by right-clicking on the control's name in the FrontPage Editor.

Because the Inches button is a normal button, it can be programmed to trigger certain actions. The other two types of buttons, Submit and Reset, are only used when submitting form data to a form handler, such as the FrontPage Save Results WebBot. You can't modify these default actions, but you can control the action of a normal button.

By default, FrontPage doesn't assign names to the forms it creates. In order to add a script to your page, though, the form(s) must have a name. Right-click on one of the controls, select Form Properties from the pop-up menu, and in the form's Properties window, enter the name Metric.

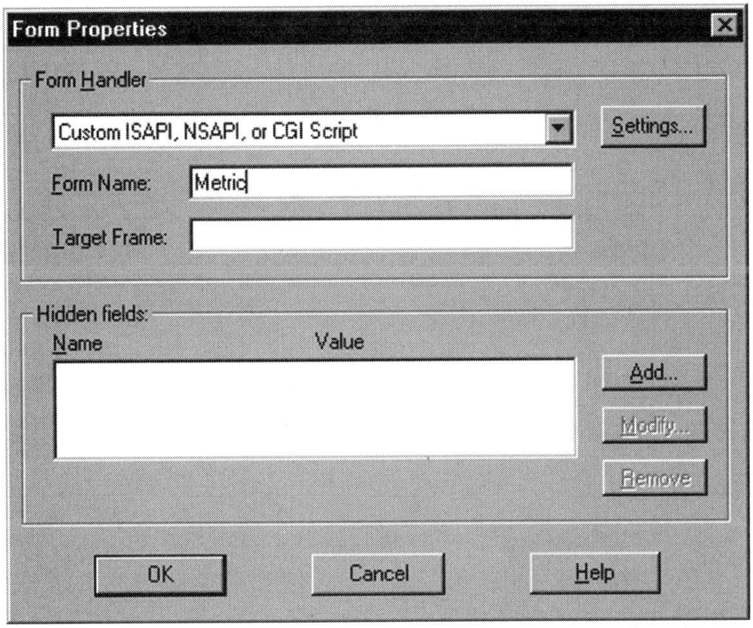

Figure 9-7: Open this Form Properties window by selecting Form Properties from any control's pop-up menu. If you plan to write a script for a form, you must give it a name.

Now you are ready to program the push buttons. Right-click on the Inches button, and from the pop-up menu, choose Script Wizard. The window shown in Figure 9-8 will appear on your screen. This is FrontPage's program editor, where you will enter the script. The Script Wizard's window has three panes:

- The Events pane (labeled Select an Event), where you select the event that will be programmed to react to user actions. Examples of events are moving the mouse, clicking a push button, typing in a text box, or completing an action.

- The Action pane (labeled Insert Actions), contains all the actions that the code can perform. An action can modify a property of a control or form field (such as changing the color of a text box). An action can also cause some process to occur, such as going to a new web page, displaying a message, or some other function specific to a particular type of control. The latter actions are called *methods*.

- The Code pane at the bottom, where the script is displayed (the Code pane is empty in the window of Figure 9-8). The Code pane can show the actions associated with events in either list form or as "raw" VBScript code.

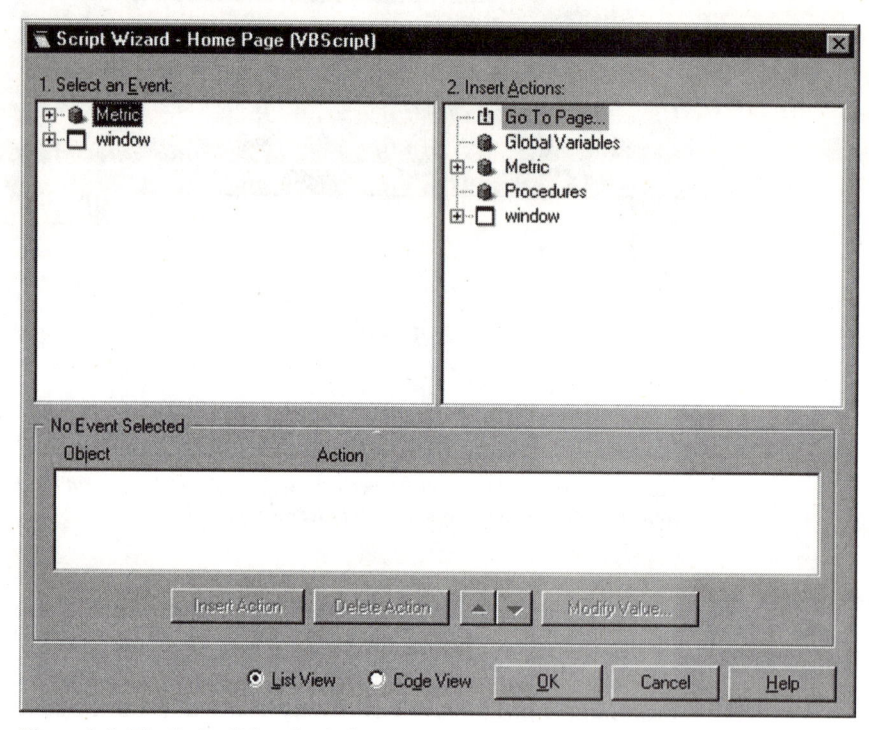

Figure 9-8: The Script Wizard window.

The two option buttons under the Code pane window determine which of the two available modes you want to work in. List View is the simple mode, where you can specify simple actions, and is seriously limited. In List View, you use point-and-click operations to specify the actions you want the script to perform, like choosing menu items a la cart at a restaurant. Hardly any typing on your part—is that too good to be true? It certainly is, as the List View of the Code window isn't the most flexible way to script a procedure. It's quite automated, but highly limited. You will see how to use the Script Wizard in List View, but most of the examples in this chapter require that you enter the script in Code View.

As you see in Figure 9-9, the Events pane contains the names of two objects, the Metric form and the Window object.

If you expand the Metric form by clicking on the plus sign in front of its name (in the window shown in Figure 9-9 the Metric form is already expanded), you will see the names of the two controls on it. Expand the names of the two push button controls by clicking on the plus sign to the left of each name and you will see the names of the events they recognize. Each push button control recognizes a single event, the onClick event, which is fired every time the user clicks on the control.

If you want your Web page to react to the onClick event, you must supply the appropriate code for this event. In other words, you must write a script that prompts the user for the number of inches to be converted, performs the conversions, and then displays the result.

Let's see how you can add VBScript commands to your page. Expand the control you want to program (the Inch or CM push buttons) and then select the name of the event to program. In other words, click on the onClick item below the Inches item. This action will activate the Code pane.

By default, the Code pane works in List mode, which is the simpler mode. Click the Code View radio button to switch to the more flexible view. In the Code View mode, you must type the commands that make up the script. This shouldn't intimidate you, however, even if you are a beginner programmer. VBScript is as simple as a programming language can get.

The definition of a subroutine will appear in the Code pane:

```
Sub Inches_Click()
```

and the Code pane will be activated.

When the Code pane is in Code View mode, enter the following lines, as shown in Figure 8-9:

```
Centimeters = InputBox("How many centimeters do you want to convert?")
MsgBox Centimeters & " cm are " & Centimeters / 2.54 & " inches"
```

The first line prompts the user to enter the amount of centimeters he or she wants to convert. The number entered by the user is stored in the variable Centimeters. A *variable* is a placeholder, a name for a value. Each time you want to access the value entered by the user, you must reference the variable Centimeters. You could have used the name cm, Number_of_Centimeters, or any other name you preferred, but once you name the variable, you have to use the same name for it throughout the script.

TIP

A variable name is valid if it starts with an alphabetic character, is less than 255 characters long, and is composed of upper- or lowercase alphabetic symbols and numbers. A variable name can also contain the underscore character, which is frequently used to separate words in a variable name. Another common convention is to use mixed case; NumberOfCentimeters, for instance. Always strive to use meaningful variable names, the better to make your code self-documenting. The only other limitation on variable names is that you can't use a reserved word as a variable—you couldn't have a line like MsgBox=10, since MsgBox is a reserved word for the Message Box function.

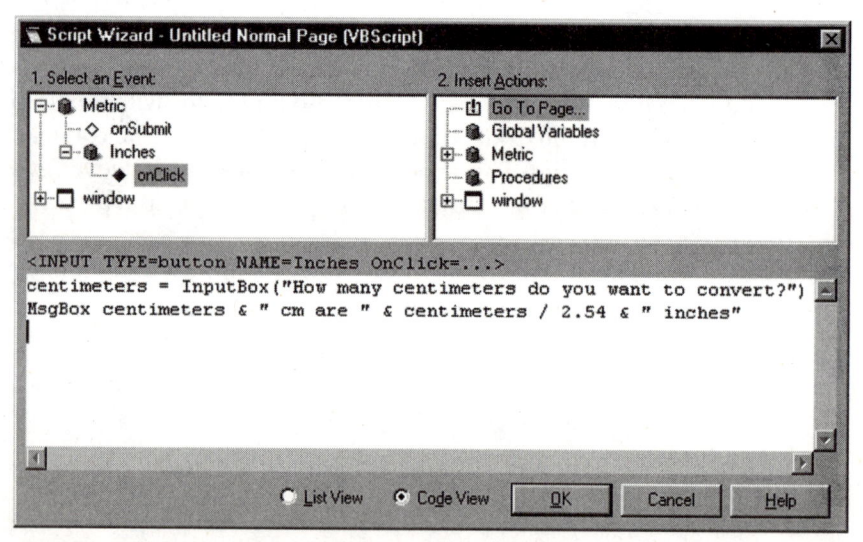

Figure 9-9: Entering the code to convert inches to centimeters.

The second line of code you entered is more complicated, so let's analyze it. The & character combines strings of text to create a longer string. Let's say the user has entered the value 10, which is stored in the variable Centimeters. The MsgBox command will display the following:

```
10 cm are 3.9370079 inches.
```

Here's what happens. The variable Centimeters is replaced by its value, 10. Then the text enclosed in quotes is displayed. Then the computer calculates an arithmetic operation: 10 / 2.54, which results in 3.9370079. The expression:

```
Centimeters / 2.54
```

will be replaced by its value, which is 3.9370079. Finally, the word "inches" is appended to the message.

> **TIP**
>
> *The rules for creating messages with VBScript are very simple:*
> *Variables are replaced by their values.*
> *Arithmetic operations are replaced by their results.*
> *Text enclosed in double quotes is displayed as is.*
> *The & operator concatenates strings of text. It puts them together, one after the other. (It will not add spaces between words joined together, so the spaces should be included in the quoted text.)*

The code behind the onClick event of the Inches push button is nearly identical. Just switch the variables Inches and Centimeters, and instead of a division, perform an addition:

```
Inches = InputBox("How many inches do you want to convert?")
MsgBox Inches & " inches are " & Inches * 2.54 & " centimeters"
```

After you have entered these two lines in the Code pane, close the Script Wizard and return to the FrontPage Editor. The page has been activated! Check it out using the Preview in Browser command from the File menu. Try clicking either of the buttons and verifying that the program runs as expected.

Building a Better User Interface

Prompting the user for input in a dialog box and displaying output in another box works OK, but it isn't the ideal method of communicating with your users—at least not in a Windows-style graphical user interface environment. There are better ways to request and convey information to the viewers of your pages. You should use elements like push buttons, text boxes, and radio buttons to build active pages that interact with the user on his or her computer, without the intervention of the server.

Let's improve our utility that converts inches to centimeters. This time you'll provide two text boxes and a push button, as shown in Figure 9-10. The user will enter the number of inches to be converted in the first text box and then click on the push button to see the result in the second text box.

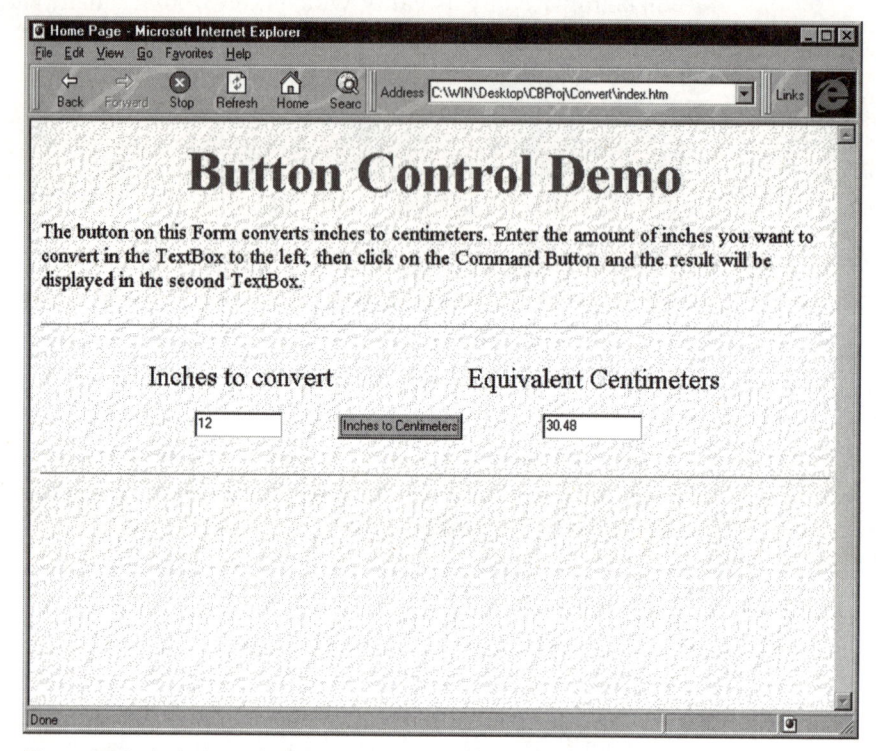

Figure 9-10: An improved version of the inches-to-centimeters conversion utility.

Metric Conversion Revisited

The project we are going to build in this example is called Convert and you will find it on this book's Companion CD-ROM in the folder \Webs\Chap09\Convert\ as index.htm.

Here's how to build the page from scratch:

1. Start a new page with FrontPage Editor and insert the three controls you see in Figure 9-10: a text box, a push button, and another text box.

All controls must be placed on the same form, as shown in Figure 9-11, which shows the Convert page open within the FrontPage Editor.

2. Change the settings for each control by double-clicking on each one. Set the width of both text boxes to 12 characters and name them T1 and T2, respectively. (These should be the default names.)

3. Change the push button to a normal button, with a name of Inches and a value/label (caption) of Inches to Centimeters.

4. Right-click within the form and choose Form Properties from the pop-up menu. Change the name of the form to Metric, since it's always good practice to name the forms you use.

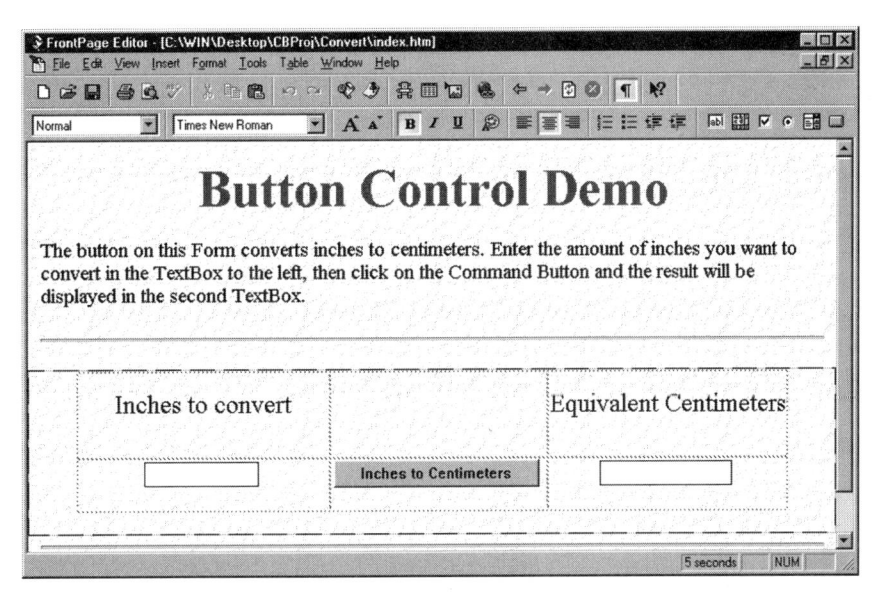

Figure 9-11: The Convert page opened in FrontPage Editor.

Designing the page is straightforward, and since you've already worked with form controls in previous chapters, we needn't belabor how to place the controls on the page. Instead, let's take a look at the page's script. All the work is done by the push button's onClick event, which reads the value in the first text box, multiplies it by 2.54, and displays the result in the second text box.

Right-click on the push button, and from the pop-up menu, choose Script Wizard. When the Script Wizard's window appears on your screen, locate the Inches push button control's onClick event, switch to Code View (if necessary) and enter the following line in the Code pane:

```
T2.Value = T1.Value * 2.54
```

The text box's Value property reads or sets the text in the text box. The expression T1.Value is the text stored in the first text box. This value is multiplied by 2.54, and the result is assigned to the T2.Value property, which causes it to be displayed in the second text box. When a property name appears to the left of the equal sign, the expression to the right of the equal sign assigns a value to it. By assigning a piece of text to the property T2.Value, this text is immediately displayed in the T2 text box. When a property name appears to the right of the equal sign, then the computer "reads out" its value. When the line:

```
T2.Value = T1.Value * 2.54
```

is executed, T1.Value is replaced with the actual contents of the T1 text box. In effect, VBScript executes the expression as:

```
T2.Value = 10 * 2.45
```

(if the value in the second text box is 10).

The code is quite simple, and you are now ready to test this page with Internet Explorer. Choose Preview in Browser from the File menu and open the Convert page in the browser. Enter a number into the Inches to Convert text box and click the Inches to Centimeter button to verify that the script works. Next, enter an invalid value to the first text box, such as ABC, and then try to convert it to centimeters by clicking on the push button. Nothing will happen. VBScript understands that this is not a numeric value and treats it like a zero.

Where Is the Script?

Now you can take a closer look at what the Script Wizard has done. Open the View menu and choose the HTML command. FrontPage will display the View or Edit HTML dialog box, as shown in Figure 9-12. In this window, locate the definition of the Inches push button. The tag for this button is:

```
<input type="button" name="Inches" value="Inches to Centimeters"
language="VBScript" onclick="T2.value = T1.Value * 2.54">
```

Chapter 9: Advanced FrontPage Techniques

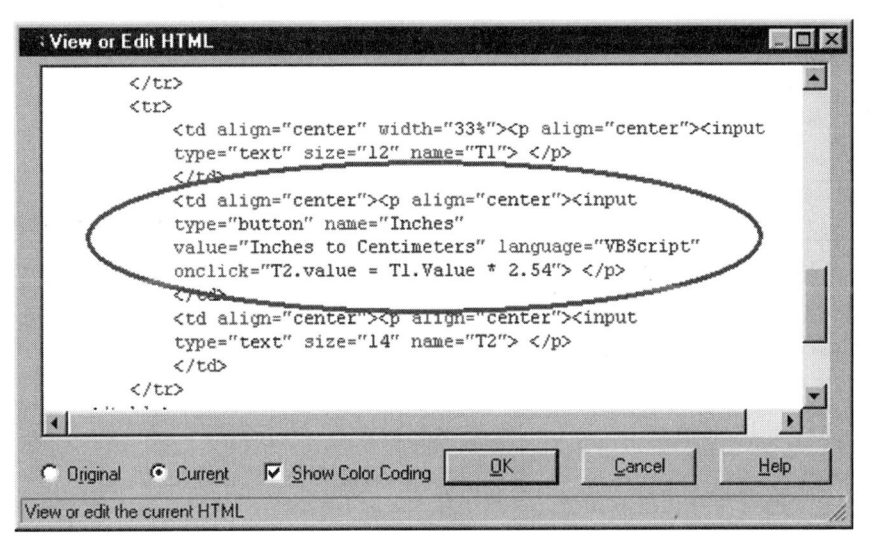

Figure 9-12: Examining the tag inserted in the HTML file by the Script Wizard.

The onClick parameter is assigned the action you entered in the Script Wizard's Code pane. The button has several parameters (properties like its type and its name). One of these parameters is the onClick parameter, which tells VBScript to execute the following command whenever the Inches push button is clicked (the onClick event is triggered):

```
T2.value = T1.Value * 2.54
```

This is how scripts are embedded in HTML code. You specify an action with VBScript commands and the event that will trigger them. The Script Wizard embeds the commands in the definition of the control.

Form Validation Techniques

One purpose of VBScript is to give web authors access to the contents of the various controls that appear on a page. For example, there's no need to submit a form to the server to verify that all text boxes have been filled by the user. The FrontPage validation rules (covered in Chapter 4) allow you to specify that certain fields are mandatory, but this isn't always the most flexible approach.

Take a look at the page shown in Figure 9-13. This form is valid if either an e-mail address or a fax number has been specified. It's not mandatory to enter both values, but at least one of the two must be filled in by the user. To check this, you must have a way to know the values of the two controls from within our script. You can then validate the form on the client's side.

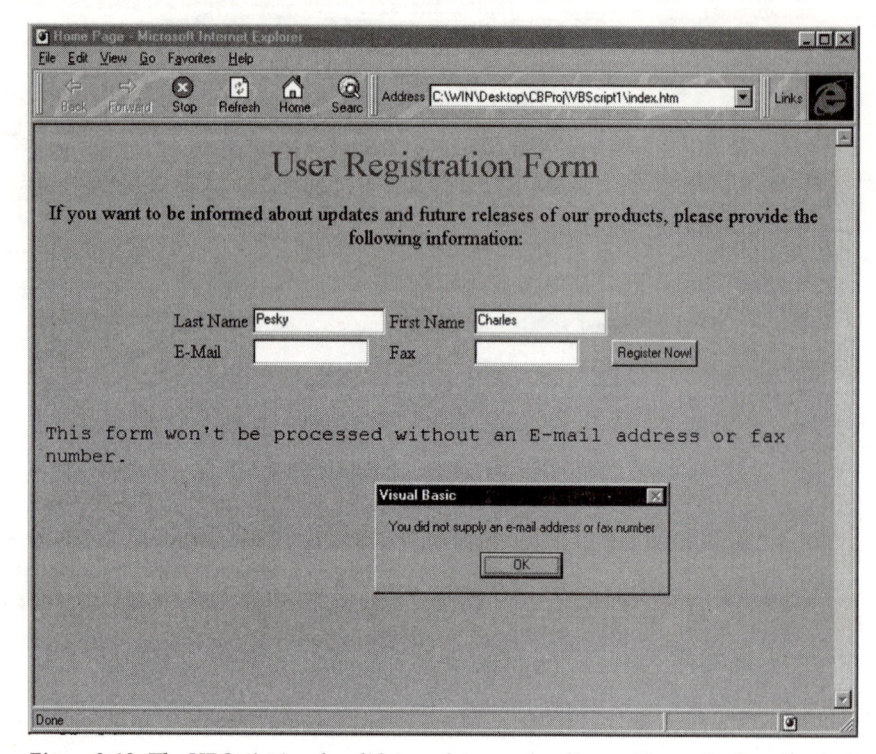

Figure 9-13: The VBScript1 web validates a form on the client with a technique that isn't possible with FrontPage's tools.

The page shown in Figure 9-13 can be found on this book's Companion CD-ROM, in the \Webs\Chap09\VBScript\ folder, as index.htm.
If you want to create this web on your own, follow these steps:

1. Start FrontPage Explorer, create a new web, and name it VBScript.

2. Open the index.htm (Home) page with the FrontPage Editor.

3. Create a form by placing four text boxes and one push button on it.

4. Insert a table (with five columns and two rows) within the form, to precisely align the controls on the page.

5. After creating the table, move the controls into the table, as shown in Figure 9-14. You can do this with Edit | Cut and Edit | Paste or by simply dragging each control with the mouse and dropping it into place on the table.

In Figure 9-14, you see the VBScript home page at design time from within the FrontPage Editor. The single button on the form is not a Submit button. If it were, it would submit the contents of the form without giving your script a chance to validate them.

Instead, after you insert the push button on the form, right-click on it and select Form Field Properties from the pop-up menu. When the Push Button Properties dialog box appears on the screen, check the Normal radio button (to make this a normal button) and change its name to DoneButton and its value/label to "Register Now!".

Right-click within the form and choose Form Properties; then set the form name to RegistrationForm. (Use one word.) Double-click on each text box control and name them (in succession): LName, FName, Fax, and EMail.

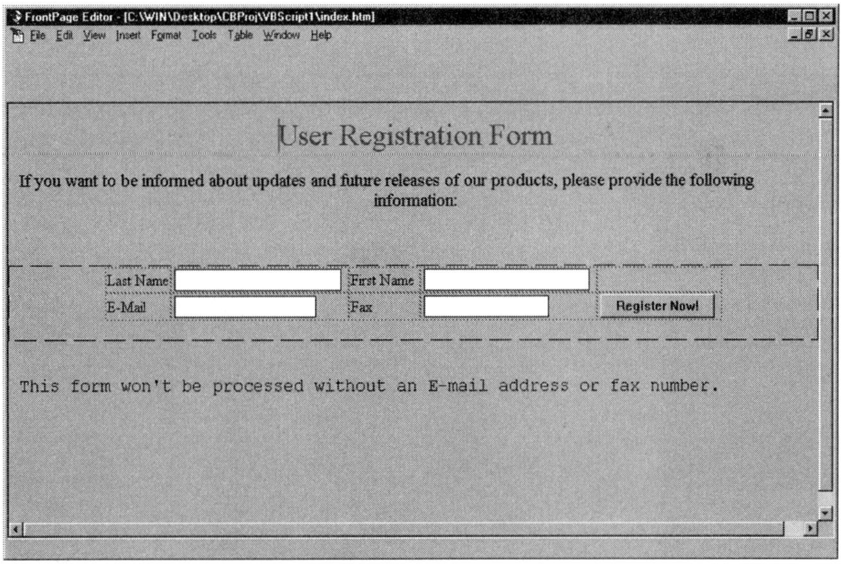

Figure 9-14: The VBScript page designed with the FrontPage Editor.

Once the controls have been placed on the page, you can open the Script Wizard to enter the validation code. Right-click on any of the controls and choose Script Wizard. The Script Wizard window for the form RegistrationForm is shown in Figure 9-15. The DoneButton push button is the only control that has a script associated with it.

Expand the DoneButton tree by clicking on the plus sign in front of its name, as shown in Figure 9-15; then select the onClick event and enter the following lines in the Code pane:

```
If EMail.Value="" and Fax.Value ="" Then
     MsgBox "You did not supply an e-mail address or fax number"
Else
     RegistrationForm.Submit()
End If
```

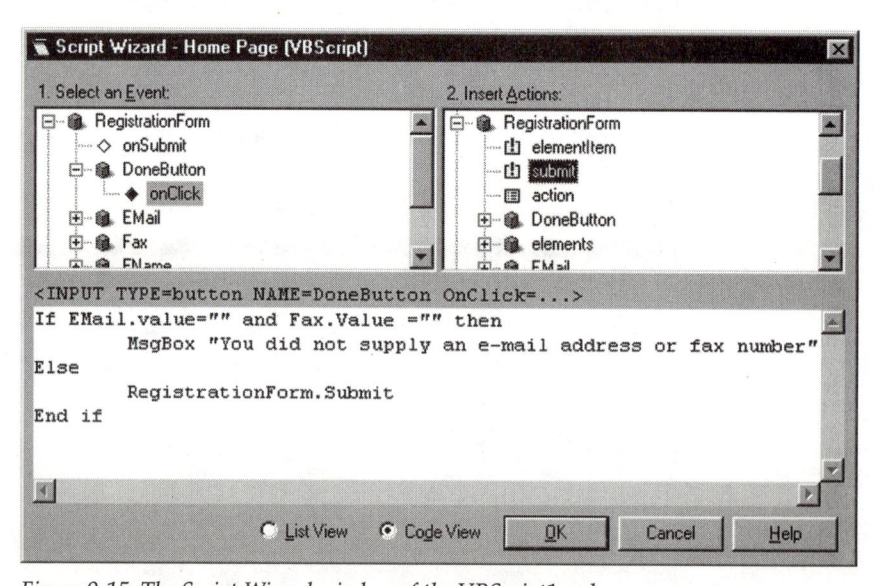

Figure 9-15: The Script Wizard window of the VBScript1 web.

This script contains a *conditional statement*. The If statement allows you to include any necessary logic in your script. By using If, you can test for a condition, and only if that condition is true, take some course of action, such as executing another statement.

The script starts by examining the values of the EMail and Fax text boxes (using the properties Email.Value and Fax.Value). If they are both equal to the empty string (""), in other words, if Email.Value is an empty string and Fax.Value is an empty string, then the MsgBox statement following the If test is executed: The MsgBox statement displays a message warning the user that the form can't be processed.

If either of the two controls has a value, the test fails and the MsgBox statement is not executed. Instead, the statement following the Else keyword is executed. This statement actually submits the form's contents to the server. Submit is the name of a *method*, which applies to the Registration form. It does exactly what the Submit push button does when it's clicked. The Submit method is an action that only the form knows how to perform; that's why it must be prefixed with the name of the form. The line:

```
RegistrationForm.Submit()
```

submits the contents of the form to the server. The benefit of using the Submit *method*, instead of relying on the Submit *button*, is that the script gets a chance to validate the form before submitting it (something that can't be done with a regular Submit button).

This form doesn't actually have a working form handler set up, but you get the idea. Whatever form handler you want to use, whether it's the FrontPage Save Results 'bot or a custom script, will be launched when the Submit method of the form is executed. To set up a form handler, right-click within the form and choose Form Properties from the pop-up menu.

Browsing For Methods

At this point, questions are probably cropping up in your mind regarding scripting and programming. You might ask, "How do I know what other methods the controls have, and how do I use them?" Each control has it own methods and properties, and you must either know them or look them up in a reference source.

One such source is the Action pane (the right pane) of the Script Wizard window, which can ease script development. So far, we have ignored the right pane of the Script Wizard. This pane contains the various actions the controls can perform (see Figure 9-16).

To see how this works, right-click on one of the buttons on the form and choose Script Wizard. When the Script Wizard appears, click on the plus sign in front of the RegistrationForm entry in the Action pane on the right, and you'll see the names of the controls on the form. Under the item RegistrationForm, you will see the item Submit, which is marked with the icon of an exclamation mark, to indicate that Submit is a method, an action that can be performed.

The Action pane is like a reminder. It contains all the controls on the form, and for each control, it can display its methods and properties.

Now select with the mouse the line:

```
RegistrationForm.Submit()
```

in your script and delete it. Then double-click on the name of the Submit method in the Action pane and the Script Wizard will reinsert this line in the code at the location of the text insertion point.

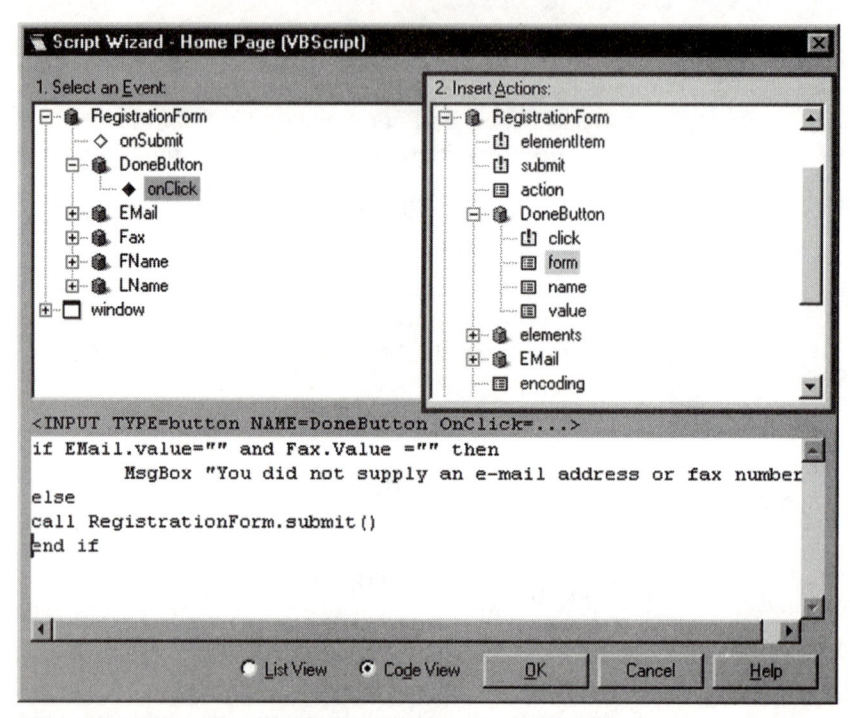

Figure 9-16: The Action pane of the Script Wizard contains the controls and their properties and methods.

Next, scroll down within the Action pane, locate the control DoneButton, and expand it by clicking on the plus sign in front of its name. You will see its properties, including the name and value properties.

To use a method or insert the property name of a control into your current script, simply double-click on the name of the desired property in the Action pane, and the Script Wizard will insert it in the Code pane for you. The Action pane is the place to go when you don't remember a property's or method's name. Expand the control whose properties you are interested in and look up its members.

Updating & Reading Form Field Controls

Our next example is a bit more complicated. It doesn't validate any user data, but it interacts with the user to update the display. Figure 9-17 shows the Order page, which lets the user specify the desired computer configuration by clicking on the various option buttons. Each time a new component is selected, the total price at the bottom of the form is updated.

The page can be found on this book's Companion CD-ROM in the folder \Webs\Chap09\Orders as order.htm, but let's see how to build this page from scratch.

Figure 9-17: This page updates the total cost of the selected configuration every time the user selects a new component.

Here's how you put together the controls on this form. Refer to Figure 9-17 as you go along:

1. Start a new page, enter the titles and the text, and then create a form by placing any form field control (a dummy control) on the page. After the form outline appears, delete the dummy control. Right-click in the form, choose Form Properties from the pop-up menu, and set the form name to OrderForm.

2. Once the form is placed on the page, create a table with eight rows and five columns and a border size of two. Once the table is on the page, select all the cells on the last row, and use Table | Merge Cells to combine them.

3. Type the labels (CPU, Memory, Hard Disk, etc.) in the first column. Also type the text for the radio button that you will place in the other cells. Use a larger typeface than the default to make the table more readable. You can also select all the text after you've typed it and click the (Increase Text Size) to change its size.

4. In the last row, type **The Current configuration costs**, select the text with the mouse, and click the Increase Text Size button twice.

5. Insert a text box just after the text you typed in the last row. Double-click on it to pop up the Form Properties dialog box, name the control as text_config, and set its value/label to 2100. Set the width to 12 characters.

6. Place the radio button controls on the table's cells, as shown in Figure 9-18, which shows the Order page at design time. To do this, position the text insertion point just prior to each label and click the (Radio Button) icon on the Forms toolbar. Leave the seventh row empty.

7. The radio buttons on each row must belong to the same group name so that clicking on one of them will reset the others. Here are the settings you should use for each row (you may also wish to refer to Table 9-1):

   - Double-click on the first radio button on the CPU row. Change its group name to CPU and its value to CPU_DX4. Repeat for the other radio buttons on that row, setting the group name for each radio button in that row to CPU and the values to CPU_P100, CPU_P166, and CPU_P200, respectively.

   - Double-click on the first radio button on the second row and set the group name to RAM and the value to RAM_8. Set the other radio buttons to the same group name (RAM) and use RAM_16, RAM_32, and RAM_64 for the values.

   - For the third row, use a group name of HDD and values of

HDD_850, HDD_1200, HDD_1600, and HDD_2000.

- For the fourth row, use CRT as the group name, and values of CRT_14, CRT_15, CRT_17, and CRT_21.

- Use a group name of MODEM for the fifth row and use MODEM_14, MODEM_28, MODEM_33, and MODEM_ISDN for the values of the buttons on that row.

- Finish up the radio button settings with the sixth row by using a group name of CD and values of CD_2X, CD_4X, CD_8X, and CD_12X.

TIP

When naming form fields (controls), you must use names that are legal in the scripting language you use. In VBScript, you can't use the hyphen character in variable names (this would be misinterpreted as a mathematical expression involving subtraction), so I used the underline character for clarity.

Restrict yourself to upper- and lowercase alphabetic characters and numbers, along with the underscore, when naming controls to which you wish to attach scripting. (You should try to reference your variables using the same case, consistently. Although the variables EatDonuts and eatdonuts are interchangeable in Visual Basic and VBScript, this is not true in other programming languages and inconsistency is bad programming practice.)

Designing the form should be a straightforward task. If you have made any mistakes, you can always double-click on a control to see the control's Properties dialog box, where you can change the control's group name and value/label.

If you like, you can select rows of the table and use Cell Properties to assign custom colors (I used yellow, lime, and aqua) as implied (but not shown, given that the figures in this book are in black and white) by Figure 9-17. Type the heading at the top of the page: **Computer Deals Online**. You'll also want to select the table (try Table | Select Table) and click the Center button on the formatting toolbar to center the table on the page.

Web Publishing With FrontPage 97

> **TIP**
>
> *If you didn't leave a blank line at the top of the page before creating your form, you'll find it impossible to insert text above the form. This problem is all too common with the FrontPage Editor. You can't even use the Ctrl+Enter trick I mentioned in earlier chapters, which inserts a blank line above or below the current item.*
>
> *Instead, type the heading below the form. Select the form by positioning the mouse pointer at the upper left corner of the form and double-clicking. Now drag the highlighted form to the line beneath the heading.*

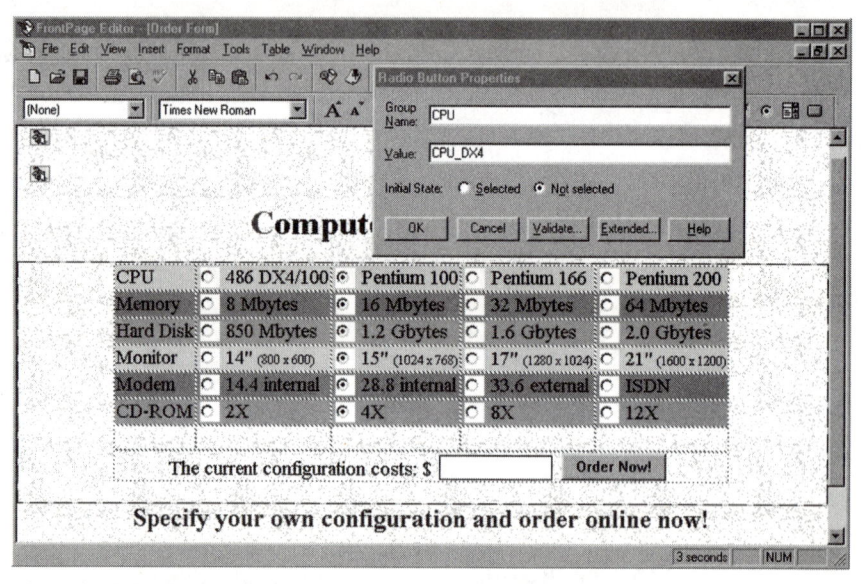

Figure 9-18: Designing the Order page with the FrontPage Editor.

While editing the form field properties for each radio button, you must also set the initial state of each control to Not Selected (see Figure 9-18), except for the ones that should be initially selected (the default configuration). For our example, set the Initial State options to Selected for the radio buttons that correspond to a Pentium/100 machine with 16MB RAM, 1.2GB hard disk, and a 15-inch monitor.

Although you won't provide a form handler for this form (it's just an example, after all), to make the form look complete, add a button to the right of the price on the last row of the table. Double-click upon the button and set its name to Order_Button, its value/label (caption) to Order Now!, and set the button type to Normal. This button could be linked to a script that submits the form, presenting a summary for the buyer before purchase.

Use File | Preview in Browser to check out the operation of this page. You should be able to change the configuration of the computer by clicking on the various radio buttons, but the total won't be updated until you add some VBScript.

Notice, however, that much of the functionality you need for the application is already there. Every time you click one of the radio buttons, the other ones on the same row are cleared automatically.

Check the operation of the form at this point to make sure that you have grouped the radio buttons correctly and no two radio buttons can be checked on the same row. Also make sure that choosing one radio button in one row won't clear a radio button in another row.

Activating the Page

Now you are ready to activate the page by adding the VBScript code that will make it react to user actions. You will want the page to react to mouse clicks on the various radio buttons by calculating a new total for the selected configuration and displaying it in the text box at the bottom of the form. Let's start by discussing our approach.

The cost of the configuration is the cost of the CPU plus the cost of the memory, hard disk, monitor, modem, and CD-ROM drive. Let's use a variable to store each component's cost. The cost of the CPU will be stored in the variable CPUCost, the cost of the memory in the variable RAMCost, the cost of the hard disk in the variable HDDCost, the cost of the monitor in the variable CRTCost, the cost of the modem in the variable ModemCost, and the cost of the CD-ROM drive in the CDROMCost. To calculate the total cost, the script must add together these variables and display the result in the text box control.

How about updating the cost each time the user clicks on a radio button? You'll exploit the Click event of each radio button control to update the cost of a component, depending on which radio button was clicked.

> **What's a Global Variable?**
> Normally, the variable names you make up are only valid for the procedure or event in which they are used. That way, you don't have to worry about using the same variable name in two different places, which can cause confusing errors when one procedure changes the value of a variable that is used in another procedure. By making variables local by default, this problem is avoided. Even if you use the same variable names in two different procedures, and even if one procedure calls another one, each variable will maintain its own local, independent value.
>
> On the other hand, this means that a variable used in one part of your program may be invisible to other parts of the program. Sometimes you want to use a variable that is valid and visible to all procedures. This is why you would declare a global variable. Since all the event procedures for the radio buttons need to communicate the monetary value of their respective component (CPU, CRT, RAM) to a common procedure that makes a calculation, global variables are used.
>
> An alternative to using global variables is to pass the *values* of the variables from one procedure (function) to another. For simplicity, we'll stick with the global variable technique for now.
>
> By declaring the global variables, these variable names are reserved so that they can't be inadvertently used as local variables in a procedure.

Variable Declaration

Right-click on one of the radio buttons, and from the pop-up menu choose Script Wizard. To see all the controls on the form, click the plus symbol to the left of OrderForm in the Events pane to expand it, as shown in Figure 9-19.

Next, you will define the variables that will hold the values of each component.

In the Action pane, there's an entry called Global Variables. Right-click on it and from the pop-up menu choose New Global Variable. You are going to define a new variable, which will be a *global* one. A global variable is one that is accessible from every event. In other words, the entire script has access to it. There's another type of variable, the *local* variable, which is local to the event that needs it and can't be accessed from the rest of the script.

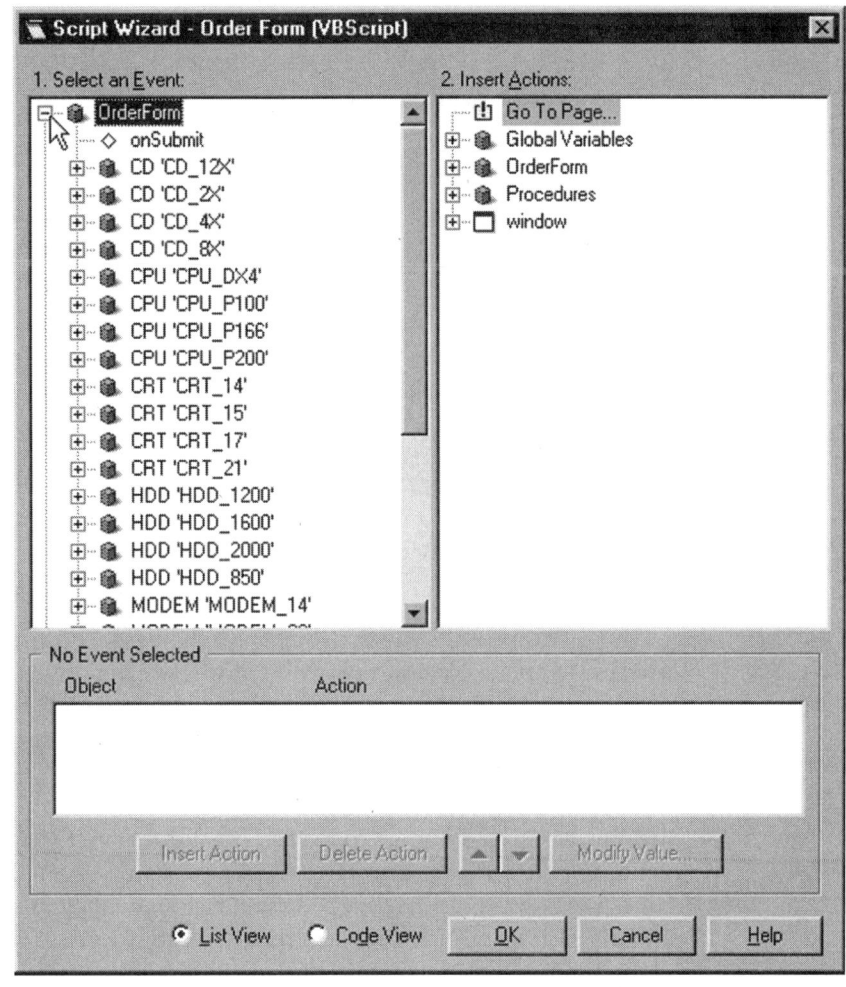

Figure 9-19: Click the symbol next to OrderForm in the Event pane to see all the events using the Script Wizard.

As soon as you click on the New Global Variable item, you'll see the New Global Variable dialog box, as shown in Figure 9-20.

Enter the name of the variable (CPUCost) and click OK to close the New Global Variable window. Repeat the same process to add these global variables: RAMCost, HDDCost, CRTCost, ModemCost, and CDCost. You have defined the script's variables; now you can proceed with the code that manipulates them.

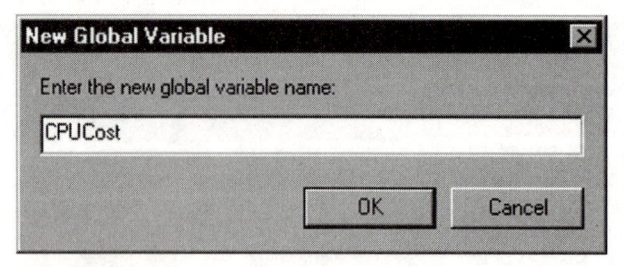

Figure 9-20: Use the New Global Variable window to enter the name of a global variable you wish to declare.

Calculating the Total

You must also define a procedure to calculate and display the total. Both steps can be taken care of with a single line of code:

```
OrderForm.text_config.Value=CPUCost+RAMCost+HDDCost+CRTCost+ModemCost+CDCost
```

This long line adds the variables with the partial costs and assigns the result to the text box control's Value property. Even if you have not programmed in the past, you can certainly understand what it does and even write similar statements of your own. This line must be executed every time the user clicks on a radio button.

Instead of typing this long line of code repeatedly for each radio button, you can create a new "command" that does exactly that. This user-defined "command" is formally called a procedure. A *procedure* is a collection of lines of VBScript code that is assigned a name. Then, instead of typing each line of code wherever you need it, you can just type the name of the procedure. In effect, you will design a new VBScript function.

Let's see how this is done.

1. In the Action pane, locate the Procedures entry and right-click on it. From the pop-up menu that will appear, choose New Procedure and the definition:

   ```
   Sub Procedure1()
   ```

   will appear in the Code pane (make sure you have Code View enabled).

2. Select the name of the procedure with the mouse and type **ShowTotal()** over the selection. What you have now is the header of the ShowTotal() subroutine.

Now you will enter the code for the ShowTotal subroutine.

3. Place the text insertion point on the line below the procedure's header, and then locate the text box control (text_config) in the Action pane (the one on the right).

4. Expand the item OrderForm (by clicking its plus symbol), then the control text_config, and you will see the properties of the text box control.

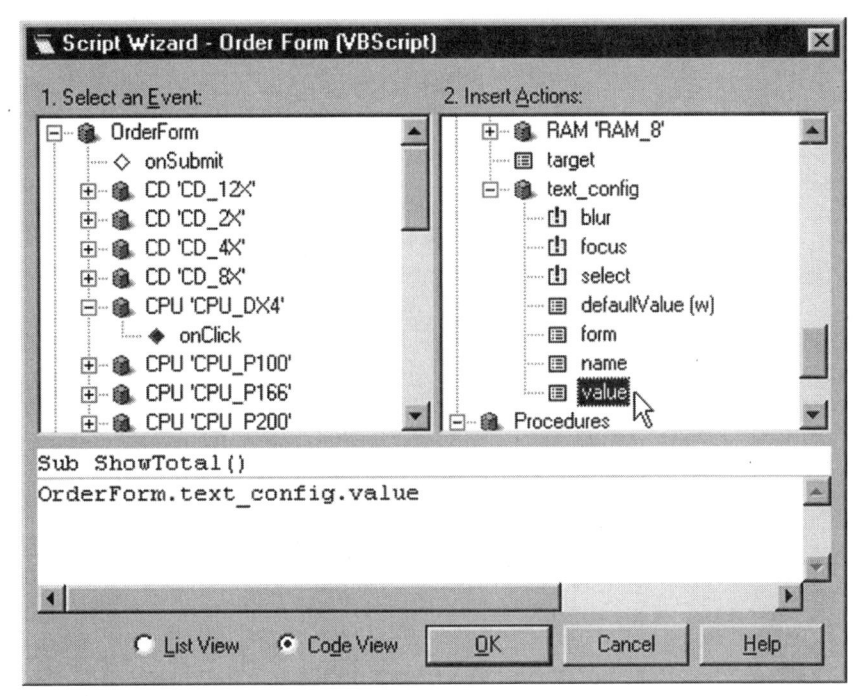

Figure 9-21. Double-click on a property name in the Action window and its complete name will appear in the Code pane.

5. Double-click on the Value property.

    The complete name of the property will appear in the Code pane (see Figure 9-21). It's the Value property of the text_config control, which belongs to the form OrderForm, which in turn belongs to the current document.

6. Now place the pointer after the property's full name and type the following:

```
= CPUCost+RAMCost+HDDCost+CRTCost+
ModemCost+CDROMCost
```

This is the value you want to assign to the text box (text_config), or more specifically, to the Value property of the text box. From now on, every time you want to calculate and display the total, you can type the name of the subroutine ShowTotal() instead of the long statement.

Responding to User Input

Now you are ready to program the radio buttons to react to the click events.

Return to the leftmost pane, the Events pane, and expand the tree OrderForm by clicking on the plus sign in front of its name. This is the form that contains all the radio button controls, and those controls appear when you expand the tree. Each control has a plus sign in front of its name, too. If you expand a control's name by clicking on the plus sign, you will see the events recognized by the control.

Let's expand the control named CPU 'CPU_DX4'. (The control name of a radio button is the group name followed by the value of that radio button selection.)

After clicking the plus symbol next to CPU 'CPU_DX4', you will see the onClick event, which is the only event radio buttons recognize. Now click on the event's name to open the Code pane for this event. The Code pane will be empty, and you must supply the code to be executed every time the user checks this radio button. You want to perform two actions from within this event:

- Set the CPUCost variable to the cost of a DX4/100 CPU.
- Recalculate and display the new total.

To implement the first action, you must assign the cost of a DX4/100 CPU to the variable CPUCost.

Follow these steps:

1. With the onClick event of CPU 'CPU_DX4' selected in the Event pane, switch to List View for the Code pane at the bottom of the window.

2. In the Action pane (the rightmost half of the window), expand the Global Variables tree by clicking on the plus sign.

3. In the Action pane, double-click on the name of the variable CPUCost.

4. In the dialog box that pops up, enter the value 350, which represents the cost of a DX4/100 CPU (for the sake of this example, $350.00). This is a numeric value, so don't prefix it with the dollar sign. The action:

    ```
    Change CPUCost to 350
    ```

    will appear in the code window. This action makes the CPUCost variable equal to 350. (If you were using Code View, you'd have to manually insert the line CPUCost=350.)

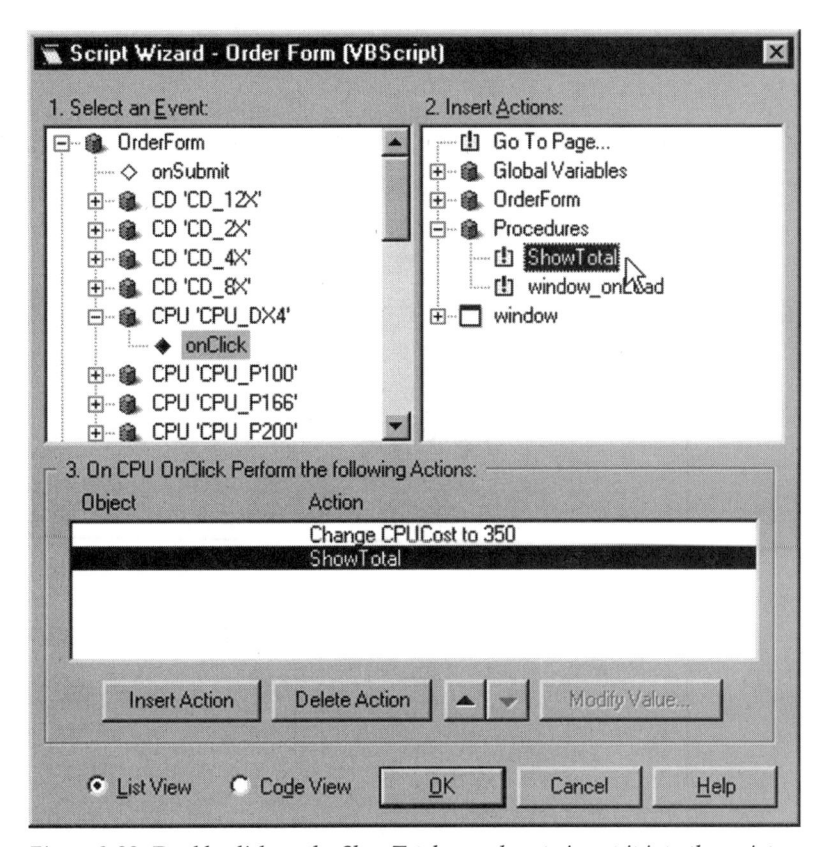

Figure 9-22: Double-click on the ShowTotal procedure to insert it into the script.

5. Expand the Procedures tree and double-click on the name of the procedure ShowTotal. This causes the action ShowTotal to appear in the Code window after the previous action.

The Script Wizard's window will look like the one shown in Figure 9-22. So far, you have programmed the page to react to a single external event: the click of the mouse on the first radio button, which corresponds to the DX4/100 CPU.

Repeat the same process for all the option buttons on the first row of the table. The only thing you must change is the value of the various CPUs; do this by assigning them to the CPUCost variable. In the example web, we used the fictional values shown in Table 9-1.

Group Name	Description	Control Name	Value ($US)
CPU	DX4/100	CPU_DX4	350
	Pentium/100	CPU_P100	450
	Pentium/166	CPU_P166	750
	Pentium/200	CPU_P200	900
RAM	8MB	RAM_8	50
	16MB	RAM_16	100
	32MB	RAM_32	200
	64MB	RAM_64	350
HDD	850MB	HDD_850	100
	1.2GB	HDD_1200	150
	1.6GB	HDD_1600	200
	2.0GB	HDD_2000	250
CRT	14-inch	CRT_14	250
	15-inch	CRT_15	350
	17-inch	CRT_17	500
	21-inch	CRT_21	1500
MODEM	14.4 int.	MODEM_14	20
	28.8 int.	MODEM_28	50
	33.6 ext.	MODEM_33	75
	ISDN	MODEM_ISDN	250
CD	2X	CD_2X	25
	4X	CD_4X	50
	8X	CD_8X	90
	12X	CD_12X	250

Table 9-1: These are the properties for the radio button controls on the form.

Now you're ready to supply the code for the memory components. As with the CPU, each time the user clicks on one of the radio buttons for Memory, you must update the cost of the variable RAMCost, calculate the new total cost, and display it in the TextBox control with the total.

Adding script code for the other radio buttons is quite similar to the process I've described already, and we need not repeat the steps again.

For each radio button, double-click on the appropriate global variable, set its value (from Table 9-1), and then double-click on the ShowTotal() procedure to complete each radio button's script.

TIP

You may wish to switch to Code View after inserting the actions for one of the radio buttons. That way, you can copy and paste the two script lines into the other onClick events for related buttons and change just the value of the variable.

After completing each radio button's onClick event, go back and double-check your work. When you close the script wizard, you return to the FrontPage Editor. Toward the top of the page open in the FrontPage Editor, you'll notice that the script you created earlier is now represented on the screen as a small yellow box. Be careful not to delete this box or all the scripting events will be removed.

Now you can open the Order page with Internet Explorer and check it out.

While testing the page, you may notice a small problem with the way the total is calculated on this form. First of all, there is no price shown for the default configuration (Pentium 100, 8MB RAM, 1.2GB hard disk, 28.8 modem, 15-inch monitor).

Also, the total cost should change every time the user clicks on a radio button to select a different component. However, the first time the page is viewed, there are no values for the variables CPUCost, RAMCost, HDDCost, CRTCost, or CDCost. Attempting to choose a radio button to change the configuration will give a misleading total until all five options have been chosen.

To fix this, you need to set the initial values of these variables (initialize them) before the page is presented to the user and call the ShowTotal() procedure to set the initial cost of the default configuration.

To accomplish this task, you'll add another script to the page to initialize the text_config text box and the values of the global variables.

To add the extra code to initialize the page, choose Script from the Insert menu. The raw script editor will appear. Type the text shown in Figure 9-23 into the script editor, and then click OK. (You could have also created the script with the Script Wizard by locating the window object in the Event pane, inserting actions to define the global variables, and finishing up by inserting an action to call the ShowTotal procedure.)

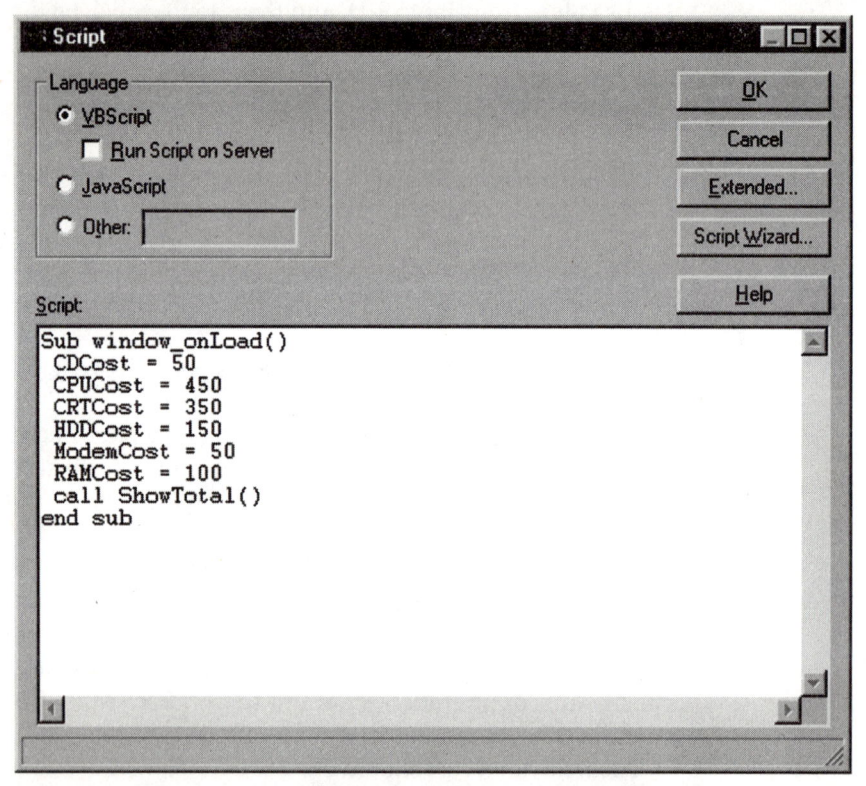

```
Sub window_onLoad()
  CDCost = 50
  CPUCost = 450
  CRTCost = 350
  HDDCost = 150
  ModemCost = 50
  RAMCost = 100
  call ShowTotal()
end sub
```

Figure 9-23: This script initializes the global variables and the Total text box.

One more script will help to solve another minor problem. Since the total is displayed in a text box, it's possible for the user to accidentally (or mischievously) change the total before the form is submitted.

To prevent this, use the Scripting Wizard to insert the ShowTotal() procedure in the onChange event of the text_config text box (see Figure 9-24). Although this doesn't prevent editing of the total, the total will be reset to the value computed by ShowTotal() as soon as the user leaves the text box control.

Here's how this works: the onChange event will be triggered if the user makes any change to the text, then moves to another field or clicks another button. Technically, when a user is using or otherwise interacting with a control on a form, that control is said to have the *focus*. When another control gets the focus, by clicking on it, tabbing to it, and so forth, the original control loses the focus and can then fire off an onChange event if there was any change made to the contents of the control. So making a change to the text and moving off the control triggers the onChange event.

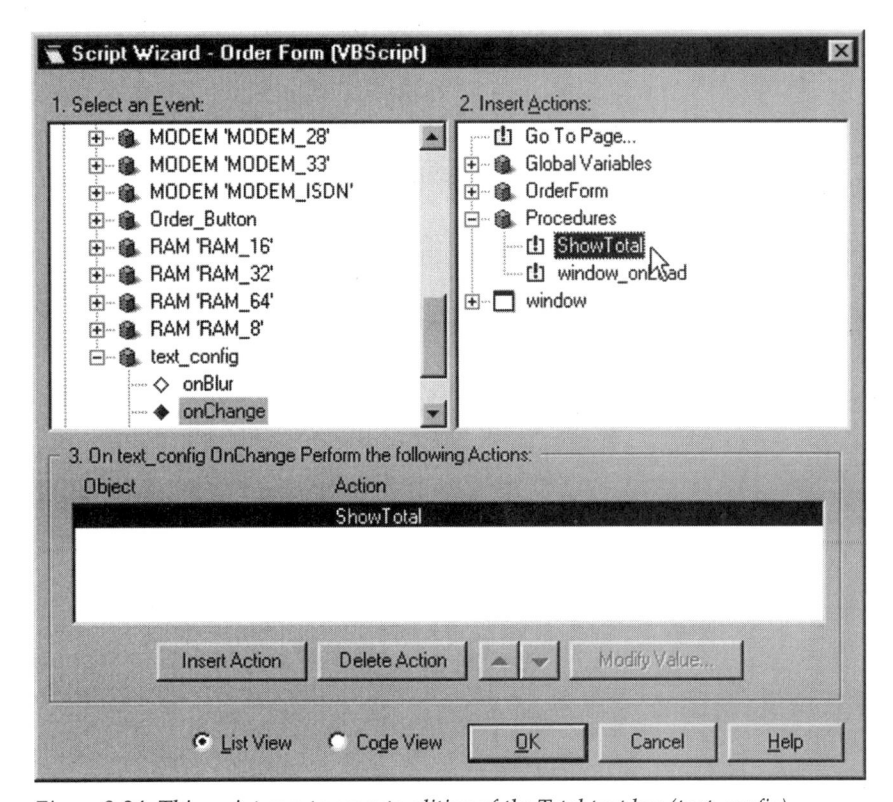

Figure 9-24: This script event prevents editing of the Total text box (text_config).

The Order Form page behaves like a small program embedded in the browser's window. It's an active page that reacts to user actions and updates the total in real-time. A page like this could be used as the starting point for an online computer store.

Floating Frames

One of the hottest features of Internet Explorer 3.0 or later, which isn't directly supported by FrontPage 97, is the floating frame. (The floating frame technique should also be supported in the Communicator version 4.0 release of Netscape Navigator.)

In Chapter 7, you learned how to build documents with frames, but the entire page needs to be built with frames to use standard framesets. *Floating frames* are similar to regular frames in the sense that they can contain any HTML page and operate independently of each other, but they can be placed anywhere on a web page. A floating frame is like an image, only instead of a bitmap, it contains an entire HTML document.

To insert a floating frame on your page, use the IFRAME tag with the following syntax:

```
<IFRAME WIDTH=500 HEIGHT=400 SRC="http://www.microsoft.com">
</IFRAME>
```

This floating frame has dimensions of 500 X 400 and displays Microsoft's home page. (You can assign any of your pages to the SRC property to display it in the floating frame.) To insert this frame on the page, select the HTML markup command of the Insert menu, and in the dialog box that will appear on your screen, type the previous tag. Figure 9-25 shows an empty page with an IFRAME tag like the previous one. Notice the scroll bars, which allow the user to view any part of a page that doesn't fit within the floating frame's area. The two scroll bars are attached automatically if they are required.

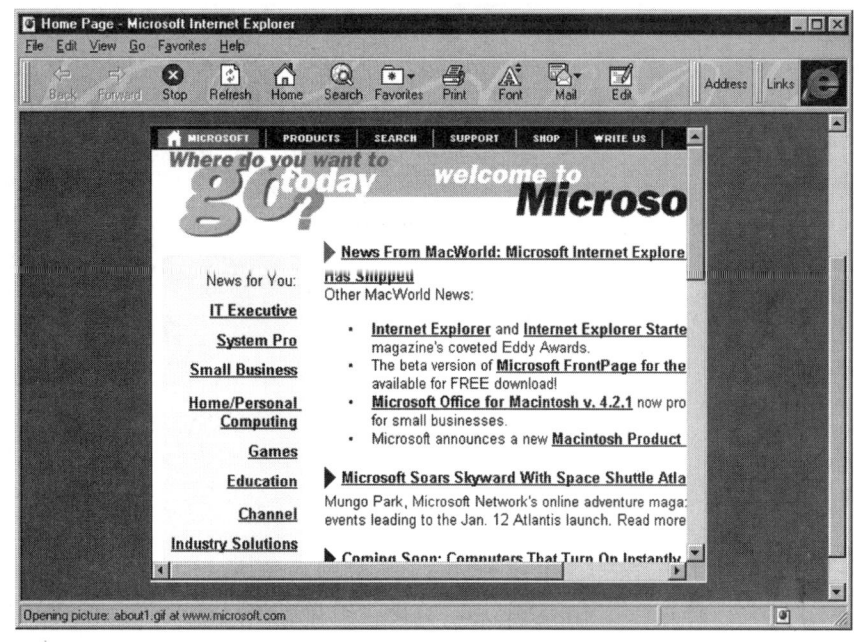

Figure 9-25: The Microsoft site is displayed on a floating frame.

Floating frames are quite interesting design elements, but there's more to them—you can control their contents from within your scripts, which is another great way to create active pages. The page shown in Figure 9-26 can be found in the \Webs\Chap09\Fframes folder on this book's Companion CD-ROM, as index.htm. It contains a floating frame and three push buttons. Each push button causes another URL to be displayed in the floating frame. The three buttons were placed on a page (using a form name of Form1) and named MS, Netscape, and Ventana, respectively. (These buttons are set as normal buttons, so they don't submit the form.) Below the form, there is a floating frame, which you can place on the page as follows.

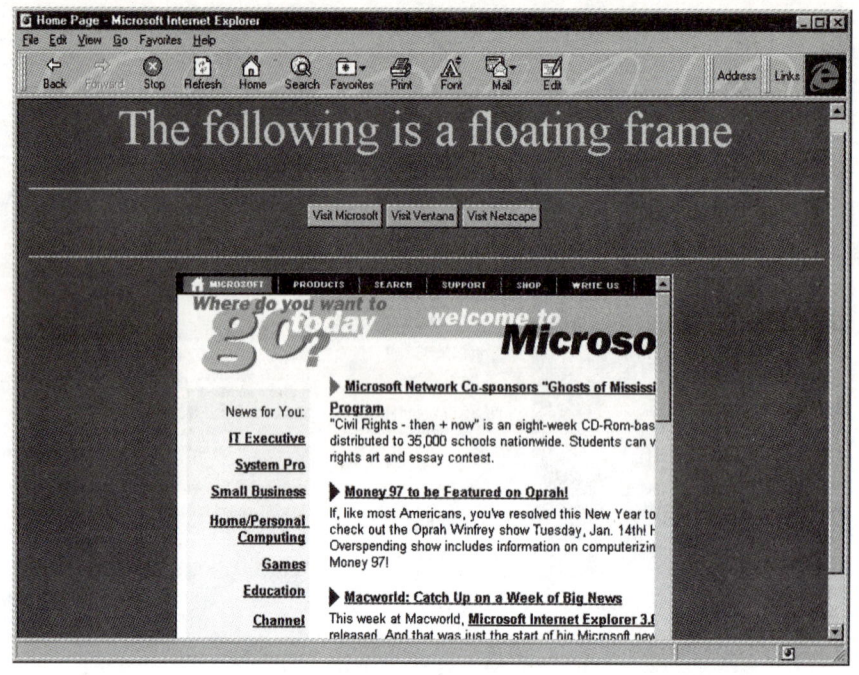

Figure 9-26: The FFrames web can display various URLs in a floating frame.

Open the Insert menu and select HTML Markup. In the HTML Markup window, type the following:

`<IFRAME WIDTH=500 HEIGHT=400 SRC="http://www.microsoft.com">`

Finally, close the HTML Markup window by clicking the OK button.

Figure 9-27 shows this page in Design mode from within the FrontPage Editor. In Design mode, this page looks odd. You have specified that the frame is 500 X 400, yet it's displayed as an icon. FrontPage ignores the HTML tags you place in an HTML Markup 'bot, so it can't display the corresponding elements. It just saves them in the HTML file it produces and lets the browser handle them.

The three push buttons on the form are normal buttons and must be programmed to change the contents of the floating frame. Open the Script Wizard window for this form by right-clicking on one of the buttons and choosing Script Wizard from the pop-up menu. Expand the entry Form1 in the left pane and expand all the controls on this form, as shown in Figure 9-28.

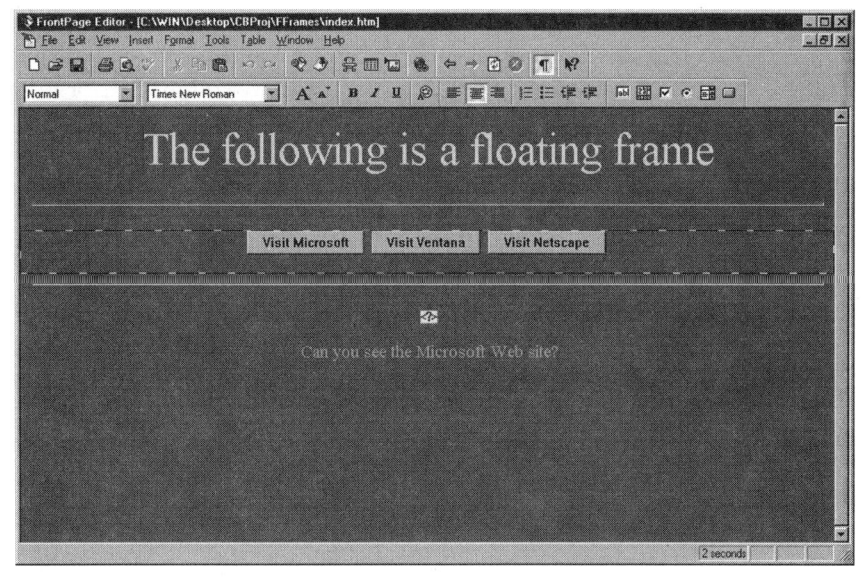

Figure 9-27: The FFrames web (from Figure 9-26) in Design mode.

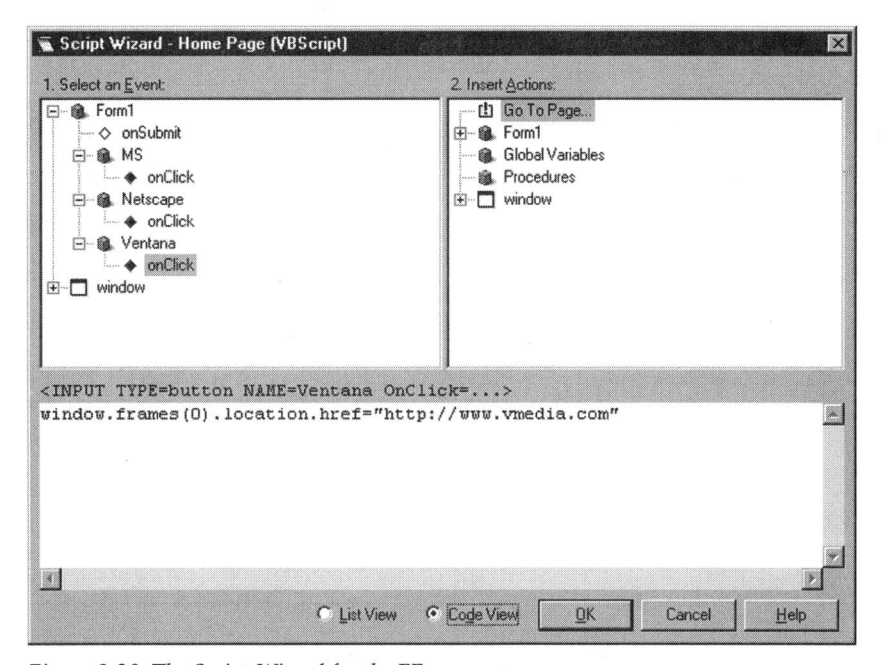

Figure 9-28: The Script Wizard for the FFrames page.

Your task is to program each button's onClick event so that it will display the corresponding URL in the floating frame. The frame belongs to the window, and each window may contain one or more frames.

Each frame is identified by an index, which starts at zero. The first frame is window.frames(0), the second one is window.frames(1), and so on. Moreover, each frame has a property called location.href, which is the URL of the site displayed in the frame. The property for the URL of the page displayed in the floating frame of the FFrames page is:

```
window.frames(0).location.href
```

To cause another URL to be displayed in the floating frame, all you have to do is assign the new URL to this property.

Select the onClick event of the button MS and switch to Code View by checking the Code View check box at the bottom of the Script Wizard window. Then type the following in the code pane:

```
window.frames(0).location.href="http://www.microsoft.com"
```

Every time the Microsoft button is clicked, the floating frame will download the page at http://www.microsoft.com and display it.

If you find this script confusing, the following is all you need to understand in order to make it work in your projects: The number in parentheses indicates the number of the frame. If the page contains a single floating frame, it is frame number 0. If the page contains two floating frames, they are numbered 0 and 1. The other item you must change in this lengthy statement is the URL of the desired page. Just supply the URL of the site you want to display on the corresponding floating frame.

You can program the onClick events of the other two command buttons with a similar line. The code behind the Netscape button's onClick event is:

```
window.frames(0).location.href="http://www.netscape.com"
```

and the code behind the Ventana button is:

```
window.frames(0).location.href="http://www.vmedia.com"
```

The active page's design is complete. You can now open the FFrames project with Internet Explorer and try it out.

Floating Images

Floating frames need not contain web pages (HTML documents). Any content that the browser can recognize (images, for instance) can be placed in floating frames. Figure 9-29 shows the FImages page, which contains three images, each one in its own floating frame. The benefit of placing images into floating frames is that you can restrict the viewing area, yet allow the viewer to bring any portion of the image into view with the help of the scroll bars.

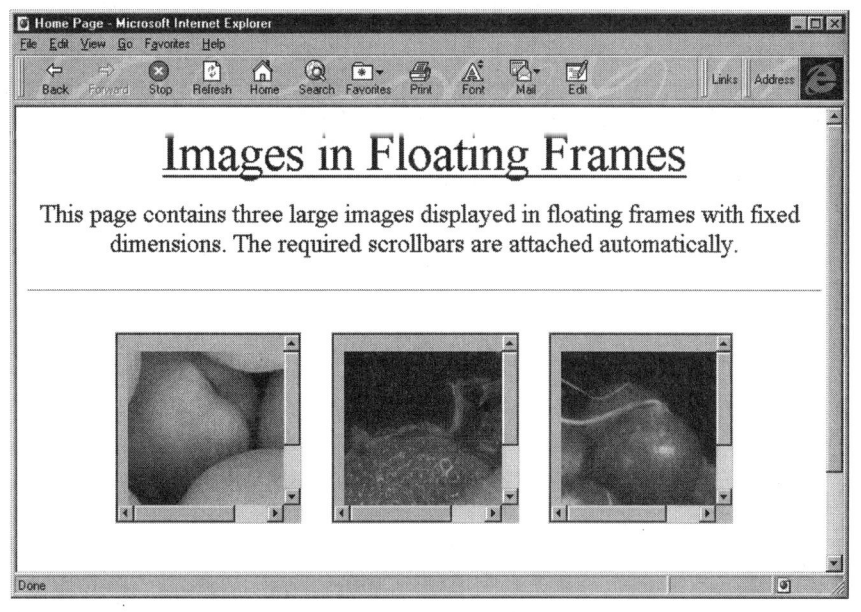

Figure 9-29: The FImages web demonstrates how to display images in floating frames.

Open the page index.htm from the folder \Webs\Chap09\Fimages on this book's Companion CD-ROM. The home page for this web contains two paragraphs of text and a table with three columns. In each one of the three cells of the table, there is an IFRAME tag.

If you want to reproduce this page, follow these steps:

1. Place the pointer in the first table cell to select it.
2. Choose HTML Markup from the Insert menu.
3. In the HTML Markup window, type the following:

```
<IFRAME width=180 height=180 src="image1.jpg"></IFRAME>
```

Repeat this process for the other two cells. Just change the name of the file to Image2.jpg and Image3.jpg, respectively. Then preview the page with Internet Explorer and check it out. You can place really large images in the floating frames, saving a lot of space on your page.

The Story of ActiveX

The controls you have been manipulating so far with VBScript are the so-called *intrinsic* controls. They are standard on most browsers, and they were supported even before VBScript was introduced. The standard controls are actually HTML elements.

With the introduction of VBScript, though, there was a need for more flexible and more functional controls than the built-in intrinsic controls. Microsoft, and soon other companies, designed new controls to be used exclusively on web pages. These are called *ActiveX Controls*, and their purpose is to help web authors make their pages far more interactive than is possible with the intrinsic controls. (There are also ActiveX Controls that duplicate the intrinsic controls, providing additional methods and events.)

ActiveX Controls didn't just pop onto existence overnight. The ActiveX Control began life as the Visual Basic Extension, or VBX, a kind of plug-in for the Visual Basic language. The VBX modules were a very convenient and powerful way to add new features to a program, such as sophisticated 3-D input controls, image viewers, spreadsheet grids, and so forth, without having to manually write any of this custom programming. Why reinvent the wheel, so to speak, when expert programmers can supply you with a Ferrari?

As Visual Basic moved into the 32-bit environment of Windows NT and Windows 95, the designers saw an opportunity to use the Object Linking and Embedding (OLE) features of the Windows operating system. After all, the plug-ins might as well be treated as live objects. This breathed new life into an already powerful method. The new OLE Custom Controls, now called OCX controls instead of VBX, had another advantage. They could be embeded like any other OLE object (a document, spreadsheet, graphic) inside other documents, and activated with scripting.

This meant that the same OLE controls designed originally for Visual Basic could also be exploited with Microsoft Access or Microsoft Excel, thanks to the built-in Visual Basic for Applications language, a much more powerful version of Visual Basic than the diminuitive VBScript.

With the rush to the Internet and the demand for more powerful web creation techniques, the OLE custom control was a natural. It could be embedded on a web page, and with a little bit of scripting thrown in, would be fully functional. The embedded control, a complete program module, could run on any computer, anywhere on the Internet.

In a stroke of marketing genius, the cumbersome term OCX or OLE Custom Control, was renamed by Microsoft as the ActiveX Control. No new technology was needed, just a sexier name.

The market for Visual Basic programming lead to the widespread availability of custom controls, but that is nothing compared to the outrageous growth of the Internet and related technologies. As soon as the specification for ActiveX was released, dozens of companies began furiously to develop ActiveX Controls for the web. Many of these were initially "ports" (translations) of existing Netscape plug-ins, or spiffed up Visual Basic custom controls.

You can now choose from hundreds of quality ActiveX Controls that add interactivity, flair, and functionality to your web pages. Furthermore, anyone with a copy of new Visual Basic 5.0 (or the freeware VB5 Custom Control Creation Edition), can design ActiveX Controls. That means that anyone who knows Visual Basic, C++, or other programming languages can now package their custom software as ActiveX Controls. The possibilities are about to explode.

Inserting ActiveX Controls

In this section, we are going to look at two ActiveX Controls that can add two different types of functionality to your pages. The first one is the *Marquee*, a control that functions like the HTML marquee, but where the standard marquee can scroll only simple text, the Marquee control can scroll images, even an entire Web page. It's an impressive control that can add a unique touch to your page.

The second ActiveX Control we'll explore is a peculiar one. The *Timer control* is like an alarm clock that notifies your program to carry out some action every so many seconds. Whereas most events are generated by the user clicking on something, the Timer control automatically generates events using a count-down timer. You can take advantage of this to update your pages at regular intervals, animate images, display a real-time clock, and so on. Where the Marquee control deals with the appearance of your page, the Timer control deals with its function.

Where to Find ActiveX Controls

FrontPage doesn't come with ActiveX Controls. You must download and install them on your computer before you can use them. It is very likely that you already have several ActiveX Controls already installed.

If at any time you have visited sites that deploy ActiveX Controls (most of the sites that require Internet Explorer 3.0 deploy ActiveX Controls), you are bound to have a few of them on your system, especially the common ones like the Marquee control and the Timer control.

One of the cool features of the ActiveX Controls is that they are downloaded only once. When you run into a page that uses an ActiveX Control that doesn't exist on your system, Internet Explorer 3.0 downloads it and installs it on the system. If you visit another page that deploys the same control, Internet Explorer doesn't download it again. It's already in the system and Internet Explorer knows where to find and use it. Unless, of course, there's a newer version of the same control, in which case Internet Explorer downloads the newer version and replaces the existing ActiveX Control.

To download the controls for the examples of this chapter, as well as a number of other interesting ActiveX Controls, visit the site http://www.microsoft.com/activex/gallery, which is shown in Figure 9-30. This is a major repository of ActiveX Controls. To download the Marquee control, select its name in the left frame, as shown in Figure 9-30, and click on the Download and Run a Working Sample of This Control hyperlink in the right frame.

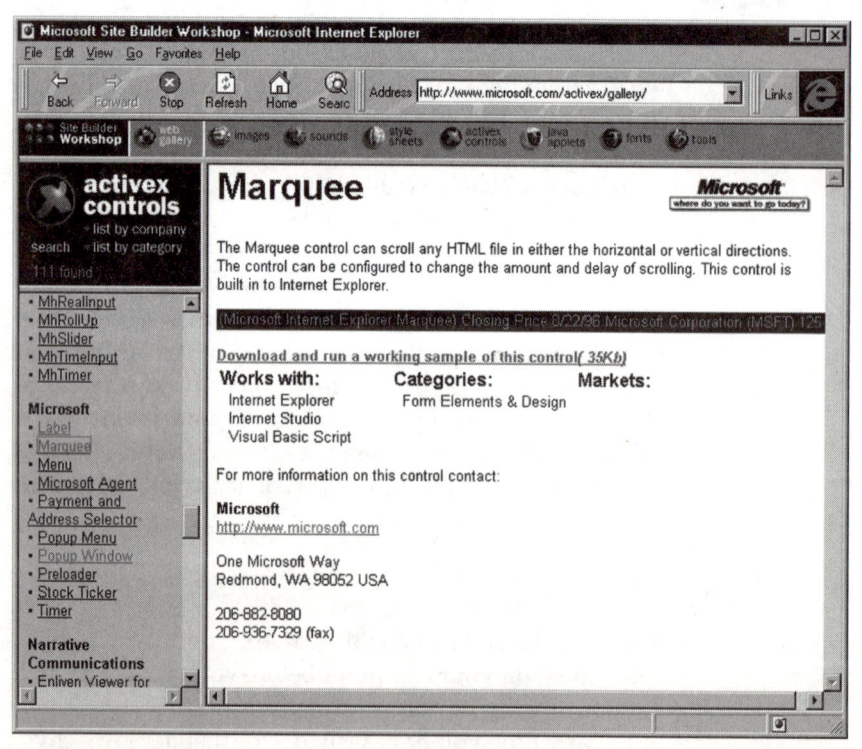

Figure 9-30: The http://www.microsoft.com/activex/gallery site is a major repository of ActiveX Controls.

The control will be downloaded automatically and you can switch to FrontPage and use it. Download the Marquee control and the Timer control, which you are going to need for the examples of the following sections.

> **TIP**
>
> *Another great place to look for ActiveX Controls is http://www.activex.com. Additional resources are listed in Appendix B.*

Using the ActiveX Marquee Control

The Marquee control lets you scroll another page within a rectangular area on your web page. The other page could be an HTML file you created with FrontPage or the URL of someone else's site. The scrolling can take place in any of four directions and you also control the scroll rate.

To see how this works, you can open the home page (index.htm) found on this book's Companion CD-ROM in the \Webs\Chap09\Axcontro folder. The home page contains two ActiveX Marquee controls (Figure 9-31). Both controls scroll the same document. The first one scrolls it horizontally and the second one vertically. While you obviously can't see the movement on the printed figure, you can open the AXControl page with Internet Explorer and check out the control's operation.

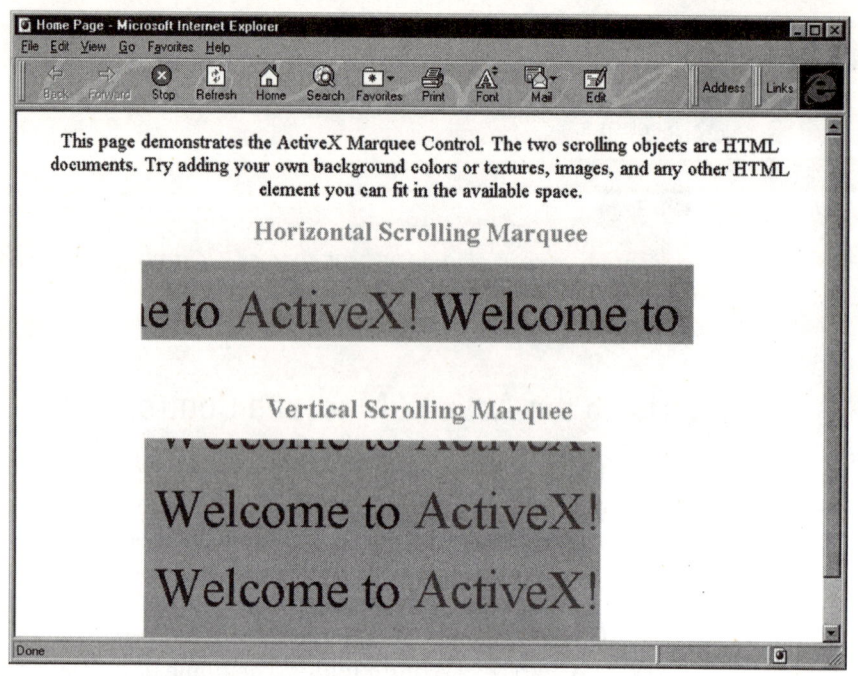

Figure 9-31: The AXControl page contains two Marquee controls that display another HTML document and scroll it.

Let's follow the steps of building this page:

1. Create a new web and open the home page with the FrontPage Editor.

2. Enter the text that appears at the top of the page (see Figure 9-31) and type the heading **Horizontal Scrolling Marquee**.

3. Open the Insert menu, choose Other Components from the submenu, and choose ActiveX Control.

    Now you'll see the ActiveX Control Properties dialog box, shown in Figure 9-32.

4. Click the arrow next to the Pick a Control drop-down list box, and choose the MarqueeCtl object.

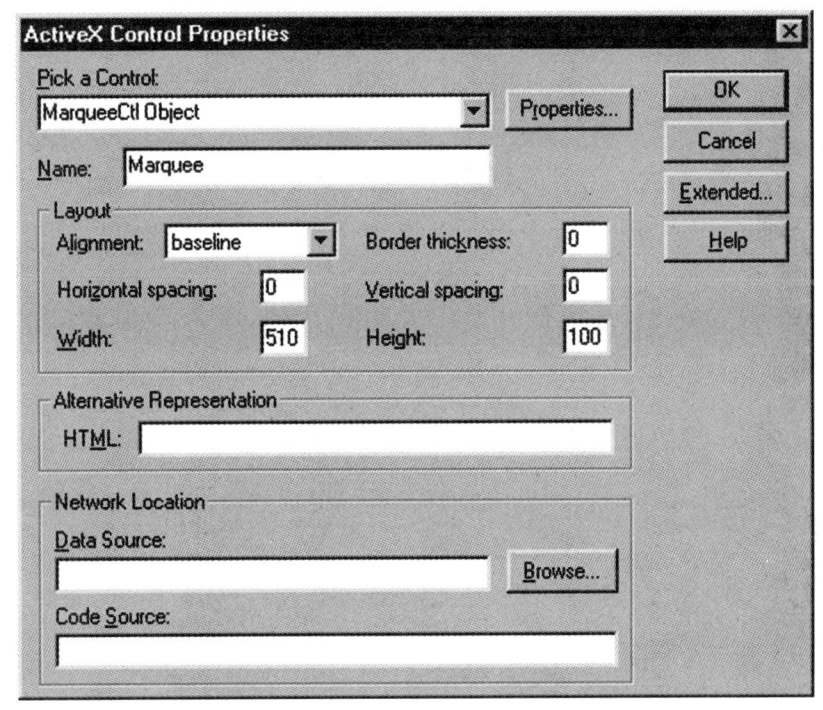

Figure 9-32: Choose MarqueeCtl from the ActiveX Control Properties window.

5. Enter a name for this control in the Name box. Name the control Marquee. Click OK to place the control on the page.

An icon appears on the page representing the Marquee control. Click the control to select it, drag the handles around the control with the mouse, and resize the control so that it will fit the page to be displayed within it. Unfortunately, you can't see the control's contents as you design it, and you have to guess its size. Previewing the page (File | Preview in Browser) will help you get the size right.

In the case of the Marquee control, you are going to set the values of the properties (parameters) that determine how the contents of the control will be scrolled. These parameters are ScrollPixelsX and ScrollPixelsY.

To set the ScrollPixelsX value to 0 and the ScrollPixelsY value to 2, follow these steps:

1. To add these properties, right-click on the control and choose ActiveX Control Properties from the pop-up menu. This opens the ActiveX Control Properties dialog box, which you already visited when you inserted the control.

2. Click the Properties button. This reveals the Object Parameters dialog box, which lets you set the properties for the control (Figure 9-33). To add a property, you add an attribute and a value.

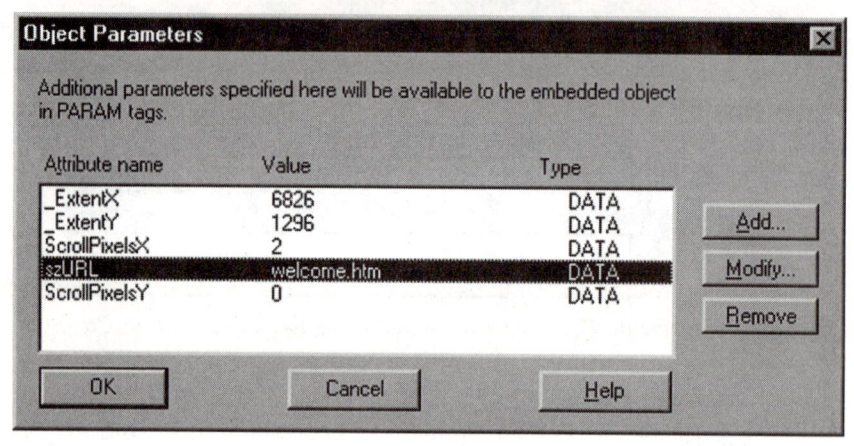

Figure 9-33: Edit the properties of an ActiveX Control by adding or modifying attributes.

3. Click the Add button, which brings up the Edit Object Parameter dialog box. Type **ScrollPixelsX** into the Name box, and type the value **0** into the Data box, as shown in Figure 9-34.

4. Click Add again. Enter the Name **ScrollPixelsY** with a Data value of **2**.

   The ActiveX Marquee control's most important property is called szURL, and it's the URL of the document to be displayed in the control.

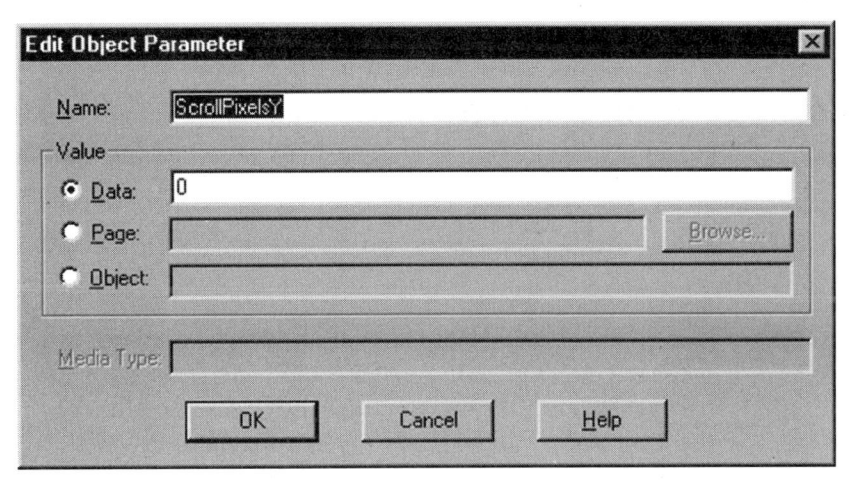

Figure 9-34: When you add a parameter, you can set its name and value.

TIP

To display an image or another object in the marquee, just "point" the URL to it, as in http://yoursite.com/images/joyride.gif. Or use a relative URL to a graphic stored on the same site, such as images/happynow.jpg.

5. Click Add, and create an attribute named szURL, with a data value of welcome.htm.

The first Marquee control on the AXControl page scrolls the welcome.htm page horizontally (along the X direction), by 2 pixels at a time, within the Marquee control on the index.htm page. Because ScrollPixelsX is set to 0 (zero), the marquee doesn't scroll vertically at all.

How often does the control scroll its contents? This is set by another property, the ScrollDelay property. Its default value is 100 milliseconds (10 times per second), and you aren't going to change this value. (This attribute can be added to the properties for the control if you want to change the rate of scrolling.)

Two more parameters of interest are the ScrollStyleX and ScrollStyleY parameters. Their values can be:

- **Circular**: The contents of the control scroll in a circular fashion. When they reach one end of the control, they come in from the other end.
- **Bounce**: The contents of the control bounce back and forth between the two ends.

As you can see, it is possible to scroll the control differently in the two directions. To use the circular scroll, you don't need to specify any values (leave the value of these two parameters as they are), because the default style for the Marquee control is the circular scroll.

Close the Edit Object Parameter dialog box by clicking the OK button. When you return to the ActiveX Control Properties window, click the OK button to place the control on the page. The Marquee control you defined will appear on your page as a gray box.

Add the heading **Vertical Scrolling Marquee** and insert another ActiveX Marquee named Marquee2. This time set ScrollPixelsX to 0 and ScrollPixelsY to -2 (see Figure 9-35) so that this marquee will scroll vertically. (Using a negative value for ScrollPixelsY causes the page within the control to scroll upward.)

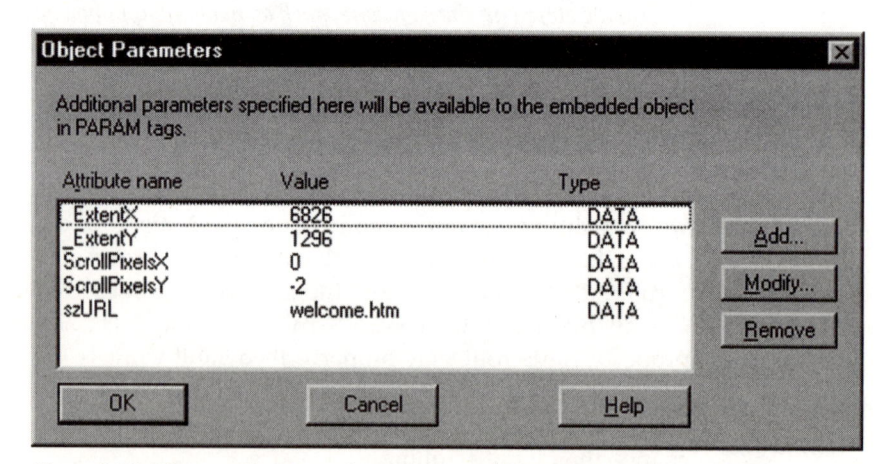

Figure 9-35: These are the properties of the second Marquee control.

Your page is done and you can use File | Preview in Browser (or just click the Preview button on the toolbar, to view your page.

Exploiting the Timer Control

Assuming that you installed the Timer control while visiting the ActiveX Gallery (http://www.microsoft.com/activex/gallery), you're ready to build a new project, called Year2000. The Year2000 application displays the number of years, months, days, hours, minutes, and seconds remaining until the turn of the century.

Open the Year2000 page (from \Webs\Chap09\Year2000 on this book's Companion CD-ROM) with Internet Explorer to see how it works. Every second, the various controls on the form are updated. The text box that displays the seconds is updated every second, the text box that displays the minutes is updated every minute (or every time the text box with the seconds is zeroed), and so on (see Figure 9-36).

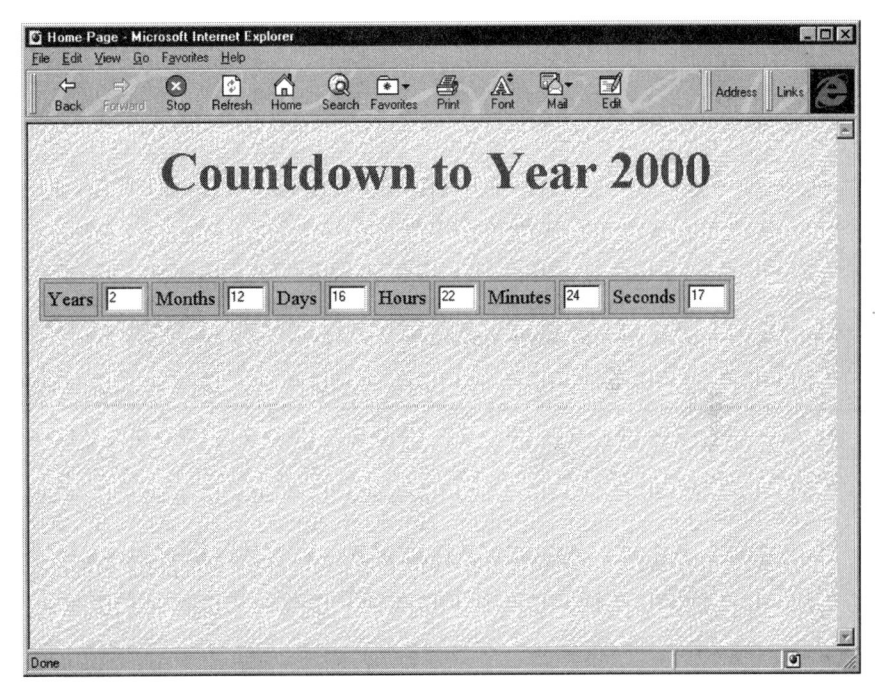

Figure 9-36: The Year2000 page displays the time left until the turn of the century and is updated every second.

As you may have guessed, the Timer control triggers a special event every second, which you use to update the page. The Timer control isn't even visible on the page. It's a special control that remains hidden, but it ticks away and notifies the script every second (or any other interval you specify) that it needs to do something. In the case of the Year2000 web, the script updates the text boxes.

In the previous examples, you have worked with the onClick event, which is triggered whenever the user clicks on a push button or other control. This is an external event, which can be caused by the viewer of the page. The Timer's event is different. It's caused by the Timer control itself and is signaled to your application via the Timer event.

To perform an action every time a push button was clicked, you had to enter the appropriate code in the onClick event of the push button by opening this event's procedure from within the Script Wizard. To perform an action every time the Timer control triggers its Timer event, you must supply the appropriate code in the Timer event. Apart from the fact that the two events are generated differently, there are no more differences.

Let's build the Year2000 web:

1. Use FrontPage Explorer to create a new Normal web, and name it **Year2000**.

2. Open the home page with the FrontPage Editor.

3. Type the title **Count Down To Year 2000** and set it to the Heading1 paragraph style.

4. Create a form by inserting a dummy control, and then delete the control. Name the form CountDown (using Form Properties).

5. Insert a table with 1 row and 12 columns.

6. Type the titles and insert the text boxes as shown in Figure 9-37. Each text box should be 4 characters wide.

Once all the elements are on the page, insert the Timer control. It doesn't make any difference where the control will be placed, as it will remain invisible when the rest of the page is viewed. In the web you'll find on the Companion CD-ROM (\Webs\Chap09\Year2000\index.htm), the timer is placed between the title and the table (the little gray square in Figure 9-37, which shows the Year2000 page during its design).

Chapter 9: Advanced FrontPage Techniques

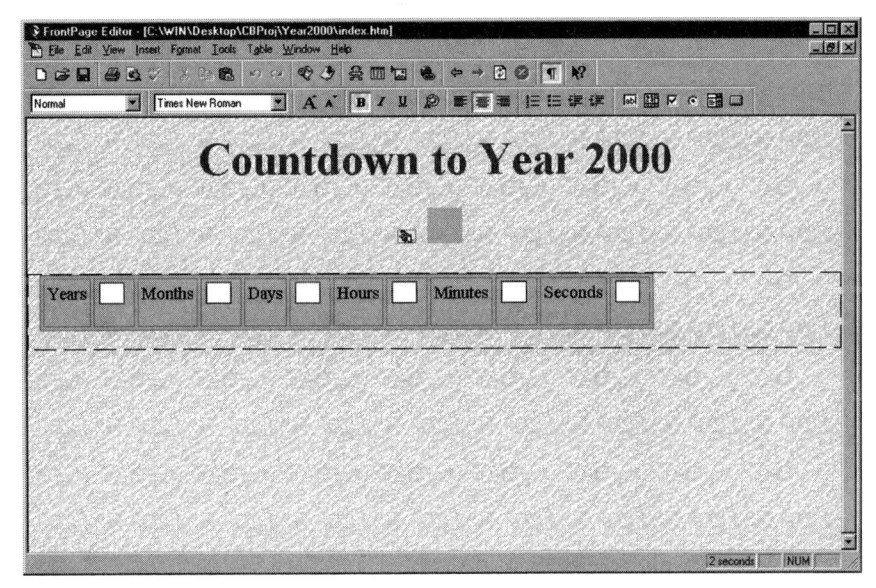

Figure 9-37: The Year2000 Web at design time.

To place a Timer control on the page:

1. Open the Insert menu and choose Other Component. From the submenu, choose ActiveX Control.

2. When the ActiveX Control Properties dialog box appears on the screen, pick the Timer Object control from the Pick a Control list.

3. Name the control SecondTimer and then click on the Properties button.

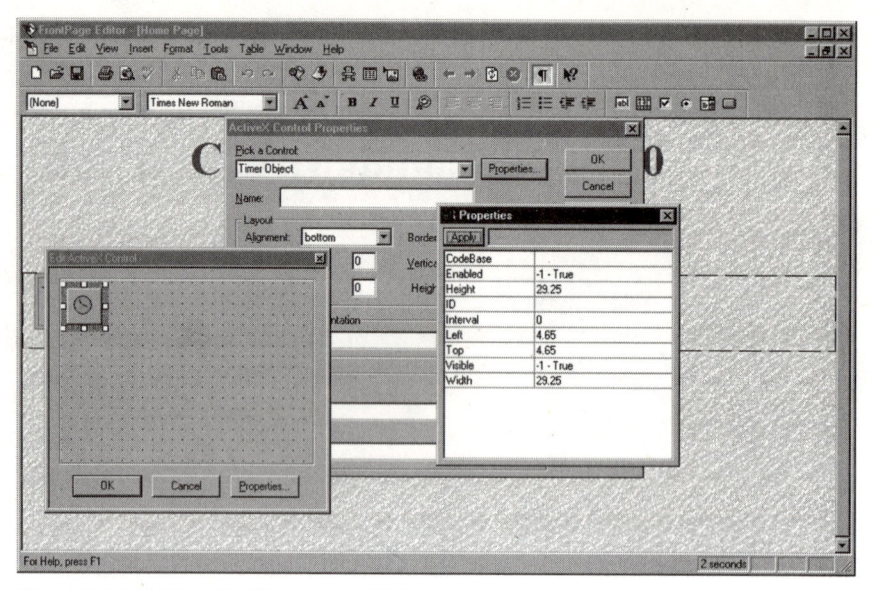

Figure 9-38: Editing the Timer ActiveX Control.

4. When you click the Properties button for the SecondTimer control, you get a very different properties dialog box, as shown in Figure 9-38. The Edit ActiveX Control dialog box shows the icon for the Timer object, a clock symbol. The second window, Properties, contains a list of properties for the control. To edit a property, click on it in the list, and enter the new value at the top of the list; then click Apply.

The Timer control has very few properties. The only property you need to be concerned with is called Interval and it determines how often the control's Timer event will be triggered. The Interval property is expressed in milliseconds and you must set it to 1000 to make an event occur every second.

5. Click the Interval property, and type **1000** into the box at the top of the property sheet.

6. Click Apply. Use the OK button to close each open dialog box. (You'll need to click the X symbol to close the Properties dialog box, since it doesn't have an OK button.)

Now you are ready to add the script that will display the time on the various controls on the Year2000 page. Right-click on one of the controls and select Script Wizard. Expand the SecondTimer control in the left pane and select the control's Timer event, as shown in Figure 9-39. Then check the Code View radio button.

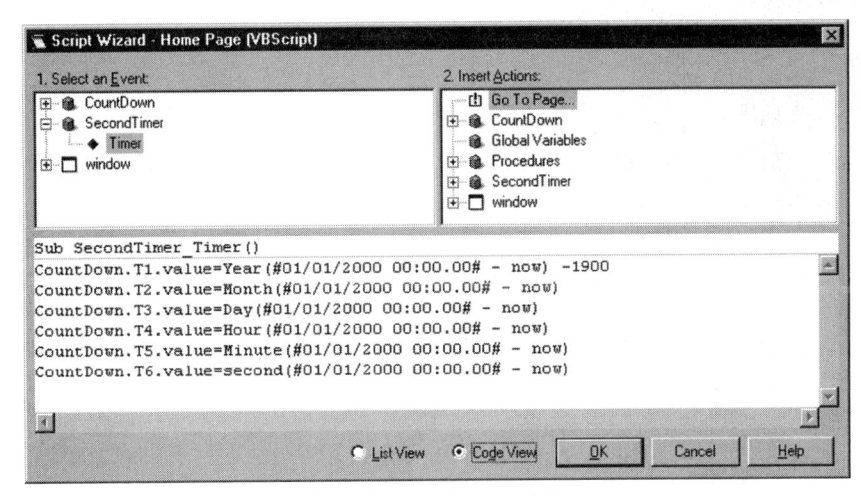

```
Script Wizard - Home Page (VBScript)

1. Select an Event:                          2. Insert Actions:
   CountDown                                    Go To Page...
   SecondTimer                                  CountDown
       Timer                                    Global Variables
   window                                       Procedures
                                                SecondTimer
                                                window

Sub SecondTimer_Timer()
CountDown.T1.value=Year(#01/01/2000 00:00.00# - now) -1900
CountDown.T2.value=Month(#01/01/2000 00:00.00# - now)
CountDown.T3.value=Day(#01/01/2000 00:00.00# - now)
CountDown.T4.value=Hour(#01/01/2000 00:00.00# - now)
CountDown.T5.value=Minute(#01/01/2000 00:00.00# - now)
CountDown.T6.value=second(#01/01/2000 00:00.00# - now)
```

Figure 9-39: The Script Wizard window for the Year2000 page.

The Code pane on your screen will be empty. Enter the following lines:

```
CountDown.T1.value=Year(#01/01/2000 00:00.00# - now) -1900
CountDown.T2.value=Month(#01/01/2000 00:00.00# - now)
CountDown.T3.value=Day(#01/01/2000 00:00.00# - now)
CountDown.T4.value=Hour(#01/01/2000 00:00.00# - now)
CountDown.T5.value=Minute(#01/01/2000 00:00.00# - now)
CountDown.T6.value=second(#01/01/2000 00:00.00# - now)
```

CountDown is the name of the form and T1 through T6 are the names of the six text box controls. The value property of each text box control is set to a different value.

Let's start by examining the expression:

```
#01/01/2000 00:00.00# - now
```

which appears in all lines. The first part is the date and time of the first second of the year 2000. The pound sign that surrounds the date and time signifies that it's a date. *Now* is a VBScript function that returns the current date and time. The arithmetic difference of the two values is the total time between any moment and the turn of the century.

The first line in the script converts this difference into years using the Year function. Year() is a VBScript function that converts a time value to the equivalent number of years. The Year function returns a number between 0 and 100; that's why the script adds 1900 to it.

The Month() function is similar. It takes a time interval and converts it to months. The Day() function returns the number of days in a time interval, the Hour() function returns the number of hours, the Minute() function returns the number of minutes, and the Second() function returns the number of seconds.

As you see, the code passes the time interval between now (which is the date and time at the moment you are viewing the page) and the first moment of the year 2000. Then, each of the VBScript functions converts this difference to years, months, days, hours, minutes, and seconds. These values are then displayed to the appropriate text boxes by assigning them to the value property of each text box.

Displaying Status Messages

The Timer web (\Webs\Chap09\Timer\index.htm on this book's Companion CD-ROM), shown in Figure 9-40, is another example of the Timer event. Open this page with Internet Explorer and watch the browser's status bar. Every 10 seconds, a message indicating how long you have been viewing this page is displayed.

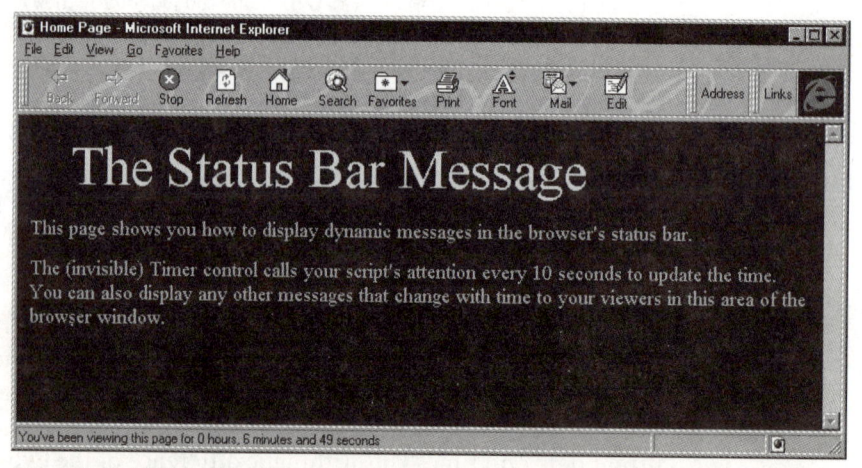

Figure 9-40: The Timer web uses a Timer control to update the message at the browser's status bar every 10 seconds.

Obviously this page contains a Timer control, which triggers a Timer event every 10 seconds. Create a new page and place the text on the page as shown in Figure 9-40, and then insert a Timer control as described in the previous section. The control's name is Timer1 and its Interval property must be set to 10000 (so that it notifies the script every 10 seconds).

The script of this page is a little more involved than the ones you've seen so far. To display how long the user has been viewing the page, you must store the time he or she opened the page somewhere. You must create a variable where the current time will be stored. Then, each time the timer triggers the Timer event, you must subtract this time from the current time to find out the difference. This result is converted to hours, minutes, and seconds with the Hour, Minute, and Second functions, as you have done in the previous example.

Let's start by creating a variable, where the time when the page was opened will be stored. Open the Script Wizard for this page, as shown in Figure 9-41.

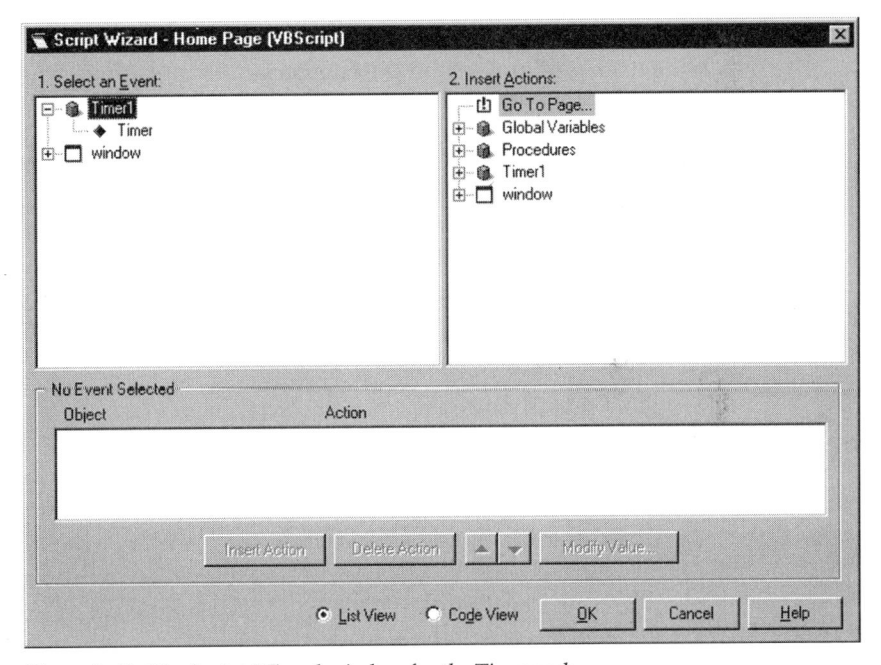

Figure 9-41: The Script Wizard window for the Timer web.

Right-click on the Global Variables entry in the Action pane, and from the pop-up menu, choose New Global Variable. The New Global Variable window will be displayed, where you can enter the name of the new variable (as shown in Figure 9-42). Click OK.

Figure 9-42: Defining a new global variable.

Now move to the Action pane of the Script Wizard's window and expand the items Timer1 and Window. The Window object (which is the browser's window) has two events, onLoad and onUnload, which are triggered when the page is loaded and unloaded respectively. When the page is loaded, you want to store the current time (that is, the time when the page was opened) in the Connected variable. Enter the line:

```
Connected = Time
```

in the Code pane (first switch to the Code view). Time is another VBScript function that returns the current time.

Next click on the Timer1 control's Timer event, and in the Code pane, enter the following line:

```
Window.Status = "You've been viewing this page for " & hour(Time-Connected) & " hours, " & minute(Time-Connected) & " minutes and " & second(Time-Connected) & " seconds"
```

Note that in this book, this line wraps to several lines, but you must enter it as a single line in the code editor.

What does this line do? It sets the value of the Window.Status property. As I mentioned, Window is the name of the browser's window. As with controls, the browser's window has its own properties. One of them is the *Status* property, which is the text displayed in the browser's status bar. To display the string "Welcome to our fabulous site" in the status bar while your page is displayed, use the line:

```
Window.Status = "Welcome to our fabulous site"
```

from within your script. In our example, you are displaying a different message, which is more complicated. Let's break up the long string to see how it displays how long the current page is open:

```
hour(time-Connected)
```

The expression (time-Connected) is the difference between the current moment and the moment this page was opened. The time when the page was opened is stored in the Connected variable. The function:

```
Hour(Time - Connected)
```

returns the number of hours that correspond to this time interval. Similarly, the function Minute(Time - Connected) returns the number of minutes and Second(Time - Connected) returns the number of seconds. These values are concatenated with text (with the & operator) to produce a message like:

```
You've been viewing this page for 2 hours, 43 minutes, and 30 seconds
```

This message is displayed on the browser's status bar. This message is also updated every 10 seconds, because the Timer control's interval was set to 10 seconds. I have chosen a complicated message for the example to demonstrate some of VBScript's functions. You can display any message you wish on the browser's status bar, such as welcoming messages, ads, and so on.

More VBScript Techniques

Before we explore another way to add complete programs to a web page (embedding a Visual Basic program as a custom control), let's explore some of the possibilities brought up by the previous examples. I'll show you how to add an animated, colored fade effect and offer some techniques for experimenting with VBScript code.

Color Animation

This project demonstrates another method of adding scripts to your pages. The script of the Colors page isn't tied to an event, like the click of a mouse or a timer's Timer event. Instead, it's executed when the page is loaded.

This web can be imported into FrontPage from the \Webs\Chap09\Colors folder of this book's Companion CD-ROM. Look for the file index.htm.

Open the Colors web (shown in Figure 9-43) and notice what happens when the page is loaded. The page's background color changes smoothly, giving the impression of a fade from black. It starts as a black page and quickly turns silvery gray. The animation lasts a second or so and stops when the page assumes the silver tone. Only then are the page's contents loaded. If the effect was too fast for you to watch, click on the Refresh button to repeat the animation. It's an interesting effect you can add to your pages.

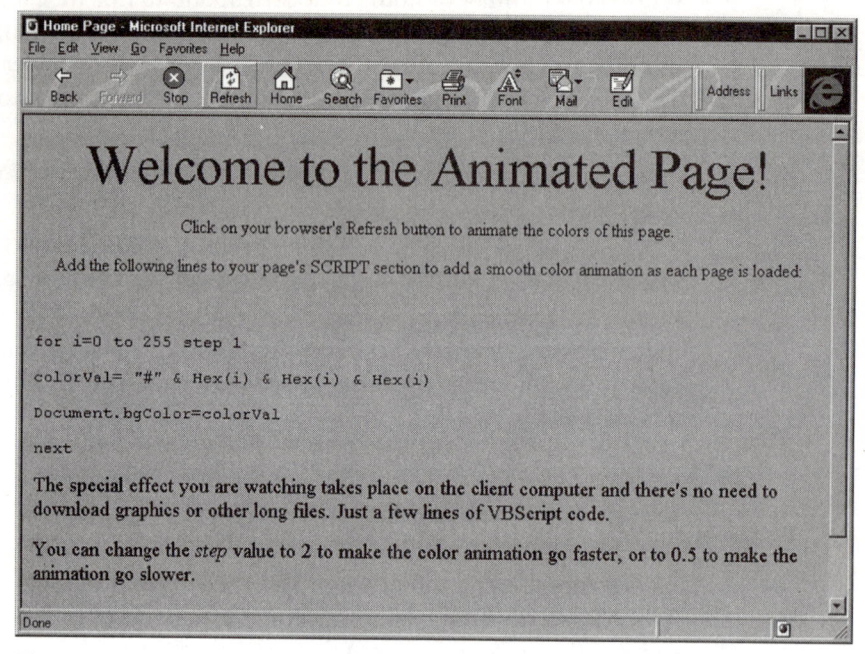

Figure 9-43: The Colors web animates the background color as the page is loaded.

Here's how to add the color fade animation:

1. Create a blank page with the text shown in Figure 9-43, or open any other page you want to add the color animation to.
   The script effect can be applied to any page, even if it has a custom background, because it takes place *before* the page is actually displayed.

2. With the page open in the FrontPage Editor, open the Insert menu and choose Script. You will see the Script window shown in Figure 9-44.

3. Check the VBScript button to indicate that your script will be written in VBScript.

   Notice that you can invoke the Script Wizard from within the Script window, but you don't need to. There are no events to program because this page doesn't contain any controls. The script you are going to enter here will be executed when the page is first opened and before its elements are downloaded and displayed.

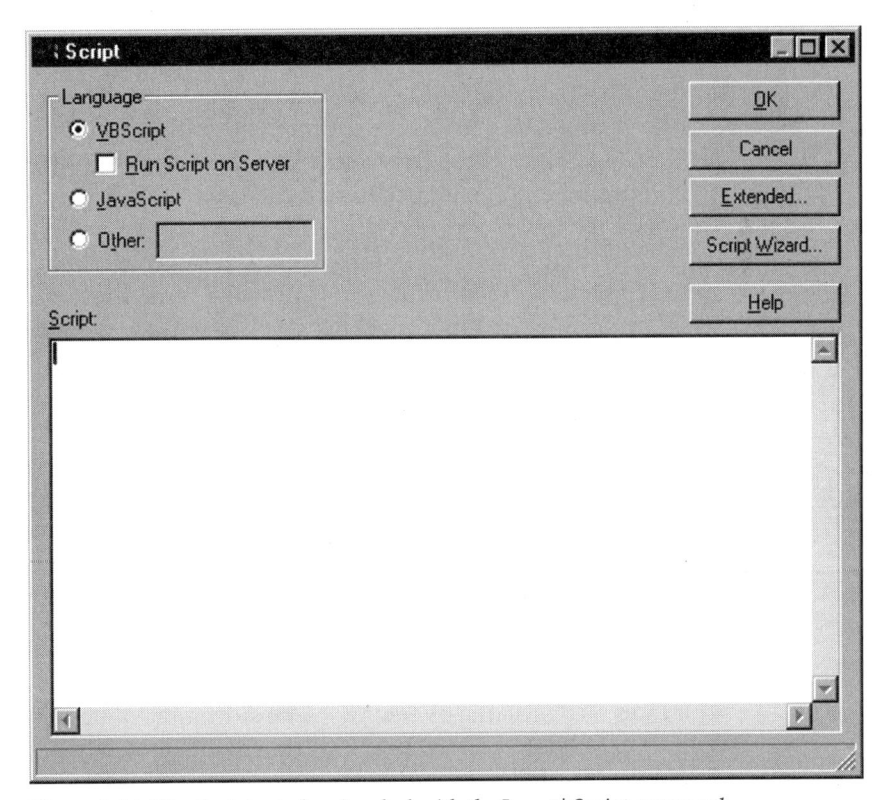

Figure 9-44: The Script window invoked with the Insert | Script command.

4. Enter the following lines in the Script window:

```
For i=0 to 255 step 1
        colorVal= "#" & Hex(i) & Hex(i) & Hex(i)
        Document.bgColor=colorVal
Next
```

This script contains a structure you have not seen so far: a For... Next loop. The For... Next loop executes a block of statements repeatedly. The loop starts with an initial value for the *i* variable equal to 0. After the statements are executed and the Next command is reached, the program increases the value of *i* by 1 and checks whether it has reached the maximum value (255). If not, it executes the statements again. When the maximum value has been reached, the loop exits.

This loop will be executed 256 times. With each successive iteration, the variable *i* is increased by 1. How about the loop's statements? What does the Hex function do and what is this bgColor property?

Document.bgColor is a property of the web document. It's the document's background color. You already know how to set a page's background color to any value from within the FrontPage Editor (using File | Page Properties); now you know that it is possible to set it from within a script. The loop assigns a different color to the Document.bgColor property at each iteration.

Let's digress for a moment to look at how color is specified. You open the Color dialog box, shown in Figure 9-45, and select a color. If you click on the Define Custom Colors button, you will see the right half of the Color box, where you can define a color value. Any color you select on the color swatch is represented by three numbers, listed in the lower right corner of the Colors box. They are the intensities of the red, green, and blue components of the color. Every color you can view on a computer monitor is made up of three values: Red, Green, and Blue.

In Web page design, colors are represented as hexadecimal numbers. It's a strange notation, but you don't really need to know anything about it short of the Hex function, which converts the values you see in the Colors dialog box in hexadecimal numbers. The line:

```
colorVal= "#" & Hex(i) & Hex(i) & Hex(i)
```

creates a color value by taking the hexadecimal value of each iteration of the *i* variable. When the previous statement is executed for i=3, it will produce the following number:

#030303

which is the value of a gray tone. All three components of the colorVal variable have equal values, and the color specified is a gray tone. You can verify this by selecting various gray tones on the color swatch of the Colors dialog box. Select colors at the bottom of the window with the color spectrum and read the values of their Red, Green, and Blue components. They all have the same value.

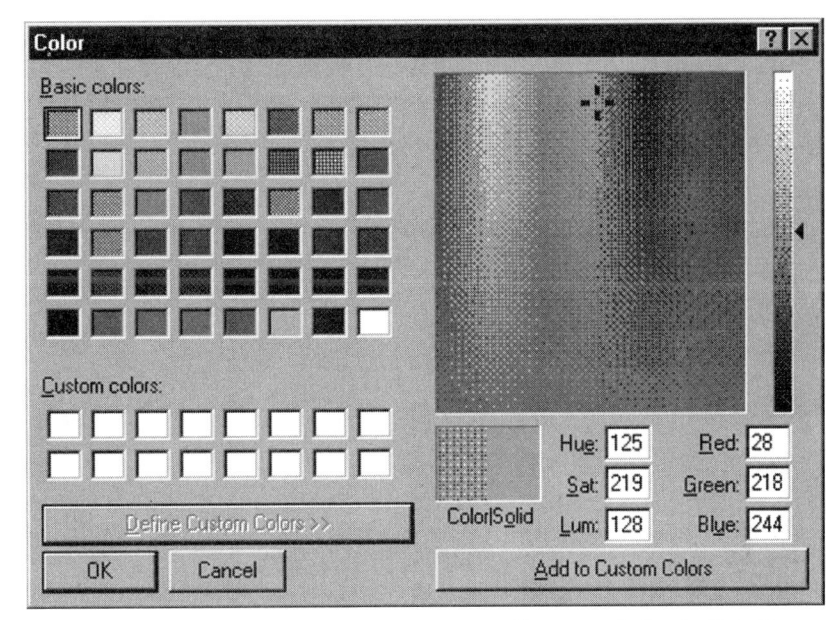

Figure 9-45: To specify custom colors, you are actually manipulating its Red, Green, and Blue components. These components for the selected color are 28, 218, and 244.

In effect, the For. . . Next loop creates successively lighter tones of gray and assigns them to the colorVal variable, which is in turn assigned to the document's background. The page's background changes colors slowly, starting with black and ending with a light gray tone.

You can try different colors, too. The line:

```
colorVal= "#" & Hex(i) & Hex(0) & Hex(0)
```

will produce variations of red colors. Notice that the intensity of the green and blue components is zero, so only the red component changes value, from black to a bright red color.

Experimenting With VBScript

The technique you used to enter the script in our last example is a good way to quickly test VBScript commands.

Create a new page, issue the Script command from the Insert menu, and in the Script window, type a few VBScript commands, like:

```
name = InputBox("Please enter your name")
MsgBox "Welcome home " & name
```

Then close the Script window, save the page, and preview it. As soon as the script is loaded, it will prompt you to enter your name, which it will use to display a personalized welcome message.

Return to the same page in the FrontPage Editor and enter a different script. This time, let's test the Date function of VBScript. Delete the script's lines and enter the following commands:

```
MsgBox Now
MsgBox Now + 1
MsgBox Now + 1/24
```

The first statement will display the current date and time, obviously. The second statement will print tomorrow's date and the same time. It's the current date and time plus 1 day. The third statement will print the current date and time, plus 1 hour (1/24 of a day). VBScript can handle date and time very well, as you can see.

The Game of Life ActiveX Control

One of the projects included on the Companion CD-ROM is the AXLife web, which is shown in Figure 9-46. The AXLife web contains a custom ActiveX Control designed for this book. This control encapsulates a complete application, a simulation of the classic game of Life. It's not really a game, per se, although it can be fun. In the game of Life, you set up some initial conditions and the program starts simulating the birth and death of cells while displaying each new generation.

The game of life is a simulation of a small cell society, where cells vanish (or are regenerated) based on a few basic rules. A cell dies of loneliness if it has less than two neighbors. If a cell has more than three neighbors, it dies of overpopulation. A new cell comes alive if it has one or two neighbors only. To play the game, you must specify the initial "inhabitants" of this cell society. Turn on a few cells on the board by clicking on the corresponding square with the mouse. To turn off a square that's on, click on it with the mouse. After the initial pattern has been defined, click on the Start button and watch the evolution of the population on the board. The game produces interesting geometric patterns and the faster your computer, the faster the display is updated.

Chapter 9: Advanced FrontPage Techniques 499

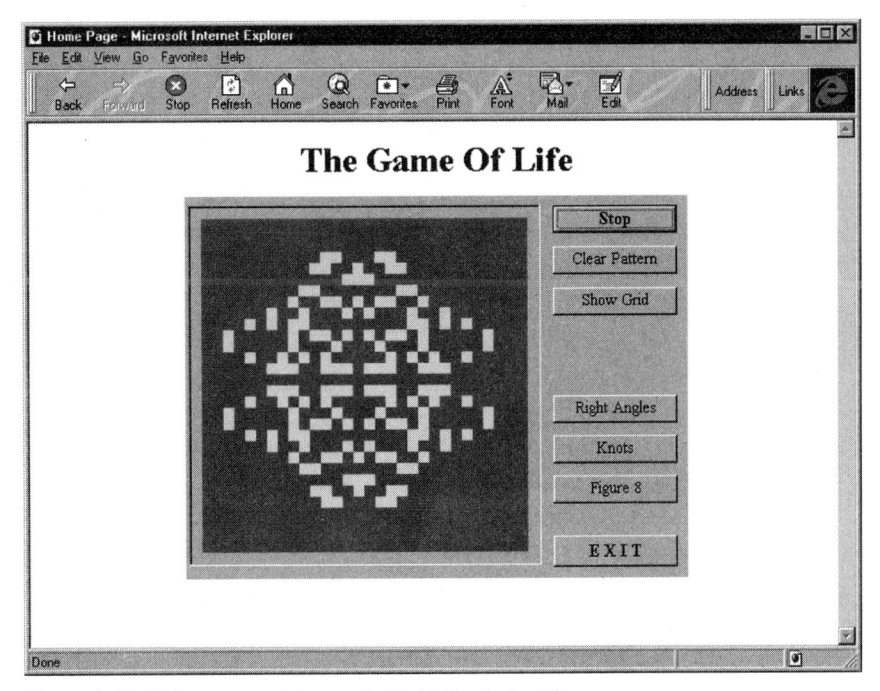

Figure 9-46: This page contains an ActiveX Control with a game.

To use the AXLife control, it must first be installed on your system. If you simply open the AXLife web on the the Companion CD-ROM, it's not going to work. To install the ActiveX Control it contains, you must do the following:

1. Use the FrontPage Explorer's File | Import command to import the AXLife web (the entire folder from the CD-ROM) as a new FrontPage web from the following folder of this book's CD-ROM: \Webs\Chap09\AXLife.

2. Start Internet Explorer and connect to your own web server. To connect to your own server, choose File | Open and enter your computer's IP address followed by the web's name. For example, use http:// localhost/AXLife, assuming you imported the page into a web named AXLife.

3. Your browser's status bar should display the message "Installing Components," and when it's done installing it, you will see the page shown in Figure 9-46.

Now you can test the game, or switch to FrontPage and create a new web that makes use of the AXLife ActiveX Control.

Once the control has been installed, you can insert the AXLife control on your own pages with the FrontPage Editor. Just use Insert | Other Components | ActiveX Control. When the ActiveX Control Properties window appears, scroll down the list of available ActiveX Controls to locate the control Project1.AXLife, as shown in Figure 9-47. Select it with the mouse and click the OK button. The AXLife control will be placed on the page at the pointer's location.

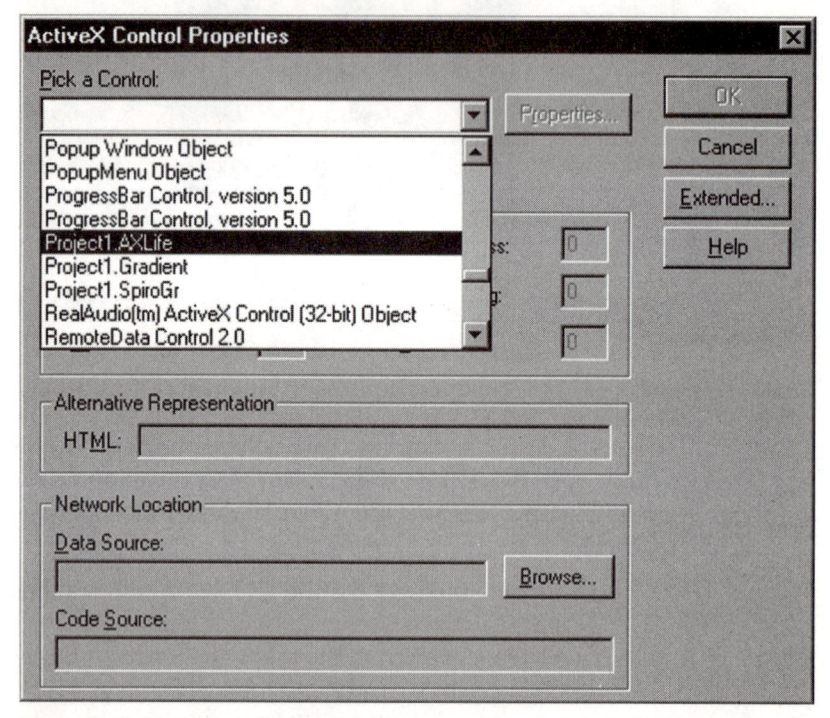

Figure 9-47: To use the AXLife control on your page, select Project1.AXLife from the list of available ActiveX Controls.

You can place text and any other design elements on the page (the game's instructions, for instance) and then preview the page with Internet Explorer. Notice that the AXLife control has no properties; all the functionality can be accessed via the various buttons on the control.

The AXLife ActiveX Control is an application that runs from within Internet Explorer just as it would run on the desktop. Developing applications that run within Internet Explorer is a bit more complicated than developing actual applications.

The AXLife control was developed with Visual Basic 5.0 Control Creation Edition, which, at the time of publication, was available for free download from Microsoft's Web site (http://www.microsoft.com/sitebuilder). You will have to register with the SiteBuilder network to gain access to the guest download area, but it's well worth it to gain access to numerous web authoring resources. You can get a free membership by simply placing the Internet Explorer logo on one of your sites.

While many web authors will find it daunting to develop ActiveX Controls, the VB5CCE tool will lead to scores of controls available for use on the Web.

Using a custom control lets you go beyond the intentionally limited feature set of VBScript. You're free to develop the same kind of application that would normally run on the desktop, yet easily distribute it by embedding it on a web page.

Note: You may get a security warning when you try to open the AXLife page, since the custom control does not have a Verisign certificate. A *certificate* ensures that the code has not been tampered with and has been developed by a trusted source. When developing projects for your own use or for a corporate intranet, you needn't bother with the cumbersome certification process. When working with or developing your own custom controls, I recommend changing the default Internet Explorer security setting to allow you to view these controls. Choose View | Options, go to the Security tab, and click the Safety Level button. Choose Medium and click OK.

You can use the controls from the Microsoft ActiveX Gallery, and the growing library of third-party controls, as basic building blocks for your projects. They add functionality to your pages that isn't available through HTML. Many of the controls are available for your own use when developing webs. Other controls in the Gallery are only demonstration controls, and you will need to purchase the developer's version of the controls to use them in your own pages.

Inserting Java Applets

Up to now, we've focused on VBScript and ActiveX Controls. They provide the easiest way to activate your pages. VBScript is the easiest web scripting language, and ActiveX Controls are the most powerful and easy-to-use modular components for use with web pages.

There are other web technologies that you may be interested in. Instead of writing your code in VBScript, which isn't supported by Netscape Navigator (although the 4.0 release of Netscape Navigator, called Communicator, should support all Internet Explorer features), you may prefer to stick with JavaScript, called JScript by Microsoft.

Jscript is very similar to VBScript, but the syntax of the code and the function names will vary.

I didn't discuss JavaScript in this book for two reasons. The first is because VBScript is easier to program and understand, so I chose to focus on it in this chapter. Second, I believe that VBScript will end up as the dominant web scripting language; this is due to the widespread popularity of Visual Basic and the clear usability advantage that VBScript offers over JavaScript.

For the time being, you may prefer to learn JavaScript if you want to design pages with simple scripting that will run on any modern web browser. On the other hand, if you use ActiveX Controls, you might as well script them with VBScript, since any browser capable of displaying ActiveX Controls will be able to interpret VBScript, the specification for which Microsoft has released into the public domain.

While Java*Script* may or may not retain its popularity, Java applets are a different matter. Like ActiveX Controls, Java applets encapsulate programs that you can insert on a web page. Unlike ActiveX Controls, which are a special technology first implemented on Windows and only recently supported by the Macintosh, Java applets are by design compatible with any computer running a web browser with Java support. Java applets are therefore *cross-platform* applications, as long as only standard Java features are deployed.

Java was created by Sun Microsystems as a replacement for the hard-to-use and hard-to-comprehend C language. Features of the C language that are difficult to decipher and potentially dangerous, such as using pointer variables to directly access system memory, are forbidden. When the idea of programmable web objects surfaced, Java became one of the leading contenders because of its platform-neutral design and security features.

Java supports a generic Windows-type graphical user interface, so that Java applets have a graphical look and feel that are nearly identical whether the program is running on a Windows 3.1, Windows 95, Macintosh, or UNIX system. It's also possible to write Java applets that take full advantage of a particular platform's features, although this means foregoing that crucial cross-platform advantage.

A Java applet is a text file called a *class*. You can insert a Java class on a web page to tap into its capabilities just like inserting an ActiveX Control. FrontPage offers a few features to make this easy.

Acquiring Java Classes/Applets

While it's possible to teach some elements of a simple scripting language like VBScript in a book of this size, a tutorial on how to program in Java is way beyond the scope of a single chapter. Instead, we'll focus on how to insert ready-to-use Java applets.

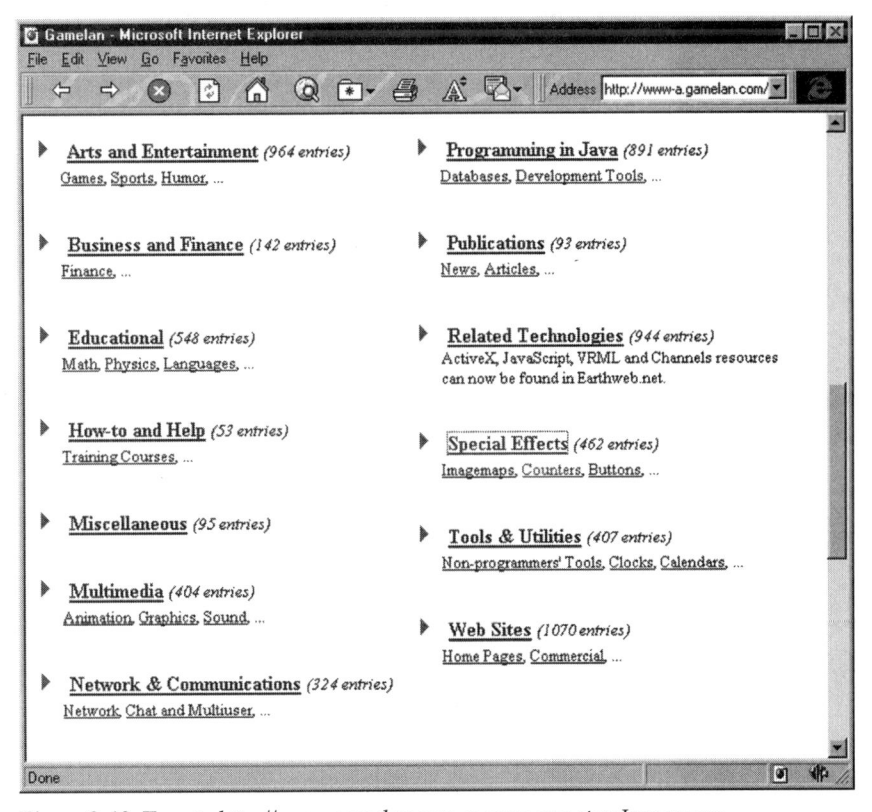

Figure 9-48: Turn to http://www.gamelan.com as your one-stop Java source.

One great source for Java applets is http://www.gamelan.com. To give you a taste of the Java applets available for your use, Figure 9-48 shows the home page of Gamelan (pronounced gamma-lan). (Many of these applets must be purchased before use, although there are demo versions to whet your appetite.)

Inserting a Java Applet

I found a cute little Java applet on Gamelan called Cam's Dynamic Counter Applet that displays a hit counter for your page. The counter, displayed as odometer, increases each time your page is accessed by someone. Go to http://www.local.com/counter to get all the details on using this applet. That page gives you information on how to insert the Java code directly into the HTML of your page. You could do this using an HTML Markup WebBot (Insert | HTML Markup).

But editing raw HTML is so *ugly*. Instead, FrontPage provides a simple GUI interface for inserting and setting the properties for a Java applet.

Follow these steps to insert Cam's Dynamic Counter Applet onto a blank web page:

1. Create a new web with FrontPage Explorer and name it JavaDemo.

2. Open the home page with the FrontPage Editor.

3. Type **This page has been accessed times.**

4. Move the text insertion point between "accessed" and "times."

5. Choose Insert | Other Component | Java Applet.

6. Fill out the Java Applet Properties dialog box as shown in Figure 9-49.

7. Save the page as Java Demo (using a URL of index.htm) and preview it.

Each time you visit this page (or click the Refresh or Reload button), the counter value increases by one. (You will have to be connected to the Internet for this to work, since the applet is loaded from an Internet web server.)

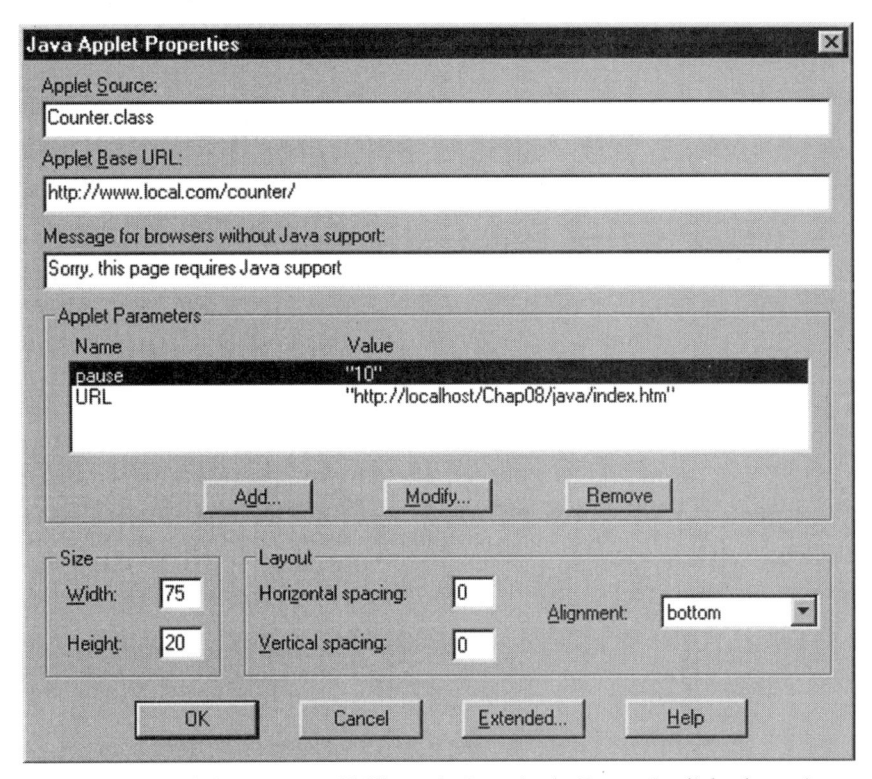

Figure 9-49: Here's how you would fill out the Java Applet Properties dialog box to insert Cam's Dynamic Counter Applet.

The Java Applet Properties dialog box (Figure 9-49) lets you fill out many of the HTML attributes for a Java applet. The HTML tag CODEBASE is represented by Applet Base URL. The HTML tag CODE is supported by the Applet Source text box.

The applet source is usually just the name of the Java applet, a text file ending with the extension *.class*. (Yes, you can have extensions longer than 3 characters with Windows 95 and NT 4, as well as with UNIX.) If you purchase a Java applet, you may be entitled to store the class on your own server. Otherwise, as in the case of the Dynamic Counter, you'll have to run the Java applet from the server operated by the applet's author, although this can lead to slower performance than hosting the code on your own site.

Another reason this applet runs from Cam's server is that the applet relies on a site database to track accesses to pages. To make this work, you have to include the URL of your site so that it can be added to the tracking database. To do so, click the Add button from the Applet Parameters section of the Java Applet Properties dialog box. This lets you add a named parameter and a value associated with the parameter.

I added a parameter named URL with the path of http://localhost/Chap09/java/index.htm—you would change this to the actual URL of your web site.

You can also add a parameter called *pause* to control how quickly the digit counter changes from one number to the next. The default value (if you don't specify it) is 30.

Unlike ActiveX Controls, which publicly expose their methods, properties, and parameters for use with the Script Wizard, there is no simple mechanism for displaying the available parameters or methods of a Java class. Instead, you'll need to rely on the documentation for the program written by its author, or attempt to deduce these if you have access to the plain-text Java source code. (Much Java code is distributed as byte-code. While byte-code is still portable between various platforms, there is no easy way to turn it back into readable source code, which protects the programmer's trade secrets.)

Once the Java applet is placed on the page, you can click on it and then drag its handles to size its region. Or you can double-click on the control to return to the Java Applet Properties dialog box and enter the size directly into the Width and Height boxes.

TIP

Some Java applet parameters aren't supported directly by the Java Applet Properties dialog box, but you can use the Extended button to insert them (for example, the ARCHIVE tag used to refer to a Java class (and associated files) stored as a PKWare PKZIP-compatible archive).

Java or ActiveX?

Only time will tell whether Java lives up to its promise as the new "operating system" of the World Wide Web. If the Java initiative succeeds, it could upset the Microsoft hegemony over software standards, which rely on the Windows operating system. This is no easy challenge for Java's proponents, since Windows runs on over 85 percent of the world's personal computers, and Java applications have a long way to go to catch up with the power and sophistication of Windows software like Microsoft Office.

> **TIP**
>
> *To see the state of the art in Java application programming, visit Corel's web site at http:/www.corel.com, and download and evaluate the Java version of Corel PerfectOffice. So far, it's a disappointing reality. Java just doesn't run quickly enough or offer enough features to programmers at this stage. Worse, incompatibilities between platforms and browsers in the implementation of the Java virtual machine have made it difficult to take advantage of one of Java's most important goals: true platform independence.*

Furthermore, Microsoft isn't resting on its laurels. The ActiveX specification has already moved to become a cross-platform standard. Microsoft voluntarily surrendered control of the ActiveX specification to a third party consortium. Support for ActiveX technology in Internet Explorer and in the operating system is now available for all Windows platforms, the Macintosh, and on many Unix systems, something even Java can't effectively deliver.

On the other front, Microsoft has added Windows-like Application Foundation Classes to the Java language that, if exploited by many programmers, could relegate Java to just another Windows programming language. (Microsoft's Visual J++ is also a superior development environment for Java, making it hard to resist these new features.)

Microsoft counters that programmers want to be able to use the tool of their choice to program, and that Java alone can't offer the richness or ease of use expected by Windows users. Microsoft also insists that the new Java AFCs it proposes will be portable to other computing platforms, subject to Microsoft licensing agreements.

When designing your own pages, consider your audience, and decide if this is an ideological issue for you. If you want to design the flashiest, most powerful, and interactive web sites, you'll go with ActiveX, even if this means excluding some users with outdated browsers or unsupported computers.

If you prefer not to support Microsoft (even though ActiveX is no longer controlled by Microsoft), you'll limit yourself to Java. But of course, if you felt that way, you wouldn't have purchased Microsoft FrontPage in the first place.

Moving On

This chapter has shown you how to develop active pages using scripting, ActiveX Controls, and Java. In the next chapter, we'll explore a visual reference guide to menus, templates, and toolbars within FrontPage 97.

chapter 10

FrontPage 97 Visual Reference Guide

It can be intimidating to learn a new software package, especially one as sophisticated as FrontPage 97. Navigating through the hundred or so menu items, dialog boxes, and property sheets is a lot like blindly pursuing an elusive quarry through a twisting maze. Would it help to have a map?

This chapter is quite unlike the others in this book, in that it is laid out as a visual map rather than taking the form of a narrative discussion. Instead of reading text and referring to figure captions, the figures themselves take center stage. On the pages that follow, you'll find a thorough reference to all the toolbars, menus, and most dialog boxes for both FrontPage Explorer and the FrontPage Editor. At the heart of each illustration is one of the menus for either FrontPage Explorer or the FrontPage Editor, with arrows radiating out from each choice, clearly showing the dialog box or property sheet that appears when you choose that menu option. You can also back-trace an arrow from a dialog box to see which menu option activates it. Or an arrow might point to another embedded illustration that depicts how a menu option works.

In addition to every menu of the two main components of FrontPage, this reference also includes an illustration of the various author-insertable WebBot components. I wrap up this chapter with a listing of every FrontPage web and page template, so that you can quickly decide which of them (if any) are useful for a new project.

To complement this chapter, turn to Appendix B, a listing of FrontPage resources (mainly hyperlinks) on the Internet and World Wide Web.

While this chapter is rather terse, you'll turn to it again and again, even after you've mastered the tutorials and techniques I offer in the rest of this book. I hope this reference section (and the appendices) will provide you with lasting value, as there will always be times when you can't quite figure out *where* to look to find a particular feature or option of FrontPage 97.

FrontPage Menu Reference

FrontPage Explorer (Link View) Toolbar Reference

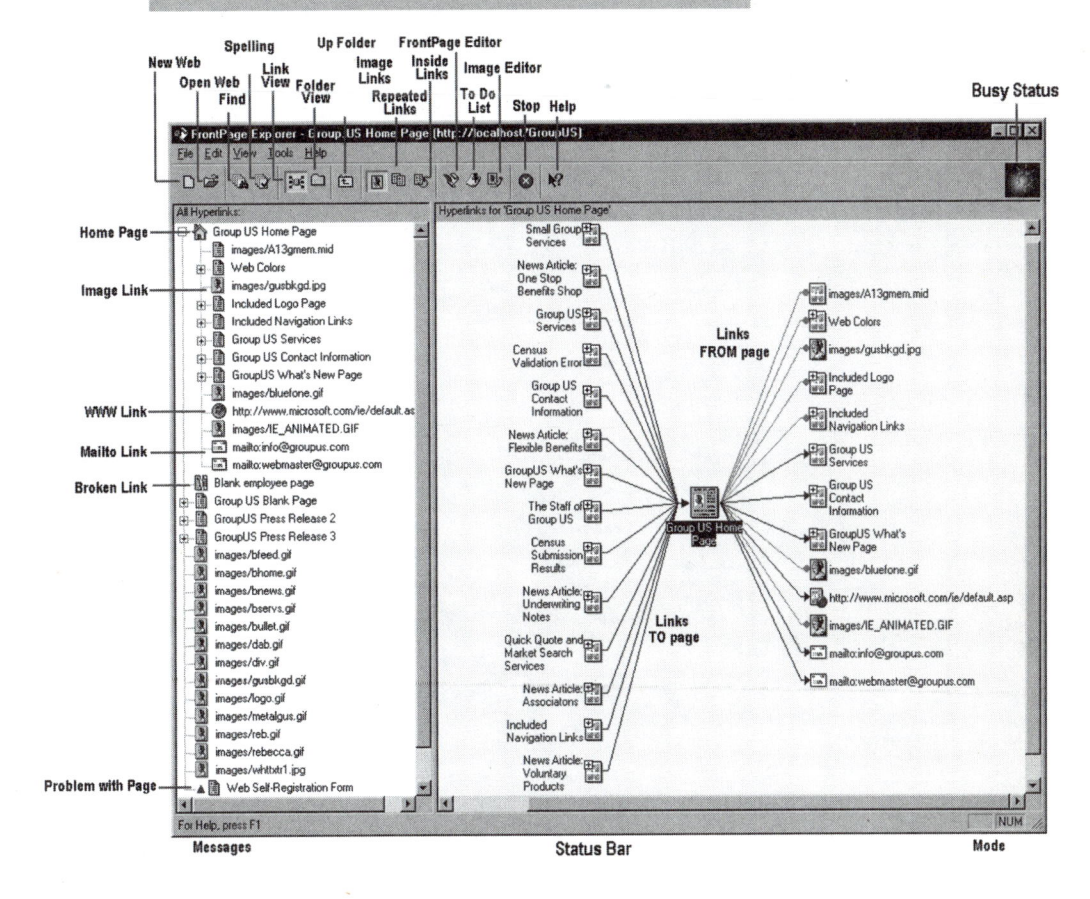

The Link View of the FrontPage Explorer gives you a visual map (an inspiration for this chapter) of the relationships (links) between the pages in your web. You can "drill down" by clicking a plus symbol to continue to follow the path of links. In this view, the lefthand pane is a hierarchical tree listing of the links, and the righthand pane is a diagrammatic view.

FrontPage Explorer (Folder View) Toolbar Reference

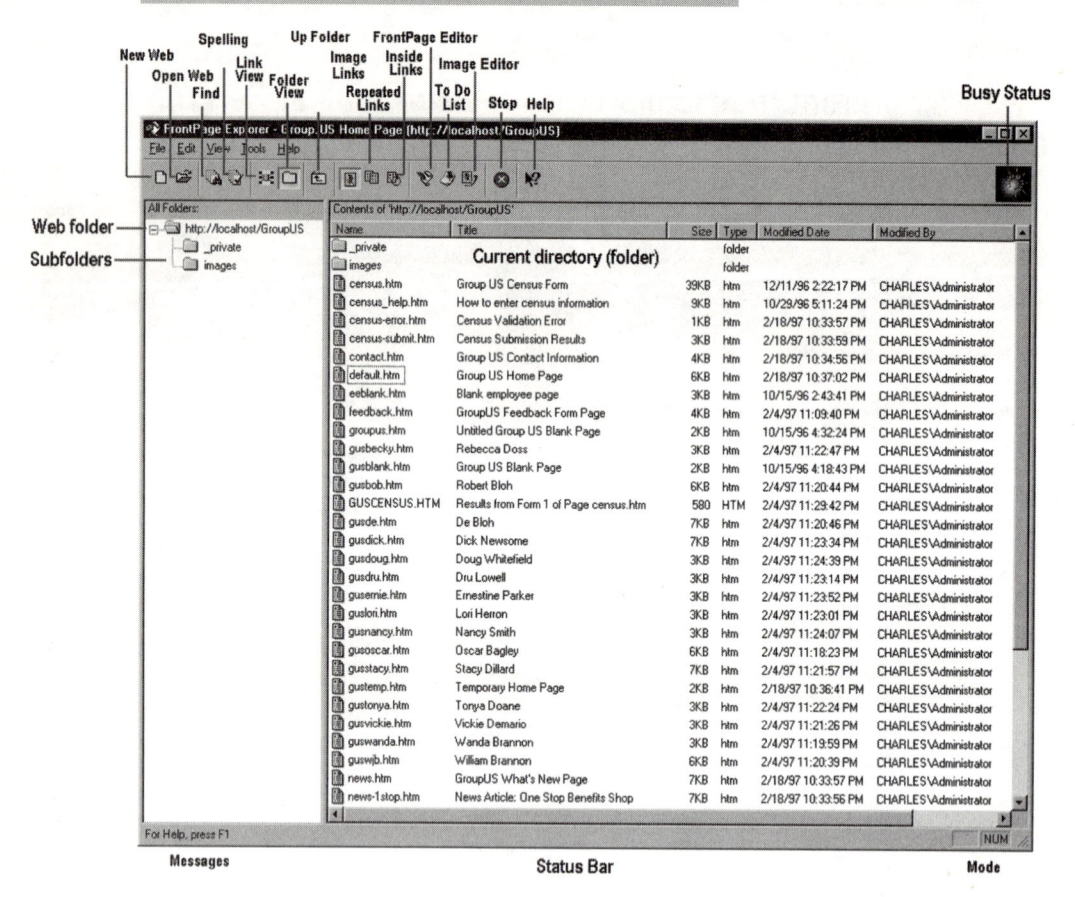

Labels (toolbar buttons): New Web, Open Web, Spelling, Link View, Find, Folder View, Up Folder, Image Links, Repeated Links, Inside Links, FrontPage Editor, Image Editor, To Do List, Stop, Help, Busy Status

Left-side labels: Web folder, Subfolders

Bottom labels: Messages, Status Bar, Mode

Name	Title	Size	Type	Modified Date	Modified By
_private			folder		
images	Current directory (folder)		folder		
census.htm	Group US Census Form	39KB	htm	12/11/96 2:22:17 PM	CHARLES\Administrator
census_help.htm	How to enter census information	9KB	htm	10/29/96 5:11:24 PM	CHARLES\Administrator
census-error.htm	Census Validation Error	1KB	htm	2/18/97 10:33:57 PM	CHARLES\Administrator
census-submit.htm	Census Submission Results	3KB	htm	2/18/97 10:33:59 PM	CHARLES\Administrator
contact.htm	Group US Contact Information	4KB	htm	2/18/97 10:34:56 PM	CHARLES\Administrator
default.htm	Group US Home Page	6KB	htm	2/18/97 10:37:02 PM	CHARLES\Administrator
eeblank.htm	Blank employee page	3KB	htm	10/15/96 2:43:41 PM	CHARLES\Administrator
feedback.htm	GroupUS Feedback Form Page	4KB	htm	2/4/97 11:09:40 PM	CHARLES\Administrator
groupus.htm	Untitled Group US Blank Page	2KB	htm	10/15/96 4:32:24 PM	CHARLES\Administrator
gusbecky.htm	Rebecca Doss	3KB	htm	2/4/97 11:22:47 PM	CHARLES\Administrator
gusblank.htm	Group US Blank Page	2KB	htm	10/15/96 4:18:43 PM	CHARLES\Administrator
gusbob.htm	Robert Bloh	6KB	htm	2/4/97 11:20:44 PM	CHARLES\Administrator
GUSCENSUS.HTM	Results from Form 1 of Page census.htm	580	HTM	2/4/97 11:29:42 PM	CHARLES\Administrator
gusde.htm	De Bloh	7KB	htm	2/4/97 11:20:46 PM	CHARLES\Administrator
gusdick.htm	Dick Newsome	7KB	htm	2/4/97 11:23:34 PM	CHARLES\Administrator
gusdoug.htm	Doug Whitefield	3KB	htm	2/4/97 11:24:39 PM	CHARLES\Administrator
gusdru.htm	Dru Lowell	3KB	htm	2/4/97 11:23:14 PM	CHARLES\Administrator
gusernie.htm	Ernestine Parker	3KB	htm	2/4/97 11:23:52 PM	CHARLES\Administrator
guslori.htm	Lori Herron	3KB	htm	2/4/97 11:23:01 PM	CHARLES\Administrator
gusnancy.htm	Nancy Smith	3KB	htm	2/4/97 11:24:07 PM	CHARLES\Administrator
gusoscar.htm	Oscar Bagley	6KB	htm	2/4/97 11:18:23 PM	CHARLES\Administrator
gusstacy.htm	Stacy Dillard	7KB	htm	2/4/97 11:21:57 PM	CHARLES\Administrator
gustemp.htm	Temporary Home Page	2KB	htm	2/18/97 10:36:41 PM	CHARLES\Administrator
gustonya.htm	Tonya Doane	3KB	htm	2/4/97 11:22:24 PM	CHARLES\Administrator
gusvickie.htm	Vickie Demario	3KB	htm	2/4/97 11:21:26 PM	CHARLES\Administrator
guswanda.htm	Wanda Brannon	3KB	htm	2/4/97 11:19:59 PM	CHARLES\Administrator
guswjb.htm	William Brannon	6KB	htm	2/4/97 11:20:39 PM	CHARLES\Administrator
news.htm	GroupUS What's New Page	7KB	htm	2/18/97 10:33:57 PM	CHARLES\Administrator
news-1stop.htm	News Article: One Stop Benefits Shop	7KB	htm	2/18/97 10:33:56 PM	CHARLES\Administrator

The more practical Folder View lets you treat your web like a hard disk directory, similar to the way Windows Explorer works. In this mode, you can drag and drop files between folders or from an Explorer folder to the FrontPage Explorer. You can rename, copy, and delete pages and other files.

Chapter 10: FrontPage 97 Visual Reference Guide

FrontPage Explorer—File Menu

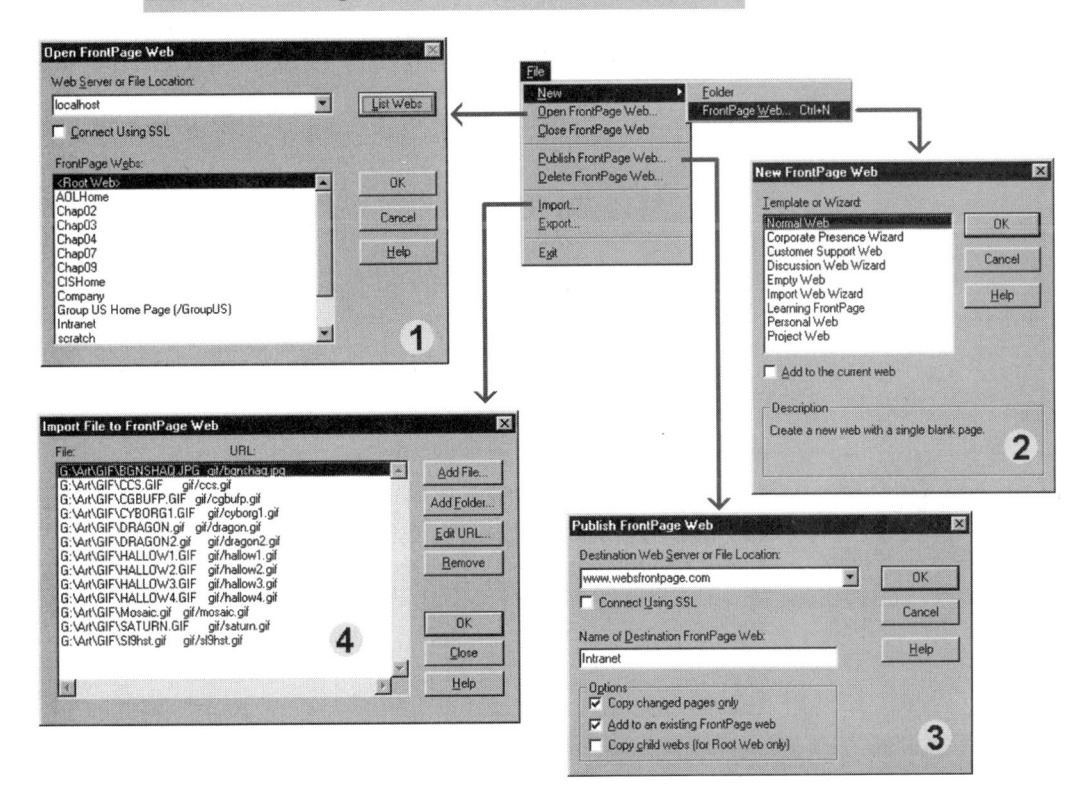

Use the FrontPage Explorer File menu to: (1) Open existing webs from the local server or Internet web server; (2) Create new webs or subfolders; (3) Publish a web to another server or Internet Web Presence Provider; and (4) Import files into the current web. You can also delete the current web (irreversible), export a file from the web to your hard disk, close the current web, and exit FrontPage Explorer.

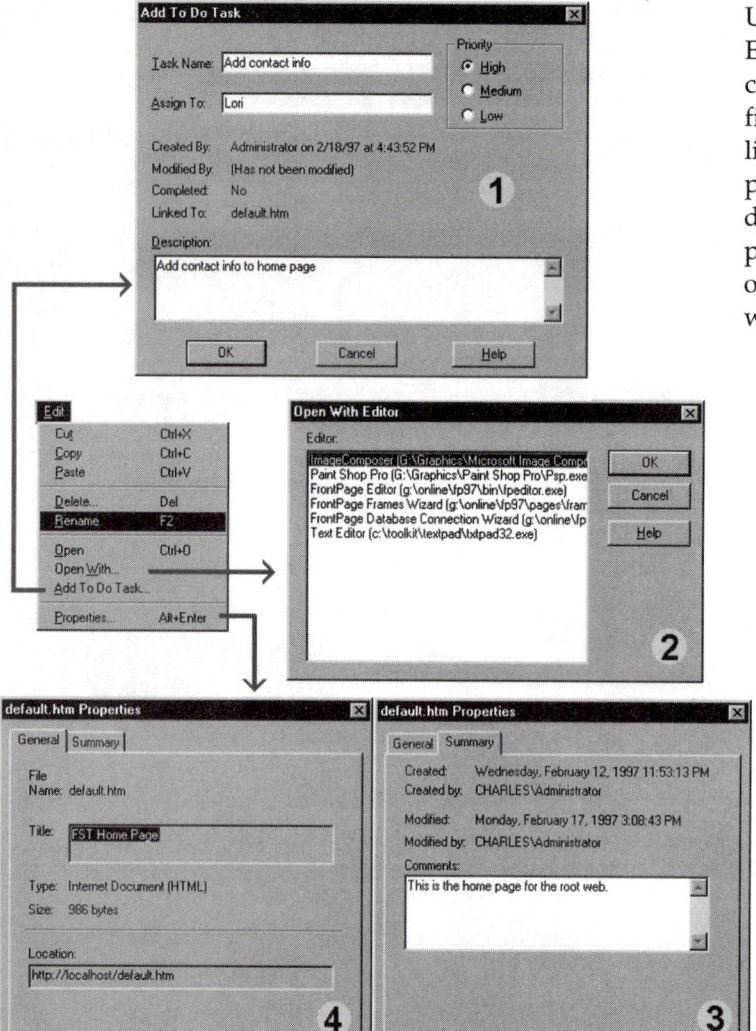

FrontPage Explorer—Edit Menu

Use the FrontPage Explorer Edit menu to cut, copy, and paste files and pages (works like Windows Explorer). You can also delete and rename pages and files. Other options include (clockwise from top-left):

(1) Use Add To Do Task to schedule work concerning the web.

(2) Use Open With to open a page or file with an alternate program (configured via Tools | Options, Configure Editors.

(3) After choosing Properties for a page, you can view file and authoring statistics, and enter comments for a page.

(4) After choosing Properties for a page, you can view (but not change) the page title and URL.

FrontPage Explorer—View Menu

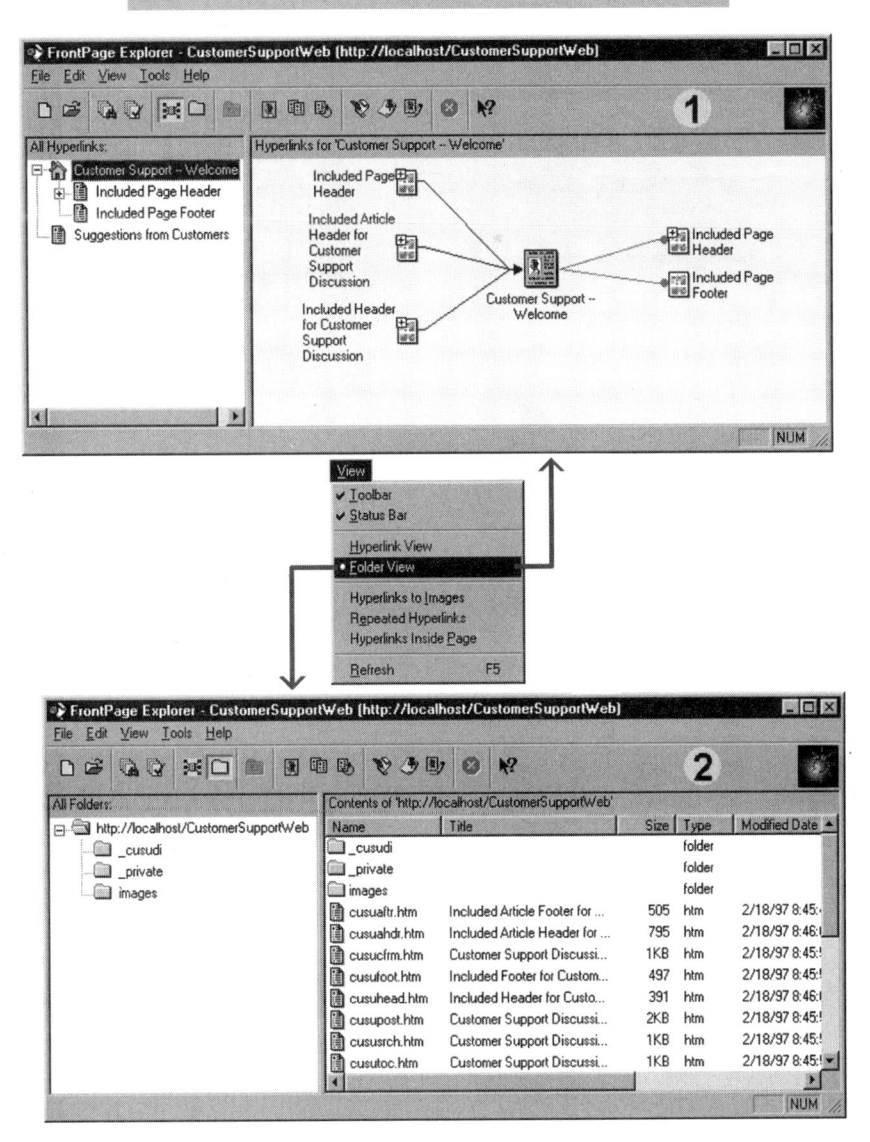

Use the FrontPage Explorer View menu to turn on and off interface elements such as the toolbar and status bar, or switch from (1) Hyperlink View to (2) Folder View or vice-versa. In Hyperlink View, turn on Hyperlinks to Images to include image files in the diagram, turn on Repeated Hyperlinks to see all links, even if multiple links point to the same page, and/or turn on Hyperlinks Inside Page if you want to see where a page points to itself, as in the case of bookmark links.

FrontPage Explorer—Tools Menu

The FrontPage Explorer Tools menu is a busy place. Here you can check spelling, find, or search and replace text across the entire web (not shown here as these dialogs are obvious). You can switch to or open the FrontPage Editor or the current Image Editor. Additional options include (clockwise from top-left):

(1) Choose Tools | Permissions to add or edit access rights for users and groups. This is normally restricted to the root web unless you enable unique permissions for a subweb. See Chapters 5 and 6.

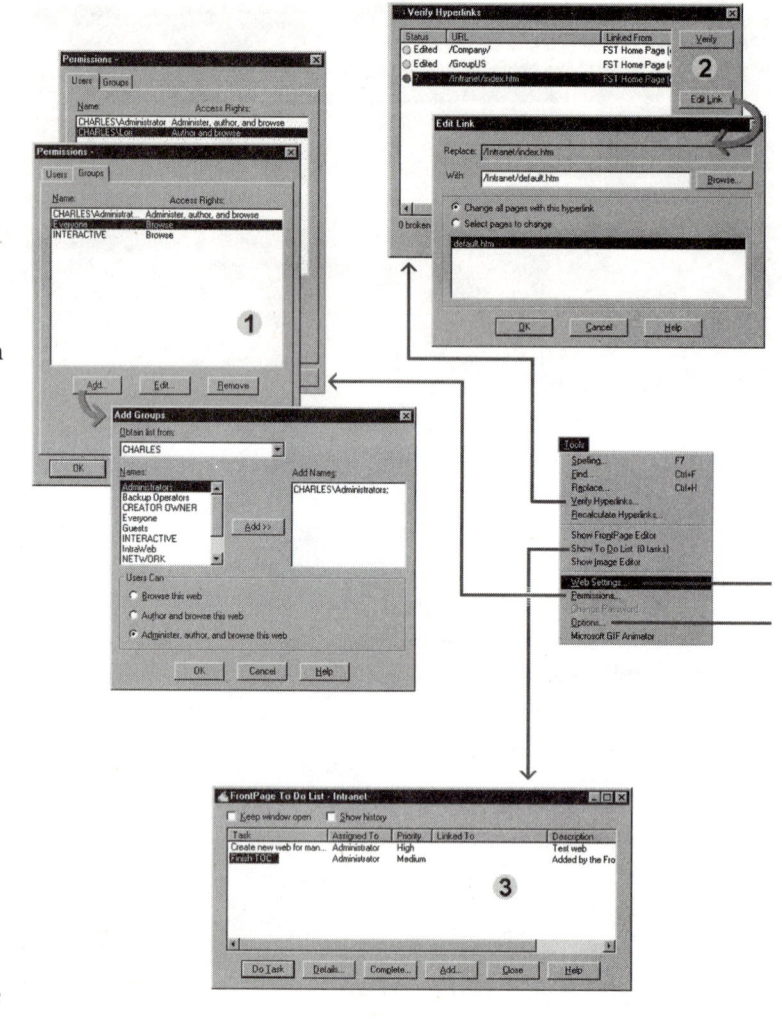

(2) Use Verify Hyperlinks to make sure that all links are intact and valid. You can then click Edit Link to make global corrections or correct only the links on a particular page.

(3) Choose Tools | Show To Do List to reveal the To Do List, which shows any tasks remaining to be completed.

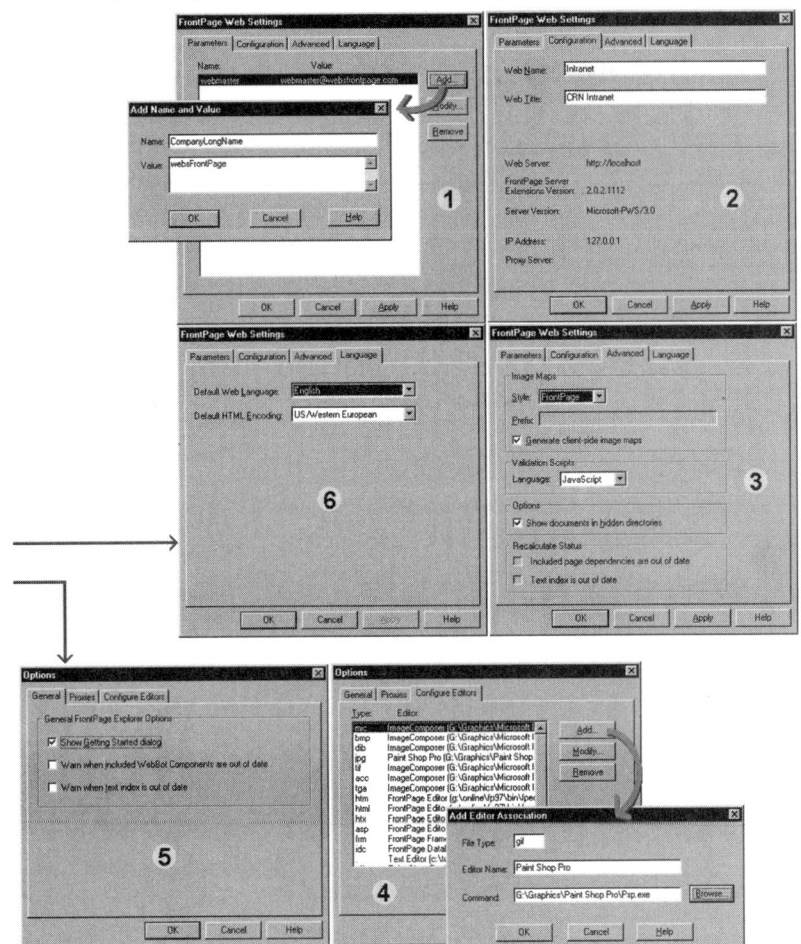

Continuing the explanation of the FrontPage Explorer Tools menu (clockwise from upper-left):

(1) Use the Parameters property sheet of Web Settings to add or edit parameters (variables) for use with the Substitution WebBot.

(2) Use the Configuration tab of Web Settings to view or change the Web Name (folder name) of the current web or the Web Title, used as the description of the web.

(3) Use the Advanced tab of Web Settings to choose the image map options (see Chapter 3), script language for validation scripts (see Chapter 4), and to enable the display of documents in folders beginning with the underscore character, which are hidden by default.

(4) Choose Tools | Options, then click the Configure Editors tab to choose your favorite programs for editing various types of files.

(5) Use the General tab of Tools | Options to decide whether to show the Getting Started dialog box or display any of two warning messages.

(6) Unless you're authoring in another language, you won't need to use the Language tab of the FrontPage Web Settings dialog box.

FrontPage Explorer & Editor—Help Menu

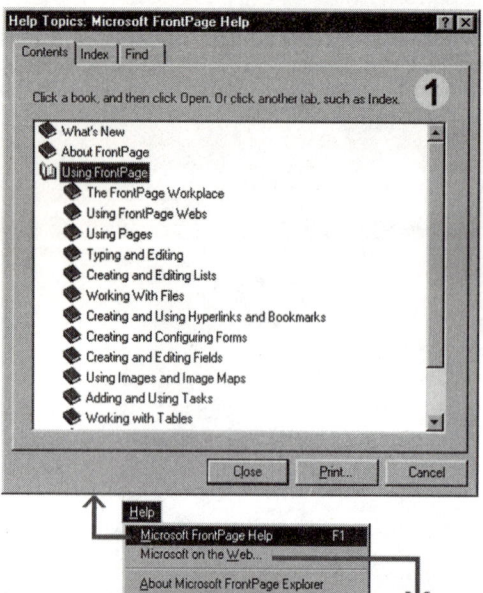

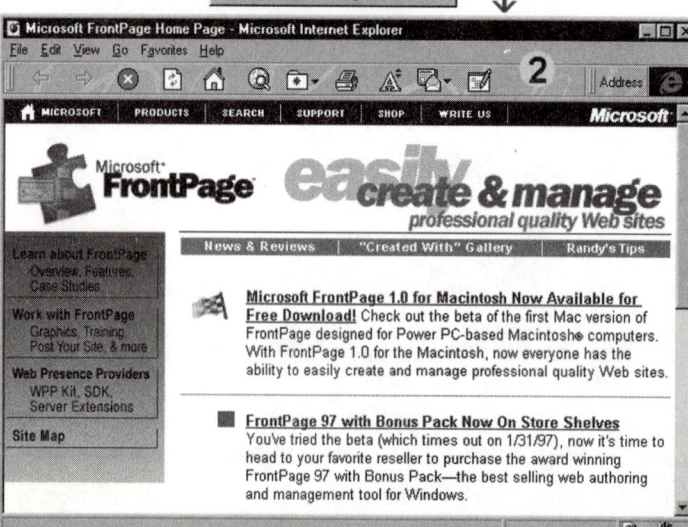

The Help menu is identical for both FrontPage Explorer and the FrontPage Editor.

(1) Choose Microsoft FrontPage Help to open the help viewer. From the help viewer, double-click on a booklet to reveal the topics in that help section. Double-click on a topic to open a help window for that topic.

(2) Choose Microsoft on the Web to open the FrontPage support area on http://www.microsoft.com/frontpage using your web browser and dial-up connection.

About Microsoft FrontPage Explorer or About Microsoft FrontPage Editor (not shown) gives the version number, copyright, and user registration information.

Chapter 10: FrontPage 97 Visual Reference Guide 519

FrontPage Editor—Toolbar Reference

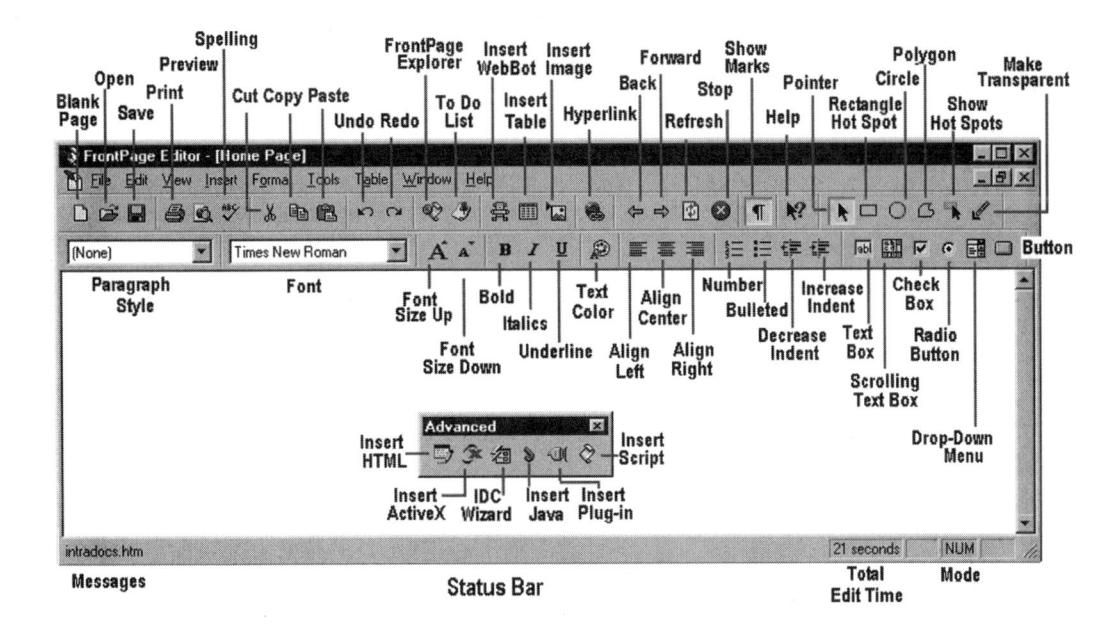

Labels (clockwise around the toolbar screenshot):

- Blank Page
- Open
- Save
- Print
- Preview
- Spelling
- Cut
- Copy
- Paste
- Undo
- Redo
- FrontPage Explorer
- To Do List
- Insert WebBot
- Insert Image
- Insert Table
- Hyperlink
- Forward
- Back
- Stop
- Refresh
- Show Marks
- Pointer
- Help
- Rectangle Hot Spot
- Polygon
- Circle
- Show Hot Spots
- Make Transparent

Second toolbar:

- Paragraph Style
- Font
- Font Size Up
- Font Size Down
- Bold
- Italics
- Underline
- Text Color
- Align Left
- Align Center
- Align Right
- Number Bulleted
- Increase Indent
- Decrease Indent
- Text Box
- Scrolling Text Box
- Check Box
- Radio Button
- Drop-Down Menu
- Button

Advanced toolbar:

- Insert HTML
- Insert ActiveX
- IDC Wizard
- Insert Java
- Insert Plug-in
- Insert Script

Bottom labels:

- Messages
- Status Bar
- Total Edit Time
- Mode

When you don't have access to this book (heaven forbid), you can reveal the pop-up tooltip help for any toolbar button by moving the mouse pointer over a toolbar without clicking and waiting for about a half-second. Once the tooltip appears, you can continue to reveal additional tooltips by moving across the toolbar. Use the Help pointer for more detailed information.

FrontPage Editor—File Menu

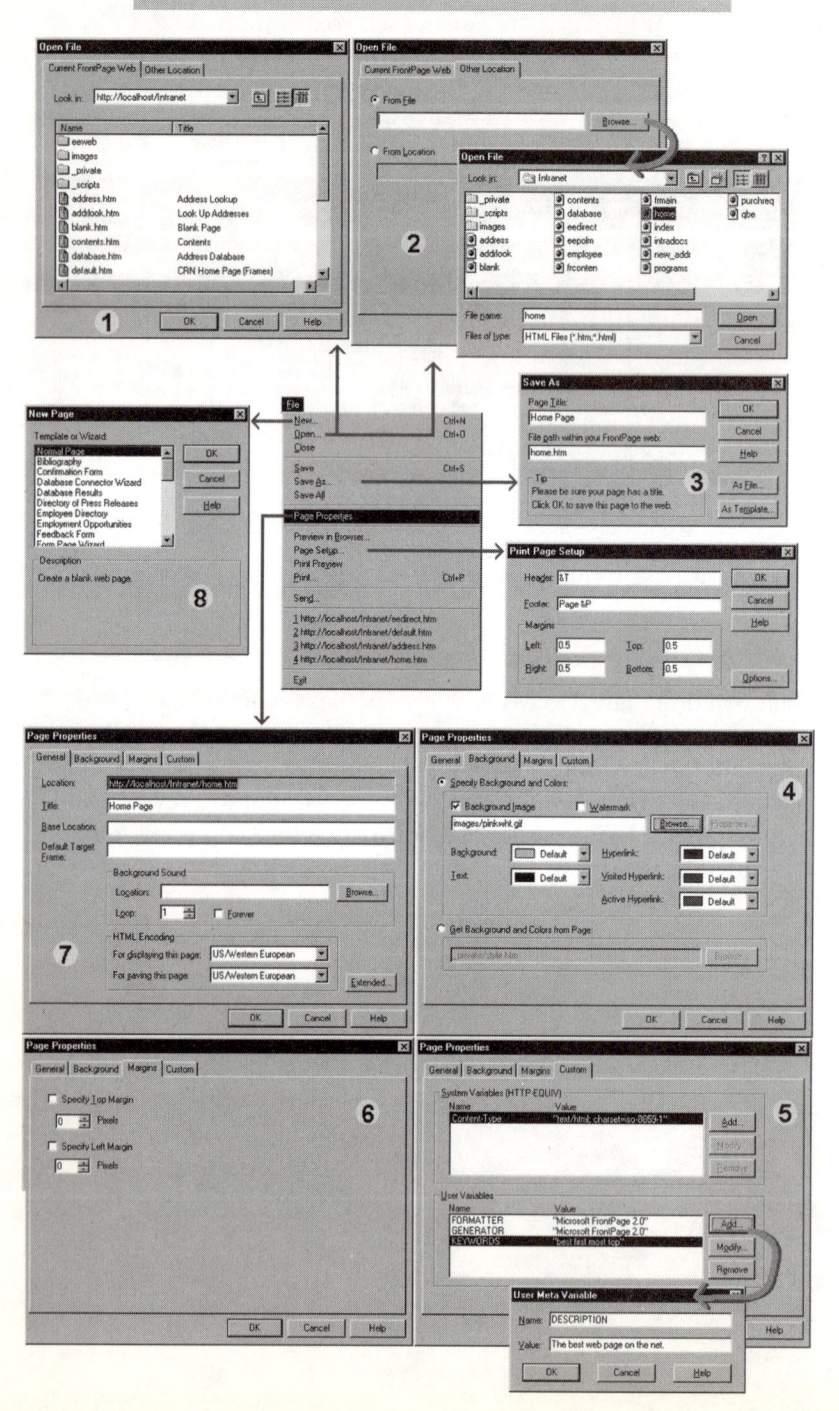

You will use the FrontPage File menu to accomplish the following (clockwise from upper-left):

(1) Choose File | Open and open a web page from the Current FrontPage Web.

(2) Open a web page as a file (use Browse to find the file), or from an Internet location.

(3) Save a web page, choosing a page title and base URL (filename). You can also save the page as a template, so that it always appears on the File | New dialog box.

(4) View the Page Properties. Use the Background tab to choose a page texture or custom colors, or obtain these settings from a "master page." (See Chapter 3.)

(5) Use the Custom tab of Page Properties to add, modify, or remove META tags. See Chapter 5 for a tip on using the META tag.

(6) Use the Margins tab of Page Properties if you want to change the default top and left margin, the offset from the inner corner of the browser window, and the content on that page. This is only supported so far by Internet Explorer.

(7) Use the General tab of Page Properties to change the page title, choose a background sound, or change HTML encoding (changing the latter is not recommended).

(8) Choose File | New to choose a web page template or web page wizard. Refer to "FrontPage Template Reference" at the end of this chapter.

FrontPage Editor—Edit Menu

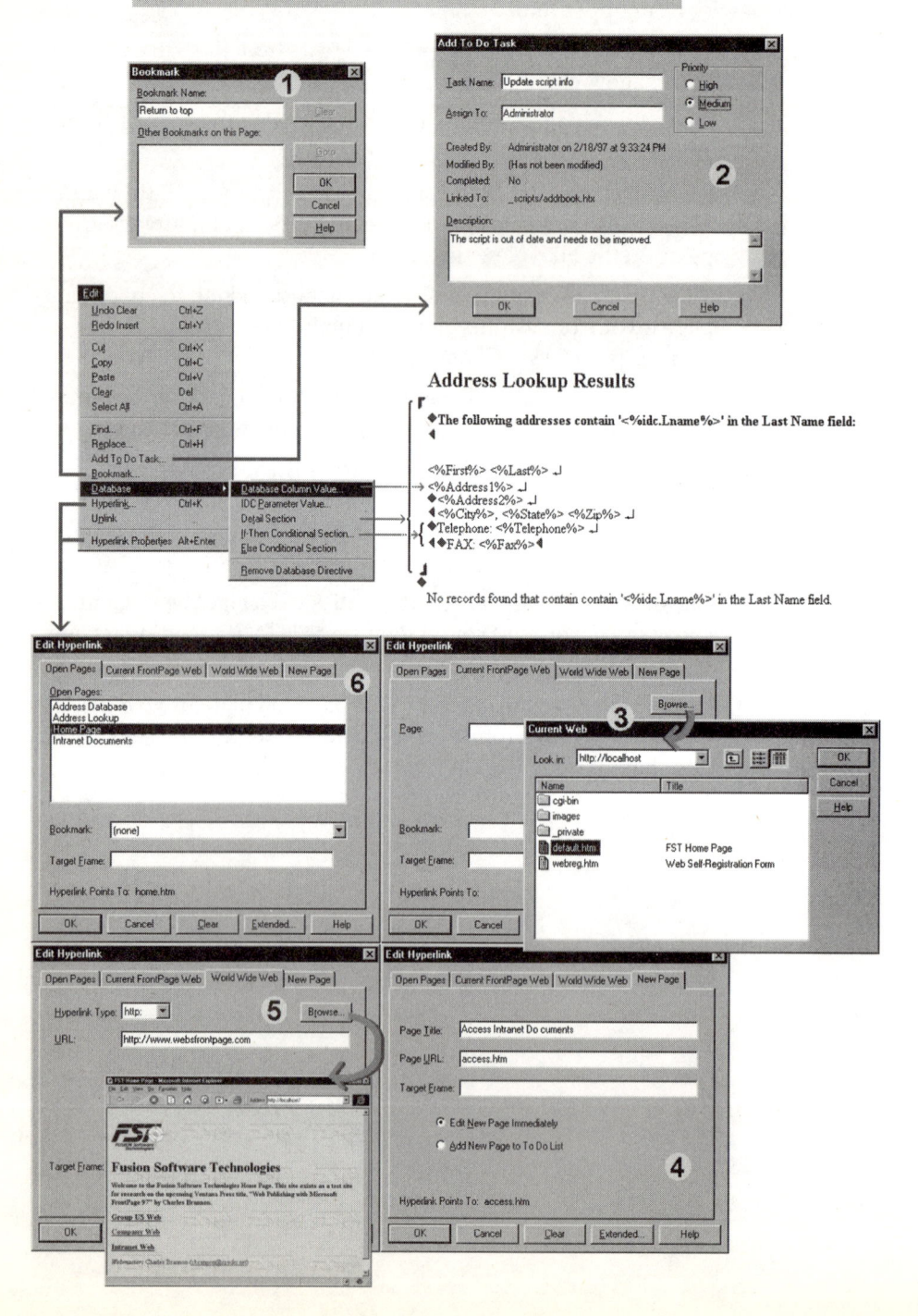

The FrontPage Editor Edit menu contains the usual gang of Undo, Redo, Cut, Copy, Clear, and Select All, used with text editing, selections, and clipboard operations. Use Find to search for text in the current page, or Replace to search and replace. You can also add or edit Internet Database Connector settings and fields (see Chapter 8). Other options include (clockwise from upper left):

(1) Choose Edit | Bookmark to attach a bookmark, a dotted underline, to the position of the text insertion point. Hyperlinks can include the bookmark to jump to that point in the page.

(2) Choose Add To Do Task if you want to add the current page to the list, with instructions on the work that should be performed to complete the page. Double-clicking on that item in the list automatically opens the page.

(3) When creating a hyperlink with Ctrl+K or when editing the properties of an existing hyperlink you can choose a page to link to in the Current FrontPage Web.

(4) You can also link to a page that doesn't exist yet, and either edit the new page immediately, or add it as a task to the To Do List.

(5) A link can point to a location on the World Wide Web (or use another Internet protocol) by choosing Browse and opening the page with the browser. Return to the FrontPage Editor and the current Internet location is inserted.

(6) You can link to any of the currently Open Pages, and choose a bookmark or target frame in a frameset.

FrontPage Editor—View Menu

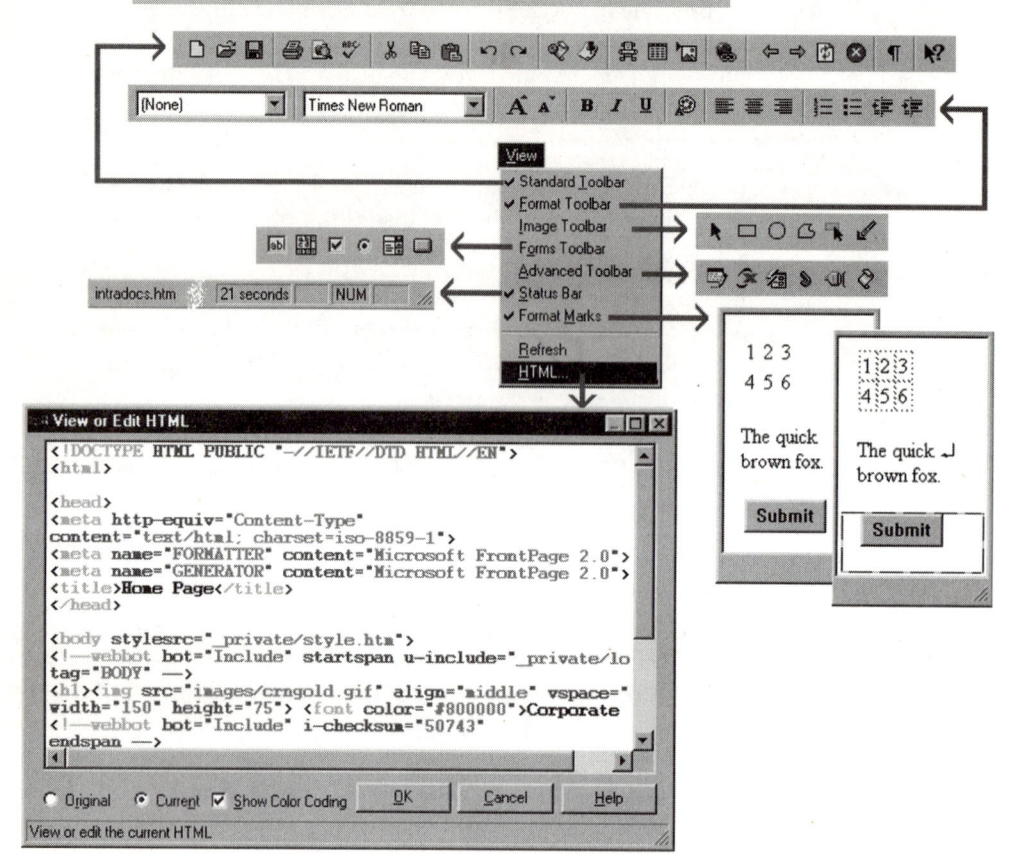

As implied by this illustration, you can use the FrontPage View menu to enable or disable individual toolbars, the status bar, and the display of formatting marks. You can also view and edit the HTML used to generate the current page.

FrontPage Editor—Insert Menu

The FrontPage Editor's Insert menu is at the heart of the enhanced web functionality offered by FrontPage 97. Following are some of the options available (clockwise from top-left, page 526). Also see the facing page.

(1) When you choose to insert an Image, Video, or Background Sound, you can use the Current FrontPage Web dialog box to choose a file from the current web (imported earlier or created in the web with the image editor), or from a file or Internet/intranet location. For images, you can also choose from the clipart installed with FrontPage 97.

(2) Use Insert | Comment to add a hidden comment that is only visible in the FrontPage Editor and invisible when browsed.

(3) Use Break Properties if you want to insert a special line break. It's most useful when you want to choose how the following line is formatted.

(4) Choose Insert | Script to add a general script (in VBScript, Javascript, or another scripting language such as Perlscript) to the page. To attach script events to controls, right-click on a form field and choose Script Wizard from the pop-up menu.

(5) Add a new hyperlink. (For more details, refer to the Edit menu on the previous page.)

(6) Choose a WebBot component.

Refering to page 527:

(1) After you choose Insert | File, you can pick a file type from the drop-down menu, and a file from your hard disk or network. FrontPage can convert many types of files to HTML automatically.

(2) To insert an ActiveX Control, choose a control from the drop-down list, position and size the control on the sample form, and use the Properties button to set the options for the control. You will need to refer to the documentation for the control; some do not offer a full-featured interface.

(3) Refer to Chapter 9 to see how to insert a Java applet.

(4) Refer to the documentation for the Netscape plug-in you want to embed on your page to see how to fill out the various options. Netscape plug-ins are also supported by Internet Explorer 3.01 or later.

(5) To add a Microsoft PowerPoint slide show to your page, choose the PPT file and decide if you want to embed it as an ActiveX control (a complete full-featured slideshow) or as a plug-in (more limited, but compatible with Netscape Navigator).

(6) Use View | HTML to view and/or edit the actual HTML code used to generate the current page. Be sure to save your page before tinkering with its code. Some types of custom HTML will be rejected or mangled by the FrontPage Editor; to overcome this, insert an HTML Markup bot containing the custom code, which will be ignored by FrontPage.

(7) It's easy to insert an Internet Explorer marquee by filling out the self-explanatory Marquee property sheet.

(8) This diagram illustrates the various form fields you can insert on a page.

(9) Choose Insert | Symbol to add a special symbol, many of which are not available from the keyboard. Some symbols are not understood by Netscape Navigator, such as the TM symbol.

Web Publishing With FrontPage 97

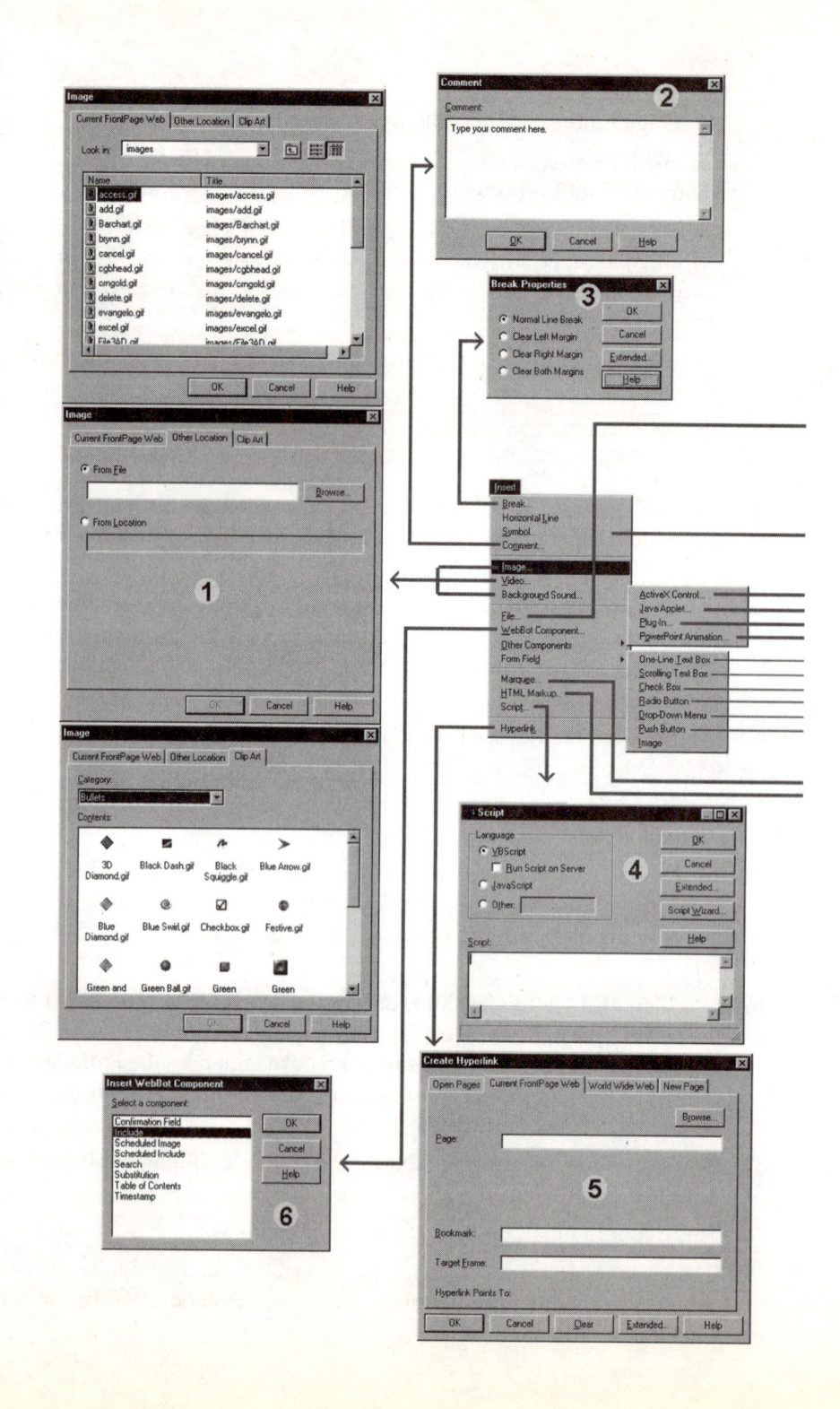

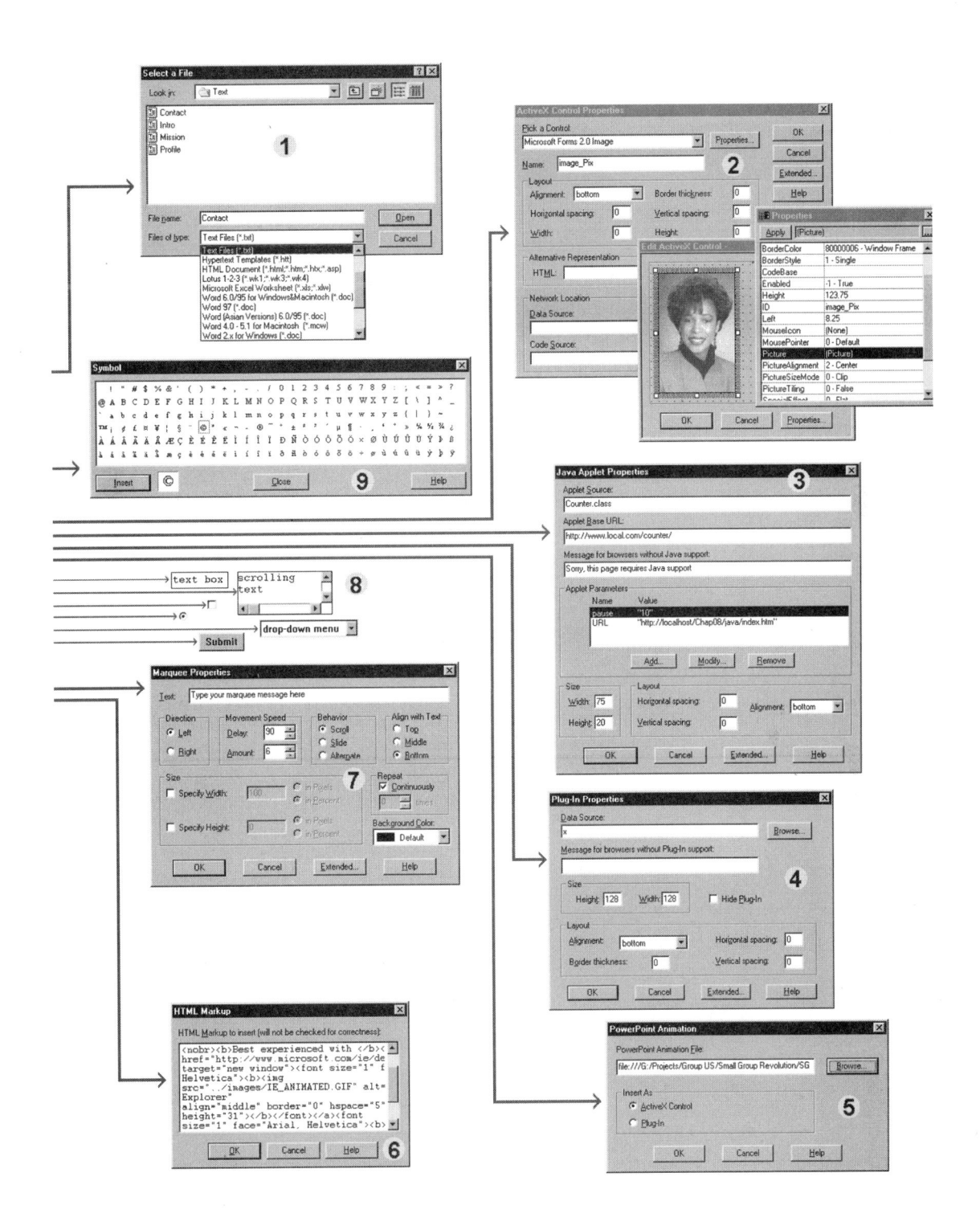

Chapter 10: FrontPage 97 Visual Reference Guide

FrontPage Editor—Tools Menu

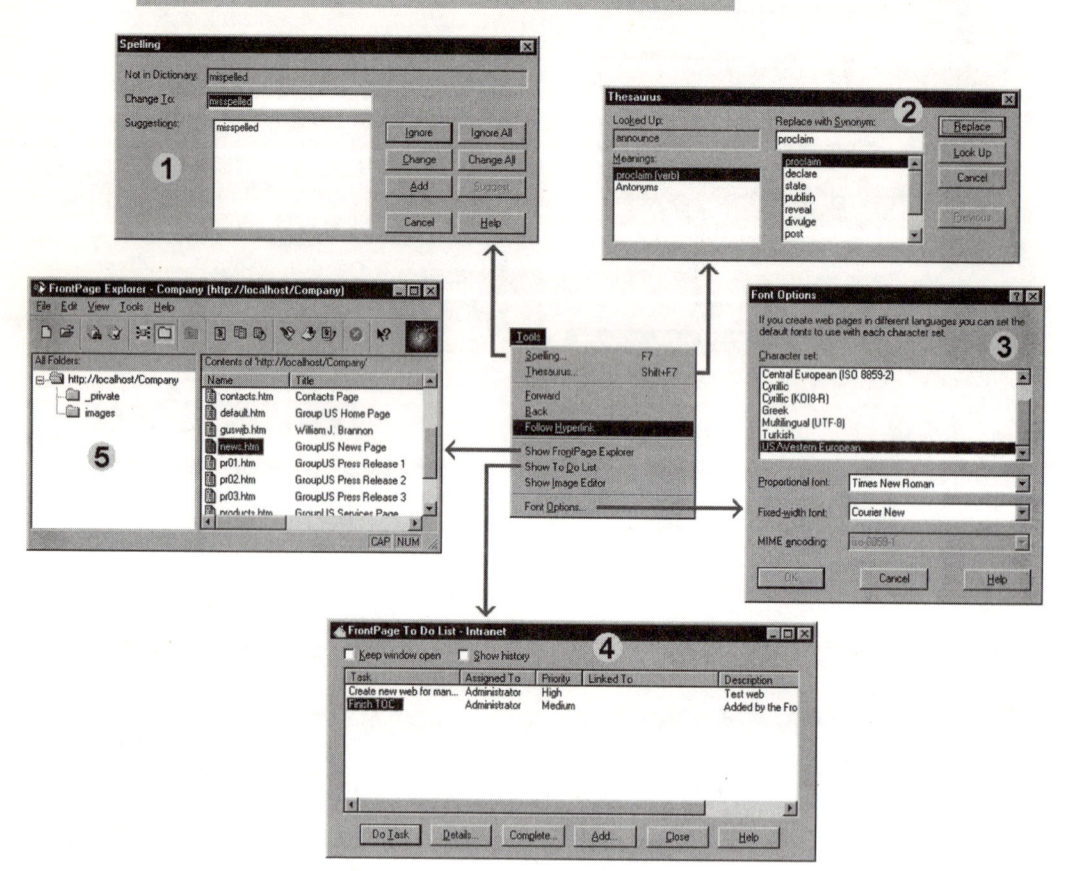

The FrontPage Editor tools are straightforward. Clockwise from upper-left:

(1) Always run a spelling check on a page before you save it. You can check an individual word or phrase by selecting it and pressing F7.

(2) To look up the current word in the thesaurus, press Shift+F7. Click the Replace button if you want to choose an alternative word.

(3) You won't need to change the Font Options unless you're developing your page in a language other than U.S. English.

(4) You can reveal the To Do List if you need to see which tasks remain to be completed.

(5) You can switch to or open the FrontPage Explorer at any time.

FrontPage Editor—Table Menu

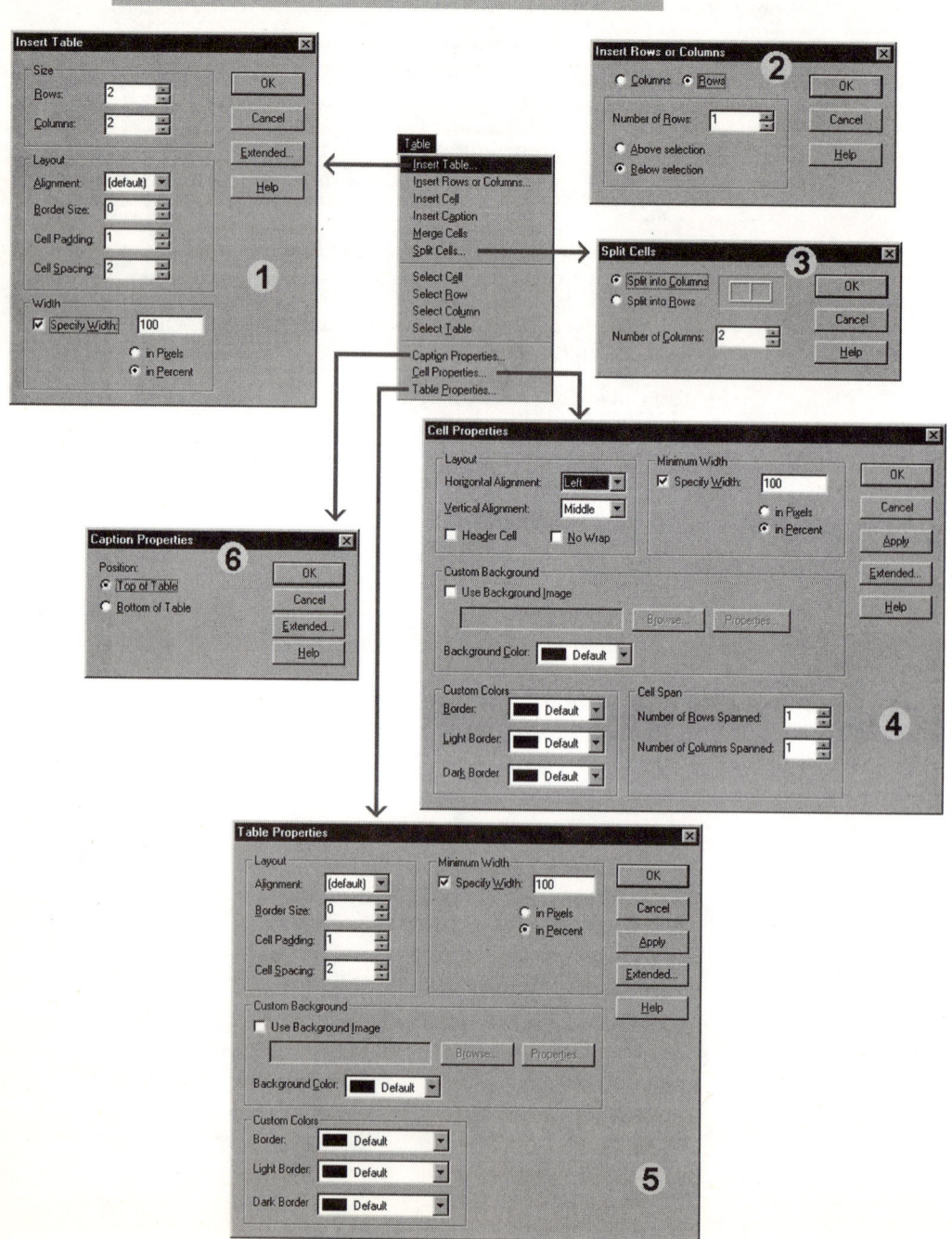

HTML tables are difficult to hand-code, but a breeze with the FrontPage Editor Table menu. Remember that primitive HTML 1.1 browsers can not properly display tables, and some table options such as background color are only supported on the most recent version of browsers. Always check your tables with both Internet Explorer and Netscape Navigator. Clockwise from upper left:

(1) Choose Table | Insert Table (or use the Insert Table toolbar button) to add a table at the text insertion point. The settings you choose here will be used for future tables you create. See Chapter 3.

(2) Choose Table | Insert Rows or Columns to add new rows or columns.

(3) You can split a single cell into subcells that together take up the same width as the original cell, but can each hold unique content.

(4) Choose Table | Cell Properties (or right-click within a cell and choose the same menu option from the pop-up menu) to format a cell. This also applies to a range of cells you've selected. See Chapter 3.

(5) Choose Table Properties to alter an existing table and set background colors or images.

(6) After choosing Insert Caption, you can choose whether the caption is aligned at the top or bottom of the table. Rarely used.

FrontPage WebBot Reference

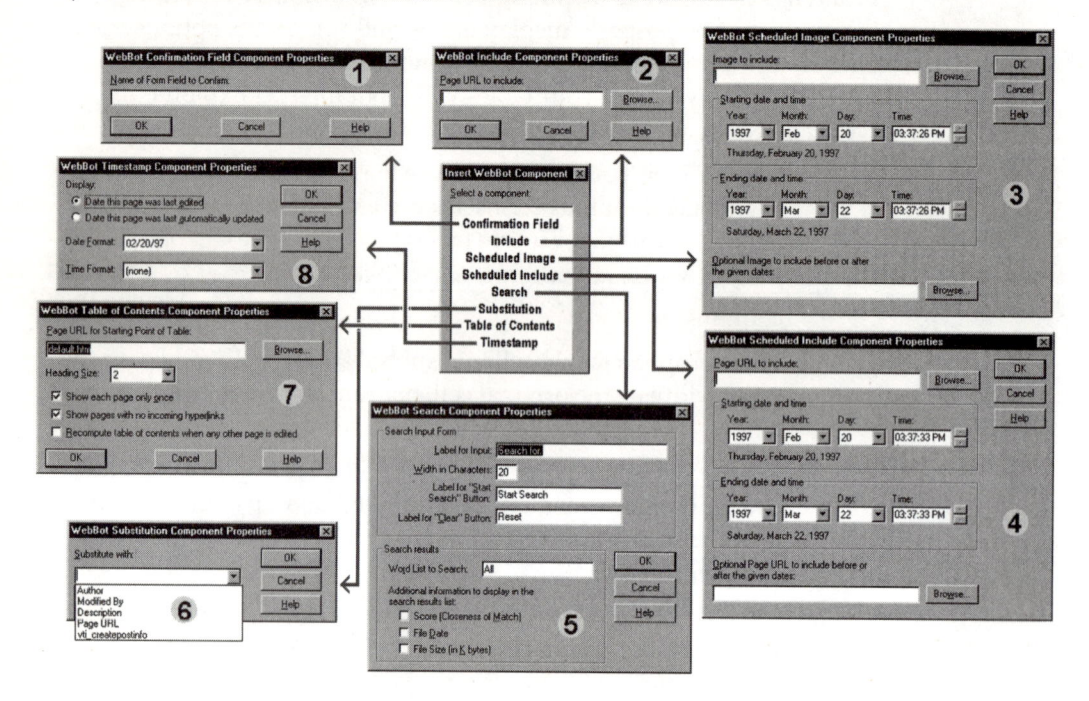

Most FrontPage WebBots only work on a web published to a server running FrontPage extensions as the pages are browsed. A few only require a local web server during authoring time. See Chapter 5 for more details. Clockwise from upper left:

(1) Insert a Confirmation Field WebBot on a custom confirmation page that you can specify with the Save Results WebBot, a form handler specified with the Form Properties of a form containing form fields on a page. See Chapter 4. (Browse-time WebBot)

(2) Use the Include WebBot to embed, in effect, the content of another page, like a master logo page, within the current page. (Authoring-time WebBot)

(3) You can choose to have an image appear on a web page during a range of dates and times. Outside of this range, the image will not appear when the page is browsed, even though it is still included on the page. Pages with this WebBot are only updated (the image shown or hidden) if the page is routinely edited, or if the FrontPage Explorer Tools | Recalculate Hyperlinks menu option is chosen. (Authoring-time WebBot)

(4) The Scheduled Include works the same way, but can include any web page content, not just an image.

(5) You can add a Search button to any page that returns pages in your web that match the user's search criteria. The search is performed against the full-text index maintained as you edit the pages in the web. For a full-featured search page, choose File | New, and pick the Search Page template. (Indexing occurs at authoring time, but Search is a Browse-time WebBot.)

(6) Insert a Substitution Parameter WebBot to show some text that is associated with a name that you have edited in FrontPage Explorer's Tools | Web Settings dialog box.

(7) You can insert an automatic table of contents listing at the position of the text insertion point. This TOC can be generated only once, from the current state of the web, or it can be recomputed whenever any page is added or edited. If you omit the latter option, the TOC is updated whenever you open the page containing the TOC WebBot. The TOC can only "see" the current web. If used on the root web, you can not include on the TOC the pages in subwebs.

(8) Use a Timestamp WebBot to mark when the page was last edited or updated. You can choose how the timestamp is formtatted.

FrontPage Template Reference

Web Self-Registration Form

Web Self-Registration Form

Fill out and submit the following form to register yourself as a member of the discussion called *Discussion*.

Comment: You selected the option to have your discussion inside a protected web. First you'll need to change the Web Permissions from the Explorer's Tools menu. Make the permissions unique for this web, and then set the End User access control so that only registered users may enter. Next, open the Root Web for this server, and save this document into it. Now users will be able to register themselves to use the protected discussion web.

Username:

Password:

Verify password:

[Register Me] [Reset Form]

Directory of Press Releases

Comment: Use this page to organize your press releases by date and title. Place the most recent entries first. Each entry should be a link to a separate press release document. Once a month, copy the contents of each section to the next section below it.

Press Release Directory

- This Month's Releases
- Last Month's Releases
- Prior Releases

This Month's Releases

Mm-Dd-Yy
   Title of Announcement 6
   Title of Announcement 5

Employee Directory

> Comment: Create an alphabetized list of employee names in the first section below. Each item should be a link to a bookmark later on the page holding contact information for the named employee. Encourage everyone to include a small photograph of themselves. If the list of employees becomes too large, try using a format like the Glossary template, with a section for each letter of the alphabet.

Company Logo

Employee Directory

Alphabetical listing, by last name:

- Alastname, Afirstname
- Blastname, Bfirstname
- Clastname, Cfirstname
-
- Zlastname, Zfirstname

Alastname, Afirstname

Employee Opportunities

> Comment: Replace the sample job descriptions and requirements presented below with ones more appropriate to your company's needs. Each position should have its own section delimited by horizontal lines, a bookmarked heading, and a link from the main Listing by Job Title. There is a form at the bottom of the page where readers can express their interest in a position with the company.

Company Logo

Employment Opportunities

Listings by Job Title:

- Software Engineer
- Technical Writer
- Publications Coordinator
- Marketing Manager
- Chief Financial Officer

If none of these positions match what you're looking for, you can write a brief statement about your skills and requirements and submit it to our personnel file using the form at the bottom of this page. The next time a position opens up, we'll look for potential matches in this file before we begin a wider search.

Feedback Form

Form Page Wizard

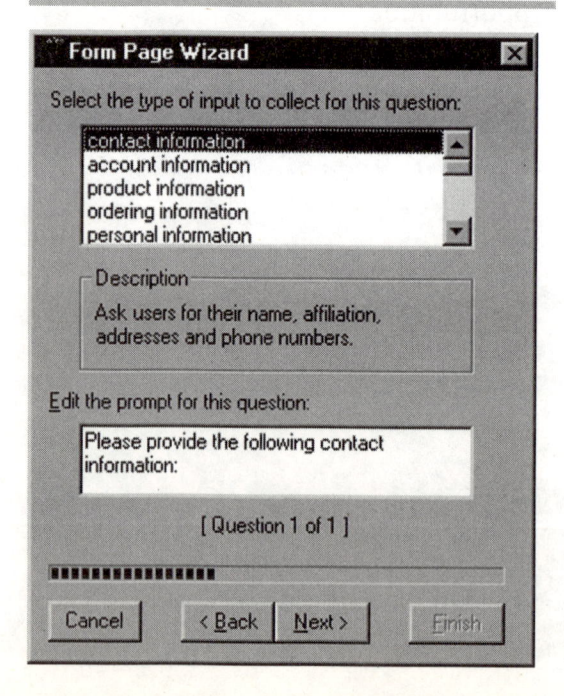

Frames Wizard

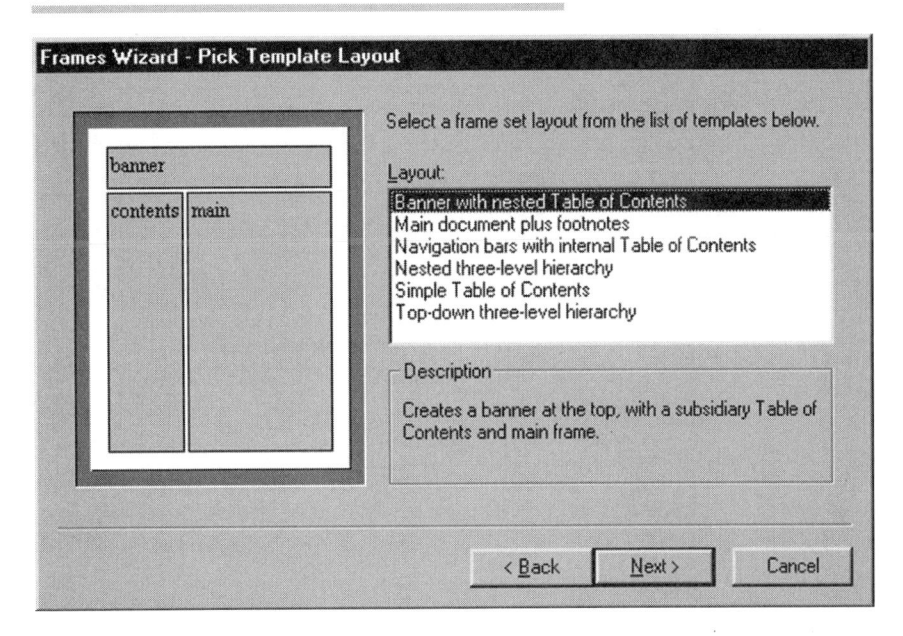

Frames Wizard - Pick Template Layout

Select a frame set layout from the list of templates below.

Layout:
- Banner with nested Table of Contents
- Main document plus footnotes
- Navigation bars with internal Table of Contents
- Nested three-level hierarchy
- Simple Table of Contents
- Top-down three-level hierarchy

Description

Creates a banner at the top, with a subsidiary Table of Contents and main frame.

< Back | Next > | Cancel

Frequently Asked Questions

Comment: Add new questions at the end of the Table of Contents list. For each new question, create a new section where the heading contains the text of the question, followed by one or more paragraphs presenting the answer.

Answers to Frequently Asked Questions

Table of Contents

1. How do I ... ?
2. Where can I find ... ?
3. Why doesn't ... ?
4. Who is ... ?
5. What is ... ?
6. When is ... ?

How do I ... ?

[This is the answer to the question.]

Back to Top

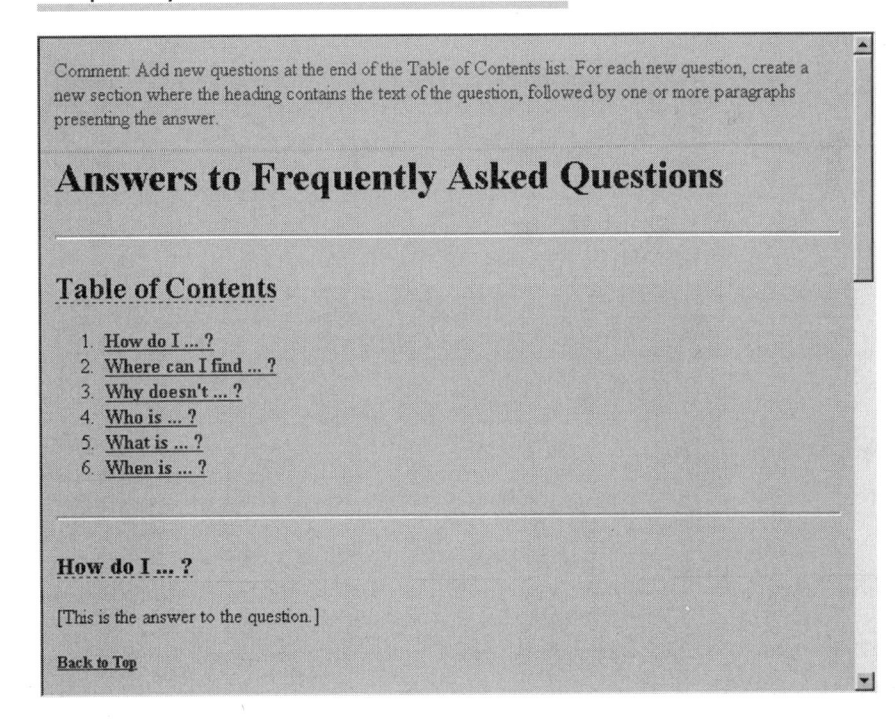

Glossary of Terms

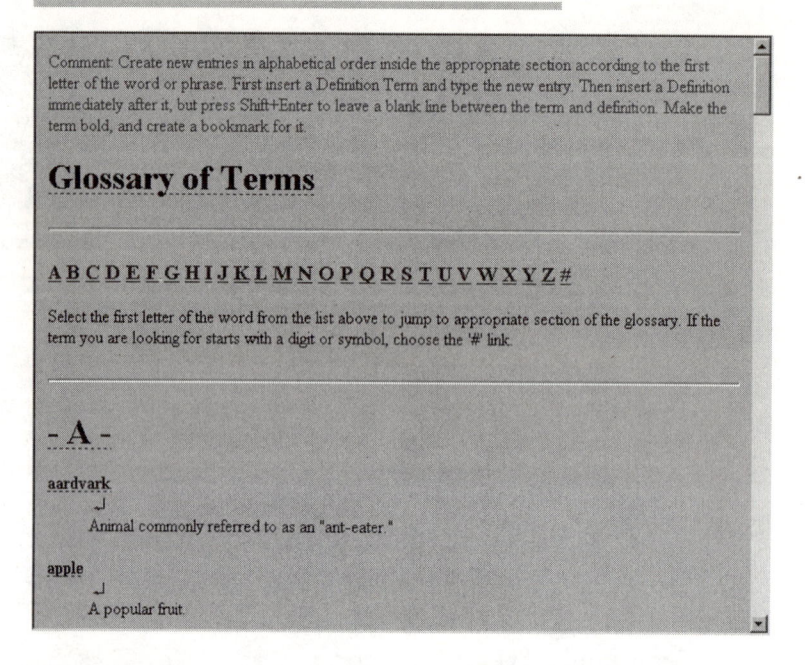

> Comment: Create new entries in alphabetical order inside the appropriate section according to the first letter of the word or phrase. First insert a Definition Term and type the new entry. Then insert a Definition immediately after it, but press Shift+Enter to leave a blank line between the term and definition. Make the term bold, and create a bookmark for it.
>
> # Glossary of Terms
>
> A B C D E F G H I J K L M N O P Q R S T U V W X Y Z #
>
> Select the first letter of the word from the list above to jump to appropriate section of the glossary. If the term you are looking for starts with a digit or symbol, choose the '#' link.
>
> - A -
>
> **aardvark**
> Animal commonly referred to as an "ant-eater."
>
> **apple**
> A popular fruit.

Guest Book

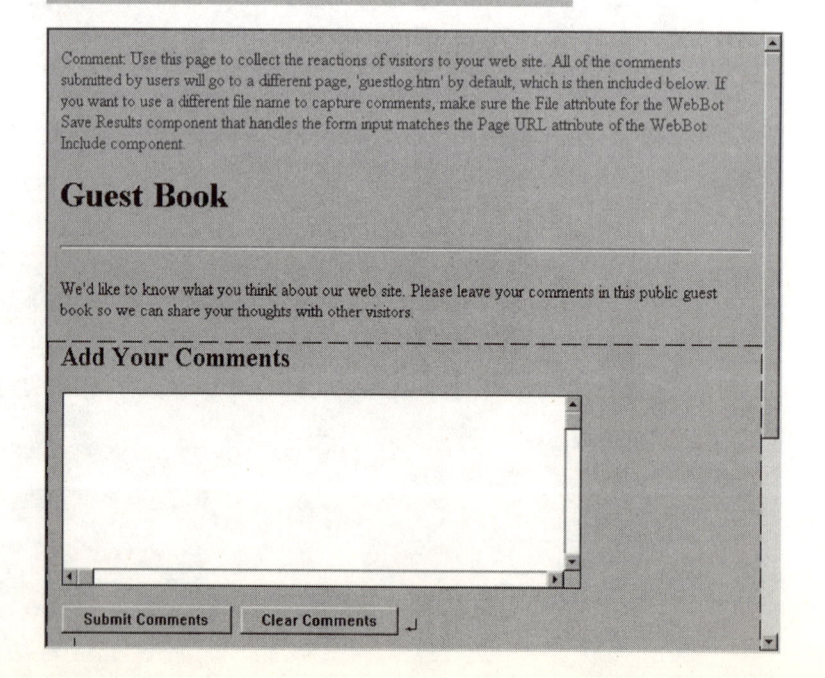

> Comment: Use this page to collect the reactions of visitors to your web site. All of the comments submitted by users will go to a different page, 'guestlog.htm' by default, which is then included below. If you want to use a different file name to capture comments, make sure the File attribute for the WebBot Save Results component that handles the form input matches the Page URL attribute of the WebBot Include component.
>
> # Guest Book
>
> We'd like to know what you think about our web site. Please leave your comments in this public guest book so we can share your thoughts with other visitors.
>
> **Add Your Comments**
>
> [text area]
>
> [Submit Comments] [Clear Comments]

Hot List

Comment: Create categories for the sites you want to present on your Hot List page. Create a link for each category in the Table of Contents section. For each category, write a few sentences explaining your rationale for including sites in the list. Each entry should be a link to a page, with the text being either the page title or a descriptive phrase.

Hot List for [Subject Area]

Table of Contents

This page contains links to web sites and pages having to do with [Subject Area]. The information is divided into the following categories:

- Category 1
- Category 2
- Category 3
- Category 4
- Category 5

Category 1

This is an explanation of what the links in this category have in common.

- Site 1

HyperDocument Page

Comment: This page is meant to be one section of a large hyperlinked manual or report. Fill in the document name and section name below, and link them to the hyperdocument's home page and Table of Contents page respectively. Replace the gray buttons with icons appropriate to each section's content.

HyperDocument Name / *Section Name*

PAGE TITLE

Subsection Title 1

[Body of Section 1]

Back to Top

Subsection Title 2

[Body of Section 2]

Back to Top

Lecture Abstract

Comment: Use this page to announce an upcoming lecture, talk, or round-table discussion. Fill in the items in square brackets, and provide a list of topics.

[Lecture Title]

[Speaker Name], [Role]
[Organization]
[Date and Time]

[The abstract for the lecture goes here; it should be no more than a couple of paragraphs.]

Topics covered include:

- Topic 1
- Topic 2
- Topic 3
- Topic 4
- Topic 5

Back to seminar or workshop schedule

[The speaker's biography goes here.]

Meeting Agenda

Comment: Fill in the correct date, time, location, and purpose of the meeting, along with a list of the major topics to be covered, and who should attend.

Meeting Agenda

Date -- August 1st, 1995
Time -- 9:15
Location -- Main Conference Room

Purpose -- This short paragraph describes the intended outcome of the meeting.

Topics for Discussion

1. Description of Topic 1
2. Description of Topic 2
3. Description of Topic 3
4. Description of Topic 4
5. Description of Topic 5

Attendees

- Department 1
- Project 1

Office Directory

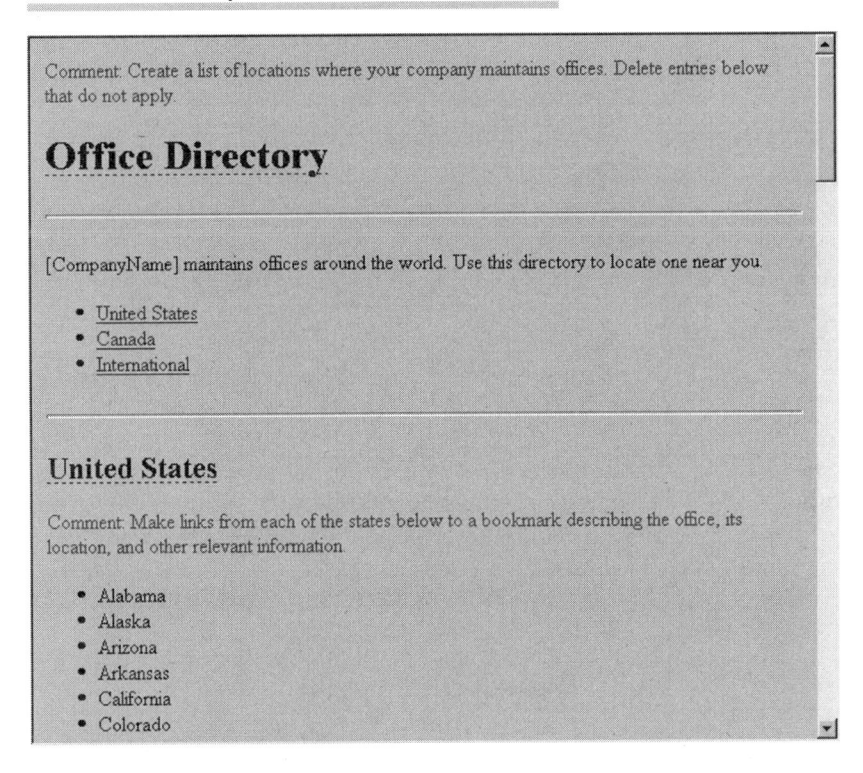

> Comment: Create a list of locations where your company maintains offices. Delete entries below that do not apply.
>
> # Office Directory
>
> [CompanyName] maintains offices around the world. Use this directory to locate one near you.
>
> - United States
> - Canada
> - International
>
> ## United States
>
> Comment: Make links from each of the states below to a bookmark describing the office, its location, and other relevant information.
>
> - Alabama
> - Alaska
> - Arizona
> - Arkansas
> - California
> - Colorado

Personal Home Page Wizard

Personal Home Page Wizard

This wizard helps you create a customized personal Home Page. Use it to tell friends and colleagues about yourself, and to publish links to information you are providing or have located.

Select the major sections for your Home Page:

- ☑ Employee Information
- ☐ Current Projects
- ☑ Hot List: Interesting Web Sites
- ☐ Biographical Information
- ☐ Personal Interests
- ☑ Contact Information
- ☑ Comments and Suggestions

[Cancel] [< Back] [Next >] [Finish]

Personal Home Page Wizard

The Employee Information section is used to describe your job role and responsibilities to other people in your organization.

Select the information to include in this section:

- ☑ Job title
- ☑ Key responsibilities
- ☑ Department or workgroup
- ☐ Manager
- ☐ Direct reports

NOTE: the wizard will create sample links to other employee web pages where appropriate. You can change these links later using the FrontPage editor.

[Cancel] [< Back] [Next >] [Finish]

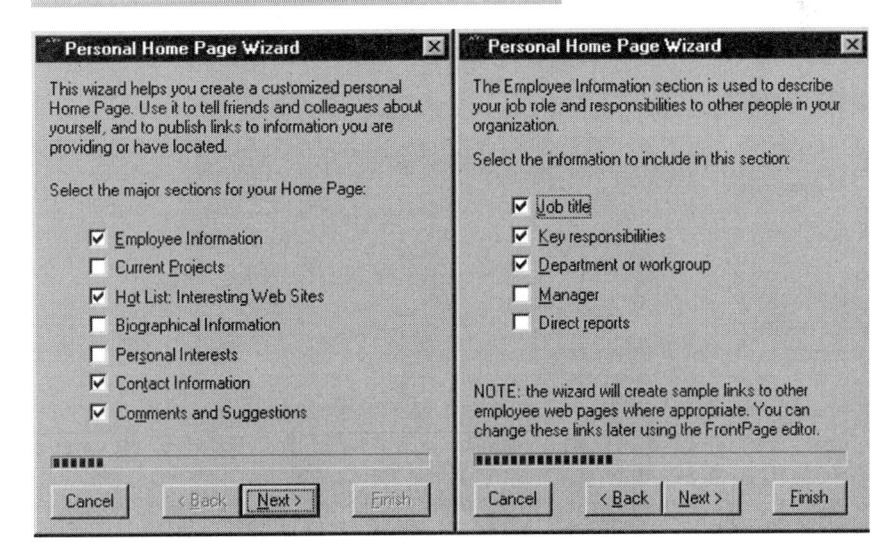

Press Release

> Comment: Replace the text in square brackets, and insert the body of your press release in the section starting with 'Dateline'.
>
> # Press Release Title
>
> ***Subtitle of Announcement***
>
> ---
>
> Dateline -- [OrganizationName] today announced ...
>
> [The body of the press release goes here.]
>
> ---
>
> [OrganizationName] is the leading supplier of a certain kind of products to a particular industry. It has a long history as a successful organization.
>
> **For Further Information Contact:**
> [OrganizationName]
> [OrganizationAddress]
> Tel: [PhoneNumber]
> FAX: [FaxNumber]
> e-mail: [EmailAdddress]
> URL: [http://www.your.org.addr]

Product Description

> Comment: Write a brief description of the product's highlights for the Summary section. Then create a list of the most important differentiating features. Finally, present the major benefits of your product in separate sections below. Some products may require a list of specifications at the end of the document.
>
> # Product Name
>
> ---
>
> ## Contents:
>
> - Product Summary
> - Key Features
> - Benefit Heading 1
> - Benefit Heading 2
> - Benefit Heading 3
> - Specifications
>
> ---
>
> ## Product Summary
>
> [PRODUCT IMAGE]
>
> [This is a brief introduction to product and its benefits from the customer's perspective.]
>
> Back to Top

Product or Event Registration

> Comment: Create a registration form for a product or event. Fill in the text in square brackets, and change the input areas to gather the information you require. If you want to change how user input is stored, edit the properties of the WebBot Save Results component that handles form input.

Registration Form

[The instructions for registration go here.]

User Information

```
    First Name: [_____]
     Last Name: [_____]
         Title: [_____]
       Company: [_____]
Street Address: [_____]
          City: [_____]
         State: [_____]
      Zip Code: [_____]
     Telephone: [_____]
           FAX: [_____]
        E-mail: [_____]
           URL: [_____]
```

Search Page

> Comment: This page lets you search through the default text index that is created whenever web pages are saved or web links are recalculated. No customization is required.

Text Search

Use the form below to search for documents in this web containing specific words or combinations of words. The text search engine will display a weighted list of matching documents, with better matches shown first. Each list item is a link to a matching document; if the document has a title it will be shown, otherwise only the document's file name is displayed. A brief explanation of the query language is available, along with examples.

Search for: [_____]

[Start Search] [Clear]

Query Language

The text search engine allows queries to be formed from arbitrary Boolean expressions containing the keywords AND, OR, and NOT, and grouped with parentheses. For example:

```
information retrieval
    finds documents containing 'information' or 'retrieval'

information or retrieval
    same as above
```

Seminar Schedule

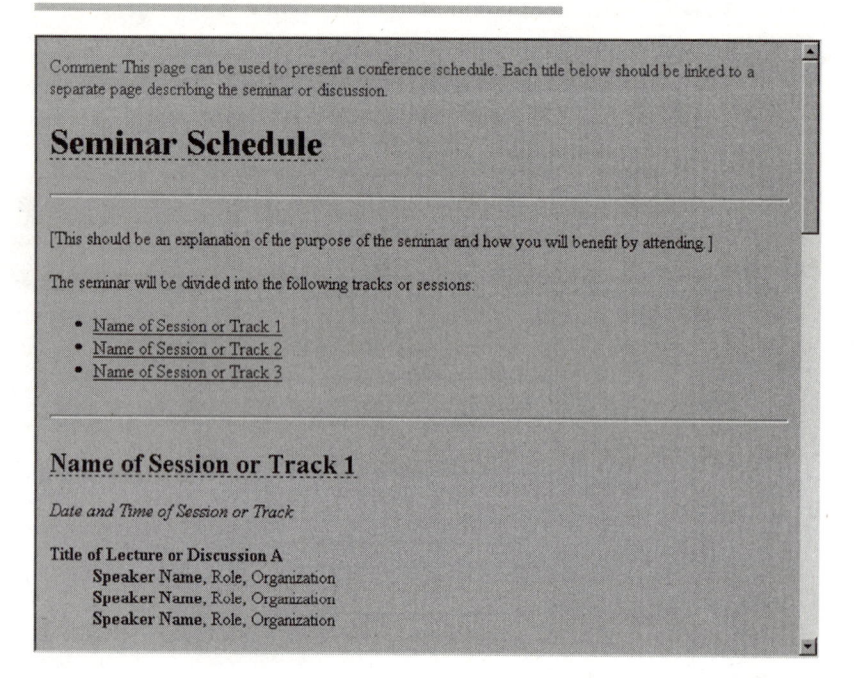

> Comment: This page can be used to present a conference schedule. Each title below should be linked to a separate page describing the seminar or discussion.
>
> # Seminar Schedule
>
> [This should be an explanation of the purpose of the seminar and how you will benefit by attending.]
>
> The seminar will be divided into the following tracks or sessions:
>
> - Name of Session or Track 1
> - Name of Session or Track 2
> - Name of Session or Track 3
>
> ### Name of Session or Track 1
>
> *Date and Time of Session or Track*
>
> **Title of Lecture or Discussion A**
>   **Speaker Name**, Role, Organization
>   **Speaker Name**, Role, Organization
>   **Speaker Name**, Role, Organization

Software Data Sheet

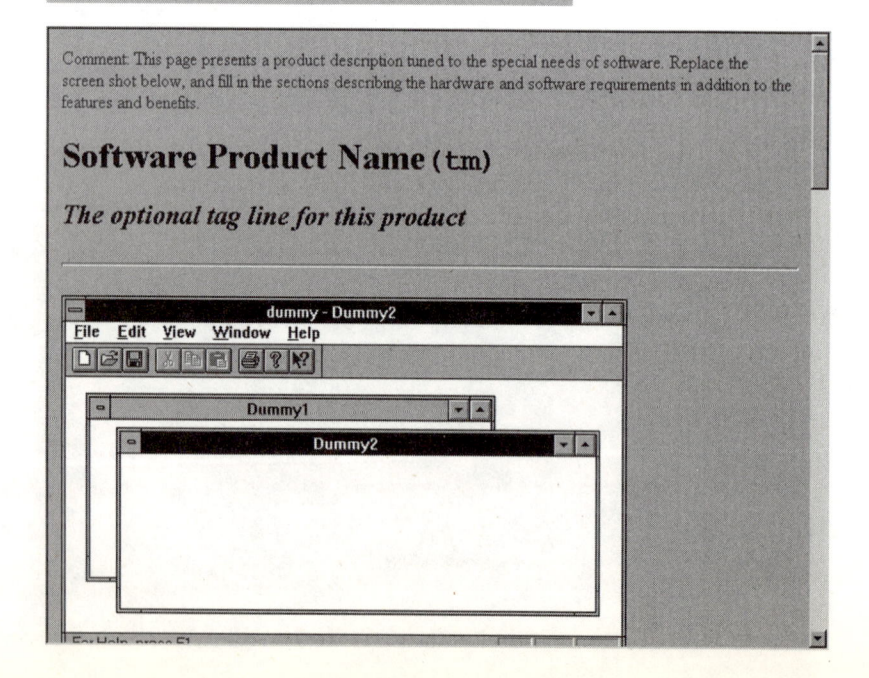

> Comment: This page presents a product description tuned to the special needs of software. Replace the screen shot below, and fill in the sections describing the hardware and software requirements in addition to the features and benefits.
>
> # Software Product Name (tm)
>
> *The optional tag line for this product*

Survey Form

> Comment: Replace the sample questions on this page with ones more appropriate to your needs. You may find the Form Page Wizard useful in this task. Adjust the WebBot Save Results component settings on the form to save the results in a text or HTML file as appropriate.
>
> **Name of Organization Requesting Information**
>
> # Information Survey
>
> The purpose of this survey is to collect information from you about something. The purpose of this survey is to collect information from you about something. The purpose of this survey is to collect information from you about something. The purpose of this survey is to collect information from you about something. The purpose of this survey is to collect information from you about something. The purpose of this survey is to collect information from you about something.
>
> This survey is divided into the following sections:
>
> - Section A
> - Section B
> - Section C
> - Form Submission
>
> Fill out the information in each section as requested. Then at the end of the form supply your name and contact information, and submit the form. You will receive a confirmation message from us shortly.

Table of Contents

> Comment: Adjust the settings for the WebBot Table of Contents component below, which shows all of the pages that can be reached from the given starting page by following links. If you choose to have the list of documents updated automatically, it can increase the amount of time it takes to save a page while editing.
>
> # Table of Contents
>
> The following is a hierarchical listing of all the pages in this web that can be reached by following links from the top-level file "index.htm". Page titles are displayed if they exist, otherwise the entries are file names. Unreachable files are shown at the bottom of the list.
>
> **Table of Contents Heading Page**
>
> - Title of a Page
> - Title of a Page
> - Title of a Page

User Registration

Comment: NOTE: Some web servers do not allow self-registration. When you save this page to a web, the FrontPage Explorer will test for this capability, and flag the page with a red triangle in the Outline view if there is a problem.

Comment: This page must be saved into the Root Web in order to function properly. After users fill out and submit the form on this page, they will become registered users of another web on the server. The target web must already exist before you save this page. First edit the form's properties to set the name of the target web, which cannot be the Root Web. Then use the Search/Replace feature to change all instances of the text [OtherWeb] on this page with the title of the target web, such as "New Ideas Web" or "Employee Discussion Web".

User Registration for [OtherWeb]

You can automatically register yourself to be a user of [OtherWeb] by filling out and submitting this form. Only registered users are allowed into [OtherWeb]. Choose a username for yourself (such as your last name) and a private password. Together these will be your "key" into [OtherWeb] from now on. This information will be kept in a registration database that is accessible only to the webmaster, not to ordinary users.

One of the main benefits of having a protected web like [OtherWeb] is that authorized users don't have to keep typing their names into form fields, such as when submitting an article to a discussion group, because the web server already knows who they are. Similarly, other users can be reasonably sure that you really sent the articles and postings attributed to you, that someone else didn't pretend to be you when posting.

After you are successfully registered, your web browser will ask you to type in your username and password the first time you try to access [OtherWeb]. The browser will remember this information for as long as it continues to run, so you can access any document in [OtherWeb] without being asked for it again.

Bibliography

Comment: Create entries in alphabetical order, each with its own unique bookmark. Make links to on-line texts whenever possible.

Bibliography

ALastName, FirstInitial. Year. *Title of publication*. City, State: Publisher.

BLastName, FirstInitial. Year. *Title of publication*. City, State: Publisher.

CLastName, FirstInitial. Year. *Title of publication*. City, State: Publisher.

Revised: February 18, 1997.

What's New

> Comment: Once you create this page, keep it up to date by making an entry here every time you make a significant change to your web site. Clear out old entries every month so it appears fresh and up-to-date for frequent visitors.
>
> # What's New?
>
> The following is a list of the major changes to this web over the last month, with the most recent changes shown first:
>
> **DateOfChanges**
>   Synopsis of change and link to relevant page
>   Synopsis of change and link to relevant page
>
> **DateOfChanges**
>   Synopsis of change and link to relevant page
>   Synopsis of change and link to relevant page
>
> **07-05-95**
>   Created this What's New page.

Customer Support Web

> # Customer Support Web
>
> [Welcome | What's New | FAQ | Bugs | Suggestions | Download | Discussion | Search]
>
> ## WELCOME
>
> Welcome to [CompanyName]. The purpose of this web is to enhance the support services we provide to our customers. We've provided a number of resources here to help you resolve problems, report bugs, and suggest improvements to our products and service.
>
> You may also obtain technical support by telephone at [CompanyPhone]; and by e-mail to [CompanyEmail].
>
> [TmName1] and [TmName2] are trademarks of [CompanyName]. All other products mentioned are registered trademarks or trademarks of their respective companies.
> Questions or problems regarding this web site should be directed to [CompanyEmail].
> Copyright © 1995 [CompanyName]. All rights reserved.
> Last modified: Tuesday February 18, 1997.

Personal Web

My Home Page

Contents

- Employee Information
- Current Projects
- Hot List
- Biographical Information
- Personal Interests
- Contact Information
- Comments and Suggestions

Employee Information

Job title
My official title

Key responsibilities
A brief explanation of my official duties

Project Web

Project Web

[Home | Members | Schedule | Status | Archive | Search | Discussions]

HOME

Welcome to the home page for Project. Take a look at What's New in our web.

Comment: Write a brief statment about the purpose and direction of the project.

What's New

The following is a list of recent additions to our web. Whenever we publish a paper, write a specification, submit a status report, or add anything else to our web, we'll put a notice here. Every month we'll remove the oldest items. The most recent changes are listed first, and each item is linked to the page with the updated content.

Date 3

- Description of Change 6

appendix A

About the Companion CD-ROM

The Companion CD-ROM included with your copy of *Web Publishing With FrontPage97* contains valuable shareware plus example files to be used in conjunction with the projects described in the book.

Navigating the CD-ROM

WINDOWS 95/NT:
If Windows "autorun" is not enabled, double-click on the LAUNCH.EXE file. Or go to START | RUN and type d:\(where d is the name of your CD-ROM drive) launch.exe in the space provided. You will see a small menu screen offering several choices. They include quitting the CD, viewing the readme, or launching the installers. For more detailed instructions on how to use the author example files, see below.

Instructions for Example Projects

Please visit the site http://www.WebsFrontPage.com, maintained independently by the author as a resource for the readers of this book and for all FrontPage users.

Also visit the Ventana web site at http://www.vmedia.com/updates for other updated information or corrections.

Book Projects on CD-ROM

The \Palettes folder contains PAL files for use with PaintShop Pro or Microsoft Image Composer when converting GIF files to web format. The \SampleDB folder contains database files used as examples. Refer to Chapter 7 to learn how to copy these to your computer and set up an ODBC32 system data source for them.

The \Webs folder contains subfolders for the projects demonstrated in this book, named according to the chapter, as in Chap01, Chap02, and so on. Inside each folder is another folder containing the files needed to import these webs into the FrontPage Editor. (The examples for Chapters 2 through 4 are included for reference, representing the Company web in various stages of completion. You will actually build the Company web from scratch as you work your way through the chapters.)

Read These Notes to Import the Sample Webs Into FrontPage Explorer

The HTML files on this CD can not be browsed as-is (with the exception of the Chapter 9 demos). If you double-click the default.htm file in each example folder, the web may appear to work, but several features, such as database access and form submission, will only work on a properly installed web.

To view the examples with a web browser or work them with FrontPage, you must first import each web's folder as a FrontPage web using FrontPage Explorer.

There are two methods to import files into FrontPage. Before you begin, back up your WWW publishing directory (e.g., c:\inetpub\wwwroot or c:\webshare\wwwroot).

Method 1

Run FrontPage Explorer and use either the Import Wizard or the File | Import command to create a new subweb. Be sure you are creating a new web for the imported files; don't copy them to the root web.

When prompted for the location of the files to import, specify one of the following directories from this CD-ROM (substitute for x: the drive letter of your CD-ROM):

- x:\Webs\Chap02\Company
- x:\Webs\Chap03\Company
- x:\Webs\Chap04\Company
- x:\Webs\Chap07\Intranet
- x:\Webs\Chap09

Be sure to turn on the checkbox for Include Subdirectories. After the import completes, you will be returned to FrontPage Explorer, ready to work with the new web.

Method 2 (Advanced)

Use Windows Explorer to drag and drop the folder you want to import (such as the folder \Webs\Chap04\Company) into the WWW publishing folder (such as c:\inetpub\wwwroot or c:\Webshare\wwwroot). Select the files after you've copied them and use File | Properties to clear the Read-Only checkbox.

Next, use FrontPage Explorer's File | New | Web command to create a new web with the SAME NAME as the folder you copied. This will register the web with FrontPage Explorer, but won't erase the files you've copied.

You can now use FrontPage Explorer and the FrontPage Editor to open, examine, and customize these webs.

Additional Preparation

For any project containing a _scripts folder (such as the intranet demo in Chapter 7), set the properties for the _scripts folder to Allow Scripts or Programs to Run. To do this, open the web with FrontPage Explorer. Switch to Folder View, and right-click on the _scripts folder and choose Properties. Once you've done this, the pages in the _scripts folder can not be previewed directly from a web browser (such as Internet Explorer), but must instead be linked to from a page in the main web folder.

This is explained in Chapters 7 and 8.

Viewing Hidden Files With FrontPage Explorer

Since the files in any folder beginning with the underscore character (such as _private or _scripts) are normally hidden, you will want to choose Tools | Web Settings, click the Advanced tab, and turn on the check box for Show Documents in Hidden Directories.

Software Descriptions

Program	Description
BMP Wizard	BMP Wizard is a script-driven image filter, which can treat BMP files in 1-4-8-24 bit format. BMP uses a basic-like script language. Version 1.81 includes 63 examples, many of which are ready to use to filter other effects. BMP Wizard's script language is compiled for the fastest execution. The basic-like script language has variables, arrays, and can treat multiple images simultaneously.
Cute FTP	The best file transfer protocol available on the Internet. This CD-ROM contains two versions: a 32-bit version and a version that works for both 32- and 16- bit operating systems.
Eudora Lite	Eudora is one of the most popular and proven electronic mail software on the Internet. Eudora's easy-to-use features save you time in composing, organizing, and replying to your electronic mail.

Program	Description
Free Agent	Free Agent is your guide to news, fun and information in the Usenet newsgroups. You can configure Free Agent for online or offline operation, to set your own balance between convenience and economy. In offline mode, it briefly connects to the server to retrieve article headers, lets you browse them offline and mark the interesting ones, and then goes online for another quick session to retrieve the marked articles. In online mode, you can browse newsgroups at will, dipping into threads as they interest you. You can still mark long articles to be downloaded later, or you can download one article while browsing others. This CD contains both the 16-bit and 32-bit versions.
Gif*gIf*giF	Gif*gIf*giF is an easy-to-use program for recording single or multiple captures of whatever is on your monitor. The animations are saved as animated GIFs, so that animations may be viewed online or off the hard drive with Web browsers or other GIF viewing tools. The produced animations are quite compact, as only the differences between capture frames are recorded. The capture area can be selected, and recordings can be 100%, 44%, or 25% of the original size (44% meaning $2/3$ the width and $2/3$ the height; 25% meaning $1/2$ the width and $1/2$ the height). With the Mac version, there is a "Fake screen" option that makes the resulting captures look like a miniature Macintosh screen, complete with rounded corners and top right process and help menus. Gif*gIf*giF is useful for software demonstrations, training, making compact animations, and also for fun!

Program	Description
Jamba	If you design or develop Web pages, Jamba is the fastest and most productive way to add the excitement and the power of multimedia and interactivity to static HTML pages. Combining an intuitive, award-winning user interface with Java's standard cross-platform deliver, Jamba eliminates the plug-in nightmare while providing an open, extensible environment for applet development. This trial version contains a serial number which is needed for upgrading at the Aimtech Web site (www.aimtech.com). For more information, consult the Jamba readme.
MapEdit	MapEdit is a WYSIWYG editor for imagemaps, available for Microsoft Windows and the X Window System. Version 2.24 for Windows 3.1, 95, and NT, as well as 10 variations of Unix, is now available. All these versions support client-side imagemaps, targeting of individual frames, and more. This version of MapEdit is shareware, not freeware. If you choose to use MapEdit beyond the 30-day trial period, please register your copy with Boutell.Com, Inc., via e-mail: mapedit@boutell.com or snail mail: PO Box 20837, Seattle, WA 98102.
mIRC	To connect to IRC you'll need a small chat program like mIRC. mIRC is the shareware IRC chat program made for Windows by Khaled Mardam-Bey. It offers a fast and clean interface to IRC and it is well equipped with options and tools. This CD-ROM contains both a 16- and a 32-bit version of mIRC. For more information, visit http://www.mirc.co.uk.
Pegasus	Pegasus Mail is an electronic mail system for use with Novell NetWare (versions 2.15A and later), and on standalone systems using the WINSOCK TCP/IP interface.

Program	Description
Thumbs Plus!	A graphic file viewer, locator, and organizer which simplifies the process of finding and maintaining graphics, clip-art files, fonts, and animations. It displays a small image (thumbnail) of each file. You can use Thumbs Plus to browse, view, crop, launch external editors, and copy images to the clipboard. Supports over 30 file types internally with the option to support more using OLE or Aldus Rev 1 graphic filters. There are two versions on this CD-ROM. Thumbs Plus v.2.0e for 16-bit operating systems and Thumbs Plus v.3.oe-s for 32-bit operating systems. For more info, go to http://www.cerious.com.
VideoCraft	VideoCraft GIF Animator features seven powerful effects editors to create stunning Web animations and video special effects. Besides animated effects such as morphing and distorting, VideoCraft can be used to convert existing ALL files to GIF animations.
WS_FTP Ltd Ed	File transfer client with a highly intuitive graphical user interface.
WinVN	WinVN is an NNTP newsreader for the Microsoft Windows family. You can use it to read and post Usenet News, and send e-mail via the SMTP or MAPI protocols. There are three versions of WinVN, all derived from a common set of source files.

Table A-1: Programs on the Companion CD-ROM.

Technical Support

Technical support is available for installation-related problems only. The technical support office is open from 8:00 A.M. to 6:00 P.M. Monday through Friday and can be reached via the following methods:

    Phone: (919) 544-9404 extension 81

    Faxback Answer System: (919) 544-9404 extension 85

    E-mail: help@vmedia.com

    FAX: (919) 544-9472

    World Wide Web: **http://www.vmedia.com/support**

    America Online: keyword *Ventana*

Limits of Liability & Disclaimer of Warranty

The authors and publisher of this book have used their best efforts in preparing the CD-ROM and the programs contained in it. These efforts include the development, research, and testing of the theories and programs to determine their effectiveness. The authors and publisher make no warranty of any kind expressed or implied, with regard to these programs or the documentation contained in this book.

The authors and publisher shall not be liable in the event of incidental or consequential damages in connection with, or arising out of, the furnishing, performance, or use of the programs, associated instructions, and/or claims of productivity gains.

Some of the software on this CD-ROM is shareware; there may be additional charges (owed to the software authors/makers) incurred for their registration and continued use. See individual program's README or VREADME.TXT files for more information.

appendix B
FrontPage 97 Internet Resources

Other than the book you're reading, the best place to get support for FrontPage 97 is on the Internet. In this appendix, I've compiled a list of some of the best places to go if you're looking for more information on FrontPage 97, as well as links to other web authoring resources, including a large list of clip-art sites.

The first place to visit is the author's official web site for the book you're reading now, at http://www.WebsFrontPage.com. Here, you can browse the sample web sites discussed in this book, access additional tutorials and resources, find updates and corrections, and take advantage of a special offer for FrontPage web hosting services.

This list was current as of February 20, 1997. For the latest list of links and to save some typing, visit http://www.WebsFrontPage.com. You can also find any online updates to this book at http://www.vmedia.com/updates/.

Special thanks to Peter Perchansky of PMP Computer Solutions for documenting some of the CGI, ActiveX, and Java links I've included below. Be sure to visit Peter's FrontPage support site listed below under General FrontPage Resources.

In addition to the WWW links listed below, also check out the following newsgroups. (To read and post articles on USENET newsgroups you need an NNTP client, such as WinVN, included on this book's Companion CD-ROM.) To find these newsgroups, set up your news server to point to msnews.microsoft.com.

- microsoft.public.frontpage.client
- microsoft.public.frontpage.extensions.unix
- microsoft.public.frontpage.extensions.windowsnt

Microsoft FrontPage Resources

Microsoft FrontPage Home
http:/www.microsoft.com/frontpage/

Work With FrontPage
http://www.microsoft.com/frontpage/work.htm

Microsoft FrontPage Web Presence Providers
http://microsoft.saltmine.com/frontpage/wpp/list/

FrontPage Bonus Pack
http://www.microsoft.com/frontpage/documents/bonus.htm

Microsoft Web Gallery
http://www.microsoft.com/gallery/

Microsoft SiteBuilder Network
http://www.microsoft.com/sitebuilder/

General FrontPage Resources

Akorn Access FAQ
http://205.217.100.14/FrontPage/FPfaq.html

Chris' FrontPage 97 Information Web
http://jazzpiano.com/frontpage97/

Dave's Unauthorized FrontPage Support Site
http://infomatique.iol.ie:8080/dave/

FrontPage 97 Java Chat
http://www.hpns.com/fpchat.htm

FrontPage 97 Q&A
http://goinside.com/96/fp97qa.html

FrontPage97 Home Page
http://www.frontpage97.com/

GRM—Welcome to the FrontPage Forum
http://www.grm.com/frontpage/

Imageworx FP FAQ—Home
http://www.xerox.francoudi.com.cy/frontpage/

Jhas FP Chat
http://www.jhas.com/chat.asp

Laura Lemay's Frequently Asked Questions
http://frontpage.flex.net/dtyler/main/faqmain.htm

Okanagan Online's FrontPage Discussion
http://www.okonline.com/frontpage/

Peter Perchansky's PMPCS Support Area for Microsoft FrontPage
http://www.pmpcs.com/support/frontpage.htm

The Incredible MS-FrontPage Linksite
http://www.cosy.sbg.ac.at/~ohaus/docs/frontpage.html

Two Hawks' Trail Guide to Microsoft FrontPage
http://www.execpc.com/~blackjon/frontpage.html

Welcome to FrontPage Live! On-line Chat Forum
http://www.thevmtbuilding.com/fpchat.htm

Yahoo's FrontPage Directory
http://www.yahoo.com/Computers_and_Internet/Software/Reviews/Individual/Internet/Web_Authoring_Tools/HTML_Editors/Microsoft_FrontPage/

Site Promotion Links

Register It!
http://www.register-it.com

100% On Target
http://www.webthemes.com/

AAA Internet Promotions
http://www.websitepromote.com/index.html

Add It!
http://www.liquidimaging.com/submit/

InfoSpace
http://www.infospace.com/submit.html

Easy-Submit
http://www.the-vault.com/easy-submit/

FreeLinks
http://www.freelinks.com/

Go Net-Wide
http://www.gonetwide.com/goguide.html

Promoting Your Page
http://www.orst.edu/aw/stygui/propag.htm

Link Exchange
http://www.linkexchange.com

Web Promote
http://online-biz.com/promote/index.cgi

Promote-It!
http://www.itools.com/promote-it/promote-it.html

Publishing and Promoting Your Web Site
http://www.desktoppublishing.com/webpromote.html

Web Top 100
http://www.mmgco.com/top100.html

Yahoo Announcement Services
http://www.yahoo.com/Computers_and_Internet/Internet/World_Wide_Web/Announcement_Services/

Scripting & Programming

ActiveWare Perl for Win32
http://www.perl.hip.com/

Miscellaneous CGI Sources
http://hcs.harvard.edu/~eekim/web/cgihtml/cgihtml.html

http://home.sol.no/jgaa/cgi-bin.htmWin

http://homepage.seas.upenn.edu/~mengwong/perlhtml.html

http://icg.resnet.upenn.edu/mailto/

http://kufacts.cc.ukans.edu/info/forms/forms-intro.html

http://kuhttp.cc.ukans.edu/info/forms/forms-intro.html

http://web.mit.edu/wwwdev/cgiemail/

http://websunlimited.com/mailit.htm

Appendix B: FrontPage 97 Internet Resources

http://wsk.eit.com/wsk/dist/doc/libcgi/libcgi.html
http://www.aa.net/~rclark/scripts/
http://www.ahg.com/listcgi.htm
http://www.behold-software.com/counter/
http://www.bio.cam.ac.uk/cgi-lib/
http://www.boutell.com/cgic/
http://www.cis.ufl.edu/perl/ftp.html
http://www.cobb.msstate.edu/chris/cgi-bin/perl_scripts.cgi
http://www.cobleskill.edu/faculty/motylw/perl/
http://www.cs.uoregon.edu/~jhobbs/guestbook
http://www.genome.wi.mit.edu/ftp/pub/software/WWW/cgi_docs.html
http://www.geocities.com/SiliconValley/6742/
http://www.hkstar.com./~west/perl/
http://www.hyperion.com/~koreth/uncgi.html
http://www.illuminatus.com/cookie
http://www.metronet.com/1/perlinfo/scripts/
http://www.perl.hip.com/man-pages/perl5.htm
http://www.prplus.com/
http://www.rcsoftware.com/scripts.html
http://www.seas.upenn.edu/~mengwong/forms/
http://www.seds.org/~smiley/cgiperl/cgi.htm
http://www.sgi.com/counter.html
http://www.stars.com/Seminars/CGI/
http://www.stars.com/Vlib/Providers/CGI.html
http://www.tardis.ed.ac.uk/~angus/Computing/Programming/Perl/
http://www.terminalp.com/scripts/
http://www.webtools.org/counter/counter.html
http://www.worldwidemart.com/scripts/
http://www2.eff.org/~erict/Scripts/
http://www59.metronet.com/cgi/

JavaScript

Cut-N-Paste JavaScript
http://www.infohiway.com/javascript/indexf.htm

JavaScript 411
http://www.freqgrafx.com/411/

JavaScript Sourcebook
http://gmccomb.com/javascript/

Netscape JavaScript Authoring Guide
http://home.netscape.com/eng/mozilla/Gold/handbook/javascript/index.html

Netscape JavaScript Resources
http://home.netscape.com/comprod/products/navigator/version_2.0/script/script_info/index.html

Yahoo's Javascript Directory
http://www.yahoo.com/Computers_and_Internet/Programming_Languages/JavaScript/

VBScript

Microsoft VBScript Resources
http://www.microsoft.com/VBSCRIPT/

Microsoft VBScript Links
http://www.microsoft.com/vbscript/us/techinfo/vbslinks.htm

Ncompass ScriptActive
http://www.ncompasslabs.com/scriptactive/index.htm

Rollins Visual Basic Script Examples
http://www.rollins-assoc.com/fvbs.html

SCRIBE
http://www.km-cd.com/scribe/

Special Edition Using Visual Basic Script - Online Version
http://www.mcp.com/29987326632933/que/developer_expert/sevbsc/index.html

ActiveX

ACTIVEX.COM
http://www.activex.com/

ActiveX Demos
http://www.bitgroup.co.uk/INT_DEV/ACTIVEX.HTM

ActiveX Files
http://the-pages.com/activex/

GameLan ActiveX
http://www.gamelan.com/pages/Gamelan.related.activex.html

Microsoft ActiveX Gallery
http://www.microsoft.com/activex/gallery/

Net Heads Inc. X-Zone
http://www.netheads.net/alink.htm

PartBank
http://www.partbank.com/cgi-bin/getNode/entrance?technology=ActiveX

Yahoo ActiveX Directory
http://www.yahoo.com/Computers_and_Internet/Operating_Systems/Microsoft_Windows/Windows_95/Technical/ActiveX/

ZDNet Whole Web Catalog: MegaSource/ActiveX
http://www5.zdnet.com/zdwebcat/content/megasource/activex/activex.html

Java

GameLan EarthWeb (The Official Directory for Java)
http://www.gamelan.com/

Jars Java Review
http://www.jars.com/

JavaWorld
http://www.javaworld.com/

Presenting Java
http://www.december.com/works/java.html

The Java Center
http://www.java.co.uk/

The Java Tutorial
http://www.javasoft.com/nav/read/Tutorial/index.html

Yahoo's Java Directory
http://www.yahoo.com/Computers_and_Internet/
    Programming_Languages/Java/

Miscellaneous Java Links
http://java.wiwi.uni-frankfurt.de/

http://www.conveyor.com/conveyor-java.html

http://www.demon.co.uk/cyba/javamain.html

http://www.digitalfocus.com/digitalfocus/faq/howdoi.html

http://www.dogtech.com/webcenter/program.htm

http://www.easynet.it/~jhl/java.html

http://www.infospheres.caltech.edu/resources/java.html

http://www.javadevelopersjournal.com/java/

http://www.j-g.com/java/

http://www.online-magazine.com/cafeconn.htm

http://www.softbear.com/people/moe/mojava.htm

Multimedia Resources

Animated GIFs

Addicted to Stuff's Animated GIFs
http://www.morestuff.com/anima/a2anim.htm

The Animation Zone
http://www.anizone.com/

Animation by Cyber-Guide
http://www.cyber-guide.co.uk/animate/homepage.htm

AVIGIF Collection
http://www.download.com/PC/Result/TitleDetail/0,4,0-15302,00.html

Microsoft GIF Animator Showcase
http://www.microsoft.com/imagecomposer/feature/samples/

Net M GIF Animations
http://www.netm.com/animations/

Ulead GIF Tips
http://www.ulead.com/new/frameimg.htm

Yahoo's Animated GIF Collections
http://www.yahoo.com/Computers_and_Internet/Graphics/
    Computer_Animation/Animated_GIFs/Collections/

Graphics and Clipart

ArcaMax
http://www.arcamax.com/

Ball Boutique Logo
http://www.octagamm.com/boutique/mainball.htm

Barry's Clip Art Server
http://www.barrysclipart.com/

Clip Art Collection
http://leviathan.tamu.edu:70/1s/clipart

The Clip Art Connection
http://www.ist.net/clipart/index.html

The Clip Art Universe
http://www.nzwwa.com/mirror/clipart/

desktopPublishing.com
http://www.desktoppublishing.com/

GIF*DOT Home Page
http://www.graphcomp.com/gifdot/gifdot.html

Go Grab My Graphic
http://home.earthlink.net/~rodt/

Icon Browser
http://www.cli.di.unipi.it/iconbrowser/icons.html

The Image Mill
http://www.theimagemill.com/

Jon's HTML Graphics Archive
http://www.pvv.org/~bratseth/icons.html

Little Men Studios
http://members.aol.com/lmenstudio/index.html

Mission Media—Free Clip Art
http://www.goshen.net/icrd/cpr/cpr033/mm/page2.html

Microsoft Web Gallery
http://www.microsoft.com/gallery/

Multimedia and Clip Art
http://www.itec.sfsu.edu/multimedia/multimedia.html

Pathways Eye Candy
http://www.satchmo.com/cheryl/eyecandy.html

Pixelsight Clip Art Library
http://beta.pixelsight.com/PS/clipart/clipart.html

Psyched Up Clip Art
http://www.econ.cbs.dk/~gemal/

Rocket Shop
http://www.rocketshop.holowww.com/

The Style Factory
http://www.geocities.com/SiliconValley/Heights/1254/

Tup's Logo
http://www.cyberspace.com/~tup/graphics.html

Turnpike Web Page Clip Art
http://metro.turnpike.net/kyee/Construction.html

Web Art Server
http://www.lenna.net/webart/

Yahoo's Clip Art Directory
http://www.yahoo.com/Computers_and_Internet/Multimedia/Pictures/Clip_Art/

Sound

Animations and Graphics for Your Website
http://www.cyberspace.com/~tup/graphics.html

Adam's Audio Archive
http://pagraphics.com/~adam/

Aristosoft's 1000 New Sounds
http://204.31.29.4/ftp/wired/sounds/

EarthStation1
http://www.attention.net/wandarer/homepage.html

Microsoft Sounds Gallery
http://www.microsoft.com/gallery/files/sounds/default.htm

Multi-Media Music
http://www.wavenet.com/~axgrindr/quimby.html

Oxford University Sound Archive
http://www.comlab.ox.ac.uk/archive/sound.html

Skokefoe's Funky Sound Archive
http://nh.ultranet.com/~skokefoe/sound.html

SoundsAmerica
http://soundamerica.com/

SoundSpace
http://members.aol.com/pucknut468/soundpg.html

The WAV Emporium
http://www.forsite.net/wav_emporium/

Yahoo's Sound Archive Directory
http://www.yahoo.com/Computers_and_Internet/Multimedia/Sound/Archives/

Video & Other

Micro Movie Mini Multiplex
http://www.teleport.com/~cooler/MMMM/index.html

MPEG Archive
http://www.powerweb.de/mpeg/

Multimedia and Clip Art
http://www.itec.sfsu.edu/multimedia/multimedia.html

Rob's Multimedia Lab
http://www.acm.uiuc.edu:81/rml/

Yahoo's Multimedia Directory
http://www.yahoo.com/Computers_and_Internet/Multimedia/

Advanced Topics

ASP Development Network
http://www.aspdeveloper.net/

FrontPage Configuration Settings for Windows NT Servers
http://www.microsoft.com/kb/articles/q162/1/45.htm

The ISAPI Developer's Site
http://www.genusa.com/isapi/

IIS, IDC & HTX Lessons
http://www.dsi.org/DSI/iis.htm

The Microsoft Internet Information Server FAQ
http://www.genusa.com/iis/

Using FrontPage 97 to Edit & Manage Active Server Pages
http://www.microsoft.com/kb/articles/q161/7/79.htm

The Wynkoop Pages
http://www.swynk.com/

Index

& (ampersand), concatenation operator   438
<> (angle brackets), results pages   414
% characters
   IDC scripts
      definition   404–405
      in SQL queries   408
   results pages   413
100% On Target submission service   255

A

<a>, </a> tags   18
AAA Internet Promotions submission service   255
AARNet (Australian Academic and Research Network)   6
Access Intranet Documents page   370–373
Active Desktop   266
Active pages
   ActiveX Controls
      countdown to year 2000   485–490
      date/time conversions   489–490
      Game of Life   498–501
      history of   476–477
      inserting in active pages   476–477
      Marquee control   479–484
      scrolling pages   479–484
      simulating life cycle of cells   498–501
      sources for   477–479
      status messages, displaying   490–493
      Timer control   485–490
      vs. Java applets   506–507
      web sites of interest   563
   Java applets   501–502
      inserting   504–506
      sources for   503
      vs. ActiveX controls   506–507
   VBScript   449–453
      activating   459
      adding VBScript to   443–445
      browsing for methods   453–455
      calculations on   434
      client-side scripting   432, 435
      color animation   493–497
      configuring a computer from   434
      creating messages   445
      definition   431
      displaying output   437–445

    floating frames   470–474
    floating images   474–475
    focus   469
    form field controls   455–459
    forms, inserting text above   458
    getting input   437–445
    InputBox function   437–439
    metric conversion example   439–448
    MsgBox function   437–439
    server scripts   432
    user input   464–469
    user interface   445–446
    user registration page, example   432–435
    variable declarations   460–462
ActiveX controls
    countdown to year 2000   485–490
    date/time conversions   489–490
    Game of Life   498–501
    history of   476–477
    inserting in active pages   476–477
    Marquee control   479–484
    scrolling pages   479–484
    simulating life cycle of cells   498–501
    sources for   477–479
    status messages, displaying   490–493
    Timer control   485–490
    vs. Java applets   506–507
    web sites of interest   563
    See also Active pages
Add It! submission service   255
Addrbook.mdb file   396
Address book   399–400
Address Database page   399–400
Administration dialog box
    See PWS Properties dialog box
Administration web page   277–278
ADSL (asymmetric digital subscriber loop) modems   215
AltaVista search engine   253
America Online, publishing to
    with FTP   229–233
    limitations   227–229
    with Web Publishing Wizard   233–234
Andreesson, Marc   8
Animation
    See Microsoft GIF Animator

Annotation WebBot   227
Apology page   239
Application servers, defined   257
ARPANet   5–6
.arts domains   215
ASP (Active Server Pages)   394–395
    directory access required   282
Audio design tips   45
Australian Academic and Research Network (AARNet)   6
Authoring-time WebBots   260
AVI files, converting to animation   140

B

Backing up web sites   251–252
Berners-Lee, Tim   8
Bibliography template, example   546
Bigfoot   219
Blank pages, creating   128–129
<BLOCKQUOTE>, </BLOCKQUOTE> tags   119
<body>, </body> tags   15

 tag   17
Browse-time WebBots   260
Buttons, forms   194–196

C

Carolina Resource network project
    See Corporate intranet project
CD-ROM
    files for projects   550–552
    navigating   549
    software descriptions   552–555
Cells
    See Tables
CGI (Common Gateway Interface)
    e-mail scripts, where to get   207–208
    and forms   207–208
    Hip Software   265
Check boxes
    defined   160
    validation rules   179
    See also Active pages
    See also Forms

Index

Client workstations, intranets   358–360
Client-side image maps
   See Image mapping
Client-side pull   239
Client-side scripting   432, 435
Clip art collections, importing   79
Color animation, VBScript   493–497
Comment WebBot   77
Companion CD-ROM
   See CD-ROM
CompuServe, publishing to
   limitations   227–229
   with Web Publishing Wizard   233–236
Concatenation, definition   438
Confirmation WebBot   202–203, 227
Controls
   defined   43–44, 439
   See also Active pages
   See also Forms
Convert Text dialog box   89
Cool Edit   45
Copyright issues
   linking to images   41
   public domain works   40
Corporate intranet project
   Access Intranet Documents page   370–373
   browser, selecting   358–360
   CD-ROM files   550–552
   client workstations, setting up   358–360
   Corel publishing   372
   Employee Resources page
      Employee Directory page   381–383
      Employee Policy Manual page   383–386
      overview   380–381
      Requisition Form page   386–388
   frames
      content   367–369
      defined   362
      Frames Wizard   363–367
      framesets, customizing   365–367
      linking   368–369
      target frames   368–370
      testing   370
   home page, designing   360–362
   Microsoft Office 97 publishing   372
   planning   356–357

Run Software page
   creating   378–380
   shortcuts to executable files   375–377
   starting programs, problems   373–375
Corporate Presence Wizard   54
   software requirements   54
   See also Corporate web project
Corporate web project
   background
      changing   85–86
      choosing   65–66
      custom, applying   116–118
      custom, creating   105–116
      watermark   87
   buttons   194–196
   CD-ROM files   103, 550–552
   census form
      analyzing with Excel   200
      blank e-mail results   207
      confirmation page, creating   201–203
      designing   161–164
      form handler, adding   194–199
      HTML code, editing   191–194
      linking to   204
      paper form, comparing to   159–160
      purpose of form   158–159
      results via CGI scripts   207–208
      results via e-mail   205–207
      results via Save Results WebBot   194–199
      rows, naming   191–194
      table for aligning introduction   164–165
      table for contact information   165–172
      table for data   179–190
      text fields, inserting   167–172
      validation rules, contact table   172–179
      validation rules, data table   188–189
   columns, creating   120–127
   company name, adding   67–68
   consistency   63–67, 87–88
   contact information   67–68
   Contacts page
      creating   129–135
      linking to home page   131–132
      linking to web   135–136
   e-mail addresses   67–68
   employee pages

creating   133–136
   linking to previous page   133–134
   linking to web   135–136
   template   134–135
FAX number   67–68
finished page, illustration   99
footers   63–64
headers   63–64
home page
   choosing topics   60
   file name   82
Included Logo Page   73–82
included pages, editing   83
Information Request form, linking to   100–102
linked pages, creating   135–136
linked pages, opening   92
logo, creating   73–74, 77–82
Microsoft Word documents, importing   88–90
music   85
navigation bar, animated
   adding to Included Navigation Links page   148–149
   building GIF animation   136–146
   deleting old   148–149
   hot spots   151–152
   moving   153
   saving to web   152–153
   testing   153
News page   91–92
opening   54–55
photographs, adding   133
press releases   92
previewing   103–104
Products/Services page
   choosing entries   61–63
   customizing   92–100
purple text, deleting   77
server, choosing   56–58
Services page   92–100
sound   85
spell checking   71
style, choosing   64–65
style pages   87–88, 116–118
subfolder, naming   58
tables
   adding to web page   120–122

blank lines, difficulty inserting   131–132
column width   125–126
content, adding   126–127
links, inserting   135–136
nested, creating   130–131
properties, setting   123–125
telephone number   67–68
testing   102–104
text
   aligning with tables   120–127
   importing   88–90
   indenting   118–120
To Do List
   Add New Page task   98
   adding tasks   71–72
   completing tasks   71
   Customize Home Page task   82–90
   Customize News Page task   91–92
   Customize Products page task   92–100
   Customizing the What's New page   91–92
   delegating tasks   72
   deleting tasks   71–72
   displaying   82
   Replace Logo Image task   73–82
   sorting   73
   turning off   69
topics, choosing from wizard   58–63
Under Construction sign
   adding   66–67
   deleting   90
uploading to web server   69
viewing in FrontPage Explorer   70
web, naming   58
Web Colors page   116–118
web pages, choosing from wizard   58–63
What's New page
   choosing topics   60–61
   customizing   91–92
wizards, choosing   55–56
word processing documents, importing   88–90
Countdown to year 2000   485–490
Create Hyperlink dialog box
   Current FrontPage Web tab   93–94
   New Page tab   97–98

Open Pages tab   94
World Wide Web tab   96–97
Create Link dialog box
    See Create Hyperlink dialog box
Ctrl+K keyboard shortcut   25
Customer Support Web template,
    example   547
CuteFTP
    uploading web pages   231–233
    where to get   230

D

Data collection forms
    See Corporate web project
Date/time conversions   489–490
Dedicated dial-up   218–219
    vs. unlimited access   216
_default.htm file   82
Design tips
    body text   36–37
    color   37
    controls   43–44
    forms   43–44
    graphics   38–41
    headings   36
    horizontal rules   38
    HTML markup, manual coding   49–51
    links   41–42
    multimedia content   44–45
    music   45
    Netscape Plug-ins   48–49
    PowerPoint animations   48
    sound, background   45
    tables   42
    text formatting   36–37
    video   44, 46–48
Detail sections   394, 415
Dial-Up Networking
    automatic reconnect   216–218
    disabling   267
    security   285
Directory of Press Releases template,
    example   534
Directory services   255
Direct-to-web publishing   372
Discussion Web Wizard   247

Discussion WebBot   227
Disk-based web (DBW)
    defined   258
    FAQ, creating   338–341
    launching   342
    limitations   343
    testing   342–343
Dithering   76
<!doctype> tag   50
Domain, defined   7
Domain names
    new top-level domains   215
    obtaining   214–215
Download directories   10
Dragging and dropping
    graphics   79
    Microsoft GIF Animator   140
    WebBots   153
Drop-down menus
    defined   160
    validation rules   179

E

Easy-Submit submission service   255
Edit Hyperlink dialog box   25–26
Edit menu
    FrontPage Editor   522–523
    FrontPage Explorer   514
Editor
    See FrontPage Editor
.edu domain names   214
E-mail
    CGI scripts   207–208
    forged headers, tracing   283
    form results   205–207
    links   94
Emergency recovery   252–253
Employee Directory page
    Corporate intranet project   381–383
    template, example   535
Employee Opportunities template,
    example   535
Employee Policy Manual page   383–386
Employee Resources page
    Employee Directory page   381–383
    Employee Policy Manual page   383–386

overview   380–381
    Requisition Form page   386–388
Employee webs
    See FTP servers
    See Intranets
Eraser tool   80
Error checking
    See Validation rules
Error diffusion   76
European Laboratory for Particle Physics (CERN)   8
Excel, analyzing form data   200
Excite search engine   253
Executing a program, definition   436
Explorer
    See FrontPage Explorer

F

FAQ (Frequently Asked Questions) template   537
Feedback Form template, example   536
File and Printer sharing   290–291
File menu
    FrontPage Editor   520–521
    FrontPage Explorer   513
File naming conventions   81
File server, defined   257
.firm domains   215
Fixed font, defined   16
Floating frames   470–474
Floating images   474–475
Focus   469
Folder view, FrontPage Explorer   31–33
Fonts, defaults   16
Form handlers
    buttons   194–196
    custom   205–207
    defined   157
    Save Results WebBot   194–199
Form Page Wizard template, example   536
Form Properties dialog box   196–197
Form Properties window   441–442
Forms
    analyzing with Excel   200
    blank e-mail results   207
    buttons   194–196

    confirmation page, creating   201–203
    controls   160–161, 455–459
    Corporate web project   101–102
    dashed lines   167
    defined   157
    design tips   43–44
    fields   157
        naming conventions   184
        types, list of   160–161
    form handler, adding   194–199
    Forms toolbar   160–161, 167
    Group US, Inc. project   101–102
    hidden fields, defined   161
    inserting text above   458
    linking to scripts   196
    results
        via CGI scripts   207–208
        via e-mail   205–207
        via Save Results WebBot   194–199
    text fields, inserting   167–172
    validation failure page   203
    validation rules   172–179
    See also Corporate web project
    See also Form handlers
Forms toolbar   160–161, 167
FQDN (fully qualified domain names)   18
Frames
    Microsoft GIF Animator   138
    web pages
        content   367–369
        defined   362
        framesets, customizing   365–367
        linking   368–369
        target frames   368–370
        testing   370
Frames Wizard   363–367
    template, example   537
Free home pages   219–220
FreeLinks submission service   255
FrontPage 1.1
    migrating to Microsoft Personal Web Server   266
    server extensions compatibility   221
FrontPage 97
    FrontPage 1.1 compatibility   221
    software requirements   10–12
    web servers

Index

included   11
recommended   11–12
WebBots, defined   12
See also FrontPage Editor
See also FrontPage Explorer
See also FrontPage server extensions
FrontPage Editor
   Eraser tool   80
   features overview   21–26
   links, automatic conversion of text   98
   marks, hiding   103
   reverting to saved page   121
   text, automatic conversion to links   98
FrontPage Explorer
   features overview   27–33
   Folder view   31–33
   hot spots, creating   149–152
   image maps, creating   147–152
   Link view   30–31
   projects, organization   27–29
   security   287–289
   templates, overview   34
   WebBots, overview   35
   webs, organization   27–29
   wizards, overview   34
FrontPage Server Administrator   269–272
FrontPage server extensions
   compatibility   221
   defined   12
   FrontPage Web Presence Providers (WPPs)   220–221
   installing
      Microsoft PWS for Windows 95   269–272
      Peer Web Services for Windows NT   310–314
   limited support   237–238
   uninstalling   252–253
   UNIX   264
FrontPage servers, Internet
   publishing to   237–242
   See also Microsoft PWS for Windows 95
   See also Peer Web Services for Windows NT
FrontPage servers, local
   choosing   264–266
   defined   11
   reason to use   258–260

FrontPage Web Presence Providers (WPPs)
   choosing   220–226
   server extensions   220–221
   special offer   226
   where to find   220
FTP Administration page (Windows 95)
   Directories tab   296–298
   Logging tab   298
   Messages tab   295
   Service tab   294
FTP (File Transfer Protocol)
   CuteFTP
      uploading web pages   231–233
      where to get   230
   servers, overview   10
   uploading to non-FrontPage servers   229–233
   Web Publishing Wizard as client   236
   See also Intranets
   See also Publishing
FTP servers
   Microsoft PWS for Windows 95   294–298
      and Microsoft Office 97   298–301
      restricting user access   302–304
      setting properties   275–276
   Peer Web Services for Windows NT   325–331
      IUSR account   334
      and Microsoft Office 97   331–334
      restricting access   334
FTP Service Properties (Windows NT)
   Directories tab   328–331
   Message tab   327–328
   Service tab   325–327
Fully qualified domain names (FQDN)   18
Functions, definition   436

G

Game of Life   498–501
GENERATOR tag   50
Geocities   219
GIF Animator
   See Microsoft GIF Animator
GIF format, when to use   74–77
GIF*GIF*GIF utility   139
Global variables, definition   460

Glossary of Terms template, example 538
Go Net-Wide submission service 255
.gov domain names 214
Graphics
    animation, creating 136–146
    backgrounds, creating custom 108–116
    client-side *vs.* server-side 148
    converting format 80–82
    converting to backgrounds 86
    copyright issues 40–41
    design tips 38–41
    dithering 76
    dragging and dropping 79
    error diffusion 76
    formats, choosing 74–77
    GIF*GIF*GIF utility 139
    image mapping 147–152
    importing 77–80
    logo, creating 73–82
    lossy compression 76
    Microsoft GIF Animator 136–146
    Microsoft Image Composer (MIC) 108–116
        Balanced Ramp palette 76
        converting images to backgrounds 86
        palettes, importing 75–76
    Paint Shop Pro, converting images 86
    palettes 75
    photographs, choosing format 77
    public domain 40
    saving 80–82
    TIFF format, importing 76
    transparent 74–75
    TrueColor 76
    Ulead GIF tools 139
    VideoCraft GIF Animator 139
Group US, Inc. project
    See Corporate web project
Guest Book template, example 538
Guslogo.gif file 77

H

<h1>, </h1> tags 15–17
<head>, </head> tags 15, 50
Headings, design tips 36
Help menu

FrontPage Editor 518
FrontPage Explorer 518
Hip Software 265
Horizontal rules 38
HOSTS file, creating 310
Hot List template, example 539
HotBot search engine 253
<html>, </html> tags 15
HTML 3.2 specification 50
HTML (HyperText Markup Language)
    cutting and pasting 50
    Greetings Page, example 13–18
    SGML 13
    tagging manually 13–21, 49–51
HTML Markup WebBot 227
HTTP (HyperText Transfer Protocol)
    defined 9
    variables 421–422
.HTX file extension 394, 413
HyperDocument Page template, example 539

I

IAB (Internet Architecture Board) 6
Icons
    FrontPage Server Administrator 269
    Microsoft PWS 273
.IDC file extension 404
IDC (Internet Database Connector)
    access restriction 399
    adding records 429
    Addrbook.mdb file 396
    address book 399–400
    Address Database page 399–400
    definition 391
    deleting records 428
    detail sections 394
    intranet database applications 392–393
    naming conventions 401
    preparing databases for 396–399
    purchase requisition form 422–426
    Purchreq.mdb file 396
    Query by Example 426–428
    results pages
        % characters 413
        <> (angle brackets) 414

Index

conditional inclusion   416–421
creating   414–415
detail sections   415
HTTP variables   421–422
inserting IDC parameters into   414
results template   394
SQL statements in   407–408
thin clients   391
updating records   428
IDC queries
creating   405–407
SQL statements
building with Access   409–412
predefined parameters   412
spaces in field names   411
IDC scripts
% characters
definition   404–405
in SQL queries   408
access restriction   403
definition   394
example   403
in hidden folders   403
percent procedures   404–405
subfolders for   402–403
IETF (Internet Engineering Task Force)   6
Image Composer
See Microsoft Image Composer (MIC)
Image fields
defined   161
validation rules   179
Image mapping   147–152
Image Properties dialog box   39–40
Image Toolbar commands   149–152
Importing
graphics   77–80
text   89–90
word processing documents   88–90
Include WebBot   153, 227
Index.htm file   82
Index.html file   82
Indexing web sites   253–254
.info domains   215
Inforeq.htm file   102
Infoseek search engine   253
InfoSpace submission service   255
InputBox function   437–439
Insert Table dialog box   121–122

Internet
history   5–6
HTTP (HyperText Transfer Protocol)   9
organizations, list of   6
Internet Architecture Board (IAB)   6
Internet connections
automatic reconnect   216–218
dedicated dial-up   218–219
leased lines   218–219
routers, defined   218
speed   215–216
T1 lines   218–219
unlimited access *vs.* dedicated access   216
Internet Database Connector WebBot   227
Internet Engineering Task Force (IETF)   6
Internet Information Server
See Peer Web Services for Windows NT
Internet Relay Chat (IRC)   213
Internet Research Task Force (IRTF)   6
Internet Service Manager   315–316
Internet Society (ISOC)   6
InterNIC   6
Interpreters, definition   436
Intranets
browser, selecting   358–360
client workstations, setting up   358–360
Corporate intranet project
Access Intranet Documents page   370–373
Employee Directory page   381–383
Employee Policy Manual page   383–386
Employee Resources page   380–381
home page, designing   360–362
Microsoft Office 97 publishing   372
planning   356–357
Requisition Form page   386–388
Run Software page   378–380
database applications
See IDC
defined   335
discussion subwebs   247
disk-based webs
FAQ (Frequently Asked Questions), creating   338–341
launching   342
limitations   343
testing   342–343

frames
    content   367–369
    defined   362
    framesets, customizing   365–367
    linking   368–369
    target frames   368–370
    testing   370
Frames Wizard   363–367
overview   336–337
planning   356–357
proxy servers   344
Registration WebBot   248–251
security   248–251
shortcuts to executable files   375–377
starting programs, problems   373–375
TCP/IP intranets
    overview   344–346
    Windows 95 setup   346–352
    Windows NT 4.0 Workstation
        setup   352–356
See also FTP servers
Intrinsic controls, definition   476
IP address
    determining   211–213
    publishing via   210–213
    tracing   283
IPCONFIG command   211–212
IRTF (Internet Research Task Force)   6
ISAPI (Internet Server Application Programming Interface)   205, 265
ISDN lines   215–216
ISOC (Internet Society)   6

J

Java
    defined   10
    web sites of interest   563–564
Java applets   501–502
    inserting   504–506
    sources for   503
    vs. ActiveX controls   506–507
JavaScript
    definition   435
    web sites of interest   562
JPEG format, when to use   74–77

K

Keyboard shortcuts
    documents, moving between   82
    links, creating   25

L

Leased lines   218–219
Lecture Abstract template, example   540
<li>, </li> tags   17
Link Exchange submission service   255
Link referral service   255–256
Link View (Explorer)   30–31
Links
    automatic   239
    client-side pull   239
    design tips   41–42
    e-mail   94
    keyboard shortcut   25
    localhost, reserved address   95
    mailto: 94
    naming conventions   94
    syntax   94–96
    targets
        FTP servers   94
        local files   95
        newsgroups   94
        parent folder   96
        planned pages   97–98
        World Wide Web pages   94, 96–97
    URLs   94–98
Local authoring, defined   260
Local User Administration page   293
Local variables, definition   460
Logo, creating   73–82
Logo.htm file   74
Lossy compression   76

M

Maintenance, web sites   242–243
MapEdit utility   148
Marquee control   479–484
Meeting Agenda template, example   540

Index

META tags 50–51
Metric conversion example 439–448
Microsoft Active Desktop 266
Microsoft Active Server Pages
   See Active pages
Microsoft Excel 200
Microsoft GIF Animator
   AVI files, converting 140
   duration 143
   frames
      adding 139–140
      defined 138
   Import Color Palette option 141
   Import Dither Method option 141
   Looping option 142
   playing animations 146
   property sheets
      Animation 142–143
      Image 143–146
      Options 140–142
   size 142, 144
   speed 146
   starting 139
   thumbnails, properties 143–144
   toolbar 138
   Transparency option 145–146
   Undraw option 145
   where to get 137
Microsoft Image Composer (MIC)
   Balanced Ramp palette 76
   color 112–114
   composition guide 109–112
   Composition Properties dialog box 109–112
   converting images to backgrounds 86
   error message, sprites will be flattened 116
   launching 109
   magnify tool 111
   overview 108
   palettes 75–76, 111
   saving images 115–116
   sketching 112–114
   sprites 108, 116
   texture 114–116
   tiling 109–112
   where to find 106

Microsoft Internet Information Server for Windows NT
   See Peer Web Services for Windows NT
Microsoft NetShow 44
Microsoft Personal Server for Windows 95
   See Microsoft PWS for Windows 95
Microsoft PowerPoint animations 48
Microsoft PWS for Windows 95
   Administration web page, launching 277–278
   File and Printer sharing, disabling 290–291
   FTP Administration page
      Directories tab 296–298
      Logging tab 298
      Messages tab 295
      Service tab 294
   FTP server 294–298
      and Microsoft Office 97 298–301
      restricting user access 302–304
      setting properties 275–276
   HTTP service, setting properties 275–276
   icon, Windows 95 system tray 273, 275
   installing 268–269
   intranet address, displaying 275
   Local User Administration page 293
   PWS Properties dialog box
      Administration tab 275
      General tab 275
      icon 273
      Services tab 275–276
      Startup tab 275
   remote administration, enabling 277
   security 284–293
   server extensions, installing 269–272
   starting 275
   stopping 275
   WWW Administration page
      Directories tab 280–282
      Logging tab 283–284
      password security 289–290
      Service tab 278–280
Microsoft Word
   See Corporate intranet project
.mil domain names 214
MIRC utility 213
Modems 215–216
MsgBox function 437–439

Multimedia
   design tips   44–45
   web sites of interest
      animated GIFs   564–565
      clipart   565–566
      graphics   565–566
      sound   566–567
      video   567

N

Naming conventions
   form fields   184
   home pages   82
   IDC   401
   links   94
   variables   444
NASA Science Internet (NSI)   6
National Center for Supercomputing Applications (NCSA)   8
.net domain names   214
Netscape plug-ins   48–49
NetShow   44
Network Information Center (NIC)   6
New FrontPage Web dialog box   55–56
NIC (Network Information Center)   6
.nom domains   215
Non-FrontPage servers
   publishing to   227–236
   and WebBots   227–229
Normal button   196
NSAPI (Netscape Applications Programming Interface)   205
NSFNET   6
NSI (NASA Science Internet)   6
NT Service Pack 2   306
NT Workstation
   See Peer Web Services for Windows NT

O

Office Directory template, example   541
100% On Target submission service   255
.org domain names   214

P

<p>, </p> tags   17
Packets, defined   7
Page Properties dialog box
   Background Sound section   85
   Background tab   85–88
   General tab   84–85
   naming web page   84
   title bar, setting text   84
   Watermark check box   87
   web page name (FrontPage Explorer)   84
Paint Shop Pro   86, 108
Peer Web Services for Windows NT
   FTP server   325–331
      IUSR account   334
      and Microsoft Office 97   331–334
      restricting access   334
   FTP Service Properties
      Directories tab   328–331
      Message tab   327–328
      Service tab   325–327
   HOSTS file, creating   310
   installing   306–310
   Internet Service Manager
      starting   315–316
   security   320–325
   server extensions, installing   310–314
   WWW Service Properties
      Directories tab   317–319
      Logging tab   319–320
      Service tab   317
Percent procedures   404–405
Personal Home Page Wizard template, example   541
Personal Server for Windows 95
   See Microsoft PWS for Windows 95
Personal Web template, example   547
Plug-In Properties dialog box   48–49
PowerPoint animations   48
<pre>, </pre> tags   16
Press Release template, example   542
_private subfolder   73–74
Private webs
   See Intranets
Procedures, definition   436
Product Description template, example   542

Product or Event Registration template,
    example   543
Programs, running in intranets   373–377
Project Web template, example   547
Projects
    CD-ROM files   550–552
    organizing   27–29
    See also Corporate intranet project
    See also Corporate web project
Promote-It submission service   256
Promoting Your Page submission service   255
Proportional font, defined   16
Protocol, defined   7, 336
Prototyping
    software requirements   10–12
    See also Corporate web project
Proxy servers   344
Public domain works   40
Publish FrontPage Web dialog box   240–242
Publishing
    America Online
        with FTP   229–233
        limitations   227–229
        with Web Publishing Wizard   233–234
    CompuServe
        limitations   227–229
        with Web Publishing Wizard   233–236
    free home pages   219–220
    FrontPage Web Presence Providers,
        finding   220–226
    from Internet to local server   251–252
    running your own server   210–219
    to FrontPage servers   237–242
    to non-FrontPage servers   227–236
    with FTP   229–233
    with IP address   210–213
    with Web Publishing Wizard   233–236
Publishing and Promoting Your Web Site,
    submission service   256
Purchase requisition form   422–426
Purchreq.mdb file   396
Push Button Properties dialog box   195–196
Push buttons, defined   160
PWS for Windows 95
    See Microsoft PWS for Windows 95
PWS Properties dialog box
    Administration tab   275
    General tab   275
    icon   273
    illustration   274
    Service tab   275–276
    Services tab   275–276
    Startup tab   275

Q

Query by Example   426–428

R

Radio buttons
    defined   160
    validation rules   179
.rec domains   215
Register It! submission service   255
Registration WebBot   227, 248–251
Relative URLs, defined   18
Remote administration, enabling   277
Requisition Form page   386–388
Reset button   160, 194–195
Restoring from backup   252
Results pages
    % characters   413
    <> (angle brackets)   414
    conditional inclusion   416–421
    creating   414–415
    detail sections   415
    HTTP variables   421–422
    inserting IDC parameters into   414
Results template   394
Root web, organizing   238–239
Routers, defined   218
Run Software page
    creating   378–380
    shortcuts to executable files   375–377
    starting programs, problems   373–375

S

Save As dialog box   88
Save Results WebBot   102, 205, 227
Scheduled Image WebBot   227
Scheduled Include WebBot   227

Scripts, definition   436
Scrolling pages   479–484
Search engines
    excluding your site   255
    promoting your web site   253–256
Search Page template, example   543
Search WebBot   227
Security
    cookies   286
    credit card transactions   285–286
    Dial-Up Networking   285
    directory browsing, prohibiting   282
    Microsoft PWS for Windows 95   284–293
    overview   261–263, 284–285
    Peer Web Services for Windows NT   320–325
    permissions, editing   244–247
    Registration WebBot   248–251
Seminar Schedule template, example   544
Server, defined   257
Server Administrator   269–272
Server extensions
    See FrontPage server extensions
Server scripts   432
Server-side image maps   41
Settings for Custom Form Handler dialog box   206–207
Settings for Saving Results of Form dialog box
    Advanced tab   199–200
    Confirmation tab   201
    Results tab   197–198
Shortcuts to executable files   375–377
Simulating life cycle of cells   498–501
Smallgrp.doc file   100
Software Data Sheet template, example   544
Sound, background   45
Speed, transmission   215–216
SQL (Structured Query Language)
    definition   394
    IDC queries   407–408
        building with Access   409–412
        predefined parameters   412
        spaces in field names   411
Status messages, displaying   490–493
.store domains   215
Strings, definition   438
Submission services, list of   255–256
Submit button   160, 194–195

Substitution WebBot   227
Subwebs, publishing   238–239
Survey Form template, example   545
Swiss Academic and Research Network (SWITCH)   6
SWITCH (Swiss Academic and Research Network)   6

T

T1 lines   216, 218–219
Table menu, FrontPage Editor   530–531
Table of Contents template, example   545
Table of Contents WebBot   227
Tables
    adding to web page   120–122
    aligning text   120–127
    blank lines, difficulty inserting   131–132
    column width   125–126
    content, adding   126–127
    design tips   42
    HTML code, editing   192–194
    links, inserting   135–136
    nested, creating   130–131
    properties, setting   123–125
    See also Forms
Tags, HTML   13–21, 49–51
Targets
    See Links
TCP/IP intranets
    overview   344–346
    Windows 95 setup   346–352
    Windows NT 4.0 Workstation setup   352–356
Team development   243–244
Templates   34, 88
Templates, examples
    Bibliography   546
    Customer Support Web   547
    Directory of Press Releases   534
    Employee Directory   535
    Employee Opportunities   535
    Feedback Form   536
    Form Page Wizard   536
    Frames Wizard   537
    Frequently Asked Questions   537
    Glossary of Terms   538

Index

Guest Book 538
Hot List 539
HyperDocument Page 539
Lecture Abstract 540
Meeting Agenda 540
Office Directory 541
Personal Home Page Wizard 541
Personal Web 547
Press Release 542
Product Description 542
Product or Event Registration 543
Project Web 547
Search Page 543
Seminar Schedule 544
Software Data Sheet 544
Survey Form 545
Table of Contents 545
User Registration 546
Web Self-Registration Form 534
What's New 547
Text, importing
  carriage returns, stripping 89
  line breaks, preserving 90
Text Box Properties dialog box 170–172
Text Box Validation dialog box 173–177
Text boxes
  defined 160
  validation rules 175–177
  See also Forms
Text formatting, design tips 36–37
Thin clients 391
Timer control 485–490
Timestamp WebBot 227
<title>, </title> tags 15
To Do List
  adding tasks 71–72
  completing tasks 71
  Customize Home Page task 82–90
  Customize News Page task 91–92
  Customize Products page task 92–100
  Customizing the What's New page 91–92
  delegating tasks 72
  deleting tasks 71–72
  displaying 82
  Replace Logo Image task 73–82
  sorting 73
  turning off 69

Toolbars
  Forms toolbar 160–161, 167
  FrontPage Editor 519
  FrontPage Explorer 511
  Microsoft GIF Animator 138
Tools menu
  FrontPage Editor 528–529
  FrontPage Explorer 516–517
<tr>, </tr> tags 193
Tracert command 283

U

<ul>, </ul> tags 17
Ulead GIF tools 139
Under Construction sign
  adding 66–67
  deleting 90
Uninstalling server extensions 252–253
UNIX, and server extensions 264
Unlimited access *vs.* dedicated access 216
Upload directories 10
Uploading
  See Publishing
URL (Uniform Resource Locator)
  absolute 95–98
  fully qualified domain names (FQDN) 18
  overview 94–95
  pronunciation 18
  relative 18, 95–96
User input, active pages 464–469
User interface, active pages 445–446
User Meta Variable dialog box 253–254
User Registration page
  example 432–435
  template 546

V

Validation failure page 203
Validation rules 172–177
  Corporate web project 177–179, 188–189
  language, choosing 173
  limitations 173
Validation WebBot 227

Variables
    definition   437–438
    naming conventions   444
VBScript   449–453
    activating   459
    adding VBScript to   443–445
    browsing for methods   453–455
    calculations on   434
    client-side scripting   432, 435
    color animation   493–497
    configuring a computer from   434
    creating messages   445
    definition   431
    displaying output   437–445
    floating frames   470–474
    floating images   474–475
    focus   469
    form field controls   455–459
    forms, inserting text above   458
    getting input   437–445
    InputBox function   437–439
    metric conversion example   439–448
    MsgBox function   437–439
    Netscape Navigator support for   435
    programming concepts   436–437
    server scripts   432
    user input   464–469
    user interface   445–446
    user registration page, example   432–435
    variable declarations   460–462
    web sites of interest   562
Versioning web sites   251–252
Video, design tips   44, 46–48
VideoCraft GIF Animator   139
VideoLive   44
View menu
    FrontPage Editor   524–527
    FrontPage Explorer   515
VivoActive   44

W

Web browsers
    fonts, defaults   16
    history   8
    intranets   358–360
    title bar, setting text   84

    vs. web servers   9
.web domains   215
Web hosting services
    See FrontPage Web Presence Providers
Web pages
    animation, creating   136–146
    apology page   239
    automatically forwarding users   239
    backgrounds, creating custom   105–116
    blank pages, creating   128–129
    columns, creating   120–127
    description, adding with Meta Variable   253–254
    design tips
        body text   36–37
        color   37
        controls   43–44
        forms   43–44
        graphics   38–41
        headings   36
        horizontal rules   38
        HTML markup, manual coding   49–51
        links   41–42
        multimedia content   44–45
        music   45
        Netscape Plug-ins   48–49
        PowerPoint animations   48
        sound, background   45
        tables   42
        text formatting   36–37
        video   44, 46–48
    file naming conventions   81
    idle users, disconnecting   279
    IP addresses, determining   211–213
    linked, creating   93–98
    linked, opening   92
    logging access attempts   283
    saving, with graphics   81
    speed   261
    tables
        adding to web pages   120–122
        aligning text   120–127
        blank lines, difficulty inserting   131–132
        column width   125–126
        content, adding   126–127
        links, inserting   135–136
        nested, creating   130–131

Index

properties, setting 123–125
templates
   creating 88, 128–129
   and custom page elements 88
   errors 88
   examples 532–547
text, aligning with tables 120–126
See also Active pages
See also Corporate web project
See also Forms
See also Intranets
See also Publishing
Web Promote submission service 255
Web Publishing Wizard
   America Online publishing 233–234
   CompuServe publishing 234–236
   stand-alone tool 236
Web Self-Registration Form template, example 534
Web servers
   defined 9, 258
   file naming conventions 81
   FrontPage servers, Internet
      client-side pull 239
      FrontPage 97 support, limitations 237–238
      Internet web server, defined 237
      publishing to 237–242
      upload times out 242
   FrontPage servers, local
      choosing 264–266
      defined 11
      reason to use 258–260
   included with FrontPage 97 11
   naming conventions, home pages 82
   non-FrontPage servers
      default home page, setting 229
      publishing to 227–236
      server-side image maps, avoiding 228
      uploading with FTP 229–233
      WebBot limitations 227–229
   recommended 11–12
   required for prototyping 10–12
   running your own 210–219
   vs. web browsers 9
   See also Intranets
   See also Microsoft PWS for Windows 95
   See also Peer Web Services for Windows NT

Web sites
   backing up 251–252
   discussion subwebs 247
   emergency recovery 252–253
   indexing, for search engines 253–254
   maintenance 242–243
   promoting 253–256
   restoring from backup 252
   security
      directory browsing, prohibiting 282
      permissions, editing 244–247
      Registration WebBot 248–251
   team development 243–244
   versioning 251–252
   See also Corporate intranet project
   See also Corporate web project
   See also Publishing
web sites of interest
   ActiveX 563
   advanced topics 568
   FrontPage resources 558–559
   Java 563–564
   JavaScript 562
   multimedia
      animated GIFs 564–565
      clipart 565–566
      graphics 565–566
      sound 566–567
      video 567
   programming resources 560–561
   scripting resources 560–561
   site promotion resources 559–560
   VBScript 562
Web Top 100 submission service 256
WebBots
   Annotation WebBot 227
   authoring-time WebBots 260
   browse-time WebBots 260
   Comment WebBot 77
   Confirmation WebBot 202–203, 227
   Discussion WebBot 227
   HTML Markup WebBot 227
   Include WebBot 153, 227
   Internet Database Connector WebBot 227
   moving 153
   with non-FrontPage servers, list of 227–229

overview   12, 35
    Registration WebBot   227, 248–251
    Save Results WebBot   102, 205, 227
    Scheduled Image WebBot   227
    Scheduled Include WebBot   227
    screen reference   532–533
    Search WebBot   227
    Substitution WebBot   227
    Table of Contents WebBot   227
    Timestamp WebBot   227
    Validation WebBot   227
WebCrawler search engine   253
Webs, organizing   27–29
Webtop publishing, defined   3–5
What's New template, example   547
Windows 95
    TCP/IP setup   346–352
    See also Microsoft PWS for Windows 95
Windows NT
    TCP/IP setup   352–356
    See also Peer Web Services for Windows NT
WINIPCFG command   211–212
Wizards
    Corporate Presence Wizard   54
    Discussion Web Wizard   247
    Frames Wizard   363–367
    overview   34
    Web Publishing Wizard   233–236
Word processing documents
    importing   88–90
    See also Corporate intranet project
World Wide Web Consortium (W3C)   19
World Wide Web (WWW)
    applications, list of   8–9
    history   8–9
    size   9
WWW Administration page (Windows 95)
    Directories tab   280–282
    Logging tab   283–284
    password security   289–290
    Service tab   278–280

WWW Service Properties page (Windows NT)
    Directories tab   317–319
    Logging tab   319–320
    Service tab   317

X

X2 modems   215–216

Y

Yahoo Announcement Services   256
Year 2000 countdown   485–490

VENTANA

http://www.vmedia.com

VENTANA

Official HTML Publishing for Netscape, Second Edition
$49.99, 800 pages, illustrated, part #: 650-5

Find out how to play to Navigator's hottest new features. Here's everything you need to know to design great web pages—from starting a page to organizing a site, creating intricate layouts and incorporating the latest technologies. This new edition features new material on style sheets, sound, multimedia and databases, along with a more extensive look at Java and JavaScript. Packed with expert advice about what works and what doesn't. The CD-ROM features author examples, sample JavaScript, clip objects (graphics, sound and animations), backgrounds, and more.

Official Multimedia Publishing for Netscape
$49.95, 512 pages, illustrated, part #: 381-6

Enhance your online documents with sound, video and interactivity. Learn how to create multimedia effects as you build power and payback into your pages. The CD-ROM features multimedia utilities; custom, one-of-a-kind fonts; fully working plug-in filter; client-side image-mapping shareware; free graphics, animations, sounds and templates; links to Internet resources.

VENTANA

Macromedia Director 5 Power Toolkit

$49.95, 800 pages, illustrated, part #: 289-5

Macromedia Director 5 Power Toolkit views the industry's hottest multimedia authoring environment from the inside out. Features tools, tips and professional tricks for producing power-packed projects for CD-ROM and Internet distribution. Dozens of exercises detail the principles behind successful multimedia presentations and the steps to achieve professional results. The companion CD-ROM includes utilities, sample presentations, animations, scripts and files.

The Comprehensive Guide to Lingo

$49.99, 824 pages, illustrated, part #: 463-4

Master the Lingo of Macromedia Director's scripting language for adding interactivity to presentations. Covers beginning scripts to advanced techniques, including creating movies for the Web and problem solving. The companion CD-ROM features demo movies of all scripts in the book, plus numerous examples, a searchable database of problems and solutions, and much more!

Shockwave!

$49.95, 400 pages, illustrated, part #: 441-3

Breathe new life into your web pages with Macromedia Shockwave. Ventana's *Shockwave!* teaches you how to enliven and animate your Web sites with online movies. Beginning with step-by-step exercises and examples, and ending with in-depth excursions into the use of Shockwave Lingo extensions, Shockwave! is a must-buy for both novices and experienced Director developers. Plus, tap into current Macromedia resources on the Internet with Ventana's Online Companion. The companion CD-ROM includes the Shockwave plug-in, sample Director movies and tutorials, and much more!

VENTANA

Web Publishing With Adobe PageMill 2
$34.99, 480 pages, illustrated, part #: 458-8

Now, creating and designing professional pages on the Web is a simple, drag-and-drop function. Learn to pump up PageMill with tips, tricks and troubleshooting strategies in this step-by-step tutorial for designing professional pages. The CD-ROM features Netscape plug-ins, original textures, graphical and text-editing tools, sample backgrounds, icons, buttons, bars, GIF and JPEG images, Shockwave animations.

Web Publishing With QuarkImmedia
$39.99, 576 pages, illustrated, part #: 525-8

Use multimedia to learn multimedia, building on the power of QuarkXPress. Step-by-step instructions introduce basic features and techniques, moving quickly to delivering dynamic documents for the Web and other electronic media. The CD-ROM features an interactive manual and sample movie gallery with displays showing settings and steps. Both are written in QuarkImmedia.

VENTANA

Interactive Web Publishing With Microsoft Tools
$49.99, 848 pages, illustrated, part #: 462-6

Take advantage of Microsoft's broad range of development tools to produce powerful web pages, program with VBScript, create virtual 3D worlds, and incorporate the functionality of Office applications with OLE. The CD-ROM features demos/lite versions of third party software, sample code.

Web Publishing With Microsoft FrontPage 97
$34.99, 624 pages, illustrated, part #: 478-2

Web page publishing for everyone! Streamline web-site creation and automate maintenance, all without programming! Covers introductory-to-advanced techniques, with hands-on examples. For Internet and intranet developers. The CD-ROM includes all web-site examples from the book, FrontPage add-ons, shareware, clip art and more.

Web Publishing With ActiveX Controls
$39.99, 688 pages, illustrated, part #: 647-5

Activate web pages using Microsoft's powerful new ActiveX technology. From HTML basics to layout, find all you need to make web pages come alive, add multimedia punch to pages and streamline work with ActiveX Controls. The CD-ROM features example files from the book, Working Scripts for using Explorer's built-in controls, 3D Viewer, HTML editor, image map editor and more!

VENTANA

Looking Good in Print, Deluxe CD-ROM Edition
$34.99, 416 pages, illustrated, part #: 471-5

This completely updated version of the most widely used design companion for desktop publishers features all-new sections on color and printing. Packed with professional tips for creating powerful reports, newsletters, ads, brochures and more. The companion CD-ROM features Adobe® Acrobat® Reader, author examples, fonts, templates, graphics and more.

Looking Good Online
$39.99, 384 pages, illustrated, part #: 469-3

Create well-designed, organized web sites—incorporating text, graphics, digital photos, backgrounds and forms. Features studies of successful sites and design tips from pros. The companion CD-ROM includes samples from online professionals; buttons, backgrounds, templates and graphics.

Looking Good in 3D
$39.99, 384 pages, illustrated, part #: 494-4

Become the da Vinci of the 3D world! Learn the artistic elements involved in 3D design—light, motion, perspective, animation and more—to create effective interactive projects. The CD-ROM includes samples from the book, templates, fonts and graphics.

VENTANA

3D Studio MAX f/x
$49.99, 552 pages, illustrated, part #: 427-8

Create Hollywood-style special effects! Plunge into 3D animation with step-by-step instructions for lighting, camera movements, optical effects, texture maps, storyboarding, cinematography, editing and much more. The companion CD-ROM features free plug-ins, all the tutorials from the book, 300+ original texture maps and animations.

Microsoft SoftImage|3D Professional Techniques
$69.99, 524 pages, illustrated, part #: 499-5

Create intuitive, visually rich 3D images with this award-winning technology. Follow the structured tutorial to master modeling, animation and rendering, and to increase your 3D productivity. The CD-ROM features tutorials, sample scenes, textures, scripts, shaders, images and animations.

LightWave 3D 5 Character Animation f/x
$69.99, 760 pages, illustrated, part #: 532-0

Master the fine—and lucrative—art of 3D character animation. Traditional animators and computer graphic artists alike will discover everything they need to know: lighting, motion, caricature, composition, rendering ... right down to work-flow strategies. The CD-ROM features a collection of the most popular LightWave plug-ins, scripts, storyboards, finished animations, models and much more.

VENTANA

TO ORDER ANY VENTANA TITLE, COMPLETE THIS ORDER FORM AND MAIL OR FAX IT TO US, WITH PAYMENT, FOR QUICK SHIPMENT.

TITLE	PART #	QTY	PRICE	TOTAL

SHIPPING

For orders shipping within the United States, please add $4.95 for the first book, $1.50 for each additional book.
For "two-day air," add $7.95 for the first book, $3.00 for each additional book.
Email: vorders@kdc.com for exact shipping charges.
Note: Please include your local sales tax.

SUBTOTAL = $ _____
SHIPPING = $ _____
TAX = $ _____
TOTAL = $ _____

Mail to: International Thomson Publishing • 7625 Empire Drive • Florence, KY 41042
☎ US orders 800/332-7450 • fax 606/283-0718
☎ International orders 606/282-5786 • Canadian orders 800/268-2222

Name _____
E-mail _____ Daytime phone _____
Company _____
Address (No PO Box) _____
City_____ State_____ Zip_____
Payment enclosed ___ VISA ___ MC ___ Acc't # _____ Exp. date _____
Signature _____ Exact name on card _____

Check your local bookstore or software retailer for these and other bestselling titles, or call toll free:

800/332-7450
8:00 am - 6:00 pm EST